A Behavioral Approach to Asset Pricing

Second Edition

Hersh Shefrin

Mario L. Belotti Professor of Finance
Leavey School of Business
Santa Clara University

AMSTERDAM • BOSTON • HEIDELBERG • LONDON
NEW YORK • OXFORD • PARIS • SAN DIEGO
SAN FRANCISCO • SINGAPORE • SYDNEY • TOKYO

Academic Press is an imprint of Elsevier

Academic Press is an imprint of Elsevier
30 Corporate Drive, Suite 400, Burlington, MA 01803, USA
525 B Street, Suite 1900, San Diego, California 92101-4495, USA
84 Theobald's Road, London WC1X 8RR, UK

Library of Congress Cataloging-in-Publication Data
Application submitted

British Library Cataloguing-in-Publication Data
A catalogue record for this book is available from the British Library.

ISBN: 978-0-12-374356-5

For information on all Academic Press publications
visit our Web site at *www.books.elsevier.com*

Printed in the United States of America
08 09 10   9 8 7 6 5 4 3 2 1

Working together to grow
libraries in developing countries

www.elsevier.com | www.bookaid.org | www.sabre.org

ELSEVIER   BOOK AID
            International   Sabre Foundation

*To my mother Clara Shefrin and
the memory of my late father Sam Shefrin.*

Contents

Preface to Second Edition

The opportunity to write a second edition of *A Behavioral Approach to Asset Pricing* enables me to reiterate a core message in the book. That message is: The future of asset pricing theory lies in bringing together the powerful SDF-based tools adopted by neoclassical asset pricing theorists and the more realistic assumptions adopted by behavioral asset pricing theorists. Put somewhat differently, I propose that neoclassical asset pricing theorists and behavioral asset pricing theorists converge to common middle ground. In this regard, I am grateful to Robert Shiller who, in endorsing the first edition of this book, stated the core message.

In the last part of the book, I point out that there has been progress in moving to common middle ground. In the main, most of this progress has come from neoclassical asset pricing theorists who have begun to adopt behavioral assumptions. As of the time I am writing this preface, behavioral asset pricing theorists have been much slower to adopt SDF-based techniques.

The second edition features the addition of new material. The most significant new material pertains to

- the extension of the log-SDF decomposition to incorporate behavioral preferences
- the connection between behavioral mean-variance portfolios and coskewness
- the sentiment of individual stocks
- the benefits of SP/A theory relative to prospect theory

- new evidence involving the disposition effect, and
- theoretical advances in developing behavioral asset pricing models in both discrete time and continuous time.

The new material covers many papers that were not part of the first edition. In this regard, I have been selective, focusing on papers that provide insights into the behavioral SDF-based approach to asset pricing. As I mentioned in the first edition, this book makes no attempt at providing comprehensive coverage of the literature. There are many interesting papers dealing with either behavioral issues or asset pricing issues that I have not included because they are not closely linked to the behavioral SDF approach. For example, I do not include papers dealing with such issues as style investing, dividends, or home bias, as interesting as these topics are.

The most important equation in the first edition of *A Behavioral Approach to Asset Pricing* is the decomposition of the log-SDF into sentiment and a fundamental component. In the second edition of the book, I have extended the analysis to demonstrate how this equation can be generalized to encompass the combination of behavioral preferences and behavioral beliefs. This generalization provides a unified approach that ties together the main ideas in the book more comprehensively than in the first edition.

In the second edition, I have made an effort to introduce the key concepts and relationships much earlier in the book. In particular, Chapters 4 and 9 of the second edition include short sections that prefigure the main results. They do so by providing simple illustrative examples of sentiment, the pricing kernel, and the log-SDF decomposition result.

Chapter 17 of the first edition describes behavioral mean-variance portfolios and behavioral risk premiums. Notably, behavioral mean-variance portfolios are more complex than weighted averages of the market portfolio and the risk-free security. Instead, behavioral mean-variance portfolios reflect the use of derivatives to exploit pockets of mispricing. This point is important. In 2006, the total outstanding amount of financial derivatives on world markets was estimated to be about $480 trillion, and growing rapidly. As a result, there is reason to expect that activity in the derivatives market spill over and impact the risk premiums in equity and bond markets. Indeed as this book goes to press, global equity markets have declined sharply, reflecting trades in collateralized debt obligations (CDOs) and structured investment vehicles (SIVs).

The second edition extends the analysis of risk and return to identify conditions under which coskewness with the market portfolio is a key variable underlying risk premiums. This analysis has empirical implications. Chapter 23 of the second edition now includes a discussion of the empirical literature on coskewness, and why the evidence supports the behavioral theory developed in Chapter 17.

The first edition introduced the concept of a sentiment function and discussed empirical evidence about the projection of that function onto the return distribution for the S&P 500. The second edition extends the discussion to the projection of the sentiment function onto the return distribution for individual stocks.

The first edition described theoretical implications for the portfolio choices of investors with prospect theory preferences. In doing so, I made the point that although prospect theory is quite rich in its descriptive power, it also possesses features that are highly unrealistic, and not supported by experimental evidence.

In the first edition, I developed the portfolio implications for investors whose preferences conform to SP/A theory, a psychologically based theory of choice developed by Lola Lopes that serves as an alternative to prospect theory. Meir Statman and I used SP/A theory as the basis for the framework we call "behavioral portfolio theory." In the second edition, I describe contributions to the literature suggesting that in key ways, SP/A theory is superior to prospect theory. Moreover, SP/A theory naturally accomodates important new insights from the emerging filed of neuroeconomics about the impact of brain structure and hormones on risk taking. For these reasons, I have augmented the discussion of SP/A theory in the second edition.

The disposition effect is the most well studied aspect of individual investor behavior in behavioral finance. In 1985, Meir Statman and I introduced the concept and coined the term. At the time, we suggested that the disposition effect reflects a series of psychological phenomena, one of which is prospect theory. At the same time, we cautioned that, by itself, prospect theory is incapable of explaining the effect. In the second edition, I review the basis for the disposition effect in greater detail than I did in the first edition. In this respect, I discuss new findings that shed light on the key role played by psychological phenomena other than prospect theory that Meir Statman and I proposed.

The first edition described the asset pricing implications associated with the disposition effect. Since the first edition appeared, several interesting papers have been published on this topic. The second edition includes a discussion of the recent literature on how the disposition effect impacts prices.

The first edition developed behavioral asset pricing theory using a discrete time framework, and included a limited discussion of continuous time models in connection with option pricing. Since the first edition was published, several important continuous time models have appeared in the literature. As a result, I have added a new chapter which surveys several of these models and links them to the core ideas in the book. In the main, these contributions focus on modeling heterogeneous beliefs instead of the representative investor assumption. This is a welcome development. A key point in this book is that the representative investor assumption tends to inject bias into asset pricing models. This message is important for asset pricing theorists, be they neoclassical or behavioral, who continue to invoke the representative investor assumption without regard to the associated biases.

Two of the major revisions discussed above resulted from conversations I had during a visit to Duke University. The conversations were with Campbell Harvey and John Payne, respectively, and I express my gratitude to both.

The conversation with Campbell Harvey occurred in connection with my having presented "On Kernels and Sentiment," the paper upon which the book is based. After I presented the theoretical implications associated with behavioral mean-variance portfolios, based on Figure 15.4, Harvey suggested a link to his work with Akhtar Siddique on coskewness. Harvey and Siddique explained their findings in a neoclassical framework involving a quadratic SDF: They associated this SDF with a representative investor utility function featuring a positive third derivative, and hence a demand for positively skewed returns. In this second edition, I suggest that their findings instead reflect behavioral phenomena, rather than neoclassical phenomena.

The conversation with John Payne occurred in connection with findings in his work which run counter to the predictions of cumulative prospect theory. In this second edition, I suggest that for the purpose of modeling behavioral preferences, Payne's findings support the use of SP/A theory over cumulative prospect theory.

The second edition of this book provides me with an opportunity to make corrections to the errors and omissions that I did not catch in the first edition. For their help in identifying errors in the first printing, I thank George Constantinides, Anke Gerber, Peter Nyberg, David Margolis, Huanghai Li, Vladimir Mlynarovic, Doruk Ilgaz, and Mei Wang. For their feedback on new material in the second edition, I thank Gurdip Bakshi, Sanjiv Das, Bernard Dumas, Elyès Jouini, Valerio Poti, Mark Seasholes, and Raman Uppal. I am especially grateful to Jens Jackwerth and Andrey Ukhov for kindly sharing data with me. I am very appreciative to *The Journal of Investment Management* and to *The Journal of Investment Consulting* for allowing me to include material, authored by me, from articles, both forthcoming and published, as part of this second edition. I would also like to express my appreciation to the Dean Witter Foundation for both their financial assistance and their longstanding support of Santa Clara University.

Special thanks to the Elsevier team for helping me put this second edition together. My editor, Karen Maloney, was incredibly supportive throughout the process. Jay Donahue, the project manager, was a joy to work with in terms of flexibility, communication, and efficiency. Greg deZarn-O'Hare smoothly facilitated file management.

Finally, I thank my wife Arna for her great patience during the time I was preparing this second edition.

Hersh Shefrin
Santa Clara University
2008

Preface to First Edition

In this book, I present a unified, systematic approach to asset pricing that incorporates the key concepts in behavioral finance. The approach represents the culmination of almost twenty years of thought about the impact of behavioral decision making on finance in general, and asset pricing in particular.

This work is neither a handbook, nor a comprehensive survey, nor a collection of previous writings. Rather, it is a treatise about how modern asset pricing theory, built around the concept of a stochastic discount factor (SDF), can be extended to incorporate behavioral elements. The book presents behavioral versions of the term structure of interest rates, option prices, mean-variance efficient portfolios, beta, and the SDF. This is not a collection of separate behavioral theories. Instead, they are all special cases of a single, unified, behaviorally based theory of asset pricing.

In order to develop the approach, I begin with what seems to me to be the most important behavioral concept for asset pricing. That concept is *representativeness*. The first several chapters introduce the concept, first from the perspective of psychologists, and then from the perspective of economists. Having introduced the concept, I then devote several chapters to explaining how representativeness affects the expectations and decisions of real investors, including academics.

I develop a sequence of models to explain the impact of representativeness on asset pricing. In an attempt to make the key features of the models as clear as possible, I have structured the first models very simply. I only add complexity on an as-needed basis.

Besides representativeness, there is a wide range of other behavioral concepts. Examples include overconfidence, prospect theory, excessive optimism, anchoring and adjustment, availability, self-attribution error, and conservatism. All of these concepts play roles in this book. Of these, overconfidence is the most important.

To my mind, the most important feature of the approach in this book is that it provides a theoretical structure to analyze the impact of behavioral beliefs and preferences on all asset prices through the SDF. In this respect, the approach in this book develops testable hypotheses about the shape of the SDF function. These hypotheses link the empirical evidence on investor expectations to the shape of the empirical SDF.

Unlike the downward sloping SDF found in traditional theory, a typical behavioral SDF oscillates. The theory developed in this book provides hypotheses for how the distribution of investor errors generates particular oscillations in the SDF. In other words, oscillations in the graph of the SDF are not arbitrary residual variables that, for lack of an alternative explanation, are attributed to investor sentiment. Rather, empirical evidence about investor errors is presented and, in conjunction with the theory, used to develop hypotheses about the oscillating patterns in the SDF. I argue that the empirical evidence about the shape of the SDF supports the hypotheses in question.

As the title of the book indicates, the body of work described therein is a behavioral approach to asset pricing. Indeed, it is not the only behavioral approach to asset pricing. Alternative approaches can be found in the pages of academic journals in finance, and in books in behavioral finance that address market efficiency. None of the alternative approaches focuses on the SDF. Instead they emphasize utility functions that exhibit constant absolute risk aversion and mean-variance principles.

In 1986 I began to develop general equilibrium models that accommodated behavioral assumptions, asking how behavioral phenomena affected the character of equilibrium prices. The core ideas in this book took shape in a paper I eventually entitled "On Kernels and Sentiment." Traditional theorists initially criticized the paper for being too behavioral, suggesting that I eliminate the focus on investor errors and concentrate on the implications of heterogeneous beliefs. Behaviorists initially suggested that the paper was insufficiently behavioral, proposing that I concentrate less on heterogeneous beliefs, and more on specific investor errors.

The contradictory criticisms of traditionalists and behaviorists reflect some of the reasons why members of both camps did not embrace the behavioral asset pricing approach that I was proposing. Traditional asset pricing theorists were reared in the tradition of rational expectations, and found the behavioral emphasis on investor error counterintuitive. Behaviorists were largely empirically focused, and not especially interested in a general asset pricing framework that was theoretically oriented rather than empirically oriented.

Interactions with critics have influenced the presentation of ideas in this book. The most common criticism from traditional asset pricing theorists is that the main theoretical results in the book are false. I learned a great deal from these interactions. For example, Richard Green suggested that I develop a behavioral binomial option pricing example to illustrate my contention that heterogeneous beliefs can give rise to smile effects in the implied volatility function for options. In doing so, I gained a deeper understanding of the model's structure, and the example can be found in Chapter 21. Kenneth Singleton, a leading asset pricing theorist, indicated that he was better able to follow a critic's argument that one of the theorems was false than the proof of the theorem. Singleton's remark led me to improve the exposition of the proof.

To my mind, the most important feature of the approach in this book is that it provides a theoretical structure to analyze the impact of behavioral beliefs and preferences on all asset prices through the SDF. Not everyone agrees. Kenneth Singleton took the position that I should be focusing on option prices, not the shape of the SDF. He also asserted that it is sufficient to assume heterogeneous risk tolerance, not heterogeneous beliefs. Although I discuss these points in the book (Chapters 16, 21), at this point let me speculate that theorists who have been reared in the tradition of rational expectations might find the idea of investor errors, meaning nonrational expectations, counterintuitive. Therefore, many avoid assuming heterogeneous beliefs in order to avoid assumptions involving investor error.

A common claim by traditional asset pricing theorists has been that the results in "On Kernels and Sentiment," which appear in this book, must be false. One critic claimed that the option pricing results in the paper violate put-call parity and therefore cannot hold. A second contended that a key bond pricing equation must be false. A third held that the main representative investor theorem would be remarkable if true, but in fact is false.

The counterarguments advanced by critics are sophisticated and interesting. The common nature of the criticisms suggests to me that they represent typical reactions by traditional asset pricing theorists. Because I suspect that the results presented here are highly counterintuitive to theorists reared in the tradition of rational expectations, I have included their major criticisms in the book. Doing so provides me with an opportunity to explain why the criticisms are incorrect. Not doing so would increase the risk that traditional asset pricing theorists will continue to believe that my results are false.

My hope is that with the publication of this book, asset pricing theorists will accept that my results are correct, and attention will shift to the application of behavioral asset pricing theory. Future work should investigate whether observed oscillations in the empirical SDF stem from investor errors, from rational sources, or from both. In this respect, observed oscillations in the empirical SDF are not tautologically attributed to sentiment. Rather, the theory developed in this book generates testable predictions that link the distribution of investor errors to the shape of the SDF. Different error distributions give rise to different shapes of SDF. These linkages can be used to structure new tests based on new data sets or new time periods. Behavioral asset pricing predicts that when the error distribution is time varying, so too will be the SDF. And the empirical evidence presented in this book indicates that the error distribution is indeed time varying.

In recent years, research has documented that the graph of the empirical SDF features an oscillating pattern. "On Kernels and Sentiment" dates back to 1996, and to the best of my knowledge, predates empirical work reporting that the SDF features an oscillating pattern. The early versions of the paper predicted that the SDF would feature an oscillating pattern that I called a "kernel smile." The point is important, in that I did not set out to produce a model whose results fit the data. As far as I can tell, my paper was the first to suggest that the SDF featured an upward sloping portion. Indeed, no reader of the early versions of the paper appeared to find the claim of much interest.

The core material in this book has not appeared in print before. In addition to the core, I have selected a body of work, some published, some unpublished, that illuminates how the core ideas apply to asset pricing in the real world. The literature that I have chosen to include relates directly to the core ideas. My purpose in selecting these works is to provide support for the core approach, and to indicate how the core ideas relate to the existing literature. In this regard, I make no effort to be comprehensive or inclusive. There are many fine works that I have chosen not to mention, simply because I did not judge their inclusion as fitting my agenda.

My apologies to readers for duplicate notation in a few places, or in order to avoid duplicate notation, unusual notation in others. Notation is consistent within chapters, but in a few instances is not consistent across chapters. For example, α is used for regression coefficients in Chapter 3, but as an exponential smoothing parameter in Chapter 18. Having used P and p to denote probability, I used q to denote price, even though p or P is more common for price.

I would like to express my gratitude to many people who provided advice and comments during the development of this work. Scott Bentley and Karen Maloney, my editors at Elsevier, provided much guidance and encouragement. I would also like to thank Elsevier staff members for their help, especially Dennis McGonagle, Troy Lilly, and Angela Dooley. Conversations with Maureen O'Hara and John Campbell persuaded me that there were too many integrated ideas in "On Kernels and Sentiment" for a single paper, and that a book might be the appropriate way to provide a unified treatment of the approach. Three reviewers provided invaluable comments and suggestions, for which I am very appreciative indeed. Wayne Ferson was kind enough to invite me to present "On Kernels and Sentiment" to his graduate asset pricing class, and to offer a series of constructive suggestions. Bing Han read through an early version of the manuscript and provided many helpful comments. Jens Jackwerth and Joshua Rosenberg read excerpts from the book, and made important comments. Ivo Welch was kind enough to share the data from his surveys of financial economists with me. My colleague Sanjiv Das, himself working on a book, shared all kinds of useful tips with me. My colleague and good friend Meir Statman engaged me in countless stimulating and productive conversations on many of the topics discussed in the book. Robert Shiller kindly provided me with one of his figures. Seminar participants at the University of Michigan, Duke University, Stanford University, Queens University, the Chicago Board of Trade, Tel Aviv University, the Interdisciplinary Center (IDC), and the Hebrew University of Jerusalem made excellent suggestions. I especially thank Alon Brav, Roni Michaely, Oded Sarig, Simon Benninga, Jacob Boudoukh, Eugene Kandel, Zvi Weiner, Itzhak Venezia, David Hirshleifer, Bhaskaran Swaminathan, Terry Odean, Ming Huang, Peter Carr, Joseph Langsam, Peter Cotton, Dilip Madan, Frank Milne, and Campbell Harvey. John Ronstadt from UBS was kind enough to help me locate data from the UBS/Gallup Survey. I am also grateful to those who have been critical of this work, whose challenges helped me achieve a deeper understanding of the ideas than would otherwise have occurred. Needless to say, none of the individuals mentioned above is responsible for any errors that remain in the book. I thank the Dean Witter Foundation for financial support. Finally, I thank my wife Arna for her strong, unwavering support during the long gestation period of this work.

Hersh Shefrin
Santa Clara University
July 2004

About the Author

Hersh Shefrin holds the Mario L. Belotti Chair in the Department of Finance at Santa Clara University's Leavey School of Business. He is a pioneer of behavioral finance, and has worked on behavioral issues for over thirty years. *A Behavioral Approach to Asset Pricing* is the first behavioral treatment of the pricing kernel. His book *Behavioral Corporate Finance* is the first textbook dedicated to the application of behavioral concepts to corporate finance. His book *Beyond Greed and Fear* was the first comprehensive treatment of the field of behavioral finance. A 2003 article appearing in *The American Economic Review* included him among the top fifteen theorists to have influenced empirical work in microeconomics. One of his articles is among the all time top ten papers to be downloaded from SSRN. He holds a Ph.D. from the London School of Economics, and an honorary doctorate from the University of Oulu in Finland.

1
Introduction

Behavioral finance is the study of how psychological phenomena impact financial behavior. As its title suggests, the subject of this book is the implications of behavioral finance for asset pricing. The long-term objective of behavioral finance is to behavioralize finance. In this vein, the objective of the book is to behavioralize asset pricing theory. Behavioralizing asset pricing theory means tracing the implications of behavioral assumptions for equilibrium prices.

Financial economists are in the midst of a debate about a paradigm shift, from a neoclassical-based paradigm to one that is behaviorally based. The basis for the debate about a paradigm shift in finance involves the way that people make decisions. In the course of making decisions, people generally make observations, process data, and arrive at judgments. In finance, these judgments and decisions pertain to the composition of individual portfolios, the range of securities offered in the market, the character of earnings forecasts, and the manner in which securities are priced through time.

In building a framework for the study of financial markets, academics face a fundamental choice. They need to choose a set of assumptions about the judgments, preferences, and decisions of participants in financial markets. The paradigmatic debate centers on whether these assumptions should be neoclassical-based or behaviorally based.

Traditionally, finance has adopted the neoclassical framework of micro-economics. In the neoclassical framework, financial decision makers possess von Neumann–Morgenstern preferences over uncertain wealth distributions, and use Bayesian techniques to make appropriate statistical judgments from the data at their disposal.

Psychologists working in the area of behavioral decision making have produced much evidence that people do not behave as if they have von Neumann–Morgenstern preferences, and do not form judgments in accordance with Bayesian principles. Rather, they systematically behave in a manner different from both. Notably, behavioral psychologists have advanced theories that address the causes and effects associated with these systematic departures. The behavioral counterpart to von Neumann–Morgenstern theory is known as prospect theory. The behavioral counterpart to Bayesian theory is known as "heuristics and biases."

1.1   Why Read This Book?

Those who read this book might be proponents of the traditional approach to asset pricing, or proponents of a behavioral approach. What will they gain by reading this book? How will investing time reading this book result in a positive net present value for their efforts? The answer to these questions might well be different for proponents of the traditional approach than for proponents of the behavioral approach. Consider first the proponents of the traditional approach to asset pricing theory.

1.1.1   Value to Proponents of Traditional Asset Pricing

The value of reading a book such as this one comes in being exposed to a point of view that is different, but expressed in a familiar framework, such as Cochrane (2005). For the purpose of clarity, the points of differentiation are organized into a series of messages.

This book has four main messages for proponents of traditional asset pricing theory. These messages pertain to the inputs and outputs of asset pricing models. The inputs into a model are its assumptions. The outputs of a model are its results. The first message relates to model inputs and the remaining three messages relate to outputs.

The traditional neoclassical assumptions that underlie asset pricing models are rationality based. The preferences of fully rational investors conform to expected utility. Notably, the expected utility model has two components: a set of probability beliefs and a utility function. In traditional models, rational investors make efficient use of information, in that their beliefs are based on the application of optimal statistical procedures. In traditional asset pricing models, utility functions are concave functions of wealth levels, with concavity reflecting risk aversion on the part of investors.

The first message for traditional asset pricing theorists relates to the behavioral character of the model inputs. Proponents of behavioral finance assume that psychological phenomena prevent most investors from being fully rational. Instead, investors are assumed to be imperfectly rational. Imperfectly rational investors are not uniformly averse to risk. In some circumstances, they act as if they are risk seeking. Moreover, imperfectly rational investors do not rely on optimal statistical procedures. Instead, they rely on crude heuristics that predispose their beliefs to bias. As to utility functions, the functional arguments used by imperfectly rational investors are changes in wealth rather than final wealth position. As a result, imperfectly rational investors can appear to exhibit intransitive preferences in respect to final asset positions.

As documented in the pages that follow, investors commit systematic errors. Pretending that investors are error-free runs counter to the empirical evidence. The most important part of the first message concerns the importance of replacing the unrealistic assumption that investors are error-free with assumptions that reflect the errors that investors actually commit.

Although traditionalists have been willing to incorporate nonexpected utility maximizing preferences into their models, they have strongly resisted incorporating errors in investors' beliefs. For example, all traditional approaches to explaining the equity premium puzzle, expectations hypothesis for the term structure of interest rates, and option smiles assume that investors hold correct beliefs.

The second message pertains to the notion of a representative investor. Proponents of traditional asset pricing theory tend to use a representative investor whose beliefs and preferences set prices. This representative investor holds correct beliefs and is a traditional expected utility maximizer who exhibits either constant risk aversion or time-varying risk aversion stemming from habit formation. This book makes the point that although a representative investor may set prices, a behavioral representative investor typically holds erroneous beliefs. In particular, heterogeneity typically gives rise to time-varying beliefs, risk aversion, and time preference on the part of the representative investor. In addition, heterogeneity of beliefs produces a representative investor who may not resemble any of the individual investors participating in the market. Readers of this book will learn how to structure a representative investor that reflects the heterogeneity across the individual investors that make up the market.

The third message for traditional asset pricing theorists pertains to the stochastic discount factor (SDF). Behavioral asset pricing theory has a coherent structure centered on the SDF. In particular, the behavioral SDF decomposes into a fundamental component and a sentiment component, where the sentiment component captures the aggregate error in the market. In contrast, the traditional SDF only has a fundamental component. The traditional SDF is a monotone declining function of the underlying state variable. In contrast the typical behavioral SDF is an oscillating function,

FIGURE 1.1. Contrasting a typical traditional SDF and a typical behavioral SDF.

where the oscillation reflects the specific structure of the aggregate market error.[1]

In order to illustrate the flavor of the argument, Figure 1.1 contrasts a traditional SDF and an oscillating behavioral SDF. The gap between the two functions reflects inefficiency in respect to the spectrum of state prices. At points where the two functions coincide, the state prices associated with the intersection are efficient. Where the functions do not coincide, the state prices are inefficient.

The fourth message for traditional asset pricing theorists concerns the empirical SDF, meaning the SDF that is estimated from market prices. It is here that the rubber meets the road. The evidence indicates that the empirical SDF has the behavioral shape depicted in Figure 1.1.

An important aspect of the approach in this book is that a behaviorally based asset pricing theory provides testable predictions about the shape of the SDF. Those predictions relate the distribution of investor errors to the specific shape of the SDF. Different distributions give rise to different

---

[1] There are rationality based models that feature an oscillating SDF, a point that is discussed in Chapter 23. Therefore, an oscillating SDF in and of itself does not imply that investors commit errors.

shapes. Moreover, if the distribution of investor errors is time-varying, then so too will be the shape of the SDF. Notably, evidence is presented that serves to document the time-varying character of the distribution of investor errors.

In particular, the empirical SDF oscillates in a manner that is consistent both with the behavioral decomposition result shown in Figure 1.1 and with the empirical evidence pertaining to the structure of investor errors. As was mentioned earlier, the oscillating shape of the empirical SDF identifies the location of mispricing in equilibrium prices. It is important for readers to understand that the oscillating pattern is not attributed to sentiment for lack of a better explanation. Rather, the empirical evidence relating to the distribution of investor errors predicts the particular shape of SDF that is observed.

Readers of this book will learn how to build asset pricing theories that feature mispricing of many securities: options, fixed income securities, equities and mean-variance portfolios. To be sure, empirical evidence about mispricing in different asset classes has been growing. Indeed, this book argues that investor errors are well documented, nonzero, and that they play an important role in explaining the puzzles involving the equity premium, the expectations hypothesis of the term structure of interest rates, and option smiles.

1.1.2 Value to Proponents of Behavioral Asset Pricing

Consider next behavioral asset pricing theorists. What can they learn by reading this book? After all, behavioral asset pricing theorists already incorporate investor errors and behavioral preferences into their models. Although true, behavioral asset pricing models lack the general SDF-based approach favored by traditional asset pricing theorists. To date, behavioral asset pricing models have been more ad hoc, mainly constructed to provide behaviorally based explanations of particular empirical phenomena, rather than to develop a general approach.[2]

The ad hoc approach that has characterized most behavioral asset pricing theories to date has a theory mining flavor, mainly building custom models to fit the empirical facts. These models have tended to combine one or two behaviorally realistic assumptions with other assumptions that are highly unrealistic. For example, the behavioral decision literature contains many studies demonstrating that people routinely violate Bayes rule. That literature also contains studies demonstrating that people overweight recent events relative to more distant events. Yet some behavioral models assume that investors act as Bayesians in some of their decisions, but that they overweight recent events in other of their decisions. In other

---

[2] The models in question are described in Chapter 18.

words, behavioral asset pricing theorists tend to pick and choose behavioral features in order to build models whose conclusions fit the established empirical patterns.

The piecemeal approach to developing behavioral asset pricing models has resulted more in a patchwork quilt of contrived examples than in a general theory of asset pricing. Some models emphasize overconfidence. Other models emphasize excessive optimism. Some models assume that investors overreact. Other models assume that investors underreact.

This book has several messages for behavioral asset pricing theorists. The first message is that theory mining is bad science, and produces a patchwork quilt of models with no unifying structure. This book develops a general approach to behavioral asset pricing.

The second message pertains to the representative investor, and is similar to the message conveyed to traditional asset pricing theorists. Some behavioral asset pricing models assume a representative investor who commits errors identified in the behavioral literature. There is considerable heterogeneity in respect to the errors committed at the individual level. Heterogeneity tends to produce a representative investor who does not resemble any of the individual investors. Therefore, the behavioral representative investor might not commit the classic errors identified in the behavioral decision literature. In other words, asset pricing models built around a "behavioral representative investor" might be misleading.

The third message for behavioral asset pricing theorists pertains to sentiment. The term "sentiment" is synonymous with error, either at the level of the individual investor or at the level of the market. Behavioral asset pricing theorists often model sentiment as a scalar variable, such as the bias to the mean of a particular distribution. That is fine for small ad hoc models, but, in general, is too simplistic. In general, sentiment is not a scalar but a stochastic process. It evolves according to a distribution that interacts with fundamental variables. In a market with heterogeneous beliefs, market sentiment might not be uniformly optimistic. The prices of some assets may feature excessive optimism while the prices of other assets feature excessive pessimism. That is the point of the oscillating SDF: nonuniform sentiment. The message here to behavioral asset pricing theorists is that by reading this book, they will learn how to develop a general approach to sentiment.

1.2   Organization: How the Ideas in This Book Tie Together

The book is organized into groups of short chapters that develop a behavioral approach to asset pricing theory. This section describes the chapter groups that combine to produce the flow of ideas.

1.2.1   Heuristics and Representativeness: Experimental Evidence

Chapters 2 through 5 are devoted to two psychological concepts, "heuristics" and "representativeness." Although there are many psychological concepts used in behavioral finance, heuristics and representativeness are the most important ones in respect to asset pricing. A heuristic is a rule of thumb, and representativeness is a principle that underlies particular rules of thumb. Representativeness is critical because it underlies the manner in which both individual investors and professional investors forecast returns.

Chapter 2 describes the key psychological studies of representativeness, focusing on the intuition that underlies the main ideas. Chapter 3 discusses how representativeness was first tested in the economics literature. Chapter 4 illustrates how representativeness can be introduced into a simple equilibrium model.

Chapter 5 emphasizes that despite the fact that people form forecasts using common principles, in practice there is a great deal of heterogeneity in their forecasts. This heterogeneity is an important part of the behavioral approach, and needs to be accommodated formally in asset pricing models. Much of the theoretical apparatus that comes later in the book is built around heterogeneity.

1.2.2   Heuristics and Representativeness: Investor Expectations

Chapters 6 and 7 are among the most important in the book. These chapters apply representativeness to the return forecasts made by individual investors, professional investors, corporate chief financial officers, and financial economists. Although all appear to rely on representativeness when forecasting returns, they do so in different ways. The differences are central and turn out to affect the nature of the empirical SDF discussed later in the book. The findings in these two chapters motivate the assumptions that underlie the models developed in later chapters. Testable predictions about the shape of the SDF are based on the empirical findings documented in Chapters 6 and 7.

1.2.3   Developing Behavioral Asset Pricing Models

Chapters 8 through 11 illustrate the implications of representativeness and heterogeneous beliefs in a log-utility model. Log-utility serves as a special case that provides some simplifying structure. Chapter 8 develops the structure of the model.

Chapter 9 is devoted to market efficiency. Discussions about market efficiency tend to be controversial, and the controversy begins with the question of how to define the term itself. Several alternative definitions are proposed, and one most suitable to the present approach is selected. The heart of Chapter 9 is the development of a necessary and sufficient condition for prices to be efficient when investors rely on representativeness to forecast returns and beliefs are heterogeneous.

Chapter 10 focuses on the structure of returns and trading volume. Heterogeneous beliefs constitute the driving force underlying trading volume. Most of the discussion in the chapter is theoretical. However, a brief empirical discussion about trading volume is provided in this chapter.

Chapter 11 addresses the issue of long-run dynamics when some investors commit errors. This chapter describes how the concept of entropy can be applied to address the question of survival. The analysis also demonstrates that in the presence of heterogeneity, prices cannot be perpetually efficient. That is, heterogeneous beliefs ultimately force prices to become inefficient.

1.2.4   Heterogeneity in Risk Tolerance and Time Discounting

Chapters 12 through 14 are devoted to generalizing the approach to accommodate heterogeneous preferences in respect to both risk tolerance and time discounting. Chapter 12 reviews the basic Arrow–Pratt framework for measuring risk aversion. Log-utility is a special case of this framework, corresponding to the case when the coefficient of relative risk aversion is unity. The chapter demonstrates how the basic equilibrium results generalize when investors have common preferences and when either the coefficient of relative risk aversion is not unity, or investors exhibit constant absolute risk aversion.

Chapter 13 describes evidence concerning the empirical distribution of risk aversion and time preference in the general population. Notably, there is considerable heterogeneity in respect to both risk aversion and time preference.

Chapter 14 develops the general equilibrium framework to accommodate heterogeneous beliefs, risk tolerance, and time preference. The core of the chapter is a representative investor characterization theorem. The theorem establishes the structure of a representative investor whose beliefs and preferences establish prices. Notably, the representative investor serves to aggregate the heterogeneous beliefs and preferences of all the investors in the market. This aggregation result provides the main building block for the characterization of a behavioral SDF.

For reasons explained in the preface, typical arguments advanced by critics are discussed and analyzed in the text. The first such argument involves a claim that Theorem 14.1 is false. Chapter 14 includes the argument and an analysis of the argument. Similar arguments, pertaining to other results, appear in later chapters as well. Because arguments of this type have been advanced with some frequency, the intent is to address them directly, for the purpose of laying them to rest, and moving the discussion to how best to apply the theory to understand the character of asset pricing.

1.2.5 Sentiment and Behavioral SDF

Chapters 15 and 16 are the core of the book. Chapter 15 develops the concept of market sentiment. Market sentiment is understood as the aggregate error in the market. When market sentiment is zero, prices are efficient, and vice versa. Chapter 15 establishes that market sentiment is a stochastic process that co-evolves with fundamentals.

Chapter 16 establishes two decomposition results involving sentiment. The first result is that the log-SDF can be decomposed into a fundamental component and sentiment. The second result is that the risk premium on any security can be decomposed into a fundamental premium and a sentiment premium. The log-SDF decomposition theorem, in combination with the analysis in Chapter 14, and empirical findings reported in Chapters 6 and 7, provides the main testable hypothesis in the book. That hypothesis states that the empirical evidence described in Chapters 6 and 7 implies that the graph of the empirical SDF will exhibit the oscillating pattern displayed in Figure 1.1. Notably, this is but one possible pattern. The chapter points out that other patterns are possible, depending on the distribution of investor errors.

The SDF underlies all asset prices. An oscillating SDF is the signature of sentiment. To say that the SDF oscillates is effectively to say that the SDF is behavioral. To say that the SDF is behavioral is to say that psychological forces operate alongside fundamental forces to determine prices. That is, asset pricing theory needs to be behavioral.

Chapter 16 also extends the discussion about long-run dynamics and entropy from the case of log-utility to more general preferences. The results are surprising, in that utility maximization has very robust long-term survival properties.

1.2.6 Applications of Behavioral SDF

Chapters 17 through 23 describe how the behavioral SDF can be viewed as the channel through which psychological forces impact the spectrum of asset prices.

Chapter 17 develops the notions of behavioral mean-variance frontier and behavioral beta. Beta and mean-variance efficiency are not meaningless concepts in a behavioral setting. They are just different. This chapter explains the nature of the differences. In particular, both mean-variance returns and beta decompose into the sum of two terms, one corresponding to fundamentals and the other to sentiment. The sentiment component of the mean-variance return is typically an oscillating function. The sentiment component of beta underlies the traditional notion of abnormal return. A key empirical feature of behavioral mean-variance portfolios involves a property known as coskewness with the market portfolio. The theory presented in the chapter implies that risk premiums are determined in a multifactor model, in which the first two factors are the return on the market portfolio, and the squared return on the market portfolio. Coskewness pertains to the factor loading associated with the squared return. The discussion in the chapter deals with conditions under which the sign is large and negative.

Chapter 18 reviews the literature dealing with the cross-section of stock returns, the so-called anomalies literature. The review is not intended to be comprehensive. Rather, the intent is to describe the role that representativeness plays in the cross-section return patterns, and to discuss evidence that suggests why the cross-sectional structure reflects sentiment premiums as well as fundamental risk components.

Chapter 19 is related to Chapter 18, and directly tests Theorem 16.2, the return decomposition result in Chapter 16. The chapter describes an empirical study that tests whether there is a second component to the risk premium besides the fundamental component.

Chapter 20 describes how behavioral elements impact the term structure of interest rates. The chapter makes several points. First, behavioral elements influence the shape of the yield curve. Second, these elements inject volatility into the time series properties of the term structure of interest rates. Third, behavioral elements serve as an obstacle to the expectations hypothesis. In particular, if expectations are based on fundamentals alone, then nonzero sentiment typically prevents the expectations hypothesis from holding.

Chapters 21 through 23 deal with options pricing. Options markets certainly provide a natural means by which heterogeneous beliefs and preferences can be expressed. More importantly, option prices provide the best means of estimating the empirical SDF.

Chapter 21 develops a behavioral analogue to the Black–Scholes formula. A continuous time example is provided for purposes of contrast. Notably, behavioral option prices give rise to smile patterns in the implied volatility functions.

Chapter 16 having made the point that irrational exuberance generates upward sloping portions of the SDF, Chapter 22 discusses the connection between irrational exuberance and index option prices. The chapter focuses on sentiment indexes and option prices during 1996, when Alan Greenspan first used the phrase "irrational exuberance" in a public address. The last part of the chapter suggests that because of price pressure, arbitrage pricing may have been violated prior to Greenspan's remark, thereby generating potential arbitrage profits.

Chapter 23 describes several studies of option prices, which combine to produce a portrait of the behavioral influences on option prices, and the implications of these influences for the empirical SDF. Chapter 23 extends the ideas developed in Chapter 22 on the combination of sentiment and price pressure, focusing on the manner in which professional investors use index put options to provide portfolio insurance. The culmination of Chapter 23 involves the literature dealing with the empirical SDF. This literature establishes that the graph of the SDF features an oscillating pattern that corresponds to the pattern derived in Chapter 16. This pattern has been called the "pricing kernel puzzle." Notably, this pattern corresponds to a particular structure for sentiment, a structure that derives from the empirical evidence on investor errors presented in Chapters 6 and 7. The chapter concludes with a discussion about the empirical evidence pertaining to coskewness. The evidence is consistent with the theoretical relationships derived in Chapter 17. Coskewness is empirically significant, and impacts risk premiums with a negative sign. In a neoclassical setting, the negative sign is viewed as an indication that investors have a preference for positive skewness. This idea receives reinforcement in the part of the book dealing with behavioral preferences. However, the nature of the empirical SDF having a behavioral shape also suggests that investor errors figure prominently.

There is a unified thread in the examples presented in Chapters 15 through 23, one that has sentiment as its core. The oscillating shape of the empirical SDF has a theoretical counterpart derived in Chapter 16, reflecting the oscillating shape of the sentiment function derived in Chapter 15. This shape also underlies the oscillating structure of the mean-variance efficient frontier discussed in Chapter 20, the fat-tailed character of risk-neutral density functions discussed in Chapter 21, and the downward-sloping smile patterns in the implied volatility functions for index options discussed in Chapter 21. In other words, these features are different facets of a single sentiment-based theory, not a disparate collection of unrelated phenomena.

1.2.7 Behavioral Preferences

Part VII discusses the nature of behavioral preference models, and how preferences and beliefs combine to influence asset prices. The book focuses on two psychologically based theories of risk, prospect theory and SP/A theory. Chapter 24 introduces prospect theory and Chapter 25 develops a portfolio selection model for an investor whose preferences conform to prospect theory. Chapter 26 introduces SP/A theory, and Chapter 27 develops a portfolio selection model for an investor whose preferences conform to SP/A theory.

A key feature of the theory developed in Chapter 27 is that investors choose to hold undiversified portfolios which combine very safe and very risky securities. The theory has empirical implications, and the chapter summarizes the empirical literature documenting this feature. Notably, Chapter 27 also suggests that SP/A theory holds important advantages over prospect theory, both from an empirical perspective and a theoretical perspective.

Chapter 28 extends the equilibrium model developed throughout the book to accommodate behavioral preferences. Because prospect theory preferences are non-convex, a key feature of markets with prospect theory investors is that equilibrium may fail to exist. In this regard, Chapter 28 develops some simple examples to demonstrate conditions under which equilibrium exists, and conditions under which equilibrium fails to exist. These examples also provide insights into how prospect theory preferences impact the shape of the SDF. In an interesting special case of the model, prospect theory preferences induce expected utility maximizing investors to choose full portfolio insurance in equilibrium.

Chapter 28 also develops the equilibrium implications associated with SP/A theory. This analysis serves to generalize the main result in the book, namely that the log-SDF decomposes into the sum of sentiment and a fundamental component. The generalization illustrates how sentiment captures the combination of behavioral preferences and beliefs, which together impact asset prices through the SDF.

Chapter 29 describes one of the main pricing implications of the "disposition effect," a phenomenon associated with the degree to which investors realize their winners relative to their losers. This effect is the most studied aspect of individual investor behavior in the literature on behavioral finance. The chapter begins by explaining the theoretical basis for the disposition effect. Notably, the disposition effect reflects additional psychological elements besides prospect theory and SP/A theory. The chapter then documents the empirical evidence for the disposition effect. Finally, the chapter describes the implications of the disposition effect for asset pricing, namely that that the disposition effect underlies momentum.

The first major application of prospect theory to asset pricing involves the equity premium puzzle. Chapter 30 discusses this puzzle. Prospect theory is a theory about the determinants of attitude toward risk, which certainly plays an important role in determining the equity premium. At the same time, both traditional explanations and behavioral explanations of the equity premium puzzle assume that investors are error-free. This chapter discusses the role of investor errors in explaining the equity premium. As in the discussion of the behavioral SDF, the empirical studies in Chapters 6 and 7 play central roles. Investor errors also contribute to two related puzzles, the interest rate puzzle and volatility puzzle.

1.2.8   Future Directions and Closing Comments

Chapter 31 surveys advances in continuous time behavioral asset pricing models that have taken place since the first edition of this book. These advances are important for two reasons. First, they are examples of models based on both behavioral assumptions and the use of SDF-based tools. Second, they represent progress in respect to the key message of this book, namely that the future of asset pricing research lies in bringing together the SDF-based approach favored by neoclassical asset pricing theorists with the behavioral assumptions favored by behavioral asset pricing theorists.

Chapter 32 recapitulates the main points in the book and offers some final remarks.

1.3   Summary

The main pillars of pricing in neoclassical finance are the efficient market hypothesis, factor models such as the capital asset pricing model, Black–Scholes option pricing theory, and mean-variance efficient portfolios. This book demonstrates how the main pillars of asset pricing are impacted when the traditional neoclassical assumptions are replaced by heuristics, biases, and behavioral preferences. There are several puzzles in traditional asset pricing: the equity premium puzzle, interest rate puzzle, volatility puzzle, expectations hypothesis, and pricing kernel puzzle. Throughout the book, the argument is advanced that these phenomena are puzzling because the attempts to explain them rely on traditional models in which investors are error-free. However, there is ample evidence that investors commit systematic errors that manifest themselves in the form of inefficient prices in the aggregate. Moreover, the phenomena associated with these puzzles are less puzzling, if puzzles at all, once investor errors and preferences are taken into account.

Part I

Heuristics and Representativeness: Experimental Evidence

2

Representativeness and Bayes Rule: Psychological Perspective

The behavioral decision literature contains a body of work known as *heuristics and biases*. When psychologists use the term "heuristic," they mean rule of thumb. When they use the word "judgment," they mean assessment. The major finding of heuristics and biases is that people form judgments by relying on heuristics, and that these heuristics bias their judgments and produce systematic errors.

This chapter describes some of the key studies that have been conducted by psychologists of a particular heuristic known as *representativeness*. Although there are many heuristics that affect financial decision makers, during the first several chapters of this book, attention is focused on representativeness. There are two reasons for doing so. First, representativeness plays a prominent role in financial forecasts. Second, proponents of traditional finance often criticize proponents of behavioral finance for a lack of rigor in applying psychological concepts. The argument here is that behaviorists select heuristics to explain empirical phenomena after the fact, but that the choice set is so large that it becomes possible to explain any phenomenon after the fact.

In order to address this issue, attention is focused almost exclusively on representativeness for the first section of this book. The discussion of representativeness begins with a review of key contributions in the psychology literature, and then describes how representativeness has been studied in the economics literature.

Traditional equilibrium models involve the use of signals. In the discussion of psychological experiments that follows, an effort is made to use the language of signals. In each experiment, subjects receive information and are asked to formulate judgments. The information received can be interpreted as a signal. In this respect, the psychological studies analyze the impact of representativeness on judgments based on signals.

2.1   Explaining Representativeness

A major class of heuristics involves a principle known as *representativeness*. Psychologists Daniel Kahneman and Amos Tversky (1972) defined representativeness as follows: A person who relies on representativeness "evaluates the probability of an uncertain event, or a sample, by the degree to which it is: (i) similar in essential properties to its parent population; and (ii) reflects the salient features of the process by which it is generated." Kahneman and Tversky hypothesized that whenever event A is more representative than event B, event A will be judged to have a higher probability than event B. Call this the *representativeness hypothesis*. Representativeness is one of the most important psychological features associated with heuristics and biases. Later in the text, the discussion is expanded to include features such as *overconfidence*.

2.2   Implications for Bayes Rule

Bayes rule states that if D and F are two events, then $P(F|D) = P(D|F)P(F)/P(D)$. The representativeness hypothesis has many implications, and one of the most important is that people will form probability judgments that violate Bayes rule. In particular, reliance on representativeness will lead people to underweight the prior probability $P(F)$ and overweight the conditional probability $P(D|F)$.

2.3   Experiment

Kahneman and Tversky (1973) present an experiment to test the implications of the representativeness hypothesis in respect to the use of Bayes rule. The experiment involves two types of events. D pertains to the *description* of a particular graduate student named Tom. In this respect, D is a signal. F pertains to a *field* of study. The subjects in the experiment were provided with a description of Tom, and asked questions to elicit their judgments about $P(D)$, $P(F)$, $P(F|D)$, and $P(D|F)$.

2.3.1   Three Groups

The experiment had a *between subjects* design, meaning that no single group provided judgments about all four probabilities: $P(D)$, $P(F)$, and $P(F|D)$ and $P(D|F)$. Three groups of students were used, called respectively *base rate*, *similarity*, and *prediction*.

Base rate refers to prior probabilities, denoted $P(F)$. The base rate group was presented with nine fields of study and asked the following question to elicit $P(F)$. The question read

> Consider all first-year graduate students in the U.S. today. Please write down your best guesses about the percentage of these students who are now enrolled in the following nine fields of specialization.

The nine fields of study were: (1) business administration, (2) computer science, (3) engineering, (4) humanities and education, (5) law, (6) library science, (7) medicine, (8) physical and life sciences, and (9) social science and social work.

The similarity group was presented with a personality sketch of Tom, and then asked a question to elicit $P(D|F)$. The description of Tom read as follows:

> Tom W. is of high intelligence, although lacking in true creativity. He has a need for order and clarity, and for neat and tidy systems in which every detail finds its appropriate place. His writing is rather dull and mechanical, occasionally enlivened by somewhat corny puns and by flashes of imagination of the sci-fi type. He has a strong drive for competence. He seems to have little feel and little sympathy for other people and does not enjoy interacting with others. Self-centered, he nonetheless has a deep moral sense.

The question posed to the similarity group read: "How similar is Tom W. to the typical graduate student in each of the nine fields of specialization?"

The prediction group was given the personality sketch of Tom W., some additional information, and a question to elicit $P(F|D)$. The information and question read

> The preceding personality sketch of Tom W. was written during Tom's senior year in high school by a psychologist, on the basis of projective tests. Tom W. is currently a graduate student. Please rank the nine fields of graduate specialization in order of the likelihood that Tom W. is now a graduate student in each of these fields.

This last task is the central one, asking subjects to form a judgment based on a signal, the description of Tom W.

2.3.2 Bayesian Hypothesis

Bayes rule states that $P(F|D)$ is the product of $P(D|F)$ and the ratio $P(F)/P(D)$. For example, suppose that F is the field of engineering. The term $P(D|F)$ is the probability that an engineering student shares the features in Tom's description. That is, $P(D|F)$ provides a measure for how representative Tom's description is of an engineering student. The ratio $P(F)/P(D)$ provides the relative proportion of engineers to graduate students who share Tom's description.

Suppose that most engineering students conform to the description of Tom, but engineering students are relatively rare in the population. Moreover, suppose that although Tom's description is not especially representative of graduate students in other fields, there are many students who do share Tom's description. In particular, assume that there are far more graduate students who share Tom's description than there are engineering students. In this case, $P(F)/P(D)$ will be a small number. What does this imply about $P(F|D)$, the probability that based on his description, Tom is an engineering student?

$P(F|D)$, being the product of $P(D|F)$ and the ratio $P(F)/P(D)$, will be small, even if $P(D|F)$ is as high as 1. That is, even if the description of Tom fit every graduate student of engineering, the probability that Tom was an engineering student would be small. There are just too many non-engineering students who look like Tom.

2.3.3 Results

Probability judgments that conform to Bayes rule require that base rate information, $P(F)$, be appropriately combined with $P(D|F)$ and $P(D)$. However, judgments based on representativeness overemphasize the representative measure $P(D|F)$. That means that people who rely on representativeness are inclined to underweight base rate information $P(F)$. Is this what Kahneman and Tversky found?

Table 2.1 describes Kahneman and Tversky's experimental results. Notice that the proxies for $P(F|D)$ and $P(D|F)$ are highly correlated (0.97), whereas the proxies for $P(F|D)$ and $P(F)$ are negatively correlated (-0.65). For example, people accord a high rank to Tom's being representative of an engineering student, and they judge it likely that Tom is an engineering student. However, they judge that only 9 percent of graduate students are engineers, well below humanities and education, social science and social work, business administration, and physical and life sciences.

2.4 Representativeness and Prediction

Besides probabilities, Kahneman and Tversky (1973) also discuss the impact of representativeness on judgments involving prediction. This body

TABLE 2.1. Judgments of Similarity and Representativeness

This table presents the mean judged base rate, mean similarity rank, and mean likelihood rank in an experiment conducted by psychologists Kahneman and Tversky relating to field of graduate study. Similarity and likelihood rankings are ordered from 1 to 9, where 1 denotes most similar or most likely and 9 denotes least similar or least likely. The rankings are inverse proxies for $P(D|F)$ and $P(F|D)$ respectively.

Graduate Specialization Area	Mean Judged Base Rate	Mean Similarity Rank	Mean Likelihood Rank
	$P(F)$	$P(D\|F)$	$P(F\|D)$
business administration	15%	3.9	4.3
computer science	7%	2.1	2.5
engineering	9%	2.9	2.6
humanities and education	20%	7.2	7.6
law	9%	5.9	5.2
library science	3%	4.2	4.7
medicine	8%	5.9	5.8
physical and life sciences	12%	4.5	4.3
social science and social work	17%	8.2	8.0

of work serves as the psychological basis for behavioral hypotheses involving long-term overreaction in respect to returns, a topic discussed in Chapter 18. The overreaction hypothesis plays a central role in behavioral finance, and so the present section is important.

The main Kahneman–Tversky prediction studies involved subjects being asked to predict college students' grade point average (GPA), based on a signal (or input). In the first study, subjects received descriptive information from college counselors about individual college students. This information comprised the signal or input. As an example, a subject might be told that a college counselor had described a particular student as "intelligent, self-confident, well-read, hard working, and inquisitive." The subjects were divided into two groups, one called the *evaluation group* and the other called the *prediction group*.

Based on each student description, the evaluation group was asked to estimate "the percentage of students in the entire class whose descriptions indicate a higher academic ability." The prediction group was asked "to predict the grade point average achieved by each student at the end of his freshman year and his class standing in percentiles."

Observe that the two tasks performed by these groups are quite different from each other. The prediction group was asked to make a prediction based on a forecast input or signal. However, the evaluation group was only asked to evaluate an input.

2.4.1   Two Extreme Cases

At the heart of the study is the manner in which subjects predict GPA based on the input information. In order to explain the impact of representativeness, consider two extreme cases. In the first case, counselors' descriptions are thought to be useless as predictors of future GPA. In the second case, counselors' descriptions are thought to be fully informative as predictors of future GPA.

Begin with the first extreme case. Suppose that the mean GPA for freshman students was 3.1. Imagine that subjects were provided with no information about individual students, but were informed that the mean GPA for the freshman class was 3.1. If asked to predict the GPA of a student about whom no information is provided, what would be a sensible prediction? Clearly, it would be 3.1, the mean for the class.

Suppose now that the information content in counselors' descriptions was totally uncorrelated with GPA. In this case, what would be a sensible prediction of GPA, conditional on the description? The prediction should be 3.1, the mean GPA for the freshman class. That is, subjects should treat the description as if they had no information.

Imagine a plot with the percentile scores from the evaluation group on the horizontal axis and the prediction scores from the prediction group on the vertical axis. If the prediction group regarded the descriptions as useless information, then the graph of points associated with the responses of the two groups should form a horizontal line. That is, the prediction group should predict the GPA value to be 3.1, and indicate that 50 percent of the class will do better than the student in question.

The case in which descriptions are treated as completely noninformative corresponds to the case of full regression to the mean. That is, all predictions coincide with the mean.

In the second extreme case, counselors' descriptions are thought to be fully informative as predictors of future GPA. Suppose that the evaluation group is efficacious at translating the counselors' qualitative descriptions into quantitative percentile rankings. In that case, what type of plot should be expected when the percentile predictions of the prediction group are graphed against the percentile responses of the evaluation group? The answer is a 45-degree line. That is because in this case, counselors' descriptions are assumed to be perfect signals of future GPA performance.

In one extreme case, counselors' descriptions are useless signals; in the other extreme case, counselors' descriptions are fully informative signals. Most situations lie somewhere in between. A plot of the predictions from the prediction group against the percentile ratings from the evaluation group should produce a line whose slope lies somewhere between the 0 from the uninformative case and the 1 from the fully informative case.

2.4.2   Representativeness and Regression to the Mean

Someone who relies on representativeness to formulate a GPA prediction for an individual student asks what GPA percentile score most closely matches the input information or signal; in this case the counselor's description. For example, if the input information indicates that 20 percent of the students in the class have higher ability, so that the student's ability lies in the 80th percentile, then a representativeness-based prediction would be for GPA to lie in the 80th percentile.

With the preceding discussion in mind, consider a hypothesis to test whether the prediction group in the study relies on representativeness to form their predictions. The hypothesis would be that a plot of predicted GPA by the prediction group against ability, as measured by the evaluation group, would conform to the second extreme case when the signal is fully informative.

2.4.3   Results for the Prediction Study

Kahneman and Tversky used two versions of the experiment to test their hypothesis. The versions differed in respect to the type of descriptive information characterizing counselors' input. One version used descriptive reports, while the second version used lists of adjectives. In both versions, the resulting plots of GPA percentile predicted against the percentile measuring academic ability were each very close to a 45-degree line. That is, subjects acted as if the counselors' descriptions of academic ability were fully informative about future GPA performance.

2.4.4   Strength of Relationship Between Signal and Prediction

A second study conducted by Kahneman and Tversky provided subjects with an input variable in the form of a percentile, similar in form to the outcome variable, percentile GPA.

Subjects were divided into three groups, and all were asked to predict the GPA for the entire year. The first group was told that the input variable was a GPA percentile for some classes taken in the year. The second group was told that the percentile score was the outcome from a test of mental concentration, and that performance on the mental concentration test was highly variable, depending on such variables as mood and amount of sleep the previous night. The third group was told that the input variable measured sense of humor. This group was also told that students who do well on the test measuring sense of humor tend to achieve high GPA scores. (In fact, sense of humor does not provide a strong basis for predicting future GPA scores.)

The design in this experiment featured identical quantitative data for the three groups. However, subjects in the three groups perceived the strength of the relationship between the input variable and prediction variable differently. The relationship was strongest for the first group, who were told that the input variable measured GPA percentile for some classes taken in the year. The relationship was weakest for the third group, who had been told that the input variable measured sense of humor.

The results from this study showed that subjects' GPA predictions based on sense of humor were more regressive than their predictions based on previous GPA percentile, or mental concentration. This is appropriate, given the weak relationship between sense of humor and future GPA scores. However, the degree of regression toward the mean is insufficient, given the information provided about the weak relationship.

2.4.5 How Regressive?

In order to assess the appropriate degree of regression toward the mean, along with the degree of regression in subjects' predictions, consider an experiment involving real GPA data. In the experiment, subjects were presented with the following question:

> Suppose that a university is attempting to predict the grade point average (GPA) of some graduating students based upon their high school GPA levels. As usual, a student's GPA lies between 0 and 4. Below are some data for undergraduates at Santa Clara University, based on students who entered the university in the years 1990, 1991, and 1992. During this period, the mean high school GPA of students who entered as freshmen and graduated was 3.44 (standard deviation was 0.36). The mean college GPA of those same students was 3.08 (standard deviation 0.40). Suppose that it is your task to predict the college GPA scores of three graduating students, based solely on their high school GPA scores. The three high school GPAs are 2.2, 3.0, and 3.8. Write down your prediction below for the college GPAs of these students upon graduation.

The three high school GPA scores have associated z-values of -3.4, -1.2, and 1.0. That is, 2.2 lies 3.4 standard deviations below the mean of 3.44, while 3.8 lies 1.0 standard deviations above the mean.

The subjects asked to answer the above question were recruited from seven different classes at Santa Clara University, of which three were undergraduate and four were MBA. An additional 41 subjects were recruited from professional investment groups, located in the United States and in Europe. In total, 183 students participated, bringing the number of participants to 224. The mean predictions for the three input values were 2.16,

2.83, and 3.46. These corresponded to z-values of -2.30, -0.63, and 0.95, respectively.

Are the subjects' predictions in this experiment regressive? Notice that the predicted z-values lie closer to zero than the corresponding input z-values. This means that the subjects' predictions were regressive. This stands in contrast to the Kahneman–Tversky results, where subjects treated the input variables as fully informative.

Are the subjects' predictions in this experiment sufficiently regressive? In order to answer that question, consider the relationship between students' high school GPAs and their college GPAs. A regression of college GPA on high school GPA produces an intercept coefficient of 1.27 and a slope coefficient of 0.53. The associated t-values are 17.1 and 24.6, meaning that these coefficients are statistically significant at the 1 percent level. The slope coefficient being less than 1 indicates the degree of regression in the relationship.

Predictions based on the regression equation lead to predicted z-values of -1.61, -0.55, and 0.51, respectively. Notice that the regression-based z-values are closer to zero than the subjects' predicted z-values. This fact indicates that the subjects' predictions are insufficiently regressive. The degree to which predictions are insufficiently regressive can be measured by the ratios of the z-values for the subjects' predictions to the z-values for the regression predictions. These are 1.43, 1.14, and 1.86, respectively. Hence, the z-scores of subjects' predictions were too high by 43 percent at one extreme and 86 percent at the other extreme, but much less in the middle.

2.5   Summary

Psychologists contend that people rely on particular heuristics to form judgments. One of the most prevalent heuristics is known as representativeness. Representativeness involves overreliance on stereotypes. Reliance on representativeness leads people to form probability judgments that systematically violate Bayes rule. Reliance on representativeness also leads people to make predictions that are insufficiently regressive relative to the mean.

3

Representativeness and Bayes Rule: Economics Perspective

Economists were initially skeptical of the Kahneman–Tversky claims that because of representativeness people's probability judgments routinely violate Bayes rule. After all, the subjects who participated in the experiment discussed in the preceding chapter had no incentive to provide accurate responses. Moreover, most questions elicited not explicit probabilities but rankings. In addition, the experimental design was between subjects, so that individual responses were not tested for violations of Bayes rule.

3.1 The Grether Experiment

3.1.1 Design

Economist David Grether (1980) used a well-designed experiment to test the representativeness hypothesis carefully. Although he paid all of his students to participate, he paid some of them an additional amount if they provided accurate responses. This enabled him to test whether representativeness is robust to the effect of incentives.

Grether used an experimental design well suited to the asset pricing models discussed in later chapters. Imagine that time is discrete, and that at each date a drawing takes place from one of two random processes called *regime processes*. Assume a binomial world, so that there are only two possible regime processes, denoted *strong* (S) and *weak* (W). Each regime process gives rise to one of two *outcomes*, respectively called *up* and *down*. The probability attached to an up outcome depends on the prevailing regime process. In the strong regime process, the probability of an up outcome is two thirds, and in the weak regime process, the probability of an up outcome is one half. The regime process is also randomly determined at the beginning of each experimental run. The experiment involved three possible conditions for the probability of a strong regime process: one third, one half, and two thirds.

Grether's experiment involved a random procedure to generate a regime process and a sample from the regime process consisting of a six-element sequence of up and down outcomes. Subjects observed the sequence of outcomes but not the underlying regime process. The actual mechanism made use of cages used to play the game of bingo, with the balls appropriately labeled. There were three bingo cages. The first cage contained six balls, numbered 1 through 6. The second cage contained six balls, of which four were labeled UP and two were labeled DOWN.[1] The third cage contained six balls, of which three were labeled UP and three were labeled DOWN.

Suppose that the probability of a strong regime process is one third. To generate the regime process, the experimenter would draw a number from the first bingo cage. If the number selected was 1 or 2, the regime would be strong and the drawing of the six-outcome sequence would be drawn, with replacement, from the second bingo cage. If the number selected from the first bingo cage was between 3 and 6, the six-outcome sequence would be drawn, with replacement, from the third bingo cage.

The same procedures were used to produce different regime process probabilities. For example, to produce a probability of one half instead of one third, choose the second bingo cage if the number selected from the first cage falls between 1 and 3 instead of 1 and 2.

All subjects in the experiment were briefed on the contents of the three bingo cages, and were informed about the regime process probabilities in effect.

3.1.2 Experimental Task: Bayesian Approach

The subjects in the Grether experiment had one task: to guess the regime process associated with each six-outcome sequence. How would a Bayesian go about this task?

A Bayesian would begin with the prior probabilities, these being the regime process probabilities and associated probabilities for up and down

---

[1] Grether actually labeled the balls N and G, rather than UP and DOWN.

regime processes. There are effectively three prior probability parameters: (1) the probability of a strong regime process; (2) the probability of an up move in a strong regime process; and (3) the probability of an up move in a weak regime process.

A Bayesian would then consider the evidence, that being the six-element sequence of up and down outcomes. Here, the sequence order is irrelevant, and therefore the key variable defining the evidence is the number of up outcomes observed. The Bayesian would then compute the probability associated with the observed evidence, conditional on the regime process being strong, and the probability associated with the observed evidence, conditional on the regime process being weak.

Finally, a Bayesian would use Bayes rule to generate the probability associated with the strong regime process, conditional on the observed evidence. If the probability of the strong regime process was greater than or equal to one half, the Bayesian would guess that the underlying regime process was strong. Otherwise, he or she would guess that the underlying process was weak.

Consider an example. Let the probability of a strong process be one third. Suppose that a Bayesian observes a sequence consisting of 4 up outcomes and 2 down outcomes. How should the Bayesian compute the probability that the underlying process is strong?

Using the notation developed earlier in the chapter, let F correspond to the event that the underlying regime process is strong. Let event D be the event in which the six-element sequence contains 4 up outcomes and 2 down outcomes. The Bayesian would begin by computing the probabilities $P(F)$, $P(D)$, and $P(D|F)$.

The probability $P(F)$ is just the prior, and in this case $P(F) = 1/3$. $P(D|F)$ is the conditional probability that 4 up outcomes and 2 down outcomes will be drawn when the regime process is strong. Since the drawing of ups and downs is accomplished with replacement, $P(D|F)$ is given by the binomial formula

$$P(D|F) = \binom{6}{4}(2/3)^4(1/3)^2 = 0.329 \qquad (3.1)$$

The probability $P(D)$ is unconditional. Event D can occur under both regime processes. As was just mentioned, in the strong regime, the probability associated with D is 0.329. An analogous computation in the weak regime results in a probability of 0.234. Given that the prior probability $P(F) = 1/3$, $P(D)$ is just given by

$$P(D) = (0.329 \times 0.333) + (0.234 \times 0.667) = 0.266 \qquad (3.2)$$

Now the Bayesian is in a position to compute $P(F|D)$, the probability that the true regime is strong, given the evidence that 4 up outcomes were observed.

$$P(F|D) = P(D|F)P(F)/P(D) = 0.329 \times 0.333/0.266 = 0.413 \qquad (3.3)$$

Notice that $P(F|D)$ is less than one half. In other words, the probability attached to the strong regime is less than fifty-fifty. Therefore, the Bayesian prediction should be that the underlying regime is weak.

3.2   Representativeness

Consider next how a person who relies on representativeness would form a judgment about which regime process generated the observed sequence containing 4 up outcomes and 2 down outcomes. The concept of representativeness involves stereotyping, basing judgments on the similarity between the observed sample and the salient features of the parent population.

The salient feature of the strong regime process is that it features a two thirds probability of an up outcome. In Grether's experiment, this is represented by a bingo cage containing four balls with the word UP and two balls with the word DOWN. Moreover, Grether's experiment involves six-element sequences to match the six elements in each bingo cage.

A person relying on representativeness would associate the observed sample sequence of 4 ups and 2 downs with the strong regime process. Why? Because the sample captures the essential features of the parent population. Therefore, a person relying on representativeness to form probability judgments would tend to predict that the underlying regime process is strong.

Notice that the representativeness-based predictions make no use of prior information, such as $P(F)$, the base rate probability associated with the regime process. Instead, they tend to act as if they rely exclusively on $P(D|F)$. As just noted, when F is the strong regime process, $P(D|F) = 0.329$, whereas when F is the weak regime process, $P(D|F) = 0.234$.

Suppose that the observed sequence consists of 3 ups and 3 downs. In this case, a person who relied on representativeness to form probability judgments would predict that the underlying regime process is weak. This is because the sample of 3 ups and 3 downs is most similar to the probabilities associated with the weak regime process.

3.3   Results

Tables 3.1 and 3.2 contain results from Grether's experiment, for the percentage predicting that the underlying regime process is strong. Table 3.1

TABLE 3.1. Results of Grether Experiment: Monetary Incentives

This table presents the mean responses from the Grether experiment for subjects who faced monetary incentives, and predicted the underlying regime to be strong.

Prior Probability for Strong	With Monetary Incentives 33%	50%	67%
School			
Number of up outcomes observed = 3			
Pasadena City College	16%	11%	50%
Occidental College	10%	12%	72%
University of Southern California	0%	5%	68%
California State University, Los Angeles	12%	15%	35%
University of California, Los Angeles	8%	0%	0%
California State University, Northridge 1	3%	23%	58%
California State University, Northridge 2	0%	8%	65%
Mean	7%	11%	50%
Standard Deviation	6%	7%	25%
Coefficient of Variation	88%	70%	50%
Number of up outcomes observed = 4			
Pasadena City College	35%	0%	76%
Occidental College	68%	88%	92%
University of Southern California	55%	73%	5%
California State University, Los Angeles	18%	82%	81%
University of California, Los Angeles	30%	80%	94%
California State University, Northridge 1	48%	55%	0%
California State University, Northridge 2	29%	87%	85%
Mean	40%	66%	62%
Standard Deviation	17%	31%	41%
Coefficient of Variation	43%	47%	66%

displays the results for subjects facing monetary incentives. Table 3.2 displays the results for subjects who did not face monetary incentives. Each table is divided into several sections. The top section pertains to the case when the number of up outcomes observed is 3, while the bottom section pertains to the case when the number of up outcomes observed is 4. Table 3.1 pertains to the case when subjects were paid to be accurate, while Table 3.2 pertains to the case when subjects were not paid to be accurate.

TABLE 3.2. Results of Grether Experiment: No Monetary Incentives

This table presents the mean responses from the Grether experiment for subjects who did not face monetary incentives, and predicted the underlying regime to be strong.

Prior Probability for Strong	Without Monetary Incentives 33%	50%	67%
School			
Number of up outcomes observed = 3			
Pasadena City College	0%	0%	48%
Occidental College	12%	19%	55%
University of Southern California	0%	0%	60%
California State University, Los Angeles	15%	0%	53%
University of California, Los Angeles	6%	0%	64%
California State University, Northridge 1			
California State University, Northridge 2			
Mean	7%	4%	56%
Standard Deviation	7%	8%	6%
Coefficient of Variation	104%	224%	11%
Number of up outcomes observed = 4			
Pasadena City College	59%	83%	91%
Occidental College	45%	77%	87%
University of Southern California	43%	0%	93%
California State University, Los Angeles	50%	70%	90%
University of California, Los Angeles	40%	86%	96%
California State University, Northridge 1			
California State University, Northridge 2			
Mean	47%	63%	91%
Standard Deviation	7%	36%	3%
Coefficient of Variation	16%	57%	4%

Finally, the prior probability associated with a strong regime process was varied, taking the values 33 percent, 50 percent, and 67 percent.

Compare the top and bottom portions of each table for the case when the prior probability associated with the strong regime process is 33 percent, and the sample comprises 4 ups and 2 downs. Recall from the previous discussion that the Bayesian prediction is to predict that the underlying regime process is weak, while the representativeness-based prediction is to predict that the underlying regime process is strong.

Averaging across groups, 40 percent of those who are paid for accuracy predict that the regime process is strong. That is, 40 percent make predictions consistent with representativeness. For groups who are not paid for accuracy, the corresponding figure is 47 percent.

Notice from Table 3.1 that when the sample consists of 3 ups and 3 downs, the proportion predicting that the underlying regime process is strong drops to 7 percent. This is consistent with representativeness, although it is also consistent with the use of Bayes rule. As for the 40 percent plus who predict a strong regime process when the sample consists of 4 ups and 2 downs, they act as if they rely on representativeness but not Bayes rule.

Additional support for the prevalence of representativeness-based predictions comes from the case when the observed sequence consists of 3 ups and 3 downs, and the prior probability associated with the strong regime process is two thirds. The Bayesian prediction in this case is for the strong regime process. Yet only half the respondents who were paid according to their accuracy predicted the strong regime process.

3.3.1   Underweighting Base Rate Information

Grether's study indicates that although people appear to underweight base rate information, they do not completely ignore it. Notice in Table 3.1 that as the prior probability associated with the strong regime process increases, so does the proportion predicting a strong regime process.

What does it mean for people to underweight, but not ignore, base rate information? Consider the conditional probabilities $P(S|D)$ and $P(W|D)$ associated with a six-element sequence denoted by D, where S is the strong regime process and W is the weak regime process. The Bayesian decision rule is to predict S if $P(S|D)/P(W|D) \geq 1$. By Bayes rule,

$$\frac{P(S|D)}{P(W|D)} = \frac{P(D|S)}{P(D|W)} \frac{P(S)}{P(W)} \tag{3.4}$$

which in logarithmic terms is

$$ln(P(S|D)/P(W|D)) = ln(P(D|S)/P(D|W)) + ln(P(S)/P(W)) \tag{3.5}$$

A Bayesian gives equal weight to both terms on the right-hand side of (3.5). However, Grether's empirical findings suggest that representativeness leads people to underweight $ln(P(S)/P(W))$ relative to $ln(P(D|S)/P(D|W))$. For example, someone who relies on representativeness might compute $ln(P(S|D)/P(W|D))$ as a linear combination of

$ln(P(D|S)/P(D|W))$ and $ln(P(S)/P(W))$, using nonnegative weights α_L and α_P respectively, but with $\alpha_L > \alpha_P$. That is, a person who underestimates base rate information might form judgments of $ln(P(D|S)/P(D|W))$ according to

$$ln(P(S|D)/P(W|D)) = \alpha_0 + \alpha_L ln(P(D|S)/P(D|W))$$

$$+ \alpha_P ln(P(S)/P(W)) \qquad (3.6)$$

Grether estimates equation (3.6) for his entire sample using a *logit* regression and reports that the estimate of α_L is 2.08 and the estimate of α_P is 1.69, with the difference of 0.39 being statistically significant at the 1 percent level.[2]

Grether also augments the specification in (3.6) by adding two dummy variables that equal 1 when the six-element sequence features either 3 up outcomes or 4 up outcomes, respectively. The addition of these dummy variables provides extra weight to the coefficient α_L associated with the likelihood ratio $ln(P(D|S)/P(D|W))$ for the two observed sequences that most closely resemble the salient features of the parent populations. Empirically, the coefficients on these dummy variables are statistically significant.

3.4   Summary

What are the general lessons from the Grether study? Many people rely on representativeness to form their probability judgments. In some situations, the reliance on representativeness leads people to violate Bayes rule. Moreover, incentives by themselves do not induce the greater majority of people to form judgments that are consistent with the application of Bayes rule.

---

[2] A reasonable hypothesis is that $\alpha_L > 1$ and $0 < \alpha_P < 1$. However, Grether does not find that this is the case, which is puzzling. He finds $\alpha_p = 1.69 > 1$. Of course, he does find $\alpha_p < \alpha_L$.

4
A Simple Asset Pricing Model Featuring Representativeness

This chapter describes a very simple complete market asset pricing model to illustrate the impact of representativeness described in Grether's experiment.

Imagine a market for two securities, one that pays off in the strong regime process and one that pays off in the weak regime process. These securities can be traded at two dates. The first date occurs at the beginning before any information is revealed. After the first trades, intermediate information is revealed as a *signal*. The six-element sequences in the Grether experiment can be interpreted as signals. A second market is held after the release of the signal.

The key issue in respect to representativeness is how its use affects market prices. This chapter develops a model to identify the channel through which representativeness operates. The discussion proceeds in two stages. In the first stage, a non-signal-based framework is presented and equilibrium asset prices derived. In the second stage, the framework is reinterpreted to bring out the signal-based features.

4.1   First Stage, Modified Experimental Structure

Consider a hypothetical complete market, based on the structure of Grether's experiment.[1] As in the actual experiment, subjects are aware that the experimenter will randomly choose a regime process, and then provide a six-element sequence drawn in accordance with the regime process probabilities. As in the actual experiment, all subjects know the probability associated with the regime process being strong, say one third.

Suppose that the experimenter will eventually reveal the true regime process as well. Therefore, subjects eventually observe the combination of a six-element sequence, followed by the revelation of the true regime process. For example, a subject may observe a six-element sequence with 4 up outcomes, followed by the revelation that the true regime process was strong. Call the combination (j, R) a signal-regime. In the example just described, (j, R) might be $(4, strong)$.

Suppose that at the beginning of the experiment, subjects have the opportunity to purchase claims that pay off in specific signal-regimes. For example, a subject will be able to purchase a claim that pays $1 in the future if the signal-regime $(4, strong)$ occurs. However, the claim pays $0 if some other signal-regime occurs, $(3, weak)$ for example.

Table 4.1 describes the prices for contingent claims. These prices are called state prices (or Arrow–Debreu prices). Notice that there are 15 state prices. In particular, there are 14 date-event combinations, because j can take on any of the 7 values between 0 and 6, and there are two possible regime processes, strong and weak. The 15th state price is fixed at 1, and allows the subject to set aside money at the beginning of the experiment.

Consider a subject with $200 to spend. This subject might put $100 aside, and spend the rest purchasing claims that pay off in the signal-regime $(4, strong)$. Since the state price associated with $(4, strong)$ is $0.0914, and the subject spends $100 on these claims, the subject will receive $1094.09 if $(4, strong)$ actually materializes. (Here, $1094.09 = $100/0.0914.)

4.2   Expected Utility Model

Here is a simple expected utility model that depicts the underlying choice problem. Let c_0 denote the amount the subject sets aside at the beginning of the experiment. Index the 14 signal-regimes from 1 through 14, and let c_κ denote the number of claims that the subject purchases in the signal-regime bearing the index k. Let ν_κ denote the state price associated with

---

[1] An Excel file *Chapter 4 Example.xls* illustrates the example discussed in this chapter. Readers may wish to consult the file after they have read through the chapter.

TABLE 4.1. State Prices

This table presents the state prices in a simple model based on the Grether experiment.

State Prices		
Date 0	$1.00	
	Regime	
j	Strong	Weak
0	$0.0004	$0.0110
1	$0.0046	$0.0658
2	$0.0229	$0.1645
3	$0.0610	$0.2193
4	$0.0914	$0.1645
5	$0.0732	$0.0658
6	$0.0244	$0.0110

the signal-regime bearing the index κ, and set $\nu_0 = 1$. Denote the amount that the subject can spend by W; in this example, $W = \$200$. Since a subject either sets aside money or uses it to purchase contingent claims,

$$\sum_{\kappa=0}^{14} \nu_\kappa c_\kappa = W \qquad (4.1)$$

Suppose that the subject has a logarithmic utility function, which is additively separable over the current payoff c_0 and future payoff c_κ, where signal-regime κ materializes. That is, the subject receives total utility $u = ln(c_0) + ln(c_\kappa)$. Of course, at the time the subject buys claims, he or she does not know exactly which signal-regime will occur. Therefore, the subject spreads the available \$200 in order to maximize the expected value of $ln(c_0) + ln(c_\kappa)$.

Let the probability associated with the signal-regime bearing the index κ be denoted by P_κ. For the sake of uniformity, set $P_0 = 1$, where 0 denotes the current date. Formally, the decision problem can be expressed as choosing $c_0, c_1, \ldots, c_{14}$ to maximize

$$E(u) = \sum_{\kappa=0}^{14} P_\kappa ln(c_\kappa) \qquad (4.2)$$

subject to

$$\sum_{\kappa=0}^{14} \nu_\kappa c_\kappa = W \tag{4.3}$$

To solve for the expected maximizing solution, form the Lagrangean

$$L = \sum_{\kappa=0}^{14} P_\kappa ln(c_\kappa) - \lambda \left(\sum_{\kappa=0}^{14} \nu_\kappa c_\kappa - W \right) \tag{4.4}$$

Differentiation of L with respect to c_κ yields

$$P_\kappa/c_\kappa = \lambda\nu_\kappa \tag{4.5}$$

which can be rewritten as

$$\lambda\nu_\kappa c_\kappa = P_\kappa \tag{4.6}$$

In view of the budget constraint $\sum_{\kappa=0}^{14} \nu_\kappa c_\kappa = W$, we obtain

$$\lambda \sum_{\kappa=0}^{14} \nu_\kappa c_\kappa = \sum_{\kappa=0}^{14} P_\kappa \tag{4.7}$$

Now $P_0 = 1$, and $\sum_{\kappa=1}^{14} P_\kappa = 1$. Therefore,

$$\lambda = 2/W \tag{4.8}$$

which in view of (4.5) implies that

$$c_\kappa = 0.5 P_\kappa W/\nu_\kappa \tag{4.9}$$

4.2.1 Bayesian Solution

A Bayesian subject would use the entries that appear in Table 4.2 for the P_κ values. In this table, the probability associated with $(j, strong)$ is computed as $P(j, strong) = P(strong|j)P(j)$, where $P(j) = P(j|strong)P(strong) + P(j|weak)P(weak)$.

Given the state prices in Table 4.1, and probabilities in Table 4.2, what would a Bayesian expected utility maximizer choose for the c_κ? The answer appears in Table 4.3, and is based on equation (4.9).

Notice that in this solution, the subject sets aside \$100 of his or her \$200 for the current payoff, and spends the remaining \$100 purchasing

TABLE 4.2. Bayesian Probabilities

This table presents the Bayesian probabilities $Pr\{j, regime\}$ in a simple model based
on the Grether experiment.

j	Probabilities Regime Strong	Weak
0	0.05%	1.04%
1	0.55%	6.25%
2	2.74%	15.63%
3	7.32%	20.83%
4	10.97%	15.63%
5	8.78%	6.25%
6	2.93%	1.04%

TABLE 4.3. Consumption Profile

This table presents the consumption profile $c = [c_\kappa]$ in a
simple model based on the Grether experiment.

Consumption plan c Date 0 j	$100 Regime Strong	Weak
0	$120	$95
1	$120	$95
2	$120	$95
3	$120	$95
4	$120	$95
5	$120	$95
6	$120	$95

contingent claims. The subject receives an additional $120 in the future if
the regime process turns out to be strong, and $95 if the regime process
turns out to be weak.

4.3 Equilibrium Prices

Consider a complete market model featuring a representative investor
whose subjective beliefs are determined in accordance with representativeness. How will representativeness influence prices? To answer this question,

reverse the logic in the preceding discussion. Imagine that there is $100 available for the present, and either $120 or $95 available in the future, depending on whether the future regime process is respectively strong or weak. Define ω_κ as the amount available in the signal-regime indexed by k. For example, $\omega_0 = 100$: ω_κ is either 120 or 95. Denote the consumption growth rate as $g_\kappa = \omega_\kappa/\omega_0$ for $\kappa > 1$. That is, g_κ is either 1.2 or 0.95 (corresponding to 20 percent or -5 percent, net).

Now, the question is how to establish the prices $\{\nu_\kappa\}$ in order to induce the subject to choose $c_0 = 100$, $c_\kappa = 120$ if the regime process associated with κ is strong, and $c_\kappa = 95$ if the regime process associated with κ is weak.

To find the requisite state prices, recall that $\nu_0 = 1$ and $P_0 = 1$. Therefore, $c_0 = 0.5W$, implying that $W = 2c_0$. In equilibrium, prices ν induce demand to coincide with supply so that $c_k = \omega_k$. Use (4.9) to obtain

$$\nu_k = 0.5 P_\kappa W/\omega_\kappa = P_k/g_\kappa \qquad (4.10)$$

Solving (4.10) for ν_κ results in the state prices portrayed in Table 4.1.

4.4   Representativeness

Subjects who rely on representativeness rather than Bayes rule have different probability beliefs. Recall that reliance on representativeness leads to different posterior probabilities $P(strong|j)$, and therefore to different probabilities for $P(j, strong)$ computed as $P(strong|j)P(j)$.

Recall from the previous chapter that representativeness leads people to underweight prior probabilities or base rate information relative to the likelihood ratio. Table 4.4 contains the representativeness induced probabilities, derived using (3.6) where $\alpha_0 = 0$, $\alpha_L = 3$, and $\alpha_P = 1$.[2]

Table 4.5 displays probability differences and state price differences, contrasting values in the representativeness-based model against their counterparts in the Bayesian-based model. Differences are measured using log-ratios, with the ratios being values in the representativeness-based model divided by their counterparts in the Bayesian-based model. A log-ratio effectively gives the percentage difference by which the representativeness-based value exceeds its Bayesian counterpart if positive, or falls short if negative. Notice that for $j < 4$, representativeness leads the representativeness investor to underestimate the probability associated with the occurrence of the strong regime process, and for $j \geq 4$ to overestimate

---

[2] For ease of exposition, the dummy variable specification, although providing a better empirical fit, is not used here.

TABLE 4.4. Representativeness-Based Probabilities

This table presents the representativeness-based probabilities $Pr\{j, regime\}$ in a simple model based on the Grether experiment.

Probabilities	Regime	
j	Strong	Weak
0	0.00%	1.09%
1	0.02%	6.78%
2	0.39%	17.98%
3	4.16%	23.99%
4	15.45%	11.15%
5	13.79%	1.24%
6	3.92%	0.04%

TABLE 4.5. Relative Differences Caused by Representativeness on Probabilities and State Prices

This table displays the percentage difference by which probabilities and state prices in the representativeness-based model differ from their respective counterparts in the Bayesian-based model. Relative differences are measured by log-ratios, the natural logarithm of a ratio of a representativeness-based variable to its Bayesian counterpart. A negative value indicates the percentage by which the representativeness-based variable lies below its Bayesian counterpart. A positive value indicates the percentage by which the representativeness-based variable lies above its Bayesian counterpart. Equation (4.10) implies that the respective log-ratio probabilities and log-ratio state prices coincide.

	Log-ratio Probabilities		Log-ratio State Prices	
	Regime		Regime	
j	Strong	Weak	Strong	Weak
0	−482.3%	4.3%	−482.3%	4.3%
1	−339.8%	8.1%	339.8%	8.1%
2	−195.3%	14.0%	−195.3%	14.0%
3	−56.5%	14.1%	−56.5%	14.1%
4	34.2%	−33.8%	34.2%	−33.8%
5	45.1%	−161.5%	45.1%	−161.5%
6	29.3%	−315.9%	29.3%	−315.9%

this probability. Because of equation (4.10), the same comment applies to the corresponding state prices. In this respect, notice from Table 4.5, that the log-ratios for probabilities are identical to the log-ratios for the corresponding state prices.

Notably, representativeness leads the probability associated with the strong regime process to be upwardly biased, at 0.377 instead of 0.333. As a result, the expected value of the future payoff will be upwardly biased for subjects who rely on representativeness.

4.5   Second Stage: Signal-Based Market Structure

Suppose that instead of allowing subjects to purchase all tickets for contingent claims in advance, the market operated a bit differently. In particular, suppose that the contingencies specified in the tickets pertain to the regime process, strong or weak, but not the intermediate information associated with the number of up outcomes (j) in the six-element sequence.

In the second stage, the intermediate information is interpreted as a *signal*. In particular, markets are held at two separate dates, one at the beginning, and one after the signal is revealed but before the actual regime process is revealed.

The prices in the alternative market structure can be derived from the original contingent claims structure as follows. Holding a claim to \$1 in the event that the regime process is strong is equivalent to holding a package of claims that pay \$1 in events $(1, strong), (2, strong), \ldots, (6, strong)$. Therefore, the price $\nu(strong)$ of such a claim is just

$$\nu(strong) = \sum_{j=1}^{6} \nu(j, strong) \tag{4.11}$$

As for the prices on the intermediate market, consider an example. Suppose that the intermediate information consists of a six-element sequence containing 4 up outcomes. In this case, the only valuable contingent claims are those associated with the date event pairs $(4, strong)$ and $(4, weak)$. Therefore, the relative price of the contract that pays off in $(4, strong)$ is just

$$\nu(strong) = \frac{\nu(4, strong)}{\nu(4, strong) + \nu(4, weak)} \tag{4.12}$$

More generally, after the intermediate signal j, the market price of a claim that pays off if the regime process is strong is given by

$$\nu(strong) = \frac{\nu(j, strong)}{\nu(j, strong) + \nu(j, weak)} \tag{4.13}$$

There is no aggregate consumption in the intermediate market. Therefore, the relevant price information is given by $\nu(strong)/\nu(weak)$. Table 4.6 displays the values of this ratio, conditional on the outcome of j, for both the

TABLE 4.6. Differences in Relative Probabilities and Relative Prices in the Signal-Based Market Structure Model

In the signal-based structure, the log-ratio for probabilities is equal to the log-ratio for prices for the market at $t = 0$. Probabilities and prices for claims to the strong regime are 12 percent higher in the representativeness-based model than the Bayesian-based model, and for claims to the weak regime 7 percent lower. As consumption is 0 at $t = 1$, the key price information is the relative price of a claim to the strong regime relative to a claim to the weak regime. The table shows that for signals 0-3, the probabilities, conditional on the outcome for j, and prices for the strong regime are reduced relative to the weak regime. For signals 4-6, the probabilities, conditional on the outcome for j, and prices for the strong regime are increased relative to the weak regime. Log-ratios indicate the percentage by which relative prices and likelihood ratios in the representativeness-based model exceed, or if negative fall short, of those in the Bayesian-based model.

| | Relative prices | | Log-ratio | Log-ratio Relative |
j	Representativeness	Bayes	Relative Prices	Conditional Probabilities
0	0.0003	0.0348	−486.6%	−486.6%
1	0.0021	0.0695	−347.9%	−347.9%
2	0.0171	0.1390	−209.3%	−209.3%
3	0.1371	0.2780	−70.7%	−70.7%
4	1.0971	0.5560	68.0%	68.0%
5	8.7765	1.1120	206.6%	206.6%
6	70.2117	2.2241	345.2%	345.2%

representativeness-based model and the Bayesian-based model. Table 4.6 also displays the log-ratio of the relative prices in the representativeness-based model to their counterparts in the Bayesian-based model. This log-ratio is effectively the percentage amount by which the relative price in the representativeness-based model exceeds its Bayesian counterpart, if positive, or falls below it, if negative.

Notice that the log-ratio difference is negative for $j < 4$, and positive for $j \geq 4$. State prices on the intermediate market reflect probabilities conditional on the outcome of j. This feature accords with intuition, because signal values from 4 to 6 are more representative of the strong regime than of the weak regime, and vice versa for signal values 0 to 3.

The right-most column in Table 4.6 pertains to differences in likelihood ratios. The likelihood ratio is the conditional probability of a strong regime to the conditional probability of a weak regime, where the conditioning value is j. The log-ratio is the log of the likelihood ratio for the representativeness-based model relative to its Bayesian counterpart. Notice that the values in the two right columns are equal to each other. This reflects the fact that state price differences completely reflect differences in probability beliefs.

4.6   Sentiment, State Prices, and the Pricing Kernel

The simple model described in this chapter provides a foretaste of the key ideas developed in the book. The key ideas involve the concept of sentiment, and the impact of sentiment on market prices.

The log-ratio probability columns displayed in Tables 4.5 and 4.6 describe the percentage probability errors induced by representativeness relative to the Bayesian case. Technically, these log-ratio probabilities constitute a log-change of measure. In behavioral finance, errors in judgment associated with market outcomes are called "sentiment." Notice that sentiment is a function. In Table 4.5, it is a function of the $(j, regime)$ pairs, and in Table 4.6, it is a function of j. For example, Table 4.5 indicates that representativeness leads the probability associated with $(0, strong)$ to be 482.3 percent too low relative to its Bayesian counterpart. Table 4.6 indicates that representativeness leads the probability of the strong regime, conditional on $j = 0$, to be 486.6 percent too low in the representativeness-based model relative to the corresponding Bayesian model.

Figure 4.1 displays the values for sentiment associated with Table 4.6. Notice that the function is increasing and linear in the signal. Linearity stems from the Grether equation (3.6). The positive slope is an indication of excessive pessimism for signal values below 4 and excessive optimism for signal values equal to 4 or more.

Consider next the manner in which probability errors impact prices, relative to the Bayesian-based model. Table 4.6 tells us that if the value of the signal j is 0, then on the intermediate market the relative price for a claim to the strong regime is 486.6 percent less in the representativeness-based model than in the corresponding Bayesian model. On the other hand, if the value of the signal is 6, then the relative price for a claim to the strong regime is 345.2 percent higher in the representativeness-based model than in the corresponding Bayesian model.

As the text to Table 4.6 indicates, the price for a claim to the strong regime on the initial market is 12 percent higher in the representativeness-based model than its Bayesian counterpart, while for a claim to the weak regime the price is 7 percent less in the representativeness-based model than its Bayesian counterpart. These values reflect the fact that the representative investor overweights the probability attached to the strong regime, and is therefore excessively optimistic on the initial market. However, as discussed above, a signal below 4 at the intermediate date will induce the representative investor to become excessively pessimistic. Figure 4.1 effectively implies that representativeness causes market prices on the intermediate date market to be excessively volatile; reflecting excessive optimism for signal values of 4 or more, and excessively pessimistic for signal values below 4.

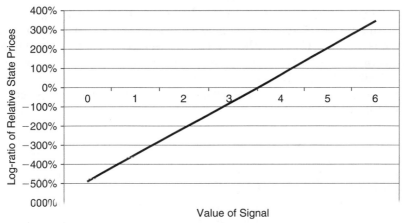

Sentiment Function
Log-ratio of conditional likelihoods in representativeness-based model to their
counterparts in the Bayesian-based model as a function of the signal value j

FIGURE 4.1. This figure displays the log-ratio function for two likelihood functions. The top likelihood is the ratio $Pr\{strong|j\}/Pr\{weak|j\}$, where the probabilities are associated with the representativeness-based model. The bottom likelihood is the ratio $Pr\{strong|j\}/Pr\{weak|j\}$, where the probabilities are associated with the Bayesian-based model. The log ratio is the natural logarithm of the ratio of these two likelihoods. The log-ratio is a measure of sentiment, the errors in probability. By definition, the zero error case occurs when the representative investor's probabilities satisfy Bayes rule.

The Bayesian-based model represents the situation when information is processed efficiently. As a result, the state prices associated with the Bayesian-based model can be termed efficient. In contrast, the state prices associated with the representativeness-based model can be termed inefficient.

Tables 4.5 and 4.6 tell us about the degree to which representativeness causes state prices to be inefficient. The tables also tell us that in this model, the root cause of the inefficiency is sentiment. In particular, for both tables, the log-ratio state price columns are exactly equal to the log-ratio probability columns which measure sentiment. The tables demonstrate exactly how the Grether representativeness equation (3.6) impacts equilibrium prices.

Consider equation (4.10). Let the symbol Π_κ be the value of P_κ for the Bayesian-based model. The ratio ν_κ/Π_κ is known as a pricing kernel and measures state price per unit probability, where the probability is correctly measured. In the representativeness-based model, the prices on the initial market for unit claims to strong and weak regimes respectively are \$0.31 and \$0.66. However, the weak regime is twice as likely to occur as the strong regime. On a per unit probability basis, the prices are much closer to each other, $0.94 and $0.98 respectively, although the claims to the weak regime are still higher than to the strong regime.

Equation (4.10) implies that in the Bayesian-based model, the pricing kernel function is $1/g_\kappa$, where g_κ is the growth rate in gross aggregate consumption. Call this the fundamental-based pricing kernel. In the representativeness-based model equation (4.10) implies that the pricing kernel is given by $(P_\kappa/\Pi_\kappa)/g_\kappa$.

For the models described in this chapter, the log of the pricing kernel, denoted by m, is given by

$$m = \ln(P_\kappa/\Pi_\kappa) - \ln(g_\kappa) \qquad (4.14)$$

That is, the log of the pricing kernel is equal to the sum of sentiment and log of the fundamental-based pricing kernel.

Equation (4.14) illustrates the most important equation in the book, that the log-pricing kernel is the sum of sentiment and a fundamental component. The reason why the equation is so important is that the pricing kernel underlies the prices of all assets. In behavioral asset pricing theory, the key issue is the degree to which asset prices reflect the sentiment term in (4.14). Indeed, most of the book is devoted to generalizing equation (4.14) for more complex models, including those that involve both errors in probability beliefs and behavioral preferences.

4.7   Summary

This chapter illustrated the impact of representativeness on equilibrium prices in a simple asset pricing model. In the model, state prices are proportional to subjective probability beliefs. Therefore, errors in probability beliefs are directly transmitted to equilibrium prices.

Bayesian-based beliefs are error-free. Therefore, state prices associated with Bayesian-based beliefs can be viewed as corresponding to fundamental value. The discussion in this chapter demonstrates how representativeness can lead prices to deviate from fundamental values.

The examples in this chapter illustrated the concept of a sentiment function, one of the key variables in the book. The examples also introduced the concept of a pricing kernel, and illustrated the most important relationship developed in the book, that the log-pricing kernel is the sum of sentiment and a fundamental component.

5

Heterogeneous Judgments in Experiments

Heterogeneity is a fact of life. People are different in the way they form judgments. Some form judgments as if they rely on heuristics such as representativeness, while others form judgments as if they use Bayes rule. Even among those who rely on representativeness, the degree of heterogeneity can be wide. The next few chapters focus on heterogeneity of beliefs in situations where people rely on representativeness. The present chapter deals with heterogeneity in the Grether experiment, the Kahneman–Tversky GPA experiment, and a stock price forecast experiment conducted by De Bondt.

5.1 Grether Experiment

The subjects in Grether's experiment were students in six different universities. Moreover, the students were enrolled in different classes. The students at the University of Southern California were enrolled in an upper division course in chemistry. The students at California State University at Northridge were enrolled in a course in logic. The students at the University of California at Los Angeles were students in an introductory economics course.

Looking back at Table 3.1, notice that the students in these different institutions responded differently from each other. For the case in which the sample featured 4 up outcomes and 2 down outcomes, the standard deviation of responses for those students who were paid for accuracy was 17 percent. This produced a coefficient of variation of 43 percent. Students at Occidental College formed judgments most in accordance with representativeness (68 percent), whereas students at California State University, Los Angeles formed judgments least in accordance with representativeness (18 percent).

In studying the heterogeneity in subjects' responses, Grether did not focus on whether a student was enrolled in a particular university or course. Instead, he focused on two variables. First, were subjects paid for accuracy? Second, when a subject made a choice, did he or she already have experience with the conditions of the experiment?

What does experience mean? Each subject faced many sample drawings during the experiment, and therefore made many predictions. Grether classified a subject as experienced in a particular choice situation if the subject had observed the outcome combination produced by the bingo cage drawings in an earlier phase of the experiment.

Grether asked whether some of the heterogeneity in subjects' responses could be explained in terms of financial incentives and subjects' experience. In order to address the issue he estimated equation (3.6) separately for groups differentiated by either financial incentives, degree of experience, or both. He also estimated equations that included dummy variables added to highlight the two cases in which the number of up outcomes j takes either value 3 or 4.

Using a likelihood ratio test, Grether tested whether the regression coefficients associated with the various groups were the same, and concluded that they were not. Statistically speaking, financial incentives make a difference. Incentives reduce reliance on representativeness. Experience also reduces reliance on representativeness, but interestingly only for those who are paid for accuracy.

One last insight that comes from the Grether experiment is that as subjects gain experience with particular outcome combinations, their responses become less variable. The reduction in variability is evidence of fixed behavioral responses. For some subjects the behavior reflects representativeness. For others the behavior reflects beliefs consistent with Bayesian judgments.

Experience and financial incentives explain some of the heterogeneity displayed in the Grether experiment. However, experience and financial incentives only explain a portion of the heterogeneity. The rest is natural variation.

5.2   Heterogeneity in Predictions of GPA

Unfortunately, Kahneman and Tversky do not present the evidence from their GPA prediction experiments in respect to heterogeneous predictions.

As a substitute, consider evidence from the variant of their experiment that uses high school GPA score as the signal or input variable and graduating college GPA as the prediction variable.

Recall the details of the experiment. Subjects were provided with the high school GPA of three students. The GPA scores lay 3.4 standard deviations below the mean, 1.2 standard deviations below the mean, and 1.1 standard deviations above the mean. The subjects' task was to predict these students' college GPAs upon graduation. Had the subjects used the information appropriately, their predictions would have been located, respectively, -1.62, -0.57, and 0.48 standard deviations from the mean. The mean predictions were, respectively, -2.28, -0.61, and 0.95 standard deviations. The conclusion was that representativeness induced predictions that were too extreme.

As was mentioned in Chapter 2, 224 subjects participated in the experiment. Of these, 85 percent predicted too low a GPA score for the student with the lowest signal. In respect to the highest signal, 81 percent predicted too high a GPA score. Of the 224 subjects, 60 percent formulated predictions that were extreme for all three inputs.

Clearly, there is heterogeneity in respect to the GPA predictions. The subjects most experienced with undergraduate GPAs were themselves undergraduate students. Their predictions were more regressive than the predictions of MBA students and the investment professionals. The mean predictions of undergraduate students were, respectively, -2.08, -0.50, and 0.82 standard deviations. Nevertheless, these predictions were insufficiently regressive. Just under half of undergraduates, 43 percent, made predictions that were too extreme in the case of all three input variables.

The input GPA for this case was 3.8, and the maximum possible GPA was 4.0. Therefore, there is an upper bound on the prediction variable. There is also a lower bound of 0 for the predictions, although in practice, graduation typically requires a minimum GPA such as 2.0.

The bounds on the prediction variable, together with the tendency for extreme predictions, suggest that differences of opinion may be widest for the intermediate input value. Yet this does not turn out to be so.

The standard deviation for predictions associated with input values of 3.0 and 3.8 was 0.34. However, the standard deviation for predictions associated with 2.2 was higher, at 0.40. That is, disagreement was strongest at the extreme input value.

Consider the coefficient of variation in respect to the three predictions. The coefficient of variation is the ratio of the standard deviation to the mean. The coefficient of variation, measured across all respondents, was 19.6 percent for the lowest GPA, 10.6 percent for the middle GPA, and 7.7 percent for the highest GPA. The reason why the coefficient of variation is lower for the highest GPA than for the middle GPA is that although both share the same standard deviation, the higher input value features a higher mean prediction.

Disagreement turns out to be widest for the lowest GPA input. Subjects' predictions display the greatest heterogeneity for students with the lowest high school GPA scores. Disagreement is also lowest among undergraduate subjects. Subjects who were MBA students or investment professionals display about the same degree of heterogeneity. Investment professionals provide the least regressive predictions for the low GPA input, and MBA students provide the least regressive predictions for the high GPA input.

As in the Grether experiment, experience serves to mitigate, but not eliminate, the extent of the bias.

5.3   The De Bondt Experiment

Do people predict future stock prices in the same way that they predict future GPA scores? In "Betting on Trends: Intuitive Forecasts of Financial Risk and Return," Werner De Bondt (1993) examines this question. De Bondt's study provides important insights about both reliance on representativeness and heterogeneity in predictions.

5.3.1   Forecasts of the S&P Index: Original Study

De Bondt conducted a study in order to determine how investors form forecasts of future stock returns. In the study, subjects were presented with a series of six stock price charts, with each chart displaying stock prices for a 48-month period. Subjects were then asked to predict the value of these stocks seven months (and again 13 months) after the last price was charted in each series.

The input information is displayed in Figures 5.1 through 5.6. De Bondt chose for his six series six time periods of prices for the S&P 500, with each series suitably scaled in order to mask its identity from subjects. He chose periods that featured the ending points for three bull markets and three bear markets. Table 5.1 provides the ending year for each series, along with an identifier to indicate whether the period conformed to a bull market or a bear market. The years and identifiers were not displayed to subjects.

In order to incentivize his subjects, De Bondt provided a prize for the most accurate predictions. The subjects were students at the University of Wisconsin-Madison. Twenty-seven subjects took part. Some were undergraduate students and some were MBA students. All had taken at least two courses in finance, and were familiar with the tenets of the efficient market hypothesis.

FIGURE 5.1. De Bondt experiment Chart 1.

FIGURE 5.2. De Bondt experiment Chart 2.

FIGURE 5.3. De Bondt experiment Chart 3.

FIGURE 5.4. De Bondt experiment Chart 4.

FIGURE 5.5. De Bondt experiment Chart 5.

FIGURE 5.6. De Bondt experiment Chart 6.

TABLE 5.1. Bull and Bear Markets

This table presents the periods used in the De Bondt (1993) experiment, along with their designations as bull market or bear market.

Designation	Year	Chart	Last Stock Price
Bull	1967	Stock 1	$95.30
Bear	1970	Stock 2	$18.01
Bear	1974	Stock 3	$22.36
Bull	1980	Stock 4	$44.49
Bear	1982	Stock 5	$21.93
Bull	1986	Stock 6	$24.86

De Bondt asked his subjects for both point forecasts and interval forecasts, where the interval forecasts corresponded to an 80 percent confidence interval. Each subject was asked to form low and high forecasts, so that there is only a 1 in 10 chance that the actual price turns out to be lower than his or her low price, and a 1 in 10 chance that the actual price turns out to be higher than his or her high price.

Consider three sets of questions. First, do people tend to forecast future stock prices in a manner that is similar to the way they predict future GPA scores? Do they respond to the information contained in the stock price charts in the same manner as they respond to the information contained in high school GPA scores? In other words, do people tend to extrapolate past price performance in a way that displays insufficient regression to the mean?

Second, do people form assessments of risk by extrapolating the amount of volatility they perceive in the stock price charts? If so, is the amount of volatility they predict different when stock prices are trending up than when stock prices are trending down?

Third, are people's interval forecasts symmetric about their point forecasts? If not, why, and what do nonsymmetric forecast intervals imply?

De Bondt's study provides intriguing answers. First, the majority of subjects forecast future stock prices by extrapolating any trends they perceive in the stock price charts. De Bondt calls this tendency "betting on trends."

Trend following, also known as *extrapolation bias*, stems from representativeness. To see why, consider Figures 5.1 and 5.3. Figure 5.1 features a clear upward trend, while Figure 5.3 features a clear downward trend. A subject who relies on representativeness to predict a future value for the series in Figure 5.1 is apt to ask: For what kind of stochastic process is Figure 5.1 representative? For most subjects, the answer is a series that involves a positive trend. Therefore, in formulating a prediction for the future value of the series in Figure 5.1, a subject is prone to predict that the series displayed in Figure 5.1 will lie above the last value shown. By the same token, a person who relies on representativeness will be prone to predict that the series displayed in Figure 5.3 will lie below the last value shown.

De Bondt calls those who predict continuation "trend followers." He divides trend followers into two groups, weak trend followers and strong trend followers. In extrapolating past trends, strong trend followers predict that the trend will continue through the 7 and 13 months out. Weak trend followers predict a trend 7 months out, but not necessarily 13 months out.

Although there are some similarities between the ways that people forecast GPA scores and stock prices, the analogy is not exact. De Bondt points out that people more readily extrapolate in the case of low GPA scores than they extrapolate stock prices that have been trending downward. About 62 percent of subjects act as trend followers in upward trending series, but only 40 percent act as trend followers in downward trending series.

Second, people do appear to associate wider interval forecasts to stock price histories that have exhibited greater volatility.

Third, people appear to construct interval forecasts that are skewed. For upward trending stock prices, they place their point forecasts closer to the high end of their confidence intervals, while for downward trending stocks they place their point forecasts closer to the low end of their interval forecasts. That is, their confidence intervals feature negative skewness when the stock has been trending upward, and positive skewness when the stock has been trending downward.

De Bondt suggests that people skew their interval forecasts because they are influenced by a behavioral bias known as *anchoring and adjustment.* To understand the bias, think about a boat with its anchor dropped. The anchor keeps the boat from moving too far. This is fine when the boat is moored but problematic if we want to go somewhere. Anchoring bias pertains to computations involving a series of numbers and operations. The bias occurs when an operation begins with a number and then makes an adjustment relative to that number. If the adjustment is too small, then the person is said to be anchored on the number. The psychological bias involves failing to adjust sufficiently from the anchor.

De Bondt hypothesizes that two anchors in the input data affect subjects as they forecast future stock prices. The first anchor is the perceived slope measuring past price changes. The second anchor is the average stock price in the input series. He suggests that people follow a three-step procedure to arrive at their interval forecasts. In the first stage, they apply the rate of past price change to the last price in order to arrive at their point forecasts. In the second stage, they establish a symmetric interval forecast, centered on their point forecasts. In the third stage, they come under the influence of the second anchor, the average stock price, and adjust both points of their interval forecast. In the case of an upward trending series, the second anchor (the average price) lies below the point forecast. This anchor exerts an effect on both the upper and lower boundaries of the interval but not the point forecast. For many predictions, the anchor will lie below the entire interval forecast. In this case, the anchor would pull both the low prediction and the high prediction down. In consequence, the resulting interval forecast would feature negative skewness. Similarly, De Bondt predicts positive skewness associated with the interval forecasts associated with negative trending series.

One of the most important findings in De Bondt's study concerns heterogeneous predictions. Not all subjects extrapolate past trends, thereby predicting continuation. Although most do, a substantial proportion of subjects predict reversals. De Bondt calls those who predict reversals "contrarians." In respect to upward trending series, he found that about 50 percent of subjects act as strong trend followers and about 11 percent as contrarians.

5.3.2   Replication of De Bondt Study

The original De Bondt study involved 27 subjects. The study was replicated using a total of 115 subjects. Some subjects were drawn from undergraduate and MBA classes at Santa Clara University. However, other subjects were drawn from investment firms in the United States and Europe.

The replicated study reinforced the findings in the original study. On average, people predict stock prices from charts by extrapolating perceived trends in the input series. In particular, the return predictions implied by the average point forecasts, and the degree of risk, as implied by the width of the average interval forecasts, suggest that extrapolation bias is at work in respect to both variables.

Tables 5.2 through 5.4 summarize the key findings from the replicated study. As can be seen from Table 5.2, interval forecasts are skewed, and in

TABLE 5.2. Bull and Bear Markets

This table describes the skewness in subjects' interval forecasts in the De Bondt (1993) experiment.

Designation	Chart	Skewness
Bull	Stock 1	−3.3%
Bear	Stock 2	0.3%
Bear	Stock 3	8.3%
Bull	Stock 4	15.5%
Bear	Stock 5	5.3%
Bull	Stock 6	−2.4%
Bull skewness		3.3%
Bear skewness		4.6%

TABLE 5.3. Bull and Bear Markets

This table shows how return predictions in the De Bondt (1993) experiment varied in respect to price change during the prior 48 months.

Designation	Chart	Increase During Prior 48 Months	Expected Return Over Prediction Period
Bull	Stock 1	24.66%	2.4%
Bear	Stock 2	6.63%	4.0%
Bear	Stock 3	−28.26%	−8.8%
Bull	Stock 4	28.58%	0.14%
Bear	Stock 5	5.57%	0.06%
Bull	Stock 6	72.32%	10.12%

TABLE 5.4. Bull and Bear Markets

This table shows how estimates of interval risk in the De Bondt (1993) experiment varied in respect to volatility during the prior 48 months.

Designation	Chart	Volatility During Prior 48 Months	Estimate of Interval Risk During Prediction Period
Bull	Stock 1	22.3%	19.5%
Bear	Stock 2	33.2%	35.2%
Bear	Stock 3	51.6%	43.6%
Bull	Stock 4	45.0%	26.0%
Bear	Stock 5	35.7%	28.0%
Bull	Stock 6	56.1%	31.6%

the predicted direction for all but one stock, stock 4. (The designation *bull market* or *bear market* indicates whether the time period involved was part of a bull market or bear market for the S&P 500 index.)

Professional investors act as trend followers in this study, just as undergraduate and MBA students. However, professional investors' predicted returns are about 70 percent greater than the predicted returns of students, for both upward trending stocks and downward trending stocks. Moreover, the proportion of trend followers to contrarians was considerably higher for those at investment firms. The general group comprised 37 percent trend followers and 16 percent contrarians. The investment firm group comprised 55 percent trend followers and 7 percent contrarians.

Table 5.3 provides some insight into the question of whether predicted stock prices are insufficiently regressive to the mean. Notice that expected returns are highest in absolute value for the stock price charts showing the largest changes rise in past stock prices, stocks 3 and 6. Table 5.4 shows that a similar remark applies to estimates of volatility based on the width of the interval forecasts. The chart featuring the greatest historical volatility also features the greatest forecasted volatility.

The replicated De Bondt study provides some important information about heterogeneity. Disagreement turns out to be stronger after downward trends (bear markets) than after upward trends (bull markets). The average coefficient of variation for bear markets is 19.2 percent, whereas after bull markets it is 18.2 percent. Notably, the coefficient of variation peaks at 23.2 percent in connection with the severe 1974 bear market (corresponding to Figure 5.3). This is an interesting feature, and is taken up again in Chapter 7.

5.3.3   Overconfidence

Recall that in the original De Bondt study, subjects were asked for 80 percent confidence intervals. In particular, subjects were asked to establish their interval forecasts so that there was a 10 percent chance that the actual stock price would exceed their high values, and a 10 percent chance that the actual stock price would fall below their low values.

In the replicated study, subjects were instead asked for a 90 percent confidence interval. If people are well calibrated, then, on average, the actual value will fall within their interval forecasts 90 percent of the time. One of the most robust behavioral findings is that people are typically overconfident about their knowledge when the issues at hand are difficult. Therefore, overconfident people establish interval forecasts that are too narrow. As a result, the true value falls within their interval forecasts less than 90 percent of the time.

The findings in the replicated study demonstrate overconfidence bias at work. The average accuracy rate across the 115 subjects and 6 stocks was 45.7 percent, well short of the 90 percent associated with well-calibrated subjects. The accuracy range across the 6 stocks was quite wide, with a high value of 77.4 percent for stock chart 2 and a low one of 6.1 percent for stock chart 5.

Odean (1998b) argues that overconfidence leads investors to underestimate risk. In the De Bondt study, increased risk in the form of volatility should lead investors to widen their interval forecasts. Therefore, establishing interval forecasts that are too narrow is equivalent to underestimating risk or volatility.

Chapters 16 and 23 make the point that misperceptions of risk affect the shape of the SDF. For this reason, it is important to understand whether investors underestimate risk in practice. This issue is addressed in both Chapters 6 and 7.

5.4   Why Some Commit "Hot Hand" Fallacy and Others Commit Gambler's Fallacy

One of the most intriguing contrasts that De Bondt (1993) offers is between the historical forecasts of individual investors and the historical forecasts of professional investors. Individual investors tend to be trend followers, predicting continuation. However, professional investors tend to predict reversals. This is a key issue in respect to heterogeneity. The next two chapters, 6 and 7, document the evidence.

It is important to understand the reason why some investors predict continuation while others predict reversal. Moreover, there is good reason to believe that both types of investors rely on representativeness, though this sounds puzzling.[1] The present section discusses the puzzle of why some investors predict continuation and other investors predict reversal.

Begin with continuation. Both in Kahneman–Tversky's GPA study and in De Bondt's stock price prediction study, representativeness predisposes people to predict continuation. In both cases, people use representativeness to form a judgment about the most likely *population* from which their sample input is drawn, and then base their predictions on those judgments. For example, in the De Bondt stock price study, people judge that the population from which a negative trending series is drawn also features negative trend. The key issue here is that people use input data to form judgments about the underlying population (or process), and then form predictions in accordance with their judgments about the population or process.

Representativeness leads people to predict reversals when they know something about the process, but to formulate incorrect judgments about the realizations generated by that process. Biased predictions of reversal stem from a phenomenon Kahneman–Tversky facetiously dubbed the "law of small numbers." This law is not a law at all, but an error people make in assuming that small samples feature the same general properties as the parent population from which they are generated. The most common example used to describe the law of small numbers involves short sequences generated from random tosses of a fair coin. Many people hold the intuitive belief that these sequences comprise 50 percent heads and 50 percent tails, with frequent alternation between heads and tails. Yet, the realized sequences that are generated by random coin tosses tend to feature longer runs than most people expect.

---

[1] After reading the last statement, some readers may infer that if representativeness underlies both positive feedback trend following and negative feedback contrarian prediction, then it is surely a vacuous concept. However, one reaches such a conclusion in haste.

Consider a person who observes a fair coin being tossed five times in a row. Suppose that the observed sequence consists of a tail followed by four heads, that is, THHHH. Now the person is asked to predict the outcome of the next toss of the coin. A person who knows that the coin is fair, and relies on representativeness, will view the sequence THHHHT as more representative of a fair coin toss than the sequence THHHHH. Therefore, representativeness would lead the observer to view tails as being more likely on the next toss than heads. This tendency has come to be called "gambler's fallacy." Of course, tails are as likely as heads, not more likely.

To predict tails after a sequence of heads is to predict reversal. A person who knows that the process is 50-50 and relies on representativeness will be prone to predict reversals. A person who does not know that the process is 50-50, but instead uses representativeness to infer the process from the realized history, will be prone to predict continuation. That is, someone who sees many more heads than tails, and does not believe that the coin is necessarily fair, might well conclude that the coin is weighted to favor heads, and predict accordingly.

One of the most interesting applications of representativeness is to basketball. As basketball fans know, basketball players' performances vary from game to game. In some games, players are hot, and miss few of their shots, while in other games the same players miss many more of their shots. Players, coaches, and fans have all observed this "hot hand" phenomenon.

Consider this question: Is a player less likely to miss a basket when he is hot than when he is not? Most people answer yes to this question. However, based on data received from the Philadelphia 76ers, Gilovich, Vallone, and Tversky (1985) conclude that the answer to this question is definitely no. A player is no more likely to sink his next basket when he appears to be hot than he is at any other time.

Why are players, coaches, and fans all vulnerable to the hot hand fallacy? Because they believe that the underlying process governing players' success rates varies from game to game. Therefore, they rely on representativeness to infer the process in place during any particular game. When they see that a player is hot during a game, they are inclined to conclude that the player has a "hot hand" during this particular game. As a result people will conclude that the player will continue to be hot during the game. Representativeness leads people to misjudge the realizations from i.i.d. processes, in that people mistakenly believe that the realizations from i.i.d. processes feature shorter runs than occur in practice.[2] When Gilovich, Vallone, and Tversky presented the results of their study to the Philadelphia 76ers, the team would not accept the conclusion that there is no statistical evidence to support a hot hand phenomenon. It was just too counterintuitive for them. Despite many follow-up studies of the hot hand,

---

[2] The term i.i.d. stands for *independent and identically distributed*.

players, coaches, and fans are adamant in their continued belief that the hot hand phenomenon is real and not a statistical illusion.

A key feature distinguishing situations that promote predictions of continuation from those that promote predictions of reversal is availability bias. When a fair coin is being tossed, the 50-50 likelihood ratio associated with the process is salient. With the GPA prediction exercise and the De Bondt prediction exercise, the input variables are salient, not the underlying process.

The next two chapters describe the prediction errors of individual investors and professional investors. Professional investors are much more aware of the statistical properties of stock prices, such as the Ibbotson charts, than are individual investors. Therefore, professional investors are more prone to have a fixed process in mind than are individual investors. In other words, professional investors are more likely to be like people who knowingly observe a fair coin being tossed, while individual investors are more likely to be like basketball fans. If so, professional investors will be prone to predict reversals (gambler's fallacy), while individual investors will be prone to predict continuation (hot hand fallacy).

The discussion in Section 5.3.2 pointed out that most professional investors who participated in the replication of the De Bondt prediction study were prone to bet on trends, predicting continuation not reversals. Yet many professional investors who perform the exercise indicate that in practice they do not rely solely on 48-month stock price histories to predict returns, but use other information. Their comments suggest that the De Bondt exercise might have an implicit framing feature that induces them to think in a particular way. Chapter 7 discusses evidence pertaining to the return predictions of professional investors where the setting is real rather than hypothetical. As shall be seen, the tendency for professional investors to predict reversals is strong.

5.5   Summary

Heterogeneity characterizes responses in both the Grether study and the De Bondt study. Some of that heterogeneity can be explained by level of experience and the presence of incentives. Both the Grether and De Bondt studies investigate the impact of representativeness on behavior. Notably, representativeness can produce both predictions of continuation and predictions of reversal, depending on the context. Indeed, some subjects in De Bondt's study predicted continuation, while others predicted reversals.

Notably, even after studies, control for experience and incentives, considerable heterogeneity remains unexplained. Even subjects in investment firms displayed heterogeneous behavior, in that some acted as trend followers and others acted as contrarians.

Part II

Heuristics and Representativeness: Investor Expectations

6

Representativeness and Heterogeneous Beliefs Among Individual Investors, Financial Executives, and Academics

The next two chapters present empirical evidence about the return expectations of individual investors, professional investors, financial executives, and academics. The current chapter focuses on individual investors, academics, and corporate financial executives. The next chapter focuses on investment professionals. These chapters are critical to the behavioral approach presented in the book, in that they underlie the assumptions used in the models developed later. In particular, the testable predictions about the shape of the SDF pertain to the distribution of investors' beliefs about return distributions. Different distributions give rise to different shapes of SDF.

Two themes developed in earlier chapters permeate the discussion about investors' return expectations. The first is that investors rely on representativeness when forming return expectations. The second is that there is considerable heterogeneity in respect to investors' expectations: Investors respond to common stimuli in diverse ways.

6.1 Individual Investors

Although the subjects in De Bondt's studies were students, De Bondt also examines the responses of individual investors, as surveyed by the

American Association of Individual Investors (AAII). AAII surveys individual investors weekly in respect to their outlook, asking them to state whether they believe that over the next six months the stock market will be bullish, bearish, or neutral.

6.1.1   Bullish Sentiment and Heterogeneity

The AAII sentiment index is defined as the ratio of bullish responses to bearish responses. Suppose that individual investors base their forecasts on the change in the Dow Jones Industrial Average during the preceding month. That is, they treat the past change in the Dow as a signal. Figure 6.1 is a scatter plot depicting the level of the AAII sentiment index against the change in the S&P 500 for the preceding eight weeks, between June 1987 and December 2003.

Notice the distinct positive correlation between the two series. The correlation coefficient is 0.39. That is, more individual investors become bullish after the S&P 500 has advanced than become bearish, and more become bearish after the S&P 500 has declined than become bullish.

Of course, the AAII sentiment index does not provide investors' predictions for the amount by which the market will advance over the subsequent six months. In this respect, the index measures the degree of heterogeneity in the distribution of bullish sentiment among individual investors.

FIGURE 6.1. Relationship between the degree of bullish sentiment and the percentage change in the S&P 500 during the preceding eight weeks.

6.1.2 The UBS/Gallup Survey

Since 1996 UBS and Gallup Organization have conducted monthly telephone surveys of about 1,000 individual investors in the United States. In order to be included in the survey, investors must have at least $10,000 in household financial assets.[1] In 1998, households with $10,000 or more in financial assets owned more than 99 percent of stocks owned directly or indirectly by U.S. households, more than 99 percent of household financial wealth, and about 95 percent of household net worth.[2]

The UBS Index of Investor Optimism is based on responses to a series of questions about optimism–pessimism regarding an investor's own investment and income outlook, as well as about the stock market and other macroeconomic variables.

The survey collects information about several variables pertaining to expectations and demographics. Of particular interest are questions asking investors about the past 1-year return for each investor's portfolio, along with the return the investor expects for stocks over a 1-year horizon and a 10-year horizon.[3] Responses to these questions are available for June, September, and December 1998, and then monthly from February 1999 to December 2002, with the exception that the expected 10-year market return is not asked in June 1998 or in various months of 2002.

6.1.3 Heterogeneous Beliefs

UBS presents the results of its survey in histogram form, placing the responses of investors into categories, and providing the mean and median of the distribution for those who provide a response. Notably, some investors respond by saying that they do not know.

Figure 6.2 shows the distribution of return expectations for the market, for surveys conducted at year-end for 1998 through 2001. The left-most histogram pertains to 1998, while the right-most histogram pertains to 2001. Notice that the distribution mass shifts right from 1998 to 1999, and then left in 2000 and 2001. An interesting feature shared in common by all

---

[1] Financial assets are defined as "stocks, bonds, or mutual funds in an investment account, or in a self-directed IRA or 401(k) retirement accounts." In 1996, about one in three households qualified as potential participants in the survey based on this criterion, increasing to about 40 percent of households by the start of 2003.

[2] Based on the 1998 Survey of Consumer Finances.

[3] The wording of these questions is as follows: 1. "What was the overall percentage rate of return you got on your portfolio in the past 12 months?" 2. "What overall rate of return do you expect to get on your portfolio in the next 12 months?" 3. "Thinking about the stock market more generally, what overall rate of return do you think the stock market will provide investors during the coming 12 months?" 4. "What annual rate of return do you think the stock market will provide investors over the next 10 years?"

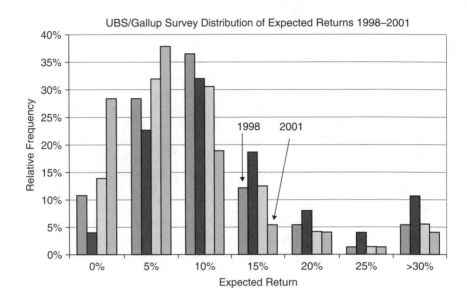

FIGURE 6.2. The distribution of individual investors' return expectations at year-end, 1998–2001, based on the survey conducted by UBS/Gallup.

these distributions is that they are bimodal, with the second mode at the extreme right. This feature plays a part in the discussion about the shape of the SDF in Chapters 16 and 23.

The histogram data are sufficiently detailed to impute both the mean and standard deviation of responses. The standard deviation and associated coefficient of variation describe the extent of disagreement among different investors.

Figure 6.3 shows how the coefficient of variation among investors' forecasts covaries with the level of their expectations and the past 12-month return on the S&P 500 index. Notice that as the return on the S&P 500 declines during the late stages of the 1990s bull market, the coefficient of variation rises. Figure 6.4 displays the same series as a scatter plot. The correlation coefficient between the two series is −0.85. That is, as the S&P 500 declines, the coefficient of variation rises. This feature is consistent with the study results described in Section 5.3.2 of the previous chapter, where the coefficient of variation was higher during bear markets than in bull markets.

6.1.4   Hot Hand Fallacy

Consider investors' expected returns for the stock market over the next 12 months. Do individual investors bet on trends? Do individual investors treat the return on the market during the preceding 12 months as a signal?

FIGURE 6.3. Time series of investors' mean return expectations, coefficient of variation, and return to S&P 500, 1998–2003, based on the survey conducted by UBS/Gallup.

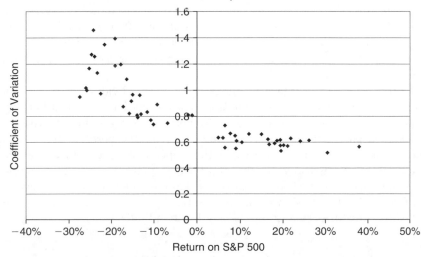

FIGURE 6.4. Scatter plot displaying the relationship between the coefficient of variation in responses to the UBS/Gallup survey and prior returns to the S&P 500.

FIGURE 6.5. Scatter plot displaying the relationship between expected returns in responses to the UBS/Gallup survey and prior returns to the S&P 500.

Is there a statistical relationship between investors' return expectations and the returns on the stock market during the previous 12 months? Figures 6.3 and 6.5 provide the answer. For the period June 1998 through April 2003, Figure 6.3 shows how investors' expected returns covaried with the return on the S&P 500 index over the prior 12 months. Figure 6.5 portrays the same data, but as a scatter plot.

Figures 6.3 and 6.5 both demonstrate that individual investors are trend followers, predicting continuation. The correlation coefficient between expected returns and past returns is 90 percent. A regression of expected returns on past returns features an intercept of 10.6 percent and a slope coefficient of 0.15. The t-statistic of the slope coefficient is 14.7, and the coefficient is statistically significant at the 1 percent level. In contrast, between 1926 and 2002, the autocorrelation coefficient for annual returns on the S&P 500 is 0.05, with an associated t-statistic of 0.45. Therefore, individual investors as a group display hot hand fallacy.

6.1.5   The Impact of Demographic Variables

Vissing-Jorgensen (2004) analyzes individual investors' responses to the UBS/Gallup survey in terms of their expectations for the overall stock market and their own portfolios.[4] Having secured the entire database from UBS, Vissing-Jorgensen supplements the answers to survey questions with background information on age, years of investing experience ("How long have you been investing in the financial markets?"), financial wealth (categorical), and household income (categorical).

Part of her paper focuses on the relationship between differences of opinion and demographic variables such as wealth. For example, Vissing-Jorgensen suggests that incentives may play a role in respect to stated expected returns. In particular, she suggests that investors having higher wealth have more of an incentive to be better informed than investors with lower wealth. Vissing-Jorgensen indicates that the cross-sectional standard deviation of expected 1-year stock market returns is 11.3 percent for those with less than $100,000 in financial assets, compared to 9.2 percent for those with $100,000 or more in financial assets.[5]

6.1.6 Own Experience: Availability Bias

Investors participating in the UBS/Gallup survey provide information about the past performance of their own portfolios. Although such self-reporting offers no control for accuracy, it is nonetheless interesting to ask about the extent to which the performance of their portfolios influences how well they expect their portfolios to perform in the future, as well as the overall market.

Begin with the returns investors expect for their own portfolios. Do investors base the return expectations for their own portfolios on the past returns from those portfolios, or the past returns from the market? Because individual investors tend to hold portfolios that do not coincide with the S&P 500, there is reason to suspect that the past returns from their own portfolios will serve as better predictors of their own future portfolio returns than the past returns from the S&P 500.

Individual investors appear to extrapolate the trends associated with the past returns from their own portfolios. Regression of their return expectations both on the past 12-month return from their own portfolio and on the past 12-month return on the S&P 500 reveals significant positive coefficients on both variables. However, the coefficient for own portfolio is similar to past market return (0.32 vs. 0.34), and is more significant (t-statistic of 7.9 vs. 2.2).

As to the investors' return expectations for the stock market, there is reason to suspect that a similar pattern would hold, except that the past

---

[4] For 1998 and 1999, responses of less than 1 percent (including negative responses) are coded as one category by Vissing-Jorgensen. She sets these values to zero. Furthermore, she drops observations of expected market or own portfolio returns and of own past portfolio returns that are below −95 percent or above 95 percent.

[5] These standard deviations are averages over time of the monthly cross-sectional standard deviations.

return on the S&P 500 would be larger and more significant than the return on their own portfolios. Surprisingly, Vissing-Jorgensen reports that this is not the case. The coefficient on the investor's own portfolio is 0.32 (*t*-statistic of 7.5), while the coefficient on the past return to the S&P 500 portfolio is 0.02 (*t*-statistic of 1.26).

The point is that individual investors appear to form their return expectations for the stock market based on the past returns from their own portfolios. That is, individual investors formulate their expectations from the market based on information that is readily available, because the performance of their own portfolios is salient for them. This tendency introduces the possibility of biased expectations at the level of the individual investor. Kahneman and Tversky refer to this bias as *availability bias*.

6.1.7   Do Individual Investors Bet on Trends? Perceptions and Reactions to Mispricing

Proponents of behavioral finance contend that equilibrium prices do not always coincide with fundamental values. They further contend that the degree of misvaluation might widen before it narrows. Consider this phenomenon in connection with the return expectations of individual investors.

The UBS/Gallup survey includes three questions that pertain to overvaluation. The three questions are:[6] 1. "Do you think the stock market is overvalued/valued about right/undervalued, or are you unsure?" 2. "Over the next three months, do you think the stock market will go up, go down, or remain about the same?" 3. "A year from now, do you think the stock market will be higher than it is now, lower, or about the same?"

Vissing-Jorgensen points out that about 50 percent of investors thought the stock market was overvalued during the last two years of the 1990s bull market. She also reports that fewer than 10 percent thought the market was undervalued. At the same time, only about 20 percent predicted that the market would decline over the short term.[7] Even among those who stated that the market was overvalued in 1999–2000, only about 25 percent predicted that it would decline. A similar pattern obtains for investors having at least $100,000 in financial assets.

---

[6] Here the overvaluation perception is available for most months of the survey since June 1998. The expected three-month market change is available from December 1998 to August 2000, and the expected one-year market change is available for September 1998 and from March 2000 onward.

[7] For the short term, Vissing-Jorgensen uses the three-month horizon from December 1998 up to February 2000, and the one-year horizon when it becomes available from March 2000 onward and for September 1998.

6.2   The Expectations of Academic Economists

Are most academic economists trend followers like most individual investors? Or do they instead rely on academic studies in forming their predictions about the market? In a series of surveys, Ivo Welch (2000, 2001) provides answers to these questions.

The equity premium is the difference between the expected return on stocks and the expected return on bonds of an equivalent horizon. Welch conducted his first survey in late 1997, asking academic economists for their estimates of the equity premium in respect to four time horizons: 1 year, 5 years, 10 years, and 30 years.

Welch's survey provided some background information. The survey stated that as of October 6, 1997, the S&P 500 stood at 965, the Dow Jones Industrial Average stood at 8,040, the 30-year Treasury bond stood at 6.3 percent, and the 3-month Treasury Bill stood at 4.9 percent. The survey also mentions that the well-known Ibbotson historical premium was 8.2 percent. To place the survey into context, Figure 6.6 provides the time series for the Dow Jones Industrial Average for the 30-year period between September 1967 and October 1997.

The results from Welch's survey are intriguing. Welch received 114 responses. For the 1-year horizon, the mean value of the equity premium provided was 5.8 percent. For the 5-year horizon the mean equity premium

FIGURE 6.6. The time series for the Dow Jones Industrial Average, September 1967 – October 1997.

was 6.7 percent, and for the 30-year horizon the mean equity premium was 7.2 percent. Hence, on average, financial economists provided a lower value than the historical Ibbotson figure.

6.2.1 Heterogeneous Beliefs

Figure 6.7 presents the histogram of responses in respect to the 1-year equity premium in Welch's first survey. Notice that there is considerable disagreement among academic economists as to the value of the equity premium. Welch points out that this is a striking finding, given that the equity premium is of fundamental importance in both asset pricing and corporate finance. The standard deviations for economists' responses straddle 2 percent, a little higher for the 1-year equity premium (2.4 percent), and a little lower for the 30-year equity premium (1.7 percent).

Did proponents of behavioral finance have different views than proponents of traditional finance? Did proponents of behavioral finance feature the same degree of disagreement as proponents of traditional finance? Table 6.1 compares the responses of six behavioral economists and six traditional economists. All 12 economists are prominent; all have made

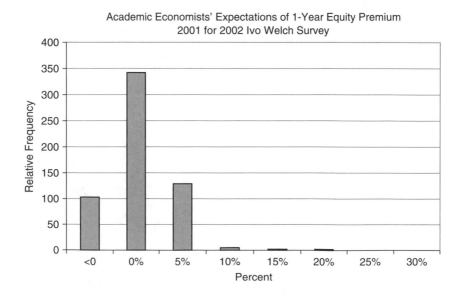

FIGURE 6.7. On the x-axis, 0% signifies the range 0-5%, 5% signifies 5-10%, etc. Distribution of responses to the survey conducted by Ivo Welch of academic economists during 2001. The negative tail is concentrated at three return levels, −2%, −5%, and −10%.

TABLE 6.1. From the Welch (2000) Survey

Contrasting the views of traditionalists and behaviorists in respect to the equity premium: Data from the Welch (2000) survey.

		M1y	M5y	M10y	M30y
Traditionalists	mean	4.5%	4.5%	5.4%	4.1%
	std dev	1.6%	1.9%	1.1%	3.3%
	median	5.0%	4.9%	5.5%	5.2%
	min	2.0%	1.0%	4.0%	−2.0%
	max	6.0%	6.0%	7.0%	7.0%
	sample size	6	6	6	6
Behaviorists	mean	2.7%	2.5%	3.0%	4.3%
	std dev	4.6%	3.8%	4.5%	3.9%
	median	2.0%	2.5%	3.5%	5.0%
	min	−3.0%	−3.0%	−5.0%	3.0%
	max	10.0%	8.0%	8.0%	8.0%
	sample size	6	6	6	6

important contributions to the asset pricing literature.[8] The column headings denote forecasts for the market equity premium, over four time horizons, 1-year, 5-year, 10-year, and 30-year.

Notice that the means for these 12 economists are considerably lower than for the entire sample. Traditionalists feature about the same standard deviations as for the entire sample, except for the 30-year horizon. Traditional asset pricing economists exhibit more disagreement amongst themselves than members of the entire sample.

Behavioral asset pricing economists provide even lower values for the equity premium than traditional asset pricing economists. In addition, they exhibit much more disagreement amongst themselves than their traditional counterparts, and members of the entire sample.

Robert Shiller's responses are among those of the six behaviorists. In 1996, a year before Welch's survey, Shiller (and his colleague John Campbell) had made a presentation to Federal Reserve chairman Alan Greenspan arguing that U.S. stocks were overvalued. A short while later, Greenspan made his famous "irrational exuberance" speech, a topic discussed further in Chapter 22. In 2000, Shiller published a book titled *Irrational Exuberance*.

In October 1997, Shiller's 1-year equity premium was 10 percent. In 1996, a year before Welch's first survey, Shiller's 5-year equity premium estimate was −3 percent, which was also his 30-year equity premium. Interestingly,

---

[8] I thank Ivo Welch for making his databases available to me.

Shiller predicted a high 1-year equity premium, despite his conviction that the market was overvalued. In this respect, his predictions were similar to those of individual investors.

In hindsight, how accurate were Shiller's predictions? In October 1997, the 1-year Treasury note rate stood at 5.46 percent. The 5-year Treasury rate stood at 5.93 percent. The return to the S&P 500 over the subsequent year was 22 percent, while the return to the S&P 500 over the subsequent 5 years was 0.7 percent (measured at an annual rate). Therefore, the 1-year equity premium between October 1997 and October 1998 was 16.5 percent, while the corresponding 5-year equity premium was −5.2 percent.

6.2.2   Welch's 1999 and 2001 Surveys

In late 1998, Welch administered a second survey, receiving back responses beginning in January 1999. He obtained similar responses to those in his first survey. However, the second survey included an interesting additional question. The question read as follows: "Presume that the stock market closed up much higher today, while interest rates remained constant. On the margin, how would today's positive stock market return influence your forecast of the 30-year arithmetic equity premium tomorrow?"

In responding to this question, most economists indicated that their estimate of the equity premium would decline. Presumably, the reason is that a higher price, in conjunction with no significant change in expected future cash flows, implies a lower future return.

In August 2001, Welch updated his survey. Figure 6.8 updates Figure 6.6, depicting the movement of the Dow Jones Industrial Average between November 1997 and August 2001. Notice that the Dow Jones Industrial Average stood at about the same level at the time of the second and third studies.

Welch sent out emails to 3,000 economists, inviting their participation in the third study, and received about 600 replies. Welch focused on the responses of the academic economists, which numbered 510.

Notably, the mean estimates of the equity premium had declined in the interim between the second and third studies. The mean 1-year equity premium declined from 5.8 percent to 3 percent. The (arithmetic) 30-year equity premium declined from 7.2 percent to 5.5 percent. That is, estimates of the equity premium had declined to figures in line with those provided by the behaviorists in the 1997 survey.

As for economists who classified themselves as experts in asset pricing, their estimates of the equity premium were higher than the estimates for the full sample. The 1-year mean for the asset pricing subgroup was 4.2 percent, and the longer-term estimates were higher by 30 to 150 basis points.

Welch asked his 2001 participants if they were more bullish or bearish in 2001 than they had been two or three years earlier. The number who

FIGURE 6.8. The time series for the Dow Jones Industrial Average, November 1997 – August 2001.

admitted to being more bearish was 154, while the number who claimed to be more bullish was 58. There were 214 respondents who claimed to have the same attitudes that they had had in the past.

In 1999, respondents indicated that a continued bull market would lower their equity premium forecasts, and by implication a bear market would raise their equity premium forecasts. Notably, many academic economists responded to the onset of the bear market by extrapolating the recent downward trend in the market, and lowered their estimates of the equity premium at all horizons.

6.3   Financial Executives

Graham and Harvey (2002) find that financial executives engage in trend following, just like individual investors. Their evidence comes from a survey that Duke University and Financial Executives International jointly conducted of chief financial officers (CFOs) during 2000 and 2001. One issue in the survey involves the CFOs' return expectations for the equity premium, the return that they expect from stocks over and above the Treasury Bill rate. It turns out that the higher the market return has been in the prior quarter, the higher their forecasts of the equity premium over the subsequent year. That is, financial executives are prone to predict continuation, just like individual investors.

In regard to optimism, the average financial executive estimated the equity premium to be between 1 and 3 percent. This range is in line with the expectations of academics, but well below the expectations of individual investors.

One of the most important features of the Duke–FEI survey is that it asks CFOs for their estimates of market volatility. Graham–Harvey report that the higher the market return has been in the prior quarter, the lower their forecasts of market volatility over the subsequent year. Notably, the combination of these beliefs leads financial executives to respond as if they believe that at the level of the market, expected returns and risk are negatively related.

6.3.1 Volatility and Overconfidence

As was discussed in Section 5.3.3, overconfidence leads people to establish confidence intervals that are too narrow, thereby leading to underestimates of risk. The financial executives surveyed by Graham–Harvey were overconfident in respect to risk. Typical market estimates for volatility are in the neighborhood of 20 percent. Financial executives' forecasts of volatility were in the neighborhood of 6 to 7 percent. Notably, overconfidence leads people to be surprised more frequently than they anticipated.

6.4 Summary

By and large, individual investors forecast future returns by engaging in trend following and predicting continuation. In this respect they display hot hand fallacy. Moreover, there is significant heterogeneity among forecasts, and the degree of heterogeneity rose as the bull market of the 1990s turned into a bear market during the early 2000s.

As a group, academic financial economists also appear to engage in trend extrapolation, at least in respect to their forecasts of the equity premium. Notably, they too exhibit considerable heterogeneity in their forecasts. Notably, during the late 1990s, proponents of traditional asset pricing appeared to hold very different views about the future equity premium than proponents of behavioral finance. However, as the bull market came to an end, the forecasts of traditional economists moved in the direction of their behavioral colleagues.

Corporate financial executives also engage in trend following, and their volatility expectations are negatively related to past returns. Notably, executives underestimated market volatility.

7

Representativeness and Heterogeneity in the Judgments of Professional Investors

This chapter discusses evidence pertaining to the impact of representativeness on the predictions of professional investors. Like individual investors, professional investors exhibit considerable heterogeneity in their beliefs. However, by and large, the evidence indicates that representativeness causes professional investors to be excessive in predicting reversals.

The data discussed in this chapter derive from three sources: (1) the Livingston survey, (2) *Business Week*, and (3) the television program *Wall Street Week with Louis Rukeyser*.

7.1 Contrasting Predictions: How Valid?

Section 5.4 pointed out that De Bondt (1993) discusses the fact that professional investors are prone to predict reversals. De Bondt bases his conclusions about the behavior of professional investors' forecasts on the Livingston data set. This data set was originally compiled by Joseph Livingston, a journalist at the *Philadelphia Enquirer*. Livingston began the survey in 1946. After his death, the Federal Reserve Bank of Philadelphia took responsibility for maintaining and updating the survey. Until 1989, Livingston surveyed economists for their predictions of the S&P 400 over the subsequent 7 months and the subsequent 13 months.

In his study, De Bondt (1991) examined the 10 most extreme bull markets and bear markets between 1952 and 1989. He concluded that professional investors tended to predict reversals after 3-year trends. For example, during the bull markets of 1980 and 1986, their 7-month forecasts and 13-month forecasts were for market declines. During the bear markets of 1970, 1974, and 1982, their 7-month and 13-month forecasts were for market advances.

In choosing the S&P index for the stock price study discussed in Chapter 5, De Bondt was able to simulate the Livingston survey conditions for the subjects in the stock market study described in the preceding chapter. This clever construction enabled him to contrast the predictions made by his subjects with the predictions made by the professionals who participated in the Livingston survey. For example, he found that although 73 percent of professionals predicted a strong upward trend after a bear market, only 32 percent of the subjects in his experiment did so.

De Bondt concludes that professional investors are inclined to predict reversals and novice investors are inclined to predict continuation. However, this conclusion is difficult to support. As was mentioned in Section 5.4, when professional investors participate in De Bondt's experiment, they too are inclined to predict continuation. Therefore, there is some other factor at work driving the difference in prediction patterns between professionals and novices.

De Bondt acknowledges that, in practice, investors base their predictions on more information than just previous prices. This other information is bound to play a key role in explaining the factors that lead professional investors to predict reversals. And, of course, not all professional investors are inclined to predict reversals. Some predict continuation. Indeed, the remainder of this chapter focuses on the nature of heterogeneous predictions among professional investors.

7.2   Update to Livingston Survey

Beginning in 1990, the Livingston survey began to use the S&P 500 index instead of the S&P 400 index. Figure 7.1 displays the time series for the annual rate of forecasted capital gains associated with the 13-month forecasts, and the actual gains.

Did the Livingston survey forecasts continue to feature predictions of reversal as they had prior to 1990? They most certainly did. A regression of predicted change against prior change reveals a slope coefficient of -0.24 and an intercept coefficient of 0.08. The t-statistic on the slope coefficient is -3.75 and is significant at the 1 percent level. The regression equation implies the following. In order to forecast the 13-month S&P predictions of the professionals participating in the Livingston survey, begin

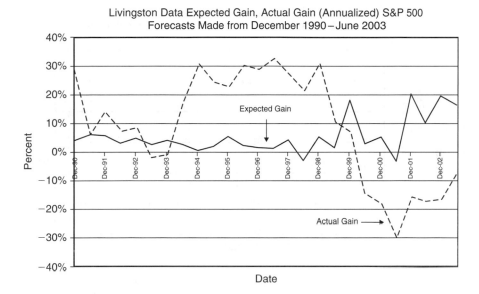

FIGURE 7.1. Time series for Livingston survey forecasts of the annual rate of change in the S&P 500 along with the actual change for the period December 1990 through June 2003.

with 8 percent and subtract 24 percent of the gain in the S&P 500 during the previous 12 months.

Figure 7.2 is a scatter plot displaying the relationship. Notice the striking contrast between Figure 6.5, which shows that individual investors are prone to predict continuation, and Figure 7.2, which shows that professional investors are prone to predict reversal.[1]

7.2.1 Heterogeneity

Figure 7.3 displays the distribution of year-end expected returns from the Livingston survey for 1998–2001. Notice that in three of the four years,

---

[1] Fama and French (2002) analyze the changing nature of the equity premium relative to underlying fundamentals. They point out that realized returns in the period 1951–2000 were much higher than realized returns were in the period 1872–1950. What makes this finding especially interesting is that the underlying fundamentals, dividend and earnings growth, appear to be consistent with realized returns in the early period, but not in the later period. Fama and French recognize that their results can be interpreted as evidence of investor irrationality. However, they suggest instead that rather than irrationality, investors' required returns fell after 1950, thereby leading to a prolonged period of unanticipated capital gains.

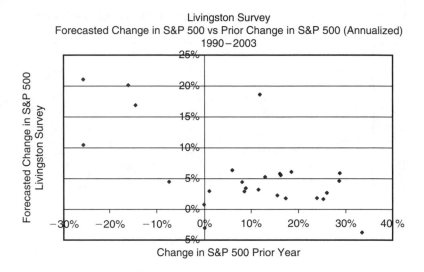

FIGURE 7.2. Scatter plot displaying the relationship between expected returns in responses to the Livingston survey and prior returns to the S&P 500.

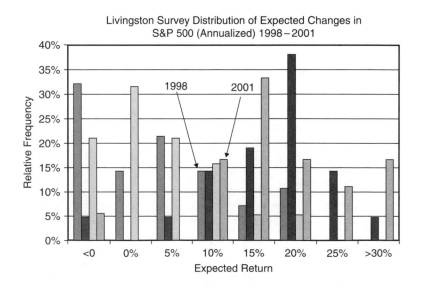

FIGURE 7.3. The distribution of professional investors' return expectations at year-end, 1998–2001, based on the Livingston survey.

the distribution is bimodal. Along with other heterogeneous features, bimodality is an issue that surfaces later in the discussion about the shape of the SDF.

The degree of heterogeneity in the Livingston survey forecasts is evident in Figure 7.3. The coefficient of variation measures the degree of disagreement among the professionals' forecasts. The range in the coefficient of variation is 4.3 percent to 10.8 percent.

Earlier chapters discussed the degree of heterogeneity in the GPA prediction study and the De Bondt stock price prediction study. In the GPA study, the coefficient of variation was a monotone declining function of the input variable "high school GPA." That is, disagreement was wider for students having lower GPA scores in high school than for students having higher GPA scores in high school.

In the replicated De Bondt study, disagreement is stronger after downward trends (bear markets) than after upward trends (bull markets). The average coefficient of variation for bear markets is 19.2 percent, whereas after bull markets it is 18.2 percent. Notably, the coefficient of variation peaks at 23.2 percent in connection with the severe 1974 bear market (corresponding to Figure 5.3).

Figure 7.4 displays the time series for the coefficient of variation in the Livingston survey data, plotted along with the prior gain in the S&P

FIGURE 7.4. Time series of the coefficient of variation in responses to the Livingston survey and prior returns to the S&P 500.

500 over the preceding year. The coefficient of variation is itself variable, but much less variable than the S&P 500. Indeed, the two variables are positively correlated, albeit weakly, with the correlation coefficient being 14.3 percent.

Notice that the coefficient of variation peaks when the gain in the S&P 500 has been extreme. The extremes occur in 1998–1999 and 2001. Indeed, the correlation between the coefficient of variation and the absolute value of the prior gain in the S&P 500 is 57 percent. A regression of the coefficient of variation on the absolute change in the prior gain to the S&P 500 features a slope coefficient of 12.2 and an intercept coefficient of 5.2 percent. The t-statistic for the slope coefficient is 3.4, and the coefficient is significant at the 5 percent level.

In all the studies discussed, disagreement is greater at one of the extremes, if not both extremes. Why is this the case? In order to understand this issue, it is useful to examine the forecasting records of individual professionals.

7.3   Individual Forecasting Records

The Livingston data identify individual forecasters by general affiliation (business, government, and so on) but not by name. *BusinessWeek* magazine has compiled an annual survey of market forecasts, but this survey only began in 1996. Still, the forecasts for the S&P 500 reported in *BusinessWeek* provide supporting evidence for the relationship between the coefficient of variation across forecasts and prior gains. The coefficient of variation for these forecasts rose sharply in 1998 and 2001, from the 9–10 percent range to about 14 percent. Figure 7.5 displays the distribution of return expectations for the *BusinessWeek* survey.

In 1983, the television program *Wall $treet Week with Louis Rukeyser* began to elicit annual forecasts for the Dow Jones Industrial Average from its panel of participants. Figure 7.6 displays the distribution of return expectations for the *Wall $treet Week* panelists. Notice the degree of heterogeneity in both figures, along with the time variation in the distributions. As was mentioned earlier, Chapter 16 discusses the ramifications of both features for the shape of the SDF.

The participants on *Wall $treet Week with Louis Rukeyser* included Frank Cappiello (of McCullough, Andrews & Cappiello) and Mary Farrell (senior investment strategist at UBS/PaineWebber) who provided annual forecasts for the Dow Jones Industrial Average from 1983 through 2001. In 2001 public television terminated the program and it moved to CNBC. Ralph Acampora (director of technical research for Prudential Financial) joined the program's panelists in 1989, and provided forecasts for the Dow Jones Industrial Average every year through 2001.

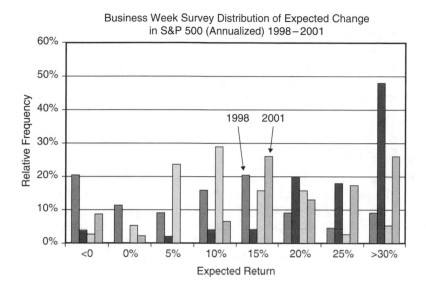

FIGURE 7.5. The distribution of professional investors' return expectations at year-end, 1998–2001, based on the *BusinessWeek* survey.

FIGURE 7.6. The distribution of professional investors' return expectations at year-end, 1998–2001, based on the *Wall $treet Week* panelists.

Cappiello, Farrell, and Acampora were well-known media personalities during the 1990s and the early part of the 21st century. All were frequently interviewed by CNBC. In this section, their forecast histories are presented and analyzed. After presentation of the numerical data, excerpts from their public statements are provided, in order to gain insight into their thought processes in preparing forecasts.

7.3.1   Frank Cappiello

Frank Cappiello is president of an investment counseling firm that manages more than $1 billion in assets, publisher of a monthly newsletter on mutual funds, author of four investing books and regular television guest on CNBC and *Wall $treet Week with Louis Rukeyser.*

At the end of every year, *Wall $treet Week* panelists made three forecasts pertaining to the Dow Jones Industrial Average (DJIA). The forecasts were for its closing value during the next year, its high during the year and its low during the year. Consider the forecasts for the percentage change in the DJIA, based on the closing price at the end of the year in which the forecasts were made.

As will become clear below, Cappiello bases his predictions on a variety of signals. However, for the moment suppose that he were to use just one signal, the percentage change in the Dow Jones Industrial Average during the year just past. Figure 7.7 portrays the scatter plot of Frank Cappiello's (implied) forecasted change against the percentage change in the Dow Jones Industrial Average during the year just past. Notice the negative relationship in Figure 7.7. The correlation coefficient between Cappiello's forecasted change and the actual change is −70 percent.

A regression of Cappiello's forecasted change against the prior change in the index features an intercept coefficient of 12.9 percent and a slope coefficient of −0.35. The *t*-statistic associated with the slope coefficient is −4.1, with the level of statistical significance being 1 percent. That is, Frank Cappiello appears to act as if he forms his forecast of the Dow Jones Industrial Average a year hence by taking 12.9 percent and then subtracting 35 percent of the change in the index during the prior year.

Interestingly, Mary Farrell's forecasts are similar to those of Frank Cappiello, but the impact of the prior year is not as strong. The correlation coefficient between her forecasts and the prior change in the index is −0.38.

Figure 7.8 displays the time series for Frank Cappiello's forecasted change in the DJIA along with the actual change in the DJIA. Notice that between 1987 and 1994, Cappiello forecasted the change in direction of the DJIA accurately. However, from 1995 on, his forecasts were less accurate, frequently moving in the opposite direction from the DJIA.

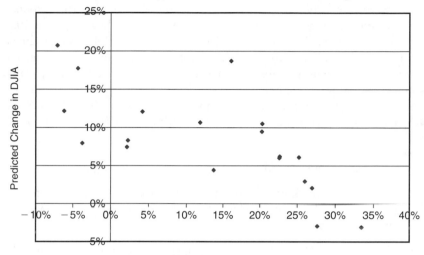

FIGURE 7.7. Scatter plot displaying the relationship between Frank Cappiello's forecasted returns and prior returns to the Dow Jones Industrial Average.

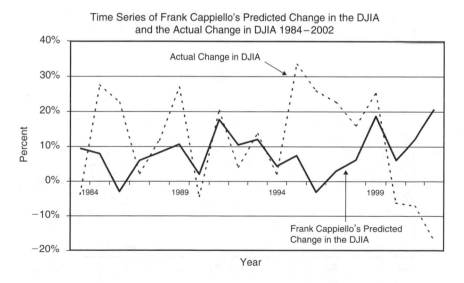

FIGURE 7.8. This figure contrasts Frank Cappiello's forecasted change in the Dow Jones Industrial Average with the actual change in the Dow Jones Industrial Average, for the period 1984–2002.

In order to gain some insight into the factors that Cappiello takes into account when preparing his forecasts, consider some of the responses he provided when being interviewed. The interviews begin in late 1994. Figure 7.9 displays the path of the Dow Jones Industrial Average during the period November 1997 through November 1998. As can be seen in Figure 7.8, Cappiello had forecast that the Dow Jones Industrial Average would increase by 18.7 percent in 1999.

The following interview took place in late November 1998. As you read the discussion, keep in mind that Figure 7.9 provides the context for the discussion.

November 27, 1998, CNNfn, interviewer is Sasha Salama:

SALAMA: It's certainly an understatement to say that the market has just really come back to life since the lows of early last month. What is your take on the sustainability of this market rally?

CAPPIELLO: Well, first a bit of perspective. This market violated all the rules, going down. Without any stops, we had a bear market in eight to nine weeks. And then, with a couple of events occurring, we had a bull market started almost immediately from the bottom of 7500.

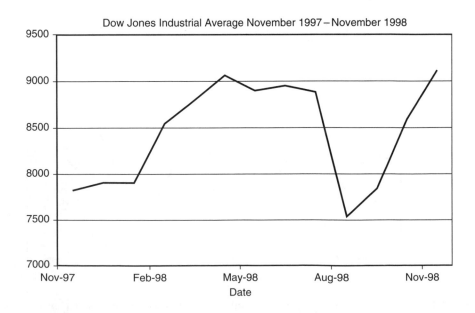

FIGURE 7.9. This figure displays the monthly closing values of the Dow Jones Industrial Average during the period November 1997 and November 1998.

And we'd broken all the rules coming up.

I think we're in a big bull market. The volume is very, very impressive. Price moves are impressive. There is a bit of, you know, mania on the Internet sector, but overall, over the next six or eight weeks, this is a powerful season for the market. Tax loss selling will end. Pension funds will start contributing early next year, massive amounts of funds, so we're in a very, very soft spot right now.

SALAMA: So you do think that this is still a bull market?

CAPPIELLO: Yes.

Notice that Cappiello's bullish forecast of 18.7 percent for 1999 took place against the backdrop of a recent bearish period. In addition, as Figure 7.8 shows, Cappiello's forecasts between 1996 and 1999 climbed as the prior return on the DJIA fell.

At year end 1999, Cappiello forecast that the Dow Jones Industrial Average would increase by 6.1 percent in 2000. His forecast was based, in part, on his views about Federal Reserve Policy. For example, on May 14, 1999, he appeared as a panelist on *Wall $treet Week with Louis Rukeyser*, and stated the market would "continue to go up." In this respect, he indicated that the Fed would not likely raise interest rates unless it perceived a clear increase in the rate of inflation.

As Figure 7.8 shows, although Cappiello forecasted that the Dow Jones Industrial Average would increase by 6.1 percent in 2000, it actually declined by 6 percent. Figure 7.8 also shows that Cappiello's forecasts were off the mark for the next two years.

On November 24, 2000, appearing as a panelist on *Wall $treet Week with Louis Rukeyser*, Cappiello attributed the market downturn to "a slowing economy, earnings warnings," and Federal Reserve policy. He pointed out that the Fed had raised interest rates six times in 2000. Cappiello correctly forecast that the Fed would begin to ease in January 2001. In this regard, he forecast that the stock market would rally twelve months later, with the DJIA going up by 12.1 percent at year end 2001. During 2001, the DJIA fell by 7.1 percent.

Cappiello's prediction for 2002 was for a 20.7 percent increase in the DJIA. Appearing as a panelist on *Wall $treet Week with Louis Rukeyser* on December 28, 2001, he described his position as "bullish," basing his prediction on a strong economy. In particular, he mentioned the Federal Reserve Board's easy money policy, President Bush's tax cuts, and the high level of consumer confidence.

Despite Cappiello's bullish forecast for 2002, the Dow Jones Industrial Average fell by 16.8 percent, the third negative year in a row. In April 2003, the index stood at 8,221.33. At that time, Cappiello predicted that it would reach 10,500 one year later, a 28 percent increase. What was his thought process? A month earlier, he had been interviewed on CNBC. Pay attention to his comments about four bad years in a row, and think about these comments in light of the law of small numbers, a phenomenon at the heart of gambler's fallacy.

March 5, 2003, CNBC, interviewer is Ron Insana.

INSANA: Now, Frank, you're a long-term veteran of environments that have been as tough or, in some cases, maybe even more difficult than this one. After three years, isn't the market ready to go up, or are we essentially, at least in modern times, in uncharted territory?

Mr. CAPPIELLO: Well, we're in somewhat uncharted territory because we've never had a recession, except the Great Depression, that really started with business spending falling off. But that being said, I think the worst period was the '30s, obviously '29 to '32. But after '32, the market never revisited the lows. So those four bad years, you know, never came back in full fury. It was still a difficult time, but we never repeated the lows of '32. I think this time, to think that we'll have four bad years is stretching it. I think we'll get through the summer and see a nice rally in the fall. But I said that last year, too, so. . .

Sadly, Louis Rukeyser passed away in 2006. Before his death, his television show had moved from PBS to CNBC, and became *Louis Rukeyser's Wall Street*. The CNBC version of the program yielded one additional set of panelist predictions, at the end of 2003 for the year 2004. This last set provides us with an opportunity to conduct an out-of-sample test.

The 2003 closing value for the Dow Jones Industrial Average was 10,453, which represented a gain for the year of 15.6 percent. This was above average for the period 1983–2002 associated with the *Wall $treet Week* data set, when the average increase in the Dow was 13.4 percent. If Frank Cappiello was subject to gambler's fallacy, then his 2004 prediction should have been lower than average. If we used the regression of his past forecasts on the percentage change in the Dow from the prior year, we would have forecast that Cappiello's prediction for 2004 would be for an increase of 7.5 percent.

Frank Cappiello's prediction for the Dow was that it would close 2004 at 10,750, an increase of only 2.8 percent. Not only is his prediction below average, it is below the regression-based forecast of his prediction which already reflects his susceptibility to gambler's fallacy.

As it happens, in 2004, the Dow rose by 3.1 percent in 2004, which made his forecast look accurate and masked the underlying bias.

7.3.2   Ralph Acampora

In 1995, the Dow Jones Industrial Average closed the year at 1546.6, having risen 27.7 percent for the year. In 1995, Ralph Acampora boldly forecast that the index would rise to 7,000 within three years. He subsequently predicted that the Dow would hit 11,000 in 1999. In 2003, he indicated that by the end of 2005, the index would break its record of 11,750.27, set in 2000.

Figure 7.10 displays his annual forecasts for the channge in the DJIA, made on *Wall $treet Week with Louis Rukeyser*. Notice that Acampora's forecasts were quite accurate between 1989 and 1992. Ralph Acampora's forecasts are positively correlated with the previous year's change in the Dow Jones Industrial Average, albeit weakly. The correlation coefficient between the two variables is 10 percent. This means that Acampora is inclined to predict continuation, rather than reversal.

What can we learn about Ralph Acampora's thought process? On April 13, 2001, Acampora appeared as a panelist on *Wall $treet Week with Louis Rukeyser*. During that program, Acampora described the key indicators he uses, focusing on the market breadth, the number of stocks advancing versus the number of stocks declining. He concluded by saying that he thought there were good buying opportunities in the market. Indeed, his

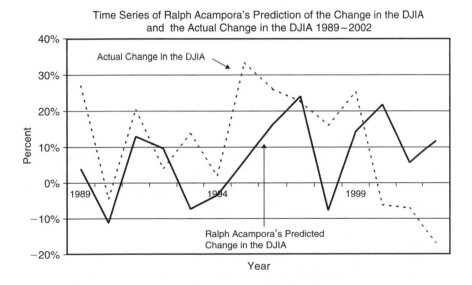

FIGURE 7.10. This figure contrasts Ralph Acampora's forecasted change in the Dow Jones Industrial Average with the actual change in the Dow Jones Industrial Average, for the period 1989–2002.

forecast later that year for 2002 was bullish. As can be seen in Figure 7.10, he predicted that the DJIA would increase by 11.8 percent in 2002.

The following passage provides insight into Acampora's thought process. In the quoted passage, Acampora identifies himself as a "momentum guy," meaning that he engages in trend following when selecting stocks.

August 21, 2002, CNNfn, Acampora was guest host, and Ali Velshi was anchor.

VELSHI: Ralph I want to talk to you about some of your picks. You like IBM.

ACAMPORA: Yes. IBM is in the Dow. As you know, late June early July stabilized. Built that little bit of a base. Not much. But I don't think there's any major supply between here and 100. A stock that has made an all time new high in all of this environment is H&R Block. I'm a momentum guy. I think we're going higher.

VELSHI: I was going to say I haven't heard that word for a while. H&R Block is coming up near its 52 high. We're going to show you a picture of that right now. It's at its 52 week highs almost.

ACAMPORA: Yes it is. Yes. And then the last one is UPS, talking about momentum from the September low of last year. This thing has been chugging along very, very nicely. Even in the throes of the decline in June and July, UPS is acting very, very well. These are three very nice stocks.

VELSHI: From a technical perspective the wisdom of buying stocks at or near their 52 week highs.

ACAMPORA: Fine. If you've got the momentum going for you no problem.

The concept of momentum underlies the positive correlation between forecasts and past changes in the DJIA. The next quotation reinforces Acampora's momentum perspective, extending it from individual stocks to the market as a whole.

May 27, 2003, CNNfn, Acampora was co-anchor with Christine Romans, and interviewing Tim Smalls from S.G. Cowen.

ACAMPORA: When these guys wake up that the market's moving away from them, volume will come in.

SMALLS: I tend to agree to you. I think one of the things we've seen, too is, after the end of the war, we had the initial push up on big volume, very quickly. And since then, we haven't had the pullback and the sell-off that everybody was expecting. I think you'll see portfolio managers and traders getting more and more comfortable with these price levels and as they look at things going forward, the next move, we may see a little bit a pullback just a little consolidation but I think the next big move probably is up to above 9,000.

ACAMPORA: Tim, a lot of us were calling for that pullback. This market doesn't want a pullback in the face of rising gold prices and oil prices. You got to go with momentum, that's your job!

7.4   Gambler's Fallacy

Gambler's fallacy is the tendency to predict reversals too frequently. People who commit gambler's fallacy tend to do so because they believe in the law of small numbers. People fall prey to gambler's fallacy when they rely on representativeness and believe they face mean reverting random processes.

Stock market indexes appear to be mean reverting. In the 53 years between 1949 and 2002, the Dow Jones Industrial Average did not quite behave as a random walk. The index was negatively autocorrelated at (annual) lags 1 and 2, and positively autocorrelated at lags 3 and 4. The autocorrelation for lag 4 was approximately 26 percent, approaching statistical significance. However, this autocorrelation structure does not appear to have been stable. For the period 1983 through 2002, the four autocorrelations were lower than in the full sample, and some coefficients flipped signs.

In order to assess whether Frank Cappiello fell prey to gambler's fallacy, consider the manner in which his forecasts correlate with changes in the Dow Jones Industrial Average at various lags. As previously mentioned, Cappiello's annual predictions feature a significant negative correlation coefficient at lag 1. The correlations at lags 2 through 4 are positive, ranging from 13 percent to 20 percent. Conclusion: Cappiello fell prey to gambler's fallacy.

The majority of panelists on *Wall $treet Week with Louis Rukeyser* fell prey to gambler's fallacy, although in varying degrees. The forecast formed by aggregating the predictions of all the panelists in any given year is negatively correlated with the previous change in the index. The correlation coefficient is −35 percent.

7.4.1   Forecast Accuracy

Ralph Acampora's predictions constitute an exception, though not the only exception. Gambler's fallacy afflicted panelists by about a two-to-one ratio. Heterogeneity prevails even among trend followers.

Consider the question of forecast accuracy. How accurate were the forecasts of Frank Cappiello, Mary Farrell, and Ralph Acampora? Let's take root mean squared error (RMS) as the measure of accuracy. Cappiello's forecast had an RMS of 17.6 percent. Mary Farrell's forecast had an RMS of 22.2 percent.

Ralph Acampora's forecasts had an RMS of 17.7 percent, computed over a smaller sample, 1989–2002. In order to compare Acampora's forecast series with those of Cappiello and Farrell, recompute the RMS of the latter two for the same sample. This leads to an RMS of 15 percent for Cappiello and 17.5 percent for Farrell. Therefore, the predictions featuring gambler's fallacy outperformed the predictions featuring extrapolation bias.

At the same time, a very simple forecasting rule would have outperformed all three, whether computed over the full period or the subperiod. The simple rule involves the prediction that the change in the Dow Jones Industrial Average will be the average annual percentage change for the years 1949 through the current year. This forecast had an RMS of 15.6 percent on the full sample and 14.5 percent on the smaller sample.

The simple forecast outperforms the others because it avoids introducing extraneous noise stemming from overweighting the contributions of the lag structure. Now it is possible to have outperformed the simple forecast rule by making proper use of the lag structure. That would have reduced the RMS by about 1 percent. More important, though, is that the simple rule would have outperformed the professionals, including the average prediction of the professionals.

7.4.2 Excessive Pessimism

Were the *W$W* panelists excessively optimistic, excessively pessimistic, or free from either bias for the overall period? Figure 7.11 depicts the time series for the predicted change in the Dow Jones Industrial Average over the period alongside the actual change.

Notice that the realized series for the Dow lies well above the predicted series. The mean value for the actual series during the period was 11.4 percent. The mean predicted value was 6.2 percent.

In a sense, excessive pessimism is not a surprise. Most of the period featured a major bull market, and panelists fell prey to gambler's fallacy. Therefore, they were overinclined to predict reversals, thereby making pessimistic predictions in respect to future growth. As was discussed earlier, similar statements apply to the Livingston forecasts.

7.4.3 Predictions of Volatility

Section 5.3.3 discussed the fact that overconfidence predisposes investors to underestimate volatility. The difference between panelists' predictions

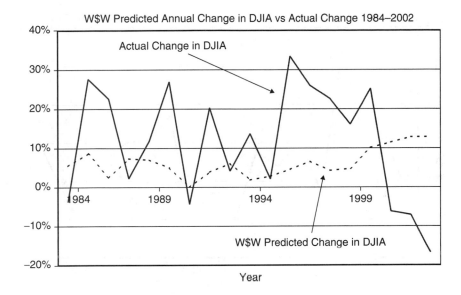

FIGURE 7.11. Time series of average *Wall $treet Week* panelist predictions for change in the Dow Jones Industrial Average and actual change in Dow Jones Industrial.

for the subsequent high and low value of the index serves as a proxy of volatility during the coming year. Do panelists underestimate volatility? In order to answer this question, contrast the actual difference between high and low with the predicted difference.

For the period 1984–2002, the actual annual difference between high and low values was 26.5 percent. The predicted difference was 24.4 percent. In other words, panelists predicted that there would be less volatility than actually occurred. Figure 7.12 displays the time series of predicted volatility and actual volatility.

The analysis in Chapter 16 suggests that the shape of the SDF depends on investor errors about both volatility and expected returns, as well as the degree of heterogeneity associated with those errors. In this respect, consider Figure 7.13. This figure indicates how the coefficient of variation in *Wall $treet Week* panelists' forecasts for the expected change in the Dow Jones Industrial Average behaved relative to the panelists' forecasts for volatility, and past volatility. Clearly, the degree of heterogeneity is strongly related to volatility.

During the period 1950–2002, volatility (measured by the difference between high and low values for the year) was distributed with a mean of 25 percent and a standard deviation of 9 percent. Notably, lagged autocorrelations for volatility changes were significant, with the first order

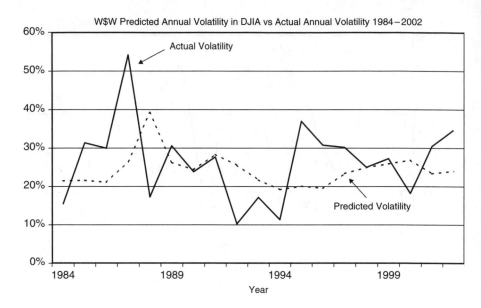

FIGURE 7.12. Time series for predicted volatility for Dow Jones Industrial Average by *Wall $treet Week* panelists and actual volatility, 1984–2002.

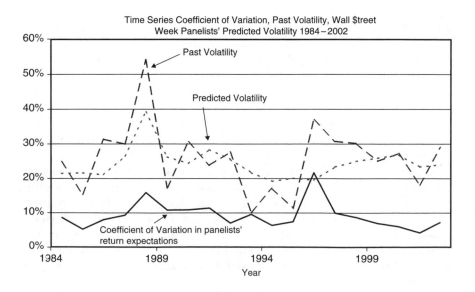

FIGURE 7.13. Time series for predicted volatility for Dow Jones Industrial Average by *Wall $treet Week* panelists, past volatility, and coefficient of variation in panelists' forecasts, 1984–2002.

autocorrelation being −0.41. At the annual level, volatility *changes* appear to depend on own lagged values and the prior change in the index.[2] A regression of volatility changes on these two variables features an R-squared of 0.34. The coefficient on lagged volatility change is −0.35 (*t*-stat equal to −2.88), and the coefficient on the lagged change in the index is −0.34 (*t*-stat equal to −3.49).

Panelists acted as if they understood the variables determining volatility. They acted as if they forecasted volatility changes by using a regression equation based on past lagged volatility and past percentage change in the Dow Jones Industrial Average. This equation features an R-squared of 0.78. The coefficient on lagged volatility change is −0.39 (*t*-stat equal to −5.98), and the coefficient on the lagged change in the index is −0.19 (*t*-stat equal to −2.52).[3]

7.5 Why Heterogeneity Is Time Varying

The earlier discussion about the Livingston forecasts and the *Business Week* forecasts pointed out that the coefficient of variation tends to be positively correlated with the magnitude of the change in the index over the prior year. Sharp moves in the index increase the degree of heterogeneity in forecasts. The purpose of this section is to explain the reason for this relationship.

The coefficients of variation for the forecasts made on *Wall $treet Week with Louis Rukeyser* exhibit a similar pattern as the forecasts for the Livingston data and the *Business Week* data. The two largest values for the coefficient of variation, 15 percent and 21 percent, occurred in conjunction with the forecasts for 1988 and 1996. The forecast for 1988 was made right after the crash of 1987. In 1995 the Dow Jones Industrial Average rose by 33.5 percent, the largest percentage change since 1976.

Frank Cappiello's forecast for 1988 was for an 8.3 percent rise. In 1987, Ralph Acampora had not yet joined the *Wall $treet Week* panelists. However, consider the forecast made by Elizabeth Dater. Like Frank Cappiello, she had been a panel member from the outset. The correlation coefficient between her forecasts and the prior change in the Dow Jones Industrial Average was 0.36. That is, like Ralph Acampora, she too tended to predict continuation. Her forecast for 1988 was for a 12.3 percent decline.

---

[2] Lagged autocorrelations for volatility *levels* were not significant at the 5 percent level.

[3] The panelists' predictions were for the period 1984–2002. During this period, actual volatility changes were not related to past changes in the index. However, the coefficient for past volatility change in a regression equation for volatility change was −0.53 (*t*-statistic of −2.53).

The extreme forecasts for 1987 came from the writers of two newsletters. Robert Nurock, a technical analyst and founder of Investors Analysis Inc., issued the highest forecast for 1988, 36.6 percent. James Grant, the editor of *Grant's Interest Rate Observer*, issued the lowest forecast for 1988, −27.8 percent. Not surprisingly, the correlation coefficient between Nurock's forecasts and the prior change in the Dow Jones Industrial Average was sharply negative, −0.54. The correlation coefficient between Grant's forecasts and the prior change in the Dow Jones Industrial Average was 0.25.

Nurock had an interesting history with *Wall $treet Week*. He was a panelist on the very first program, and eventually designed the program's Technical Market Index, a stock market indicator. That index had been successful during the 1970s and first half of the 1980s. However, it had failed to call the 1987 stock market crash or the 1989 minicrash, and in between had given a "sell" signal in January 1989, before the Dow Jones Industrial Average rallied 500 points. During a program that aired on October 13, 1989, Rukeyser questioned the accuracy of Nurock's index. The two disagreed on the air about the future direction of the market. In some post-program volatility, Nurock resigned from the program.

For 1996, the year after the Dow had risen 33.5 percent, Frank Cappiello had issued a forecast of −3.1 percent. Ralph Acampora had issued a forecast of 16.3 percent. Being a trend follower like Acampora, Elizabeth Dater issued a forecast of 13.6 percent. The maximum forecast was 17.3 percent (John Dessauer), and the minimum forecast was −12.1 percent (Lazlo Birinyi). Not surprisingly, Dessauer's forecasts were positively correlated with the prior change in the Dow, and those of Birinyi were negatively correlated.

The forecast rules used by Frank Cappiello and Ralph Acampora share an important characteristic in common. They are both overly sensitive to past history, and are excessively volatile. When that history features extreme movements, both rules make bold predictions. However, because the coefficients for their rules have opposite signs, their forecasts will tend to be far apart.

7.5.1   Heterogeneity and Newsletter Writers

A counterpart to the AAII sentiment index discussed in Chapter 6 is the sentiment index reported in *Investor's Intelligence* (II). On the basis of stock market newsletters, Chartcraft, Inc. compiles the II index. In the II system, advisor opinion falls into one of three groups: (1) bullish, (2) bearish, or (3) correction. *Investor's Intelligence* reports the percentage of advisors that fall into each group on a weekly basis. The II sentiment index is the ratio of the bullish percentage to the sum of the bullish and bearish percentages.

Clarke and Statman (1997) have identified an interesting property of the II index. High returns over a period of 26 to 52 weeks lead to what they call "nervous bullishness." Bullishness increases, bearishness decreases, but a significant proportion of newsletter writers migrate to the correction group. Specifically, Clarke and Statman report that over short periods of approximately four weeks, an advance in stock prices leads to an increase in bullish sentiment, a decrease in bearish sentiment, and no effect on the proportion of those in the correction group. For longer periods, between 26 and 52 weeks, a stock price advance leads both the proportion of bulls and the proportion of those anticipating a correction to increase.

7.6 Summary

Nature appears to favor heterogeneity, even in the forecasts of professional investors. The degree of heterogeneity in investors' beliefs is nontrivial, and has a time-varying structure that increases with the magnitude of past changes in the index. Why is this the case? The answer is that different investors use different forecasting rules, and these rules are overly sensitive to past changes. Moreover, some rules predict continuation while other rules predict reversals. Therefore, large changes in the index induce extreme forecasts among investors, and many lie in opposite directions.

There are several data sets providing market forecasts by professional investors. The Livingston data set is the oldest. However, the forecasts in that particular data set mask the identity of the forecaster in every year, and are not provided in panel format. One data set providing panel data stems from the television program *Wall $treet Week with Louis Rukeyser.* This particular data set enables three conclusions to be drawn about the general nature of professional investors' market forecasts. (1) Professional investors exhibit gambler's fallacy. (2) Between 1983 and 2002, professional investors were unduly pessimistic, underestimating market returns. (3) Between 1983 and 2002, professional investors underestimated market volatility.

Part III

Developing Behavioral Asset Pricing Models

8

A Simple Asset Pricing Model with Heterogeneous Beliefs

This chapter extends the asset pricing model of Chapter 4 in order to include heterogeneous beliefs. The simplest such model features two agents with different beliefs, trading over time in a market for two securities, a risk free security and a risky security, which can be viewed as the market portfolio. As in Chapter 4, the formal analysis focuses on underlying state prices. The state price model is first developed in this chapter, and then extended to develop the two-securities model in Chapter 10.

8.1 A Simple Model with Two Investors

Consider a financial market with two investors. Time is discrete, with a set of dates indexed $t = 0$ through T. At date 0 an aggregate amount ω_0 is available for consumption by the two investors. At each subsequent date, the aggregate amount available will unfold through a binomial process, growing by either $u > 1$ or $d < 1$. Therefore, at date 1, the aggregate amount available will be either $\omega_1 = u\omega_0$ or $\omega_1 = d\omega_0$. Denote the sequence of up and down moves between dates 1 and t by the symbol x_t. As in Chapter 4, x_t is a *date–event pair*. Define the cumulative growth rate between dates 0 and t by $g(x_t) = \omega(x_t)/\omega(x_0)$.

8.1.1   Probabilities

There are two traders in the model; index these traders by the symbol j, where j is either 1 or 2. Suppose that investor j attaches probability $P_j(x_t)$ to the date–event pair x_t. More precisely, at date 0, investor j attaches probability $P_j(x_t)$ to the occurrence of date–event pair x_t at date t. Because exactly one date–event pair x_t occurs at each date, summing probabilities for each fixed date t requires $\sum_{x_t} P_j(x_t) = 1$.

Later, attention focuses on the structure of these probabilities, in respect to the discussion in prior chapters about the predictions of investors, both individual and professional. However, at this stage the formulation is more generic.

8.1.2   Utility Functions

Suppose that both traders derive utility from consumption, and only consumption. Define $c_j(x_t)$ to be the number of units that investor j consumes at the end of date–event pair x_t. As in Chapter 4, the utility associated with consumption is assumed to be logarithmic. However, unlike with the model in Chapter 4, assume that investors treat the near future as more important than the distant future. Therefore, the utility associated with $c_j(x_t)$ is discounted, using discount factor δ^t, where $\delta \leq 1$. That is, investor j associates utility $\delta^t ln(c_j(x_t))$ to the consumption level $c_j(x_t)$ in date–event pair x_t. (To simplify matters, assume that the two investors share the same discount factor.)

Consider the vector c_j whose components are the values of $c_j(x_t)$ in the various date–event pairs. Call c_j investor j's consumption plan. Investor j is assumed to judge between alternative consumption plans on the basis of their respective expected utilities. The expected utility that investor j associates with consumption plan c_j is just $E(u_j) = \sum_{t,x_t} P_j(x_t)\delta^t ln(c_j(x_t))$.

8.1.3   State Prices

Imagine a contingent futures market that takes place at date 0. The objects of trade on this market are contracts for delivery of consumption, contingent on the occurrence of date–event pairs. Contracts involving delivery of consumption contingent on the date–event pair x_0 are spot contracts, since the market takes place at date 0. All other contracts are contingent futures contracts. Let $\nu(x_t)$ denote the price of a contract that promises delivery of one unit of consumption, should date–event pair x_t occur at date t. Because the key attribute of prices is their value relative to each other, and not their level, without loss of generality, we may set $\nu(x_0) = 1$. In other words, the numeraire is date 0 consumption. Write the vector of state prices as ν, where the components of ν correspond to date–event pairs.

8.1.4 Budget Constraint

Recall that $\omega(x_t)$ denotes the amount of aggregate consumption available in date–event pair x_t. This aggregate amount is jointly held by the two investors. Denote the amount held by investor j as $\omega_j(x_t)$. If the state prices are given by ν, then the value of holding an initial amount $\omega_j(x_t)$ is just $\nu(x_t)\omega_j(x_t)$. Therefore, the initial wealth level of investor j is given by $W_j = \sum_{t,x_t} \nu(x_t)\omega_j(x_t)$.

The budget constraint for investor j states that the value of the claims $\sum_{t,x_t} \nu(x_t)c_j(x_t)$ cannot exceed j's wealth W_j.

To simplify the discussion, assume that the initial holdings of investors vary from the aggregate amounts by a factor of proportionality. That is, $\omega_j(x_t)$ is given by

$$\omega_j(x_t) = w_j\omega(x_t) \tag{8.1}$$

for $j = 1, 2$. Therefore, the initial wealth of investor 1 relative to the initial wealth of investor 2 is w_1/w_2.

8.1.5 Expected Utility Maximization

Investor j faces state prices ν and chooses consumption c_j in order to maximize expected utility subject to the budget constraint. That is, investor j's decision problem involves choosing consumption vector c_j in order to maximize

$$E(u_j) = \sum_{t,x_t} P_j(x_t)\delta^t ln(c_j(x_t)) \tag{8.2}$$

subject to the budget constraint

$$\sum_{t,x_t} \nu_j(x_t)c_j(x_t) \leq W_j \tag{8.3}$$

To solve the optimization, define the Lagrangean

$$L_j = E(u_j) - \lambda_j \left(\sum_{t,x_t} \nu_j(x_t)c_j(x_t) - W_j \right) \tag{8.4}$$

or, substituting for $E(u_j)$,

$$L_j = \sum_{t,x_t} P_j(x_t)\delta^t ln(c_j(x_t)) - \lambda_j \left(\sum_{t,x_t} \nu(x_t)c_j(x_t) - W_j \right) \quad (8.5)$$

Differentiating with respect to $c_j(x_t)$ leads to the first order condition

$$\frac{\delta^t P_j(x_t)}{c_j(x_t)} = \lambda_j \nu(x_t) \quad (8.6)$$

Rearranging (8.6), obtain

$$\lambda_j \nu(x_t)c_j(x_t) = \delta^t P_j(x_t) \quad (8.7)$$

Summing (8.7) over all (t, x_t), and using the fact that for each fixed t, $\sum_{x_t} P_j(x_t) = 1$, leads to

$$\lambda_j \sum_{t,x_t} \nu(x_t)c_j(x_t) = \sum_{t=0}^{T} \delta^t \quad (8.8)$$

Substituting W_j for $\sum_{t,x_t} \nu(x_t)c_j(x_t)$ into (8.8) implies that

$$\lambda_j = \frac{\sum_{t=0}^{T} \delta^t}{W_j} \quad (8.9)$$

Therefore, substituting for λ_j into (8.6) and solving for $c_j(x_t)$, obtain

$$c_j(x_t) = \frac{\delta^t}{\sum_{\tau=0}^{T} \delta^\tau} \frac{P_j(x_t)}{\nu(x_t)} W_j \quad (8.10)$$

8.2   Equilibrium Prices

The most important equation in this book is the equilibrium pricing equation for the case of investor heterogeneity. This section derives a special case of that equation, when there are two investors whose utility functions are logarithmic.

The equilibrium pricing equation involves the state price vector ν. The equation indicates that a state price is a ratio of a discounted probability to the cumulative consumption growth rate. Notably, the state price embodies heterogeneity through the discounted probability. The discounted probability is a relative wealth-weighted convex combination of the individual investors' probabilities.

8.2.1   *Formal Argument*

Consider the formal argument. The condition defining equilibrium is that demand equal supply. For date–event pair x_t, demand is given by the sum of the demands of the individual investors, that being

$$c_1(x_t) + c_2(x_t) \tag{8.11}$$

Supply is given by the aggregate amount available, $w(x_t)$. Use (8.10) to obtain the following expression for aggregate demand:

$$c_1(x_t) + c_2(x_t) = \frac{\delta^t}{\sum_{\tau=0}^{T} \delta^\tau} \frac{(P_1(x_t)W_1 + P_2(x_t)W_2)}{\nu(x_t)} \tag{8.12}$$

Using the equilibrium condition $c_1(x_t) + c_2(x_t) = w(x_t)$, obtain

$$w(x_t) = \frac{\delta^t}{\sum_{\tau=0}^{T} \delta^\tau \nu(x_t)}(P_1(x_t)W_1 + P_2(x_t)W_2) \tag{8.13}$$

Solve (8.13) for $\nu(x_t)$ to obtain

$$\nu(x_t) = \frac{\delta^t}{\sum_{\tau=0}^{T} \delta^\tau w(x_t)}(P_1(x_t)W_1 + P_2(x_t)W_2) \tag{8.14}$$

Define aggregate wealth at $t = 0$ by $W = W_1 + W_2$, and relative wealth w_j at $t - 0$ by $w_j - W_j/W$ for $j = 1, 2$. By construction (see subsection 8.1.4, *Budget Constraint*), w_1 and w_2 are exogenously given.

Define the probability $P_R(x_t)$ as the following wealth-weighted convex combination:

$$P_R(x_t) = w_1 P_1(x_t) + w_2 P_2(x_t) \tag{8.15}$$

Notice that being a convex combination of probabilities, $P_R(x_t)$ is non-negative and for fixed t, $\sum_{x_t} P_R(x_t) = 1$.

Substitution of $P_R(x_t)$ and $W_j = w_j W$ into (8.14) implies

$$\nu(x_t) = \frac{\delta^t}{\sum_{\tau=0}^{T} \delta^\tau w(x_t)} P_R(x_t)W \tag{8.16}$$

By assumption, date 0 serves as numeraire. Therefore, $\nu(x_0) = 1$. Moreover, because there is no uncertainty at date 0, $P_j(x_0) = 1$. Therefore,

$$c_j(x_0) = \frac{1}{\sum_{\tau=0}^{T} \delta^\tau} W_j \tag{8.17}$$

Now $c_1(x_0) + c_2(x_0) = \omega(x_0)$. Therefore, summing (8.17) over $j = 1, 2$ implies

$$\sum_{j=1}^{2} c_j(x_0) = \omega(x_0) = \frac{1}{\sum_{\tau=0}^{T} \delta^\tau} \sum_{j=1}^{2} W_j \tag{8.18}$$

That is,

$$W = \left(\sum_{\tau=0}^{T} \delta^\tau \right) \omega(x_0) \tag{8.19}$$

Substitute (8.19) into (8.16) to obtain

$$\nu(x_t) = \frac{\delta^t P_R(x_t) \omega(x_0)}{\omega(x_t)} \tag{8.20}$$

Since cumulative aggregate consumption growth is defined as $g(x_t) = \omega(x_t)/\omega(x_0)$, (8.20) implies

$$\nu(x_t) = \frac{\delta^t P_R(x_t)}{g(x_t)} \tag{8.21}$$

8.2.2 Representative Investor

Suppose that investor 1 has 100 percent of the wealth. In that case, $w_1 = 1$ and $w_2 = 0$. Therefore, in (8.21), P_R is just P_1. In other words, in the case of a single investor, the state price reflects the investor's probability density functions directly through the equation

$$\nu(x_t) = \frac{\delta^t P_1(x_t)}{g(x_t)} \tag{8.22}$$

In the case of investor heterogeneity, equilibrium state prices are established *as if* there were a single investor whose probability density function corresponds to a wealth-weighted convex combination of both investors' probability density functions.

8.3 Fixed Optimism and Pessimism

Between 1947 and 2003, real personal consumption in the United States grew at the rate of 3.5 percent per year. Mean quarterly consumption growth during this period was 0.87 percent, with a standard deviation of 0.86 percent.

The percentage of quarters that featured positive consumption growth was 91.6 percent. For quarters in which consumption growth was positive, mean consumption growth was 0.95 percent. For quarters in which consumption growth was negative, mean consumption growth was −0.07 percent.

Consider a binomial model that captures the essential features of the consumption growth process. In this respect, let consumption growth g evolve according to a binomial process in which g takes on the values $u = 1.0095$ or $d = 0.9993$. Let the probability associated with an up-move be 0.916, and the probability associated with a down-move be 0.084.

In terms of model heterogeneity, suppose that the two investors agree about the values of u and d, but disagree about the probabilities. In particular, let investor 1 be excessively optimistic, and investor 2 be excessively pessimistic. For example, suppose that investor 1 believes that the probability associated with an up-move is 0.95, and that investor 2 believes that the probability associated with an up-move is 0.85.

If the two investors' levels of initial wealth are the same, then (8.21) and (8.15) imply that the equilibrium state price associated with an up-move at $t = 1$ is based on a probability of 0.90, the wealth-weighted average of 0.95 and 0.85. Moreover, an analogous statement applies to date event pairs occurring for $t > 1$. For example, investor 1 associates a probability of $0.9025 = 0.95^2$ to the occurrence of two consecutive up-moves, while investor 2 assigns a probability of $0.7225 = 0.85^2$ to the same event. The equilibrium state price associated with the occurrence of two consecutive up-moves will be based on the wealth-weighted average of 0.9025 and 0.7225, namely 0.8125.

Figure 8.1 displays the probability density functions associated with a multinomial version of this example when the objective density function, denoted by Π, is approximately log-normal (that is, corresponds to the logarithm of gross consumption growth being normally distributed), and both investors hold beliefs that are approximately log-normal. Viewed from the central area of the figure, the density function furthest to the left belongs to investor 2, the pessimistic (bearish) investor. The density function furthest to the right belongs to investor 1, the optimistic (bullish) investor. There are two density functions between the extremes. One is the density function associated with the equilibrium state prices. The second is the objective density function, the one associated with the true process (in the model) that governs the evolution of aggregate consumption growth.

Figure 8.2 displays the probability distributions for the log-normal example when the differences in beliefs are magnified (by a factor of 10).[1]

---

[1] Magnifying by a factor of 10 is like changing the time horizon from 3 months to 30 months. Therefore, Figure 8.1 can be understood as depicting the representative investor's probability density function associated with short time intervals, while Figure 8.2 can depict the density function associated with longer time intervals.

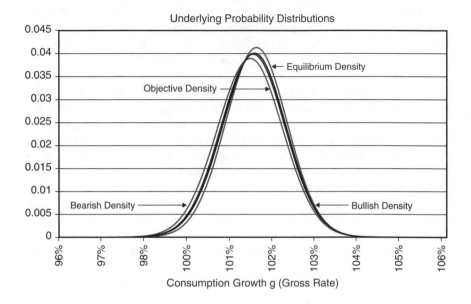

FIGURE 8.1. This figure depicts the four probability density functions in the Chapter 8 example: the bullish density of investor 1, the bearish density of investor 2, the equilibrium density (heavy line), and the objective density.

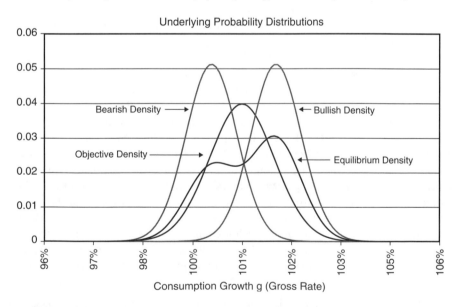

FIGURE 8.2. This figure is an exaggerated version of Figure 8.1, to show the effect of severe disagreement.

This figure brings out the structure of the model more clearly. In contrast to Figure 8.1, where the equilibrium density P_R appears to be close to the objective density Π, in Figure 8.2 P_R is not close to Π. Clearly, P_R is multimodal with fat tails, and does not correspond to a log-normal density function.

8.3.1 Impact of Heterogeneity

Investors 1 and 2 both have binomial beliefs; that is, they both believe that aggregate consumption growth evolves as a binomial process. Therefore, their subjective probability density functions are both binomial. Their density functions share the same general shape, but differ because they use different branch probabilities. Indeed, the true probability density function is also binomial, and because one investor is optimistic and one is pessimistic, the probability mass of the true density function lies between the probability masses of the two investors' density functions.

Equation (8.21) tells us that state prices are proportional to P_R, the objective density function in Figure 8.1. Notice that P_R does not correspond to any of the other three density functions. Most noticeably, the equilibrium price density function is not even binomial. Being a convex combination of binomial density functions, it features fatter tails and possibly more than one local maximum. This property is critical to asset pricing, and is discussed more thoroughly in subsequent chapters.

8.4   Incorporating Representativeness

Investor 1 is always optimistic. Investor 2 is always pessimistic. Think back to Chapter 7, which discussed the market forecasts of Wall Street strategists. Was Elizabeth Dater uniformly optimistic? Was Frank Cappiello uniformly pessimistic?

The answer is no. In the wake of the stock market crash of 1987, Cappiello was optimistic and Dater was pessimistic. However, after the runup in market prices in 1995, Cappiello was pessimistic while Dater was optimistic. This is because Cappiello's forecasts conform to gambler's fallacy, while those of Dater conform to trend following. One's forecasts conform to positive feedback, the other's to negative feedback. As was discussed in earlier chapters, both trend following and gambler's fallacy derive from representativeness, but applied to different initial premises.

In order to model trend following and gambler's fallacy, let investors 1 and 2 both have Markovian beliefs. For example, suppose that investor 1 is a trend follower. Investor 1 believes that the probability that an up-move follows an up-move is 0.95, and the probability that a down-move follows a down-move is 0.15. In contrast, investor 2 believes that the probability that an up-move follows an up-move is 0.85, and the probability that a down-move follows a down-move is 0.05.

Let P_j^* denote the Markov transition matrix associated with investor j. Associated with each P_j^* is an Ergodic (or invariant) distribution, p_j, where $p_j(u)$ denotes the fraction of time spent in up-states. As usual, p_j satisfies $p_j P_j^* = p_j$.

In this example, both p_1 and p_2 are unique, and obtained by solving the equations $p_j P_j^* = p_j$ together with the requirement that the components of p_j sum to unity. In particular, $p_1(u) = 0.944$ and $p_2(u) = 0.864$. That is, on average investor 1 is excessively optimistic and investor 2 is excessively pessimistic.[2]

The Ergodic theorem for Markov chains tells us that the probability that an up-move occurs at date t converges to the Ergodic probability as t approaches infinity. Imagine that at $t = 0$ investor j attaches the (invariant) probability $p_j(u)$ to the occurrence of an up-move at $t = 1$. Using the invariant distribution for the first transition produces a stationary Markov case. That is, the probability that investor j assigns to an up-move at date t will be $p_j(u)$ for every t. In other words, the Ergodic probability applies not just asymptotically, but exactly at all times. However, this means that the probabilities $P_j(x_t)$ conform to an *independent and identically distributed* (*i.i.d.*) process, as in the previous section.

As noted, the representative investor's probability density function is a wealth-weighted convex combination of the individual investors' probability density functions. For example, the probability that investor 1 assigns to two consecutive up-moves is 0.897. Now, 0.897 is just the product of $p_1(u)^2$ where $p_1(u) = 0.944$. In other words, investor 1 acts as if his beliefs were *i.i.d.*, with probabilities given by p_1. A similar remark applies to investor 2. Therefore, the equilibrium density function in this example conforms to a convex combination of binomial density functions. In the numerical example, investor 1 attaches probability 0.897 to the occurrence of two consecutive up-moves during the first two dates, while investor 2 attaches probability 0.734. According to the representative investor's beliefs, the probability of this event is just the wealth-weighted convex combination of the two, which turns out to be 0.816.

Although the example features two investors, it is easily generalized to accommodate an arbitrary number of investors. In this case, the representative investor's probability density function will also be a wealth-weighted convex combination of the individual investors' probability density

---

[2] In this example, the investor who predicts continuation is optimistic, and the investor who predicts reversal is pessimistic. This happens largely because an up-move is more probable than a down-move. It is not true as a general matter that predicting continuation signals excessive optimism and predicting reversals signals excessive pessimism.

functions. The resulting density function can assume many shapes. For example, the representative investor's density function might be quite flat and fat-tailed, a state of affairs that occurs if wealth is uniformly distributed across the population, and investors hold a wide spectrum of beliefs with little polarization. Polarization tends to produce multimodality in the representative investor's probability density function.

8.5   Summary

This chapter presented a simple equilibrium model to analyze the impact of heterogeneous beliefs on equilibrium prices. The model features two investors, each with logarithmic utility. In equilibrium, prices are set as if there is a representative investor whose probability density function is a wealth-weighted convex combination of the individual investors' density functions.

The model can be structured to reflect the major empirical findings described in Chapters 6 and 7, where one investor predicts continuation and the other investor predicts reversal. In this case, the representative investor's probability density function might well be bimodal in respect to long time horizons.

9
Heterogeneous Beliefs and Inefficient Markets

This chapter has two parts. The first part of the chapter is short, describing alternative notions of market efficiency, and then identifying one that is best suited to the ideas developed in this book. The second part of the chapter develops necessary and sufficient conditions for prices to be efficient according to the definition adopted.

9.1 Defining Market Efficiency

Market prices are often described as efficient when they *fully reflect* available information. This description is vague, in that the notion of reflection can be very weak. For example, reflection can be understood to mean that prices do not ignore information, but little more than that.

A major source of confusion in the debate between proponents of market efficiency and proponents of behavioral finance has been the definition of market efficiency. Proponents of efficient market theory have tended to focus on definitions based on the absence of arbitrage. Proponents of behavioral finance have tended to define market efficiency in terms of objectively correct prices, rather than the absence of arbitrage profits.

An example of the confusion can be found in a side-by-side debate conducted on the pages of *The Wall Street Journal* on December 28, 2000. The Journal published two opinion pieces: "Are Markets Efficient?: Yes, Even if

They Make Errors" by Burton G. Malkiel, and "No, Arbitrage Is Inherently Risky" by Andrei Shleifer. A key difficulty with that debate was that the two authors did not subscribe to a shared definition of market efficiency. Shleifer focused on the mispricing of particular securities, whereas Malkiel focused on the absence of abnormal profits being earned by those he took to be informed investors.

In this section, three alternative definitions for market efficiency are discussed, one based on the absence of riskless arbitrage opportunities, a second based on the absence of risky arbitrage opportunities, and a third that requires prices to coincide with fundamental values.

Figure 9.1 displays the cumulative returns between 1988 and 2004 to the three major U.S. market indexes, the Dow Jones Industrial Average, the S&P 500, and the Nasdaq Composite Index. The figure suggests that there was a bubble (in technology stocks) during 1999 and 2000. Consider the following question: Did irrational exuberance on the part of some investors lead technology stocks to be overvalued in the late 1990s? Answering this question requires being precise about what "overvalued" means. Is a technology stock overvalued because its market price lies above

FIGURE 9.1. Cumulative returns to the Nasdaq Composite, S&P 500, and Dow Jones Industrial Average during the period January 1988 through March 2004. The figure assumes that on January 1, 1988 $100 was invested in each market index.

its objective value? Or is a technology stock overpriced when an informed investor chooses not to exploit a perceived profit opportunity?

The preceding questions are different questions. Perhaps both merit attention and discussion. Perhaps it makes better sense to address both questions as separate questions than to become bogged down in a debate over which definition of market efficiency is the more appropriate one.

The discussion below focuses on the first type of question, and examines the nature of divergences between market prices and objectively correct values.

9.1.1   Riskless Arbitrage

In the framework developed in previous chapters, all market securities are priced in accordance with state prices. This condition eliminates the possibility of any investor's being able to earn a nonzero profit through riskless arbitrage. For those who use the absence of riskless arbitrage-based profits as defining market efficiency, prices will always be efficient in the present framework.

9.1.2   Risky Arbitrage

The definition of market efficiency in terms of zero riskless arbitrage profits is weak. A stronger definition is to assume that there are no nonzero profits to be earned from risky arbitrage. Typically, this is taken to mean that it is not possible for an investor to use available information in order to earn abnormal expected returns. Notably, the notion of abnormality requires a model that relates expected return and risk.

To make the notions of risky arbitrage and abnormal returns more precise, define an informed investor as someone holding correct beliefs. Formally, investor j is an informed investor if $P_j = \Pi$. Think about equilibrium from the perspective of an informed investor. Keep in mind that this investor is an expected utility maximizing agent with correct beliefs. Given market prices, an informed investor chooses a dynamic trading strategy that is objectively optimal for her, not just subjectively optimal. In that sense, she correctly balances risk and return in choosing her trades.

Can there be unexploited risky arbitrage opportunities in equilibrium when there are informed investors in the market? If there were, then why would the informed investors not exploit these opportunities? The point is that informed investors properly balance risk and return. If they choose to avoid a trading opportunity, then it must be because they judge that the marginal risk does not justify the marginal return. That is, informed investors, who hold correct perceptions of both risk and return, trade to the point where all objective risky arbitrage opportunities are exploited. Therefore, as long as there are informed investors in the model, any equilibrium will be efficient in the sense of no risky arbitrage profits.

9.1.3 Fundamental Value

Fama (1965) states that in an efficient market, prices will be good estimates of intrinic, or fundamental, values. In this respect, imagine a market with two investors, an informed investor and an investor whose beliefs feature major biases. Consider the case when the initial wealth of the informed investor is small relative to the total wealth. Because the representative investor's beliefs are a wealth-weighted combination of the beliefs of the individual investors, the representative investor will have erroneous beliefs in the sense that $P_R \neq \Pi$.

From the perspective of the informed investor, the prices of some securities will not coincide with their fundamental values. In this sense, the informed investor will judge that some securities are mispriced in equilibrium. Yet, the informed investor will only seek to exploit a portion of the mispricing, not the full mispricing. Why does an informed investor choose to stop short? Because the expected rewards associated with full exploitation are not worth the attendant risks. This property has come to be known as the "limits of arbitrage."

Now were the initial wealth of the informed investor larger, then the informed investor would be willing to take a larger position in order to exploit the mispricing she perceives. It is in this sense that because of a wealth constraint, an abnormal return may potentially be unexploited. In order for informed investors to perceive that there is no mispricing to be exploited, even if they had more wealth, prices must be set so that $P_R = \Pi$. In other words, the representative investor must hold objectively correct beliefs. When $P_R = \Pi$, the prices of all securities coincide with their fundamental values, where fundamental values are computed using objectively correct probabilities Π.

The definition of market efficiency used in this book is based on fundamental value, that prices are objectively correct. *A market is termed efficient if and only if state prices correctly reflect the preferences of investors and underlying risk.* Equilibrium state prices are used because, as was seen in Chapter 4, they serve to generate the prices of all other assets. In this respect, there is an implicit no-arbitrage condition at work, either riskless or risky. For the moment, attention is focused only on state prices. In the next chapter, attention shifts to the pricing of other assets such as bonds, and equities.

9.1.4 When Π Is Nonexistent

Suppose that there is no objective stochastic process Π governing the evolution of the consumption growth g. In that case, it makes no sense to speak of objective expected returns, objective risk measured by second moments, and fundamental value. Individual investors might still hold subjective density functions, and the notion of equilibrium will be just as before. Indeed, the notion of a representative investor will continue to be a valid concept. However, the notion of fundamental value will be undefined, as will the notion of risky arbitrage. In this case, the only definition of market efficiency that remains valid is the definition based on the absence of risk-free arbitrage.

9.2   Market Efficiency and Logarithmic Utility

Consider what the definition of market efficiency means in the context of the model developed in the preceding chapter. In Chapter 8, *aggregate consumption growth g* evolves according to a binomial process in which g takes on either value, $u = 1.0095$ or $d = 0.9993$. The probability associated with an up-move is 0.916, and the probability associated with a down-move is 0.084. Let $\Pi(x_t)$ denote the probability density function that is associated with this binomial process.

Do equilibrium prices correctly reflect investors' logarithmic utility functions and the objectively correct stochastic process Π? Recall that equation (8.21) stipulates that for the model developed in Chapter 8, equilibrium state prices satisfy

$$\nu(x_t) = \frac{\delta^t P_R(x_t)}{g(x_t)} \tag{9.1}$$

where $P_R(x_t)$ is the probability assigned by the representative investor to date–event pair x_t. Therefore, for state prices to correctly reflect the underlying stochastic process Π, state prices must satisfy

$$\nu(x_t) = \frac{\delta^t \Pi(x_t)}{g(x_t)} \tag{9.2}$$

In other words, for this model, market efficiency requires that

$$P_R(x_t) = \Pi(x_t) \tag{9.3}$$

9.2.1   Example of Market Inefficiency

Consider one of the examples provided in Chapter 8. In the example, two investors agree about the values of u and d, but disagree about the probabilities. In particular, investor 1 is excessively optimistic, and investor 2 is excessively pessimistic. Specifically, investor 1 believes that the probability associated with an up-move is 0.95 and investor 2 believes that the probability associated with an up-move is 0.85.

As was discussed in Chapter 8, the equilibrium state price associated with an up-move at $t = 1$ is based on a probability of 0.90, the wealth-weighted average of 0.95 and 0.85. That is, the probability of an up-move at $t = 0$ is 0.90 under the representative investor's probability density P_R. Yet, the objective probability associated with an up-move under Π is 0.916, not 0.90. Therefore, (9.3) does not hold. The market is not efficient under the definition of efficiency employed here.

9.2.2   Sentiment and the Log-Pricing Kernel

Sentiment and the pricing kernel (also known as the stochastic discount factor or SDF) are the core concepts in the book. The relationship between market sentiment and the pricing kernel lies at the heart of the behavioral approach to asset pricing. This subsection relates the discussion in the present chapter to these core concepts.

Begin with market sentiment, by which I mean the error structure associated with equilibrium prices. Consider Figure 9.2, which is similar in structure to Figure 8.2, but features a probability density function P_R which is symmetric and unimodal. Figure 9.2 depicts the probability density functions (pdfs) for a complete market model featuring two log-utility investors, whose initial wealth levels are equal. In the figure, the log of consumption growth is normally distributed, and both investors believe it to be normally distributed. However, one investor is excessively bullish about mean consumption growth, while the second investor is excessively bearish about mean consumption growth. At the same time, both investors hold correct beliefs about the second moment of log-consumption growth rate.

As in the case of Figure 8.2, Figure 9.2 demonstrates how in equilibrium the market aggregates the pdfs of the two investors. The figure displays four probability density functions over aggregate consumption growth. The two extreme pdfs belong to the two investors. The middle pdf, labeled Objective Density, is indeed the objective pdf, and is denoted by the symbol Π. By assumption, the first moment of Π in this example is set equal to the simple average of the two investors' first moments for consumption growth. The fourth pdf is the market pdf P_R, the equilibrium density defined by equation (8.15) used to price assets.

Section 4.6 introduced the notion of a sentiment function, based on the log-ratio $ln(P_R/\Pi)$. This log-ratio measures the percentage by which, in equilibrium, the representative investor's pdf exceeds the objective pdf. Technically, the ratio P_R/Π is a Radon-Nikodym derivative.

Figure 9.3 provides a graphical illustration of the market sentiment function in this example. The inset in the middle of Figure 9.3 is a reproduction

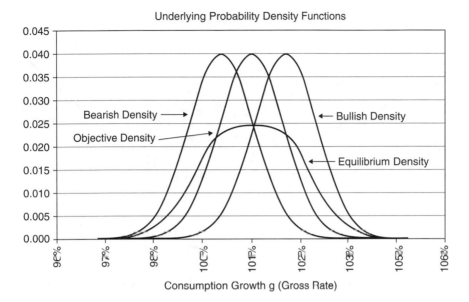

FIGURE 9.2. Underlying probability density functions. The bullish probability density function (pdf) and bearish pdf describe investor beliefs in a two-investor complete market example where both investors have erroneous beliefs about the growth rate of gross consumption, the source of fundamental uncertainty in the model. The true pdf is the objective density Π. In equilibrium, prices are set as if there is a representative investor whose beliefs are given by the pdf P_R, which is a wealth weighted average of the bullish pdf and bearish pdf.

of Figure 9.2. The U-shaped function is the sentiment function. In the region of the domain where the representative investor's pdf lies above the objective pdf, market sentiment is positive. In the region of the domain where the representative investor's pdf lies below the objective pdf, market sentiment is negative. Sentiment must have both positive and negative regions, except for the case when it is the zero function.

The downward sloping portion at the left of the sentiment function in Figure 9.3 reflects pessimism of the bearish investor. The upward sloping portion at the right reflects the optimism of the bullish investor. In this example, market sentiment is neither uniformly optimistic nor uniformly pessimistic.

Consider next the pricing kernel which measures state price per unit probability, ν/Π. Denote the state prices in (9.2) by ν_Π. Consider the ratio $ln(\nu/\nu_\Pi)$, where ν corresponds to (9.1). As was discussed in section 4.6, this log-ratio denotes the percentage by which the equilibrium state price exceeds its efficient counterpart. It follows from equations (9.1) and (9.2)

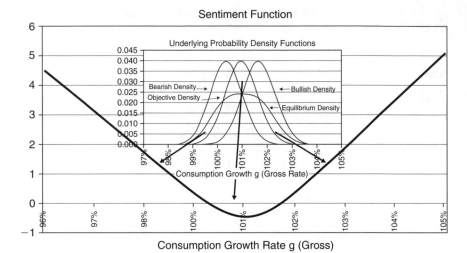

FIGURE 9.3. Illustration of log-ratio $ln(P_M/\Pi)$. The arrows in the figure indicate the three regions of the sentiment function. In the middle region, sentiment is negative because in the inset, the equilibrium density P_M lies below the objective density Π. In the left and right regions, sentiment is positive because in the inset, the density P_M lies above the density Π.

that $ln(\nu/\nu_\Pi) = ln(P_R/\Pi)$. This last equality can also be expressed as $ln(\nu/\Pi) = ln(P_R/\Pi) + ln(\nu_\Pi/\Pi)$. That is, in equilibrium, the log-pricing kernel can be decomposed into the sum of sentiment and a fundamental component that corresponds to the efficient log-pricing kernel.

The log-pricing kernel decomposition equation indicates that prices are efficient if and only if sentiment is zero. In the remainder of the chapter, I derive necessary and sufficient conditions for sentiment to be zero. These conditions apply to the model analyzed in this chapter.

9.3   Equilibrium Prices as Aggregators

One of the main points of Chapter 2 is that many people rely on representativeness to form probability judgments, and that such reliance predisposes them to systematic biases. That is, the direction of the average error is predictable. One of the main points in Chapters 5 through 7 is that there is heterogeneity in the errors: different groups of investors are prone to different errors. Moreover, within the same group, different investors commit different errors. For example, although most professional investors appear to suffer from gambler's fallacy, some suffer from hot hand fallacy, an error that is opposite in direction to gambler's fallacy.

Because P_R is a wealth-weighted convex combination of the investors' probability density functions, equations (8.15) and (8.21) tell us that market prices effectively aggregate investors' beliefs. Of course, if every investor is error-free, and holds objectively correct beliefs, then $P_j = \Pi$ for all j. In this case, the aggregation is trivial, and $P_R = \Pi$ trivially. That is, when all investors hold objectively correct beliefs, the market is efficient.

Now consider a situation when some investor holds erroneous beliefs. As was discussed earlier, prices may be inefficient in such a case. However, that does not mean that prices must be inefficient. The question is, might the errors be self-canceling in the aggregate?

Errors may well be self-canceling. Nevertheless, this does not necessarily imply that prices must be efficient whenever errors are unsystematic. In this respect, consider the following question: What are the necessary and sufficient conditions for market efficiency, at least in the model developed in Chapter 8?

9.4   Market Efficiency: Necessary and Sufficient Condition

One way of describing the market error in respect to date–event pair x_t is through the ratio $P_R(x_t)/\Pi(x_t)$. This ratio provides the relative value of the market error. Consider an alternative measure of the market error, a measure based on the absolute size of the error rather than the relative size of the error.

For each x_t, define the discounted investor error by

$$\epsilon_j(x_t) = \delta'(t)(P_j(x_t) - \Pi(x_t)) \tag{9.4}$$

where

$$\delta'(t) = \frac{\delta^t}{\sum_{\tau=0}^{T} \delta^\tau} \tag{9.5}$$

Notice that ϵ_j measures the difference between j's discount-weighted subjective probability and the corresponding objective probability. Let w_j denote j's relative wealth share $w_j = W_j/\sum_k W_k$, and define the covariance $cov\{w_j, \epsilon_j(x_t)\}$ by

$$cov\{w_j, \epsilon_j(x_t)\} = \sum_k (w_k - (1/J))(\epsilon_j(x_t) - \bar{\epsilon}(x_t))/J \tag{9.6}$$

where J denotes the number of investors (in this case $J = 2$), and

$$\bar{\epsilon}(x_t) = \sum_k \epsilon_k(x_t)/J \tag{9.7}$$

The main conclusion of this section is that prices are efficient if and only if the sum of the error–wealth covariance plus the product of the average error and mean wealth is equal to zero. The formal statement of this result is as follows:

Theorem 9.1 *The necessary and sufficient condition for market efficiency in this model is that*

$$cov\{W_j, \epsilon_j(x_t)\} + \bar{\epsilon}(x_t)\left(\sum_j W_j/J\right) = 0 \tag{9.8}$$

The condition can also be expressed in the following dot product form:

$$\sum_j w_j \epsilon_j(x_t) = 0 \tag{9.9}$$

Proof of Theorem   By the definitions of ϵ and P_R, obtain

$$P_R(x_t) = \frac{\sum_j w_j[(\delta'(t)\Pi(x_t)) + \epsilon_j(x_t)]}{\sum_j w_j \delta'(t)} \tag{9.10}$$

so that

$$P_R(x_t) = \Pi(x_t) + \frac{\sum_j w_j \epsilon_j(x_t)}{\sum_j w_j \delta'_j(t)} \tag{9.11}$$

It follows that in order for the efficiency condition $P_R(x_t) = \Pi(x_t)$ to hold, the sum $\sum_j w_j \epsilon_j(x_t)$ must be zero.

Define the covariance $cov\{w_j, \epsilon_j(x_t)\}$ by

$$cov\{w_j, \epsilon_j(x_t)\} = \sum_j (w_j - (1/J))(\epsilon_j(x_t) - \bar{\epsilon}(x_t))/J \tag{9.12}$$

where

$$\bar{\epsilon}(x_t) = \sum_j \epsilon_j(x_t)/J \tag{9.13}$$

Multiplying out the terms in the covariance yields the equivalent covariance expression

$$(1/J)\left[\sum_j w_j\epsilon_j - \bar{\epsilon}\right] \tag{9.14}$$

for each x_t. Recall that prices are efficient if and only if $\sum_j w_j\epsilon_j = 0$ for all x_t. This is equivalent to

$$cov\{w_j, \epsilon_j(x_t)\} + \bar{\epsilon}(x_t)/J = 0 \tag{9.15}$$

Multiplication of this last expression by $\sum_j W_j$ yields the equivalent condition

$$cov\{W_j, \epsilon_j(x_t)\} + \bar{\epsilon}(x_t)\left(\sum_j W_j/J\right) = 0 \tag{9.16}$$

which implies that prices are efficient if and only if the sum of the error–wealth covariance plus the product of the average error and mean wealth is equal to zero. This completes the proof. ∎

9.5   Interpreting the Efficiency Condition

Equation (9.16) provides a necessary and sufficient condition for market efficiency in the log-utility model. Notice that the equation consists of two terms, which must add to zero. The easiest way to interpret the condition is to focus on the case when both terms are zero individually. In this case, there are two conditions required for markets to be efficient. Both conditions involve the distributions of investors' errors.

9.5.1   When the Market Is Naturally Efficient

Consider some special cases for which market efficiency holds. In the first case, the error term $\epsilon_j(x_t)$ is zero for all investors and every date–event pair. This is the error-free case. Hence, both terms in equation (9.16) are zero. The error–wealth covariance is zero because there is no variation in investors' errors. And trivially, the mean error $\bar{\epsilon}$ is zero for all date–event pairs.

Consider a second case where markets are efficient. Some investors make errors, but the mean error $\bar{\epsilon}$ is zero for every date–event pair. In addition, initial wealth is uniformly distributed across the investor population.

Therefore, although there is positive variation in investors' errors, there is zero variation in their initial wealth levels. Consequently, the error–wealth covariance will be zero. Therefore, both the first and second terms in equation (9.16) are zero. Hence, the market is efficient in this case.

The case just described conforms to the idea that although some investors commit errors at the individual level, these errors wash out at the level of the market. In other words, the market efficiently aggregates the errors committed at the individual level.

9.5.2   Knife-Edge Efficiency

The first two cases feature nonsystematic errors, meaning that $\bar{\epsilon} = 0$. Table 9.1 describes the parameters of a case where the mean error $\bar{\epsilon}$ is nonzero and yet the market is efficient.[1] The table pertains to an example of the log-utility binomial model when $T = 2$. For simplicity, the discount factor $\delta = 1$, and initial wealth is nonuniformly distributed, being split 60/40 between the two investors. The first two events on the left, u and d, are the two date 1 event pairs. The other four events, uu through dd, are the date–event pairs for date 2. The true probabilities Π appear in the top row of the table. These are followed by the probabilities for the two investors: the wealth-weighted convex combination of the investors' probabilities $(P_R(x_t))$, the individual errors $\epsilon_j(x_t)$, the $\bar{\epsilon}$ error in each date–event pair, and the initial wealth ratios.

Comparison of the first and fourth rows shows that the representative trader's probabilities coincide with the true probabilities. That is, the market is efficient in this example. However, notice that the average investor error is nonzero in every date–event pair. That is, errors are systematic. In addition, wealth is not uniformly distributed. Investor 1 has 60 percent of the initial wealth, while investor 2 has 40 percent of the investor wealth.

In the example depicted in Table 9.1, neither the average error nor the covariance is zero in any date–event pair. However, the sum of twice the covariance and average investor error equals zero. This is a knife-edge case that produces market efficiency. Either a slight change in an investor's errors or a shift in the initial wealth distribution leads to a violation of the efficiency condition (9.16).

Consider two additional points about this example. The first point is that although investor 1's probabilities for $t = 2$ conform to conjunction, investor 2's probabilities do not. For example, the probability that investor 1 attaches to the event in which two successive up-moves occur is 0.95^2, the product of the probability associated with a single up-move.

---

[1] The example is presented in the accompanying file *Chapter 9 Example.xls*.

TABLE 9.1. Probability Density Functions

This table presents the probability density functions, errors, and initial wealth levels used in the example discussed in Chapter 9.

	Pr(u)	Pr(d)	Pr(uu)	Pr(ud)	Pr(du)	Pr(dd)
True Probability	91.59%	8.41%	83.89%	7.70%	7.70%	0.71%
Investor 1 Probability	95.00%	5.00%	90.25%	4.75%	4.75%	0.25%
Investor 2 Probability	86.48%	13.52%	74.36%	12.13%	12.13%	1.39%
Wealth-Weighted Investor Probability	91.59%	8.41%	83.89%	7.70%	7.70%	0.71%
Error Investor 1	3.41%	−3.41%	6.36%	−2.95%	−2.95%	−0.46%
Error Investor 2	−5.11%	5.11%	−9.54%	4.43%	4.43%	0.69%
Average Investor Error	−0.85%	0.85%	−1.59%	0.74%	0.74%	0.11%
W_1	0.6					
W_2	0.4					

However, the probability that investor 2 attaches to the event in which two successive up-moves occur, 0.7436, is not equal to 0.8648^2, the latter being the square of the probability that investor 2 associates with a single up-move.

9.5.3   When the Market Is Naturally Inefficient

The second point about this example is that the magnitudes of investor 2's errors are larger than those of investor 1. In effect, because investor 2 has less wealth than investor 1, market efficiency requires that investor 2's errors be more serious. Were investor 1 to hold more than 92.7 percent of the wealth, investor 2's errors would have to be so large that his probabilities could not remain positive. In other words, in that case no beliefs on the part of investor 2 would lead the market to be efficient.

Because (9.16) constitutes a knife-edge case as a single condition for efficiency, it is best regarded as two conditions. The first condition is that the mean investor error must be zero across all date–event pairs. That is, errors cannot be systematic, in that the unweighted average of the distributional errors across the investor population must be zero.

The second condition is that any errors must be smoothly distributed across the investor population. Technically, the covariance between investor errors and investor wealth must be zero.

The presence of either (1) systematic errors, or (2) wealthy investors who are prone to a particular error, will cause some state prices to deviate from their fundamental values.

In respect to the first condition, remember that a key point in the behavioral psychology literature (one emphasized in Chapters 2, 3, 5, 6, and 7) is that errors are indeed systematic. The average error in the population is not zero. Heuristics produce biased judgments. Nonzero bias leads to systematic errors.

Despite the strong evidence that errors are systematic, suppose for the moment that they were indeed nonsystematic. What are the implications for efficiency? Equation (9.16) tells us that efficiency now requires the error–wealth covariance to be zero in all date–event pairs. This is asking for a lot.

Why is it asking for a lot? The reason is that over long runs, wealth tends to shift back and forth between investors. Therefore, at any time, the errors of successful investors will tend to predominate. That interferes with the condition that errors and wealth are statistically unrelated over time. Indeed, over time the identity of successful investors will typically change. Of course, if wealth shifts to one particular investor in the long run, then the error–wealth covariance will converge to zero. This important issue is the subject of Chapter 11.

9.6   Summary

This chapter defined market efficiency as state prices correctly reflecting investors' preferences and the true stochastic process underlying aggregate consumption growth. The key result in the chapter is a necessary and sufficient condition for market efficiency in a log-utility framework. The condition implies that the market is efficient when investors' errors are nonsystematic and the error–wealth covariance is zero at all times.

10

A Simple Market Model of Prices and Trading Volume

This chapter studies the evolution of prices and trading volume in a model involving two securities, a risky security (the market portfolio) and a risk-free security. One of the central questions in the book is how representativeness affects security prices and trading volume. The model in this chapter addresses this question, based on the framework developed in Chapters 8 and 9. The model also serves to set the stage for the discussion of long-run survival that is the subject of Chapter 11.

The chapter is divided into four main portions. The first portion develops the model. The second portion focuses on security prices. The third portion focuses on trading volume. The fourth portion provides an example.

10.1   The Model

Imagine two investors, designated 1 and 2, who occupy a three-date economy featuring markets at two dates, $t=0$ and $t=1$. As in the models of Chapters 8 and 9, aggregate consumption grows at the random rate g according to a binomial process.

10.1.1   Expected Utility Maximization

At the outset of $t=0$, investor j has to decide how to allocate wealth W_j between current consumption $c_j(x_0)$ and a portfolio ϕ_j consisting of holdings of two securities, a risky security and a risk-free security priced at $q_R(x_0)$ and $q_F(x_0)$, respectively. Let $\phi_{j,R}(x_0)$ denote the number of units of the risky security that investor j chooses to hold in his portfolio at $t=0$, and $\phi_{j,F}(x_0)$ denote the number of units of the risk-free security that investor j chooses to hold in his portfolio at $t=0$.

Let l denote either u or d. Define $r_{k,l}(x_t)$ as the gross return (one plus the net return) earned in date–event pair x_t in respect to a single unit of security k. Here, l denotes the most recent up- or down-move in respect to date–event pair x_t.

If an up-move occurs at $t=1$, investor j's wealth will be

$$q_R(x_0)\phi_{j,R}(x_0)r_{R,u}(x_1) + q_F(x_0)\phi_{j,F}(x_0)r_{F,u}(x_1) \tag{10.1}$$

which for general x_t can be compactly written in general matrix notation as

$$W_j(x_t) = \phi_j(x_{t-1})q(x_{t-1})r(x_t) \tag{10.2}$$

Here, the product of q and ϕ gives the value in x_{t-1}-dollars, which gets converted into x_t-dollars by the return r.[1]

As in Chapter 8, the expected utility that investor j associates with consumption plan c_j is $E(u_j) = \sum_{t,x_t} P_j(x_t)\delta^t ln(c_j(x_t))$. Define the return matrix r, as the submatrices $\{r(x_t)\}$. Given the return matrix r, investor j's portfolio problem is to choose a consumption plan c_j and portfolio strategy ϕ to maximize $E(u_j)$ subject to the sequence of budget constraints. Associated with each date–event pair is a market that imposes a budget constraint on every investor. The budget constraint stipulates that the sum of consumption and security holdings at the end of the period cannot exceed the investor's wealth at the beginning of the period. Formally, the budget constraint for investor j in date–event pair x_t is given by

$$c_j(x_t) + q_R(x_t)\phi_{j,R}(x_t) + q_F(x_t)\phi_{j,F}(x_t) \leq W_j(x_t) \tag{10.3}$$

At the end of the terminal date $t=T$, both securities become worthless, and so by assumption their values are set to zero.

The Lagrangean associated with investor j's maximization problem is

$$L_j = \sum_{t,x_t} P_j(x_t)\delta^t ln(c_j(x_t))$$

$$- \sum_{t,x_t} \lambda_{j,t,x_t}(c_j(x_t) + q_R(x_t)\phi_{j,R}(x_t) + q_F(x_t)\phi_{j,F}(x_t) - W_j(x_t))$$

$$\tag{10.4}$$

---

[1] In (10.2), $\phi_j(x_{t-1})$ is a row matrix, $q(x_{t-1})$ is a diagonal matrix, and $r(x_t)$ is a column matrix.

Differentiating L_j with respect to $c_j(x_t)$ leads to the first order condition:

$$\frac{\delta^t P_j(x_t)}{c_j(x_t)} = \lambda_{j,t,x_t} \tag{10.5}$$

Differentiating L_j with respect to $\phi_{j,R}(x_t)$ and making use of (10.2) yields the following condition:

$$\lambda_{j,t,x_t} - \sum_{x_{t+1}} \lambda_{j,t+1,x_{t+1}} r(x_{t+1}) = 0 \tag{10.6}$$

A similar set of equations holds for $\phi_{j,F}(x_t)$.

Equation (10.5) is the familiar condition requiring that the contribution to marginal expected utility from a dollar of wealth expended in any date–event pair be the same across all date–event pairs. Equation (10.6) concerns the impact of a marginal increase in the holdings of security R. This marginal increase is financed by a reduction in consumption at x_t, thereby resulting in a loss to expected utility in respect to this particular date–event pair. However, consumption in the date–event pairs associated with $t+1$ will increase. Equation (10.6) stipulates that the increased contribution from all date $t+1$ date–event pairs to expected utility must exactly offset the reduction in utility to the contribution stemming from x_t.

Combining the two first order conditions leads to a series of Euler equations. For example, using (10.5) to substitute for λ_{j,t,x_t} in (10.6) yields the following equation, in this case for $l=0$ and $t=1$:

$$q_R(x_0) = \delta \left[P_j(u) \frac{c_j(x_0)}{c_j(u)} q_R(x_0) r(u) + P_j(d) \frac{c_j(x_0)}{c_j(d)} q_R(x_0) r(d) \right] \tag{10.7}$$

where u and d refer to the two possible date–event pairs at $t=1$. Since the $q_R(x_0)$ terms cancel, the last equation can be expressed as

$$1 = \delta E_{x_0} \left[\frac{c_j(x_0)}{c_j(x_1)} r(x_1) \right] \tag{10.8}$$

The Euler equation plays a role in Chapter 16 and is easily explained. If investor j were to substitute consumption in date–event pair x_1 for consumption at date–event pair x_0, then his marginal rate of substitution specifies the maximum amount of x_0-consumption he would be willing to sacrifice in order to receive a marginal (unit) increase in x_1-consumption. Multiplying this marginal rate of substitution by the actual increase in x_1-consumption provides a measure of the benefit in date–event pair x_1, measured in units of x_0-consumption. It measures how much

x_0-consumption investor j is willing to sacrifice in exchange for the additional x_1-consumption.

Suppose that investor j increases his holdings of security R by decreasing his consumption at $t=0$ by a marginal unit. In so doing, investor j increases his consumption in the various date–event pairs that occur at $t=1$. Therefore, summing the products of marginal rates of substitution and marginal increases in x_1-consumption across *all* the x_1-events provides a measure for the total amount of x_0-consumption that investor j is willing to sacrifice in exchange for the additional consumption at $t=1$.

The Euler equation specifies that at the margin, the amount of x_0-consumption that investor j is willing to sacrifice in exchange for the additional consumption at $t=1$ should be the same as the amount investor j must, in fact, sacrifice. Of course, the amount investor j must sacrifice is 1, since the increased purchase of security R is financed by a reduction of consumption at $t=0$ by exactly one unit.

10.2   Analysis of Returns

This section discusses the relationship between the underlying state prices and the prices and returns associated with the risky and risk-free securities.

10.2.1   Market Portfolio

The market portfolio is a security entitling its holder to the entire consumption stream in each date–event pair. Aggregate consumption in date–event pair x_t is $w(x_t)$. Recall that $w(x_t) = g(x_t)w(x_0)$. Recall from equation (8.21) that the equation for the equilibrium state prices is given by

$$\nu(x_t) = \frac{\delta^t P_R(x_t)}{g(x_t)} \tag{10.9}$$

where P_R denotes the probability density function of the representative investor. As in Chapter 8, P_R is a wealth-weighted convex combination of the individual investors' probability density functions. In view of (10.9) at date $t=0$, the value of the future uncertain consumption stream can be valued using state prices. Call the latter variable $q_w(x_0)$. Observe that

$$q_w(x_0) = \sum_{t=1}^{T} \sum_{x_t} \nu(x_t)w(x_t) = \sum_{t=1}^{T} \sum_{x_t} \frac{\delta^t P_R(x_t)}{g(x_t)} g(x_t)w(x_0) \tag{10.10}$$

Canceling the terms in $g(x_t)$, and noting that the probability terms $P_R(x_t)$ sum to unity for each t, implies that

$$q_\omega(x_0) = \sum_{t=1}^{T} \sum_{x_t} \nu(x_t)\omega(x_t) = \omega(x_0) \sum_{t=1}^{T} \delta^t \tag{10.11}$$

Analogously,

$$q_\omega(x_1) = \omega(x_1) \sum_{t=2}^{T} \delta^{t-1} \tag{10.12}$$

The return to holding the market portfolio is easily obtained. In date–event pair x_1, the holder of the market portfolio receives a dividend of $\omega(x_1)$ along with the ex-dividend value $q_\omega(x_1)$. The gross return is the sum of the two, $\omega(x_1) + q_\omega(x_1)$. The gross rate of return is the return divided by the original price $q_\omega(x_0)$. Define the return $r_\omega(x_1)$ as the gross rate of return to the market portfolio in date–event pair x_1. Using (10.11) and (10.12), obtain

$$r_\omega(x_1) = \frac{\omega(x_1) + q_\omega(x_1)}{q_\omega(x_0)} = g(x_1)/\delta \tag{10.13}$$

In the example presented later in this chapter, the risky security is the market portfolio.

10.2.2   Risk-Free Security

Consider a security that is traded on the x_0-market and promises to deliver a single unit of the consumption good at every x_1 date–event pair. Using state prices to value this security at $t = 0$, obtain

$$q_F(x_0) = \sum_{x_1} \nu(x_1) = \sum_{x_1} \frac{\delta P_R(x_1)}{g(x_1)} \tag{10.14}$$

That is, the price of the risk free security, effectively the risk-free discount factor, is the product of δ and the expected inverse growth rate under the representative investor's probability density function. The gross risk-free rate of interest, i_1, is simply the inverse of the risk-free discount factor. That is,

$$i_1(x_0) = [\delta E_R(1/g(x_1))]^{-1} \tag{10.15}$$

10.3   Analysis of Trading Volume

What are the main determinants of trading volume? This portion of the chapter suggests that representativeness is key. Representativeness is the root cause of the fact that some investors are prone to predict continuation while other investors are prone to predict reversals. When these two groups of investors meet in the market, trading volume ensues. The key to understanding trading volume is not so much heterogeneous beliefs, but the process governing *the rate of change in heterogeneity*. Recall the discussion of overconfidence in Chapter 5. Odean (1998b) argues that overconfidence is the key determinant of trading volume. In the present approach, overconfidence serves to amplify the effects of representativeness in generating trading volume. However, representativeness is the primary determinant, with overconfidence playing a supporting role.

In order to motivate the discussion, consider a study by Kandel and Pearson (1995), who focus on the heterogeneity in the earnings forecasts of security analysts.[2]

Kandel–Pearson contain two empirical findings. Their first finding relates to the degree of heterogeneity in analysts' forecasts. Their second finding relates to the relationship between realized returns and trading volume, in connection with earnings announcements.

Just to review context, Chapter 7 emphasizes the heterogeneous nature of heuristics that professional investors use when forecasting future market returns. The theoretical nature of volume discussed previously emphasizes that trading volume stems from changes in investor beliefs associated with new information.

In order to illustrate the heterogeneous manner in which security analysts respond to new information, Kandel–Pearson discuss an example involving the stock of Apple Computer. In 1993, Apple Computer announced a decline in its earnings for the second quarter of its fiscal year. In response, several analysts revised their earnings forecasts. Some analysts revised their forecasts down. But not all: Others raised their forecasts, and indeed some even issued new buy recommendations. Those who revised their estimates downward pointed to a history of negative earnings surprises in the past, and indicated that competitive pressures would become more intense in the future, not weaker. Those who revised their estimates upward pointed to new product lines that would be available later in the year, thereby leading to less price pressure facing the firm.

Kandel–Pearson suggest that if analysts formulated earnings forecasts in accordance with Bayes rule, then there would be less heterogeneity in

---

[2] There are many studies of trading volume. The Kandel–Pearson study has been selected because of its explicit focus on heterogeneity.

their responses to earnings announcements. They suggest that for any two analysts, an earnings announcement will either lead them to revise their forecasts in the same direction, or lead them to revise their forecasts so as to reduce the forecast difference. They describe a situation where analysts make revisions in different directions as a "flip" and a situation where the forecast difference gets larger rather than smaller as a "divergence." They use the term "inconsistency" to describe a situation where either a flip or a divergence occurs.

Flips and divergences are common. Kandel–Pearson use data from 1992 and 1993 to document the extent of flips and divergences. They divide their sample into windows, with a window before and including an earnings announcement, a window that begins immediately following an earnings announcement, and two other windows later in time, but before the next earnings announcement. In the general sample, flips occur about 8 percent of the time, and divergences occur about 9 percent of the time.

Earnings announcements serve as major information events. However, information generation also takes place between earnings announcements. The second finding reported by Kandel–Pearson concerns the question of whether trading volume is different around earnings announcements. In studying this question, they control for return, in that returns and volume are known to be related.

Kandel–Pearson match events by return, where one event includes an earnings announcement and the other does not. For every matched pair, they report that trading volume is higher during windows that include earnings announcements than in windows that exclude earnings announcements. In terms of the theoretical model discussed above, earnings announcements generate increased heterogeneity in respect to analysts' beliefs.

Notably, trading volume during periods that do not include earnings announcements is roughly 75 percent of trading volume during periods that include earnings announcements. That is, even in the absence of major fundamental information, investors appear to exhibit significant degrees of heterogeneity in respect to changes in their beliefs.

10.3.1 Theory

Recall from Chapter 8 that the optimal consumption choice for investor j is given by

$$c_j(x_t) = \frac{\delta^t}{\sum_{\tau=0}^{T} \delta^\tau} \frac{P_j(x_t)}{\nu(x_t)} W_j \tag{10.16}$$

Substituting the equilibrium prices for ν, from (10.9), into (10.16) indicates how investor j's choice of $c_j(x_t)$ is determined in equilibrium. The substitution yields

$$c_j(x_t) = \frac{P_j(x_t)}{P_R(x_t)} \frac{W_j(x_0)g(x_t)}{\sum_{\tau=0}^{T} \delta^\tau} \tag{10.17}$$

Consider investor j's portfolio at dates $t=0$ and $t=1$. In the binomial example, $g(x_1)$ is either u or d. The return to the risky portfolio, that being the market portfolio, is either u/δ or d/δ. How does investor j choose his portfolio at each date, as a function of the evolution of aggregate consumption process?

In order to answer the latter question, observe that equation (10.16) indicates that in date–event pair x_t, investor j's consumption is directly proportional to his initial wealth. This equation also implies that at the end of x_1, investor j's wealth will be proportional to his consumption during x_1. This is because investor j's wealth is just the value of his future uncertain consumption stream. This implies that investor j's wealth $W_j(x_1)$ is proportional to the expression in (10.17). Specifically,

$$W_j(x_1) = \frac{P_j(x_1)}{P_R(x_1)} \frac{(\sum_{\tau=1}^{T} \delta^\tau)W_j(x_0)g(x_1)}{\sum_{\tau=0}^{T} \delta^\tau} \tag{10.18}$$

In particular, investor j's wealth will depend on aggregate consumption growth (u or d) and the likelihood ratios $P_j(u)/P_R(u)$ and $P_j(d)/P_R(d)$.

For simplicity, assume that $q_R(x_0) = q_F(x_0) = 1$. The x_0-portfolio $\phi_j(x_0)$ that provides j with outcome $W_j(u)$ or $W_j(d)$ is obtained by solving the matrix equation $\phi_j(x_0)r(x_1) = W_j$ to obtain $\phi_j(x_0) = W_j r(x_1)^{-1}$. As was mentioned earlier, the return to the risky portfolio is either u/δ or d/δ. The return to the risk-free security is i. Using matrix algebra to solve for $r(x_1)^{-1}$ yields the following:

$$\phi_{j,R}(x_1) = \frac{W_j(u) - W_j(d)}{u/\delta - d/\delta} \tag{10.19}$$

and

$$\phi_{j,F}(x_1) = \frac{uW_j(u) - dW_j(d)}{i(u - d)} \tag{10.20}$$

Trading volume for investor j at date–event pair x_2 can be measured as number of units traded of the risky security. That would be given by

$$Vol_{j,R}(x_2) = \phi_{j,R}(x_2) - \phi_{j,R}(x_1) \tag{10.21}$$

where $\phi_{j,R}(x_t)$ is given by (10.19). Market volume would then measure the number of units trading hands and would be given by

$$Vol_{M,R}(x_2) = \sum_{j=1}^{J} |Vol_{j,R}(x_2)|/2 \qquad (10.22)$$

where division by 2 is used to adjust for double counting. A similar definition holds for the risk-free security. However, because in this model investors trade the risky security for the risk-free security, using the volume associated with the risk-free security would be redundant.

Equations (10.19), (10.20), and (10.22) demonstrate the channel through which the transition likelihood ratios $P_j(u)/P_R(u)$ and $P_j(d)/P_R(d)$ in the W_j vector affect portfolio composition. The ratio $\phi_{j,R}(x_1)/\phi_{j,F}(x_1)$ describes the portfolio mix. Equation (10.18) implies that this mix is independent of the initial wealth level. Since the possible growth rates are constant over time, it follows that a change in portfolio mix only occurs in respect to a change in the interest rate and the transition likelihood ratios.

The key variable that determines the manner in which investor j changes the weights assigned to the risky security and risk-free security in his portfolio depends on the manner in which $P_j(u)/P_R(u)$ changes over time, where the probabilities all refer to the next transitions. If investor j has the same probabilities as the representative investor, then $P_j(u) = P_R(u)$, and so $P_j(u)/P_R(u) = 1$ at all times. In this case, investor j only adjusts his portfolio in respect to changes in the underlying interest rate.

The manner in which $P_j(u)/P_R(u)$ changes over time is primarily driven by representativeness. In this model representativeness impacts $P_j(u)$ at the individual level, and therefore also affects $P_R(u)$ at the aggregate level. Recall from the discussion in Chapters 6 and 7 that individual investors and professional investors react to past market movements in opposite ways, and by more than is justified. Taken together, the combination of hypersensitivity and opposing directions provides the basis for high trading volume.

10.4   Example

Consider a numerical example to illustrate the features of the preceding model. (The computations for the example can be found in the accompanying Excel file *Chapter 10 Example.xls*.)

As was mentioned in Chapter 8, between 1947 and 2003, real personal consumption in the United States grew at the rate of 3.5 percent per year. Mean quarterly consumption growth during this period was 0.87 percent, with a standard deviation of 0.86 percent. The percentage of quarters that featured positive consumption growth was 91.6 percent. For quarters in which consumption growth was positive, mean consumption growth was 0.95 percent. For quarters in which consumption growth was negative, mean consumption growth was −0.07 percent.

10.4.1 Stochastic Processes

For the purpose of the model, imagine that aggregate consumption at $t=0$ is 100 units. Let consumption growth g evolve according to a binomial process in which g takes on the values $u=1.0095$ or $d=0.9993$. Let the true probability associated with an up-move be 0.916, and the probability associated with a down-move be 0.084. These probabilities reflect the historical rates associated with positive and negative consumption growth in the U.S.

In terms of model heterogeneity, suppose that the two investors agree about the values of u and d, but disagree about the probabilities. Notably, one investor subscribes to trend following and the other investor subscribes to gambler's fallacy. Therefore, both investors hold Markovian beliefs.

Suppose that investor 1 is a trend follower. Investor 1 believes that the probability that an up-move follows an up-move is 0.95, and that the probability that a down-move follows a down-move is 0.15. In contrast, investor 2 believes that the probability that an up-move follows an up-move is 0.85, and the probability that a down-move follows a down-move is 0.05. As in Chapter 8, the two investors use their respective Ergodic density functions for the initial transitions at $t=0$. Investor 1 assigns a probability of 0.944 to the occurrence of an up-move, while investor 2 assigns a probability of 0.864 to the occurrence of an up-move.

Table 10.1 displays the underlying probabilities $\Pi(x_t)$ and $P_j(x_t)$ for the model. The table also includes aggregate consumption and cumulative aggregate consumption growth rates. Notice that, being a trend follower, investor 1 overestimates the probabilities associated with the extreme events, uu and dd. In contrast, investor 2, who succumbs to gambler's fallacy, overestimates the probabilities associated with events that feature reversal, ud and du.

10.4.2 Available Securities

Assume that at each date two securities can be traded. One security offers a risky return and the other offers a risk-free return. At $t=0$, the prices of the risky and risk-free security are normalized at \$1.[3] Assume that at

---

[3] That is, the number of shares of each is established in order that the price of each share is equal to \$1 at $t=0$.

TABLE 10.1. Probability Density Functions

This table presents probability density functions, cumulative growth rates, and aggregate consumption used in the example in Chapter 10.

	Pr(u)	Pr(d)	Pr(uu)	Pr(ud)	Pr(du)	Pr(dd)
True Process	91.59%	8.41%	83.89%	7.70%	7.70%	0.71%
Investor 1	94.44%	5.56%	89.72%	4.72%	4.72%	0.83%
Investor 2	86.36%	13.64%	73.41%	12.95%	12.95%	0.68%
	u	d	uu	ud	du	dd
Cumulative Growth Rates	0.95%	−0.07%	1.90%	0.87%	0.87%	−0.15%
Aggregate Consumption	100.95	99.93	101.90	100.87	100.87	99.85

$t=0$, the risky security offers a total return of either 1.97 percent or 0.94 percent, depending respectively on whether aggregate consumption grows or contracts (up-move or down-move). The total return consists of a dividend yield and capital gain. At $t=0$ the risk-free security offers a single period return of 1.84 percent.

The gross returns earned at $t=1$, for securities traded at $t=0$, are either 1.0197 or 1.0094 for the risky security, and 1.0184 for the risk-free security. At $t=1$, the prices of both the risky and risk-free security will change to reflect the fact that the number of remaining periods has fallen, with the next date being the terminal date. After an up-move, the price of each security falls to $0.5073. After a down-move, the price of each security falls to $0.5022. Denote the price of security l on the x_t-market by $q_l(x_t)$.

Table 10.2 displays the returns per unit security associated with all date–event pairs. On a per dollar basis, the rates of return for the risky security continue to be either 1.97 percent or 0.94 percent, depending respectively on whether aggregate consumption grows or contracts (up-move or down-move). After an up-move, the interest rate at $t=1$ will be 1.83 percent. After a down-move, the interest rate at $t=1$ will be 1.91 percent.

10.4.3 Initial Portfolios

At $t=0$, investor 1 receives a dividend consisting of 20 units of the consumption good, and holds $39.40 worth of the risky security (ex-dividend). Similarly, investor 2 receives an 80 unit dividend and holds $157.61 worth of the risky security (ex-dividend). Let the unit price of each consumption be $1. Therefore, investor 1 has initial wealth of $W_1(x_0) = \$59.40$ and investor 2 has initial wealth of $W_2(x_0) = \$237.61$.

TABLE 10.2. Returns

This table presents the gross return process, per unit security, used in the example.

$t = 0$	u	d
Market	$1.0197	$1.0094
Risk-free security	$1.0184	$1.0184

u	u	d
Market	$0.5173	$0.5120
Risk-free security	$0.5166	$0.5166

d	u	d
Market	$0.5120	$0.5069
Risk-free security	$0.5117	$0.5117

Together, the two investors hold 100 units of the consumption good, and 197.01 units of the risky security. Notice that the initial portfolio held by each investor features a zero holding of the risk-free security. That is, the risk-free security is in zero net supply.

Recall that investor 1 is a trend follower, whereas investor 2 succumbs to gambler's fallacy. The discussion in Chapter 7 made the point that among professional investors, gambler's fallacy is more prevalent than trend following. To capture this feature, investor 2 is assumed more wealthy than investor 1.

10.4.4   Equilibrium Portfolio Strategies

In this model, equilibrium occurs when the aggregate demand for consumption, the risky security, and the risk-free security coincide with the supply of each. Because the price of every security is normalized to be $1, the return matrix r plays the role of the variable that adjusts to induce equilibrium. As will be seen shortly, the numerical values for the return matrix r described earlier induce equilibrium behavior on the part of the two investors.

Consider how the equilibrium unfolds. At $t = 0$ each investor receives a dividend payment based on his respective holdings of the risky security. Investor 1 receives 20 units of the consumption good, and investor 2 receives 80 units. Both investors choose to consume these amounts, and adjust their portfolios.

Notice from Table 10.1 that investor 1 is more optimistic than investor 2. Investor 1 attaches a probability of 94.44 percent to an up-move occurring at $t = 1$, whereas investor 2 attaches a probability of 83.36 percent. Given these differential beliefs, investor 1 chooses to increase his holdings of the risky asset, whereas investor 2 does the opposite. Notably, investor 1 finances the acquisition of the additional risky security by borrowing, not by selling units of the consumption good. That is, investor 1 purchases the additional risky security on margin. Investor 2 does the opposite, taking a short position in the risky security, and parking the proceeds in the risk-free security.

Table 10.3 summarizes the activity on the market at $t = 0$. Investor 1 increases his holdings of the risky security from 39.40 units to 2,402.28 units, a change of 2,362.88 units. Notice that this trade is financed by the borrowing of the same number of units (2,362.88) of the risk-free security. The trading activity of investor 2 is the mirror image of that of investor 1.

Suppose next that an up-move occurs at $t = 1$, that being the most likely event. Based on the portfolio investor 1 selected at $t = 0$, his initial wealth will be \$43.13. This represents an increase of 9.45 percent from the \$39.40 that the portfolio was worth at the end of $t - 0$. Moreover, investor 1 now holds 21.5 percent of the aggregate wealth, an increase from his initial 20 percent. Of this amount, investor 1 finances the purchase of 21.67 units of consumption, and invests the remainder.

Investor 1 is a trend follower. Since an up-move occurred at $t = 1$, investor 1 attaches a high probability that an up-move will also occur at $t = 2$. That probability is 95 percent. In contrast, investor 2 succumbs to gambler's

TABLE 10.3. Portfolio Holdings

This table presents the portfolio holdings at $t = 0$ in the Chapter 10 example.

Investor 1	Risky security	Risk-free security
Portfolio beginning of period	39.40	0.00
Portfolio end of period	2,402.28	−2,362.88
Investor 2	Risky security	Risk-free security
Portfolio beginning of period	157.61	0.00
Portfolio end of period	−2,205.27	2,362.88
Aggregate Holdings	Risky security	Risk-free security
Portfolio beginning of period	197.01	0.00
Portfolio end of period	197.01	0.00
	Risky security	Risk-free security
Trading Volume	2,362.88	2,362.88

fallacy, and attaches a probability of 85 percent to an up-move occurring at $t = 2$. The true probability that an up-move occurs at $t = 2$ (given that it occurred at $t = 1$) is 91.59 percent.

It follows that after an up-move at $t = 1$, investor 1 remains optimistic and investor 2 remains pessimistic. But notice that investor 1 actually becomes even more optimistic at $t = 1$ than he was at $t = 0$. The probability he attaches to an up-move occurring at the next transition has increased from 94.44 percent to 95 percent. As a result, investor 1 chooses to increase his holdings of the risky security, and does so by increasing his level of borrowing. In contrast, investor 2 does exactly the opposite.

After an up-move at $t = 1$, investor 1 consumes $1.47 of portfolio wealth, financed by selling 2.9 units of the risky security. In this respect, his end-of-period portfolio is worth less than his beginning-of-period portfolio, where both portfolios are measured using the ex-dividend prices at $t = 1$. Therefore, investor 1 consumes more than the net dividends and interest of his portfolio. By the same token, investor 2 saves $1.47 after an up-move at $t = 1$, so that his savings exactly offset investor 1's dissaving.

Table 10.4 summarizes the activity on the market at $t = 1$, given the occurrence of an up-move. Notably, the volume of trading at $t = 1$ reflects the change in beliefs of the two traders, not the degree of difference in these beliefs. That is, trading volume stems from changing beliefs, not differences in beliefs. This point was discussed earlier in the chapter.

TABLE 10.4. Portfolio Holdings

This table presents the portfolio holdings at $t = 1$ in the Chapter 10 example, in the event of an up-move.

Investor 1	Risky security	Risk-free security
Portfolio beginning of period	2,402.28	−2,362.88
Portfolio end of period	2,951.69	−2,909.39
Investor 2	Risky security	Risk-free security
Portfolio beginning of period	−2,205.27	2,362.88
Portfolio end of period	−2,754.68	2,909.39
Aggregate Holdings	Risky security	Risk-free security
Portfolio beginning of period	197.01	0.00
Portfolio end of period	197.01	0.00
	Risky security	Risk-free security
Trading Volume	549.41	546.51

Suppose that a down-move occurs at $t = 1$. This would be bad news for investor 1, who had purchased the risky security on margin. After a down-move at $t = 1$, investor 1's share of the wealth would decline from 20 percent to 9.2 percent. In this event, investor 1, the trend follower, would become pessimistic, assigning a probability of 15 percent to the occurrence of a down-move at $t = 2$. In contrast, investor 2 would now become optimistic, assigning a probability of only 5 percent to the occurrence of a down-move at $t = 2$. What are the implications for trade?

Investor 1 would then take a short position in the risky security, and go long in the risk-free security. Investor 2 would do the opposite. Trading volume would be large; 5,291.4 units of the risky security would change hands, with investor 1 liquidating his position in the risky security and then going short. As before, it is the relative change in beliefs that produces trading volume. Table 10.5 summarizes the activity on the market at $t = 1$, given the occurrence of a down-move.

At $t = 2$, the terminal date, the two investors would consume the value of their respective portfolios. Not surprisingly, after two successive up-moves, investor 1 increases his share of wealth, to 23.4 percent. A down-move at $t = 1$ followed by an up-move at $t = 2$ represents the worst possible scenario for investor 1, in that his initial optimism is proved wrong at $t = 1$, and his subsequent pessimism is proved wrong at $t = 2$. In this scenario, investor 1's share of wealth declines to 8.4 percent.

TABLE 10.5. Portfolio Holdings

This table presents the portfolio holdings at $t = 1$ in the Chapter 10 example, in the event of a down-move.

Investor 1		
	Risky security	Risk-free security
Portfolio beginning of period	2,402.28	−2,362.88
Portfolio end of period	−2,889.13	2,907.34
Investor 2		
	Risky security	Risk-free security
Portfolio beginning of period	−2,205.27	2,362.88
Portfolio end of period	3,086.14	−2,907.34
Aggregate Holdings		
	Risky security	Risk-free security
Portfolio beginning of period	197.01	0
Portfolio end of period	197.01	0
	Risky security	Risk-free security
Trading Volume	5,291.41	5,270.22

Interestingly, investor 1 does as badly if the sequence is reversed, with an up-move taking place at $t = 1$ and a down-move taking place at $t = 2$. In addition, investor 1 ends up with the same wealth share after two successive down-moves as with two successive up-moves.

10.4.5 Markov Structure, Continuation, and Asymmetric Volatility

In the example just discussed, personal consumption growth was assumed to be independent and identically distributed. However, historically, the estimated transition probabilities conditional on positive growth are different from the probabilities conditional on negative growth. Given an up-move, the probability of a subsequent up-move is 92.7 percent. Given a down-move, the probability of a subsequent up-move is 78.9 percent. Although up-moves are generally more likely to occur, they are less likely to occur once consumption has turned down.

The associated Markov structure naturally gives rise to asymmetric volatility. There are two reasons why this is the case. First, the standard deviation of consumption growth increases as the transition probabilities shift in the direction of equiprobability. Second, the magnitudes of the average up- and down-moves are different after up-moves than after down-moves. Historically, the difference between up- and down-moves after an up-move is 1.85 percent, whereas after a down-move the difference is 2.03 percent. Taking the two effects together, the standard deviation is higher after a down-move than after an up-move. In fact, it almost doubles, from 0.48 percent to 0.84 percent.

In view of equation (10.13), the essential features of the stochastic process on consumption growth carry through to the return on the market portfolio. Therefore, the return on the market portfolio will exhibit asymmetric volatility. In this regard, the market risk premium will be higher after a down-move. For reasons discussed in Chapter 12, the difference in risk premiums is proportional to the difference in return variances.

At daily and monthly frequencies, the S&P 500 also features asymmetric volatility, with the effect effectively disappearing at the annual frequency. Given a positive return (up-return), the probability associated with a subsequent up-return is 55.9 percent at the daily frequency and 60 percent at the monthly frequency. Given a down-return, the corresponding probabilities are 47.9 percent and 55.1 percent. At both frequencies, the average down-return is lower after a down-return than after an up-return. At the monthly frequency, the average up-return is higher after a down-return than after an up-return; however, the two are about the same at the daily frequency.

Because the S&P 500 comprises levered equity with limited liability, it is not a perfect proxy for the market portfolio. In the above example, levered equity with limited liability might correspond to a security that pays off in up-states but not in down-states. Asymmetric volatility in the return distribution for such a security can stem from investors' beliefs as well as from economic fundamentals. For volatility to be higher after down-states than after up-states, investor wealth needs to be concentrated among trend followers. For the 20/80 wealth split in the example, where gambler's fallacy is assumed to be the dominant belief, volatility is actually higher after up-states than down-states.

The subjects in the De Bondt S&P 500 experiment that were discussed in Chapter 5 also predict higher volatility after bear markets than after bull markets. Evidence reported in Bange (2000) and Bange and Miller (2003) suggests that in the aggregate both individual investors and professional investors choose asset allocations that are consistent with trend following.

10.5   Arbitrage

Imagine that at $t = 0$, an investor forms a position that features 97.07 units of the risky security, with a corresponding short position (borrowing) in the risk-free security of -96.21 units. At $t = 1$ such a position would be worth $1 in the event of an up-move and $0 in the event of a down-move. Because both securities are priced at $1 at $t = 0$, the value of the position at $t = 0$ would be $0.86 = 97.07 - 96.21$.

The price of a unit of consumption in a particular date–event pair is a state price. Therefore, the state price associated with a single unit of consumption in the date–event pair u at $t = 1$ is $0.86. The object to which a state price refers is called a *contingent claim*. For example, $0.86 is the state price associated with the contingent claim that pays $1 at date $t = 1$ if u occurs, and $0 otherwise. In similar fashion, consider the contingent claim that pays $1 at date $t = 1$ if d occurs, and $0 otherwise. It is easily verified that the state price of this contingent claim is $0.119.

In this model, contingent claims can be construed as the primary building blocks of all securities. For example, the risky security can be viewed as the combination of two contracts, one that pays 1.0197 units of consumption if u occurs at $t = 1$, and the other that pays 1.0094 units of consumption if d occurs at $t = 1$. The price of the combination is just $(1.0197 \times 0.86) + (1.0094 \times 0.119)$, which equals 1.00. This should come as no surprise, in that the price of the risky security is $1.00.

The point is that when a security is constructed as a combination of contingent claims, the price of the security is just the sum of the values of the ingredients that it comprises. Moreover, the decomposition into contingent claims is unique. There is only one way to construct security payoffs from contingent claims.

Pure arbitrage profits occur when there are two different ways to arrive at the same portfolio position, but the two ways have associated with them

TABLE 10.6. Growth Rates and State Prices

This table presents the probability density functions, cumulative growth rates, and state prices used in the Chapter 10 example.

	Pr(u)	Pr(d)	Pr(uu)	Pr(ud)	Pr(du)	Pr(dd)
Investor 1	94.44%	5.56%	89.72%	4.72%	4.72%	0.83%
Investor 2	86.36%	13.64%	73.41%	12.95%	12.95%	0.68%
Representative Investor	87.98%	12.02%	76.67%	11.31%	11.31%	0.71%
	u	d	uu	ud	du	dd
Cumulative Growth Rates	0.95%	−0.07%	1.90%	0.87%	0.87%	−0.15%
State Prices	$0.863	$0.119	$0.737	$0.110	$0.110	$0.007

different values. When all securities are priced in terms of underlying state prices, there is no possibility for pure arbitrage profits. This is because all securities can be decomposed into their primary building blocks, the contingent claims. Since identical positions must feature the same decomposition into contingent claims, the values of those positions must also be identical.

10.5.1   State Prices

Equilibrium state prices can be inferred directly from (10.9). Table 10.6 displays the probability density functions and state prices for this example. For example, notice that the state price associated with an up-move at $t = 1$ is

$$\nu(x_t) = \frac{\delta^t P_R(x_t)}{g(x_t)} = \frac{0.99 \times 0.8798}{1.0095} = 0.86 \qquad (10.23)$$

10.6   Summary

This chapter described the equilibrium portfolio strategies for a market involving trade in a risky security and a risk-free security, when one investor is a trend follower, and the other investor succumbs to gambler's fallacy. The chapter illustrated the main concepts through a numerical example. A key issue in the chapter involved the relationship between trading volume and the changes in beliefs stemming from the different transition probabilities employed by the investors.

11
Efficiency and Entropy: Long-Run Dynamics

Imagine that some investors predict continuation and other investors predict reversals. Consider two related questions. First, in terms of wealth share, which investors vanish in the long run, those that predict continuation, those that predict reversal, or neither? Second, if prices are initially inefficient, will the inefficiency be eliminated over time?

These questions are important, and are addressed in two parts. The first part is found in this chapter, and the issues are discussed in the context of the model presented in Chapter 10. The second part is discussed in Chapter 16, after the model has been generalized to accommodate heterogeneous risk tolerance, in addition to heterogeneous beliefs.

The key to answering the two main questions in the chapter involves an entropy variable. The entropy variable is like a distance measure, indicating how close investors' beliefs P_j are to objectively correct beliefs Π. In the model described in this chapter, any investor whose beliefs are perpetually too far away from Π is prone to vanish in the long run.

Notably, beliefs are but one variable affecting long-run survival. A second variable is the rate at which investor j consumes his wealth. An investor who consumes wealth too rapidly can vanish in the long run, even if the entropy measure of his beliefs is low (even zero).

This chapter describes a condition for long-run survival that involves the sum of two terms, one related to the entropy measure of beliefs and the other to the rate that wealth is consumed. This sum serves as a vulnerability index. The higher the index, the more vulnerable the investor is to vanish in the long run.

11.1   Introductory Example

The two-investor model described in Chapter 10 described the stochastic structure of a market that evolved over a three-date time horizon. Consider a slight modification to the model, in which one investor is always optimistic (or bullish) and the other investor is always pessimistic (or bearish). Table 11.1 displays the probability beliefs in question. Otherwise, the parameters of the model are the same as in Chapter 10. Notably, prices are inefficient in this example. This is easily seen through a comparison of the stochastic processes corresponding to the representative investor (P_R) and the true process Π. As can be seen in Table 11.1, the two processes are not the same.

In respect to market efficiency, the present chapter asks, what happens over time in this example, as the horizon grows? The answer to this question is bound up with the manner in which wealth shifts between the two investors as they trade. Recall that in the example, investor 1 is a trend follower while investor 2 succumbs to gambler's fallacy. Notably, investor 1's wealth share increases along the extreme scenarios uu and dd, but decreases along the intermediate scenarios ud and du.

The evolution of wealth share plays a central role in respect to market efficiency. The representative trader's probability density functions are

TABLE 11.1. Probability Density Functions

This table presents the true end equilibrium probability density functions, growth rates, and consumption used in the Chapter 11 example.

	Pr(u)	Pr(d)	Pr(uu)	Pr(ud)	Pr(du)	Pr(dd)
True Process	91.59%	8.41%	83.89%	7.70%	7.70%	0.71%
Representative Investor	87.98%	12.02%	76.67%	11.31%	11.31%	0.71%
	u	d	uu	ud	du	dd
Cumulative Growth Rates	0.95%	−0.07%	1.90%	0.87%	0.87%	−0.15%
Aggregate Consumption	100.95	99.93	101.90	100.87	100.87	99.85

a wealth-weighted average of the individual investors' probability density functions. Consider the manner in which market prices evolve. At the outset, the state price vector ν is determined as a function of the process that begins at $t=0$. However, after the first transition the event at $t=0$ becomes irrelevant. If the first transition happened to be an up-move at $t=1$, then the model could be reinitialized, conditional on this event. That is, $t=1$ could be taken as the initial date (instead of $t=0$), with initial aggregate consumption being $\omega(x_1)=\omega(u)$. Likewise, the probabilities Π, P_R, and P_j, $j=1,2$ associated with the various stochastic processes can all be reinitialized by conditioning on the first transition.

If the first transition was an up-move, then investor 1's wealth share increases. Therefore, at $t=1$, in the reinitialized model, investor 1's probability densities are accorded additional weight in the determination of the representative investor's probability densities. Therefore, the influence of investor 1's trades on market prices increases.

To illustrate the issue, consider how the numbers work out in the example from Chapter 10. As was mentioned in that chapter, the occurrence of an up-move at $t=1$ leads investor 1's share of total wealth to increase from 20 percent to 21.47 percent. At $t=1$, investor 1 attaches a probability of 95 percent to occurrence of a second up-move at $t=2$. At $t=1$, investor 2 attaches a probability of 85 percent to occurrence of a second up-move at $t=2$. The wealth-weighted average of the two probabilities is 87.15 percent. Notably, this is the same value implied by P_R. From Table 10.1, the probability attached to the occurrence of an up-move at $t=2$, given an up-move at $t=1$, is $P_R(uu)/P_R(u)=0.7667/0.8798=0.8715$. The point is that the wealth shift at $t=1$ affects the state prices that prevail on the market held at $t=1$.

What will happen over time? Will wealth shift back and forth between investor 1 and investor 2? Will state prices oscillate, occasionally approaching market efficiency, and then departing? Or will one investor almost surely accumulate most of the wealth over time, thereby leading market prices to reflect his beliefs? Those are the key issues addressed in the present chapter.

11.1.1   The Market

The discussion of wealth share dynamics is more easily analyzed using primitive securities instead of the risky security and risk-free security used in Chapter 10. In this respect, consider two risky securities that can be traded at every date. Call the two securities the up-security and down-security, respectively. A single unit of the up-security pays $\omega(x_t)$ units of consumption at the next date if the transition is up, and 0 otherwise. A single unit of the down-security pays $\omega(x_t)$ units of consumption at the next date if the transition is down, and 0 otherwise.

The two risky securities are short-lived, with a maturity of one period. They are purchased at the end of one period, say $t-1$, and pay off at the beginning of the subsequent period (t). Investors can use the proceeds from their security holdings to purchase either current consumption or new securities that pay off in the subsequent period $(t+1)$. (Assume that the two risky securities have terminal values equal to zero.)

11.1.2 Budget Share Equations

A central issue underlying the dynamics of wealth share involves budget share. Recall from (8.10) in Chapter 8 that investor j chooses his consumption plan to satisfy

$$c_j(x_t) = \frac{\delta^t}{\sum_{\tau=0}^{T} \delta^\tau} \frac{P_j(x_t)}{\nu(x_t)} W_j \tag{11.1}$$

This equation can be rewritten in budget share form as

$$\frac{\nu(x_t)c_j(x_t)}{W_j} = \frac{\delta^t P_j(x_t)}{\sum_{\tau=0}^{T} \delta^\tau} \tag{11.2}$$

Equation (11.2) stipulates that investor j follows a fixed budget share rule, where the share of expenditure on consumption in date–event pair x_t is proportional to the product of $\delta^t P_j(x_t)$. This implies that on the market at date 0, investor j will divide his wealth into three portions. The first portion is for current consumption, and represents $1/\sum_{\tau=0}^{T} \delta^\tau$ of investor j's date 0 wealth W_j. The second portion is for future consumption in the date–event pairs where an up-move occurs at $t=1$. This portion represents $P_j(u)(\sum_{\tau=1}^{T} \delta^\tau / \sum_{\tau=0}^{T} \delta^\tau)$ of j's date 0 wealth W_j. The third portion is for future consumption in the date–event pairs where a down-move occurs at $t=1$. This portion represents $P_j(d)(\sum_{\tau=1}^{T} \delta^\tau / \sum_{\tau=0}^{T} \delta^\tau)$ of j's date 0 wealth W_j. Notice that investor j's savings rate at $t=0$ is $\sum_{\tau=1}^{T} \delta^\tau / \sum_{\tau=0}^{T} \delta^\tau$, this being the fraction of his wealth that he saves rather than consumes. Define j's saving ratio $B_{j,t} = \sum_{\tau=t+1}^{T-t} \delta^\tau / \sum_{\tau=t}^{T} \delta^\tau$.

11.1.3 Portfolio Relationships

Blume and Easley (1992) provide an entropy-based analysis of long-term dynamics. Their argument, described below, relies on the following variables. Define $W_j(x_t)$ as investor j's wealth at the outset of date–event pair x_t, after x_t has been revealed to all investors. Define $V_j(x_t) = B_{j,t}W_j(x_t)$ as investor j's portfolio wealth in x_t. Define $w_j(x_t)$ to be investor j's portfolio wealth share $V_j/\sum_k V_k$. Let $\alpha_{j,u}(x_t)$ denote the portion of j's portfolio that is allocated to the up-security during date–event pair x_t. Let $\alpha_{j,d}(x_t)$

denote the portion of j's portfolio that is allocated to the down-security during date–event pair x_t. Denote by $q_u(x_t)$ and $q_d(x_t)$ the market prices for the up-security and down-security during the market that takes place in date–event pair x_t. Denote by $\phi_{j,u}(x_t)$ and $\phi_{j,d}((x_t)$ the number of shares respectively of the up-security and the down-security that investor j holds at the end of date–event pair x_t.

At the end of date–event pair x_t, the value of investor j's holdings of the up-security is $q_u(x_t)\phi_{j,u}(x_t)$. The latter will constitute fraction $\alpha_{j,u}(x_t)$ of investor j's portfolio wealth $V_j(x_t)$. Equating the two expressions implies that $\phi_{j,u}(x_t) = \alpha_{j,u}(x_t)V_j(x_t)/q_u(x_t)$.

Because, by definition, one unit of the up-security pays the entire amount of aggregate consumption available, in equilibrium it must be that

$$\sum_j \phi_{j,u}(x_t) = \sum_j \alpha_{j,u}(x_t)V_j(x_t)/q_u(x_t) = 1 \qquad (11.3)$$

or

$$q_u(x_t) = \sum_j \alpha_{j,u}(x_t)V_j(x_t) \qquad (11.4)$$

Divide (11.4) by total wealth $V(x_t) = \sum_j V_j(x_t)$ to obtain

$$q_u(x_t)/V(x_t) = \sum_j \alpha_{j,u}(x_t)w_j(x_t) \qquad (11.5)$$

Notice that

$$\sum_{k=u,d} q_k(x_t)/V(x_t) = \sum_{k=u,d}\sum_j \alpha_{j,k}(x_t)w_j(x_t) = 1 \qquad (11.6)$$

The last portion of the equation follows because the partition of wealth share across investors and securities at each date–event pair is both mutually exclusive and exhaustive. Define $q*_k(x_t) = q_k(x_t)/V(x_t)$. It follows that $\sum_{k=u,d} q*_k(x_t) = 1$.

11.1.4   Wealth Share Equations

Consider the manner in which investor j's wealth evolves over time. Investor j's initial wealth is $W_j(x_0)$, of which he will consume a portion, and invest the remainder. At the end of x_0 investor j will have portfolio wealth equal to $V_j(x_0) = B_{j,0}W_j(x_0)$. He will invest the fraction $\alpha_{j,u}(x_0)$ of his portfolio in the up-security, purchasing $\phi_{j,u}(x_0)$ units. As was mentioned earlier, $\phi_{j,u}(x_0) = \alpha_{j,u}(x_0)V_j(x_0)/q_{j,u}(x_0)$. Investor j will invest the remainder of his portfolio in the down-security.

Suppose that an up-move occurs at $t=1$. In this case, j's wealth $W_j(x_1)$ will be $\phi_{j,u}(x_0)\omega(x_1)$. Investor j will apply the savings rate $B_{j,1}$ to his wealth, saving $V_j(x_1) = B_{j,1}W_j(x_1)$. Of this amount, j invests fraction $\alpha_{j,u}(x_1)$ in the up-security and $\alpha_{j,d}(x_1)$ in the down security, resulting in $\phi_{j,u}(x_1)$ units of the up-security and $\phi_{j,d}(x_1)$ units of the down-security.

Consider the equation that defines the evolution of investor j's portfolio wealth from $t = 0$ through $t = 2$ in the preceding scenario, where an up-move occurs at $t = 1$ and a down-move occurs at $t = 2$. At the end of x_0, investor j holds $\phi_{j,u}(x_0) = \alpha_{j,u}(x_0)V_j(x_0)/q_u(x_0)$ shares of the up-security; this implies his portfolio wealth in x_1 to be $V_j(x_1) = B_{j,1}W_j(x_1) = B_{j,1}\phi_{j,u}(x_0)\omega(x_1) = B_{j,1}(\alpha_{j,u}(x_0)V_j(x_0)/q_u(x_0))\omega(x_1)$. Therefore, the following equation links portfolio wealth in consecutive periods:

$$V_j(x_1) = B_{j,1}\frac{\alpha_{j,u}(x_0)V_j(x_0)}{q_u(x_0)}\omega(x_1) \qquad (11.7)$$

Equation (11.7) is easily generalized to relate $V_j(x_t)$ to $V_j(x_{t-1})$.

$$V_j(x_t) = B_{j,t}\frac{\alpha_{j,l}(x_{t-1})V_j(x_{t-1})}{q_l(x_{t-1})}\omega(x_t) \qquad (11.8)$$

where $l = u, d$.

The variable $V(x_t) = \sum_j V_j(x_t)$ is the aggregate portfolio wealth at the end of x_t. Therefore, the ratio $B(x_t) = V(x_t)/\omega(x_t)$ is the aggregate savings rate. Invert this relationship to obtain $\omega(x_t) = V(x_t)/B(x_t)$. Now substitute for $\omega(x_t)$ in (11.8) to obtain

$$V_j(x_t) = \frac{B_{j,t}}{B(x_t)}\frac{\alpha_{j,l}(x_{t-1})V_j(x_{t-1})}{q_l(x_{t-1})}V(x_t) \qquad (11.9)$$

Moreover, the general equation can be applied recursively. For example, begin with the equations for $V_j(x_1)$ and $V_j(x_2)$ and substitute the expression for $V_j(x_1)$ into the equation for $V_j(x_2)$. Assuming that an up-state occurs at $t=1$ and a down-state occurs at $t=2$ leads to the following equation:

$$V_j(x_2) = \frac{B_{j,1}}{B(x_1)}\frac{\alpha_{j,u}(x_0)V_j(x_0)}{q_u(x_0)}V(x_1)\frac{B_{j,2}}{B(x_2)}\frac{\alpha_{j,d}(x_1)}{q_d(x_1)}V(x_2) \qquad (11.10)$$

Consider one other set of substitutions into equation (11.10). Multiply (11.10) by $V(x_0)/V(x_0)$, and move a $V(x_0)$-term to divide $q_u(x_0)$, thereby giving rise to $q*_u(x_0) = q_u(x_0)/V(x_0)$. Similarly, place the $V(x_1)$-term so that it divides $q_d(x_1)$, thereby giving rise to $q*_d(x_1)$. These substitutions imply that $V_j(x_2)/V(x_2)$ is the product of $V_j(x_0)/V(x_0)$ and the product of a sequence of terms, each having the form

$$\frac{B_{j,t+1}}{B(x_{t+1})} \frac{\alpha_{j,k}(x_t)}{q *_k (x_t)} \tag{11.11}$$

The expression for $V_j(x_t)/V(x_t)$ based on $V_j(x_0)/V(x_0)$ and the product of terms in (11.11) implies that

$$ln(V_j(x_t)/V(x_t)) = ln(V_j(x_0)/V(x_0)) + \sum_{\tau, x_t} ln(B_{j,\tau}/B(x_\tau))$$

$$+ \sum_{\tau, x_t} ln(\alpha_{j,k}(x_\tau)/q *_k (x_\tau)) \tag{11.12}$$

Equation (11.12) is the fundamental equation derived by Blume and Easley to analyze the evolution of wealth shares over time.

11.2   Entropy

Consider the wealth ratio $V_1(x_t)/V_2(x_t)$. The long-term behavior of this variable can be analyzed using equation (11.12), by subtracting $ln(V_2(x_0)/V(x_0))$ from $ln(V_1(x_0)/V(x_0))$. Because investors share the same time discount parameter δ, their savings rates will be the same. Therefore, in (11.12), the terms involving savings rates and prices will cancel, leaving only terms in $\alpha_{j,k}(x_t)$ (for $j = 1, 2$) and the initial portfolio wealth shares.

Divide $ln(V_1(x_t)/V_2(x_t))$ by t. Notice that this variable is a random number, consisting of a sum of differences of the form $ln(\alpha_{1,k}(x_t)) - ln(\alpha_{2,k}(x_t))$, divided by t, plus the difference in the logarithms of the initial portfolio wealth shares, again divided by t.

As t becomes large, the time average of the initial wealth share differences will approach zero. However, the time averages of the differences $ln(\alpha_{1,k}(x_t)) - ln(\alpha_{2,k}(x_t))$ will be governed by the strong law of large numbers. Recall that the portfolio proportions $\alpha_{j,k}(x_t)$ are given by the subjective transition probabilities. The objective probability density function Π indicates the relative frequency with which the bet associated with each $\alpha_{j,k}(x_t)$ pays off. For the purpose of this example, these are independent of x_t. Therefore, the long-term time average of $ln(\alpha_{1,k}(x_t)) - ln(\alpha_{2,k}(x_t))$ is just

$$\Pi(u)(ln(\alpha_{1,u}) - ln(\alpha_{2,u})) + \Pi(d)(ln(\alpha_{1,d}) - ln(\alpha_{2,d})) \tag{11.13}$$

Equations (11.12) and (11.13) give rise to an entropy measure. Define

$$I_\Pi(\alpha_j) = \sum_k \Pi(k) ln(\Pi(k)/\alpha_{j,k}) \tag{11.14}$$

and call this variable the relative entropy of α_j with respect to Π.

Equations (11.12), (11.13), and (11.14) tell us the following: $ln(V_1(x_t)/V_2(x_t))/t$ converges to $I_\Pi(\alpha_2) - I_\Pi(\alpha_1)$. That is, the time average of the ratio of investor 1's wealth to investor 2's wealth is determined by the difference between the two entropy measures: investor 2's entropy minus investor 1's entropy. If the entropy difference is positive, then investor 1's wealth at date t will tend to the product of t and a positive constant. In this case, investor 1's wealth will grow much more rapidly than investor 2's wealth. Indeed, the relative wealth share of investor 1 will grow to positive infinity, and the relative wealth share of investor 2 will go to zero.

11.3   Numerical Illustration

Table 11.2 illustrates the application of the entropy function to the numerical probabilities in the example.[1] All processes are *i.i.d.* Hence, the branch probabilities govern the evolution of the system. Table 11.2 displays the entropy measures for the transition probabilities of the two investors. Notice that investor 1 has the lower entropy, 0.010 as opposed to 0.019. Therefore, investor 1 will dominate in this example. Over time, investor 2's share of the wealth will almost surely decline to zero.

An alternative criterion is simply to compare the expected values of the two investors' log-portfolio shares. Table 11.2 shows that the expected value of investor 1's log-portfolio share choice (-0.29883)) is greater than that of investor 2's (-0.30835). Equation (11.13) implies that the investor with the higher expected log-portfolio share dominates the investor with the lower expected log-portfolio share.

The analysis also tells us that if an investor were to have objectively correct beliefs, then the entropy measure of his portfolio allocation rule would in fact be zero. An investor for whom the entropy measure is zero will not see his wealth share decline to zero over time.

This example offers one additional insight. If investor 2's share of wealth declines to zero, then over time, market prices will be determined by the probability beliefs of investor 1. Unless his beliefs are correct, market prices will be inefficient.

---

[1] The calculations are found in the accompanying file *Chapter 11 Example.xls*.

TABLE 11.2. Entropy

This table presents the probabilities and entropy values used in the Chapter 11 example.

	Pr(u)	Pr(d)
True Process	92%	8%
Investor 1	95%	5%
Investor 2	85%	15%
ln(True Prob/Inv 1 Prob)	−0.036523	0.51964
ln(True Prob/Inv 2 Prob)	0.07470	−0.57898
Entropy Investor 1	0.01023	
Entropy Investor 2	0.01975	
ln(α) Investor 1	−0.0512933	−2.99573
ln(α) Investor 2	−0.1625189	−1.89712
Expected Value Ln(α) Inv 1	−0.29883	
Expected Value Ln(α) Inv 2	−0.30835	

11.4 Markov Beliefs

The preceding argument assumes that all processes are *i.i.d.* However, what happens when some of the processes are Markovian as, for example, occurs when some investors' beliefs conform to trend, following or gambler's fallacy? In this case, the general argument carries through, and relies on the strong law of large numbers for Ergodic Markov Chains.

The key issue is that the expected value of $ln(\alpha_j(x_t))$ be well defined. To see that it will indeed be well defined, observe that $\alpha_j(x_t)$ will correspond to a transition probability. For example, consider the example in Table 11.3, that being the Markov example discussed in Chapter 10. In this example, investor 1 believes that if the most recent event was an up-move, then the probability of a second up-move is 95 percent. Therefore, after an up-move, investor 1 will allocate 95 percent of his portfolio wealth to the up-security. Now consider the following question: What fraction of the time will such a bet pay off? The answer is the relative frequency with which an up-move actually follows an up-move. From Table 11.3, the answer to the latter question is 83.89 percent.

The argument associated with the event in which two consecutive up-moves occur carries over to the other three sequences (*ud*, *du*, and *dd*). Moreover, the true probabilities associated with these sequences can be used to compute the expected value of the portfolio shares associated with the two investors' portfolio trading rules.

TABLE 11.3. Markov Probabilities

This table presents the Markov probabilities and entropy values used in Section 8.4 and in the Chapter 11 Markov example.

	Pr(u)	Pr(d)	Pr(uu)	Pr(ud)	Pr(du)	Pr(dd)
True Process	91.59%	8.41%	83.89%	7.70%	7.70%	0.71%
Investor 1	94.44%	5.56%	89.72%	4.72%	4.72%	0.83%
Investor 2	86.31%	13.63%	73.41%	12.95%	12.95%	0.68%
α Investor 1			95%	5%	85%	15%
α Investor 2			85%	15%	95%	5%
$\ln(\alpha$ Investor 1)			−5.13%	−299.57%	−16.25%	−189.71%
$\ln(\alpha$ Investor 2)			−16.25%	−189.71%	−5.13%	−299.57%
Expected Value $\ln(\alpha)$ Inv 1			−0.299630			
Expected Value $\ln(\alpha)$ Inv 2			−0.307548			

Table 11.3 illustrates the findings. Notice that the expected log-portfolio share values are similar for investors 1 and 2 in this example, as they were in the *i.i.d.* example discussed earlier. In particular, investor 1 is dominant in this example as well.

Remember that the difference between the two examples is that in the *i.i.d.* case investor 1 is always optimistic, whereas in the Markov case, investor 1 is optimistic after up-moves but pessimistic after down-moves.

It is by no means true that optimists always thrive at the expense of pessimists, nor that trend followers always thrive at the expense of investors who succumb to gambler's fallacy. In the *i.i.d.* case, the key to understanding which beliefs are more fit for the long run is the entropy measure. The lower the entropy, the fitter are the beliefs. Of course, the beliefs that are most fit are those where the portfolio shares coincide with the true probabilities.

11.5   Heterogeneous Time Preference, Entropy, and Efficiency

An important feature of the preceding examples is that the two investors' savings rates were taken to be the same. In general, this need not be the case. This section discusses the implications attached to heterogeneous time preference. Empirical evidence relating to heterogeneous time preference appears in Chapter 13. The analysis makes clear that differential beliefs and differential portfolio sharing rules are both important determinants of long-run fitness.

11.5.1 Modeling Heterogeneous Rates of Time Preference

In order to introduce heterogeneous rates of time preference into the model, index the discount rate δ by j. That is, investor j uses discount rate δ_j.

Consider how the model of Chapter 8 is impacted by this modification. Focus on Section 8.1.5, dealing with expected utility maximization. Notably, equation (8.10) can be expressed as

$$c_j(x_t) - \frac{\delta_j^t}{\sum_{\tau=0}^{T} \delta_j^\tau} \frac{P_j(x_t)}{\nu(x_t)} W_j \tag{11.15}$$

Next, consider the modified equilibrium condition (8.14), which now reads

$$\nu(x_t) = \left(\left(\frac{\delta_1^t}{\sum_{\tau=0}^{T} \delta_1^\tau} P_1(x_t) W_1 \right) + \left(\frac{\delta_2^t}{\sum_{\tau=0}^{T} \delta_2^\tau} P_2(x_t) W_2 \right) \right) \frac{1}{\omega(x_t)} \tag{11.16}$$

Using relative wealth w_j defined in Section 8.2.1, define the variable

$$D_t = \left(\frac{\delta_1^t}{\sum_{\tau=0}^{T} \delta_1^\tau} w_1 \right) + \left(\frac{\delta_2^t}{\sum_{\tau=0}^{T} \delta_2^\tau} w_2 \right) \tag{11.17}$$

Consider the ratio $\nu(x_t)/\nu(x_0)$. In view of (11.16), this ratio is equal to

$$\nu(x_t) = \frac{1}{D_0} \left[\frac{\delta_1^t}{\sum_{\tau=0}^{T} \delta_1^\tau} P_1(x_t) w_1 + \frac{\delta_2^t}{\sum_{\tau=0}^{T} \delta_2^\tau} P_2(x_t) w_2 \right] \frac{1}{g(x_t)} \tag{11.18}$$

Divide the numerator and denominator of (11.18) by D_t. With this modification, equation (11.18) implies that state prices are established by a representative investor whose probability density function is a convex combination of the probability density functions of the individual investors, with the weight associated with density function P_j being the discounted wealth factor

$$\frac{1}{D_t} \frac{\delta_j^t}{\sum_{\tau=0}^{T} \delta_j^\tau} w_j \tag{11.19}$$

The discount factor associated with the representative investor is just $\delta_R(t) = D_t/D_0$. That is,

$$\nu(x_t) = \frac{\delta_R(t)P_R(x_t)}{g(x_t)} \tag{11.20}$$

The introduction of heterogeneous time preferences alters the weights that determine the representative investor's probabilities. For example, suppose that investor 1's discount factor declines from 0.99 to 0.9 in the *i.i.d.* example described earlier. In other words, investor 1 is less patient than previously, and prefers to shift his consumption from $t = 2$ to the earlier dates. As a result, investor 1's probability density functions will carry less weight at $t = 3$ and more weight at $t = 2$.

11.5.2 Market Portfolio

As was discussed in Chapter 10, when investors share the same rate of time preference, the return on the market portfolio at x_t is simply $g(x_t)/\delta$. This implies that the objective one-period return distribution to the market portfolio is time-invariant, in that both the one-step transition probabilities and the underlying distributional support are time-invariant.

This time-invariance property fails to hold once heterogeneous time preference parameters are admitted into the analysis. This is because the discount rate function $\delta_R(t; x_0) = D_t/D_0$ is nonexponential in general. (When investors share the same time preference parameter, and have exponential discount functions, then so will the representative investor.)

To illustrate the preceding point, consider the preceding numerical example, where investor 1's discount rate declines from 0.99 to 0.9, and his relative share of the initial wealth is 20 percent. It is straightforward to compute $\delta_R(t; x_0)$, and observe that $\delta_R(0; x_0) = 1$, $\delta_R(1; x_0) = 0.97064$, and $\delta_R(2; x_0) = 0.94352$. If δ_R satisfied the exponential property, then $\delta_R(2; x_0)$ would equal $\delta_R(1; x_0)^2 = 0.94215$. However, the latter equality fails to hold.

Allowing for heterogeneous time preference implies that the generalized version of (10.11) is

$$q_\omega(x_0) = \omega(x_0)\sum_{t=1}^{T}\delta_R(t; x_0) \tag{11.21}$$

Define $\delta_R'(t; x_0) = \delta_R(t; x_0)/\delta_R(1; x_0)$. The associated equation for the return to the market portfolio generalizing (10.13) is

$$r_\omega(x_1) = \frac{g(x_1)}{\delta_R(1; x_0)}\frac{\sum_{t=1}^{T}\delta_R(t; x_1)}{\sum_{t=1}^{T}\delta_R'(t; x_0)} \tag{11.22}$$

Equation (11.22) indicates that the return to the market portfolio depends on the three terms: the dividend growth rate, the market discount factor $\delta_R(1; x_0)$, and a ratio that reflects the impact of a time-varying rate of time preference for the representative investor. If $\delta_R(0; x_t) = 1$ for all t, then the market return is equal to the dividend growth rate. If $\delta_R(0; x_t) < 1$, then the market return is the sum of the dividend growth rate and a capital appreciation term. If the representative investor becomes more patient with time, then the capital appreciation term is enhanced, as reflected by the ratio on the right of equation (11.22).

The key feature to notice about equation (11.22) is the time-varying constant of proportionality. In the three-date example above, the constant is 1.028 during x_0, 1.034 after an up-move at $t = 1$, and 1.014 after a down-move at $t = 1$.

The differences between these proportionality constants reflect the wealth shifts that take place at $t = 1$. The optimistic but impatient investor 1 plays a more dominant role in pricing after an up-move when his bet on optimism pays off than after a down-move when his bet on optimism fails. When his bet on optimism pays off, his impatience produces a higher expected return distribution at $t = 2$. When his bet on optimism fails, it is the patient investor 2 who dominates in pricing, leading to a lower return distribution at $t = 2$.

11.5.3 Digression: Hyperbolic Discounting

Exponential discounting has featured prominently in economics, because it corresponds to a property known as "dynamic consistency." Dynamic consistency is associated with the reconditioning of the time discount parameter as time moves forward. For instance, suppose that at date 0 an investor discounts the future by applying the discount function $\delta(t)$ to utility $u(c_t)$. If s' and s'' are two dates, $s' < s''$, then the relative weights used in discounting can be expressed by the ratio $\delta(s')/\delta(s'')$.

Now consider the passage of time, and suppose that the current date is s'. Typically, the weighting function at s' is conditioned, meaning that the discount function applied at s' is $\delta_{s'}(t) = \delta(t)/\delta(s')$ for $t \geq s'$. Dynamic consistency requires that the relative weights applied to consumption at the two dates s' and s'' be the same at s' as the weights used at 0 for identical time differences. That is, dynamic consistency requires that $\delta_{s'}(s')/\delta_{s'}(s'') = \delta(0)/\delta(s'' - s')$. Notably, the only discount function consistent with dynamic consistency is the exponential function. Therefore, even if all investors employ exponential discounting, heterogeneity leads the representative investor to violate dynamic consistency.

A nonexponential discount function that has received considerable attention in the behavioral economics literature is known as the hyperbolic discount function. This function has the form

$$\delta_\tau(t) = \frac{1}{K + L(t - \tau)} \tag{11.23}$$

where K and L are parameters. With the passage of time, an investor who uses hyperbolic discounting shifts the relative discounting weight between two dates in the direction of the earlier date.

11.5.4   Long-Run Dynamics When Time Preference Is Heterogeneous

Equation (11.12) provides the basis for ascertaining the impact of heterogeneous beliefs *and* heterogeneous time preference on long-term wealth dynamics. This equation implies that the time average of investor wealth shares is the sum of the difference in expected portfolio shares plus the difference in savings rates.

It follows from (8.10) that investor j consumes the fraction $1/\sum_{t=0}^{T} \delta_j^t$ of his wealth at $t = 0$. Letting T tend to infinity leads to the limiting value $1 - \delta_j$. Therefore, in the limit, investor j saves δ_j of his wealth at each date.

In the preceding numerical example, the time average of investor 1's log-portfolio share was -0.29883, while investor 2's was -0.30835. The difference between the two is 0.00952. In the earlier example, this difference implied that investor 1 would dominate investor 2 over time, in that wealth would shift from investor 1 to investor 2. Will this still be the case when investor 1 becomes less patient than investor 2?

If investor 1's rate of time preference decreases from 0.99 to 0.9, then his savings rate will likewise decrease. This will tend to retard the transfer of wealth from investor 2 to investor 1. Will the direction also be changed?

To answer the last question, recall equation (11.12):

$$ln(V_j(x_t)/V(x_t)) = ln(V_j(x_0)/V(x_0)) + \sum_{\tau, x_t} ln(B_{j,\tau}/B(x_\tau))$$

$$+ \sum_{\tau, x_t} ln(\alpha_{j,k}(x_\tau)/q *_k (x_\tau))$$

Use this equation to compare the difference in the time average of the log-portfolio shares with the difference in the log-savings rates. The difference in the time average of the portfolio shares is equal to 0.00952. The difference in the log-savings rates is $ln(0.9) - ln(0.99) = -0.09531$. Adding the two differences together leads to a sum of -0.08579. The negative sign implies that investor 1 will lose wealth share to investor 2 over time.

11.6   Entropy and Market Efficiency

A key point of emphasis in Chapter 9 is that heterogeneous beliefs can be compatible with market efficiency. Specifically, equation (9.16) provides a necessary and sufficient condition for market efficiency in the log-utility model. Table 9.1 provides an example in which this is the case.

Now consider a slight modification to the example associated with Table 9.1. Imagine that instead of there being two investors, there are three investors. The third investor holds objectively correct beliefs, meaning $P_3 = \Pi$. In addition, let investor 3 hold half the initial wealth, while investor 1 holds 30 percent of the wealth and investor 2 holds 20 percent of the wealth. Let all investors share the same discount rate.

Table 11.4 displays the key probability density functions associated with this example. Notice that the wealth-weighted stochastic process, P_R, coincides with the objective process, Π. Therefore, the market is efficient in this example.

Suppose that the market is organized along the lines of the examples in Chapter 10. That is, in each date–event pair x_t, a market is held for trade in a risky security and a risk-free security. Recall that investor 3 holds objectively correct beliefs, and uses a portfolio-sharing rule that features zero entropy at each date. Will investor 3 come to dominate the market?

TABLE 11.4. Growth Rates and State Prices

This table presents the probability density functions, investor errors, and wealth shares used in the Chapter 11 example.

	Pr(u)	Pr(d)	Pr(uu)	Pr(ud)	Pr(du)	Pr(dd)
True Probability	91.59%	8.41%	83.89%	7.70%	7.70%	0.71%
Investor 1 Probability	95.00%	5.00%	90.25%	4.75%	4.75%	0.25%
Investor 2 Probability	86.48%	13.52%	74.36%	12.13%	12.13%	1.39%
Investor 3 Probability	91.59%	8.41%	83.89%	7.70%	7.70%	0.71%
Wealth-Weighted Investor Probability	91.59%	8.41%	83.89%	7.70%	7.70%	0.71%
Error Investor 1	3.41%	−3.41%	6.36%	−2.95%	−2.95%	−0.46%
Error Investor 2	−5.11%	5.11%	−9.54%	4.43%	4.43%	0.69%
Error Investor 3	0.00%	0.00%	0.00%	0.00%	0.00%	0.00%
Average Investor Error	−0.57%	0.57%	−1.06%	0.49%	0.49%	0.08%
w_1	0.3					
w_2	0.2					
w_3	0.5					

The answer to this question turns out to be no: Market efficiency prevents investor 3 from exploiting the other two investors, and extracting wealth from them over time. This may seem paradoxical, in that the argument advanced earlier suggests that zero entropy investors gain wealth share from positive entropy investors.

However, before analyzing the apparent paradox, consider first the main claim that investor 3 does not appropriate wealth from investors 1 and 2. To see that this is so, consider the equation for state prices when the market is efficient, along with investor 3's consumption equation.

According to equation (8.21), equilibrium state prices satisfy

$$\nu(x_t) = \frac{\delta^t \Pi(x_t)}{g(x_t)} \tag{11.24}$$

According to equation (8.10), investor 3 chooses a consumption plan satisfying

$$c_3(x_t) = \frac{\delta^t}{\sum_{\tau=0}^{T} \delta^\tau} \frac{\Pi(x_t)}{\nu(x_t)} W_3 \tag{11.25}$$

Substitute from (11.24) for $\nu(x_t)$ into (8.10), and compute the value of $c_3(x_0)$. This yields an expression for W_j in terms of $c_3(x_0)$. Substitute for W_j to obtain

$$c_3(x_t) = g(x_t)c_3(x_0) \tag{11.26}$$

Notably, all investors' initial portfolios are held in the risky security, that being the market portfolio. Equation (11.26) indicates that investor 3's consumption simply grows at the same rate as the market portfolio. Therefore, investor 3 does not trade, but instead consumes the dividend from his initial portfolio at every date. For that reason, investor 3's wealth share over time will remain at 50 percent, its initial value.

The preceding argument establishes that as long as prices are efficient, investor 3's wealth share remains invariant. Investors 1 and 2 effectively trade with each other, with wealth passing back and forth between them. However, with market prices being efficient at all dates, neither investor 1 nor investor 2 dominates. The main activity involves positive trading volume, but no inefficiency.

The entropy-based argument advanced earlier established that in the long term, as the number of dates t goes to infinity, investor 3's wealth share must approach 100 percent. How can this be if investor 3's wealth share persists at 50 percent? The answer is that it cannot persist at 50 percent forever. That is, the market cannot be efficient forever.

What will cause the market to become inefficient? The answer is that investors 1 and 2 cannot maintain positive wealth share forever. Over long enough horizons, every investor will experience a run of bad luck, and see his or her wealth decline. Recall from Chapter 10 that the maintenance of market efficiency requires some investors' errors to increase as their wealth declines. That has to be the case as long as some other investors' errors stay finite, and the other investors' wealth increases.

However, there is a limit to how large an investor's error can be. Probabilities are bounded from above by 1 and from below by 0. These bounds prevent investors' errors from being bounded from below by some positive number and also being self-canceling.

The upshot is that when beliefs are heterogeneous, market efficiency can persist for a long time. However, it cannot persist indefinitely. Ultimately, investor 1 will appropriate investor 2's wealth, or vice versa. When that happens, investor 1, say, will hold 50 percent of the wealth and investor 3 will hold 50 percent of the wealth. Then, prices will be inefficient, as Table 11.5 demonstrates. In that case, trader 3 will begin to trade, and in the long run wealth will pass from investor 1 to investor 3. As that happens, investor 3's beliefs will dominate prices, and since investor 3 has correct beliefs, market efficiency will be restored.

TABLE 11.5. Growth Rates and State Prices

This table presents the probability density functions, investor errors, and wealth shares used in the Chapter 11 example.

	Pr(u)	Pr(d)	Pr(uu)	Pr(ud)	Pr(du)	Pr(dd)
True Probability	91.59%	8.41%	83.89%	7.70%	7.70%	0.71%
Investor 1 Probability	95.00%	5.00%	90.25%	4.75%	4.75%	0.25%
Investor 2 Probability	86.48%	13.52%	74.36%	12.13%	12.13%	1.39%
Investor 3 Probability	91.59%	8.41%	83.89%	7.70%	7.70%	0.71%
Wealth−Weighted Investor Probability	93.30%	6.70%	87.07%	6.23%	6.23%	0.48%
Error Investor 1	3.41%	−3.41%	6.36%	−2.95%	−2.95%	−0.46%
Error Investor 2	−5.11%	5.11%	−9.54%	4.43%	4.43%	0.69%
Error Investor 3	0.00%	0.00%	0.00%	0.00%	0.00%	0.00%
Average Investor Error	−0.57%	0.57%	−1.06%	0.49%	0.49%	0.08%
w_1	0.5					
w_2	0.0					
w_3	0.5					

11.7 Summary

The main point of the chapter is that some trading rules are fitter than others insofar as long-run survival is concerned. The fittest trading rule is that of a log-utility investor with correct beliefs. That investor's trading rule has associated with it zero entropy.

Beliefs are not the only determinant of long-term fitness. Investors who choose savings rates that are too small may see their long-term wealth shares go to zero even when they have correct beliefs. This issue is extremely important; it is the subject of further discussion in Chapter 16.

Heterogeneity in respect to time preference has other implications for asset pricing as well. Notably, the return distribution of the market portfolio, while time-invariant under homogeneous rates of time preferences, loses that invariance when investors have different rates of time preference.

Finally, market efficiency prevents informed investors from exploiting investors whose beliefs feature errors. At the same time, when beliefs are heterogeneous, market efficiency is at best transitory.

Part IV

Heterogeneity in Risk Tolerance and Time Discounting

12
CRRA and CARA Utility Functions

To this point, all the examples have featured logarithmic utility. For many reasons, log-utility is a special assumption. In order to place log-utility into context, this chapter presents a short review of the theory of risk aversion, and describes how the key results associated with log-utility generalize. The chapter focuses on the Arrow–Pratt measure of risk aversion and families of utility functions that display some form of constant risk aversion. A key portion of the discussion involves the nature of the representative investor in these more general cases.

12.1   Arrow–Pratt Measure

Imagine that an investor has an initial certain payoff x, and is exposed to a lottery whose payoff is a random variable z. Hence, the investor's payoff will end up to be the random variable $x + z$. Let $E(z) = 0$ so that z is actuarially fair. Consider how much the investor would be willing to pay in order to avoid taking on the additional risk associated with z. Call this amount the premium P. Then P satisfies

$$u(x - P) = E(u(x + z)) \tag{12.1}$$

Next, take a Taylor expansion of both sides of (12.1) to obtain

$$u(x - P) = u(x) - Pu'(x) + o(x) \tag{12.2}$$

where $o(x)$ stands for higher order terms. Continuing, (12.2) equals

$$= E(u(x) + zu'(x) + 1/2z^2 u''(x) + o(x)) \tag{12.3}$$

$$= u(x) + u'(x)E(z) + 1/2u''(x)E(z^2) + E(o(x)) \tag{12.4}$$

$$= u(x) + u'(x)0 + 1/2u''(x)var(z) + E(o(x)) \tag{12.5}$$

Now solve the last equation in order to obtain an approximate expression for P.

$$P = -1/2(u''(x)/u'(x))var(z) \tag{12.6}$$

Designate the function $-u''/u'$ as the Arrow–Pratt risk attitude measure and denote it by $r_{AP}(x)$. Therefore, $P = 1/2r_{AP}(x)var(z)$.

12.2   Proportional Risk

Suppose that the lottery features proportional risk, meaning that z has the form $z = yx$, where y is a random variable and x is initial wealth. Recall that $var(z) = x^2 var(y)$.

Now look at the expression for P once again:

$$P = -1/2u''(x)/u'(x)var(z) = 1/2r_{AP}(x)x^2 var(y) \tag{12.7}$$

Consider P expressed as a proportion p of x. For example, if $p = 0.05$, then the investor would be willing to pay 5 percent of his payoff in order to avoid taking on the proportional risk z. Substituting px for P, obtain

$$px = 1/2r_{AP}(x)x^2 var(y) \tag{12.8}$$

which implies that

$$p = 1/2xr_{AP}(x)var(y) \tag{12.9}$$

12.3   Constant Relative Risk Aversion

Consider the particular utility function $u(x) = x^{1-\gamma}/(1-\gamma)$. The product $xr_{AP}(x)$ is very simple:

$$xr_{AP}(x) = -xu''(x)/u'(x) \tag{12.10}$$

where

$$u'(x) = x^{-\gamma} \tag{12.11}$$

and

$$u''(x) = -\gamma x^{-\gamma-1} \tag{12.12}$$

so that

$$xr_{AP}(x) = -x(-\gamma x^{-\gamma-1})/x^{-\gamma} = \gamma \tag{12.13}$$

Recall from the above discussion that the investor is willing to pay a proportion p of x in order to avoid the proportional risk $z = yx$, where $p = -1/2xr_{AP}(x)var(y)$. However, in the case of this utility function, $xr_{AP}(x) = \gamma$. Therefore, the proportional risk premium p in this case is $1/2\gamma var(y)$. In other words, the premium for facing proportional risk $z = yx$ in this case is $1/2\gamma var(y)$.

Because $xr_{AP}(x)$ is constant for all x for this utility function, the utility function is said to exhibit constant relative risk aversion (CRRA).

12.3.1 Graphical Illustration

Figure 12.1 illustrates CRRA utility in the case of four values of γ, $\gamma = 0, 0.5, 1, 2$. The case of $\gamma = 0$ features risk-neutral utility, in that the function is linear. The case of $\gamma = 1$ features log-utility, in that by (12.11) $u'(x) = 1/x$, which equals $dln(x)/dx$. When $\gamma = 0.5$, the investor is risk averse, but more tolerant of risk than in the case of log-utility. When $\gamma = 2$, the investor is risk averse, but less tolerant of risk than in the case of log-utility.

12.3.2 Risk Premia

As was mentioned earlier, the premium for facing proportional risk $z = yx$ is $1/2\gamma var(y)$. For example, suppose that an investor's coefficient of relative risk aversion, γ, is 2, and the investor faces a risk whose standard deviation is 1 percent. In particular, the risk leaves the mean of the investor's wealth unchanged, but increases the standard deviation. How much would the investor be willing to pay as a premium in order to avoid the risk? The answer is $var(y) = 0.0001$, since the 1/2 and value of γ cancel. That is, the investor would be willing to give up 1/10,000 of his wealth in order to avoid the risk. An investor with a γ of 4 would be willing to give up more, in this case twice as much, or 1/5,000 of his wealth.

For small risks, the risk premium is completely determined by the variance of the risk and r. Therefore, the principle of expected utility implies

FIGURE 12.1. Illustration of CRRA utility function for $\gamma = 0, 0.5, 1, 2$.

that investors act in accordance with mean-variance principles in respect to small risks. Tolerance for risk can be measured as $1/\gamma$, the inverse of the coefficient of relative risk aversion.

12.4   Logarithmic Utility

CRRA utility has the form $u(x) = x^{1-\gamma}/(1 - \gamma)$. Logarithmic utility is identified with the special case in which $\gamma = 1$.

Strictly speaking, $u(x)$ is undefined when $\gamma = 1$, in that the denominator $(1 - \gamma) = 0$, and so is undefined. However, demand functions are determined in terms of marginal utility, rather than utility itself.

Consider the marginal utility function associated with $u(x) = x^{1-\gamma}/(1 - \gamma)$. The marginal utility function is given by $u'(x) = x^{-\gamma}$. Notice that $u'(x)$ is defined when $\gamma = 1$. In fact, when $\gamma = 1$, $u'(x) = dln(x)/dx$. For this reason, $u(x)$ is associated with log-utility when $\gamma = 1$.

12.4.1   Risk Premium in a Discrete Gamble

Let y be a random variable that takes on one of two equally probable values, 1 or -0.5. Specifically, either the investor doubles his payoff $(x + z = 2x)$ or the investor sees his payoff cut in half $(x + z = 0.5x)$. Is this a gamble that a log-utility investor would take?

In order to answer this question, compute the expected utility of the gamble. It is

$$0.5ln(2x) + 0.5ln(0.5x) = 0.5(ln(2) + ln(x)) + 0.5(ln(0.5) + ln(x)) \tag{12.14}$$

$$= ln(x) + 0.5(ln(2) + ln(0.5)) = ln(x) + 0.5(ln(2/2)) = ln(x) \tag{12.15}$$

That is, a log-utility investor is indifferent between a certain payoff of x and an equiprobable gamble whereby his payoff either doubles or is cut in half.

By the same logic, a log-utility investor is indifferent to an equiprobable binary gamble in which his payoff either increases to Kx, where $K > 1$, or decreases to x/K. In this case, the incremental expected payoff, $((K-1) - 1/K)x$, exactly compensates for the additional risk. This property plays a key role in Chapter 13.

12.5 CRRA Demand Function

Consider an investor whose coefficient of relative risk aversion is γ. Define the discounted probability $D_j(x_t) = \delta_j^t P_j(x_t)$. Every investor is assumed to choose his consumption plan c_j by maximizing the sum of probability-weighted discounted utilities

$$E(u_j) = \sum_{t=1}^{T} \sum_{x_t} D_j(x_t) u_j(c_j(x_t)) \tag{12.16}$$

subject to the lifetime budget constraint $\sum_{t,x_t} \nu(x_t) c_j(x_t) \leq W_j$.

To obtain investor j's demand function, form the Lagrangean

$$L_j = E(u_j) - \lambda_j \left(\sum_{t,x_t} \nu(x_t) c_j(x_t) - W_j \right) \tag{12.17}$$

and differentiate with respect to $c_j(x_t)$. Doing so leads to the first order condition

$$c_j(x_t) = (D_j(x_t)/\nu(x_t))^{1/\gamma} \lambda_j^{-1/\gamma} \tag{12.18}$$

Since $\sum_{t,x_t} \nu(x_t) c_j(x_t) = W_j$, and $c_j(x_t)$ is given by (12.18), it follows that

$$\lambda_j^{-1/\gamma} = \frac{W_j}{\sum_{t,x_t} \nu(x_t)(D_j(x_t)/\nu(x_t))^{1/\gamma}} \tag{12.19}$$

Therefore, j's demand function is

$$c_j(x_t) = \frac{(D_j(x_t)/\nu(x_t))^{1/\gamma}W_j}{\sum_\tau \nu(x_\tau)(D_j(x_\tau)/\nu(x_\tau))^{1/\gamma}} \tag{12.20}$$

Note that in (12.20) the pattern of the consumption profile is keyed from wealth W_j, in that (12.20) specifies the fraction of wealth W_j that is to be consumed in each date–event pair x_t. In the discussion that follows, it will be useful to consider the consumption profile as being keyed to initial consumption $c_j(x_0)$ rather than to W_j. Note that $\nu(x_0) = 1$, since x_0 is taken as numeraire. Hence the denominator of (12.20) is equal to $W_j/c_j(x_0)$, so that by substitution, j's consumption growth rate is given by

$$c_j(x_t)/c_j(x_0) = (D_j(x_t)/\nu(x_t))^{1/\gamma} \tag{12.21}$$

12.6   Representative Investor

When all investors have log-utility, then the equilibrium prices are set by a representative investor. Notably, the discount function and probability density functions are respectively obtained as weighted averages of the discount functions and probability density functions of the individual investors. This section discusses how the result for log-utility generalizes to the case when all investors have CRRA utility functions with the same coefficient of relative risk aversion γ.

To begin with, suppose there was only one investor, R. In this case, prices ν would induce this investor's consumption growth rate to be the same as the exogenously given growth rate of aggregate consumption. That is, ν would induce (12.21) to be equal to $g(x_t)$. This implies that

$$g(x_t) = (D_R(x_t)/\nu(x_t))^{1/\gamma} \tag{12.22}$$

Next, suppose that there are J investors. Equation (12.21) implies that

$$c_j(x_t) = (D_j(x_t)/\nu(x_t))^{1/\gamma}c_j(x_0) \tag{12.23}$$

Aggregate consumption in date–event pair x_t is $\sum_{j=1}^{J} c_j(x_t)$. The growth rate $g(x_t)$ is just $\sum_{j=1}^{J} c_j(x_t)/\sum_{j=1}^{J} c_j(x_0)$. Therefore, (12.23) implies that

$$g(x_t) = \sum_{j=1}^{J} \frac{c_j(x_0)}{\sum_{k=1}^{J} c_k(x_0)}(D_j(x_t)/\nu(x_t))^{1/\gamma} \tag{12.24}$$

Equations (12.21) and (12.24) together imply that the rate of growth of aggregate consumption is a convex combination of the different investors' rates of consumption growth.

Compare equations (12.22) and (12.24). Both provide expressions for $g(x_t)$. Therefore, the two equations together imply that in the case when there are actually J investors, prices ν are set as if there is a representative investor R for whom

$$D_R(x_t) = \left(\sum_{j=1}^{J} \frac{c_j(x_0)}{\sum_{k=1}^{J} c_k(x_0)} D_j(x_t)^{1/\gamma} \right)^{\gamma} \tag{12.25}$$

Equation (12.25) is central to both the probability density functions P_R and the time preference parameter $\delta_R(t)$. For fixed t, the discount function is simply

$$\delta_R(t) = \sum_{x_t} D_R(x_t) \tag{12.26}$$

and the probability density function is given by

$$P_R(x_t) = D_R(x_t)/\delta_R(t) \tag{12.27}$$

12.7 Example

Consider a numerical example to illustrate the representative investor property in the case of CRRA utility. Assume that $\gamma = 2$ and the time preference parameter $\delta = 0.99$ for all investors. As in prior examples, aggregate consumption growth evolves according to a binomial process, with the growth rate being either \$0.999 or 1.009.

The example features two investors with different probability density functions. Investor 1, the trend follower, believes that the probability that an up-state follows an up-state is 0.95, and the probability that an up-state follows a down-state is 0.85. Investor 2 succumbs to gambler's fallacy, and believes that the probability that an up-state follows an up-state is 0.85, and the probability that an up-state follows a down-state is 0.95. For the sake of simplicity, both investors believe that the probability that an up-state occurs at $t = 1$ is 0.9. Assume that both investors initially hold the market portfolio, and have equal initial wealth.

Table 12.1 describes the cumulative growth rates and aggregate consumption levels for all date-event pairs. Table 12.2 describes the equilibrium consumption levels of the two agents. Notice that for $t = 2$, the trend following investor 1 consumes more than his gambler's fallacy counterpart in

TABLE 12.1. Sample CRRA Utility

This table presents the cumulative growth rates and aggregate consumption associated with all date–event pairs in the Chapter 12 example.

Date	Sequence	Cumulative Growth Rate	Aggregate Consumption
0	0	1.000	1000
1	u	1.009	1009
1	d	0.999	999
2	uu	1.019	1019
2	ud	1.009	1009
2	du	1.009	1009
2	dd	0.999	999
3	uuu	1.029	1029
3	uud	1.018	1018
3	udu	1.018	1018
3	udd	1.008	1008
3	duu	1.018	1018
3	dud	1.008	1008
3	ddu	1.008	1008
3	ddd	0.998	998

TABLE 12.2. Sample CRRA Utility

This table presents the individual consumption levels associated with all date–event pairs in the Chapter 12 example.

Date	Sequence	Investor 1	Investor 2
0	0	500	500
1	u	505	504
1	d	500	500
2	uu	524	495
2	ud	369	639
2	du	490	518
2	dd	633	365
3	uuu	543	486
3	uud	386	632
3	udu	360	659
3	udd	504	504
3	duu	509	509
3	dud	356	652
3	ddu	626	382
3	ddd	748	249

the two states that feature continuation (uu and dd) and less in the two states that feature reversal (ud and du).

The key issue in the example concerns the nature of the representative investor, whose beliefs and preferences set prices. The representative investor's utility function will be CRRA, with coefficient of risk aversion γ_R equal to 2, the same as for the two individual investors.

The probability density functions of the representative trader will have the form of a weighted average. However, the items being weighted and the weights used are a bit different from the log-utility case. Formally, the weights in this example are based on consumption at $t = 0$, rather than wealth at $t = 0$ (as was the case for log-utility).[1]

Notice that the (discounted) probabilities derived from (12.25) involve the γ-power of a weighted sum of probabilities, each of which is raised to the power $1/\gamma$. This form of average is known as a Hölder average. When $\gamma = 1$, the case of log-utility, this computation involves the exponents' all being unity, and the interpretation is straightforward. However, when $\gamma = 2$, as is the case here, the representative investors aggregate the individual investors' probabilities by first taking the square root of each, then forming the weighted average, and finally taking the square of the weighted average. The above procedure is analogous to the computation of a standard deviation. To compute a standard deviation, take a weighted sum of squares to form the variance, and then take the square root of the variance to form the standard deviation. The representative investor does something similar, but in this example the roles of the square and square root are reversed.

12.7.1 Aggregation and Exponentiation

An important fine point associated with the representative investor's discounted probabilities is that they need not sum to the discount factor δ. This is because the function $f(x) = x^{1/\gamma}$ is strictly convex when $\gamma > 1$. The γ-power of a weighted average of probabilities raised to the power $1/\gamma$, summed over date–event pairs and investors, need not be unity when $\gamma \neq 1$. Therefore, the representative investor may not have an exponential discount function, even when the individual investors have identical exponential discount functions.[2] See Jouini and Napp (2006) who show that the resulting adjustment term can be interpreted as an additional time discount factor which is nonincreasing in $1/\gamma$ and less than unity for $\gamma > 1$, and nondecreasing in $1/\gamma$ and greater than unity for $\gamma < 1$.

---

[1] In this particular example, the distinction is immaterial. In later examples, the distinction is material.

[2] Why is the point important? As will be seen, it plays an important role in the definition of sentiment in Chapter 15.

TABLE 12.3. Sample CRRA Utility

This table presents the probabilities associated with all date–event pairs for the individual investors and the representative investor in the Chapter 12 example.

Date	Sequence	Investor 1	Investor 2	Representative Investor
0	0	1.000	1.000	1.000
1	u	0.900	0.900	0.900
1	d	0.100	0.100	0.100
2	uu	0.855	0.765	0.815
2	ud	0.045	0.135	0.085
2	du	0.085	0.095	0.091
2	dd	0.015	0.005	0.009
3	uuu	0.812	0.650	0.740
3	uud	0.043	0.115	0.075
3	udu	0.038	0.128	0.078
3	udd	0.007	0.007	0.007
3	duu	0.081	0.081	0.081
3	dud	0.004	0.014	0.009
3	ddu	0.013	0.005	0.008
3	ddd	0.002	0.000	0.001

In this example, the representative investor will not use an exponential discount function. Rather, the representative investor uses a discount factor of 0.99 to consumption at $t = 1$, a discount factor of 0.97 to consumption at $t = 2$, and a discount factor of 0.96 to consumption at $t = 3$. If the representative investor were to use exponential discounting, then he would apply discount factors of 0.98 and 0.97 to consumption at $t = 2$ and $t = 3$ respectively. (Here we use the approximations $0.98 = 0.99^2$ and $0.97 = 0.99^3$.)

In the case of homogeneous beliefs, the representative investor will have the same probability density functions and discount function as the individual investors. Technically, taking a convex combination of terms $x^{1/\gamma}$ leads to the value $x^{1/\gamma}$. Taking $x^{1/\gamma}$ to the power γ simply produces x.

12.8 CARA Utility

CRRA denotes constant relative risk aversion, and pertains to proportional risks $z = yx$. In the case of constant relative risk aversion, preferences over proportional risks are independent of the initial payoff level x.

Notably, the absolute magnitude of the risk $z = yx$ increases with the level of x. Because $x r_{AP}(x) = \gamma$, the Arrow–Pratt risk measure $r_{AP}(x)$ is

FIGURE 12.2. Illustration of CARA utility function for A = 1 and A = 2.

equal to γ/x, and therefore declines with x. Therefore, an investor with a CRRA utility function exhibits decreasing absolute risk aversion. This means that the investor becomes less averse to accepting a fixed absolute risk z as his initial certain payoff increases.

Consider next the case of constant absolute risk aversion (CARA). What type of utility function exhibits CARA? To answer this question, integrate the equation $-u''/u' = A$, where A is a constant. Doing so leads to the solution

$$u(x) = -Ae^{-Ax} \tag{12.28}$$

An investor with utility function $u(x) = -Ae^{-Ax}$ has an associated Arrow–Pratt risk aversion parameter of A, no matter what the initial level of x. It is easy to check that

$$-u''(x)/u'(x) = A^3 e^{-Ax}/A^2 e^{-Ax} = A \tag{12.29}$$

When $A < 0$, a CARA investor is risk seeking. The remainder of the chapter focuses on the case of risk aversion, where $A > 0$. In this case, it is sufficient to use $u(x) = -e^{-Ax}$. Figure 12.2 illustrates a CARA utility function for two values of A, A = 1 and A = 2.

12.8.1 CARA Demand Function

In order to derive the demand function associated with maximizing an expected CARA utility function, form the Lagrangean

$$L_j = -\sum_{t,x_t} D_j(x_t)e^{-Ac_j(x_t)} - \lambda_j\left(\sum_{t,x_t} \nu(x_t)c_j(x_t) - W_j\right) \qquad (12.30)$$

Differentiating with respect to $c_j(x_t)$ leads to the first order condition

$$e^{-Ac_j(x_t)} = \lambda_j \frac{\nu(x_t)}{AD_j(x_t)} \qquad (12.31)$$

Taking logarithms leads to the following equation for $c_j(x_t)$:

$$c_j(x_t) = 1/A(ln(AD_j(x_t)/\nu(x_t)) - ln(\lambda_j)) \qquad (12.32)$$

Since $\sum_{t,x_t} \nu(x_t)c_j(x_t) = W_j$, multiply (12.32) by $\nu(x_t)$, sum, and solve for $ln(\lambda_j)$ to obtain

$$ln(\lambda_j) = \frac{A}{\sum_{t,x_t}}\left(\sum_{t,x_t} ln(AD_j(x_t))\right) \qquad (12.33)$$

Substituting for $ln(\lambda_j)$ into (12.32) yields j's demand function:

$$c_j(x_t) = c_j(x_0) - \frac{ln(\nu(x_t)/D_j(x_t))}{A} \qquad (12.34)$$

and

$$c_j(x_0) = \frac{W_j}{\sum_{t,x_t} \nu(x_t)} + \frac{\sum_{t>0,x_t} \nu(x_t)ln(\nu(x_t)/D_j(x_t))}{A\sum_{t,x_t} \nu(x_t)} \qquad (12.35)$$

12.8.2 Aggregate Demand and Equilibrium

Consider the aggregate demand function $\sum_j c_j(x_t)$. Notice that by (12.34), the aggregate demand function involves the sum

$$\sum_{j=1}^{J} (1/A)ln(\nu(x_t)/D_j(x_t)) \qquad (12.36)$$

Observe that the preceding term can be written as a log-product

$$A^{-1}ln(\nu(x_t)^J \prod_j P_j(x_t)) \qquad (12.37)$$

In combination with (12.35), this implies that when traders share the same CARA coefficients, equilibrium prices are invariant to shifts in traders' beliefs, as long as the shift preserves the value of the probability-products. This is a different condition than the one embodied within the CRRA-based aggregate demand function.

When traders have the same coefficient of absolute risk aversion, A, then ν is a ratio of the representative trader's discounted probability to the following ratio: $e^{A\omega(x_t)}/e^{A\omega(x_0)}$. Contrast this with the corresponding CRRA condition $\nu(x_t) = \delta_R^t P_R(x_t) g(x_t)^{-\gamma}$, where δ_R and P_R are given in Section 12.6. The point is that the level sets associated with the aggregate demand function are different for different utility functions.

In (12.34), the term $ln(\nu(x_t)/D_j(x_t))$ is actually $ln((\nu(x_t)/D_j(x_t))/(\nu(x_0)/D_j(x_0)))$, where $\nu(x_0) = D_j(x_0) = 1$ because date 0 consumption is the numeraire and there is no uncertainty at date 0. In a single date binomial setting where there is no date 0 consumption, choose one of the two date 1 nodes as numeraire. In this case the equal product condition described earlier is a product of likelihood ratios. Suppose there are just two traders with the same wealth, and the objective probability of both states is $1/2$. This is an interesting special case, because maintaining the value of the product is the same as maintaining the arithmetic average. The product of the likelihood ratio remains at 1, as beliefs are altered to maintain a constant arithmetic average. This means that for this special case, the CARA efficiency condition is the same as the CRRA efficiency condition.

Notice that (12.34) and (12.35) feature the property for which CARA utility is well known

$$\partial c_j(x_t)/\partial W_j = 1/\sum_t \nu(x_t) \qquad (12.38)$$

where the notation $\sum_t$ means summation over all nodes in the tree. Observe that equations (12.34) and (12.35) imply that the CARA-demand function satisfies the Gorman polar form (Gorman, 1953)

$$c_j(x_t) = K(\nu, j) + G(\nu)W_j \qquad (12.39)$$

where in the case of CARA utility,

$$G(\nu) = 1/\sum_{t,x_t} \nu(x_t) \qquad (12.40)$$

and $K(\nu, j)$ is the second term on the right-hand-side of equation (12.35). Therefore, the aggregate demand function is

$$\sum_j c_j(x_t) = \sum_j K(\nu, j) + G(\nu)\sum_j W_j \qquad (12.41)$$

Condition (12.38) stipulates that each trader allocates every marginal dollar of portfolio wealth to the risk-free security. However, this means that wealth distribution plays no role in determining equilibrium prices, since the aggregate excess demand function $\sum_j (c_j(\nu) - \omega_j)$ is invariant to wealth redistribution. This last property is highly unrealistic. Few investors respond to an increase in their wealth by investing 100 percent of the increase in the risk-free security. For this reason, little attention will be paid to CARA utility after this chapter.

12.9   Summary

The examples used in the preceding chapters feature logarithmic utility. Log-utility is a special case, belonging to the family of functions that exhibit constant relative risk aversion (CRRA).

The notion of risk aversion reflects the idea that investors are willing to pay some positive amount in order to avoid facing a risk. For small risks, willingness to pay is proportional to the variance of the incremental payoff, where the constant of proportionality is one half of the Arrow–Pratt risk aversion measure $r_{AP}(x) = -u''(x)/u'(x)$. Risk tolerance is the inverse of risk aversion.

In terms of risk premium, investors with CARA utility functions are willing to forgo the same premium to avoid a fixed risk z, regardless of the initial payoff x.

Investors with CRRA utility functions are willing to forgo the constant fraction p of their current payoff in order to avoid taking on an incremental proportional risk, regardless of the initial payoff x.

If all investors have CRRA utility functions featuring the same coefficient of risk aversion γ, then equilibrium prices are established as if set by a representative investor. The representative investor aggregates the probability density functions of the individual investors using a moment-based function paramaterized by γ.

CARA utility functions give rise to similar aggregation properties as CRRA functions, but with some differences. CARA utility has some very unattractive properties as well.

13
Heterogeneous Risk Tolerance and Time Preference

To this point, the discussion of investor heterogeneity has focused on beliefs. This chapter extends the discussion to relative risk aversion, describing the associated survey evidence.

13.1 Survey Evidence

Meyer and Meyer (2005, 2006) survey the empirical literature on measures of relative risk aversion. This literature is characterized by wide differences in estimates. Meyer and Meyer point out that the coefficient of relative risk aversion is the percentage change in marginal utility divided by the percentage change in the argument of the utility function; in other words, relative risk aversion is the elasticity of marginal utility with respect to its underlying argument. They demonstrate that this elasticity is sensitive to how the underling argument is defined. Specifically, it matters whether the argument of utility is wealth or consumption. After adjusting for the various functional arguments studied in the literature, they conclude that the various empirical estimates are mutually consistent.

The models developed in this book involve utility functions whose arguments are consumption. One of the most comprehensive studies in the literature on relative risk aversion with respect to consumption is Barsky, Juster, Kimball, and Shapiro (1997), hereafter BJKS. BJKS surveyed investors' attitude toward risk through the Health and Retirement Study

(HRS) that was conducted in 1992. The survey yielded 11,707 responses to a series of questions about attitude to risk and risky activities. The age range of respondents was 51 to 62 years of age, with the average age being 55.6 years.

13.1.1 Questions to Elicit Relative Risk Aversion

Chapter 12 pointed out that a log-utility investor would be indifferent between having wealth level W for sure, or facing a 50–50 gamble in which his wealth would be either $2W$ or $W/2$. An investor with CRRA utility for whom the relative risk aversion parameter $\gamma > 1$ would prefer the certain W to the uncertain gamble.

With the above property in mind, BJKS added the following series of questions to the HRS.

1. Suppose that you are the only income earner in your family, and you have a good job guaranteed to give you your current (family) income every year for life. You are given the opportunity to take a new and equally good job, with a 50–50 chance it will double your (family) income and a 50–50 chance that it will cut your (family) income by a third. Would you take the new job?

If the respondent answered "yes" to question 1, the survey continues as follows:

2. You answered YES to question 1. Suppose the chances were 50–50 that it would double your (family) income, and 50–50 that it would cut it in half. Would you still take the new job?

If the respondent answered "no" to question 1, the survey continues as follows:

3. You answered NO to question 1. Suppose the chances were 50–50 that it would double your (family) income and 50–50 that it would cut it by 20 percent. Would you then take the new job?

An investor with CRRA utility places himself into one of four categories through his answers to the above questions. Specifically,

1. Someone who answers yes to question 1 and yes to question 2 has a coefficient of relative risk aversion γ that lies between 0 and 1.

2. Someone who answers yes to question 1 and no to question 2 has a coefficient of relative risk aversion γ that lies between 1 and 2.

3. Someone who answers no to question 1 and yes to question 3 has a coefficient of relative risk aversion γ that lies between 2 and 3.76.

TABLE 13.1. Conditional Means and Relative Frequencies
of Risk Aversion and Risk Tolerance

This table presents the conditional means of the coefficients
of relative risk aversion and relative risk tolerance, along
with their associated relative frequencies, in the BJKS study.

Category	Coefficient of Risk Aversion	Coefficient of Risk Tolerance	Relative Frequency
0-1	0.7	1.61	12.80%
1-2	1.5	0.68	10.90%
2-3.76	2.9	0.36	11.60%
above 3.76	15.8	0.11	64.60%

4. Someone who answers no to question 1 and no to question 3 has
   a coefficient of relative risk aversion γ that lies above 3.76.

The preceding questions serve to categorize respondents, in that an
investor with CRRA utility and a coefficient of relative risk aversion equal
to 2 would be indifferent between having wealth level W for sure, or facing a
50–50 gamble in which his wealth would be either $2W$ or $2W/3$. Similarly,
an investor with CRRA utility and a coefficient of relative risk aversion
equal to 3.76 would be indifferent between having wealth level W for sure,
or facing a 50–50 gamble in which his wealth would be either $2W$ or $4W/5$.

Call the variable $1/\gamma$ the coefficient of risk tolerance. An investor with a
high value of γ is very risk averse, and so his coefficient of risk tolerance,
$1/\gamma$, is very low.

BJKS make the assumption that the coefficient of relative risk aversion γ
is lognormally distributed in the population. Based on this assumption, and
the relative frequencies of the responses to the preceding three questions,
BJKS compute conditional means for the value of γ associated with each
category interval. Table 13.1 presents the values for the conditional means
for the coefficient of risk aversion, the coefficient of risk tolerance, and the
relative frequencies associated with the four categories.

There are several features to notice in connection with Table 13.1. First,
the conditional mean for the coefficient of risk tolerance is not the reci-
procal of the conditional mean for the coefficient of risk aversion. Jensen's
inequality implies that $E(1/\gamma)$ is greater than or equal to $1/E(\gamma)$.

Second, well over half of respondents are in the most risk averse category.

13.1.2 Two Waves

An interesting feature of the HRS survey methodology is that it is conducted in two waves, called Waves I and II. Notably, a subset of respondents

answered the four risk tolerance questions in both waves. In this respect, many respondents did not provide the same answer in the two waves, which BJKS interpret as noise in the responses.

BJKS assume that the structure of the noise error term is multiplicative, with a mean of 1. They apply an errors-in-variable analysis to adjust for the noisiness in the responses. Effectively, the procedure removes noise by imposing regression to the mean, meaning that the adjusted responses are closer to the unconditional mean than are the actual responses.

Table 13.2 displays the adjusted conditional means. Notice that the adjusted means for the coefficient of relative risk aversion do not necessarily conform to the definition of the category. For example, the adjusted value of 3.8 for category 1 clearly lies outside the interval [0, 1].

13.1.3   Status Quo Bias

Changing jobs is costly. The wording of the four risk tolerance assessment questions involves the comparison between a current job with a safe income stream and an alternative job with a risky income stream. *Status quo bias* is the tendency to prefer the status quo, not just because it offers a certain income stream, but because changing jobs involves adjustment costs.

BJKS suggest that status quo bias may predispose an individual to reject the risky alternative. They conducted a pilot study at the University of Michigan, rewording the questions as a choice between two alternative new jobs, one with a certain income stream, and the other with a safe income stream. The reworded questions led to higher coefficients of risk tolerance. In the HRS, the unconditional mean for the coefficient of risk tolerance was 0.24. In the pilot study, the unconditional mean for the coefficient of risk tolerance was 0.34. This finding supports the view that status quo

TABLE 13.2. Adjusted Conditional Means and Relative Frequencies of Risk Aversion and Risk Tolerance

This table presents the adjusted conditional means of the coefficients of relative risk aversion and relative risk tolerance, along with the corresponding values in Table 13.1.

Category	Survey Coefficient of Risk Aversion	Adjusted Coefficient of Risk Aversion	Survey Coefficient of Risk Tolerance	Adjusted Coefficient of Risk Tolerance
0-1	0.7	3.8	1.61	0.57
1-2	1.5	5.7	0.68	0.35
2-3.76	2.9	7.2	0.36	0.28
above 3.76	15.8	15.7	0.11	0.15

bias increases the estimates for the coefficient of relative risk aversion, in that people are more tolerant of risk than their responses suggest. Notably, BJKS also administered the original form of the questions in their pilot study as a control. The pilot responses to the original form of the questions were similar to the HRS responses.

Brunnermeier and Nagel (2004) provide evidence to show that relative risk aversion appears to be largely invariant to changes in wealth. Their findings appear to stem from status quo bias, in that investors are slow to rebalance their portfolios to changing market conditions. They point out that although the invariance finding is consistent with CRRA utility, the latter does not explain the failure to rebalance.

13.1.4   Risky Choice

In theory, people who are more tolerant of risk are prone to engage in riskier activities. For example, those who are more tolerant of risk would hold more equities in their portfolios than those who are less tolerant of risk. Similarly, the risk tolerant would tend to choose self-employment, consume more alcohol, and smoke more than those who were less tolerant.

Because the HRS asks a variety of questions about consumption of alcohol and tobacco products, and demographic information pertaining to employment, education, age, income, and immigrant status, BJKS were able to relate individuals' choices and characteristics with their responses to the risk tolerance assessment questions.

The overall findings indicate that choices and characteristics are related to risk tolerance. Those who are more tolerant of risk do indeed hold more equities in their portfolios, and are more inclined to be self-employed.

Interestingly, the relationship between risk tolerance and age is U-shaped. Those over the age of 70, and those under the age of 50, are more tolerant of risk than are those between the ages of 50 and 70. Risk tolerance is highest among people whose ages are less than 50. A similar U-shaped pattern holds in respect to income. Those whose incomes are at the extremes are more tolerant of risk than those with incomes in the middle.

The respondents to the HRS with at least $1,000 in financial wealth held about 14.1 percent of their portfolios in equities. The difference in percentage equity holdings between the most risk tolerant group and the least risk tolerant group was 4.1 percent.

Although the signs of the relationships between reported risk tolerance and choices involving risk are in the anticipated direction, the strength of the relationships is far from strong. BJKS indicate that risk tolerance generally explains only a small proportion of choice among risky alternatives.

13.2   Extended Survey

A separate study by this author replicated the BJKS risk tolerance assessment survey, but added a fourth question to elicit a value for γ. The additional question read as follows:

> 4. Questions 1, 2, and 3 are based on the same data, with one exception: the size of the cut to your (family) income if you take the new job and are unlucky. Having answered these questions, please indicate exactly what the percentage cut x would be that would leave you indifferent between keeping your current job or taking the new job and facing a 50–50 chance of doubling your income or cutting it by x percent.

The extended survey was administered to several small groups at different times between 1997 and 2002. Respondents were undergraduate students at Santa Clara University, MBA students at Santa Clara University, employees of a hedge fund firm (including money managers, analysts, and administrative staff), and employees of a financial services software firm that was founded by a financial economist and Nobel laureate. In all, 154 responses appear in the pooled data.

Notably, the respondents in the extended study are younger than the respondents in the HRS survey. The undergraduate students were mostly 20 years of age. The MBA students ranged in age from 25 to 40, but most were in their late twenties and early thirties. The employees at the two firms ranged in age from 25 to 50.

The responses to the extended study differed in two key respects from the BJKS responses in their HRS survey. First, as a group, respondents in the extended study appear to be more tolerant of risk. This is not especially surprising, in that the respondents to the extended survey are considerably younger than those participating in the HRS. And as BJKS find, younger people are more tolerant of risk than older people. Second, the distribution of risk tolerance appears to be bimodal, and therefore is not lognormal.

Table 13.3 contrasts the relative frequencies associated with the four risk tolerance categories. Notice that the relative frequency associated with the least risk tolerant category is about twice as high in the HRS as in the extended study. On the other hand, the relative frequency of those for whom γ lies between 2 and 3.76 in the extended study is three times the relative frequency of their counterparts in the HRS study, and it is also greater in the extended study for those still more risk tolerant.

The extended study was administered to five separate groups. Notably, the shape of the histogram associated with every one of these groups was similar. The modal category featured γ lying between 2 and 3.76.

TABLE 13.3. Relative Frequencies of Responses

This table contrasts the relative frequencies of the four risk
tolerance categories in the HRS and the extended study.

Category	HRS Relative Frequency	Extended Survey Relative Frequency
0-1	12.80%	19.7%
1-2	10.90%	14.5%
2-3.76	11.60%	33.6%
above 3.76	64.60%	32.2%

TABLE 13.4. Conditional Means and Relative Frequencies of Risk Aversion and
Risk Tolerance

This table contrasts the conditional means of the coefficients of relative risk
aversion and relative risk tolerance, for the HRS and the extended study.

Category	HRS Coefficient of Risk Aversion	Extended Coefficient of Risk Aversion	HRS Coefficient of Risk Tolerance	Extended Coefficient of Risk Tolerance
0-1	0.7	0.69	1.61	11.41
1-2	1.5	1.79	0.68	0.56
2-3.76	2.9	2.79	0.36	0.38
above 3.76	15.8	10.71	0.11	0.12

A surprising finding from the extended study is that the distribution
of the coefficient of relative risk aversion is bimodal. The second mode
occurs at $\gamma = 7.52$, the value associated with a cut in income of 10 percent.
For cuts between 5 percent and 20 percent, people tend to respond to
question 4 with responses that are in increments of 5 percent. The number
of responses with 10 percent is considerably higher than the number of
responses with 15 percent or with 5 percent.

The above finding leads the conditional means associated with the
extended study to differ from those of the HRS for the least tolerant
category. Table 13.3 contrasts the two. Interestingly, the conditional values
are similar across the three other categories.

In Table 13.4, notice that the risk tolerance coefficient is much higher
for the most risk tolerant category in the extended study than in BJKS.
This occurs because there are a fair number of respondents in the extended
study whose responses suggest values of γ much less than 1, thereby leading

to large values for $1/\gamma$. As a result, the unconditional mean of $1/\gamma$ in the extended study is considerably higher than in BJKS: 2.14 as opposed to 0.14 (or 0.24 in the errors-in-variables analysis). The unconditional mean for γ is 6.02 in the extended study, is close to 7.1, the inverse of mean risk tolerance in BJKS. Interestingly, the median value for $1/\gamma$ in the extended study is 0.34, the same value that BJKS obtain in their pilot study after adjusting for status quo bias.

13.3   Time Preference

BJKS provide additional insights into heterogeneous time preference. In Wave II of the HRS, they asked a small subset of respondents a series of questions that were designed to elicit their rates of time preference and elasticities of intertemporal substitution.

For CRRA utility, the elasticity of intertemporal substitution is given by $1/\gamma$, the coefficient of relative risk tolerance. BJKS report that virtually no respondents answered in a manner consistent with log-utility. The average elasticity of intertemporal substitution was 0.18. Moreover, there is no discernable statistical relationship at the level of the individual between the elasticity of intertemporal substitution and the coefficient of relative risk tolerance.

The questions that BJKS ask of respondents involve the choice of a future consumption profile, given a particular rate of interest. When the interest rate is zero, discount factors less than unity imply that individuals will prefer negatively sloped consumption streams over flat and positively sloped consumption streams. However, the most common response features the choice of a flat consumption stream. The next most common response features the choice of a moderately increasing consumption stream. These two choices constitute 72 percent of the sample. The remaining 28 percent did not fall into tight groupings. Notably, the overall average slope of the desired consumption stream at a zero rate of interest featured a slope of 0.78 percent a year. That is, on average people appear to display negative rates of time preference.

Additional evidence about implicit discount rates derives from the purchase of consumer durables. Hausman (1979) finds that rates of time preference are inversely related to income. The mean discount rate for households whose incomes exceeded $50,000 was 5.1 percent. However, the discount rate was higher for households with lower incomes. For example, households with incomes of about $25,000 acted as if they used discount rates of 17 percent. Low-income households with incomes below $10,000 used discount rates that were 40 percent or higher.

Additional evidence is survey based. For example, participants in the Seattle and Denver Income Maintenance Programs were asked the following question: "What size bonus would you demand today rather than collect a bonus of $100 in one year?" The range of responses to this question was wide, with answers such as $45 and $75 being typical. Notably, all the respondents to this survey were able to borrow at least $500, so the answers were not a result of credit rationing by the market.

Weitzman (2001) reports the results of a survey of the opinions of over 2,000 professional Ph.D.-level economists, in respect to determining the appropriate social discount rates advocated by these experts. He reports a range from −3 percent to +27 percent, with a sample mean of about 4 percent and a standard deviation of about 3 percent. Weitzman's article, titled "Gamma Discounting," stems from his observation that the empirical marginal distribution of discount rates appears to conform to the shape of a gamma probability density function. However, for the purpose of the present discussion, the key empirical insight is that individual expert opinions about discount rates vary rather substantially.

13.4 Summary

Survey evidence suggests a wide variation in the degree of relative risk aversion in the general population. Risk aversion appears to increase with age up to age 70, and then decline. Most of those above age 50 have coefficients of relative risk aversion that lie above 3.76. There is some evidence to suggest that for those under age 50, the modal coefficient of relative risk aversion lies between 2 and 3.76.

Survey evidence also suggests a wide variation in the degree of time preference, with the mean rate of time preference being negative.

14

Representative Investors in a Heterogeneous CRRA Model

Recall that the idea underlying a representative investor is that equilibrium prices are established *as if* the representative investor is the only investor in the economy who chooses to consume the aggregate supply of consumption as an expected utility maximizing solution. That is, equilibrium prices $\nu(x_t)$ have the form

$$\nu(x_t) = \delta_R^t P_R(x_t) g(x_t)^{-\gamma_R} \tag{14.1}$$

The discussion in prior chapters about pricing by a representative investor involved homogeneous risk preferences. Specifically, all investors were assumed to feature the same degree of risk aversion. As the prior chapter emphasized, the assumption that investors are homogeneous in their attitudes toward risk is unrealistic. Indeed, the general population features considerable heterogeneity in terms of relative risk aversion.

This chapter establishes a general theorem concerning the existence and nonuniqueness of a representative investor. The theorem applies to the case when investors hold heterogeneous beliefs, heterogeneous rates of time preference, *and* heterogeneous coefficients of relative risk aversion (CRRA utility). It is very important to understand that there are several notions of what constitutes a representative investor. The notion used in the present approach is different from the notion of a representative investor used in the traditional approach to asset pricing. In fact, the following section discusses why the traditional notion is inappropriate for studying the impact of behavioral heterogeneity on asset prices.

14.1 Relationship to Representative Investor Literature

The present chapter is the most important in this book insofar as characterizing the representative investor is involved. There is a longstanding body of literature in finance and economics about the manner in which financial markets aggregate the beliefs and risk preferences of individual investors. This section reviews the highlights of that literature and describes the manner in which the approach adopted here follows the literature, and the manner in which it departs from the literature.

The modern economics literature on aggregation begins with Gorman (1953). Gorman was interested in developing necessary and sufficient conditions under which the aggregate demand function depends on total wealth, but not on the manner in which total wealth is distributed among agents. Therefore, wealth shifts among agents do not impact aggregate demand. He established a necessary and sufficient condition that has come to be known as the *Gorman polar form*. In the Gorman polar form, demand is a linear function of wealth (or income), and consumers have a common slope coefficient.

The Gorman polar form enables prices to be determined by a representative investor, no matter the distribution of wealth among investors. In other words, the same representative investor sets market prices, regardless of how initial wealth is distributed among investors.

Lintner (1969) was the first to frame the question systematically in a finance setting. He uses a general equilibrium framework in which the returns to all securities are normally distributed, and the preferences of investors feature constant absolute risk aversion (CARA). Lintner permits his investors to disagree about security return means and the return covariance matrix. He establishes that securities can be priced as if there is a representative investor whose mean forecast of security value is a wealth-weighted convex combination of the individual investors' means. Notably, the representative investor's risk premia do not exactly conform to the wealth-weighted convex combination property. As to risk preferences, the risk tolerance parameter in Lintner's framework is the mean of the risk tolerance parameters of the individual investors.

Lintner's article, although seminal, seems to have faded from view. Rubinstein (1974) develops an aggregation approach along the lines of Gorman. Instead of assuming normality, as Lintner had done, Rubinstein uses a discrete state space, and arbitrary probabilities. He establishes an aggregation theorem for the case in which the Arrow–Pratt measure of risk aversion for individual investors, and most importantly for the representative investor, has a particular form. That form is $1/(A + Bc)$, where A and B are parameters, and c is the level of consumption. Notice that utility functions that exhibit either constant absolute risk aversion (CARA) or constant relative risk aversion (CRRA) satisfy the $1/(A + Bc)$ condition.

Rubinstein's work, which deals with sufficient conditions for aggregation, was later extended by Brennan and Kraus (1978) to establish necessary as well as sufficient conditions. Roughly speaking, the Rubinstein/Brennan–Kraus conditions require either that investors possess homogeneous beliefs and a common B-parameter, or that their utility functions feature constant absolute risk aversion ($B = 0$).

In Lintner, market prices are a function of the underlying wealth distribution. However, Gorman aggregation requires that prices be independent of the wealth distribution. As a result, the aggregation conditions in Rubinstein/Brennan–Kraus are stringent.

Both Rubinstein and Brennan–Kraus impose the Gorman restriction, namely that the parametric specification of the representative investor be invariant to wealth shifts among individual investors.[1] Yet, in the general case of Theorem 14.1 (developed in section 14.4), the Gorman conditions typically fail. This means that the representative investor that sets equilibrium prices in the theorem is different for different initial wealth distributions. Given the discussion in previous chapters, this should not be a surprise. The representative investor's time discount factor δ_R is consumption-weighted. Changing the initial wealth distribution changes the weights used to aggregate the individual coefficients δ_j into δ_R.

A very important issue is whether or not the conditions of Gorman aggregation hold. Theorem 14.1 characterizes a representative investor who sets prices along the entire equilibrium path. Along the equilibrium path, trading by investors leads to wealth shifts. Typically, these wealth shifts drive price changes and returns along the equilibrium path. Heterogeneity is important for prices precisely because aggregate demand depends on the underlying wealth distribution.

By its nature, Gorman aggregation limits the impact of heterogeneity on aggregate demand and therefore equilibrium prices. Brennan and Kraus argue that a necessary condition for (Gorman) aggregation is that investors either have constant absolute risk aversion (CARA utility), or have homogeneous beliefs and homogeneous CRRA coefficients (constant relative risk aversion). These conditions are extremely unrealistic, severely limit the

---

[1] See footnote 4, p. 230 in Rubinstein and the top of p. 410 in Brennan–Kraus.

degree of heterogeneity, and are therefore stronger than the conditions used in Theorem 14.1.

The key difference between the representative investor approach taken here and the Gorman-based approach taken in the past is the following. In the approach taken here, the representative investor sets prices for an equilibrium based on a particular initial distribution of investor portfolios. The representative investor is identified with an intertemporal equilibrium path. However, changing the initial portfolios typically changes the parameters defining the representative investor. In contrast, Gorman aggregation requires that the representative investor be the same for all initial portfolios.

In the approach taken in this book, the rationale for using the representative investor is to understand the character of equilibrium prices, not to simulate an economy that behaves as if there is only one investor. Indeed, one of the main points in this book is that the world is too complex to be modeled as if prices are set by a single, traditional investor.

14.1.1   Additional Literature

Subsequent treatments of heterogeneity have been varied. Jaffee and Winkler (1976), Figlewski (1978), Feiger (1978), and Shefrin (1984) study partial equilibrium models in which investors hold heterogeneous beliefs, but share the same tolerance for risk. Mayshar (1983) and Dumas (1989) focus on a two-investor general equilibrium model where the investors hold the same beliefs, but have different tolerances for risk. Benninga and Mayshar (2000) extend the Dumas approach to many investors, and focus on how the representative investor serves to aggregate the risk tolerance parameters of the individual investors. Their article analyzes the impact of heterogeneity, especially in respect to risk tolerance, on option prices. Similar to Dumas, Wang (1996) uses a model with heterogeneous investors to analyze the term structure of interest rates.

Detemple and Murthy (1994) develop a continuous time, incomplete market, log-utility model in which investors hold differential beliefs about diffusion process parameters. Shefrin and Statman (1994) analyze a model similar to that of Detemple and Murthy, but where time is discrete. At the heart of their analysis is a representative investor whose beliefs are a wealth-weighted combination of the individual investors' probability beliefs.

Cuoco and He (1994a, 1994b) also use the notion of a representative investor in their analysis of a continuous time dynamic equilibrium with heterogeneous investors. Kurz (1997) develops a model in which investor disagreements conform to a rational framework. Basak (2000) builds on Detemple–Murthy in analyzing a model with both fundamental risk and nonfundamental risk. His framework has several features that are similar to the features in this book. Treynor (1998, 2001) develops a model composed of both bullish investors and bearish investors to explain speculative bubbles.

There is a parallel literature in noisy rational expectations models that also features heterogeneous beliefs. These models are based on the Diamond and Verecchia (1981) model, whereby investors form their beliefs by combining their own private signals with partially revealing prices. For the purpose of tractability, these models eliminate the impact of wealth distribution on prices, by assuming CARA utility. As in Lintner, these models tend to impose normality, so that the heterogeneity is in respect to the value of the underlying distribution parameters.

14.2   Modeling Preliminaries

Consider the special case where investors all have CRRA utility functions, heterogeneous coefficients of relative risk aversion, and heterogeneous rates of time preference, but homogeneous probability density functions. Benninga and Mayshar characterized the representative investor under these conditions when $T = 1$. The analysis to follow builds on that characterization.

Let ν_π be the equilibrium price vector ν, and $c_{j,\pi}$ be the equilibrium value of c_j for the case when $P_j = \Pi$ for all j. In the Benninga–Mayshar characterization, the representative investor shares the same beliefs and time discount factor as the individual investors. In this book, equilibrium prices are said to be efficient when they are established *as if* all investors have correct beliefs, meaning $P_j = \Pi$ for all j. Benninga–Mayshar implicitly establish their result in the case of efficient prices, although formally the result does not require that investors' beliefs be correct, only that they be the same.

In Benninga–Mayshar, the representative investor's coefficient of relative risk aversion is given by a weighted harmonic mean, with the weights $\{\theta_j\}$ corresponding to consumption shares in date–event pair x_t. Notably, the variable

$$\theta_j(x_t) = \frac{c_{j,\pi}(x_0)}{\omega(x_t)}[\delta_j^t \Pi(x_t)/\nu_\pi(x_t)]^{1/\gamma_j} \tag{14.2}$$

is investor j's share of consumption in date–event pair x_t. The analysis in Benninga and Mayshar can be extended to identify a stochastic process for the representative investor's coefficient of relative risk tolerance. Specifically,

$$1/\gamma_R(x_t) = \sum_j \theta_j(x_t)(1/\gamma_j) \tag{14.3}$$

Theorem 14.1 (in section 14.4) establishes that there are other functions for γ_R besides (14.3). However, (14.3) has a very appealing property. When investors all share the same coefficient of relative risk aversion γ, then (14.3) implies that $\gamma_R = \gamma$.

The formal argument extending the Benninga–Mayshar result is straight-forward. Note first that applying (12.21) here means that j's consumption growth rate is given by

$$c_j(x_t)/c_j(x_0) = (D_j(x_t)/\nu(x_t))^{1/\gamma_j} \tag{14.4}$$

Note also that, as (12.21) and the equilibrium condition $\sum_j c_j(\nu) = \sum_j \omega_j$ imply, $\theta_j(x_t)$ is indeed investor j's share of consumption in date–event pair x_t, so that $\sum_j \theta_j(x_t) = 1$ for all x_t. Based on (12.21), the equilibrium condition $\sum_j (c_j(\nu) - \omega_j) = 0$, and the variable $V = \nu/\Pi$, Benninga–Mayshar define the implicit function

$$F(C, V) = \sum_j (c_j(x_0)/C)[\delta_j^t/V]^{1/\gamma_j} = 1 \tag{14.5}$$

Benninga and Mayshar observe that by the principle of expected utility maximization, the representative investor's marginal utility at C will be proportional to V. In turn, this implies that γ_R, the Arrow–Pratt coefficient of relative risk aversion, can be defined locally by $-CV'(C)/V(C)$. By computing $\partial F/\partial C$ and $\partial F/\partial V$, they show that

$$V'(C) = \frac{-\partial F/\partial C}{\partial F/\partial V} = \frac{(V'(C)/C)}{\sum_j \theta_j(x_t)/\gamma_j} \tag{14.6}$$

which, taken together with the local Arrow–Pratt measure, establishes the result.

14.3   Efficient Prices

Efficiency plays a key role in the derivation of the general aggregation result to follow. For this reason, consider a numerical example that illustrates the case of market efficiency. The example is equivalent to the two-investor example provided in Section 12.6, but with two modifications.

The first modification is that both investors hold objectively correct beliefs. Specifically, both investors believe that aggregate consumption growth evolves as an *i.i.d.* process, where the probability of an up-move is 0.9.

The second modification is that investor 1 has log-utility ($\gamma_1 = 1$), and investor 2 has a coefficient of relative risk aversion of 2 ($\gamma_2 = 2$).

In this example, investors hold the same beliefs, employ the same time discount factor, and have the same initial wealth levels. They differ only in respect to their coefficients of relative risk tolerance $1/\gamma_j$. The representative investor will share the beliefs and time discount factor of the two investors. However, the representative investor's coefficient of risk tolerance $1/\gamma_R$ will be a convex combination of the individual investors' coefficients of risk tolerance $1 = 1/\gamma_1$ and $0.5 = 1/\gamma_2$.

Given that the two investors have the same initial wealth, intuitively one would expect that the representative investor's coefficient of relative risk aversion would be the simple average of 1 and 0.5; that is, $1/\gamma_R = 0.75$. However, (14.3) indicates that $1/\gamma_R$ is actually a stochastic process, through its dependence on x_t. In this example, the variation in $1/\gamma_R$ is nonzero but small. This point is discussed again later, in Section 14.5.

14.4   Representative Investor Characterization Theorem

Consider the situation when investors all have CRRA utility functions, but can differ in respect to their beliefs, coefficients of risk tolerance, and time discount factors. What are the features of the representative investor in such a case?

The theorem to follow establishes a result for one such representative investor. As it happens, the representative investor is not unique. However, the representative investor described here has attractive properties not shared by other representative investors.

The starting point for the representative investor is the function $1/\gamma_R(x_t)$. We obtain what this function is by applying the result described earlier, using the function (14.3) that applies in the efficient market case. That is, even if investors have heterogeneous beliefs, and $P_j \neq \Pi$ for some investor j, the function $1/\gamma_R(x_t)$ is still taken to be (14.3). In terms of the example provided in the previous section, $1/\gamma_R$ would be approximately 0.75. Once we have nailed down $1/\gamma_R$, the remaining tasks are to identify the functions P_R and δ_R.

Theorem 14.1 *Let ν be an equilibrium state price vector for a complete market involving investor heterogeneity in respect to $\{P_j, \gamma_j, \delta_j\}$, that is, beliefs, coefficients of relative risk aversion, and time preference parameters. Then,*

(1) ν is also an equilibrium price vector for a market involving a single representative investor whose expected utility function has the form

$$\sum \delta_R(t)\, P_R(x_t)\, a(x_t)\, c(x_t)^{1-\gamma_R(x_t)}$$

where the summation is over all date-event pairs $\{x_t | t = 0, \ldots, T\}$. In particular, ν satisfies

$$\nu(x_t) = \delta_{R,t}^t P_R(x_t) g(x_t)^{-\gamma_R(x_t)} \tag{14.7}$$

where γ_R, δ_R, and P_R have the structure described below:

$$1/\gamma_R(x_t) = \sum_j \theta_j(x_t)(1/\gamma_j) \tag{14.8}$$

$$\delta_{R,t}^t = \sum_{x_t} \nu(x_t)\zeta(x_t)^{\gamma_R(x_t)} \tag{14.9}$$

where the summation in (14.9) is over all investors and x_t-events at date t.

$$P_R(x_t) = \frac{\nu(x_t)\zeta(x_t)^{\gamma_R(x_t)}}{\delta_{R,t}^t} \tag{14.10}$$

where

$$\zeta(x_t) = \sum_{j=1}^{J} \frac{c_j(x_0)(D_j(x_t)/\nu(x_t))^{1/\gamma_j}}{\sum_{k=1}^{J} c_k(x_0)} \tag{14.11}$$

(2) The representative investor is not unique. Any two representative investors, denoted $R, 1$ and $R, 2$, giving rise to (14.7) are related through the expression

$$\frac{\delta_{R,1}^t P_{R,1}}{\delta_{R,2}^t P_{R,2}} = g^{\gamma_{R,1} - \gamma_{R,2}} \tag{14.12}$$

(3) If $a(x_t) = 1/(1 - \gamma_R(x_t))$, then the representative investor's expected utility maximizing solution supports the equilibrium growth trajectory $<g(x_t)>$ for aggregate consumption. If

$$a(x_t) = (1/1 - \gamma_R(x_t)) \frac{\omega(x_0)^{\gamma_R(x_0)}}{(\omega(x_t)g(x_t))^{\gamma_R(x_t)}}$$

then the representative investor's expected utility maximizing solution supports the equilibrium trajectory $<\omega(x_t)>$ for aggregate consumption.

Proof of Theorem The plan of the proof is to derive expressions for P_R, δ_R, and γ_R, by equating two different expressions for $g(x_t)$. The first expression for $g(x_t)$ stems from the equilibrium condition $\sum c_j = \sum \omega_j$, where c_j is given by (12.21). The second expression for $g(x_t)$ stems from (14.1), which expresses equilibrium prices ν in terms of $g(x_t)$ and the representative investor's parameters P_R, δ_R, and γ_R.

Begin the proof by defining

$$\zeta_j(x_t) = \frac{c_j(x_0)D_j(x_t)^{1/\gamma_j}}{\sum_{k=1}^{J} c_k(x_0)} \tag{14.13}$$

and

$$\zeta(x_t) = \sum_{j=1}^{J} \zeta_j(x_t)\nu(x_t)^{-1/\gamma_j} \tag{14.14}$$

which is equivalent to the expression for $\zeta(x_t)$ that appears in the statement of the theorem.

Next, turn to the two expressions for $y(x_t)$. The first uses (12.21) to compute the equilibrium value of $g(x_t)$. By definition,

$$g(x_t) = \frac{\sum_j c_j(x_t)}{\sum_j c_j(x_0)}$$

and substituting for c_j from (12.21), obtain

$$= \sum_{j=1}^{J} \frac{c_j(x_0)(D_j(x_t)/\nu(x_t))^{1/\gamma_j}}{\sum_{k=1}^{J} c_k(x_0)}$$

which, using the definition of ζ_j, yields

$$= \sum_{j=1}^{J} \zeta_j(x_t)\nu(x_t)^{-1/\gamma_j} \tag{14.15}$$

$$= \zeta(x_t) \tag{14.16}$$

by the definition of ζ.

The second expression for $g(x_t)$ is obtained by inverting equation (14.1). Doing so yields

$$g(x_t) = (\delta_R^t P_R(x_t)/\nu(x_t))^{1/\gamma_R(x_t)} \tag{14.17}$$

Now equate the two expressions for $g(x_t)$ to obtain

$$g(x_t) = (\delta_R^t P_R(x_t)/\nu(x_t))^{1/\gamma_R(x_t)} \tag{14.18}$$

$$= \sum_j \zeta_j(x_t)\nu(x_t)^{-1/\gamma_j} \tag{14.19}$$

$$= \zeta(x_t) \tag{14.20}$$

In the remainder of the proof, use the last set of equations to establish the expressions for P_R, δ_R, and γ_R that appear in the statement of Theorem 14.1.

Notice that the preceding equation, equating the two terms for $g(x_t)$, implies that

$$\delta_{R,t}^t P_R(x_t) = \nu(x_t)\zeta(x_t)^{\gamma_R(x_t)} \tag{14.21}$$

Hence, the preceding equation defines $\delta_{R,t}^t P_R(x_t)$ in terms of γ_R. Define $\delta_{R,t}^t$ as the following sum, for fixed t:

$$\sum_{x_t} \nu(x_t)\zeta(x_t)^{\gamma_R(x_t)} \tag{14.22}$$

Then define $P_R(x_t)$ as the ratio

$$P_R(x_t) = \frac{\nu(x_t)\zeta(x_t)^{\gamma_R(x_t)}}{\delta_{R,t}^t} \tag{14.23}$$

In view of the normalization implicit in the last equation, $\sum P_R(x_t) = 1$, for each t. Nonnegativity of P_R follows from the fact that all variables involved in the construction are nonnegative.

With $\delta_{R,t}^t$ and $P_R(x_t)$ defined in terms of γ_R, it remains to specify γ_R. In this respect, let γ_R be (14.3). Notice that (14.8) is a function of Π, and is derived from Benninga–Mayshar. In particular, (14.8) is not dependent on P_R or δ_R. Hence, there is no issue of simultaneity in determining $\delta_{R,t}^t$, $P_R(x_t)$, and γ_R.

The preceding argument establishes the first part of the theorem. In order to establish the nonuniqueness claim, observe that we are free to specify the function γ_R. One alternative definition of γ_R features $\{\theta_j\}$ defined using actual consumption shares instead of the consumption shares associated with the case when $P_j = \Pi$ for all j. A second alternative is for $\gamma_R(x_t)$ to be set equal to an arbitrary constant for all x_t. In both alternatives, P_R and δ_R can be obtained as functions of γ_R. Equation (14.12) follows from (14.7).

Part (3) of the theorem follows directly from the first-order conditions for the representative investor's expected utility maximization problem. ∎

14.4.1 Discussion

Theorem 14.1 provides insight into how the market combines the beliefs, coefficients of risk tolerance, and time preference parameters of individual investors into corresponding market aggregates associated with the representative investor. The market weights the contribution of an individual investor's characteristics according to the degree to which the investor trades. For example, the representative investor's risk tolerance function is a consumption weighted average of the risk tolerance parameters of the individual investors. The greater an individual investor's relative share of consumption in a date-event pair, the greater will be that investor's weight in determining the market's risk tolerance.

The representative investor's stochastic process (beliefs) P_R is determined as a generalized Hölder average. Here the weights are given by initial consumption share, risk tolerance, and time preference. Equations (14.11) and (14.21) in Theorem 14.1 indicate that the degree to which the characteristics of investor j are reflected in P_R increases in respect to j's initial consumption, risk tolerance, and rate of time preference.

Because relative wealth shifts over time, the representative investor's beliefs, risk tolerance, and time preference tend to be volatile. When an investor becomes relatively wealthier, the weight of his contribution to the representative investor's characteristics increases. That is why the representative investor's coefficient of risk tolerance is stochastic in the general case, even when the individual investors each have constant coefficients of relative risk tolerance.

Heterogeneity leads the features of the representative investor to differ from those of the individual investors. The representative investor's coefficient of relative risk aversion is typically stochastic, whereas the individual investors have deterministic coefficients of relative risk aversion. Figures 8.2 and 9.2 demonstrate how the probability density functions associated with the representative investor's stochastic process typically differ from those of the individual investors. Section 12.7.1 discusses why the time preference function for the representative investor can be nonexponential, even when all investors have exponential discount functions.

One point about P_R worth emphasizing is that markets aggregate probability density functions, not moments. This property is most easily seen in Figure 9.2. If markets aggregated moments, instead of density functions, P_R would equal Π in the example underlying Figure 9.2. Theorem 14.1 indicates that it is typically inappropriate to develop asset pricing theories that feature a single representative investor who corresponds to an average investor.

Theorem 14.1 has a key message. That message reads: Do not develop asset pricing models based on a single representative investor who is a priori assumed to represent an average investor in the market. This message applies both to neoclassical asset pricing models and to behavioral asset pricing models.

Theorem 14.1 provides insight into the determinants of investor j's rate of consumption growth. Equations (12.21) and (14.7) imply that investor j's rate of consumption growth is given by the following expression:

$$c_j(x_t)/c_j(x_0) = g(x_t)^{\gamma_R/\gamma_j} (D_j(x_t)/D_R(x_t))^{1/\gamma_j}$$

where $D_R(x_t)$ is the representative investor's discounted probability (14.21).

The above expression for $c_j(x_t)/c_j(x_0)$ indicates that investor j's consumption growth rate is a product of two functions. The first function is a power function in the growth rate of aggregate consumption. In order to interpret this function, consider the case when investor j has the same discounted beliefs as the representative investor.

If investor j's coefficient of relative risk aversion γ_j exceeds $\gamma_R(x_t)$, then the power function is concave: An example is the square root function. In this case, the power function moves investor j's consumption growth rate closer to unity than the aggregate consumption growth rate. That is, because investor j is more risk averse than the representative investor, his consumption growth rate is less volatile than the growth rate of aggregate consumption. His consumption growth rate lies below the aggregate consumption growth rate in favorable states when $g(x_t) > 1$, and lies above the aggregate consumption growth rate in unfavorable states when $g(x_t) < 1$. If investor j's coefficient of relative risk aversion γ_j is less than $\gamma_R(x_t)$, then the power function is convex: An example is the quadratic function. In this case, the power function moves investor j's consumption growth rate further from unity than the aggregate consumption growth rate. That is, because investor j is less risk averse than the representative investor, his consumption growth rate is more volatile than the growth rate of aggregate consumption. His consumption growth rate lies above the aggregate consumption growth rate in favorable states when $g(x_t) > 1$, and lies below the aggregate consumption growth rate in unfavorable states when $g(x_t) < 1$.

The second function captures the impact of investor j's beliefs and discount factor on his consumption growth rate, relative to those of the representative investor. The key variable here is the discounted likelihood ratio $D_j(x_t)/D_R(x_t)$. Suppose that investor j attaches more probability to the occurrence of x_t than does the representative investor. In this case, the second function indicates the extent to which j's consumption growth rate will be higher relative to the case when his beliefs coincide with those of the representative investor. If investor j attaches less probability to the occurrence of x_t than does the representative investor, the second function indicates the extent to which j's consumption growth rate will be lower relative to the case when his beliefs coincide with those of the representative investor. Notice that the magnitude of the adjustment due to heterogeneous beliefs depends on j's coefficient of relative risk aversion. If investor j is more risk averse than a log-utility investor ($\gamma_j > 1$), then the second function is concave, which implies that the difference of opinion between investor j and the representative investor will be muted. If investor j is less risk averse than a log-utility investor ($\gamma_j < 1$), then the second function is convex, which implies that the difference of opinion between investor j and the representative investor will be exaggerated. If investor j has log-utility preferences ($\gamma_j = 1$), then the second function is linear in the discounted likelihood ratio.

14.4.2   Nonuniqueness

Although this book uses the term *the* representative investor instead of *a* representative investor, Theorem 14.1 establishes that the representative investor is not unique. Yet, for the most part, the approach in this book will continue to speak of *the* representative investor, referring to the functions P_R, δ_R, and γ_R identified in Theorem 14.1.

There is a simple reason for doing so. Other representative investors tend to have eccentric properties, in that they accentuate confounding effects from heterogeneous risk tolerance and heterogeneous beliefs, especially attributing effects arising from beliefs to risk aversion. For example, Theorem 14.1 mentions a specification whereby $\{\theta_j\}$ is defined using actual consumption shares instead of the consumption shares associated with the case when $P_j = \Pi$ for all j. This alternative specification has the potential to attribute effects to risk aversion that stem from heterogeneous beliefs. Therefore, the alternative specification would inject more variability into the γ_R function than the specification used in the first part of Theorem 14.1, in that the actual consumption shares would reflect heterogeneity in beliefs.

An example of an eccentric representative investor is provided in Chapter 16. In contrast, the representative investor identified in the first part of Theorem 14.1 will share the same beliefs and coefficient of risk aversion as the individual investors when the individual investors are homogeneous in those respects.

14.5   Comparison Example

The example developed earlier in this chapter is a modified version of the example developed in Section 12.6. The key difference between the two examples is that in the Chapter 12 example, the investors shared the same coefficient of risk tolerance, $\gamma_j = 2$ for $j = 1, 2$. In the example developed in this chapter, $\gamma_1 = 1$ and $\gamma_2 = 2$. The Excel file *Chapter 14 Example.xls* contains the details of the example.

Consider a comparison of three examples: the one in this chapter, the one in Chapter 12, and one in which both investors have log-utility ($\gamma_1 = 1$ and $\gamma_2 = 1$). The key issue of interest is how the representative investor's probability density functions differ from each other across the three examples. Keep in mind that in all these examples, the two investors' respective probability density functions are the same. That is, the density functions for each investor are the same across the three examples, although the two investors have different probability density functions.

Figure 14.1 illustrates the differences. The bar chart shows the respective ratios of the representative investor's probabilities in the two homogeneous risk tolerance examples to the representative investor's probabilities in the heterogeneous risk tolerance example.

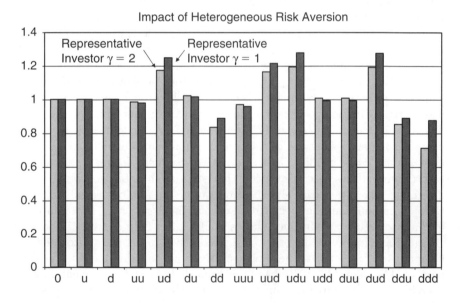

FIGURE 14.1. This figure shows the impact of heterogeneous risk tolerance on the representative investor's probability density function. In the example, the two individual investors have heterogeneous probability density functions. The variable being displayed is the likelihood ratio where the representative investor probability for a homogeneous risk tolerance example is divided by the representative investor probability for the heterogeneous risk tolerance example.

When a ratio lies above unity, the heterogeneous risk tolerance example features a lower probability than the corresponding homogeneous risk tolerance example. Notably, heterogeneous risk tolerance lowers the representative investor's probabilities for events ud, du, uud, udu, dud, relative to both homogeneous risk tolerance examples.

Figure 14.2 displays the ratio of the representative investor's probability density functions for the case when $\gamma = 2$ relative to $\gamma = 1$. Notice that the two probability density functions are similar to one another. The representative investor holds similar beliefs in the example featuring homogeneous $\gamma = 2$ as in the example homogeneous $\gamma = 1$. However, in view of Figure 14.1, the introduction of heterogeneous risk tolerance results in the representative investor's exhibiting probability density functions that are decidedly different than the two homogeneous risk tolerance examples.

Consider the shape of the γ_R function. Because the weights used to compute $1/\gamma_R(x_t)$ are consumption shares that vary across x_t, γ_R itself will vary across x_t. That is, γ_R will vary across aggregate consumption growth g. Figure 14.3 displays the γ_R function for this example. All the values for γ_R shown correspond to a value for $1/\gamma_R$ that is approximately 0.75, the midpoint between the coefficients of risk tolerance for the two investors,

FIGURE 14.2. This figure displays the ratio of the representative investor's probability density functions for the case when $\gamma = 2$ relative to $\gamma = 1$.

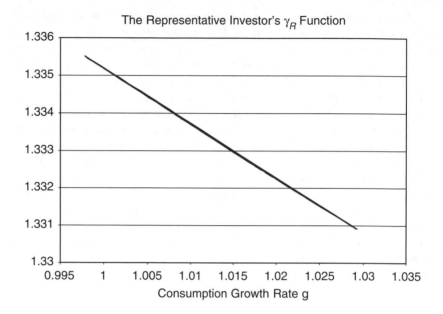

FIGURE 14.3. γ_R as a function of aggregate consumption growth g.

those being 1 and 0.5 respectively. At the same time, the γ_R function is clearly downward sloping. The downward-sloping feature arises because when prices are efficient ($P_j = \Pi$ for all j), the more risk tolerant investor 1 has a higher consumption share in high growth states than investor 2. Therefore, investor 1's coefficient of risk tolerance receives more weight in the higher growth states.

The general point brought out by this example is that heterogeneous beliefs and heterogeneous risk tolerance interact with one another. The effects of the two sources of heterogeneity are not separable. Even though the representative investor has a coefficient of risk tolerance $1/\gamma_R$ that is approximately equal to 0.75, the representative investor would hold different beliefs if all investors actually had coefficients of risk tolerance equal to 0.75.

14.6   Pitfall: The Representative Investor Theorem Is False

As was mentioned in the preface, traditional asset pricing theorists have advanced arguments to show that the main results presented in this book are false. In the hope of laying these claims to rest, the main counter arguments that have been advanced are presented at intermittent points and discussed. The counter arguments are subtle, and readers are encouraged to try and identify the pitfalls.

14.6.1 Argument Claiming That Theorem 14.1 Is False

Based on the analysis in Chapter 12, the first order condition associated with investor j stipulates that marginal expected utility per dollar of wealth expended is equal across all date–event pairs. Consider the initial date $(t = 0)$ and an arbitrary date–event pair x_t. The condition for equality between values for marginal expected utility per dollar is

$$\nu(x_t)c_j(x_0)^{-\gamma_j} = \delta_j^t P_j(x_t)c_j(x_t)^{-\gamma_j} \tag{14.24}$$

Solve this equation for $c_j(x_t)$ to obtain

$$c_j(x_t) = c_j(x_0)[\delta_j^t P_j(x_t)]^{1/\gamma_j}\nu(x_t)^{-1/\gamma_j} \tag{14.25}$$

The equilibrium condition equates aggregate demand $\sum_{j=1}^{J} c_j(x_t)$ and aggregate supply $\omega(x_t)$ for each x_t. Therefore, (14.25) implies that in equilibrium,

$$\omega(x_t) = \sum_{j=1}^{J} c_j(x_0)[\delta_j^t P_j(x_t)]^{1/\gamma_j}\nu(x_t)^{-1/\gamma_j} \tag{14.26}$$

Without loss of generality, let $\omega(x_0) = 1$. Theorem 14.1 claims that

$$\nu(x_t) = \left(\sum_{j=1}^{J} c_j(x_0)[\delta_j^t P_j(x_t)]^{1/\gamma_j}\right)^{\gamma_R} \omega(x_t)^{-\gamma_R} \tag{14.27}$$

where γ_R is a consumption-share weighted harmonic mean of the individual γ_j coefficients that is independent of the P_j values.

Fix a value of x_t and let $y = \nu(x_t)^{-1}$, $\beta_j = 1/\gamma_j$, and $k_j = (c_j(x_0)/\omega(x_t))[\delta_j^t P_j(x_t)]^{1/\gamma_j}$. Then Theorem 14.1 is equivalent to the statement that the arbitrary polynomial

$$\sum_{j=1}^{J} k_j y^{\beta_j} = 1 \tag{14.28}$$

that being (14.26) has the solution $y = (\sum_j k_j)^{-\gamma_R}$, that being (14.27). This is clearly false unless γ_j takes on the same value for all j. Therefore, except for the case of homogeneous risk tolerance, Theorem 14.1, the central aggregation result in the book, is false.

14.6.2   Identifying the Flaw

The flaw in the argument lies in the use of equation (14.27). Theorem 14.1 does not exactly imply equation (14.27), but a variant in which a term $\nu(x_t)$ is inserted into the right-hand side immediately after the equality sign, and a term $\nu(x_t)^{-1/\gamma_j}$ is inserted just to the left of the right bracket. See equation (14.21). Now, raise (14.26) to the power γ_R and substitute into the modified (14.27) as described above. The terms $\nu(x_t)$ on both sides of the equation cancel, leaving the product $\omega(x_t)^{\gamma_R}\omega(x_t)^{-\gamma_R}$, implying that both sides of the equation are equal to unity. The polynomial-based argument is itself flawed, and does not imply that theorem 14.1 fails.

Theorem 14.1 is true. One reason for including software with this book is to provide readers with examples they can work through in order to develop intuition about the way the model works. It might be the case that past readers came to the conclusion that the results must be false because their intuition was rooted in models featuring homogeneous beliefs, and that this intuition does not carry over fully to the case of heterogeneous beliefs.

14.7   Summary

This chapter presented the fundamental aggregation theorem for CRRA utility when investors might exhibit heterogeneous beliefs, heterogeneous risk tolerance parameters, and heterogeneous time discount factors. The theorem characterizes a representative investor who sets prices. The representative investor has features that are similar to, but may not be equivalent to, CRRA utility. The theorem also establishes that the representative investor is not unique.

Traditional aggregation theorems require that the representative investor be invariant to wealth distributions. This requirement is singularly unsuited for understanding the impact of heterogeneity on asset pricing. Notably, heterogeneous beliefs and heterogeneous risk tolerance interact with each other.

Part V

Sentiment and Behavioral SDF

15
Sentiment

This chapter defines *market sentiment*, a concept that lies at the core of the book. In finance, sentiment is synonymous with error. This chapter develops a formal definition of market sentiment, and discusses the manner in which the errors of individual investors, particularly representativeness and overconfidence, combine to produce market sentiment.

Notably, the concept of sentiment described here is formally modeled as a stochastic process. In this respect, sentiment is typically time-varying, with random components. One of the key points made in the chapter is that sentiment is best understood as a distribution rather than as a scalar. For example, describing market sentiment as being either only excessively bullish or only excessively bearish can result in an oversimplified characterization.

15.1 Intuition: Kahneman's Perspective

In January 2000, psychologist Daniel Kahneman gave a presentation at a conference on behavioral finance that was held at Northwestern University. In that talk, Kahneman asked whether it makes sense to speak about the evolution of market prices in terms of a representative investor. Below is an excerpt from his talk.

This talk is meant to be about Psychology and the Market. If you listen to financial analysts on the radio or on TV, you quickly learn that the market has a psychology. Indeed, it has a character. It has thoughts, beliefs, moods, and sometimes stormy emotions.

The main characteristic of the market is extreme nervousness. It is full of hope one moment and full of anxiety the next day. It often seems to be afraid of economic good news, which make it worry about inflation, but soothing words from Greenspan make it feel better.

The market is swayed by powerful emotions of like and dislike. For a while it likes one sector of the economy, but then it may become discouraged, suspicious, and even hostile. The market is generally quite active, but occasionally it stops to take a breather. And sometimes it catches its breath and takes profits.

In short, the market closely resembles a stereotypical individual investor ... The tendency to ascribe states of mind to entities that don't have a mind is a characteristic of an early phase of cognitive development, as when a child says that the sun sets because it is tired and going to bed. And we can recognize it in ourselves as grown-ups.

Why do adults engage in this kind of animistic thinking about the market? What does it do for them? I am arguing, of course, that this thinking happens automatically. But it also has a function, as a way of making sense of the past, which creates an illusion of intentionality and continuity.

Analysts are not the only ones who think of the market as a person. People who write models with representative agents obviously do something of the same general kind. Some of my best friends have written such models. As a psychologist I have always liked these models, especially when they are written in a language I understand.

But this is an instance in which my friends do something that they oppose and even ridicule in other contexts. They make assumptions that they know are not true, just because these assumptions help them reach conclusions that make sense. In fact, of course, agents are not all alike and the differences among them surely matter.

15.1.1   Relationship to Theorem 14.1

Both traditional asset pricing theorists and behavioral asset pricing theorists develop models that begin with a single representative investor. Kahneman suggests that it is natural to think of the market as an individual, with corresponding thought processes, emotions, and actions. However, he suggests that this line of thinking can be misleading, in that not all agents are alike, and modeling them as if they were leads to an "illusion of intentionality and continuity." Notice that Kahneman is critical of the use of representative investor-based thinking in behavioral asset pricing models as well as traditional asset pricing models. Indeed, he criticizes behavioral asset pricing theorists for adopting practices that they criticize others for following.

There are at least three distinct ways to build models with representative investors. The first is simply to make the outright assumption that prices are set by a single representative investor. The second is to structure a set of assumptions that imply Gorman aggregation, in order to justify the assumption of a representative investor. The third is to identify a representative investor who acts as if he sets market prices, but not require Gorman aggregation. The present volume adopts the third approach.

Think about these points in light of Kahneman's comments. Essentially Kahneman criticizes the first two approaches, because in those approaches differences among agents are irrelevant. In contrast, he suggests that in practice differences are relevant.

The representative investor in Theorem 14.1 is an amalgam of individual investors. This representative investor reflects the heterogeneity in beliefs, coefficients of relative risk tolerance, and time discount factors. That is why the beliefs of the representative investor may feature multimodal probability density functions, even when the individual investors have unimodal probability density functions. That is why the representative investor may not use exponential time discounting, even though every individual investor uses exponential time discounting. That is why the representative investor's coefficient of relative risk aversion may follow a stochastic process, even though every individual investor has a time-invariant coefficient of relative risk aversion. Moreover, as the discussion in Chapter 14 emphasized, the different types of heterogeneity can interact with one another, leading the representative investor's beliefs to depend on both the individual investors' beliefs and the individual investors' coefficients of risk tolerance. A similar statement applies to the representative investor's time preference function $\delta_{R,t}$.

In short, the representative investor of Theorem 14.1 may not resemble any of the individual investors that make up the market. That means that thinking about the market as being priced by a traditional investor may be misleading, especially for those whose intuition is based on the kind of thinking Kahneman describes at the beginning of his remarks.

In traditional finance, there is a concept known as the "marginal trader." The marginal trader is regarded as the investor who sets prices at the margin. Somehow, the view has emerged that even if some investors make mistakes in the market, there is some rational marginal trader who effectively determines prices.

Theorem 14.1 establishes that to the extent the notion of a marginal trader makes sense, it is the representative investor who is the marginal trader. And the representative investor may not be any single individual investor in the market.

15.1.2   Defining Market Efficiency

In order to make the connection between sentiment, the key concept in the chapter, and market efficiency, recall the definition of market efficiency used in this book. Prices are said to be efficient when set *as if* all investors were informed and held objectively correct beliefs, meaning that $P_j = \Pi$ for all j. Notice the phrase *as if* in this definition. The definition does not require that all investors actually have correct probability beliefs. What is required is that the representative investor hold correct probability beliefs. Specifically, prices are said to be efficient when the representative investor's probability density function is objectively correct in the sense that $P_R = \Pi$, where P_R is given by (14.10) in Theorem 14.1.

15.2   Sentiment

Chapter 6 contains a discussion about the sentiment index maintained by the American Association of Individual Investors. Recall that the AAII index measures the percentage of individual investors who are classified as bullish. Data about "sentiment indexes" are regularly reported in financial publications such as *Barron's*. These indexes are used to gauge the aggregate level of investor optimism (bullishness). The phrase "irrational exuberance" suggests excessive optimism on the part of many investors. To suggest that the prices of technology stocks display irrational exuberance is to suggest that those prices are excessively high, relative to fundamental values.

When proponents of behavioral finance speak of "sentiment," they are speaking about the aggregate errors of investors being manifest in security prices. In the case of irrational exuberance and technology stocks, the sentiment of investors was regarded as having been excessively optimistic.

The purpose of this chapter is to define sentiment formally. A starting point for this task is the evaluation of the first moments of investors' probability density functions. The literature in behavioral finance has tended to define sentiment in terms of first moments. To be sure, first moments are important. However, first moments cannot capture the structure of all investor errors. Other moments too can be important. Second moments capture errors about risk perceptions. Third moments capture whether investors, while optimistic, are also concerned about a major downturn. Fourth moments capture whether investors attach high probabilities to extreme events such as stock market crashes.

The point is that investors' errors are not confined to first moments alone. Therefore, the present approach defines sentiment in terms of entire distributions, rather than in terms of one or two moments.

15.2.1 Formal Definition

Consider a formal definition of a sentiment variable Λ. This variable is based on two terms. The first term, and the more important of the two, is the likelihood ratio $P_R(x_1)/\Pi(x_1)$. The second term involves the value of δ_R that arises from Theorem 14.1 when all investors hold objectively correct beliefs. Call this value (of δ_R) $\delta_{R,\Pi}$. Define

$$\Phi(x_t) = \frac{P_R(x_t)}{\Pi(x_t)} \frac{\delta_R(t)}{\delta_{R,\Pi}(t)} \tag{15.1}$$

The variable Φ reflects two of the deviations that can arise because of investors' errors. One deviation stems from the beliefs of the representative investor, what one might call the "market's beliefs," relative to objective beliefs. The second deviation stems from the representative investor's equilibrium time discount factor, relative to the situation when all investors hold objectively correct beliefs. As the discussion in subsection 12.7.1 explained, the process of aggregation can introduce distortions into the $\delta_{R,t}$ function. That is the reason for including the time preference term in (15.1). When all investors hold objectively correct beliefs, $\Phi = 1$.

Define the sentiment function by $\Lambda = ln(\Phi)$. Formally,[1]

$$\Lambda \equiv ln(P_R/\Pi) + ln(\delta_R/\delta_{R,\Pi}) \tag{15.2}$$

15.3 Example Featuring Heterogeneous Risk Tolerance

Figures 14.1 and 14.2 indicate that the investors' risk tolerance parameters can impact the beliefs of the representative investor. Consider the same example described in Chapter 14, in which investor 1 has a coefficient of relative risk aversion equal to 1 (log-utility), and investor 2 has a coefficient of relative risk aversion equal to 2. What does the sentiment function look like in that example?

---

[1] Although the sentiment function is the sum of two terms, the second term is typically close to zero. It can be ignored for all practical purposes, except for events for which $P_R(x_t) \approx \Pi(x_t)$. The file *Chapter 15 Example.xls* contains a table in the worksheet *Sentiment Table* illustrating the relative magnitudes of the two terms. See columns F and G in the table displayed in the worksheet.

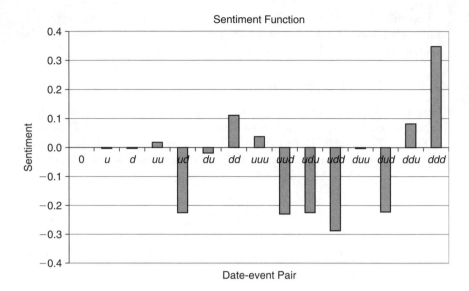

FIGURE 15.1. This figure shows the sentiment function for the two-investor binomial example featuring heterogeneous beliefs and heterogeneous risk tolerance.

Figure 15.1 is a bar chart depicting the sentiment function. Notice that sentiment is zero or nearly zero for events at $t = 1$. However, sentiment is nonzero thereafter. Consider the sentiment value associated with event dd. This value is highest among all events at $t = 2$. What does it mean? It means that the representative investor attaches too high a probability $P_R(dd)$ to this event, relative to the objective probability $\Pi(dd)$. In doing so, the representative investor is excessively pessimistic in respect to event dd.

In this example, the representative investor has a somewhat different discount factor than would be the case if investors all held correct probabilities. However, the ratio of those two factors is close to 1, and does not have much of an impact on the sentiment function in this example.

Interestingly, the representative investor is mildly optimistic about the opposite extreme, event uu. However, the excessive pessimism takes probability mass away from the less extreme outcomes, ud and du. This is a Markov setting, and hence there is no reason to expect the representative investor to assign the same probabilities to events ud and du.

In examining events at $t = 3$ it is clear that the same general pattern of pessimism prevails. The extreme negative outcome, ddd, is most overweighted. Again, the extreme positive outcome is also overweighted, with most of the intermediate outcomes being underweighted.

This example makes clear that sentiment is more complex a concept than the first moment of an expectation's function. Market sentiment is a collage of different investor's beliefs, attitude toward risk, and time preference.

15.4   Example Featuring Log-Utility

When investors are error-free in the aggregate, the sentiment function is the zero function. Conversely, a nonzero sentiment function indicates nonzero aggregate errors on the part of investors. In this respect, the shape of the sentiment function carries a lot of information about the distribution of investors' aggregate errors.

This section discusses how the shape of the sentiment function is affected by two behavioral phenomena discussed earlier in the book, representativeness and overconfidence. Recall that representativeness predisposes some investors to predict unwarranted continuation and other investors to predict unwarranted reversals. Overconfidence leads investors to underestimate future volatility.

In order to develop an understanding of how different investor errors give rise to different shapes for the sentiment function, consider a simple two-investor example when both investors have log-utility, and have time discount factors equal to unity. For this example, consider a time frame corresponding to a quarter (three months).[2]

15.4.1   Representativeness: Errors in First Moments

Both representativeness and overconfidence impact the shape of the sentiment function. Consider first the effect of representativeness. In this respect, assume that no investor is overconfident, meaning that all investors hold correct beliefs about volatility (the second moment).

Suppose that aggregate consumption growth evolves according to a distribution that is approximately log-normal, with mean 0.87 percent and standard deviation equal to 0.86 percent.[3]

Among the possible shapes for the sentiment function are monotone increasing, monotone decreasing, U-shaped, inverted U-shaped, and oscillating. What do these various shapes mean?

In order to understand the meaning behind these shapes, consider some special cases. Suppose first that all investors are excessively optimistic. In particular, let all investors believe that aggregate consumption growth

---

[2] The file *Chapter 15 Example 2.xls* was used to generate the figures discussed here.

[3] The model is discrete, but a large number of states are used in order to approximate a continuous state space.

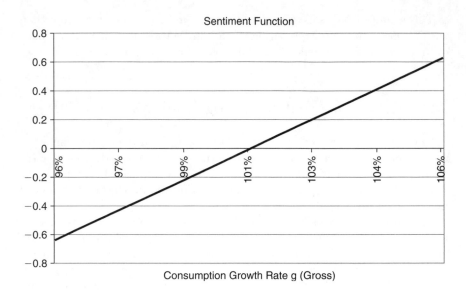

FIGURE 15.2. This figure shows the sentiment function for the two-investor log-utility example when all investors are excessively optimistic.

is (log-normally) distributed with mean 0.96 percent and standard deviation 0.86 percent. Figure 15.2 illustrates a sentiment function for this case. Notice that the function is upward sloping, with sentiment negative at the left and positive at the right. This pattern shows that low rates of consumption growth are assigned probabilities that are too small. Conversely, high rates of consumption growth are assigned rates of consumption growth that are too large. Technically, Figure 15.2 portrays sentiment as a change of measure which is log-linear, that being the form appropriate to normal distributions.

By the same token, the graph of the sentiment function is negative when all investors are excessively pessimistic, assigning probabilities to low consumption growth outcomes that are too large and probabilities to high consumption growth outcomes that are too small. Figure 15.3 shows the case when investors believe the mean of the growth rate distribution to be 0.79 percent. As with Figure 15.2, the change of measure in Figure 15.3 is log-linear.

Chapter 7 discussed the reason why representativeness typically leads individual investors to predict unwarranted continuation and professional investors to predict unwarranted reversals. Suppose that the market is populated by both types of investors. What will the shape of the sentiment function be in this case? When some investors are excessively optimistic and some investors are excessively pessimistic, the sentiment function aggregates the two as a wealth-weighted convex combination.

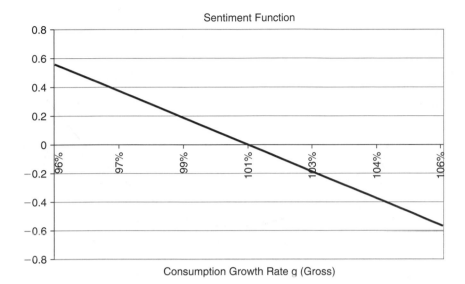

FIGURE 15.3. This figure shows the sentiment function for the two-investor log-utility example when all investors are excessively pessimistic.

Typically, sentiment does not average to the zero function. Instead, the pessimistic investors drive the left-hand side of the sentiment function, and the optimists drive the right-hand side. The result is a U-shaped function, or a "smile." Figure 15.4 provides an example that displays the graph of a sentiment function in the case where the optimistic investor and pessimistic investor have the same initial wealth.

Figure 15.2 effectively illustrates the sentiment of investor 1, the optimist (or bull). Figure 15.3 effectively illustrates the sentiment of investor 2, the pessimist (or bear). Λ, the U-shaped variable in Figure 15.4 that defines market sentiment, is a wealth-weighted mixture of the sentiments of the individual investors.

15.4.2 Overconfidence: Errors in Second Moments

In the previous example, investors erred in respect to the first moment of the distribution of aggregate consumption growth but used the correct value for the second moment. Consider how the shape of the sentiment function is impacted by errors in the second moment.

Figure 15.5 displays the sentiment function for an overconfident optimist who uses an upward-biased value for the mean, and a downward-biased estimate for the standard deviation (0.83 percent). Notice that the graph is not monotone increasing as it was in the previous subsection. By underestimating the riskiness of aggregate consumption growth, the optimistic investor underweights the probabilities at both tails.

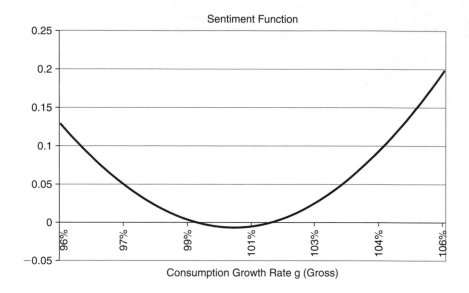

FIGURE 15.4. This figure displays the sentiment function for the two-investor log-utility model populated for excessively optimistic investors and excessively pessimistic investors.

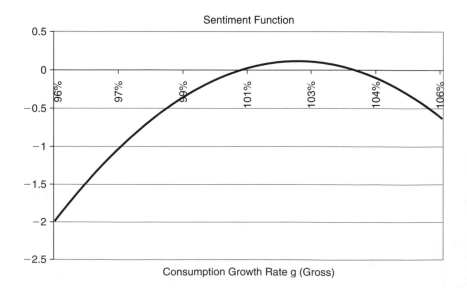

FIGURE 15.5. This figure displays the sentiment function for the two-investor log-utility example when all investors are overconfident optimists.

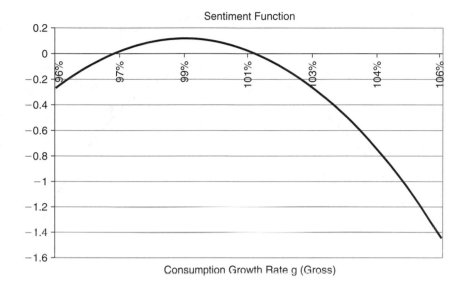

FIGURE 15.6. This figure displays the sentiment function for the two-investor log-utility example when all investors are overconfident pessimists.

Figure 15.6 displays the counterpart sentiment function for an overconfident pessimistic investor who underestimates the standard deviation at 0.84 percent. Notice that the function in Figure 15.6 has the same general shape as in Figure 15.5, but is left-shifted.

Figure 15.7 displays the market sentiment function in the case where the overconfident optimistic investor and overconfident pessimistic investor have the same initial wealth. Notice that the sentiment function has an inverted U-shape. The sentiment function is negative at the left tail, negative at the right tail, and positive in the mid-range of consumption growth. Overconfidence leads both investors to underestimate the probabilities associated with tail events, and the "market" to overestimate midrange events.

Consider one last shape. Suppose that the pessimist is underconfident rather than overconfident. Therefore, the pessimist attaches too much probability to left-tail events. This modification will tend to pull up the left portion of the sentiment function in Figure 15.7. In order to accentuate the pattern that results, suppose that the initial wealth share of the overconfident optimistic investor, investor 1, is 58 percent instead of 50 percent.

Figure 15.8 illustrates the market sentiment function for this case. Notice that the sentiment function oscillates. It is positive at the left, then dips below the axis, rises, and becomes positive, before dipping below the axis at the right.

In Figure 15.8, the overall shape of the sentiment function reflects pessimism, with the degree of market inefficiency small in the middle portion.

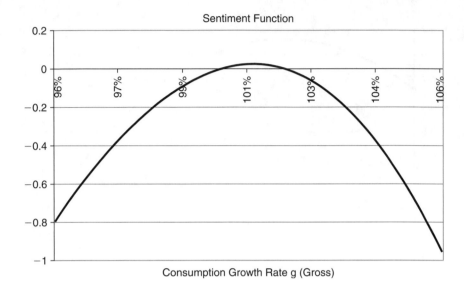

FIGURE 15.7. This figure displays the sentiment function for the two-investor log-utility example when one investor is an overconfident optimist, the other investor is an overconfident pessimist, and both have the same wealth.

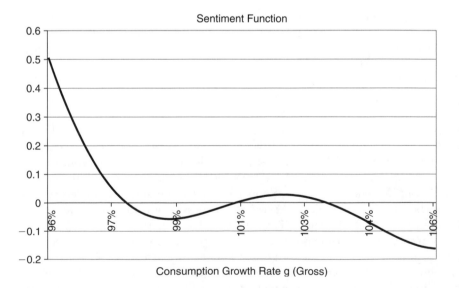

FIGURE 15.8. This figure displays the sentiment function for the two-investor log-utility example when one investor is an overconfident optimist, the other investor is an underconfident pessimist, and the optimist has 58 percent of the wealth.

This means that errors in probabilities for the mid-range are relatively small. However, relative errors for tail events are much larger. The market attaches too high a probability to extreme negative outcomes, and too low a probability to extreme positive outcomes.

Adding investors to the model is a straightforward procedure. For example, adding a third overconfident investor whose beliefs lie between those of the overconfident optimist and overconfident pessimist, and assuming that all investors have the same wealth, produces a sentiment shape that is the same as Figure 15.7. Adding an overconfident investor who is even more optimistic than the optimist, a super bull, pulls the sentiment function depicted in Figure 15.8 up at the right, with some additional oscillation before eventually turning negative far to the right.

15.4.3 Link to Empirical Evidence

What does the sentiment function look like in practice? Chapters 6 and 7 document evidence concerning the beliefs of individual investors and the beliefs of professional investors. Recall that in the aggregate individual investors engage in trend following, predicting unwarranted continuation. In contrast, professional investors largely succumb to gambler's fallacy in the aggregate, predicting unwarranted reversals.

The UBS/Gallup data demonstrate that individual investors were excessively optimistic during the bull market of the 1990s, but their optimism waned when the bull market came to an end. Survey data of corporate financial executives establish that like individual investors, they are trend followers, who predict continuation. Data from the same survey also establish that financial executives were overconfident, having underestimated volatility.

In contrast, data from the Livingston survey, *Business Week*, and *Wall $treet Week with Louis Rukeyser* indicate that as a group professional investors were unduly pessimistic during the bull market, having underestimated expected returns. The evidence from the *Wall $treet Week* panelists is that in the main, professional investors were overconfident between 1984 and 2002, having underestimated volatility. However, professional investors actually overestimated volatility in the subperiod 1988–1994. During this interval, actual volatility averaged 19.7 percent, whereas professional investors predicted 26.4 percent.

The findings described in the last paragraph suggest that the shape of the sentiment function might change shape over time. For instance, the sentiment function might have had the shape depicted in Figure 15.7 between 1984 and 1987, then shifted to the shape depicted in Figure 15.8 between 1988 and 1994, and shifted back to the shape depicted in Figure 15.7 after 1994.

Both individual investors and professional investors exhibit considerable heterogeneity in their return expectations. However, suppose that in the aggregate, investors essentially cluster into two groups, a group of optimists (bulls) and a group of pessimists (bears). In that case, the sentiment function would have the general character displayed in Figures 15.7 and 15.8.

Measuring the sentiment function directly is difficult. However, it is possible to measure the sentiment function indirectly, using a technique developed in Chapters 16 and 23. That technique suggests that for the period 1991–1995, the sentiment function had the shape indicated in Figure 15.8.

15.4.4   Evidence of Clustering

Most of the preceding examples involve just two investors. Is this realistic? To the extent that there are many more than two investors in the world, the answer is obvious. However, for the purpose of modeling the shape of the sentiment function, the real issue is not so much how many investors there are, but to what extent investors cluster in their beliefs. If investors are polarized, and fall into either a bullish camp or a bearish camp, perhaps because of representativeness, then it might be possible to explain the shape of the sentiment function using a two-investor model.

Are investors polarized? Consider Figure 15.9, which juxtaposes investors' expected return distributions from the four data sources

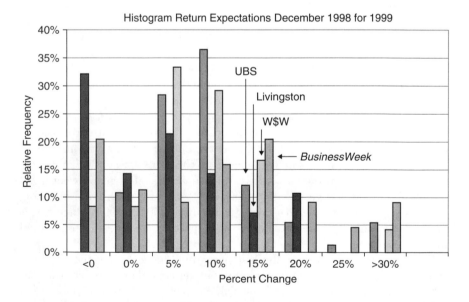

FIGURE 15.9. This figure juxtaposes investors' expected return distributions from UBS/Gallup, Livingston, *Wall $treet Week* panelists, and *BusinessWeek*, for year-end annual forecasts made in 1998 for the year 1999. Note that the data for professional investors do not include the expected dividend yield.

discussed in Chapters 6 and 7: UBS/Gallup, Livingston, *Wall $treet Week* panelists, and *BusinessWeek*. Figure 15.9 pertains to the year-end annual forecasts made in 1998 for the year 1999.

The Livingston distribution and *BusinessWeek* distribution are distinctly trimodal. The UBS distribution is bimodal with a second peak occurring at the right tail. An unweighted average of the four distributions is displayed in Figure 15.10. Notice that the unweighted average is trimodal.

Figure 15.11 shows how the unweighted average distribution of return expectations evolved between 1998 and 2001. Observe that the distributions for all years are trimodal, except for 2000, which is bimodal. Notably, there is a peak at the extreme right for all four years.

Figure 15.9 is suggestive of what the components of the representative investor's probability density function P_R might be like. Figures 15.10 and 15.11 are suggestive of what P_R itself might be. In this regard, keep in mind that the three figures display distributions of expected returns, not distributions of realized returns. P_R is a density function over realizations of consumption growth g. In addition, the weights used in Figures 15.10 and 15.11 were equal. Theorem 14.1 makes clear that the aggregating weights

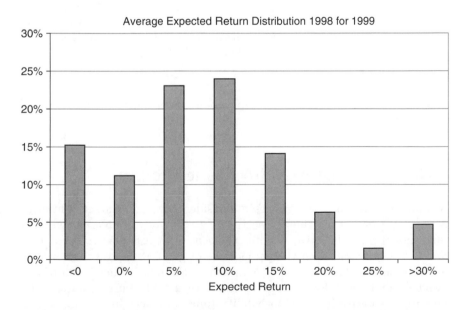

FIGURE 15.10. This figure displays an unweighted average of four expected return distributions: UBS/Gallup, Livingston, *Wall $treet Week* panelists, and *BusinessWeek*. Expected returns are for year-end annual forecasts made in 1998 for the year 1999. Note that the data for professional investors do not include the expected dividend yield.

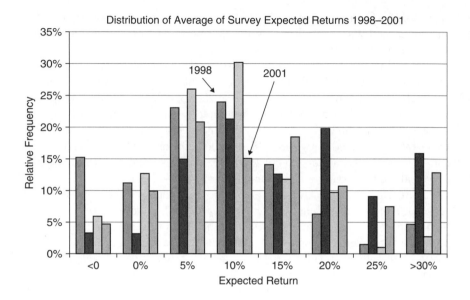

FIGURE 15.11. This figure shows how the unweighted average distribution of return expectations for UBS/Gallup, Livingston, *Wall $treet Week* panelists, and *Business Week* evolved between 1998 and 2001, in respect to year-end annual forecasts made between 1998 and 2001 inclusive. Note that the data for professional investors do not include the expected dividend yield.

used to construct P_R reflect a combination of wealth, risk tolerance, and time preference.

15.5   Sentiment as a Stochastic Process

Sentiment is a stochastic process. Consider how the market sentiment process Λ evolves from the perspective of $t = 0$. For example, in the binomial model the value $\Lambda(u)$ denotes the sentiment attached to event u at $t = 1$, when viewed from the perspective of $t = 0$. Suppose that event u actually occurs. Then at $t = 1$, Λ measures the relative likelihood of this event in hindsight. Moreover, $t = 1$ then becomes the current date, and a new representative investor probability function comes into being, conditional on u having occurred at $t = 1$. Likewise, a new sentiment function comes into being, also conditional on the occurrence of u at $t = 1$. If event ud occurs at $t = 2$, then $\Lambda(d|u)$ is the sentiment associated with d from the perspective of $t = 1$. The sequence of short-term conditional sentiment values constitutes a stochastic process.

Sentiment Λ is the aggregate reflection of investors' errors in the market. The degree to which an individual investor's error process affects market sentiment depends on the size of the investor's trades, a point stressed by Lintner (1969). Λ depends on risk tolerance and wealth because these variables provide the weights used to aggregate investor errors. Investors who are wealthier and more tolerant of risk take larger positions than investors who are less wealthy and less tolerant of risk.

Sentiment is time-varying, and reflects the evolution of the error–wealth covariance. The magnitude of Λ varies as wealth shifts between investors who have taken the opposite sides of trades. This is because the weight attached to an investor's beliefs is an increasing function of his trading success. Along a high consumption growth sequence, those who predict continuation will become unduly optimistic, and sentiment will move in the direction of excess optimism. Along a low consumption growth sequence, the reverse will occur. In a volatile segment, with frequent alternation between high and low consumption growth, weight will shift to the investors who are prone to predict reversals. These investors overestimate the degree of volatility. During those segments when consumption growth is volatile, the market will accord the beliefs of those predicting reversal greater weight, and returns will amplify the volatility in consumption growth.

What determines the relative occurrence of the different types of segments? The answer is the objective process $\{g, \Pi\}$, where g is the value of consumption growth and Π serves as the probability density sequence. In this regard, the stochastic process governing sentiment can be expressed as $\{\Lambda, \Pi\}$, in that Λ provides the value of the process, and Π serves as the probability density sequence.

15.6 Summary

The behavioral approach to asset pricing is centered on the role of sentiment. Loosely speaking, sentiment measures the degree of excessive optimism or pessimism among investors. A key point made in the chapter is that sentiment is more complex than average optimism or pessimism. Rather, sentiment pertains to the entire distribution of investors' errors. Notably, heterogeneous beliefs give rise to smile patterns in the shape of the sentiment function.

The chapter provided a formal definition for the sentiment function. Zero sentiment corresponds to the case of zero errors at the level of the market.

16

Behavioral SDF and the Sentiment Premium

This chapter is the heart of the book, in that it establishes how sentiment is manifest within asset prices through the stochastic discount factor (SDF). The main result in the chapter is a decomposition theorem for the log-SDF.

The theorem states that the log-SDF is the sum of a fundamental component and sentiment. If sentiment is small relative to the fundamental component, then investor errors exert a minor effect on asset prices. If sentiment is large relative to the fundamental component, then investor errors exert a major effect on asset prices. Whether sentiment is small or large relative to the fundamental component is an empirical question. Some of the empirical evidence is discussed in Chapter 23.

This chapter addresses two other issues. The second issue also involves a decomposition theorem, but for expected returns rather than the log-SDF. The theorem stipulates that the risk premium for any security is the sum of a fundamental premium and a sentiment premium. When the sentiment premium is large relative to the fundamental premium, risk premiums reflect both mispricing and compensation for bearing sentiment-based risk. When sentiment is small or zero, the sentiment premium is also small or zero, in which case all risk premiums are determined by fundamentals alone.

The third issue addressed in the chapter pertains to long-run survival. Chapter 11 discussed how entropy measures the fitness of an individual investor's behavior in terms of long-run survival. The discussion in Chapter 11 assumed that all investors had logarithmic utility functions. The present chapter removes the log-utility restriction.

16.1   The SDF

In a discrete time, discrete state model, a stochastic discount factor (SDF), also known as a pricing kernel M_t, measures state price per unit probability. That is, M_t has the form ν/Π. Notice that the probability used to define M_t is the objective density Π rather than the representative investor's probability P_R. Although either probability density may be used, the objective density is better suited to the purpose at hand.

Let $r(Z)$ denote the (gross) return vector for security Z. In general, a pricing kernel M_t satisfies $E_t(M_{t+1}r_{t+1}(Z)) = 1$. In effect, the SDF serves to discount the stochastic $t+1$ payoff $r_{t+1}(Z)$ and bring it back one period to t. Since the return $r_{t+1}(Z)$ is earned by purchasing \$1 of security Z at t, the SDF effectively prices the security at t.

The properties of the SDF are well known. Take Z to be the risk-free security with a maturity of one period. This security pays exactly 1 unit of consumption in every contingency. Using the SDF, the value of the payoff to this security is $E_t(M_{t+1}1) = E_t(M_{t+1})$. Let the gross real interest rate be denoted i_1. Since the price of a one-period bond that pays off 1 unit of consumption in every date–event pair is $1/i_1$, it follows that the first moment of the SDF is given by $E_t(M_{t+1}) = 1/i_1$.

The risk premium on any security Z is determined by the covariance of its return with the SDF. The risk premium is given by

$$-i_1 cov(r(Z), M) \tag{16.1}$$

To see why, consider a risky security Z and a risk-free security F, both of which are priced at one unit at t. Observe that

$$E_t(M_{t+1}r_{t+1}(Z)) = 1$$

and

$$E_t(M_{t+1}r_{t+1}(F)) = 1$$

so that

$$E_t(M_{t+1}(r_{t+1}(Z) - r_{t+1}(F))) = 0$$

Now use the fact that for random variables X and Y,

$$E(XY) = E(X)E(Y) + cov(X, Y)$$

which implies

$$E(Y) = (E(XY) - cov(X, Y))/E(X)$$

Let X be M_{t+1} and Y be $r_{t+1}(Z) - r_{t+1}(F)$. Notice that in this case $E(XY) = 0$. Therefore,

$$E_t(r_{t+1}(Z) - r_{t+1}(F)) = -i_1 cov(r(Z), M)$$

The correlation coefficient is bounded below by -1. Therefore the correlation between the SDF and the risk premium must be greater than or equal to -1. It follows that the negative covariance in the expression for the risk premium must be less than or equal to the product of the standard deviations of the risk premium and the SDF. That is,

$$\frac{\sigma(M_{t+1})}{E_t(M_{t+1})} \geq \frac{E_t(r_{t+1}(Z) - r_{t+1}(F))}{\sigma_t(r_{t+1}(Z) - r_{t+1}(F))} \tag{16.2}$$

The above inequality indicates that the maximum Sharpe ratio in the market is bounded from above by the coefficient of variation of the SDF.

16.2   Sentiment and the SDF

Chapter 15 provides a formal definition of sentiment $\Lambda = ln(\Phi)$, where Φ is given by (15.1) as

$$\Phi(x_t) = \frac{P_R(x_t)}{\Pi(x_t)} \frac{\delta_R(t)}{\delta_{R,\Pi}(t)} \tag{16.3}$$

Recall that Φ reflects two of the deviations that can arise because of investors' errors. One deviation stems from the beliefs of the representative trader, what one might call the "market's beliefs," relative to objective beliefs. The second deviation stems from the representative investor's equilibrium time discount factor, relative to the situation when all investors hold objectively correct beliefs. When all investors hold objectively correct beliefs, $\Phi = 1$, and sentiment $\Lambda = 0$.

The state price vector ν provides the present value, at date 0, of a contingent claim to one x_t-dollar. For this reason, focus on $M(x_1)$ as the prototypical case.[1] Using (14.7), obtain

$$M_1 \equiv M(x_1) = \delta_R(P_R(x_1)/\Pi(x_1))g(x_1)^{-\gamma_R} \tag{16.4}$$

---

[1] $M(x_t)$ is more correctly written $M(x_t|x_0)$. To obtain the stochastic process for the SDF, define $M_t \equiv M(x_{t+1}|x_t)$, where $M(x_{t+1}|x_t)$ is conditioned on x_t. There are two aspects to conditioning in respect to $M = \nu/\Pi$. The first involves the numerator (price) and the second involves the denominator (probability). The conditional state price $\nu(x_{t+1}|x_t)$ is $\nu(x_{t+1})/\nu(x_t)$. The conditional probability is, of course, $\Pi(x_{t+1}|x_t)$.

where the notation indicating that both δ_R and γ_R are time- and state-dependent respectively has been suppressed.

Define the log-SDF $m = ln(M)$. Then

Theorem 16.1 *The log-SDF can be expressed as a sum of sentiment and two fundamental terms, as follows:*

$$m = \Lambda - \gamma_R ln(g) + ln(\delta_{R,\Pi}) \qquad (16.5)$$

where m, Λ, γ_R, and g are functions of x_1.

Proof of Theorem   Prices are efficient if and only if $P_R = \Pi$. For the case $P_R = \Pi$, denote the state prices in (14.7) by ν_Π. Consider the ratio $ln(\nu/\nu_\Pi)$, where ν is given by (14.7) and corresponds to general P_R. It follows from equation (14.7) that $ln(\nu/\nu_\Pi) = ln(P_R/\Pi) + ln(\delta_R/\delta_\Pi)$. This last equality can also be expressed as $ln(\nu/\Pi) = \Lambda + ln(\nu_\Pi/\Pi)$. Equation (16.5) follows by substituting for $ln(\nu_\Pi/\Pi)$ from equation (14.7).   ■

Theorem 16.1 states that the log-SDF is the sum of two stochastic processes, a sentiment process and a fundamental process based on aggregate consumption growth. Note that prices are efficient when the sentiment variable Λ is uniformly zero, meaning that its value is zero at *every* node in the tree. Hence, when prices are efficient there is neither aggregate belief distortion nor discount factor aggregation bias, in which case there is only one effective driver in (16.5), the fundamental process.

Section 14.4.2 discusses two alternative specifications for the γ_R-function. The first specification uses the consumption weights associated with the case when all investors hold correct beliefs. The second specification uses the consumption weights associated with the equilibrium. The first specification is a bit more tractable than the second. This is because in the first specification, the term involving consumption growth g cancels when forming the ratio ν/ν_Π. However, in the second specification, the terms in g involve different exponents and do not cancel. Therefore, in the second specification, the sentiment function would have to include an additional term $ln(g)(\gamma_{R,\Pi} - \gamma_R)$. One might argue that for the purpose of measuring risk aversion at the market level, the second alternative is the more accurate. If so, then heterogeneous beliefs will exert a direct effect through P_R along with indirect effects, through δ_R and γ_R. In the first specification for γ_R, P_R measures both the direct effect and the indirect effect associated with the interaction between heterogeneous beliefs and heterogeneous risk aversion, but there is only one explicit indirect effect, namely through δ_R.

16.2.1   Example

Consider the last example described in Chapter 15. In the example, there are two investors, both of whom have log-utility and time discount factors equal to unity. Suppose that aggregate consumption growth evolves according to a distribution that is approximately log-normal, with mean 0.87 percent and standard deviation equal to 0.86 percent. Investor 1, the optimist, believes that aggregate consumption growth is (log-normally) distributed with mean 0.96 percent and standard deviation 0.83 percent. Investor 2, the pessimist, believes that aggregate consumption growth is log-normally distributed with mean 0.79 percent and standard deviation 0.88 percent. As with Figure 15.8, let investor 1 hold 58 percent of the initial wealth.

Figure 16.1 displays three functions: $-ln(g)$, which is monotone decreasing, the sentiment function depicted in Figure 15.8, and the log-SDF function which according to Theorem 16.1 is the sum of these two functions and a deterministic term. (The deterministic term happens to be zero in this example, since $\delta_j = 1$ for all j.)

Figure 16.2 displays the functions $1/g$ and the SDF. In effect, Figure 16.2 contrasts a traditional SDF and a behavioral SDF. When sentiment is equal to zero, market prices are efficient. In this case, the SDF just corresponds to the function $1/g$. When sentiment is nonzero, market prices are inefficient, and the SDF is behavioral. In this example, the SDF oscillates instead of declining monotonically. Some portions of the SDF are downward sloping, and other portions of the SDF are upward sloping.

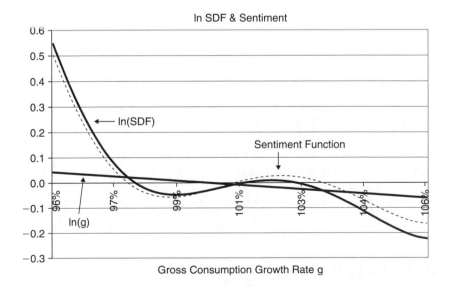

FIGURE 16.1. This figure illustrates Theorem 16.1, showing the decomposition of the log-SDF.

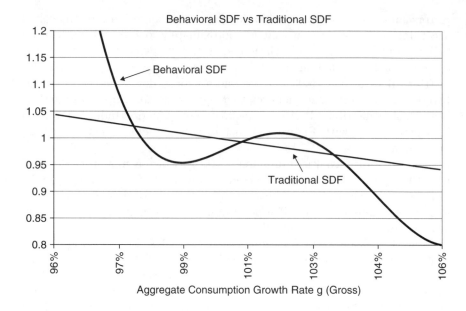

FIGURE 16.2. This figure contrasts a traditional SDF and a behavioral SDF.

The difference between the efficient SDF and the behavioral SDF effectively pinpoints the locus and magnitude of market mispricing. For growth states when the behavioral SDF lies above the efficient SDF, state prices are too high. For growth states when the behavioral SDF lies below the efficient SDF, state prices are too low.

Figure 16.2 displays the main difference between a traditional SDF and a behavioral SDF. The traditional SDF is monotone decreasing, while the behavioral SDF oscillates. Since the SDF serves to generate the prices of all assets in a no-arbitrage market, Figure 16.2 can be said to capture the most important point of this book.

The file *Chapter 16 Example 1.xls* illustrates Theorem 16.1, including the preceding figures. See the tab *Chart Illustrating Theorem 16.1*. The file *Chapter 16 Example 2.xls* also contains a demonstration of Theorem 16.1, for the binomial example discussed in Chapters 14 and 15. See the worksheet *Sentiment and Theorem 16.1*.

16.3   Pitfalls

Because the SDF underlies the pricing of all assets in a no risk-free arbitrage environment, Theorem 16.1 is the most important result in the book. Theorem 16.1 is a formal statement about the manner in which the aggregate errors that investors commit are embodied within market prices. Perhaps for this reason, traditional asset pricing theorists have had difficulty accepting the result and its implications. This section presents three examples of counter arguments offered by past readers. The counter arguments are considered and subtle, and they share a common theme, namely that investor errors have no major role to play in asset pricing models. Whether investor errors play a major role or a minor role in asset pricing is key. Therefore, these arguments need to be addressed squarely and put to rest.

16.3.1 Pitfall: The Behavioral Framework Admits a Traditional SDF

Consider the following argument, which suggests that Theorem 16.1 is a ruse. Theorem 16.1 establishes that the log-SDF decomposes into a fundamental component and a sentiment component. The fundamental component has the form $ln(\delta_{R,\Pi}) - \gamma_R ln(g)$, where g is the consumption growth rate. Implicit in the proof of the theorem is the definition of the SDF as ν/Π. However, the SDF could have been defined instead as ν/P_R. Doing so results in a log-SDF that is equal to $ln(\delta_{R,\Pi}) - \gamma_R ln(g)$. That is, the SDF being defined slightly differently, the log-SDF only consists of the fundamental component, as in the traditional framework. There is no need to deal with a sentiment component.

The preceding argument seems valid enough. Where is the flaw? It is true that if the SDF were defined relative to P_R instead of relative to Π, then the SDF would assume the traditional form. However, using this form for the purpose of pricing assets requires the use of P_R as the basis for the expectation of the product of the SDF and asset payoffs. This does not eliminate the impact of investor errors on prices, but indicates their being directed through a different channel. In the alternative definition of SDF, the channel from errors to prices would just get transferred to the probability density function P_R from the SDF that includes a sentiment component. The impact of errors does not disappear. In this respect, remember that P_R may well be multimodal and fat-tailed, rather than log-normal.

16.3.2 Pitfall: Heterogeneity Need Not Imply Sentiment

Consider a somewhat different objection to the analysis in subsection 16.2.1. The objection begins with the observation that heterogeneous beliefs may simply stem from investors' possessing different priors or different information, rather than different errors.

Moreover, heterogeneous beliefs are compatible with efficient prices. The argument in subsection 16.2.1 is that sentiment produces oscillations in the SDF even when bulls and bears have equal wealth in the market. The claim seems to be that bullish beliefs dominate the determination of prices in high consumption states while bearish beliefs dominate the determination of prices in low consumption states. Focus on high consumption states that are purported to be overpriced, where bullish beliefs are claimed to dominate. Would not bears short claims to these states? And if bears have the same wealth, would their beliefs not be as important as those of bulls? Therefore, would not bearish beliefs cancel bullish beliefs, leading to zero sentiment, and no oscillation? That is what intuition would surely suggest.

The above counter argument involves two pitfalls. The first involves the general reluctance to admit that most investors are non-Bayesians who hold erroneous return expectations. Most of the figures in Chapters 6 and 7 document wide ranges of opinions expressed by individual investors, professional investors, financial executives, and academics. What private information could possibly account for such a wide range of views in a Bayesian environment? In this respect recall that subsection 7.4.1 pointed out that a simple forecasting rule outperformed the forecasts of the *Wall $treet Week* panelists, both individually and collectively. This suggests that if the panelists had access to private information, either it was useless or they used it inappropriately.

The second pitfall in the argument pertains to error cancellation. As Chapter 9 pointed out, there are conditions under which the errors of bearish investors do indeed cancel the errors of bullish investors. The necessary and sufficient condition for full cancellation to occur in a log-utility environment is given in Theorem 9.1. Chapter 9 discussed why this condition constitutes a knife-edge case in the presence of heterogeneous beliefs. Therefore, it is the exception rather than the rule. Moreover, the discussion in Section 11.6 established that the knife-edge condition cannot hold perpetually. It is, by nature, temporary.

16.3.3   Pitfall: Heterogeneity in Risk Tolerance Is Sufficient to Explain Asset Pricing

As the work of Benninga–Mayshar (2000) shows, heterogeneous risk tolerance by itself can explain pricing effects that appear puzzling in a traditional representative investor model. In this respect, it is not clear how one would disentangle the effects of heterogeneous beliefs from those of heterogeneous risk tolerance in the asset pricing equations. Therefore, there is little reason to focus on investor errors, since models that only assume heterogeneous risk tolerance are parsimonious.

If the counter argument just advanced were valid, then effects stemming from heterogeneous beliefs could masquerade as effects stemming only from risk tolerance. In other words, we could pretend that investors always held homogeneous beliefs that were correct, and explain the SDF by appeal to heterogeneous risk tolerance alone. The question is, is it possible to do so in a plausible manner?

To address the last question, consider the log-SDF at date 0,

$$m = \Lambda - \gamma_R ln(g) + ln(\delta_{R,\Pi}) \tag{16.6}$$

where m, Λ, γ_R, and g are functions of x_1. Suppose that the true log-kernel is given by m, but we treat Λ as zero, and ask that heterogeneous risk tolerance explain the structure of the pricing kernel.[2] In order to do so, seek a risk tolerance function $\gamma_\Pi(x_t)$ to satisfy

$$-\gamma_\Pi ln(g) + ln(\delta_{R,\Pi}) = m \tag{16.7}$$

$$= \Lambda - \gamma_R ln(g) + ln(\delta_{R,\Pi}) \tag{16.8}$$

and solve for γ_Π to obtain

$$\gamma_\Pi = \gamma_R - \frac{\Lambda}{ln(g)} \tag{16.9}$$

Equation (16.9) describes the distortion that results from falsely attributing the impact of heterogeneous beliefs to heterogeneous risk tolerance. The magnitude of the distortion is $\Lambda/ln(g)$, that being the wedge between γ_Π and γ_R. In this regard, recall that $1/\gamma_R(x_t)$ is a convex combination of the individual traders' risk tolerances $\{1/\gamma_j\}$, with weights θ_j given by (14.2).

To understand the nature of the wedge between γ_R and γ_Π, return to the example depicted in Figures 16.1 and 16.2. In the example $\gamma_R(x_t) = 1$, because all traders have logarithmic utility ($\gamma_j = 1$). Consider the following question: Given the structure of the γ_R-function, is it plausible for $-\gamma_\Pi g(x)$ to capture the impact of Λ?

As a general matter, the answer to the previous question is no. To see why, consider Figure 16.3, which displays how the function in (16.9) varies across g, for the example underlying Figure 16.1. Notice that γ_Π decreases from above 13 to -42, before rising to $+\infty$, as g approaches 1 from the left.[3] To the right of the singularity at $g = 1$, γ_Π falls and then rises from 0 to a value of about 4. What Figure 16.3 illustrates, rather dramatically, is that although it is possible to find a γ_Π-function to capture the impact of sentiment, γ_Π may differ markedly from $\gamma_R = 1$. Hence, although it is formally possible to capture the impact of nonzero sentiment through

---

[2] Use the nonuniqueness property discussed in Theorem 14.1, and redefine the representative trader's beliefs by the objectively correct distribution Π. We are free to do so, even when $P_R \neq \Pi$ for the P_R of the theorem. In the notation of equation (14.12), $P_{R,1} = P_R$ and $P_{R,2} = \Pi$.

[3] Note the singularity at $g = 1$ in (16.9).

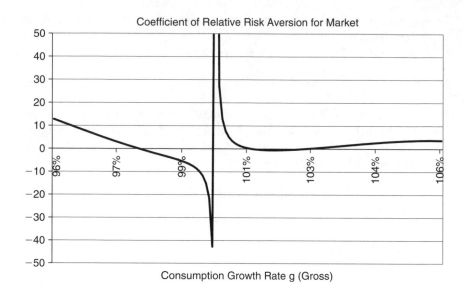

FIGURE 16.3. This figure displays how the function in (16.9) varies across g, for the example underlying Figure 16.1.

heterogeneous risk tolerance, it is not particularly meaningful, in that γ_Π does not capture the underlying risk tolerances of the individual traders.

16.4 Sentiment and Expected Returns

Theorem 16.1 captures the manner in which sentiment manifests itself within security prices. The theorem indicates that the log-SDF is the sum of a fundamental component and sentiment. Consider whether a similar structure holds in respect to the risk premium on any security. That is, can the risk premium be decomposed into the sum of a fundamental premium and a sentiment premium? This section establishes that the answer to this question is yes. The resulting relationship is called the behavioral risk premium equation.

In order to develop the behavioral risk premium equation, consider the Euler equation that was derived in Chapter 10, for $t = 0$ and $t = 1$:

$$1 = \delta E_0 \left[\frac{c_j(x_0)}{c_j(x_1)} r_Z(x_1) \right] \qquad (16.10)$$

for security Z with associated return distribution r_Z.

The preceding Euler equation was derived in the case of log-utility. As was discussed in Chapter 10, the Euler equation specifies that at the margin, the amount of x_0-consumption that investor j is willing to sacrifice in exchange for the additional consumption at $t = 1$ must be the same as the amount investor j must, in fact, sacrifice. Of course, the amount investor j must sacrifice is 1, since the increased purchase of security Z is financed by the reduction of consumption at $t = 0$ by exactly one unit.

For general γ_j, the ratio of marginal utilities in (16.10) is replaced by $(c_j(x_0)/c_j(x_1))^{\gamma_j}$, to yield

$$1 = \delta_j E_{x_0} \left[\left(\frac{c_j(x_0)}{c_j(x_1)} \right)^{\gamma_j} r_Z(x_1) \right] \tag{16.11}$$

Notably, the Euler equation will hold for the representative investor, whose equilibrium consumption choice will be total consumption, (or more precisely the growth rate of consumption). Therefore, taking $j = R$, it follows that

$$1 = E_{R,0}[\delta_R g(x_1)^{-\gamma_R} r_Z(x_1)] \tag{16.12}$$

By the definition of Φ, $P_R = (\delta_\Pi/\delta_R)\Pi\Phi$. Substitute $(\delta_\Pi/\delta_R)\Pi\Phi$ for P_R into the Euler equation $1 = F_{R,0}[\delta_R g(x_1)^{-\gamma_R} r_Z(x_1)]$ to obtain

$$1 = E_{\Pi,0}[\delta_\Pi \Phi g(x_1)^{-\gamma_R} r_Z(x_1)] \tag{16.13}$$

Next define[4]

$$h_{Z,0} = \frac{E_{\Pi,0}[\delta_\Pi \Phi g(x_1)^{-\gamma_R} r_Z(x_1)]}{E_{\Pi,0}[\delta_\Pi g(x_1)^{-\gamma_R} r_Z(x_1)]} \tag{16.14}$$

and note that

$$1 = E_{\Pi,0}[\delta_\Pi \Phi g(x_1)^{-\gamma_R} r_Z(x_1)] = h_{Z,0} E_{\Pi,0}[\delta_\Pi g(x_1)^{-\gamma_R} r_Z(x_1)] \tag{16.15}$$

or

$$1 = h_{Z,0} E_{\Pi,0}[\delta_\Pi g(x_1)^{-\gamma_R} r_Z(x_1)] \tag{16.16}$$

Rewrite the last equation to read

$$E_{\Pi,0}[g(x_1)^{-\gamma_R} r_Z(x_1)] = \frac{1}{\delta_\Pi h_{Z,0}} \tag{16.17}$$

---

[4] The 0 noted in the h-function in (16.14) denotes the time period. The arguments in this section generalize to arbitrary t. In general, the analysis applies to $h_{Z,t}$.

As before, use the fact that for random variables X and Y, $E(XY) = E(X)E(Y) + cov(X,Y)$, where $X = g(x_1)^{-\gamma_R}$ and $Y = r_Z(x_1)$. This portion of the derivation is taken from Anderson, Ghysels and Juergens (2004). Obtain

$$E_{\Pi,0}[g(x_1)^{-\gamma_R} r_Z(x_1)] = E_{\Pi,0}[g(x_1)^{-\gamma_R}] E_{\Pi,0}[r_Z(x_1)]$$
$$+ cov[g(x_1)^{-\gamma_R}, r_Z(x_1)] \qquad (16.18)$$

which can be rearranged to read

$$E_{\Pi,0}[r_Z(x_1)] = \frac{E_{\Pi,0}[g(x_1)^{-\gamma_R} r_Z(x_1)] - cov[g(x_1)^{-\gamma_R}, r_Z(x_1)]}{E_{\Pi,0}[g(x_1)^{-\gamma_R}]} \qquad (16.19)$$

Now use (16.17) to substitute for $E_{\Pi,0}[g(x_1)^{-\gamma_R} r_Z(x_1)]$, leading to

$$E_{\Pi,0}[r_Z(x_1)] = \frac{(1/\delta_\Pi h_{Z,0}) - cov[g(x_1)^{-\gamma_R}, r_Z(x_1)]}{E_{\Pi,0}[g(x_1)^{-\gamma_R}]} \qquad (16.20)$$

Recall that the expected value of the SDF is equal to the price of the risk-free security. That is, $E_t(M_{t+1}) = 1/i_1$. Therefore, when prices are efficient, $1/i_{1,\Pi} = \delta_\Pi E_\Pi(g(x_1)^{-\gamma_R})$. Here $1/i_{1,\Pi}$ is just the value of i_1 when prices are efficient. Combine the last two equations to obtain

$$E_{\Pi,0}[r_Z(x_1)] = \frac{i_{1,\Pi}}{h_{Z,0}} - \frac{cov[g(x_1)^{-\gamma_R}, r_Z(x_1)]}{E_{\Pi,0}[g(x_1)^{-\gamma_R}]} \qquad (16.21)$$

Define $r_{b,1} = i_{1,\Pi} h_{Z,0}^{-1}$ so that $i_{1,\Pi} = r_{b,1} h_{Z,0}$. Substituting $r_{b,1} h_{Z,0}/h_{Z,0}$ for $i_{1,\Pi} h_{Z,0}^{-1}$, obtain

$$E_{\Pi,0}[r_Z(x_1)] = r_{b,1} \frac{h_{Z,0}}{h_{Z,0}} - \frac{cov[g(x_1)^{-\gamma_R}, r_Z(x_1)]}{E_{\Pi,0}[g(x_1)^{-\gamma_R}]} \qquad (16.22)$$

so that

$$E_{\Pi,0}[r_Z(x_1)] = i_{1,\Pi} - \frac{cov[g(x_1)^{-\gamma_R}, r_Z(x_1)]}{E_{\Pi,0}[g(x_1)^{-\gamma_R}]} + (i_{1,\Pi}) \frac{(1 - h_{Z,0})}{h_{Z,0}} \qquad (16.23)$$

Subtract the equilibrium interest rate i_1 from both sides of (16.23). The left-hand side, so obtained, is $E_{\Pi,0}[r_Z(x_1)] - i_1$, the true risk premium associated with security Z. The right-hand side is the sum of three terms, one corresponding to fundamental value, and the other two corresponding to the impact of sentiment. Specifically, we have

Theorem 16.2 *The risk premium on any security Z is given by*

$$E_{\Pi,0}[r_Z(x_1)] - i_1 = (i_{1,\Pi} - i_1) - \frac{cov[g(x_1)^{-\gamma_R}, r_Z(x_1)]}{E_{\Pi,0}[g(x_1)^{-\gamma_R}]} + (i_{1,\Pi})\frac{(1 - h_{Z,0})}{h_{Z,0}}$$

$$(16.24)$$

16.4.1   Interpretation and Discussion

Consider the interpretation of (16.23). This equation indicates that the expected return of any security Z is the sum of three components. The first component is the interest rate that would have emerged if prices were efficient. The second term is the risk premium that would apply to the security return distribution r_Z were prices to be efficient.[5] The third term is a sentiment premium that captures mispricing in respect to both the risk-free rate and the price dynamics associated with security Z. Notably, when sentiment $\Lambda = 0$, then $h_{Z,0} = 1$ and therefore the sentiment premium is zero.

The interpretation of (16.24) is similar to that of (16.23). The risk premium associated with the return distribution r_Z is the sum of three terms. The first term is the extent to which the equilibrium interest rate is mispriced. The second term is the fundamental risk premium. The third term is the premium associated with the extent of mispricing in respect to the security return itself (including the effect of the interest rate).

Next, consider the issue of the sign of the sentiment premium component $(i_{1,\Pi})(1 - h_{Z,0})/h_{Z,0}$. Looking at $h_{Z,0} = E_{\Pi,0}[\delta_\Pi \Phi g(x_1)^{-\gamma_R} r_Z(x_1)]/E_{\Pi,0}[\delta_\Pi g(x_1)^{-\gamma_R} r_Z(x_1)]$, $h_{Z,0}$ is clearly nonnegative, since all terms are nonnegative. Notice that $h_{Z,0}$ can be either less than or equal to 1 or greater than 1. In one case the sign of the sentiment premium component will be nonnegative, and in the other case it will be negative.

The variable P_R/Π in Φ serves to reweight the product $g(x_1)^{-\gamma_R} r_Z(x_1)$ in the expectation of $g(x_1)^{-\gamma_R} r_Z(x_1)$. If, at t, the representative investor is excessively optimistic about the return to Z at $t + 1$, then events x_{t+1} at $t + 1$ that feature high realizations of $g(x_1)^{-\gamma_R} r_Z(x_1)$ receive more emphasis in $E_{\Pi,0}[\delta_\Pi \Phi g(x_1)^{-\gamma_R} r_Z(x_1)]$ than they do in $E_{\Pi,0}[\delta_\Pi g(x_1)^{-\gamma_R} r_Z(x_1)]$. In this case, we have $h_{Z,0} > 1$.

When $h_{Z,0} > 1$, Z will be overpriced at t. Observe that as a result, the sentiment premium component $(i_{1,\Pi})(1 - h_{Z,0})/h_{Z,0}$ will be negative. That is, overpriced portfolios feature negative expected abnormal returns, which

---

[5] This result takes the return distribution r_Z as given. Notably, sentiment can alter the return distribution associated with security Z, and such alteration is not captured by (16.23).

accords with intuition. Or, more precisely, the expected return to Z will be less than the value based on fundamentals alone.

16.4.2   Example Illustrating Theorem 16.2

The file *Chapter 16 Example 2.xls* features an example to illustrate Theorem 16.2. The example is found in the worksheet *Theorem 16.2*. The security Z, corresponding to levered equity, is defined so that it pays g at $t = 1$ if consumption growth $g > 1$ and \$0 otherwise. At $t = 0$, the price of this security is \$0.86; it is obtained by multiplying the state price vector ν by the payoff vector Z. Therefore r_Z will be 0 if $g \leq 1$ and greater than 1 if $g > 1$. The expected (gross) return to holding Z for one period is 1.001 under the representative investor's probability density P_R but 1.011 under the objective probability density Π.

The risk-free rate of interest, which can be obtained from the equilibrium price vector ν, is 1.009. Therefore, the objective risk premium associated with Z is -0.0082. Because its risk premium is negative, Z is overpriced at $t = 0$. The overpricing can be confirmed by using (16.14) to compute $h_{Z,0}$, which the worksheet shows to equal 1.010. Recall that when $h_{Z,0} > 1$, the sentiment premium is negative. The worksheet displays the values of the terms in (16.24), whose sum is -0.0082, the risk premium attached to Z.

16.5   Entropy and Long-Run Efficiency

Will sentiment disappear in the long run? Will information investors drive out investors who commit errors, or do not learn quickly enough? If so, then Theorem 16.1 implies that prices will be efficient in the long run.

The question of what happens in the long run was first raised in Chapter 11, and receives a two-part answer in this book. The first part involves log-utility; it was the subject of Chapter 11. The second part is the subject of this section, where the log-utility restriction is dropped. In the discussion to follow, the critical assumption is that marginal utility approaches $+\infty$ as consumption goes to zero, a property that holds for CRRA utility as long as the coefficient of relative risk aversion is greater than or equal to unity.

The example of heterogeneous beliefs discussed in this chapter and the last features $T = 3$. Suppose that T becomes large. Which of the two investors will dominate, the log-utility investor with $\gamma = 1$ or the more risk averse investor with $\gamma = 2$? Recall that both investors share the same time discount factor.

In order to answer this question, consider a simple case in which the beliefs of the two investors are correct. The commonly held view for this situation is that in the long term, the ratio of the more risk averse investor's wealth to that of the log-utility investor will go to zero. That is, the log-utility investor will eventually dominate, and the more risk averse investor will vanish.

As it happens, the risk averse investor does not vanish (nor does the log-utility investor vanish). Neither investor acquires all the wealth. Both investors survive in the long term. Given the discussion about entropy in Chapter 11, this statement may come as a surprise. (The surprise involves the survival of the more risk averse investor; after all, the entropy associated with a log-utility investor with correct beliefs is zero.)

An explanation for why both investors survive in the long term has been developed by Sandroni (2000) and extended by Blume and Easley (2004). The key to understanding the reason why the more risk averse investor survives involves the comparison of the two investors' savings rates. Consider a modification to the preceding example, the modification being that both investors have correct beliefs. Computation shows that in the equilibrium associated with the modified example, the more risk averse investor saves more of his wealth than the log-utility investor in every date–event pair.[6] Moreover, the more risk averse investor chooses a higher savings rate after a down-move than after an up-move.

One of the key points in Chapter 11 is that correctness of beliefs and savings rates are both central to long-run survival. Although the more risk averse investor has a higher entropy than his log-utility counterpart, and higher entropy is detrimental to survival, the more risk averse investor overcomes this disadvantage through a higher savings rate.

16.5.1 Formal Argument

Blume and Easley provide a formal argument that identifies the key issues underlying survival. The argument begins with the two fundamental theorems of welfare economics. The first theorem states that every competitive equilibrium is Pareto-efficient. The second theorem states that every Pareto-efficient allocation can support a competitive equilibrium, subject to some initial distribution of endowments.

Consider the first order conditions associated with a Pareto-efficient allocation. These are obtained by maximizing a weighted sum of expected utilities subject to a resource allocation constraint. The associated Lagrangean is

$$L = \sum_j \eta_j E(u_j) - \sum_{t,x_t} \lambda(x_t)\left(\sum_j c_j(x_t) - \omega(x_t)\right) \tag{16.25}$$

---

[6] See the file *Chapter 16 Example.xls*, worksheet *Demands*.

The first order condition associated with this Lagrangean is

$$\eta_j \frac{\partial E(u_j)}{\partial c_j(x_t)} = \lambda(x_t) \tag{16.26}$$

Let investor j have utility function u_j. Then j's marginal expected utility is $\delta_j^t P_j(x_t) u_j'(c_j(x_t))$. Divide the right-hand side of (16.26) for investor j by its counterpart for investor k to obtain

$$\frac{\eta_j \delta_j^t P_j(x_t) u_j'(c_j(x_t))}{\eta_k \delta_k^t P_k(x_t) u_k'(c_k(x_t))} = 1 \tag{16.27}$$

Now rearrange the last equation to obtain

$$\frac{u_j'(c_j(x_t))}{u_k'(c_k(x_t))} = \frac{\eta_k}{\eta_j} \frac{\delta_k^t}{\delta_j^t} \frac{P_k(x_t)}{P_j(x_t)} \tag{16.28}$$

Take the logarithm of the last equation, and divide by t to obtain

$$(1/t)ln\frac{u_j'(c_j(x_t))}{u_k'(c_k(x_t))} = (1/t)ln\frac{\eta_k}{\eta_j} + ln\frac{\delta_k}{\delta_j} + (1/t)ln\frac{P_k(x_t)}{P_j(x_t)} \tag{16.29}$$

Let t become large. Consider the right-hand side of (16.29). Notice that the first term goes to zero. The second term is constant and is unaffected. For *i.i.d.* processes and Ergodic Markov processes, the third term converges in probability to the entropy difference $I_\Pi(P_k) - I_\Pi(P_j)$. In other words, the time average of investor j's marginal utility to investor k's marginal utility is given by

$$[ln(\delta_k) - I_\Pi(P_k)] - [(ln(\delta_j) - I_\Pi(P_j)] \tag{16.30}$$

Blume and Easley call the difference $[ln(\delta_j) - I_\Pi(P_j)]$ investor j's *survival index*. If investor j has a lower survival index than investor k, then with probability one, the ratio of investor j's marginal utility approaches $+\infty$. However, given CRRA utility with $\gamma \geq 1$, this implies that investor j's consumption goes to zero.

In the preceding example, both investors have identical time discount factors and common beliefs. Therefore, they have identical survival indexes. Neither dominates the other in the long run, despite the fact that one investor is more risk averse than the other.

16.6   Learning: Bayesian and Non-Bayesian

The entropy-based argument above suggests that in the long run, investors who do not learn to correct their mistakes will either need to save more than informed investors or see their wealth share decline to zero. Can we expect investors to learn from their mistakes? To address this question, consider a contrast between the manner in which a Bayesian forms her beliefs and the manner in which an investor who engages in extrapolation bias forms his beliefs. For simplicity, assume that aggregate consumption growth evolves as an *i.i.d* binomial process, where Π_u is the unknown true probability attached to the occurrence of an up-move at every t.

Begin with the Bayesian. At $t=0$, the Bayesian begins with an initial prior density $Q_{B,0}(\Pi_u)$ over $\Pi_u \in [0,1]$. If the Bayesian observes the occurrence of an up-move at $t = 1$, the Bayesian forms posterior density

$$Q_{B,1}(\Pi_u) = \frac{\Pi_u Q_{B,0}(\Pi_u)}{\int_0^1 \Phi_u Q_{B,0}(\Phi_u)d\Phi} \tag{16.31}$$

At the end of $t = 1$, the Bayesian replaces $Q_{B,0}$ with $Q_{B,1}$. If the Bayesian observes the occurrence of a down-move at $t = 2$, then she forms posterior density

$$Q_{B,2}(\Pi_u) = \frac{\Pi_u Q_{B,1}(\Pi_u)}{\int_0^1 \Phi_u Q_{B,1}(\Phi_u)d\Phi} \tag{16.32}$$

Notice that if $Q_{B,0}$ is uniform, then $Q_{B,1}(\Pi_u) = 2\Pi_u$ and $Q_{B,2}(\Pi_u) = 6\Pi_u(1 - \Pi_u)$. Applying the argument recursively implies that if after t observations, a Bayesian has observed n_u up-moves, then her posterior density has the form of a beta function. That is,

$$Q_{B,t}(\Pi_u) = \frac{(t + 2)!}{(n_u + 1)!(t - n_u + 1)!}\Pi_u^{n_u}(1 - \Pi_u)^{t-n_u} \tag{16.33}$$

At t a Bayesian assigns probability $\int_0^1 \Pi_u Q_{B,t}(\Pi_u)d\Pi$ to the occurrence of an up-move at $t + 1$. The value of this integral is $(n_u + 1)/(t + 2)$. By the strong law of large numbers, $(n_u + 1)/(t + 2)$ converges to the true probability Π_u.

Blume–Easley establish that Bayesian expected utility maximizers learn quickly enough so as not to vanish over time. What about non-Bayesians?

Although there is a multitude of non-Bayesian learning rules, consider a rule that features extrapolation bias. Define $1_u(t) = 1$ if an up-move occurs at t, and zero otherwise. Notice that $n_u = \sum_{\tau=1}^t 1_u(\tau)$. Extrapolation bias stems from overweighting recent events relative to more distant events.

In order to capture the bias stemming from overweighting recent events, let $\alpha > 1$, and suppose that a non-Bayesian learner uses $m_u = \sum_{\tau=1}^{t} \alpha^\tau 1_u(\tau) / \sum_{\tau=1}^{t} \alpha^\tau$ in place of n_u. If recent events have been up-moves, then m_u will tend to exceed n_u.

When α is not close to 1, recent realizations will strongly dominate in determining m_u. A key feature of this learning rule is that it need not converge over time, but may instead be volatile. Investors who use a learning rule of this sort overreact to recent events. They become excessively optimistic after a recent run of up-moves, and excessively pessimistic after a recent run of down-moves. As was mentioned above, unless their rates of saving are high, non-Bayesian learners will vanish in the long run.

16.7 Summary

This chapter described how sentiment is manifest in the SDF and risk premia. The chapter presented two central decomposition results. The first result is that the log-SDF can be expressed as the sum of a fundamental component and sentiment. The second result is that the expected excess return (or risk premium) on any security can be expressed as the sum of a fundamental premium corresponding to efficient prices and a sentiment premium to reflect sentiment-based risk. When prices are efficient, sentiment is zero and the sentiment premium is zero. In this case the SDF is only equal to a fundamental premium, and the risk premium only reflects fundamental risk.

In the long term, an investor's survival is determined by a survival index that combines his time discount factor and the entropy of his beliefs. The result establishes that when investors share the same discount factor and the same beliefs, and $\gamma_j \geq 1$ for all j, then no investor vanishes in the long term. However, investors who violate Bayes rule and do not learn quickly enough will typically vanish in the long run.

Part VI

Applications of Behavioral SDF

17

Behavioral Betas and Mean-Variance Portfolios

The central question to be addressed in this chapter concerns the nature of beta and mean-variance efficiency when sentiment is nonzero and prices are inefficient. The chapter establishes that both mean-variance efficiency and beta are meaningful concepts when prices are inefficient. However, both reflect sentiment. Since a mean-variance portfolio is a special case of a security, Theorem 16.2 (the return decomposition result) implies that mean-variance returns decompose into a fundamental component and a sentiment premium. This chapter demonstrates that the sentiment component oscillates. The chapter also demonstrates that beta decomposes into a fundamental component and a sentiment component. The sentiment component underlies the traditional concept of expected abnormal return.

17.1 Mean-Variance Efficiency and Market Efficiency

As was mentioned in Chapter 16, the risk premium on any security Z is determined by the covariance of its return with the SDF. That is, the risk premium is $-i_1 cov(r(Z), M)$. Notably, the relationship

$$Er(Z) - i_1 = -i_1 cov(r(Z), M) \qquad (17.1)$$

does not imply that prices are efficient in the sense of coinciding with fundamental values. Indeed, Chapter 16 established that the expected return to any security can be expressed as the sum of a fundamental component that applies when prices are efficient and a sentiment premium.

The traditional approach to characterizing risk premiums uses the concepts of beta and mean-variance frontier. Beta is just the covariance between $r(Z)$ and the return to a mean-variance benchmark portfolio, divided by the variance of the benchmark return. The Capital Asset Pricing Model (CAPM) is valid when the market portfolio is mean-variance efficient.

As was mentioned earlier, the relationship (17.1) does not imply that prices are efficient in the sense of coinciding with fundamental values. By the same token, being able to express the risk premium $Er(Z) - i_1$ in terms of beta and a mean-variance efficient portfolio does not imply that prices are efficient in the sense of being objectively correct.

Are prices efficient as long as risk premia can be explained in terms of a suitably chosen beta or SDF? The answer depends on the definition of market efficiency being employed. Recall the discussion from Chapter 9. If market efficiency is defined as the absence of risky arbitrage, then the answer may well be yes. Those who adopt this definition of market efficiency do not regard situations where security prices are driven up by irrational exuberance as inefficient.

For those subscribing to this view, prices are inefficient only if informed investors fail to engage in expected utility maximizing (risky) arbitrage. If expected utility maximizing informed investors find the benefits of going short too risky, despite their view that security prices are excessively high, then prices will be efficient. As was mentioned in Chapter 9, through our defining market efficiency in this way, market efficiency and equilibrium are essentially synonymous.

If market efficiency is defined as prices' coinciding with fundamental values, then the answer is not necessarily. When market efficiency is defined as prices' coinciding with (objective) fundamental values, then market efficiency and irrationally exuberant security prices are incompatible. In other words, market efficiency is essentially equivalent to market sentiment's being equal to zero.

17.2   Characterizing Mean-Variance Efficient Portfolios

Identifying a mean-variance efficient benchmark involves maximizing the expected quadratic utility of the return r to a one dollar investment. This maximization underlies the next theorem.

Theorem 17.1 *The return $r_{MV}(x_1)$ to a mean-variance efficient portfolio is*

$$r_{MV}(x_1) = \xi - \left[M(x_1) \frac{(\xi/i_1) - 1}{E_{\Pi}(M^2)} \right] \tag{17.2}$$

where ξ is a nonnegative parameter whose variation generates the mean-variance efficient frontier.

Proof of Theorem To prove Theorem 17.1, compute the first-order-condition associated with maximizing expected quadratic utility.

$$\sum_{x_1} \Pi(x_1)(2\xi' c(x_1) - c(x_1)^2) \tag{17.3}$$

subject to the constraint

$$\sum_{x_1} \nu(x_1)c(x_1) = 1 \tag{17.4}$$

Form the Lagrangean

$$L = \sum_{x_1} \Pi(x_1)(2\xi' c(x_1) - c(x_1)^2) - \lambda \left(\sum_{x_1} \nu(x_1)c(x_1) - 1 \right)$$

The first order condition for this optimization is

$$c(x_1) = [2\xi' - \lambda\nu(x_1)/\Pi(x_1)]/2 \tag{17.5}$$

Use the constraint (17.4) to solve for λ, obtaining

$$\lambda = 2\frac{(\xi' \sum_{x_1} \nu(x_1)) - 1}{\sum_{x_1} \nu(x_1)^2/\Pi(x_1)} \tag{17.6}$$

Observe that Sections 10.2.2 and 16.1 imply that

$$\sum_{x_1} \nu(x_1) = 1/i_1 \tag{17.7}$$

where i_1 is the single period rate of interest. Multiply the denominator of (17.6) by $\Pi(x_1)/\Pi(x_1)$ and substitute $M(x_1)$ for $\nu(x_1)/\Pi(x_1)$. The substitution implies that the denominator of (17.6) is given by

$$\sum_{x_1} \nu(x_1)^2/\Pi(x_1) = E_{\Pi}\{M(x_1)^2\} \tag{17.8}$$

Substitute (17.8) and (17.7) into (17.5). Define $\xi = 2\xi'$ and substitute $M(x_1)$ for $\nu(x_1)/\Pi(x_1)$ into (17.5). This completes the proof. ∎

Equation (16.1) implies that for the risk premium on a security to be high, its return must covary negatively with the SDF. Alternatively, the security must covary positively with respect to a benchmark mean-variance efficient portfolio (17.2). Therefore, the SDF and return to a mean-variance efficient portfolio must be negatively related.

17.3   The Shape of Mean-Variance Returns

The discussion in Chapter 16 suggested that heterogeneous beliefs can impart an oscillating pattern to the SDF function. In view of the preceding paragraph, it is reasonable to hypothesize that the return distribution of a mean-variance efficient portfolio would also feature oscillation.

Theorem 17.1 expresses the mean-variance return in terms of the SDF. Notice that the return r_{MV} is linear in the kernel $M(x_1)$, and has a negative coefficient.[1] Hence, the return is low in a state that bears a high price per unit probability.

Sentiment can alter the shape of the relationship between the mean-variance return r_{MV} and aggregate consumption growth g.[2] In an efficient market, $\Lambda \equiv 0$, in which case r_{MV} is a monotone increasing, concave function of g, for a suitably low value of ξ.[3] This follows from (14.7) and the proof of Theorem 17.1. When prices are efficient, a mean-variance portfolio earns very low returns in low consumption growth rate states. Indeed, gross mean-variance returns can fall below 100 percent: there is no limited liability attached to a mean-variance efficient portfolio.[4]

---

[1] The coefficient is time-varying, and stochastic. Note that equation (17.2) is general, whereas the equation that follows it is specific to CRRA utility.

[2] Dybvig and Ingersoll (1982) discuss the mean-variance pricing in complete markets. Their work points out some of the weaknesses associated with quadratic utility. Dybvig and Ingersoll are primarily interested in CAPM pricing, which occurs when the market portfolio is mean-variance efficient. In their paper, they identify a number of reasons why CAPM pricing may fail. In contrast, the focus here is in understanding the impact of investor errors on mean-variance returns, because the mean-variance efficient frontier underlies risk premia and beta.

[3] As $\xi \to 0$, the mean-variance utility function approaches the linear risk-neutral function.

[4] Hence, gross returns can be negative, which is an important feature of benchmark portfolios used in the calculation of correct betas. Concavity implies that the marginal return to consumption growth is declining. For very high consumption growth rates, the return peaks, and can decline.

Gross Return to Mean-variance Portfolio:
Behavioral Mean-Variance Return vs Efficient Mean-Variance Return

FIGURE 17.1. This figure contrasts a traditional mean-variance return pattern and a behavioral mean-variance return pattern for the sentiment function depicted in Figure 15.8.

However, sentiment can distort the shape of the relationship between r_{MV} and aggregate consumption growth g, by introducing local extrema.[5] To see how an oscillating pattern in the sentiment function can affect the shape of the r_{MV} function, consider Figure 17.1, which involves the same example that underlies Figures 16.1 and 16.2.

Theorem 16.2 establishes that the risk premium associated with any security is composed of a fundamental component and a sentiment premium. Figure 17.1 displays two functions. The concave function corresponds to the return to a mean-variance efficient portfolio as a function of g, when sentiment is zero. It is the sum of the short-term interest rate and the fundamental component. Here the function is concave and monotone increasing. The oscillating function corresponds to a mean-variance efficient portfolio as a function of g, when sentiment is nonzero. The difference between the two functions is the sentiment premium.

To understand what drives the shape of the r_{MV} function in this example, recall that by Theorem 17.1, r_{MV} is a linear function of M with a negative coefficient. Moreover, the equilibrium log-SDF displays an

---

[5] In the relevant range.

oscillating pattern. The combination of these two features leads the graph of r_{MV} to feature oscillation.

Looking at the issue more closely, observe that there are four regions in Figure 17.1, corresponding to which function has the higher value, the function corresponding to efficient prices or the function corresponding to inefficient prices. Call these four regions left, left–middle, right–middle, and right.

The behavioral mean-variance return lies below its efficient counterpart when in the left region and in the right–middle region. These are regions where investors overweight probabilities. A mean-variance efficient portfolio, constructed using objectively correct probabilities, will respond to the attendant mispricing by tilting toward underpriced states, and away from overpriced states.

In the left region, pessimistic investors attach too high a probability to the occurrence of very low consumption growth. They might purchase out-of-the-money put options that pay off only when consumption growth is very low. An informed mean-variance investor takes the opposite side of this trade, selling out-of-the-money put options. Therefore, when consumption growth turns out to be very low, the informed mean-variance investor earns very low returns, lower than when prices are efficient.

By the same token, optimistic investors attach too high a probability to consumption growth rates in the right–middle region. Therefore, an informed mean-variance investor takes the opposite side of the trade with optimistic investors, and earns lower returns when consumption growth lies in this region.

In contrast, the informed mean-variance investor earns superior returns in the left–middle and right regions. In both the left–middle and right regions, optimistic investors underweight the probabilities of the associated events, because they underestimate the second moment of the distribution. Pessimistic investors also underestimate the probability of events in the left–middle region, because they underestimate the mean of the distribution.

Figure 17.1 contrasts the benchmark portfolios to be used in computing appropriate betas. When prices are efficient, the return to the benchmark portfolio is an increasing function of the market portfolio. However, when prices are inefficient, then the appropriate benchmark portfolio to use for beta features the oscillating property.[6]

The discussion in Section 15.4 made the point that the shape of the SDF could be time-varying, for example reflecting changes in investor confidence.

---

[6] Theorem 17.1 pertains to one-period returns. There is a counterpart result for t-period returns. But the benchmark portfolio used to price risk for t-period returns is not equivalent to compounded one-period mean-variance returns. In other words, from a theoretical perspective, betas based on monthly returns should not be used to price annual returns.

FIGURE 17.2. This figure contrasts a traditional mean-variance return pattern and a behavioral mean-variance return pattern for the sentiment function depicted in Figure 15.7.

A sentiment function such as Figure 15.7 produces a different mean-variance pattern than the one displayed in Figure 17.1. Specifically, the mean-variance pattern associated with Figure 15.7 is U-shaped. Figure 17.2 displays the mean-variance return pattern for this case. Notice that the behavioral mean-variance return exceeds the efficient mean-variance return in the extremes, but lies below it in the mid-range.

17.4   The Market Portfolio

How sensitive is the objective return distribution of the market portfolio to sentiment? The answer to this question depends on the representative investor's risk tolerance, as the following theorem demonstrates.

Theorem 17.2 *The x_0-price q_ω of the market portfolio has the form*

$$q(Z_\omega) = \omega(x_0)E_R\left\{\sum_{t=1}^{T}\delta_{R,t}^t g(x_t)^{\gamma_R(x_t)-1}\right\} \qquad (17.9)$$

Let $r_\omega(x_1)$ denote the return to holding the market portfolio from x_0 to the beginning of x_1. Then

$$r_\omega(x_1) = \frac{g(x_1)}{\delta_{R,1}} \frac{\sum_1^T E_R\{\delta_{R,1}^t g(x_t)^{1-\gamma_R(x_t)}|x_1\}}{\sum_1^T E_R\{\delta_{R,0}^{t'} g(x_t)^{1-\gamma_R(x_t)}|x_0\}} \tag{17.10}$$

where $\delta^{t'}$ is defined in Section 11.5.2.

In (17.10) the base from which growth is measured in the numerator is $\omega(x_1)$, whereas in the denominator the base is $\omega(x_0)$.

Proof of Theorem   The proof of this theorem is computational. The one-period return to the market portfolio is the sum of the date 1 dividend and date 1 price, divided by the date 0 price, i.e., $(\omega(x_1)+q_1(Z_\omega))/q_0(Z_\omega)$. Use (14.7) to compute the present values of the two future aggregate consumption streams: the value of the unconditional process under ν, and the value of the process conditional on x_1. The present value of each of these two streams appears, respectively, in the denominator and numerator of (17.10), with the numerator value divided by $\nu(x_1)$. This completes the proof. ■

The probabilities that underlie the return distribution for the market portfolio are given by Π. The support of the distribution is given by (17.10). Theorem 17.2 establishes how beliefs affect the support. The return to the market portfolio is a product of three terms, the growth rate in aggregate consumption, the inverse of δ_R, and the ratio of two expectations. The role of the ratio is to augment returns to reflect increasing patience, increasing risk tolerance, or increasing optimism. The role of increasing patience was discussed in section 11.5.2, so attention below is focused on the latter two variables.

To interpret expression (17.10), consider the case of log-utility, meaning the case when $\gamma_R = 1$. Here, the expectation ratio in (17.10) is unity, so the return to the market portfolio is $g(x_1)/\delta_R$. This implies that the return on the market portfolio is the consumption growth rate, scaled by the inverse discount factor.

Take the logarithmic situation as the base case, and consider how r_ω changes relative to the base case as we increase the value of γ_R. When $\gamma_R > 1$, the expectation ratio in (17.10) is not unity. Notice that the numerator of the expectations ratio is conditional on x_1, while the denominator is the same expectation conditional on x_0. Because of the different bases from which growth is measured in numerator and denominator, a positive trend in expected growth rates leads the expectation ratio in (17.10) to lie above unity. Hence, Theorem 17.2 implies that a shift in risk tolerance or optimism about consumption growth causes the return

r_ω to be higher than its value under logarithmic utility. In particular, Theorem 17.2 demonstrates how the value of γ_R affects the sensitivity of the return distribution of the market portfolio to investors' beliefs.

Under log-utility, the support of the return distribution is independent of traders' beliefs. Theorem 17.2 makes clear that the log-utility case is special. The lower the representative investor's risk tolerance, the greater the influence of expectations on the value of r_ω.

17.5   Risk Premiums and Coskewness

In Section 16.4 I established an equation that shows how sentiment impacts risk premiums. In neoclassical asset pricing, where sentiment is zero, the risk premium for every security is based on its return covariance with the return to any risky mean-variance portfolio. For example, in the CAPM, the market portfolio is mean-variance efficient, and this is why risk premiums are based on the covariance between the security's returns and the returns to the market portfolio.

How does sentiment impact the relationship between risk and return? The short answer is in the same way as in neoclassical asset pricing. Because risk premiums for all securities are based on return covariance with mean-variance (MV) portfolios, even when sentiment is nonzero, the key to understanding risk and return lies in the impact of sentiment on the return distributions for both MV portfolios and individual assets. This section uses the shape of the mean-variance return function to shed light on the impact of sentiment on risk premiums.

It is important to appreciate that in a behavioral framework, risk has both a fundamental component and a sentiment component. Readers whose intuition is based on neoclassical finance might be inclined to think of risk as comprising only the fundamental component, with abnormal returns being associated with the portion of returns that are not compensation for bearing fundamental risk. However, in the behavioral SDF-based framework, sentiment impacts both expected returns and risk, and of course the relationship between them.

Figure 17.1 contrasts the return pattern for a behavioral mean-variance portfolio to the return pattern for a neoclassical mean-variance portfolio. There are three points to notice about Figure 17.1. First, the return to a traditional MV portfolio is approximately, but not exactly, linear in aggregate consumption growth. In view of Theorem 17.2, this implies that the return to a neoclassical mean-variance portfolio can be approximated by a combination of the market portfolio and the risk-free security. (Figure 17.4 displays the closeness of the approximation.)

Second, the return to a behavioral MV portfolio is more volatile than the return to a traditional MV portfolio. This is because the peaks and valleys in the behavioral MV portfolio correspond to exposure from risky arbitrage. A behavioral MV portfolio is a true MV portfolio, meaning that it is based on the objective pdf Π. Therefore, maximizing expected return involves the exploitation of nonzero sentiment.

The sentiment function underlying Figure 17.1 is depicted in Figure 15.8. Notice that in Figure 15.8, sentiment is positive at the extreme left and negative at the extreme right. This means that extreme out-of-the-money put options on the market portfolio are overpriced, while extreme out-of-the-money call options are underpriced. As a result, a true mean-variance portfolio would feature a naked short position in extreme out-of-the-money put options on the market portfolio and a long position in extreme out-of-the-money call options on the market portfolio.

That a behavioral mean-variance portfolio is more volatile than its traditional counterpart is a natural consequence of a behavioral SDF being more volatile than its traditional counterpart. See Figure 16.2. The difference in volatility has profound implications for the magnitudes of risk premiums and Sharpe ratios. Sharpe ratios are bounded from above by the coefficient of variation of the SDF: see equation (16.2). As a result, the more volatile behavioral SDF admits higher risk premiums and Sharpe ratios than does the less volatile neoclassical SDF. As implied by the previous paragraph, achieving these higher risk premiums and Sharpe ratios involves the use of financial derivatives.

Third, MV-returns are very negatively skewed relative to the market portfolio because returns to a behavioral MV-portfolio are not only extremely low in low growth states, but fall off quickly as the rate of consumption growth declines. Some readers might be surprised that skewness is an issue at all in a discussion about mean-variance portfolios. After all, skewness pertains to the third moment, and mean-variance preferences are neutral in respect to all moments higher than the second. The reason why skewness can be an issue for a behavioral MV portfolio involves the risky arbitrage feature of true MV portfolios. An MV portfolio that features a large naked short position in extreme out-of-the-money put options on the market portfolio will earn a very low return when the return on the market portfolio is very low. An MV portfolio that features a long position in extreme out-of-the-money call options on the market portfolio will earn a high return when the return on the market portfolio is very high.

A classic result in asset pricing theory is that the risk premium to any asset can be expressed as the product of the asset's beta with respect to any risky MV portfolio and the risk premium of the MV portfolio. Of course, this result continues to hold when the MV frontier has a behavioral structure, because it is an equilibrium property, not a property that depends on whether sentiment is zero or nonzero.

To understand the implications that the behavioral MV shape in Figure 17.1 has for the nature of risk premiums of individual securities, consider what systematic risk entails. Systematic risk is risk associated with the returns to an MV portfolio. Securities whose returns are highly correlated with the returns to an MV portfolio will be associated with high degrees of systematic risk. In this regard, remember that the returns to the behavioral MV portfolio depicted in Figure 17.1 are negatively skewed relative to the market portfolio. Therefore, securities whose returns are high in systematic risk will feature negative skewness relative to the market portfolio.

Harvey and Siddique (2000) study the cross-section of stock returns using coskewness relative to the market portfolio. They propose several definitions of coskewness. One definition of coskewness is the beta of the security's return relative to the squared market return, controlling for covariation with the market return. To control for the market return, Harvey–Siddique compute coskewness beta using the residuals of the security's return on the market return. With this definition, coskewness measures the extent to which a security's return covaries with the squared market return.

The definition of coskewness is particularly appropriate when the SDF has a quadratic-like U-shape. Recall that the SDF will be U-shaped when the sentiment component has the U shape depicted in Figure 15.4, and is large relative to the fundamental component of the SDF. In this case, the shape of the MV function is an inverted U. Figure 17.3 depicts the log-SDF decomposition associated with Figure 15.4. Figure 17.4 depicts

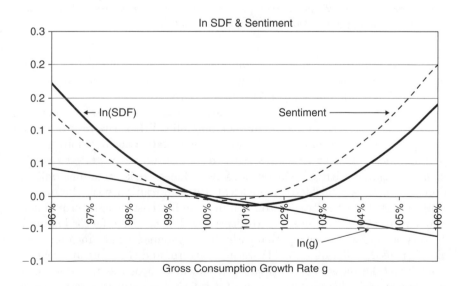

FIGURE 17.3. Decomposition of log-SDF function associated with Figure 15.4. The dotted line in the figure is a sentiment function with a U-shape similar to a quadratic function. The associated log-SDF is also U-shaped.

FIGURE 17.4. Behavioral MV Return Function Associated with U-Shaped SDF Function. The figure displays the inverted U-shape of a behavioral MV return function associated with the log-SDF function displayed in Figure 17.3. The efficient, or neoclassical, MV return function is approximately equal to the return from a combination of the market portfolio and risk-free security. The return pattern for the approximation is displayed as a dotted line.

the behavioral MV return function associated with Figure 15.4, along with a neoclassical MV return function and the return function for the combination of the market portfolio and risk-free security.

Observe that this type of MV return function will feature negative coskewness with respect to the market portfolio. When the return to the MV portfolio is a quadratic function of aggregate consumption growth g, then the coefficient associated with g will be positive, and the coefficient associated with g^2 will be negative. Hence, risk premiums will be determined by a multifactor model featuring covariation with the market portfolio (with a positive factor loading) and a coskewness term reflecting covariation with the squared return (with a negative factor loading). In this situation, a security that is high in systematic risk, meaning risk that is priced, will mimic the MV-return pattern, and therefore also feature negative coskewness. This is because coskewness measures the amount of covariance with the squared market return that a security's return adds to an investor's portfolio. Coskewness plays a role analogous to a factor loading in a multifactor asset pricing model. Notably, there is a negative premium to holding stocks whose returns exhibit positive coskewness relative to the market portfolio.

Dittmar (2002) develops a flexible nonlinear pricing kernel approach in the tradition of a zero sentiment representative investor model. Notably, he finds that the empirical SDF in his analysis is not monotone decreasing over its range, but instead has a U-shaped pattern. In this regard, Poti (2006) uses a quadratic U-shaped SDF to extend the Harvey–Siddique analysis.

Notably, the shape of the behavioral MV return pattern depicted in Figure 17.1 is not an inverted U. In the right portion of Figure 17.1, the behavioral MV-return pattern does not have the same feature as an inverted-U. However, in the left portion, the patterns are similar. This suggests that when sentiment has the shape depicted in Figure 17.1, negative coskewness with respect to the market portfolio will capture some, but not all, aspects of systematic risk.

Keep in mind that there are no mean-variance investors in the model, only investors with CRRA utility functions. Even though MV portfolios serve to price risk, no investor in the model actually chooses to hold an MV portfolio. In this regard, consider an investor with log-utility whose holds objectively correct beliefs. Chapter 11 indicates that such an investor holds a zero entropy portfolio featuring maximum long-term fitness. Figure 17.5 illustrates the difference between the return to a log-utility portfolio and to a comparable MV-portfolio.

Notice that the log-utility portfolio features higher returns than the MV portfolio in both very unfavorable states and very favorable states. The log-utility portfolio performs better in very unfavorable states because when consumption goes to zero, marginal utility for the log-utility investor goes to

FIGURE 17.5.

infinity, whereas for quadratic utility it stays finite. The log-utility portfolio performs better than the MV portfolio in very favorable states because as consumption increases, marginal utility for the quadratic utility function declines below zero: but, for log-utility, marginal utility stays positive.

17.6   Behavioral Beta: Decomposition Result

The behavioral risk premium equation (16.24) stipulates that the risk premium associated with any security is the sum of a fundamental component and a sentiment premium. This section describes this relationship from the vantage point of beta, meaning how beta decomposes into a fundamental component and a sentiment component. The argument establishing the decomposition is divided into three parts, an informal argument to provide some intuition, a formal derivation, and a short example.

17.6.1   Informal Discussion: Intuition

To fix ideas, return to Figure 17.1. This figure displays two mean-variance return patterns, one when prices are efficient and one when prices are inefficient. When prices are efficient, the mean-variance (MV) return pattern is very close to the return from a portfolio consisting of the market return and a small position in the risk-free security. When prices are inefficient, the MV return pattern oscillates in g.

Consider an observer who falsely believes that prices are efficient when they are inefficient, and seeks to use an MV factor model to compute expected returns. How would this person go about the task? He would select a benchmark MV portfolio return distribution, such as the efficient MV return displayed in Figure 17.1, and compute security betas relative to this benchmark. Then he would compute expected returns as the sum of the risk-free rate of interest and the product of beta and the excess return on the benchmark portfolio.

If the observer knows the true return distribution for a security, he will be able to compute its beta correctly, relative to the MV benchmark. He will know the risk-free rate of interest, since that is determined in the market. And since he knows the true probability density function Π, he will be able to compute the risk premium on the MV benchmark. Therefore, he will be able to apply the MV factor pricing model to compute the expected return to any security. However, the expected return that his model produces will typically be incorrect.[7]

Why will the observer miscalculate expected return using his MV factor model? The answer is that he selected the wrong MV benchmark. In order

---

[7] For a discussion that is similar in spirit, see Gibbons and Ferson (1985) and Ferson and Locke (1998).

to compute expected returns correctly, he will have to select a benchmark portfolio that is a true MV return. That is, because prices are inefficient, he will have to select a behavioral MV return distribution, such as the oscillating pattern in Figure 17.1.

If the observer selects the efficient MV return as his benchmark, then he will view the difference between the expected return produced by his model and the true expected return as being abnormal. If he persists in believing that the efficient MV return is an appropriate benchmark, then he will have to adjust his betas in order to make his model work. Such adjustments to beta are adjustments for sentiment, and can therefore be called beta sentiment components. Because his original beta would produce the correct expected return if prices were efficient, the original beta is effectively a fundamental beta component. Therefore, the betas that produce correct expected returns with misspecified MV benchmarks can be decomposed into a fundamental component and a sentiment component.

If the observer is able to find beta adjustments that work, he might be tempted to conclude that because his factor model now produces correct expected returns, prices must be efficient. Such a conclusion would be reached in error. Traditional asset pricing theorists have been conditioned to believe that finding factor loadings that explain expected returns corresponds to identifying measures of risk in an efficient market. However, the beta adjustments that correct the observer's misspecified model stem from mispricing due to sentiment, not fundamental risk. Of course, a portion of the true risk premium may also serve as compensation for risk, be that risk induced by fundamentals or by sentiment.

17.6.2   Formal Argument

Let $\beta(Z)$ be the mean-variance beta of any portfolio Z relative to r_{MV}: $\beta(Z)$ is the "true" beta. Let r_{MV}^π be a mean-variance factor r_{MV} for the case in which prices are efficient ($P_R = \Pi$). Call r_{MV}^π the *market factor*. Let $\beta_\Pi(Z)$ be the beta of security Z measured relative to the market factor. Call $\beta_\Pi(Z)$ the *market beta* of Z.

When prices are efficient, the expected return $E_\Pi(r(Z))$ to security Z is given by the sum

$$E_\Pi(r(Z)) = i_1 + \beta_\Pi(Z)(E_\Pi(r_{MV}^\pi) - i_1) \qquad (17.11)$$

where i_1 is the single period risk-free rate of interest in equilibrium.

Suppose that sentiment is nonzero, meaning prices are inefficient. In this case, (17.11) may not hold. Instead, the difference

$$A(Z) = E_\Pi(r(Z)) - i_1 - \beta_\Pi(Z)(E_\Pi(r_{MV}^\pi) - i_1) \qquad (17.12)$$

may be nonzero. Call $A(Z)$ *the expected abnormal return* to Z. The point is that when market prices are inefficient, risk is not fully priced by the market factor r_{MV}^π.

Consider the structure of the abnormal return function. There are many mean-variance return distributions r_{MV}, all parameterized by λ. Choose a risk factor r_{MV} that conforms to (17.2) and has the same standard deviation as the market factor r_{MV}^π. If prices are inefficient, then r_{MV} is a true risk factor, whereas r_{MV}^π is not.

The beta $\beta(r_{MV}^\pi)$ of r_{MV}^π, relative to the mean-variance efficient return r_{MV}, is $cov(r_{MV}^\pi, r_{MV})/var(r_{MV})$. Effectively, $\beta(r_{MV}^\pi)$ measures the degree to which r_{MV}^π is mean-variance efficient when sentiment is nonzero. Because r_{MV} has been selected to have the same standard deviation as r_{MV}^π, $\beta(r_{MV}^\pi) \leq 1$. If $\beta(r_{MV}^\pi) = 1$, r_{MV}^π is mean-variance efficient. If $\beta(r_{MV}^\pi) = 0$, then all of the risk in r_{MV}^π is unpriced.

Consider the ratio $\beta(Z)/\beta(r_{MV}^\pi)$. Observe that this ratio has the same units as the efficient beta $\beta^*(Z)$, namely the return on Z divided by the return r_{MV}^π. Both $\beta(Z)$ and $\beta(Z)/\beta(r_{MV}^\pi)$ relate the premium on Z to the premium on r_{MV}^π. However, keep in mind that as a general matter, not all the risk in r_{MV}^π is priced. What the market beta $\beta_\Pi(Z)$ measures is the amount of r_{MV}^π risk in the return $r(Z)$, both priced and unpriced. But $\beta(Z)/\beta(r_{MV}^\pi)$ reflects all priced risk in $r(Z)$, relative to the premium in r_{MV}^π. Therefore, the difference

$$(\beta(Z)/\beta(r_{MV}^\pi)) - \beta_\Pi(Z) \tag{17.13}$$

can be interpreted as a "correction" to the market beta. Call it the "beta correction."

Notice that $\beta_\Pi(Z)$ can be interpreted as the fundamental component of beta, and the beta correction (17.13) can be interpreted as the sentiment component. In other words, the true beta decomposes into a fundamental component and a sentiment component. The following theorem summarizes the result.

Theorem 17.3 *i) The expected abnormal return $A(Z)$ to Z, associated with the sentiment component of beta, is given by*

$$A(Z) = \left(\frac{\beta(Z)}{\beta(r_{MV}^\pi)} - \beta_\Pi(Z))(E_\Pi(r_{MV}^\pi) - i_1 \right) \tag{17.14}$$

ii) If prices are efficient, then $A(Z) = 0$.
iii) If the return $r(Z)$ is perfectly correlated with r_{MV}^π, then $A(Z) = 0$.

Theorem 17.3 provides a different perspective to return decompositions than the return decomposition result (16.24) described in Theorem 16.2.

Both theorems imply that a security's risk premium is the sum of a fundamental component and a sentiment component. Theorem 17.3 indicates how the sentiment premium is given by the sentiment component of beta. Theorem 17.3 indicates that abnormal returns are proportional to the risk premium on the mismeasured risk factor r_{MV}^{π}. Notably, the factor of proportionality is the "beta correction," which provides a link between market beta and perceived abnormal returns. At the same time, keep in mind that part iii) of Theorem 17.3 indicates that the beta correction will be small for securities whose returns are closely correlated with the mismeasured benchmark r_{MV}^{π}.

Theorem 17.3 indicates that the misspecified mean-variance benchmark can be used for the purpose of computing expected returns. However, a suitable correction to beta is required, where the correction term is the sentiment component. As was mentioned earlier, the possibility of finding a beta correction factor in practice does not imply that prices are efficient.

17.6.3 Example

Subsection 16.4.2 provided an example to illustrate the decomposition of expected return into a fundamental component and a sentiment component. As was mentioned earlier, Figure 17.1 depicts the mean-variance return distribution for that example. Therefore, consider the same example used in Subsection 16.4.2, including the security Z whose return was decomposed into a fundamental component and a sentiment component.

Worksheet *Beta* of the file *Chapter 17 Example.xls* establishes that the behavioral MV (gross) return distribution in Figure 17.1 has a mean equal to 1.0092, and a variance equal to 0.0001. Relative to the behavioral MV benchmark, the return r_Z has a beta equal to -34.5. The risk-free rate is 1.009. Therefore, the risk premium associated with holding Z is $-34.5(1.0092 - 1.0090) = -0.0082$ (subject to rounding error). That is, the MV factor model produces the same risk premium for Z as the SDF-based procedure discussed in Chapter 16.

Remember the observer who was discussed in Subsection 17.5.1. That observer used the efficient MV return as his benchmark, not the behavioral MV return. Relative to the efficient MV benchmark, Z has a beta equal to 99.43. Using the wrong MV benchmark and associated beta leads the observer to associate an expected risk premium to Z of -0.027, which is not the correct value. The observer would view the difference, 0.019, as an abnormal return. If the observer were to adjust his beta by -99.13, and continue to use the efficient MV return as his benchmark, then he would compute the correct expected return.

In terms of the model, the fundamental component of beta is 99.43 and the sentiment component is -99.13. The two together total 0.30.

17.7 Summary

Both the SDF and the mean-variance efficient frontier provide a basis for obtaining the expected return to a security. The two concepts are essentially mirror-image duals of each other. For this reason, sentiment-induced oscillation in the SDF function is paired with a sentiment-induced oscillation in the mean-variance efficient return function.

Sentiment also impacts the return distribution to the market portfolio. The higher the rate of risk aversion, the greater the impact of sentiment on the distribution. Notably, when all investors possess log-utility, the return distribution for the market portfolio is not impacted by sentiment.

Misspecifying a mean-variance benchmark can give rise to the perception of abnormal returns. If the benchmark would be appropriate in an efficient market setting, then the abnormal returns must relate to the sentiment premium. Notably, the misspecified mean-variance benchmark can be used for the purpose of computing expected returns; however, a suitable correction to beta is required, one that reflects sentiment as an omitted variable.

18
Cross-Section of Return Expectations

Chapter 16 established that a security's risk premium is the sum of a fundamental-based premium and a sentiment-based premium. In other words, the risk premium is not determined by fundamental risk alone. The traditional explanation for risk premiums is through beta. In this respect, a key lesson from Chapter 17 is that investor errors do not prevent risk premiums' being determined by beta. Rather, the concepts of beta and mean-variance efficiency are as applicable in inefficient markets as in efficient markets. At the same time, nonzero sentiment alters the character of the mean-variance portfolio.

Figure 17.1 contrasts the return profile of a mean-variance efficient portfolio when prices are inefficient with the return profile of a mean-variance efficient portfolio when prices are efficient. Notice that when prices are efficient, mean-variance returns approximately correspond to a weighted average of the market portfolio and the risk-free security. However, when prices are inefficient, mean-variance returns oscillate. This is important, because when prices are inefficient, the risk premium associated with any security depends on how the security's return distribution covaries with the oscillating mean-variance return profile, not the market portfolio. Recall that the oscillations correspond to market mispricing. Therefore, the return premium to any security depends on the degree to which the return profile of that security reflects the same mispricing pattern as the mean-variance profile.

The concepts just stated serve as the backdrop for discussing the literature on the cross-section of expected returns, or the characteristics literature.

This literature has been the focal point of a debate between proponents of market efficiency and proponents of behavioral finance. Proponents of market efficiency argue that characteristics explain returns because they proxy for risk. Proponents of behavioral finance argue that characteristics explain returns because they reflect investor errors.

18.1   Literature Review

This section reviews the characteristics literature, focusing on the nature of investor errors and the extent to which these errors affect risk premiums.

18.1.1   Winner–Loser Effect

The winner–loser effect is one of the central pillars of behavioral finance. Based upon Tversky–Kahneman's work on representativeness-based predictions (discussed in Section 2.4), De Bondt and Thaler (1985) conjectured that investors overreact to earnings, and as a result stock prices temporarily depart from fundamental values. Here the base rate refers to the tendency of extreme performance to be mean reverting. De Bondt and Thaler suggest that investors overreact to extreme earnings because they fail to recognize the extent to which extreme earnings revert to the mean.[1]

Empirically, De Bondt–Thaler identified a pattern suggesting that extreme prior losers tend to be undervalued and extreme prior winners tend to be overvalued. They suggest that a "winner–loser" effect occurs during the period that the mispricing gets corrected. De Bondt–Thaler (1985) document that prior losers subsequently earn positive risk-adjusted excess returns, while prior winners subsequently earn negative risk-adjusted excess returns.

De Bondt–Thaler (1987) investigate a series of important issues, involving the impact of time varying betas, the presence of a January seasonal, momentum, the roles played by size, book-to-market, and earnings announcements, and the asymmetry between returns to winners and returns to losers. These issues lie at the heart of the debate about under- and overreaction, and set the stage for many of the topics discussed in the remainder of this chapter.

The winner–loser effect is now an established fact. But there remain differences of opinion about whether risk or mispricing constitutes the cause of this effect. In their 1985 treatment, De Bondt–Thaler argue that the winner–loser effect cannot be explained by risk, when risk is measured by CAPM betas that are constant over time. Yet, CAPM beta varies with the degree of leverage, which in turn varies with the market value of equity.

---

[1] The material for the first portion of this chapter is drawn from the introductory essays in Shefrin (2001c).

To test for the effects of time-varying risk, De Bondt–Thaler construct an arbitrage portfolio that finances the purchase of prior losers with short sales of prior winners. In the arbitrage portfolio, the decline in market value of prior losers is offset by the increase for prior winners. A regression of the excess return to the arbitrage portfolio on the market risk premium produces an alpha of 5.9 percent, and a beta of 0.22. Hence, prior losers appear to be riskier than prior winners, but the 0.22 difference in betas is insufficient to explain 5.9 percent of the return differential.

Think about what happens if the difference in beta tends to be high at the same time that the market risk premium is high, and low when the risk premium is low. In this case, the small difference in beta can be a misleading indicator as far as the return on the arbitrage portfolio is concerned. Yet De Bondt–Thaler find that in periods when the market has been up, the loser portfolio has a higher beta than the winner portfolio, and when the market has been down, the loser portfolio has a lower beta. They suggest that such a pattern does not support the contention that prior losers outperform prior winners because losers are riskier than winners.

A key aspect of the risk-mispricing debate involves size and book-to-market. Since prior losers tend to get smaller and prior winners tend to get larger, it is natural to ask whether the winner–loser effect is a manifestation of the well-known size effect, in which small firms outperform large firms. De Bondt–Thaler argue not, because market value of equity for the extreme losers is in the fourth size quintile, and has a magnitude about 30 times that of the smallest firms.

18.1.2   Book-to-Market Equity and the Winner–Loser Effect

What De Bondt–Thaler point out is that the winner–loser effect is closer to the book-to-market effect described by Rosenberg, Reid, and Lanstein (1985) than the size effect. Book-to-market equity is the ratio of book market of equity to market value of equity. Firms featuring higher book-to-market equity ratios have historically earned higher returns as adjusted for risk, measured by CAPM beta. De Bondt–Thaler argue that both the winner–loser effect and the book-to-market effect stem from misvaluation. That is, they suggest that both effects arise in connection with sentiment. Proponents of market efficiency offer the counterargument that these effects reflect risk that is not captured by CAPM beta.

If investors overreact, to what do they overreact? Is it prior returns? After all, prior returns are the basis on which De Bondt–Thaler sort stocks. Actually, De Bondt–Thaler argue that investors overreact to earnings. As was mentioned earlier, empirically, there is evidence that earnings are mean reverting in the tails. But investors failing to recognize the tendency for earnings to revert to the mean predict that a recent pattern of low earnings is more likely to continue than is actually the case. This leads

De Bondt–Thaler to predict that stock price changes will be predictive of future earnings reversals. They present evidence confirming this prediction. De Bondt–Thaler identify winners and losers by looking back in time for five years, what they call the formation period. Prior winners earned positive excess returns during the formation period; prior losers earned negative excess returns. De Bondt–Thaler evaluate prior winners and losers by looking forward in time, what they call the test period.

The winner–loser effect is highly concentrated in the month of January. The January seasonal is prominent during the formation period, when losers are being losers, as well as the subsequent test period, when the reversal occurs. Why this is so remains a puzzle, and is part of a wider issue involving the turn of the year.

De Bondt–Thaler (1985, 1987) pose a challenge to the weak form of the efficient market hypothesis, that prices make efficient use of the information in current and past prices. Evidence presented by Ou and Penman (1989) presents the same challenge to the semi-strong form of the efficient market hypothesis, which maintains that prices make efficient use of all publicly available information. Ou–Penman argue that abnormal returns can be earned on the basis of information contained in firms' financial statements. They describe a zero net investment strategy that earned 12.5 percent during the period 1973–1983, or 7.0 percent on a size-adjusted basis. Unlike with De Bondt–Thaler, the Ou–Penman effect stems primarily from "winner" stocks, and is not driven by a January effect.

18.1.3   January and Momentum

Ritter (1988) studies an important issue about the behavior of individual investors in early January: the abrupt switch from being net sellers of small stocks to being net buyers of those stocks. Ritter points out that the portfolios of individual investors tend to be more intensive in low-priced, low-capitalization stocks than those of institutional investors. His findings suggest that in the prior December, individual investors sell stocks that have declined in order to realize losses for tax purposes. However, they do not immediately reinvest the proceeds from those sales. Instead, they "park" the proceeds in cash until January. At this time, they invest in a broad spectrum of small stocks, which adds to other January activity such as the sale of stocks of larger firms to realize long-term capital gains.

Ritter argues that the behavior of individual investors can explain why the turn-of-the-year effect is strongest following bear markets (there are more losers), and concerns small stocks rather than all stocks. He also points out that his interpretation explains why small stocks display a turn-of-the-year effect, and why the effect is strongest among stocks that are good candidates for tax-loss selling. It is also possible that the January seasonal stems from window dressing by institutional investors, in that these may reframe their portfolios at year-end to deceive investors about their contents. Sias and Starks (1997) provide evidence that suggests that the influence of individual investors is stronger than that of institutional investors when it comes to the January seasonal.

Is the winner–loser effect caused by overreaction? In this respect, the fact that the effect is concentrated in January is certainly puzzling. Do investors overreact only in January? Or recognize the extent of prior overreactions primarily in January? Parking the proceeds can explain the temporal nature of trading in small stocks. But it does not explain why small stocks should outperform larger stocks, and it is not clear that it explains why tax-loss motivated trading should have a significant price effect. De Bondt–Thaler (1987) conclude that they have no explanation for the January seasonal, rational or otherwise.

The winner–loser effect features a combination of overreaction and under-reaction. De Bondt–Thaler stress the return reversal pattern, which they attribute to overreaction. But they also identify elements involving momentum that suggest underreaction. For example, in examining the returns earned in the first January of the test period, De Bondt–Thaler find a momentum effect for winners. Prior winners continue to be winners during the first January, an observation in conflict with overreaction.

18.1.4   General Momentum Studies

Perhaps the most striking momentum pattern in the winner–loser effect is that it takes five years for the mispricing to correct itself. The length of the correction horizon would seem to suggest underreaction. Jegadeesh and Titman (1993) document the momentum effect for U.S. stocks, and Rouwenhorst (1998) provides independent corroboration by doing the same for international stocks.

Jegadeesh–Titman study portfolios that they describe by the term "J-month/K-month," where stocks are held for K months based on the return earned during the preceding J months. They partition stocks into deciles, and focus on the top and bottom deciles, meaning extreme "losers" and extreme "winners." They then examine the performance of a zero-cost trading relative strength strategy where they buy past winners and sell past losers, replacing 1/K of the portfolio every month. Here J and K are in multiples of 3, and do not exceed 12.

Jegadeesh–Titman focus special attention on the case J=K=6, where returns were approximately 1 percent per month during the period 1965 through 1989. They note that this return cannot be explained in terms of CAPM risk, since the post-ranking beta of the zero-cost "winners minus losers" portfolio is negative. Likewise the return cannot be explained by time-varying risk, by size (the losers are smaller than the winners), or by serial covariance or lead-lag effects in the underlying factor structure.

How can one reconcile the momentum-based findings of Jegadeesh–Titman with those of De Bondt–Thaler that emphasize long-term reversal? It turns out that in the Jegadeesh–Titman study, the portfolio based on returns realized in the prior six months generates an average cumulative return of 9.5 percent over the subsequent 12 months. But it loses more than half this return over the following 24 months, and the combined result is not statistically different from zero. The resulting pattern seems to feature short-term momentum, but long-term reversal. Moreover, January plays a prominent role in the Jegadeesh–Titman study. The relative strength strategy *loses about 7 percent on average in each January period, although it achieves positive abnormal returns in all of the other months.* The issue of January arises in later chapters as well.

18.1.5   Glamour and Value

As was mentioned earlier, earnings announcements play a role in the De Bondt–Thaler explanation of the winner–loser effect. Earnings also play a role in the relative strength effect analyzed by Jegadeesh–Titman. They point out that the returns around the earnings announcements constitute about 25 percent of the returns to a zero-cost relative strength strategy. However, earnings growth is not the only fundamental variable involved in these issues. Lakonishok, Shleifer, and Vishny (1994) (LSV) use the term "glamour stocks" to refer to the stocks of firms that (1) performed well in the past, and (2) are expected to perform well in the future. They use the term "value stocks" for the stocks of firms that have had poor past performance and are expected to have poor future performance. How do investors measure performance? Those who employ a relative strength strategy hold prior winners, where the performance measure is prior returns. As discussed above, although winners earn positive abnormal returns in the short term, they underperform in the long term.

Notably, performance can also be measured using other criteria, such as sales growth. LSV suggest using past sales as a measure of past performance, and price-to-earnings or price-to-cash flow as a measure of expected future performance. Using these criteria, they study how an investor fared if he or she purchased glamour stocks and shunned value stocks. To the extent that most investors favor glamour over value, the latter strategy can be regarded as conventional. Put another way, LSV study how a contrarian investor fared, one who held value stocks and shunned glamour stocks.

There are three main results in LSV. The first result is that during the period 1963–1990, a portfolio of value stocks held for five years outperformed a portfolio of glamour stocks, in the sense of returning 10 to 11 percent more per year, or between 8 and 9 percent more on a size-adjusted basis. LSV consider a variety of alternative definitions of glamour and value, and focus on a definition of glamour that features high past sales growth and high price to cash flow.

The second LSV result is that the superior performance of value over glamour cannot be explained by risk. LSV argue that if risk were to explain the relationship just described, then value stocks should have underperformed glamour stocks in "bad" states like recessions. However, they find that between 1963 and 1990, value stocks outperformed glamour stocks in three of four recessions, and did somewhat worse in one recession. They also find that value stocks outperformed glamour stocks in the stock market's worst 25 months. Hence, they conclude that risk does not explain why value stocks have outperformed glamour stocks.

LSV's third result sheds some additional light on the combined findings of Jegadeesh–Titman and De Bondt–Thaler. LSV examine how the growth rates of fundamental variables such as sales and cash flow change between the period prior to portfolio formation and the period after portfolio formation. They find that growth rates for glamour exceed those for value in the five years prior to portfolio formation, and in the first two years after portfolio formation. However, thereafter, the inequality reverses. For example, in years 3 through 5 of the postformation period, the cash flows from the value portfolio grew at 11.1 percent, whereas those from the glamour portfolio grew at 8.6 percent. LSV suggest that the market mistakenly extrapolates the growth rate of fundamentals such as sales, and only learns its mistake slowly because it takes several years for the growth rate of glamour stocks to slip below the growth rate of value stocks. This feature serves as a bridge between the short-term momentum finding by Jegadeesh–Titman and the long-term reversal finding by De Bondt–Thaler.

There is no single explanation for return patterns that feature short-term momentum but long-term reversals. Several theories have been put forward, and are discussed in the following sections.

18.2   Factor Models and Risk

Fama and French (1996) provide a three-factor model that accommodates reversals within the efficient market paradigm. In their model, the risk premium on a security is determined by the way the premium loads onto the following three factors: (1) the market risk premium; (2) a size factor *SMB* defined as the return difference between the smallest firms and biggest firms, where size is measured by market value of equity; and (3) the return difference *HML* between stocks with the highest and lowest ratio of book-to-market equity.

Fama and French contend that their three-factor model captures the De Bondt–Thaler reversal effect, and most of the effects of sales growth and cash flow-to-price identified by LSV. They also contend that the factors in their model proxy for risk, so that long-term reversals can be explained by risk rather than mispricing. The argument is that book-to-market equity and slopes on HML proxy for relative distress, and that weak firms with persistently low earnings have high book-to-market equity and positive slopes on HML, with the opposite pattern for strong firms. However, Fama–French note that their model cannot accommodate the momentum effect identified by Jegadeesh–Titman. They describe this failure as the "main embarrassment of the three-factor model" (page 81). Specifically, stocks that have recently declined in price load positively onto HML, and therefore the three-factor model predicts short-term reversal rather than the continuation that Jegadeesh–Titman find. Indeed, many authors now use a four-factor structure, adding a momentum factor UMD (up minus down) to the Fama–French model.[2]

The existence of a factor structure by no means implies that risk premiums are determined by fundamental risk alone. This is the point of Chapters 16 and 17. Both chapters establish that a risk premium is generally the sum of a fundamental component and a sentiment premium. In this respect, consider the Fama–French book-to-market equity factor HML. For a stock whose returns load positively onto HML, the return tends to be high when value stocks outperform growth stocks, and low when growth stocks outperform value stocks. In other words, the stock's return reflects a portion of the oscillation associated with the mean-variance efficient portfolio.

18.3   Differentiating Fundamental Risk and Investor Error

The broad debate between proponents of market efficiency and proponents of behavioral finance is centered on the cross-sectional structure of realized returns. There is general agreement that realized returns have a cross-sectional structure involving characteristics such as size, book-to-market equity, past three-year returns, and past sales growth. However, there is disagreement about the forces that give rise to this cross-sectional structure. Proponents of market efficiency mostly argue that these characteristics are proxies for fundamental risk. In contrast, proponents of behavioral finance argue that the characteristics reflect mispricing stemming from investor bias, particularly overreaction. This is not to say that sentiment premiums

---

[2] The material for this section is based on Shefrin (2001).

do not reflect risk. However, that risk stems from investor error rather than fundamental variables.

Statman (1999) described the debate between proponents of market efficiency and proponents of behavioral finance, describing past battles and predicting future engagements. Statman predicted that future engagements would begin to focus on preferences, as well as return expectations. That prediction appears to be prophetic. Fama and French (2004) develop a model that highlights two issues, investor preferences and heterogeneous beliefs. In their model, some investors have a taste for low book-to-market stocks. In addition, they assume that some investors are informed, but other investors hold erroneous expectations.[3]

The acknowledgment by Fama–French of investor error, or irrationality, being reflected in market prices represents a significant shift in their position. This shift was the subject of a front page article in the *Wall Street Journal* that appeared on October 18, 2004. Although Fama contends that his position has remained consistent over time, Thaler claims that Fama has gone behavioral.

Fama–French suggest that the preference for stocks associated with low book-to-market equity might lower the returns for these stocks relative to stocks associated with high book-to-market equity. They point out that it might be difficult to disentangle the effects of tastes and errors on the part of some investors.

The issue of whether it is possible to disentangle preference effects from belief effects is not new. Indeed, that is essentially the issue discussed in Subsection 16.3.3. The discussion in that subsection involved disentangling the effects of heterogeneous risk tolerance from those of heterogeneous beliefs. The main point made there is that the SDF can be used to address this type of question. This issue is the main theme in Chapter 23, where the argument is advanced that the shape of the SDF can serve as a discriminating variable.

A more direct route to assessing whether errors in return expectations underlie the roles of variables such as size and book-to-market equity is to look at expectations data. Chapters 6 and 7 presented data that pertain to market forecasts. What about data dealing with return expectations for individual stocks?

18.3.1   Psychology of Risk and Return

The relationship between risk and return lies at the heart of modern finance. This relationship is embodied within such core concepts as the capital

---

[3] Fama–French develop their argument in terms of the mean-variance frontier, and it is similar in spirit to the discussion in Chapter 17.

market line and the security market line.[4] Both of these graphs feature a positive slope, meaning that the higher the risk, the higher the expected return. Is it possible that even though investors may state that in principle, risk and expected return are positively related, in practice many form judgments in which the two are negatively related?

18.3.2   Evidence About Judgments of Risk and Return

In 1997, the author began to elicit judgments about one-year return expectations and perceived risk. For reasons that are explained in a later subsection, the survey instrument also included questions that make up *Fortune* magazine's annual survey on corporate reputation. Since 1999, this survey has been administered to financial professionals, mainly portfolio managers and analysts. (Before 1999, the survey was administered only to advanced MBA students.)

In the survey, eight technology companies are used: Dell, Novell, Hewlett-Packard, Unisys, Microsoft, Oracle, Intel, and Sun Microsystems.[5] The instructions in the survey ask respondents to specify the return they expect for each of the eight stocks over the next 12 months, expressed as a percentage. The survey also asks respondents to rate their perception of the riskiness of each stock on a scale of 0 to 10, with 0 being risk-free and 10 being extremely speculative. As to the *Fortune* reputation questions, the response to each is a rating on a 0-to-10 scale, exactly as in the actual survey.

The return expectations of survey respondents are consistently negatively correlated with their risk perceptions. That is, respondents appear to expect that riskier stocks will produce lower returns than safer stocks. This finding is robust, and has also been found by Ganzach (2000). The responses of portfolio managers, analysts, and MBA students all feature a negative correlation between expected return and perceived risk. For purpose of illustration, Figure 18.1 depicts the risk-return scatter plot from a 1999 survey that was administered to a group of hedge fund managers.

Because perceived risk is measured on a scale of 0 to 10, rather than in terms of a well-defined variable such as beta or return standard deviation, some readers may be skeptical of Figure 18.1. There are both advantages and disadvantages to measuring perceived risk on a scale from 0 to 10. The main disadvantage is that such a scale is inherently subjective, and not as well defined as return standard deviation or beta. The main advantage is that because of the debate about whether or not characteristics such

---

[4] The capital market line indicates the maximum expected return associated with any given return standard deviation, while the security market line indicates how the expected return to a security varies with its beta.

[5] In the actual *Fortune* survey, a single respondent typically rates 8 to 10 companies in a particular industry.

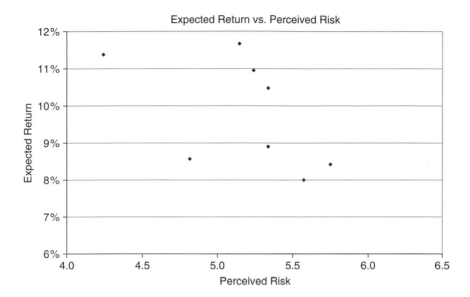

FIGURE 18.1. This figure demonstrates that investors perceive risk and expected return to be negatively correlated.

as book-to-market equity proxy for unobserved risk variables, the 0-to-10 scale imposes no strict definition of risk. Therefore, consider the security market line in Figure 18.2 that depicts the same hedge fund managers' expected returns plotted against beta.

The general result is the same with beta as it is with perceived risk. These investors formed judgments as if they believed that risk and expected return were negatively related. The correlation coefficient between beta and expected return in Figure 18.2 was −0.59. This magnitude is typical for the seven years in which the survey has been conducted. In addition, the negative relationship is not the result of the outlier at the bottom right. When this outlier is excluded, the correlation coefficient is −0.56.

18.3.3   Psychology Underlying a Negative Relationship Between Risk and Return

A cornerstone principle in traditional finance is that expected return is positively related to risk, not negatively related.[6] Why then do investors judge the relationship to be negative? Consider the hypothesis that investors

---

[6] Subsequent realized returns are noisy, and eight stocks offer few degrees of freedom when it comes to testing hypotheses that compare expected returns and realized returns. The correlation coefficient between hedge fund managers' return expectations and realized returns over the subsequent 12 months is −0.03.

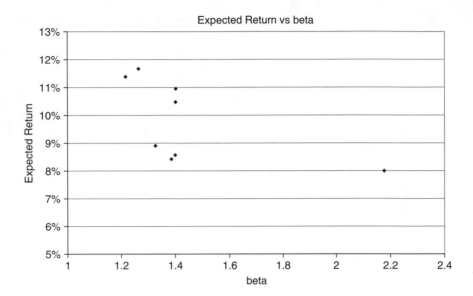

FIGURE 18.2. This figure demonstrates that investors perceive expected return and beta to be negatively correlated. That is, investors perceive the security market line to have a negative slope.

form a negative association between risk and return because they rely on representativeness.

Recall that representativeness involves over-reliance on stereotypes. The hypothesis being proposed is that investors rely on the representativeness-based heuristic "stocks of good companies are representative of good stocks." In order to test this hypothesis, Shefrin and Statman (1995) use data from the annual reputation survey conducted by *Fortune* magazine. Notably, the eight-question *Fortune* survey contains two questions that relate to the key variables of interest, (1) the goodness of a company and (2) the goodness of the company's stock. Most of the survey questions pertain to the quality of the company, asking about quality of management, quality of products, financial soundness, and so on. However, one question asks survey respondents to rate the company's stock in terms of long-term value.[7]

Shefrin–Statman suggested that *value as a long-term investment* (VLTI) seemed to be a decent proxy for the quality of the company's stock, and that quality of management seemed to be a decent proxy for the quality of the company. Therefore they tested the hypothesis that investors judge

---

[7] The survey began in 1982, when *Fortune* began asking corporate executives and analysts to rate firms in major industries.

that good stocks are stocks of good companies by comparing the responses to these two questions. The correlation coefficient is 90 percent, which they interpret as evidence in support of the hypothesis.

Consider next why investors who rely on representativeness might expect the returns to safer stocks to be higher than the returns to riskier stocks. In this respect, note that one of the questions in the *Fortune* reputation survey asks respondents to rate each company for "soundness of financial position." Shefrin–Statman find that in the *Fortune* survey, the correlation coefficient between quality of management and financial soundness is 85 percent. In other words, investors judge that good companies are safe companies. As for the company's stock, the correlation coefficient between VLTI and financial soundness is 91 percent, suggesting that investors also judge good stocks to be the stocks of financially sound companies.[8]

There is one more part to the argument that is needed to explain why investors judge that risk and return are negatively related. This last part involves the relationship between a company's financial soundness and the perceived risk of its stock. In the surveys, these turn out to be negatively correlated. For the hedge fund managers discussed earlier, the correlation coefficient between financial soundness and perceived risk is −85 percent. Therefore, investors appear to identify good stocks with companies that are both well run and financially sound. Representativeness leads investors to associate high expected returns to the stocks of companies that are well run, and low risk to companies that are financially sound. Because investors judge well-run companies to be financially sound, representativeness leads them to expect high returns from safe stocks.

18.4   Implications for the Broad Debate

Because the survey data records reported expected returns, the survey holds implications for the previously mentioned debate. Note that in setting out the efficient market position, Fama and French (1992, 1996) implicitly speak of mean realized returns as if they are expected returns. In the efficient market view, the negative relationship between realized returns and book-to-market equity serves to proxy for the relationship between expected returns and true risk. According to this line of thought, mean realized returns coincide with expected returns, and book-to-market equity proxies for the risk associated with financial distress.

In treating mean realized returns as expected returns, Fama and French make an implicit assumption. One way of testing the validity of this

---

[8]In the case of the hedge fund managers' judgments for the eight stocks, the correlation coefficient between VLTI and financial soundness was 61 percent.

assumption is to analyze the cross-sectional structure of expected returns, and compare the results with the cross-section of realized returns. In doing so, one finds that the same characteristics that Fama and French identify as being related to realized returns are also related to the expected returns in the survey data. Yet, there is one major difference between realized returns and expected returns: Namely, the signs in the two cross-sectional relationships are opposite. For example, book-to-market equity is positively related to realized returns, but negatively related to expected returns. By the same token, size is negatively related to realized returns, but positively related to expected returns.[9]

The opposite-sign pattern just described leads to the conclusion that investors form erroneous judgments about future returns. Is the same true for risk? In this respect, note that in the survey data, perceived risk is positively correlated both with book-to-market equity and with beta, and is negatively correlated with size.[10] These sign patterns are indeed consistent with the efficient market position.

To say that the sign pattern conforms to the market efficiency position is not to suggest that risk perceptions are correct. As mentioned earlier Lakonishok, Shleifer, and Vishny (1994) argue that the superior performance of high book-to-market (value) stocks over low book-to-market (glamour) stocks cannot be explained by risk. The key error in investors' judgments, then, has less to do with the nature of risk and more to do with the perception that risk and expected return are negatively related.

The approach to sentiment developed in Chapter 15 is a "bottom up" approach, in that it derives the market-level sentiment function from the sentiments of individual investors. Likewise, the analysis of survey data discussed above is bottom up. In contrast, most of the measures of sentiment used in the behavioral finance literature are "top down."

Baker and Wurgler (2006, 2007) discuss various measures of sentiment that have been used in behavioral studies. They then develop a new index of sentiment based on the following six specific measures: closed-end fund discount, detrended log-turnover, number of IPOs, first-day return on IPOs, dividend premium, and equity share in new issues.

Figure 18.3 displays the time series of the Baker-Wurgler sentiment index for the period 1966–2005. The series is consistent with speculative periods during the late 1960s, the early and mid-1980s, and the dot-com bubble in

---

[9] Past sales growth and past three-year returns are negatively related to realized returns but positively related to expected returns. This pattern supports the contention that the characteristic structure of realized returns reflects long-term overreaction rather than risk, as argued by De Bondt and Thaler (1985) and Lakonishok, Shleifer, and Vishny (1994).

[10] Perceived risk is also negatively correlated with past sales growth and past three-year returns.

FIGURE 18.3. Time series of Baker-Wurgler Sentiment Measure, January 1996–December 2005. The figure shows that the Baker-Wurgler sentiment index is consistent with speculative periods during the late 1960s, the early and mid-1980s, and the dot-com bubble in the late 1990s and 2000. It is also consistent with a bear market during the mid-1970s, and the late 1980s/early 1990s. Data downloaded from <http://www.stern.nyu.edu/~jwurgler>.

the late 1990s and 2000. It is also consistent with a bear market during the mid-1970s, and the late 1980s/early 1990s.

Baker and Wurgler suggest that sentiment will impact prices of some stocks more than others. They suggest that the returns to stocks which are difficult both to value and to arbitrage will be more sensitive to sentiment than stocks which are both easier to value and easier to arbitrage.

The heart of their argument involves the concept of a sentiment seesaw. When sentiment is high, speculative difficult-to-arbitrage stocks become overvalued, and safe easy-to-arbitrage stocks become undervalued. When sentiment is low, the reverse occurs. A notable feature of the analysis is that because of mispricing, stocks that appear to be riskier in terms of fundamentals can feature lower expected returns than safer stocks.

In Baker-Wurgler, a stock's sensitivity to sentiment is measured in terms of a sentiment beta. A sentiment beta explains the sentiment component of the risk premium. Conditional on the risk-free rate, this component effectively corresponds to the third term in the right-hand side of equation (16.24); unconditionally, it corresponds to the sum of the first and third terms. Sentiment beta is effectively given by equation (17.13).

Empirically, Baker-Wurgler report that returns are predictable, conditional on the value of sentiment in the prior month. When past sentiment has been high, subsequent returns to speculative, more difficult-to-arbitrage stocks are indeed lower than returns to safer stocks which are easier to arbitrage. Conversely, when past sentiment has been low, subsequent returns to speculative, more difficult-to-arbitrage stocks are higher than to safer stocks which are easier to arbitrage.

There is work to be done in reconciling the top-down and bottom-up approaches to sentiment. Chapters 6 and 7 demonstrate that individual investors are prone to different errors than investment professionals, but that both types of investors make errors. Chapters 14 and 15 describe a theoretical bottom-up framework to explain how these errors are manifest within market sentiment as the two types of investors interact in the market.

There is conflicting evidence about which errors are more serious, those made by individual investors or those made by investment professionals. San (2007) suggests that the errors of investment professionals might be more serious. However, Barber, Odean, and Zhu (2006) suggest that in the aggregate, investment professionals exploit the errors made by individual investors.

Part VII of this book discusses a series of behavioral issues in respect to the portfolio choices of individual investors. These issues pertain to underdiversification, skewed returns, bipolar risk profiles, and the disposition to sell winners too early and ride losers too long. In addition, Barber and Odean (forthcoming) document that individual investors appear to rely on the availability heuristic when purchasing stocks. In particular, Barber-Odean suggest that individual investors purchase stocks which catch their attention. Attention-grabbing stocks feature abnormal trading volume, extreme one-day returns, and whether or not a firm is in the news.

18.5 Analysts' Return Expectations

Brav, Lehavy, and Michaely (2005) study the return expectations of two groups of analysts. The first group comprises the Wall Street analysts tracked by First Call. The second group are Value Line analysts. The First Call data involve over 7,000 stocks over a 5-year period. The Value Line data cover approximately 2,900 stocks over a 15-year period.

Analysts do not issue forecasts of returns directly. Instead, they provide price targets, essentially price forecasts for particular time frames. These target prices provide implicit forecasts of returns. The data on Wall Street analysts pertain to a one-year horizon, whereas the Value Line horizon is four years.

Unlike for the investors whose expectations were just described, analysts' return expectations are positively related to beta. Moreover, analysts expect higher returns from small cap stocks than from large cap stocks. In this respect, the return expectations of analysts conform to the empirical cross-section of realized returns.

Because investment banks use analyst coverage as a means to attract business from firms, analysts have an incentive to generate forecasts that the firms' managers will view as favorable. For this reason, the forecasts of Wall Street analysts are likely to feature bias. Value Line analysts are not engaged in investment banking, and therefore their forecasts are not likely to be self-serving in this regard.

The return expectations of Wall Street analysts are negatively related to book-to-market equity. In other words, Wall Street analysts expect higher returns from growth firms than from value firms. Value Line analysts' return expectations are not statistically related to book-to-market equity.

The return expectations of Wall Street analysts are negatively related to prior returns. In other words, Wall Street analysts expect short-term reversals. Perhaps analysts judge the stocks of recent winners to be less risky than the stocks of recent losers. Or perhaps analysts succumb to gambler's fallacy. Given the finding described in Chapter 7, that professional investors succumb to gambler's fallacy when predicting the overall market, it seems more plausible that the explanation for analysts' predictions of reversal is gambler's fallacy.

Consider the contrast between the return expectations of analysts and the return expectations of investors. What is to be concluded from such a comparison? Just as individual investors form different forecasts from Wall Street strategists, as discussed in Chapters 6 and 7, the expectations of analysts are not the same as the expectations of investors. Beliefs are heterogeneous. In some respects, the aggregate beliefs feature similar relationships: Both Wall Street analysts and investors expect glamour stocks to outperform growth stocks. However, when it comes to beta, analysts view the relationship as positive, whereas investors view the relationship as negative.

18.6 How Consciously Aware Are Investors When Forming Judgments?

Over the 10 years of administering the expectations survey, characteristics such as past returns, book-to-market equity, and past sales growth have consistently proven correlated with return expectations. Yet, in post-survey debriefing sessions, respondents have consistently indicated that they did not consciously take any of these characteristics into account when formulating their return expectations, even though the data were readily available. All are amazed by the cross-sectional structure of their expectations. Professional investors, all educated in the tradition of risk and return being positively related, are astonished to see scatter plots (like Figures 18.1 and 18.2) showing that they implicitly expect higher returns from safer stocks. In principle, they accept that the relationship between risk and return is positive, but in practice form judgments in which the relationship is negative.

If investors do not consciously use characteristics to form their judgments about risk and return, then what do they use? What is representative of a good company, if not its characteristics? Work on these questions has only begun, but a promising route involves the role of the affect heuristic in explaining the finding that in general people perceive a negative relationship between risks and benefits (Finucane, Alhakami, Slovic, and Johnson, 2000), as well as the influence of imagery (MacGregor, Slovic, Dreman, and Berry, 2000). Affect refers to emotion, and a good stock is associated with positive affect.

18.7   How Reliable Is the Evidence on Expected Returns?

The data that have been presented about investors' expected returns and perceived risk come from a survey involving eight stocks, administered over seven years. Of course, eight is a small number of stocks. At the same time, there are good reasons to treat these data seriously. Shefrin and Statman (2003) analyze the cross-sectional structure of the actual *Fortune* variable VLTI, and find that the relationship between VLTI and firms' characteristics parallels the relationship between expected returns and characteristics. Notably, the actual *Fortune* reputation survey covers several hundred stocks, and has been administered since 1982.[11]

Shefrin–Statman find a positive and statistically significant relationship between past returns and expectations about returns, consistent with the hypothesis of De Bondt and Thaler (1985). They also find a negative and statistically significant relationship between expectations about returns and book-to-market, and a positive and statistically significant relationship between expectations and size. The signs of these relationships are not only strong, but consistent on a year-by-year basis. In addition, the signs of the relationships are contrary to the hypothesis of Fama and French (1992). Again, if one accepts the Fama–French factor structure as accurate, then in the main investors hold erroneous expectations. Interestingly,

---

[11] In the actual *Fortune* reputation surveys studied by Shefrin and Statman, the number of publicly traded firms ranges from 156 in 1982 to 335 in 1995.

Shefrin–Statman find no statistically significant relationship between cash-flow-to-price and expectations, as hypothesized by Lakonishok, Shleifer, and Vishny (1994).

Additional support for the reliability of the data comes from comparing the VLTI responses in the small-scale survey with two variables: (1) judgments of expected returns in the small-scale survey, and (2) the VLTI responses in the actual *Fortune* survey.

In the ten years that the small-scale (eight-stock) survey has been conducted, expected returns have always been positively correlated with VLTI. In addition, the responses to the *Fortune* reputation questions in the survey replication are quite close to the responses in the actual survey. For example, in the 1999 survey of hedge fund managers, the correlation coefficient between the hedge fund managers' VLTI responses and the actual Fortune VLTI responses was 81 percent.[12] The correlation coefficient between the hedge fund managers' VLTI responses and their expected returns was 70 percent. These responses are typical of the small-scale surveys.[13]

Fortune magazine bases its reputation ranking on an overall score of eight questions. The overall score is what *Fortune* publishes. It does not publish the results of the individual questions, although these data can be purchased. An interesting feature of the actual *Fortune* data is that the mean VLTI rating assigned by respondents differs from the mean overall rating. In 1999, the mean value of VLTI for the eight stocks was 6.88, whereas the mean overall score was 7.06. Notably, this same pattern emerged in the replication with hedge fund managers. The hedge fund managers' mean VLTI score was 6.80, and their mean overall score was 7.16.

Because *Fortune* does not publish the results involving individual questions, the proximity of the replicated results and the actual results gives credibility to the responses involving risk and return. There are other available data related to return expectations. These include the earnings forecasts and stock recommendations of analysts. In this respect, LaPorta (1996) explicitly uses earnings forecasts to proxy for expected returns. Barber, Lehavy, McNichols, and Trueman (2001) show that realized returns are positively related to analysts' stock recommendations. The return expectations that respondents express in the surveys are positively correlated with their earnings forecasts. However, the relationship between return expectations and actual analyst recommendations at the time is weaker. For the 1999 survey with hedge fund managers, the correlation coefficient not only was close to zero, but had the wrong sign.

---

[12] The correlation coefficient was 91 percent for overall reputation.

[13] The 1999 responses are used because 1999 was the last year that data on VLTI responses were made available by *Fortune*. The firm with which *Fortune* subcontracts to manage the data altered its policy that year and no longer offers an academic package.

The findings in Ganzach (2000) suggest that investors who devote conscious thought to the risk-return profile of stocks will form judgments consistent with the two being positively related. However, those who make quick, snap judgments will be inclined to form judgments consistent with the view that the two are negatively related.

Anginer, Fisher, and Statman (2007) report the results of an interesting experiment. They surveyed 501 high net-worth investors, asking them to rate companies from "bad" to "good" on a 10-point scale. Survey respondents only received company names as information. In addition, those responding were asked to provide their quick intuitive feelings, but not spend time thinking about their responses. The authors conducted the survey in June 2005: This was after *Fortune* magazine conducted the survey published in 2005 but before they conducted the survey published in 2006. The authors find that the average survey affect scores for companies are highly correlated with the corresponding scores for reputation published by *Fortune*. (The R^2 of a regression of affect scores on *Fortune* scores was 0.32.)

There is good reason to believe that reliance on the affect heuristic provides an important explanation for why some investors form judgments as if they believe the relationship between risk and return to be negative. However, some of the evidence reported above indicates that even investors who spend time analyzing stocks appear to form judgments as if they believe that risk and return are negatively related. In Shefrin (2006), I suggest that the affect heuristic and representativeness operate in the same direction. For investors who do spend time analyzing stocks, and rely on representativeness, there is reason to believe that the affect heuristic and representativeness are mutually reinforcing.

18.8 Alternative Theories

The phenomena just discussed appear to exhibit long-term reversals in combination with short-term continuation. What might explain this duality?

Barberis, Shleifer, and Vishny (1998) (BSV) develop an explanation that combines insights from the psychology literature on conservatism, representativeness, and salience with the literature in accounting on post–earnings announcement drift. Their explanation features an underreaction explanation for short-term momentum, and an overreaction explanation for long-term reversals.

Consider the psychology. Edwards (1968) documents that in particular situations people underreact to recent evidence; that is, they tend to be conservative. Yet the contribution by Tversky and Kahneman (1982) shows that in other situations representativeness leads people to overreact to recent evidence, and to ignore base rates. What distinguishes situations where they underreact to recent evidence from situations where they overreact to that evidence? Griffen and Tversky (1992) propose a theory to explain when people underweight base rates and when they overweight them. BSV develop a model that crudely captures the Griffen–Tversky (1992) argument. They postulate that investors believe earnings growth to be determined in one of two regimes: (1) a mean reverting regime that applies most of the time, and (2) a trend regime. A representative investor never knows exactly which regime applies, but uses Bayes rule to infer the likelihood of the prevailing regime from the history of earnings growth.

In the BSV model, actual earnings growth follows a random walk. This means that when the representative investor holds the strong belief that earnings growth is mean reverting, he underreacts to an earnings surprise. Yet, consider what happens after a string of earnings surprises. In this case, the representative investor adjusts his belief about the prevailing regime, believing it more likely that earnings growth is determined in the trend regime. Since actual earnings follow a random walk without trend, the representative investor overreacts to the most recent surprise.

Daniel, Hirshleifer, and Subrahmanyam (1998) (DHS) provide a behaviorally based explanation for short-term momentum combined with long-term reversals that is different in character from that of BSV. The DHS framework emphasizes the roles of overconfidence and biased self-attribution in the way investors react differently to private and public information. Biased self-attribution means that individuals take credit for positive events, attributing them to their own skill, but attribute negative events to bad luck or others.

In the DHS model, informed investors receive noisy signals about the true value of a security. If the signal is private, they react to the signal with overconfidence by overestimating its precision. Think of the private signal an investor receives as the outcome of his own security analysis. If the signal is public, then assume the investor is not overconfident and correctly estimates its precision. Biased self-attribution operates by rendering the degree of overconfidence endogenous. When an investor makes an assessment, and a subsequent public signal confirms that initial assessment, he becomes even more overconfident.

The DHS model has two important features. The first concerns the security price impulse function associated with a private signal. If the signal is positive, informed investors immediately overreact and the security becomes overpriced. However, because of biased self-attribution, the security will tend to become even more overpriced on average as public information continues to arrive shortly thereafter. But as public information continues to flow, investors will see that their initial optimism was unfounded. Hence, a correction phase will ensue, and the price will subsequently reverse. The resulting time series for price features initial momentum, meaning positive autocorrelation, and then a reversal pattern, as public information fails to corroborate the initial assessment.

Although the price pattern is the same as described by BSV, the valuation profile is markedly different. Consider an event that leads to a price rise with momentum. In BSV, the momentum phase features underreaction, as investors are slow to react to good news. Hence, the security is undervalued during the early stage when momentum builds. The DHS framework works differently. In DHS, the momentum phase stems from overreaction. Underreaction does occur, but it occurs during the correction phase. Underreaction is why it takes the market a long time to correct the initial overreaction, a feature discussed earlier in connection with the De Bondt–Thaler winner–loser effect.

The second important feature in DHS involves the relationship between the character of information (private or public) and the market reaction. In the DHS model, investors may underreact to public information about a firm, and yet this need not lead to drift. This happens when the public information is received simultaneously by the firm's managers and the investors. However, if the firm's managers previously received the information privately, and chose to release it publicly at a later date, then the resulting underreaction by investors will typically occur in conjunction with price drift.

Although Hong and Stein (1999) (HS) seek to explain the same empirical phenomena as BSV and DHS, they do not base their model on specific behavioral elements, as do BSV and DHS. Rather Hong–Stein focus on the interaction between two groups of boundedly rational traders, "newswatchers" (fundamentalists) and "momentum traders" (technical analysts). Notably, newswatchers do not condition their beliefs on past prices, and momentum traders do not condition their beliefs on fundamental information. In the Hong–Stein framework, newswatchers base their trades on information that slowly diffuses through the trading population. Momentum traders base their trades on simple trend extrapolation rules. Because information diffuses slowly, newswatchers underreact to new fundamental information. Their underreaction leads to price drift, a pattern that momentum traders perceive and trade upon. Hence, the actions of momentum traders reduce the degree of underreaction in the market, up to a point. Because they use crude extrapolation rules, the behavior of momentum traders ultimately produces overreaction; and price reversals occur as a correction to the overreaction.

There are some issues in the BSV, DHS, and HS frameworks that merit discussion. First, the evidence that BSV and DHS seek to explain involves the cross-section of stocks. Yet, their models feature only one security. Second, the investors in BSV and DHS apply Bayes rule correctly when drawing inferences about the prevailing regime. Yet, the failure by individuals to apply Bayes rule correctly lies at the heart of Edwards' (1968) analysis of conservatism and Tversky–Kahneman's (1982) discussion of base rate underweighting.

Third, the BSV model assumes a single representative investor whose beliefs exhibit the bias attributable to individuals. Hong–Stein point out that the DHS model is effectively a representative investor model, in that prices are set by risk-neutral traders who suffer from a common overconfidence bias. As pointed out in Chapters 14 and 15, because of heterogeneity, the traits of the representative investor typically differ from those of individual investors.

Fourth, a key area of difference between BSV and DHS concerns the basis for overreaction and underreaction. Odean (1998b) suggests that people overvalue salient events, cases, anecdotes, and extreme realizations, and overweight irrelevant data. They underreact to abstract statistical information, underestimate the importance of sample size, and underweight relevant data. In contrast, DHS postulate that investors overreact to private information and underreact to public information.

In the DHS model, the second stage of momentum phase features drift that stems from a public signal that confirms an earlier private signal. For example, suppose an overconfident trader gets a private positive signal and in response purchases a stock. If that signal is subsequently confirmed by a public signal, the trader will grow increasingly overconfident and will buy additional shares of the stock. This suggests that investors who already own a stock are more likely to buy additional shares if the stock price goes up (in response to positive public information) than if it goes down. However, Odean (1999) finds that the opposite pattern is true for individual investors. Investors are more likely to purchase additional shares of stocks that have declined in price since their initial purchase than to buy more of those that have gone up.

Fifth, in Hong–Stein newswatchers are inconsistent in the way they develop trading plans. They respond to fundamental information as if they plan to trade only in the short term, but then trade with momentum traders later in time. All three models seek to explain the same empirical phenomena involving momentum and reversals. Yet, these models differ markedly from one another.

18.8.1 The Dynamics of Expectations: Supporting Data

Despite the issues raised in the previous subsection, the various approaches discussed all appear to capture some aspect of the manner in which investors form return expectations. This subsection indicates how the time series of responses in the annual *Fortune* magazine reputation survey provides supporting evidence.

Continuations of returns over short periods and reversals over longer periods suggest that expectations about stock returns follow a dynamic process. Barberis, Shleifer, and Vishny (1998), Daniel, Hirshleifer, and

Subrahmanyam (1999), Hong and Stein (1999), Hong, Lim, and Stein (1999), and Shefrin (1999a) all use the language of overreaction and underreaction to describe the features of the expectations process and offer hypotheses. Consider an empirical examination of some of these features and hypotheses, using the VLTI data from the *Fortune* magazine surveys.[14]

One way of testing for overreaction in the *Fortune* survey data is to examine how VLTI is adjusted in response to realized returns. Consider an exponential smoothing framework whereby survey respondents formulate their new VLTI assessments by taking a linear combination of their past VLTI assessment and the most recent returns.[15] The optimal weighting parameter in the exponential smoothing model is one that minimizes the sum of squared forecast errors in the sequence of past returns. The optimal value can be computed from the data; it turns out to have a value of 0.071. That is, in an optimal forecast the weight assigned to past returns is 0.071 and the weight assigned to past VLTI is 0.929.

Regression analysis can be used to infer the implicit weight, α, that survey respondents attach to past returns when formulating their judgments of VLTI. It turns out that the mean implicit α across stocks is 0.174, indicating that, on average, *Fortune* respondents form their forecasts of returns by assigning a weight of 0.174 to past returns and a weight of 0.826 to past forecasts. Because the weight of 0.174 is higher than the optimal value of 0.071, survey respondents appear to overreact to past returns. That is, they assign past returns too much weight when revising their forecasts.

Support for the overreaction hypothesis can be found in the relationship between VLTI and subsequent returns. Consider the stocks for which VLTI has declined over a three-year period. (These are stocks for which *Fortune* respondents have reduced their assessments of value as a long-term investment.) In the spirit of De Bondt–Thaler, subsequent one-year returns are higher for these stocks than for stocks for which VLTI has been revised upward.

The above findings suggest that on average, investors in the Barberis, Shleifer, Vishny framework (BSV 1998) believe that they are in the continuation regime. BSV hypothesize that while returns follow the process $r_t = \mu + \epsilon_t$, in reality investors believe, in error, that returns vary by regime. In particular, investors believe that returns in the reversal regime revert to the mean, while returns in the continuation regime continue past trends. The finding here, that the mean implicit weight is 0.174, implies that the *Fortune* respondents believe, on average, that they are in a continuation regime; a reversal regime implies a negative implicit α.

---

[14] Data used span the time frame 1982–1995.

[15] In order to make units comparable, standardize both VLTI and returns.

Next, consider the hypotheses of Daniel, Hirshleifer, and Subrahmanyam (DHS 1998, 2001). Investors in the DHS model overreact to private information as they forecast returns, and become increasingly overconfident in their forecasts when their past forecasts turn out to be accurate. This pattern of expectations leads to a combination of short-term continuations of realized returns, long-term reversals, and a positive relationship between realized returns and book-to-market equity.

If the DHS hypotheses hold, the *Fortune* respondents should overreact when they turn out to be accurate. Specifically, greater past accuracy should lead the *Fortune* respondents to assign greater weight to past returns as they form their forecast of future returns. Measure overreaction by the extent to which the implicit weight exceeds the optimal weight. Measure accuracy by the degree to which above-average past VLTI values are associated with above-average past returns and below-average past VLTI values are associated with below-average past returns. Also, DHS (2001) hypothesize that overreaction is greater for stocks associated with high book-to-market equity than for stocks with low book-to-market equity. If the DHS hypotheses hold, there should be a positive relationship between the implicit weight and book-to-market equity.

To test these hypotheses, estimate an equation where each stock's implicit weight is determined by a linear function that combines an intercept (base weight) with three terms that capture the effects of size, book-to-market equity, and past accuracy on the implicit weight. It turns out that the implicit weight increases with accuracy, consistent with DHS (1998); it increases with book-to-market equity, consistent with DHS (2001); and it increases with size.

The connection to size in the preceding analysis may occur because size proxies for analyst coverage. Hong, Lim, and Stein (2000) argue that the rate of information diffusion is greater for firms that are followed by many analysts than for firms followed by few analysts.[16]

---

[16] The regression associated with the analysis is an augmented version of the regression used to estimate the exponential smoothing weight α, with interaction terms that capture how α is affected by size, book-to-market equity, and a variable measuring ex-post accuracy from the prior year. The accuracy variable is given by the product $z(VLTI_{t-1}) \times z(r_{t-1})$, the normalized values of VLTI and return. There are four regression coefficients. The first is a base value for α, giving the value of α when the other three variables are zero. Its estimated value is 0.02, with the associated t-statistic being 26.1. The t-statistics of the three other coefficients are 4.2 (size), 10.3 (book-to-market equity), and 7.1 (past accuracy). The signs of the three interaction coefficients indicate that larger firms, having higher book-to-market equity feature more weight being attached to α, the weight attached to the most recent return. The negative coefficient attached to the accuracy interaction term indicates that higher accuracy also leads to a higher value for α.

18.9 Summary

Although a central tenet of modern finance is that the relationship between risk and return is positive, many investors appear to form judgments to the contrary. Evidence suggests that investors' reliance on the representativeness heuristic is the key reason why they expect high returns from safe stocks. Investors who judge that good stocks are stocks of good companies will associate good stocks with both safety and high future returns.

The variables that enter into the cross-section of realized returns also enter into the cross-section of return expectations. However, many investors erroneously attach the opposite sign to return expectations, relative to the sign that applies to realized returns. Wall Street analysts appear to make fewer errors than most investors. They too, though, attach the wrong sign to prior short-term returns and to book-to-market equity.

19
Testing for a Sentiment Premium

The debate between proponents of market efficiency and proponents of behavioral finance that was described in the previous chapter rests on the following question: If risk premia are determined by the Fama–French factors and momentum, then do those factors proxy for risk that is fundamental, or do they reflect investor sentiment as well?

Proponents of behavioral finance argue that the Fama–French factors and momentum reflect sentiment as well as fundamental risk. Fama and French (1992, 1996) appear to argue that book-to-market equity and size proxy for risks associated with distress, presumably a fundamental factor. Some proponents of market efficiency may well say that it does not matter whether the factor reflects fundamentals alone or a mix of fundamentals and sentiment, that it is all risk.

Theorem 16.2 established that expected returns decompose naturally into a fundamental component and a sentiment premium. Chapter 17 established that risk premiums can also be expressed in terms of a mean-variance efficient benchmark portfolio and beta, where beta admits a similar decomposition. The focus in these chapters is general and structural. Daniel, Hirshleifer, and Subrahmanyan (2002) focus on more specific issues, and propose a beta-based theory that explains the relationship between returns and valuation measures such as book-to-market equity in the presence of mispricing stemming from overconfidence. The point is that the identification of factors and betas should not be interpreted as necessarily implying that prices are efficient in the sense of being objectively correct.

Chapter 11 made the point that prices cannot be perpetually efficient in the face of heterogeneous beliefs. Chapter 9 made the point that in the presence of heterogeneous beliefs, efficiency is a knife-edge case. Therefore, it is natural to ask, is there an empirical link between heterogeneous beliefs and inefficient markets?

Work by Diether, Malloy, and Scherbina (2002) and Anderson, Guysels, and Juergens (2005) (hereafter AGJ) establishes such a link. Diether–Malloy–Scherbina establish that the Fama–French three-factor model, augmented by momentum, cannot fully capture the manner in which dispersion in analysts' forecasts impacts asset prices. AGJ conduct two related, but separate, exercises. Their first exercise is to construct a factor to measure dispersion, and ask whether such a factor holds any explanatory power in respect to realized returns. The second exercise is to estimate an aggregate consumption-based asset pricing model that features heterogeneous beliefs on the part of investors. This chapter is devoted to a discussion of a factor structure associated with heterogeneous beliefs.

19.1   Diether–Malloy–Scherbina: Returns Are Negatively Related to Dispersion

In a seminal article, Miller (1977) emphasized that the asymmetric costs of taking short positions relative to long positions, when combined with heterogeneous beliefs, would lead some securities to be overpriced. His point is straightforward. When investors hold sharply differing points of view, those who are optimistic about a particular security take long positions. However, those investors who are pessimistic about the same security may refrain from trading instead of taking short positions. As a result, the security will be overpriced, and on average earn negative abnormal returns.

Diether–Malloy–Scherbina (2002) study Miller's hypothesis. They examine the period January 1983 through November 2000, combining analyst forecast data from I/B/E/S, return data from CRSP, and financial characteristics data from Compustat.

Diether–Malloy–Scherbina report a series of findings. The most straightforward finding stems from sorting stocks into five quintiles based on degree of dispersion in analysts' earnings forecasts. Stocks are sorted based on dispersion in the prior month, and the resulting portfolio is held for one month. Consider a long–short portfolio, where the long position corresponds to stocks that feature the least dispersion, and the short position corresponds to stocks that feature the greatest dispersion. The annual return from holding such a portfolio is 9.48 percent. Notably, 68.4 percent of the return stems from the short side of the trade.

On the surface, the findings reported by Diether–Malloy–Scherbina appear to support Miller's hypothesis. Yet it is possible that the reason why stocks associated with the greatest dispersion underperform stocks associated with the least dispersion is that stocks featuring more dispersion are associated with less risk. In order to control for this possibility, Diether–Malloy–Scherbina sort stocks by size, book-to-market equity, and momentum. They also conduct tests whereby they control for the Fama–French factors and for the momentum factor developed by Carhart (1996).

Consider the general findings. The return differential between high and low dispersion stocks is not captured by size. However, the return differential decreases with size, and is statistically insignificant for the two largest I/B/E/S-based market capitalization quintiles. When the analysis is done with NYSE-based market capitalization deciles, the return differential is significant for the fifth through ninth size deciles (all but the largest cap stocks).

In respect to book-to-market equity, there is more dispersion associated with value stocks than with growth stocks. Despite this feature, the return differential between low and high dispersion value stocks is only slightly higher than the return differential between low and high dispersion growth stocks.

As for momentum, the return differential between low and high dispersion stocks is largest for recent losers, meaning stocks that have performed poorly in the past year.

The Fama–French factors comprise returns on (1) the market portfolio, denoted r_m, (2) a size factor, denoted *SMB* (for "small minus big"), and (3) a book-to-market equity factor, denoted *HML* (for "high minus low"). The Carhart factor captures momentum, denoted *UMD* (for "up minus down"). Factors SMB, HML, and UMD share a common structure. Stocks are sorted three ways, first by size, then by book-to-market equity, and then by past returns. The return to the decile of largest firms is subtracted from the return to the decile of smallest firms; the difference is SMB. The factor HML is the analogous return difference, but based on sorting firms by book-to-market equity instead of size. An analogous statement applies to stocks sorted by past six-month return: returns on those stocks featuring the highest returns (up) minus the returns on those stocks featuring the lowest returns (down).

In running a four-factor regression model, featuring the three Fama–French factors and momentum, Diether–Malloy–Scherbina find a large negative unexplained return for stocks in the highest dispersion quintile. Stocks in the highest dispersion quintile appear to behave like small, distressed losers.

19.2   AGJ: Dispersion Factor

19.2.1   Basic Approach

AGJ's study is similar to Diether–Malloy–Scherbina, but has a somewhat different focus. They ask whether dispersion actually gives rise to another factor, alongside the Fama–French factors and momentum.

For raw data, AGJ use analyst earnings predictions and recommendations. Based on these data, they construct a factor specification for short-term and long-term earnings growth forecasts. They measure these as the standard deviation of month-end forecasts. The previous chapter mentioned the work of Brav–Lehavy–Michaely. Those authors imputed expected returns from target prices established by analysts. AGJ instead use analyst earnings predictions, and construct expected returns using an earnings-based valuation model.

The basic strategy involves the construction of dispersion factors that will be included in expected return equations, along with the Fama–French factors and momentum factor developed by Carhart (1996). The nature of the exercise is to ascertain whether the inclusion of a dispersion-based factor provides additional explanatory power in respect to expected returns. As was mentioned earlier, the existence of a factor structure does not imply that prices are efficient in the sense of being objectively correct.

19.2.2   Factor Structure

AGJ study the period 1991 through 1997.[1] They report that during this period the average monthly firm and market excess returns were 1.23 percent and 1.16 percent, respectively.[2] In the AGJ study, the average monthly size factor (SMB) was 0.14 percent, the book-to-market factor (HML) averaged 0.47 percent, and the momentum factor (UMD) averaged 0.78 percent.[3]

How might a dispersion factor be constructed from analyst earnings forecasts? A natural procedure is to sort stocks on the basis of the dispersion in these forecasts, and then form the return difference between the top decile

---

[1] AGJ indicate that their sample time period is limited to 1991–1997 because of limitations in the First Call data. Firms in the Index are identified from *Standard & Poor's Stock Market Encyclopedia* in the December prior to the year of interest (for example, 1991 firms are identified from the December 1990 *Stock Market Encyclopedia*).

[2] The time period 1991–1997 was special, in that the average value for the market was higher during this period than during the long-term period originally studied by Fama and French (1993), where the corresponding values are 0.67 percent and 0.43 percent, respectively.

[3] The results for SMB, HML, and UMD were similar to those found in other research that used substantially longer time series.

and bottom decile. The two measures of heterogeneity of beliefs that AGJ study are the dispersion of analysts' short-term (one-year) dollar earnings forecasts and long-term (five-year) earnings growth rate forecasts. They obtain their data from First Call.

AGJ measure forecast dispersion of forecasts by the standard deviation of analyst earnings forecasts. They only use the last available dispersion measure in each month. Observations above the median are designated as high dispersion forecasts, while observations at or below the median are low dispersion forecasts. Value-weighted returns are then calculated each month for high and low dispersion observations. A zero-investment strategy is realized through the purchase of high dispersion observations and the sale of low dispersion observations. The two factors are respectively labeled DISP and LTGDISP, for short-term and long-term forecasts.

19.2.3   General Properties of the Data

AGJ report that the average monthly level of short term forecast dispersion is \$0.20, and approximately 15 analysts furnish short-term forecasts per firm in the S&P 500 Index. They report that the average monthly level of long-term forecast dispersion is 4.14 percent, and approximately 19 analysts furnish long-term forecasts per firm in the S&P 500 Index.[4]

There have been many studies of analysts' earnings forecasts, and particular features appear to be well known. For example, DISP is positively correlated with SMB, suggesting that high dispersion stocks outperform low dispersion stocks when small stocks outperform large stocks, perhaps because larger firms tend to have less disagreement about earnings expectations than smaller firms. LTGDISP is negatively correlated with HML, implying returns to high dispersion firms increase when glamour outperforms value. AGJ report that there is greater institutional participation and more analyst coverage for high dispersion firms than for low dispersion firms.[5] Analysts' forecasts are known to be excessively optimistic when first issued, but to decline towards the end of the fiscal year.

Notably, AGJ measures of dispersion are significantly and negatively correlated with contemporaneous returns. However, neither measure is significantly related to one-month lagged or one-month ahead returns. Interestingly, long-term dispersion is actually positively correlated with each of these return measures. The average monthly return for the short-term dispersion factor, DISP, is −0.28 percent.

---

[4] The number of analysts covering firms in the S&P 500 is substantially higher than the average of three analysts per firm for the entire First Call database.

[5] This finding is opposite to the findings in Chen, Hong, and Stein 2000 mentioned in the previous chapter, who report that disagreement and breadth of ownership are negatively related.

AGJ report that the market factor and UMD, and HML and DISP, are marginally significant at the 10 percent level. They report that the average returns for SMB and LTGDISP are insignificantly different from zero, and that DISP is insignificantly positively correlated with both the market factor and HML.

19.2.4   Expected Returns

Analysts do not forecast future returns per se. Instead, analysts provide both short-term and long-term earnings growth forecasts, as well as investment recommendations based on expected future price performance. In order to impute expected returns from earnings forecasts, AGJ implement a modified constant dividend growth model. In the traditional Gordon equity model, expected return is equal to the sum of the expected dividend yield and the long-term growth rate of the firm. Because of data limitations associated with the dividend policies of firms, AGJ use expected earnings in place of dividends. This approach ignores the dividend payout ratio, and therefore provides an upwardly biased estimate of expected returns. However, the bias is uniform across firms, and the key issues pertain to the cross-sectional comparisons.

As described in Chapter 16, expected returns can be computed in terms of the SDF. Although the SDF is an unobserved process, consider projecting the SDF onto each factor. Doing so provides a structure to obtain expected returns in terms of loadings onto the SDF-projected factors.

AGJ first estimate an expected return model in which the factors are traditional: the three Fama–French factors and the Carhart momentum factor. They interpret these factors as fundamental, although this is (strictly speaking) unnecessary. They then relate the residuals from this process to their two dispersion factors. Doing so minimizes the extent to which the dispersion factors are able to explain realized returns.

19.2.5   Findings

AGJ report that the market factor is the dominant factor explaining realized returns. Notably, each of the other factors is generally statistically significant. In particular, both measures of the dispersion factor are highly statistically significant, and the coefficients are positively related to the S&P 500 Index returns. In other words, treating dispersion as a proxy for the sentiment premium, AGJ find that the sentiment premium is nonzero. They note that a factor for dispersion cannot fully capture the explanatory power of fundamental factors, but the inclusion of dispersion improves the predictive ability of their models. They estimate several models and find that depending on the model, dispersion captures 9 to 26 basis points of excess return.

AGJ report that excess return is positively and significantly related to SMB; however, the magnitude and significance of SMB decreases when either DISP or LTGDISP is included. Excess return is significantly and positively related to HML, but UMD is significantly and negatively related to excess returns.

Overall, none of the estimated models did a good job of predicting out-of-sample returns. AGJ indicate that larger estimates of returns were obtained in models that included the market factor. However, these estimates in the models had greater deviations than models that excluded the market return. AGJ generated slightly lower forecast mean absolute errors in their more parsimonious models. Nevertheless, they found the correlation coefficients and corresponding regression slopes to be negative. In other words, the estimated returns underestimated the actual returns. These findings stem from the strong market that prevailed in 1998 and 1999, relative to the lower returns in the period 1991–1994 and thus to the whole of the 1991–1997 estimation period.

19.2.6   Volatility

Chapter 7 contains a discussion about the nature of time-varying heterogeneity and its relationship to return volatility. AGJ study this relationship in their model. They find the following: Of their various models involving factor combinations, out-of-sample volatility, as measured by individual security return variance, is best explained when short-term dispersion is the only factor. The market model and the market factor accompanied by short-term dispersion are also good models for predicting volatility.

Interestingly, models that contain the Fama–French three-factor specification tend to underestimate individual firm volatility. This might be construed as evidence that these factors do not proxy for fundamental risk. AGJ point out that this finding may occur because earnings forecasts are forward-looking expectations, whereas the other factors rely upon historical data.

19.2.7   Direction of Mispricing

One of the points mentioned earlier is that both the short-term and long-term measures of dispersion are significantly and negatively correlated with contemporaneous returns. Similarly, the coefficients on the short-term dispersion variable in the return regressions turn out to be negative as well. What does the negative sign mean?

The stocks of firms with high dispersion of earnings forecasts have associated with them lower returns than the stocks of firms with low dispersion of earnings forecasts. This finding is consistent with the results reported by Diether–Malloy–Scherbina, who suggest that the negative relationship reflects Miller's hypothesis regarding asymmetric trading in respect to long and short positions.

In terms of factor structure, think about the risk premium decomposition developed in Theorem 16.2. Recall that when the sentiment premium is negative, the security is overpriced. Plausibly, the stocks of firms associated with low dispersion involve less mispricing than the stocks of firms associated with high dispersion. In this case, the negative sign on DISP suggests high dispersion stocks tended to be overpriced, though some might suggest an explanation involving less risk. However, the risk argument would be at odds with the positive relationship between dispersion and volatility. Diether–Malloy–Scherbina make this point.

For dispersion to emerge as a priced factor, high dispersion needs to be associated with a preponderance for either excessive optimism or excessive pessimism. If there is a preponderance for neither, then there is no reason to expect loadings on either dispersion factor to be informative. Miller's argument provides one reason why high dispersion can be associated with excessive optimism.

19.2.8   Opposite Signs for Short and Long Horizons

The difference in signs in respect to short-term dispersion and long-term dispersion is curious. In a sense, one would expect Miller's argument to apply whether dispersion was measured using a short-term horizon or a long-term horizon. Might there be additional behavioral phenomena at work?

As noted in Section 18.5, analysts exhibit gambler's fallacy in respect to their return expectations, a feature that is inconsistent with momentum. De Bondt (1992) finds that although analysts' one-year forecasts exhibit gambler's fallacy, their five-year growth rate forecasts exhibit extrapolation bias. See also La Porta (1996). That is, analysts are overprone to forecast that past long-term growth rates will continue into the future. This might explain the opposite signs associated with the short-term dispersion factor and long-term dispersion factor.

19.3   Estimating a Structural SDF-Based Model

In their second exercise, AGJ estimate a structural simultaneous version of equation (16.16), in the aggregate consumption model with five securities. They assume that all investors share the same coefficient of relative risk aversion γ, so that $\gamma_R = \gamma$, where γ_R pertains to the representative investor setting R prices. The basis for the estimation is

$$1 = E_{\Pi,0}[\delta_\Pi h_{Z,0} g(x_1)^{-\gamma} r_Z(x_1)] \tag{19.1}$$

The five securities are the market portfolio, a risk-free bond, a portfolio of stocks with a high degree of past volatility, a portfolio of stocks with a high degree of dispersion among analysts' short-term forecasts, and a portfolio of stocks with a high degree of dispersion among analysts' long-term forecasts. All asset returns and consumption growth are in real terms. AGJ use the monthly CPI for inflation.

19.3.1 Proxy for $h_{Z,0}$

The estimation equation uses real consumption growth, realized returns on the five portfolios, and variables that proxy for $h_{Z,0}$. The proxy variables are derived from analysts' earnings estimates and stock recommendations.

The first step in computing the AGJ proxy for $h_{Z,0}$ is to compute two terms for each analyst. The first of these terms is the ratio of the specific analyst's forecasted portfolio return to the average forecasted portfolio return for all analysts. The second term is similar, but applies to consumption growth. Form the ratio of the analyst's forecast of consumption growth to the corresponding average forecast, and then take this ratio to the power $-\gamma$. Then form the product of the two terms. The AGJ proxy for $h_{Z,0}$ is a weighted average of these products, over analysts. The weights are wealth proxies.

AGJ introduce two parameters that control for analysts' errors. The first parameter serves to adjust the dispersion of forecasts. The second parameter allows investors to adjust their return expectations according to the strength of recommendations in analysts' recommendations. In this respect, First Call codes analysts' recommendations on a five-point scale, where $2 =$ strong buy, $1 =$ buy, $0 =$ hold, $-1 =$ sell, and $-2 =$ strong sell. Using the associated numerical five-point scale, the mean recommendation is 0.8118. In other words, the average stock recommendation is a weak buy. AGJ permit investors to adjust their return expectations according to the difference between the average recommendation for the portfolio and 0.8118.

19.3.2 Findings

AGJ use a general method of moments (GMM) procedure to estimate several versions of their system. In most cases, their estimates for γ and δ_Π are barely significant. Estimates of γ are unrealistically high, mainly because actual consumption growth is much smoother than security returns. Therefore, the covariance between security returns and consumption growth is bound to be low, forcing a high estimate of relative risk aversion in order to explain high equity returns. This issue has come to be known as the "equity premium puzzle;" it is discussed in Chapter 30.

Notably, although there is considerable dispersion in forecasts of the high short-term portfolio, there is less dispersion in forecasts of the market portfolio. AGJ use the return on the S&P 500 as a proxy for consumption growth. Because the dispersion in market forecasts is low, $h_{Z,0}$ is close to 1 for all assets. This forces the model to treat the sentiment premium as being small.

Finally, AGJ report that both dispersion and bias seem to be important. Allowing investors to act as if their beliefs are more dispersed than analyst forecasts, and to adjust for analyst recommendation bias, produces better fits.

19.4   Summary

This chapter discussed the relationship between dispersion and realized returns. In theory, returns and dispersion are related through the sentiment premium described in Chapter 16. However, theory is silent about the sign of the relationship. Diether, Malloy, and Scherbina (2002) report a negative relationship between dispersion and returns, and suggest that it stems from restrictions on short selling.

The chapter reported on two other exercises involving the sentiment premium, both conducted by AGJ (2004). The first exercise involves the identification of a dispersion factor. This factor offers additional explanatory power in respect to realized returns and volatility. The second exercise involves estimating a structural system involving the SDF and consumption growth. This exercise features a weak sentiment component, largely because there is limited dispersion in respect to the proxy for aggregate consumption growth. Notably, both dispersion and bias appear to be germane variables.

20

A Behavioral Approach to the Term Structure of Interest Rates

This chapter derives the prices of default-free bonds of varying maturities, that is, the term structure of interest rates. After having described the general pricing formula for the term structure, the discussion shifts to the implications of nonzero sentiment for excess volatility in rates and the failure of the expectations hypothesis. When expectations are formed on the basis of efficient prices, nonzero sentiment typically causes the expectations hypothesis to fail.

20.1   The Term Structure of Interest Rates

Theorem 16.2 indicates that all security returns decompose into fundamental components and sentiment premiums. This statement also applies to fixed income securities. Theorem 20.1, which follows, describes the relationship between the term structure of interest rates and the representative investor's parameters.

Theorem 20.1 *Let i_t^t denote the gross return to a default-free investment in which one real dollar is invested at date 0 and pays off t periods later. The discount factors, which are based upon (14.1) and define the term structure of interest rates, have the form*

$$(1/i_t)^t = \delta_{R,t}^t E_R\{g(x_t)^{-\gamma_R(x_t)}|x_0\} \tag{20.1}$$

where E_R is the expectation under the representative investor's probability density function.

Equation (20.1) follows directly from (14.7) and the fact that the term structure is based on securities that offer a fixed payoff across all states for date t. This equation makes explicit the connection between the yield curve and the beliefs of the representative investor.[1] The equation captures how interest rates evolve in terms of the discount factor $\delta_{R,t}$, the parameter γ_R, and the expectations E_R of the representative investor.

20.2 Pitfall: The Bond Pricing Equation in Theorem 20.1 Is False

Past readers of this work have suggested that Theorem 20.1 is false, except for the case when beliefs are homogeneous. The argument provided is sophisticated, and offers some interesting lessons. Current readers may wish to see if they can spot the flaw in the argument that follows.

Let ν_1 denote the state prices that would prevail if all investors held investor 1's beliefs. Likewise let ν_2 denote the state prices that would prevail if all investors held investor 2's beliefs. Subsection 8.2.2 implies that in a two-investor model, where both investors have log-utility and share the same rate of time preference, state prices satisfy a convex combination property. If $w_{0,j}$ is investor j's share of aggregate wealth at $t = 0$, then in this model equilibrium prices ν satisfy

$$\nu = w_{0,1}\nu_1 + w_{0,2}\nu_2$$

The contention is that this last equation cannot hold, and that in turn the bond pricing equation in Theorem 20.1 is false. The argument goes as follows.

Consider the equation for the term structure of interest rates (20.1). This equation implies that if all investors hold investor j's beliefs, then the bond pricing equation that defines the term structure of interest rates is given by

$$(1/i_{j,t})^t = \delta^t E_j\{g(x_t)^{-1}|x_0\} \tag{20.2}$$

where E_j is the expectation under investor j's probability density function. Were it the case that $\nu = w_1\nu_1 + w_2\nu_2$ then it would follow that the

---

[1] This equation treats x_0 as the current event. The expression is easily generalized when the current event is x_t.

equilibrium bond price $(1/i_t)^t$ would satisfy

$$q(0,t) = (1/i_t)^t = (w_{0,1}(1/i_{1,t})^t) + (w_{0,2}(1/i_{2,t})^t) \qquad (20.3)$$

For sake of argument, set $w_{0,j} = 0.5$. Let $w_{t,j}$ be investor j's share of aggregate wealth at t. In general, $w_{t,j} = w_{x_t,j}$, in that wealth shares are random variables. In this case

$$q(0,1) = (1/i_1)^1 = (w_{0,1}(1/i_{1,1})^1) + (w_{0,2}(1/i_{2,1})^1) \qquad (20.4)$$

and

$$q(0,2) = (1/i_2)^2 = (w_{0,1}(1/i_{1,2})^2) + (w_{0,2}(1/i_{2,2})^2) \qquad (20.5)$$

If all investors' beliefs conform to an *i.i.d.* binomial model, and beliefs are homogeneous, then the short-term interest rate is time invariant and the term structure is flat. In this case, $q(1,2)$, the date 1 price of a bond maturing at date 2, is given by

$$q(1,2) = (w_{1,1}(1/i_{1,1})^1) + (w_{1,2}(1/i_{2,1})^1) \qquad (20.6)$$

Consider the cumulative return $i_c(x_t)$ to the investment strategy in which the single period risk-free bond is held, with continued reinvestment between dates 0 and t. That is, the product of the single-period interest rates defines the cumulative return $i_c^t(x_t) = i_1(x_0)i_1(x_1)\cdots i_1(x_{t-1})$ to holding the short-term risk-free security, with reinvestment, from date 0 to date t. Let $S(x_{t-1})$ be the set of successor nodes x_t to x_{t-1}. The risk-neutral density $\eta(x_t)$ associated with event $\{x_t\}$, conditional on x_{t-1}, is defined by

$$\eta(x_t) = \frac{\nu(x_t)}{\sum_{y_t \in S(x_{t-1})} \nu(y_t)} \qquad (20.7)$$

Computation shows that $q(0,t)$ is equal to the expectation $E_\eta(1/i_c(x_t))$, where the expectation is taken with respect to the risk-neutral density function η.[2] Consider the equation

$$q(0,t) = E_\eta(1/i_c(x_2)) \qquad (20.8)$$

---

[2] This point is discussed in detail in the proof of Theorem 21.1, which establishes that $\nu(x_t) = \eta(x_t)/i_c(x_t)$.

Here, $q(0,2)$ is given by (20.4), and $E_\eta(1/i_c(x_2))$ is the expectation of the product of (20.4) and (20.6). Setting these two expressions equal to each other implies

$$(i_{2,1}/i_{1,1})[1 - E_\eta(w_1)] + (i_{1,1}/i_{2,1})E_\eta(w_1) = 1 \qquad (20.9)$$

Define $r_{j,t} = ln(i_{j,t})$ so that $i_{j,t} = e^{r_{j,t}}$. Substitute $e^{r_{j,t}}$ for $i_{j,t}$ in equation (20.9). Because the exponential function is convex (20.9) cannot hold in general, except for the special case when $r_{j,t}$ is the same for both investors. Therefore the bond pricing equation in Theorem 20.1 holds only in the special case of homogeneous beliefs.

20.2.1 Identifying the Flaw in the Analysis

Theorem 20.1 is valid. The flaw in the preceding argument lies in the manner in which equation (20.9) is used. The variables in this equation are not free. The interest rates, wealth shares, and risk-neutral probabilities are all determined together. The Excel file *Chapter 20 Example.xls* develops the bond pricing expressions in the preceding argument, and uses an example to show that these expressions do indeed provide the same values. In particular, (20.9) holds when the $r_{j,t}$ are not the same for both investors.

20.3   Volatility

The present section uses examples developed in previous chapters to explore the manner in which sentiment induces volatility into the time series of spot rates and into the yield curve. To illustrate this point, consider the example, developed in Chapter 14, where consumption growth evolves according to an *i.i.d.* process, and investors have heterogeneous coefficients of relative risk aversion ($\gamma = 1$ and $\gamma = 2$). When prices are efficient in that example, interest rate volatility is effectively zero, and the yield curve is flat at 2.15 percent. Table 20.1 displays the equilibrium term structure in the case of heterogeneous beliefs for that example. Notice that short-term interest rates exhibit time variation, fluctuating between 2.15 percent and 2.75 percent. Table 20.2 displays the yield curve at $t = 0$. Notice that it is positively sloped (rising from 2.15 percent to 2.44 percent).

To understand the manner in which heterogeneity of beliefs affects the shape of the yield curve, begin with the case of log-utility. Let the basic parameters correspond to the example in Chapter 12 except to let $\gamma_j = 1$ for all investors j. Begin with the case of efficient prices. The equilibrium one-period interest rate will turn out to be 1.86 percent in every date–event pair, and the yield curve will be flat at 1.86 percent as well. The reason for both is that consumption growth evolves as an *i.i.d.* process.

TABLE 20.1. Short-Term Interest Rates

This table presents the stochastic process governing short-term interest rates from the example developed in Chapter 14.

Date	Sequence	Short-Term Interest Rate
0	0	2.151%
1	u	2.581%
1	d	2.619%
2	uu	2.571%
2	ud	2.745%
2	du	2.590%
2	dd	2.408%

TABLE 20.2. Yield Curve

This table presents the yield curve from the example developed in Chapter 14.

Date	Rate
1	2.151%
2	2.368%
3	2.440%

The time discount factor for the representative investor will be 0.99, the same as for the individual investors. By Theorem 20.1, the one-period interest rate is given by the inverse expectation of δ/g with respect to Π, where $g = g(x_{t+1}, |x_t)$. Because both δ and the conditional expected value of g are time invariant, the expected value of δ/g will be the same in every x_t, namely 0.9817. That is, the one-period interest rate assumes the same value in each date–event pair.

Next, consider what happens in the case of heterogeneous beliefs. Because both investors are assumed to hold correct beliefs about the first transition, the equilibrium interest rate will be 1.86 percent, just as in the efficient market case. However, in the case of heterogeneous beliefs, the shape of the yield curve at $t = 0$ will not be flat throughout. It will be flat for one more period, but then slope upward.

In order to understand why the yield curve takes the shape that it does, one needs to examine the equilibrium one-period interest rates at $t = 1$ and $t = 2$. At $t = 1$, the equilibrium one-period interest rate will be 1.86 percent regardless of whether an up-move or down-move occurred. That is why the shape of the initial portion of the $t = 0$ yield curve remains flat. However, at $t = 2$, the interest rate need not be 1.86 percent. In date–event pair ud, the interest rate will be 1.89 percent. In date–event pair dd, the interest rate will be 1.84 percent. That is why the $t = 0$ yield curve does not stay flat.

The point is that heterogeneous beliefs impact interest rate volatility and the shape of the yield curve. In order to understand why this occurs, consider the different investors' beliefs as date–event pairs unfold. Suppose that an up-move occurs at $t = 1$. On the $t = 1$ market, investors 1 and 2 hold different beliefs. Investor 1 assigns a conditional probability of 95 percent to the occurrence of a subsequent up-move at $t = 2$, whereas investor 2 assigns a probability of 85 percent to the occurrence of a subsequent up-move at $t = 2$.

Notice that the expectation of δ/g under investor 1's probabilities is 0.9812, whereas the expectation of δ/g under investor 2's probabilities is 0.9822. At $t = 0$ and $t = 1$, the equilibrium expected value of δ/g, effectively the price of the one-period default-free bond, turns out to be 0.9817. Notice that this value lies between the values associated with the two investors' expected values, 0.9812 and 0.9822. That is, the equilibrium balances the investors' expected values in arriving at the discount factor for the one-period bond. However, at $t = 2$, wealth shifts associated with trading lead the weights to shift in balancing the two expected values, 0.9812 and 0.9822.

When investor 1 gains wealth share, the one-period discount factor shifts in the direction of his beliefs. When investor 2 gains wealth share, the one-period discount factor shifts in the direction of her beliefs. This means that the discount factor is effectively bounded by those two values. Therefore the extent of heterogeneity restricts the amount of interest rate volatility and the amount of slope in the yield curve.

The preceding example assumes that the objective process (II) is $i.i.d.$ If the process is Markovian and Ergodic, then even in the case of market efficiency, the yield curve need not be flat.[3] However, rates on long-term default-free bonds will have to be given by the Ergodic (invariant) distribution. This implies that when prices are efficient, the tail of the yield curve will have to be (asymptotically) flat.

When beliefs are heterogeneous, wealth shifts inject volatility into the weights used to form the representative investor's beliefs. If the relative contribution of the investor's beliefs does not converge to a stable value, then the tail of the yield curve need not be flat. In other words, heterogeneous beliefs inject volatility into long-term rates.

---

[3] See Beja (1978) for a thorough treatment of the term structure in a Markov setting.

Of course, heterogeneous beliefs also inject volatility into short-term rates. However, because long-term rates are stable in an efficient market, the contrast is more striking.

Evidence presented in Brown and Schaefer (1994) suggests that heterogeneous beliefs describes the real term structure better than homogeneous belief, the Cox, Ingersoll, and Ross (1985) (CIR) case. Brown and Schaefer find positive volatility in long-term real rates and unstable parameters in their CIR estimates. Moreover, they find that the market underestimates the rate at which short rates revert to their long-run mean. This finding is consistent with base rate underweighting on the part of the representative investor. Brown and Schaefer's observation leads them to propose a simple market timing rule that exploits the market's underestimation.

20.3.1   *Heterogeneous Risk Tolerance*

Consider the impact of the coefficient of risk aversion γ on the term structure. In the case of log-utility, the price of a default-free bond is the expectation of δ/g under the probability density function of the representative investor. If all investors share the same value of γ, then this price is the expectation of $\delta g^{-\gamma}$ under the probability density function of the representative investor.

Think about how an increase in γ affects $E_R(\delta g^{-\gamma})$, the expected value of $\delta g^{-\gamma}$. For $g > 1$ and $\gamma > 1$, a higher value of γ will have a negative impact on $g^{-\gamma}$. For $g < 1$ and $\gamma > 1$, a higher value of γ will have a positive impact on $g^{-\gamma}$.

As for the impact of a higher value of γ on $E_R(\delta g^{-\gamma})$, that will depend on the probability mass associated with the events $\{g < 1\}$ and $\{g > 1\}$. In the preceding example, the P_R attaches considerably more probability to $\{g > 1\}$ than to $\{g < 1\}$. Therefore, an increase in γ will decrease the value of $E_R(\delta g^{-\gamma})$. In other words, a higher value of γ leads to lower bond prices and higher interest rates.

Consider the example, described in Chapter 12, where all investors have the same coefficient of relative risk aversion ($\gamma_j = 2$ for all investors j). In the case when all investors hold correct beliefs, the one-period interest rate is about 2.6 percent, and the yield curve is quite flat.[4] When the two investors have heterogeneous beliefs, as in the example in Chapter 12, then the interest rate rises to about 3.5 percent, but the yield curve remains quite flat. These rates are higher than the 1.86 percent that prevailed for the case of log-utility discussed earlier.

The impact of heterogeneity for the case $\gamma = 2$ is qualitatively similar to that under log-utility. Interest rates become more volatile, and the term structure moves from being flat to having a nonzero slope. Notably, a

---

[4] The computation of the term structure of interest rate follows from Theorem 20.1.

higher value of γ increases the sensitivity of changes in investors' beliefs to bond prices. That is, changes in P_R typically have a more pronounced effect on $E_R(\delta g^{-\gamma})$ for higher values of γ.[5] For instance, when $\gamma = 2$ the same heterogeneous beliefs used for the log-utility example above cause the interest rate at $t = 2$ to be 3.5 percent, a 100 basis point jump. In contrast, the impact of heterogeneity in the log-utility model was about 1 basis point.

The impact of heterogeneous risk aversion in this example is straight-forward. Suppose that investor 1 has a coefficient of risk aversion equal to 1, and investor 2 has a coefficient of risk aversion equal to 2. Recall that the representative investor forms a weighted average of coefficients of risk tolerance. Hence, the representative investor will have a coefficient of risk tolerance equal to 0.75, and a corresponding coefficient of risk aversion equal to 1.5. Therefore, in this example, interest rates will be determined as if all investors had a coefficient of risk aversion equal to 1.5. That is, interest rates will lie between their values achieved under log-utility and the values achieved when $\gamma = 2$. For example, the interest rate at $t = 0$ will be 2.1 percent, between the 1.86 percent associated with log-utility and the 2.7 percent associated with $\gamma = 2$.

In general, γ_R is a function of x_t, and so it varies randomly. For instance, consider the preceding example when all investors have correct probabilities but heterogeneous risk tolerance. Then the entropy argument developed in Chapter 16 will lead the wealth share of the investors to fluctuate over time. As wealth shifts back and forth between investors, the weight assigned by the representative investor to the respective coefficients of risk tolerance will fluctuate as well. This introduces an additional source of volatility into interest rates.

20.4   Expectations Hypothesis

Economists have long been puzzled by the fact that the expectations hypothesis of the yield curve fails to hold. See Campbell (1995).[6] The remainder of this chapter briefly discusses the role of sentiment in respect to the expectations hypothesis.

As Ingersoll (1987) points out, there are several definitions for the expectations hypothesis of the term structure. Consider two versions. The first is the pure version in which the forward rate equals the expected future

---

[5] More precisely, the statement should read, "for values of γ further from 1."

[6] Campbell points out that many of the term structure studies during the 1960s did not impose rational expectations, and therefore allowed systematic profit opportunities to exist. Although that may be the case in this model, I note that these opportunities are not riskless. There may well be investors who do have objectively correct beliefs, and yet refrain from seizing these opportunities because of the risk involved. See footnote 17, Campbell (1995).

spot rate. The second version states that subject to a time-invariant risk premium, the expected return to holding short-term default-free securities is the same as the return to holding long-term default-free securities. This version appears in the empirical work of Backus, Foresi, Mozumdar, and Wu (2001), and Roberds and Whiteman (1997).

The representative investor holds the market portfolio and consumes its dividends. Notably, a representative investor for whom $c_R(x_0) = 1$ consumes at the cumulative dividend growth rate $g_t = g(x_t)$. The expectations hypothesis is driven by the fact that at the margin, the representative investor is indifferent to substituting default-free bonds with long-term maturities for default-free bonds with shorter maturities in his portfolio. For example, if we consider $t = 2$ as the long term and $t = 1$ as the short term, then indifference at the margin implies that

$$\delta_R^2 E_R\{g_2^{-\gamma_R}\}i_2^2(x_0) = \delta_R^2 E_R\{g_2^{-\gamma_R}i_1(x_1)\}i_1(x_0) = 1 \qquad (20.10)$$

That is, the marginal utility of a dollar invested in either the short-term bond or the long-term bond is equal to the marginal utility of a dollar, which is unity. For ease of notation the x_2 argument in γ_R is suppressed. Define the date 2 forward rate by

$$f_2(x_0) = \frac{i_2(x_0)^2}{i_1(x_0)} \qquad (20.11)$$

Notice that (20.10) can be rewritten to obtain a condition that relates the spot and forward interest rates, a relationship often used to test the expectations hypothesis. When equation (20.14) (to be developed shortly) holds, the representative investor is indifferent to substituting a long bond for a short bond in his portfolio.[7] This condition is derived using (12.18), (20.1), and the fact that the representative investor consumes at the cumulative growth rate of the market portfolio.

The focal point of the expectations hypothesis is the difference between the forward rate $f_2(x_0)$ on the x_0 market and the expected spot rate on the x_1 market, $E_\Pi(i_1(x_1)|x_0)$. Equation (20.10) implies that

$$f_2(x_0) = \frac{(i_2(x_0))^2}{i_1(x_0)} = \frac{E_R(g_2^{-\gamma_R}i_1(x_1))}{E_R(g_2^{-\gamma_R})} \qquad (20.12)$$

In view of (20.1), $E_\Pi(i_1(x_1))$ is given by the expression

$$E_\Pi(i_1(x_1)|x_0) = E_\Pi\{\frac{1}{\delta_R}\frac{1}{E_R(g_2(x_2|x_1))^{-\gamma_R}}\} \qquad (20.13)$$

---

[7] The equation, which was derived for the case of $t = 1$ and $t = 2$, is easily generalized.

Therefore,

$$f_2 - E_\Pi(i_1(x_1)|x_0) = \frac{E_R(g_2^{-\gamma_R}i_1(x_1))}{E_R(g_2^{-\gamma_R})} - E_\Pi\left\{\frac{1}{\delta_R}\frac{1}{E_R(g_2(x_2|x_1))^{-\gamma_R}}\right\}$$

(20.14)

The pure expectations hypothesis states that equation (20.14) is equal to zero. In other words, the forward rate and expected spot rate coincide. A weaker version of the expectations hypothesis recognizes that when the future spot rate is uncertain, investors might require a risk premium to compensate them for bearing this risk. Such a risk premium would drive a wedge between the forward rate and expected spot rate. In the weak form of the expectations hypothesis, the risk premium is constant over time.

In this model, the greatest impediment to the expectations hypothesis holding is price inefficiency. That is, it is inequality between P_R and Π that is most significant in respect to (20.14) not holding (up to a fixed constant) over time. The expectations hypothesis is formed on the basis of the true probability density Π, not the market beliefs P_R. The representative investor is indeed indifferent to substituting default-free bonds with long-term maturities for default-free bonds with shorter maturities. That is, (20.10) holds when the expectations are taken with respect to P_R, but may not hold if the expectations are taken with respect to Π, when $P_R \neq \Pi$. In order to make these ideas more concrete, consider the following example.

20.4.1 Example

Consider the example featuring heterogeneous beliefs and heterogeneous risk tolerance from Chapter 14. This example was discussed in the previous section.

Table 20.3 summarizes the equilibrium term structure of interest rates from that example, along with the associated forward rates for $t = 1$ and $t = 2$ associated with the yield curve on the x_0 market. The two right-most columns display the expected spot rates at $t = 1$ and $t = 2$, conditional on x_0, under two probability density functions. One density function corresponds to the representative investor (P_R), and the other density function corresponds to the objective density (Π). Notice that the expected spot rate under P_R equals the corresponding forward rate in all circumstances. However, the same statement does not apply for the expected spot rate at $t = 2$, computed under Π.

The point of this example is that most discussions of the expectations hypothesis implicitly assume efficient prices, in the sense that the representative trader has correct beliefs. Therefore these discussions focus on the fundamental component associated with fixed income securities, but ignore

TABLE 20.3. Test of Expectations Hypothesis

This table presents the yield curve from the example developed in Chapter 14, along with the forward rates and expected spot rates, where the expectations are taken with respect to both P_R and Π.

Date	Yield Curve $t = 0$	Fwd Rates	Rep Investor Exp Spot Rate	Objective Exp Spot Rate
1	2.151%	2.151%	2.151%	2.151%
2	2.368%	2.585%	2.585%	2.585%
3	2.440%	2.583%	2.583%	2.587%

the sentiment component. As the preceding example illustrated, when expectations are formed on the basis of efficient prices, nonzero sentiment can cause the expectations hypothesis to fail.

20.5 Summary

This chapter contained a discussion of the determinants of the term structure of interest rates. Theorem 20.1 provides a characterization result. This result serves as the context for discussing the impact of sentiment on the term structure. Sentiment injects volatility into the term structure both at the short end of the yield curve and at the long end. The impact of sentiment at the long end is especially pronounced, in that in a Markov setting, market efficiency implies that there should be very little volatility attached to long-term bond prices. Higher degrees of risk aversion accentuate the impact of sentiment. Heterogeneous coefficients of risk aversion inject additional volatility into the term structure.

Although the expectations hypothesis of the term structure holds when prices are efficient, nonzero sentiment can cause the expectations hypothesis to fail.

21
Behavioral Black–Scholes

Sentiment measures the degree of bias in the representative investor's probability density function. Because options are naturally structured as contingent payoffs, they provide an important direct window into the sentiment function.

The present chapter develops a behavioral approach to option pricing. The discussion begins with some general characterization results, which are analogous to Theorem 20.1 for the term structure of interest rates. Several examples are presented in order to provide insight into the manner in which sentiment impacts the prices of options. Two of the examples illustrate how the Black–Scholes formula, lying at the center of option pricing theory, extends to a behavioral setting.

21.1   Call and Put Options

Let Z be a security that pays $Z(x_t)$ in event x_t. A European call option on Z that is issued at x_t, has an exercise price of K, and expires on date $t + \tau$ provides its holder with the right, but not the obligation, to purchase Z on date $t + \tau$ at price K. Assume that the holder of the call option is rational, and will exercise the call option if and only if the price of Z at $t + \tau$, $q_Z(x_{t+\tau})$ is at least K. Then the payoff function for the call option is $max\{q_Z(x_{t+\tau}) - K, 0\}$.

A European put option on Z that is issued at x_t, has an exercise price of K, and expires on date $t + \tau$ provides its holder with the right, but not the obligation, to sell Z on date $t + \tau$ at price K. The date τ payoff to the put option is $max\{0, K - q_Z(x_{t+\tau})\}$.[1]

21.2   Risk-Neutral Densities and Option Pricing

This section presents three equivalent option pricing expressions. The first expression is developed in Theorem 21.1. This expression, based on the standard risk-neutral density approach, involves the arguments used to demonstrate how discrete time option pricing formulas converge to the Black–Scholes formula in the limit. See Cox, Ross, and Rubinstein (1979), Madan, Milne, and Shefrin (1989), and He (1990). The next section extends the argument to establish why sentiment prevents the conditions that underlie Black–Scholes from holding.

Theorem 21.2 presents a second option pricing expression that demonstrates how investors' beliefs, operating through the beliefs of the representative investor, affect option prices. The risk-neutral-based option pricing expression in Theorem 21.1 obscures the relationship between investors' beliefs and the prices of options. And the traditional risk-neutral approach to option pricing appears to have led researchers to the view that option prices are independent of investors' beliefs, since that is the case in partial equilibrium option models. However, as will be demonstrated shortly, investors' beliefs impact option prices.

The third option pricing expression reflects a "snapshot in time" approach. The "snapshot in time" expression, described in Theorem 21.3, depends only on variables associated with the expiration date. In particular it relies on the long-term interest rate and the risk-neutral density at the expiration date. This contrasts with the first expression, in Theorem 21.1, which relies on the co-evolution of the short-term interest rate process and the risk-neutral process over the life of the option. The "snapshot in time" approach is useful for pointing out that the differences between continuous time option pricing models and discrete time option pricing models are less important than the character of the risk-neutral process. This approach serves to provide a link between the two modeling techniques.

21.2.1   Option Pricing Equation 1

Theorem 21.1 describes the first option pricing formula, expressed in terms of the risk-neutral process and the process for short-term interest rates.

---

[1] For readers who are not familiar with options, a good introduction is Hull (2004).

Theorem 21.1 *Given (14.7), the general expression for the price of a European call option on a security Z, featuring exercise price K and expiration date t, is determined as follows.*

(1) Let $S(x_{t-1})$ be the set of successor nodes x_t to x_{t-1}. The risk-neutral density $\eta(x_t)$ associated with event $\{x_t\}$, conditional on x_{t-1}, is defined by

$$\eta(x_t) = \frac{\nu(x_t)}{\sum_{y_t \in S(x_{t-1})} \nu(y_t)} \tag{21.1}$$

(2) Let A_E denote the event $\{q_z(x_t) \geq K\}$, in which the call option is exercised, and $P_\eta\{A_E\}$ be its probability under the risk-neutral density P_η. The product of the single-period interest rates defines the cumulative return $i_c^t(x_t) = i_1(x_0)i_1(x_1) \cdots i_1(x_{t-1})$ to holding the short-term risk-free security, with reinvestment, from date 0 to date t. Then the x_0 price of the call option is given by

$$q_c(x_0) = E_\eta\{(q_z(x_t) - K)/i_c^t(x_t)|A_E, x_0\}P_\eta\{A_E|x_0\} \tag{21.2}$$

Proof of Theorem Equation (20.1) in Theorem 20.1 implies that the η in (21.1) is the product of a compounded interest rate and a state price. Since a state price is a present value associated with a state claim, from the perspective of x_{t-1}, $\eta(x_t)$ is the future value of a contingent x_t real dollar payoff. Given x_{t-1}, the future value of a contract that delivers a certain dollar at date t must be one dollar. This is why $\sum_{y_t \subset S(x_{t-1})} \eta(y_t) = 1$. In other words, the future values of y_t claims are nonnegative and sum to unity. Hence, they constitute a probability distribution. Since they deal with the transition from x_{t-1}, $\{\eta(y_t)\}$ are one-step branch probabilities of a stochastic process.

Under the stochastic process, the probability attached to the occurrence of x_t is obtained by multiplying the one-step branch probabilities leading to x_t. To interpret this product, consider the denominator of (21.1). This term can be matched with the numerator of the x_{t-1} one-step branch probability to form $\nu(x_{t-1})/\sum_{y_t \in S(x_{t-1})} \nu(y_t)$. The latter term is simply one plus the single-period risk-free interest rate $i_1(x_{t-1})$ that applies on the x_{t-1} market. Therefore, the probability of the branch leading to x_t is the product of the single-period stochastic interest rates and the present value of an x_t claim: $i_1(x_0)i_1(x_1) \cdots i_1(x_{t-1})\nu(x_t)$. The product of the single-period interest rates defines the cumulative return $i_c^t(x_t)$ to holding the short-term risk-free security, with reinvestment, from date 0 to date t.

A call option pays $q_z(x_t) - K$ at date t, if $x_t \in A_E$, the set of date–event pairs where the option expires in-the-money. The present value of the claims that make up the option payoff is computed using state prices ν. But the present value of an x_t-contingent dollar is its future value discounted back by the product of the one-period risk-free rates. The discounted contingent future dollar is simply the ratio of a risk-neutral probability $\eta(x_t)$ to a compounded interest rate $i_c(x_t)$. Finally, the risk-neutral probability $\eta(x_t)$ is unconditional. To convert to a distribution conditional on exercise, divide $\eta(x_t)$ by $P_\eta\{A_E|x_0\}$. Using the conditional expectation in place of the unconditional expectation leads to the appearance of $P_\eta\{A_E|x_0\}$ in (21.2). ■

21.2.2   Option Pricing Equations 2 and 3

Risk-neutral density pricing equations such as (21.2) tend to obscure how the properties of the representative investor's beliefs affect asset prices. As was mentioned previously, two alternative option pricing expressions are presented.

Theorem 21.2 *(1) Given (14.7), the price of a European call option on a security Z, featuring exercise price K and expiration date t, is determined as follows. Let A_E denote the event $\{q_z(x_t) \geq K\}$, in which the call option is exercised, and $P_R\{A_E\}$ be its probability under the representative investor's probability distribution P_R. Then q_c satisfies*

$$q_c(x_0) = \delta_{R,t}^t E_R\{(q_z(x_t) - K)g(x_t)^{-\gamma_R(x_t)}|A_E\}P_R\{A_E\} \qquad (21.3)$$

(2) Define the t-step probability distribution $\phi(x_t)$ over date t events x_t, conditional on x_0, as follows:

$$\phi(x_t|x_0) = \frac{\nu(x_t)}{\sum_{y_t} \nu(y_t)} \qquad (21.4)$$

Then q_c satisfies

$$q_c(x_0) = E_\phi\{(q_z(x_t) - K)|A_E, x_0\}P_\phi\{A_E|x_0\}/i_t^t(x_0) \qquad (21.5)$$

The proof of Theorem 21.2 is similar to that of Theorem 21.1, and is omitted.

Equations (21.3) and (21.5) describe the direct impact of the representative investor's beliefs on call option prices. (21.3) prices the option using the state price representation (14.7).[2] (21.5) indicates the connection between the term structure and option prices, in that the t-period bond is used to price the option.

---

[2] Equation (21.2) makes use of the definition of conditional probability, $Prob\{x_t|\eta, A_E\} = Prob\{x_t|\eta\}/Prob\{A_E|\eta\}$, where $P_\eta(A_E) = Prob\{A_E|\eta\}$.

21.3   Option Pricing Examples

Consider two examples that illustrate why heterogeneity causes interest rates and volatility to be stochastic, and how this affects option prices. In the examples, both interest rates and volatility are constant under homogeneous beliefs, but stochastic under heterogeneous beliefs. In the limit, Black–Scholes holds in the homogeneous case, but not in the heterogeneous case. Of course, the limit involves continuous time.

The continuous time example provides an opportunity to discuss the emergence of so-called "option smiles." Notably, the example demonstrates that heterogeneity introduces smile effects into equilibrium option prices, and leads implied volatilities for call options to differ from implied volatilities for put options, even when both share the same exercise price.

21.3.1   Discrete Time Example

Assume that there is a single physical asset that produces a single consumption good at each date. The amount of the good available for consumption at date 0 is 1 unit. Thereafter, aggregate consumption will grow stochastically from date to date, either at rate u (with probability Π_u) or at rate $d = 1/u$ (with probability $1 - \Pi_u$). The market portfolio is a security that pays the value of aggregate consumption at each date. Let $u = 1.05$, and $\Pi_u = 0.7$.

Let there be two investors in the model, and assume that each initially holds one half of the market portfolio. There is also a risk-free security available for trade at each date. Because of the binomial character of uncertainty, these two securities will be sufficient to complete the market.

Both investors are assumed to have additively separable preferences, logarithmic utility, and discount factors equal to unity (zero impatience). They also hold beliefs about the branch probability in the binomial tree. Investor 1 assumes that the value of the branch probability P_u is $P_{1,u}$, while investor 2 believes the value to be $P_{2,u}$. Each investor seeks to maximize subjective expected utility subject to the condition that the present value of lifetime consumption be equal to initial wealth. The single budget constraint here stems from markets' being complete.

When $P_{1,u} \neq P_{2,u}$ investors have heterogeneous beliefs. As was discussed in Chapters 8 and 14, equilibrium prices can be characterized through the beliefs of a representative investor R, whose tree probabilities are a convex combination of the tree probabilities of the individual investors, where the weights are given by relative wealth. Because the two investors in this example have the same wealth at date 0, the representative investor attaches probability

$$P_{R,u} = (P_{1,u} + P_{2,u})/2 \tag{21.6}$$

to the occurrence of an up-move at the end of date 0. The probability that the representative investor attaches at date 0 to two successive up-moves, occurring at the end of date 0 and the end of date 1 respectively, is

$$P_{R,u}(2) = (P_{1,u}^2 + P_{2,u}^2)/2 \tag{21.7}$$

which is the (relative wealth-weighted) average of the two investors' binomial probabilities attached to the node in question.

For general $P_{1,u}$ and $P_{2,u}$, the equilibrium state price ν_u in this example satisfies[3]

$$\nu_u = P_{R,u}/u = 0.5((P_{1,u}/u) + (P_{2,u}/u)) \tag{21.8}$$

The preceding equation illustrates the fact that in equilibrium, state prices can be expressed as weighted sums of state prices derived from corresponding homogeneous belief cases. It follows that all security prices can be expressed as weighted sums of security prices derived from corresponding homogeneous belief cases.[4] For ease of reference, call this the *weighted average property*.

In the log-utility binomial example, the equation for the equilibrium interest rate is[5]

$$i = [P_{R,u}/u + (1 - P_{R,u})/d]^{-1} \tag{21.9}$$

This equation implies that in the case of homogeneous beliefs, the short-term interest rate will be constant over time. However, as was discussed in Section 20.3, in the case of heterogeneous beliefs about the true value of the binomial branch probability, the equilibrium short-term interest rate will be stochastic.

To illustrate the impact of heterogeneity on interest rates, consider four cases. In three of the cases, the two investors agree about the value of P_u. In the first case, both investors correctly believe its value to be 0.7. In the second case, both believe its value to be 0.8. In the third case, both believe its value to be 0.6. And in the fourth case, investor 1 believes its value to be 0.8 while investor 2 believes its value to be 0.6. Some computation shows that the interest rate in case 1 is a constant 1.87 percent, in case 2 it is a constant 2.9 percent, and in case 3 it is a constant 0.87 percent. And

---

[3] ν_u is a conditional one-period state price. When beliefs are homogeneous, the conditional state prices are time invariant. The discussion to follow addresses why heterogeneity interferes with stationarity in conditional state prices.

[4] This follows because, as usual, the absence of arbitrage profits implies that every security price is a linear combination of state prices. The result is a feature of both Shefrin–Statman (1994) and Detemple–Murthy (1994).

[5] The price of a contract that pays one real unit with certainty in the next period is $(\nu_u + \nu_d)$. Hence, the risk-free interest rate is $(\nu_u + \nu_d)^{-1}$.

what will the interest rate be in case 4, where the two investors disagree? To answer this question, compute the discount factors associated with each of the other interest rates. For 2.9 percent, the one-period discount factor (bond price) is $1/1.029 = 0.9719$. For 0.87 percent, the discount factor is 0.9914. Because of the weighted-average property, the discount factor in case 4 will be a convex combination of the discount factors 0.9719 and 0.9914, with weights given by relative wealth.

At date 0, the relative wealth levels are 0.5, so the equilibrium one-period interest rate is 1.87 percent, the same value as in case 1. However, because the investors disagree about the value of Π_u, they bet against each other on the date 0 market. Investor 1 is more optimistic than investor 2. As a result, investor 1 bets more aggressively on the occurrence of an up-move leading to date 1 than investor 2. If an up-move does occur in the first period, relative wealth will shift from investor 2 to investor 1. As a result, investor 1's beliefs will exert more of an impact on pricing on the date 1 market, and the interest rate will climb above 1.87 percent (in the direction of 2.89 percent). In this specific example, an up-move in the first period results in investor 1's holding 57 percent of overall wealth, and investor 2's holding the residual. In consequence, the one-period interest rate at date 1 rises from 1.87 percent to 2.01 percent. Notice that if we condition on an up-move at the end of date 0, then the conditional error–wealth covariance terms described in Chapter 9 will no longer be uniformly zero along the tree.[6]

The technique used to find the equilibrium interest rate for the heterogeneous case, based on four cases, applies to all securities, including options. It is simply a matter of invoking the weighted-average property, and taking a weighted average of prices for corresponding homogeneous cases. Here is a brief illustration. Take the first of the four cases, the case when both correctly believe the value to be 0.7, and the equilibrium interest rate is 1.87 percent. Consider an underlying asset for the option that pays a zero dividend. Define a security Z so that it has the same (dividend) payoff as the market portfolio for the four dates 2 through 5 inclusive, but pays no dividend prior to date 2. By constructing the state prices from ν_u, one can easily verify that this security has a price of 4.00 at date 0, and that its price changes by a factor of either u or d in every period before the option expiration date. Figure 21.1 shows the standard procedure for computing the price of a European call option on this security that expires at $t = 2$ and has an exercise price $K = 3.80$. The price of the option at date 0 is 0.355. The same procedure can be employed to compute the option price for the second and third of the four cases. Note that in each of these cases, a different set of common beliefs gives rise to a different value for the equilibrium interest rate.

---

[6] "Uniformly zero" means zero at every node in the tree.

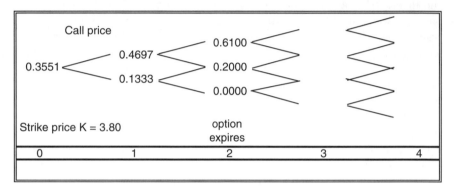

FIGURE 21.1. This figure shows the standard procedure for computing the price of a European call option on the security depicted in the top panel, that expires at $t = 2$ and has an exercise price $K = 3.80$. The price of the option at date 0 is 0.355.

In addition to causing interest rates to be volatile, heterogeneity alters the representative investor's probability density, which in turn alters the return standard deviation of the asset underlying the option. That is, heterogeneity induces both stochastic interest rates and stochastic volatility. Notice that these are the primary channels through which heterogeneity would be seen to impact option prices in traditional partial equilibrium reduced form frameworks. For this example, heterogeneity implies no impact through the return distribution of the underlying asset. The discussion in Chapter 10 established that when utility is logarithmic, the equilibrium price of the market portfolio at any node in the uncertainty tree is independent of investors' underlying beliefs. Therefore, the only impact of different beliefs on the option price here occurs through the interest rate and volatility.

21.3.2 Continuous Time Example

Consider the implications of heterogeneity for option pricing in continuous time. In the standard binomial option pricing model, the interest rate is constant, and under a suitable limiting argument, the binomial option price converges to the Black–Scholes formula. Notice that when investors are homogeneous, the standard limiting argument applies to the general equilibrium binomial example discussed above. However, as noted, heterogeneity leads interest rates to be stochastic. In turn, the volatility of short-term interest rates implies that the one-period conditional binomial state prices do not remain invariant over time. Notably, this disrupts the usual limiting argument developed by Cox, Ross, and Rubinstein (1979), where the Black–Scholes pricing equation is achieved as a limiting case of the binomial option pricing formula. Put another way, heterogeneity tends to prevent the conditions necessary for Black–Scholes pricing from holding.[7]

Notice that the weighted-average property holds in continuous time, just as it does in discrete time. In their two-agent continuous time log-utility model, Detemple–Murthy (1994) establish that when markets are complete, the price of any contingent claim is a weighted average of the prices that would prevail in two single agent economies. This implies that in the continuous time version of the preceding example, the equilibrium option price is a weighted average of Black–Scholes functions.

To state this condition formally, consider the Black–Scholes formula C_{BS} for the price of a call option

$$C_{BS}(q_Z, K, \sigma, t, r) = q_Z N(d_1) - K e^{-rt} N(d_2) \qquad (21.10)$$

where

$$d_1 = [\ln(q_Z/K) + (r + \sigma^2/2)t]/\sigma\sqrt{t} \quad d_2 = d_1 - \sigma\sqrt{t} \qquad (21.11)$$

Note that q_z is the initial price, K is the strike price, σ denotes the return standard deviation of the underlying asset, t is the time to expiration, and r is the continuous compounding rate of interest.

Consider a continuous time limiting version of the binomial example above, in which there are two log-utility investors with equal initial wealth. Imagine a European option on a security Z, whose price at $t=0$ is q_Z, and whose return is log-normally distributed with standard deviation σ. Given that Black–Scholes may fail to hold in equilibrium, how will the

---

[7]Heterogeneous beliefs do not prevent the option from being priced by arbitrage. However, the binomial-distribution for state prices that gets used in the standard binomial option pricing model with fixed i, u, and d does not apply. The binomial-distribution property will fail because the conditional state prices in the standard framework stay the same over time, but under heterogeneous beliefs, they vary. And remember, Black–Scholes emerges from the binomial framework because by the central limit theorem the binomial distribution converges to the normal. Heterogeneous beliefs will stand in the way of that argument when we seek to apply the central limit theorem in the manner of Cox, Ross, and Rubinstein (1979): see the middle of page 252 of their article.

option be priced? To answer this question, invoke the weighted-average property. That is, consider two situations. In the first situation, all investors agree with investor 1, the equilibrium value of Z is q_Z, its return standard deviation is σ, and the equilibrium continuously compounded interest rate is r_1. In the second situation, all investors agree with investor 2, the equilibrium value of Z is q_Z, its return standard deviation is σ, and the equilibrium continuously compounded interest rate is r_2. Notice that because of the general equilibrium framework, the interest rate is endogenous. The weighted-average property implies that

$$C_{eq} = [C_{BS}(q_Z, K, \sigma, t, r_1) + C_{BS}(q_Z, K, \sigma, t, r_2)]/2 \qquad (21.12)$$

Consider an example with extreme values to highlight the properties of the previous equation. Specifically, let $r_1 = 50$ percent and $r_2 = -50$ percent. Equation (3.8) on p. 302 of Detemple–Murthy implies that the weighted-average property applies to the instantaneous interest rate. Hence, $r_{eq} = 0$ percent. Let $q_Z = 4$ and $\sigma = 30$ percent.

Figure 21.2 shows how four call option prices discussed in this example vary as a function of K. The top curve pertains to the case $r_1 = 50$ percent, while the bottom curve pertains to the case $r_2 = -50$ percent. The curves in the middle are for the equilibrium option prices (solid curve) and Black–Scholes prices (dashed curve). Figure 21.3 provides another view of how the difference between the equilibrium call option price and the Black–Scholes

FIGURE 21.2. This figure shows how four call option prices discussed in the continuous time example vary as a function of K.

Difference Between Black–Scholes Call Price
and Equilibrium Call Price

FIGURE 21.3. This figure shows how the difference between the equilibrium call option price and Black–Scholes price varies as a function of the exercise price K.

price varies as a function of the exercise price K. Notice that the pattern is cyclical, and is negative for low values of K.

The Black–Scholes formula for the price of a put option is

$$P_{BS}(q_Z, K, \sigma, t, r) = Ke^{-rt}N(-d_2) - q_Z N(-d_1) \qquad (21.13)$$

The equilibrium price of a put option can be obtained in the same manner as that of a call option, with an analogous expression:

$$P_{eq} = [P_{BS}(q_Z, K, \sigma, t, r_1) + P_{BS}(q_Z, K, \sigma, t, r_2)]/2 \qquad (21.14)$$

Figures 21.4 and 21.5 are the counterparts to Figures 21.2 and 21.3.

21.4 Smile Patterns

Consider what happens when, for an interval of exercise prices, we infer the implied Black–Scholes volatilities from the equilibrium prices of options. To do so, we solve

$$C_{BS}(4.00, K, \sigma, 1, r) = C_{eq} \qquad (21.15)$$

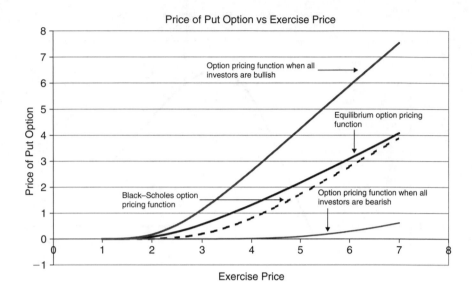

FIGURE 21.4. This figure shows how four put option prices discussed in the continuous time example vary as a function of K.

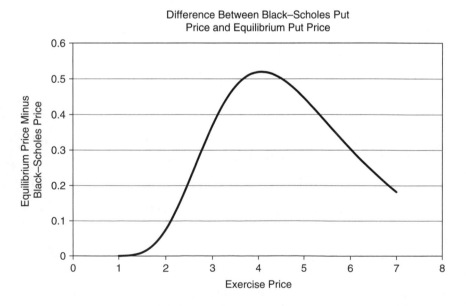

FIGURE 21.5. This figure shows how the difference between the equilibrium put option price and Black–Scholes price varies as a function of the exercise price K.

and

$$P_{BS}(4.00, K, \sigma, 1, r) = P_{eq} \qquad (21.16)$$

for σ as implicit functions of K, to obtain the implied volatility function (IVF). In equations (21.15) and (21.16), r is the equilibrium rate $r = -(\ln(e^{-r_1} + e^{-r_2}))$.

Consider a group of call options, on the S&P 500, which have different exercise prices but expire on the same date. For any specific date, the implied volatility graph has the exercise price on its horizontal axis and the Black–Scholes implied volatility on its vertical axis. Before the stock market crash that took place in October 1987, the graph of the implied volatility function (IVF) resembled the letter U. For that reason, the associated pattern came to be called a smile. After October 1987, the shape of the implied volatility function changed, and its predominant shape was to be downward sloping.

Figure 21.6 illustrates the shape of the theoretical implied volatility functions (IVFs) associated with the implicit functions just described. Notice several features about the volatility patterns. First, the IVF is not flat. Although Figure 21.6 illustrates neither the "U-shape" that led to the term

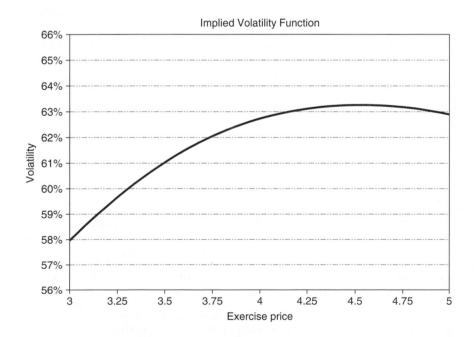

FIGURE 21.6. This figure illustrates the shape of the theoretical implied volatility function (IVF) in the example.

"smile," nor the downward-sloping pattern that emerged empirically after 1987, a smile is now generally understood to mean not flat. In a world where Black–Scholes holds, both curves would coincide with one another and be flat. Second, the implied volatility lies above the actual volatility for most of the range, including the case when options are at-the-money.

The above discussion describes how smile patterns can emerge in an equilibrium model with sentiment. This approach to option smiles is not traditional. The traditional approach involves specifying reduced form models involving stochastic processes for the underlying asset, volatility, and perhaps the interest rate. These models feature a combination of stochastic volatility and jump processes.[8]

21.4.1 Downward-Sloping Smile Patterns in the IVF Function

Although the smile pattern in the preceding discussion is upward sloping, empirical smile patterns tend to be downward sloping. Downward-sloping smile patterns emerge in the model generating the oscillating SDF in Figure 1.1. That model features three investors who disagree about the values of both first and second moments. In particular, pessimists overestimate volatility and underestimate expected returns, while optimists underestimate volatility and overestimate expected returns.

As in the example developed in Subsection 21.3.2, equilibrium option prices are wealth-weighted convex combinations of Black–Scholes functions. However, unlike the example in Section 21.3.2, the Black–Scholes functions here have different volatility arguments.[9] Specifically, the equilibrium call option pricing equation is the wealth-weighted convex combination

$$C_{eq} = \sum_{j=1}^{J} w_j C_{BS}(q_Z, K, \sigma_j, t, r_j) \qquad (21.17)$$

---

[8] For instance, Emmanuel and MacBeth (1982) use a constant elasticity of variance (CEV) model to explain the cross-sectional distribution of stock option prices, but conclude that out of sample, CEV does no better than the Black–Scholes model. Similar remarks apply to the implied binomial tree framework of Dupire (1994), Derman and Kani (1994), and Rubinstein (1994), which while flexible, has been shown by Dumas, Fleming, and Whaley (1998) to exhibit highly unstable parameters. Jump processes have been added to diffusion models: work by Jorion (1989), Bakshi, Cao, and Chen (1997), Bates (2000), Anderson, Benzoni, and Lund (2002), indicates that randomly arriving jumps are required to capture the time-series dynamics of index returns.

[9] The conditions for Black–Scholes do not require that stock prices evolve according to a Brownian motion diffusion process. Black–Scholes can hold in a discrete time model, as long as returns are log-normally distributed.

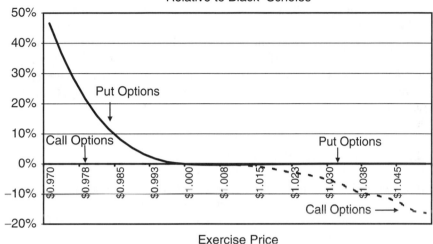

FIGURE 21.7. This figure illustrates the shape of the theoretical implied volatility functions (IVFs) for the oscillating SDF example depicted in Figure 1.1.

where $J = 3$. In this regard, it is the volatility arguments, more than the interest rate arguments, which are paramount.

Figure 21.7 displays the associated downward-sloping smile patterns for this example. The values of the vertical axis are the perceived errors in equilibrium option prices relative to their theoretical Black–Scholes counterparts: Here volatility in the Black–Scholes equation is associated with the representative investor's probability density function. The downward-sloping portion for put options in Figure 21.7 reflects the fact that pessimists overestimate future volatility. Likewise, the downward-sloping portion for call options in Figure 21.7 reflects the fact that optimists underestimate future volatility.[10] In the weighted average of three Black–Scholes functions in the example, the overestimate of volatility associated with pessimists dominates prices of out-of-the-money puts, and the underestimate of volatility associated with optimists dominates

---

[10] The IVF has a similar shape. For example, 50 percent overpricing of a put option relative to Black–Scholes corresponds to a 3 percent volatility premium, meaning that the IVF is 1.03 times the representative investor's volatility estimate. The function relating the equilibrium Black–Scholes percentage price difference to the IVF is generally an increasing, concave function. Graphs depicting the IVF are interesting, but do not display the extent of mispricing as effectively as does Figure 21.7. As in the example developed in Subsection 21.3.2, when prices are efficient, equilibrium option prices are given by the Black–Scholes formula.

prices of out-of-the-money calls. Notice that prices of neither deep in-the-money put options nor deep in-the-money call options substantially reflect the oscillating mispricing pattern associated with Figure 1.1. Rather, these oscillations are smoothed when viewed from the extreme right (put options) and extreme left (call options). In the weighted-average function, the various volatility biases effectively offset each other. The file *Chapter 21 Example.xls* develops the computations for a discrete time example, although Theorem 21.2 can be used to extend the example to continuous time.

21.5   Heterogeneous Risk Tolerance

Benninga and Mayshar (2000) explain that heterogeneous risk tolerance can be a cause of smile patterns in the IVF. Heterogeneous risk tolerance gives rise to smile patterns in the IVF through variation in the function $\gamma_R(x_t)$. The source of variation in γ_R stems from the manner in which the consumption share $\theta_j(x_t)$ varies across x_t in forming the convex combination $\sum_j \theta_j(x_t)1/\gamma_j$ to obtain $1/\gamma_R(x_t)$. Figure 14.3 depicts a typical $\gamma_R(x_t)$ function.

In contrast, when investors share the same risk tolerance parameter, as in the example just discussed, then $\gamma_R(x_t) = \gamma_j$ and so is constant across x_t. When investors share the same beliefs, homogeneous risk tolerance leads the IVF to be flat in the example.

The evidence presented in Chapter 13 indicates that investors exhibit heterogeneous risk tolerance. The evidence presented in Chapters 6 and 7 indicates that investors exhibit heterogeneous beliefs. Therefore, there is reason to suspect that both sources of heterogeneity contribute to smile patterns in the IVF. Indeed, the option pricing expression developed in Theorems 21.1 and 21.2 reflect both heterogeneous beliefs and heterogeneous risk tolerance.

Is one source of heterogeneity likely to be more important than the other? The empirical evidence presented in Chapters 6, 7, 13, and 15 suggests that the risk tolerance distribution is more stable than the distributions associated with investor beliefs. In addition, the analysis in Section 14.5 suggests that the risk tolerance function $1/\gamma_R(x_t)$ is relatively stable. See Figure 14.3 in this regard. Other examples support this general conclusion.[11]

---

[11] Consider an example where investors' risk tolerance parameters lie between 0.2 and 1, and there are four investors, with wealth divided evenly. In this example, it turns out that for fixed t, γ_R varies from 0.48 to 0.52, as consumption growth rate varies from 0.95 to 1.06.

Because of wealth shifts stemming from trading, the conditional one-period function γ_R may vary over time. For instance, suppose that wealth is initially concentrated in the hands of the investor with the lowest risk tolerance parameter, but over time he loses his wealth to the investor with the highest risk tolerance. Then over time, the conditional $1/\gamma_R$ function will move from the region around the lowest risk tolerance parameter to that around the highest. Notice that this intertemporal instability in conditional $1/\gamma_R$ contrasts with the stability of the $1/\gamma_R$ function for fixed t that generates smile effects in the SDF.

21.6 Pitfall: Equation (21.12) Is False

In the continuous time example presented in Subsection 21.3.2, the equilibrium call option price (21.12) is a convex combination of Black–Scholes functions associated with different interest rates. An analogous relation holds for put options. The example demonstrates the case of a behavioral Black–Scholes equation giving rise to option volatility smiles.

Past readers of this work have argued that the example can hold only when $r_1 = r_2$ so that the interest rate arguments in (21.12) and (21.14) are the same. Otherwise, they claim, equilibrium option prices will violate the put-call parity condition

$$C = S - e^{-rt}K + P \tag{21.18}$$

where C is the price of the call option, S is the price of the underlying stock, r is the continuous compounding risk-free rate of interest, t is the time to expiration, K is the exercise price, and P is the price of the put option.

Recall that r_j refers to the equilibrium rate of interest when all investors share the beliefs of investor j. The subscript BS denotes Black–Scholes. Put-call parity implies

$$C_{BS}(S, K, \sigma, t, r_1) = S - e^{-rt}K + P_{BS}(S, K, \sigma, t, r_1) \tag{21.19}$$

and

$$C_{BS}(S, K, \sigma, t, r_2) = S - e^{-rt}K + P_{BS}(S, K, \sigma, t, r_2) \tag{21.20}$$

Assuming equal weights ($w_j = 0.5$), form one half of the sum of (21.19) and (21.20). This convex combination is equal to

$$S - [e^{-r_1 t} + e^{-r_2 t}]K/2 + [P_{BS}(S, K, \sigma, t, r_1) + P_{BS}(S, K, \sigma, t, r_2)]/2$$

$$(21.21)$$

Taken together, equations (21.18) and (21.21) imply that

$$e^{-r_t t} = [e^{-r_1 t} + e^{-r_2 t}]/2 \qquad (21.22)$$

for all t.

There are two possibilities. First, equation (21.22) is false. In this case, by (21.21), put-call parity is violated. Second, equation (21.22) is true. In this case, there is no arbitrage opportunity, and $r_1 = r_2$.

21.6.1   Locating the Flaw

Put-call parity holds in the behavioral Black–Scholes example whether or not $r_1 = r_2$. Moreover, it is easy to see that this is the case. Consider (21.22), the condition that is necessary and sufficient for put-call parity. Notice that this condition stipulates that bond prices in the heterogeneous beliefs model be convex combinations of the bond prices that would prevail in models featuring homogeneous beliefs. However, this property is automatically implied by the convex-combination property for state prices that holds in the example.

21.7   Pitfall: Beliefs Do Not Matter in Black–Scholes

The setting in this book is discrete time, not continuous time. However, the setting for Black–Scholes theory is continuous time. Past readers have argued that effects that arise in discrete time models, such as volatility smiles in option prices, effectively disappear through the magic of continuous time.

Recall that in the standard Black–Scholes model, option prices are independent of the true mean μ of the underlying security. In this respect, assume that the process B for the risk-free asset satisfies

$$\frac{dB}{B} = rdt \qquad (21.23)$$

Suppose that the investors agree on the risk-free asset process, and agree on the volatility of the risky asset, but disagree on the drift term for the risky asset. That is, let investor 1 believe that the stock price S obeys the process

$$\frac{dS}{S} = \mu_1 dt + \sigma dZ \qquad (21.24)$$

where Z is a Wiener process. Let investor 2 believe that the stock price S obeys the process

$$\frac{dS}{S} = \mu_2 dt + \sigma dZ \qquad (21.25)$$

How will options be priced in this framework? They will be priced according to Black–Scholes. Therefore, heterogeneity will not impact option prices, and will not give rise to volatility smiles.

21.7.1   Locating the Flaw

The magic of continuous time does not prevent heterogeneous beliefs from creating volatility smiles in the IVF. The preceding argument implicitly assumes that interest rates are time invariant. However, in the continuous time example presented in Subsection 21.3.2, heterogeneous beliefs cause interest rates to be stochastic, and that is sufficient to generate volatility smiles in the IVF.

21.8   Summary

The present chapter presented some general pricing expressions for options. These options serve to identify how investor beliefs affect option prices in equilibrium. In particular, the expressions make clear the manner in which sentiment is manifest in option prices.

The chapter also developed an example to illustrate a behavioral counterpart to the Black–Scholes formula. Although simple, the example develops a closed-form solution for a behavioral version of Black–Scholes, and illustrates that option smiles are a feature of the behavioral framework. Both heterogeneous beliefs and heterogeneous risk tolerance can interfere with options being priced by the Black–Scholes formula. However, the impact of heterogeneous beliefs has the propensity to be more severe for short horizons.

22
Irrational Exuberance and Option Smiles

The previous chapter describes how sentiment can induce smile patterns in the *implied volatility functions* (IVFs) associated with option prices. The present chapter is the first part of a two-part discussion about smile patterns in practice. The chapter is based on a study of index option prices done in late 1996.[1] The original intention of the study was to conduct an exploratory investigation into the connection between option smiles and sentiment. For present purposes, the study will serve to introduce a body of work to be discussed in the next chapter.

This chapter discusses the impact of "irrational exuberance" on smile patterns in the IVF for index options. An argument is advanced that index option smiles can be understood in terms of heterogeneous beliefs, in that underconfident pessimistic investors predominantly affect the prices of out-of-the-money puts, and overconfident optimistic investors predominantly affect the prices of out-of-the-money calls. Recall that Chapters 6 and 7 suggested that the beliefs of most professional investors exhibit gambler's fallacy, while the beliefs of most individual investors exhibit extrapolation bias.

The previous paragraph makes mention of underconfident pessimists and overconfident optimists. Recall that the sentiment function displayed

---

[1] See Shefrin (1999).

in Figure 15.8 is based on a market featuring both underconfident pessimists and overconfident optimists. In this regard, Section 21.4 of Chapter 21 makes the point that heterogeneous beliefs about volatility, meaning second moments, are a critical component of option smile patterns. This property is reflected in equation (21.17), the behavioral Black–Scholes formula. For this reason, the discussion about optimism and pessimism in this chapter is to be understood as a discussion about the impact of overconfident optimistic investors and underconfident pessimistic investors.

The present chapter also suggests that prices as a whole appeared to permit arbitrage profits. Recall that the absence of pure arbitrage profits is the weakest form of market efficiency. In previous chapters, equilibrium was assumed to exclude the possibility of arbitrage profits. The present chapter presents evidence suggesting that because of price pressure and sentiment, the no-arbitrage condition might intermittently fail.

22.1   Irrational Exuberance: Brief History

Figure 9.1 graphically illustrates the stock market bubble of the 1990s and its collapse in 2000. Five years before the bubble burst, Federal Reserve chair Alan Greenspan used the phrase "irrational exuberance" to warn that stocks were overpriced. Consider the events that led up to his pronouncement in December 1996.

Following a mere 1.3 percent gain in the S&P 500 during 1994, the index returned 34 percent in 1995 and 20 percent in 1996. Notably, stocks rose by about 7 percent in November 1996. As was mentioned in Chapter 5, professional economists predict reversals after three-year trends in the market, while individual investors tend to engage in naive extrapolation and predict continuation. This suggests that there would have been considerable heterogeneity in the beliefs of investors at the end of 1996, because the market had been rising dramatically for two years.

On December 3, 1996, John Campbell and Robert Shiller expressed their views about the market in joint testimony before the Board of Governors of the Federal Reserve System. See Campbell and Shiller (1998). Campbell and Shiller explained that historically, when the dividend yield has been low and the price-to-earnings ratio (P/E) has been high, the return to holding stocks over the subsequent 10 years has tended to be low. The earnings yield is just E/P, the inverse of P/E. In a rationally priced market, dividend yields and earnings yields form the basis of stock returns, along with interest rates, inflation, and tolerance for risk. The future course of earnings and dividends would have to be dramatically better than the past in order to rationalize high subsequent stock returns in a low D/P and E/P environment. Shiller and Campbell predicted that

Price Earnings Ratio Predicting Subsequent 10 Year Real Returns
Annual January Data, 1881–1990 (1891–2000 Returns)

FIGURE 22.1. This figure shows the relationship between the price earnings ratio and subsequent 10-year real returns.

over the subsequent 10-year period, stocks would lose almost half their real value.

Figure 22.1 displays the Campbell–Shiller relationship between the price/earnings ratio and subsequent 10-year real returns for stocks making up the S&P 500 index. The data are annual, for the time periods 1881–1990 for P/E ratios and 1891–2000 for returns.[2]

On December 5, 1996, two days after Campbell and Shiller's testimony, Federal Reserve chair Alan Greenspan delivered a speech at the American Enterprise Institute where he used the phrase "irrational exuberance" in connection with security prices. This phrase evokes the notion of investors naively extrapolating a recent trend and predicting continuation. Greenspan's remark induced an immediate decline on global equity markets. The excerpt from his speech below is the portion where he talked about "irrational exuberance."

> Clearly, sustained low inflation implies less uncertainty about the future, and lower risk premiums imply higher prices of stocks and other earning assets. We can see that in the inverse relationship exhibited by price/earnings ratios and the rate of inflation in the past.
>
> But how do we know when irrational exuberance has unduly escalated asset values, which then become subject to unexpected and prolonged contractions as they have in Japan over the past decade? And how do we factor that assessment into monetary policy?

---

[2] I thank Robert Shiller for providing this figure.

22.1.1   Sentiment

"Irrational exuberance" is one aspect of sentiment, in that it suggests investors' naively extrapolating the upward market trend into the future.[3] How can we tell if this was the case? Are there any direct measures of investors' predictions, as opposed to the indirect measure contained in market prices?

There are many measures of sentiment. Two of the most prominent are the advisory sentiment index reported in *Investor's Intelligence* (II), and the sentiment index compiled by the American Association of Individual Investors (AAII). The II index is compiled by Chartcraft, Inc., based on stock market newsletters. In the II system, advisor opinion falls into one of three groups: (1) bullish, (2) bearish, or (3) correction. *Investor's Intelligence* reports the percentage of advisors that fall into each group on a weekly basis. The II sentiment index is the ratio of the bullish percentage to the sum of the bullish and bearish percentages. The AAII index was described in Chapters 5 and 6. Based on surveys of individual investors, the AAII is similar to the II, except that the former uses a neutral category instead of a correction category.

These two indicators are published on a weekly basis in *Barron's*, and historical data are available from *Investor's Intelligence* and the AAII. Clarke and Statman (1997) report that the II index experienced a permanent downward shift after the stock market crash of 1987. Therefore, the discussion focuses on the period after December 1987.[4] Figure 22.2 depicts the path of four time series discussed in this section: the S&P 500 index and three sentiment indicators, the II, AAII, and call-put ratio (CPR).

What can we learn from the manner in which the first two sentiment indicators changed during the weeks leading up to December 5, 1996? Were there indications that investors were irrationally exuberant? The index climbed steadily from the end of October through the beginning of December, beginning at a level of 54 percent, peaking at 66 percent at the end of November, and ending the period at 63 percent, just prior to Greenspan's announcement.[5] At its maximum, the index was 1.53 standard

---

[3] Investor exuberance has been an issue of longstanding concern to Alan Greenspan. In 1958, the return to the S&P 500 was a remarkable 43 percent. In the March 1959 issue of *Fortune* magazine, when Greenspan was a consulting economist, he expressed concern about investors' "over exuberance." On August 27, 1999, in a speech to a conference of international central bankers in Jackson Hole, Wyoming, Greenspan described the "extraordinary increase in stock prices over the last five years" as "inexplicable."

[4] Data on the II index runs from June 1969 through October 1997. The AAII series begins in July 1987. I thank Meir Statman for kindly sharing some of his historical data on the two series with me.

[5] Notably, the percentage of bulls began the month below 50 percent (at 45 percent) and ended the month at 56 percent.

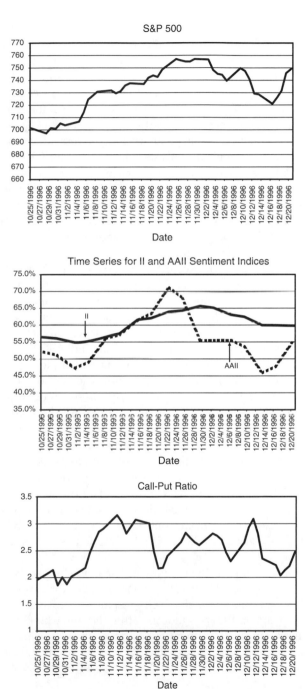

FIGURE 22.2. This figure depicts the path of four time series discussed in this section.

deviations above its 10-year mean of 52 percent. The week after the announcement, the index fell below 60 percent. The AAII index followed a similar trajectory. It rose from 47 percent at the beginning of November to a peak of 71 percent on November 22. It stood at 56 percent at the time of Greenspan's announcement, and fell to 46 percent a week later.

Option markets also provide information to gauge market sentiment. The call-put ratio is defined as the ratio of open daily call option volume to open daily put option volume, aggregated across all exchange-traded options in the U.S. Technical analysts who follow the CPR suggest that when investors become more optimistic, option traders increase their holding of call options relative to put options. Hence, an abnormally high reading of this index signals optimistic sentiment. See Mayers (1989, 1994). Data on the daily values of the call-put ratio for the period January 1995 through August 1999 were obtained from Bridge Information Systems, Inc.[6]

The call-put ratio tells a slightly different story than the II and AAII. Although the CPR also rose during the first part of November, it then peaked and began to meander and decline. At the beginning of November it stood at 2.0, rising to a maximum of 3.15 on November 11. After that it declined, rose, and declined again, essentially drifting down to 2.6 on December 5. The day after the announcement, it fell further to 2.3. For the month of November 1996 the mean value of the index was 2.67, 0.93 standard deviations above 2.24, its mean for the entire sample. At its November peak, the call-put ratio was 1.93 standard deviations above the mean.

Taken together, the evidence indicates the presence of substantial heterogeneity during November and December 1996. As the market soared in November, the predominant prediction of newsletter writers and individual investors was for continuation. But there was a substantial group predicting reversal. Even when the bullish sentiment index peaked, 44 percent of all advisors were either bearish or predicting a correction. Moreover, the call-put ratio drifted downward from November 11 on, meaning that option traders were moving into puts. This suggests that some option traders were changing their predictions from continuation to reversal. Still, between November 11 and December 6, the CPR never fell as far as its mean over the sample period.

Section 18.4 of Chapter 18 includes a discussion of the Baker-Wurgler sentiment index. Figure 22.3 displays the time series for this index between January 1995, 23 months before Greenspan's "irrational exuberance" remark and December 1997, 13 months after the remark. The figure shows that the Baker-Wurgler sentiment index trended up during 1996, reaching a peak at the end of October 1996. The index declined slightly during November, and fell dramatically in December after Greenspan's speech.

---

[6] Unless otherwise indicated, securities data and prices furnished herein are provided by Bridge Information Systems, Inc.

FIGURE 22.3. Time series of Baker-Wurgler sentiment measure, January 1995–December 1997. The figure shows that the Baker-Wurgler sentiment index trended up during 1996, reaching a peak at the end of October 1996. The index declined slightly during November, and fell dramatically in December after Greenspan's speech. It then drifted downward in 1997. Data downloaded from <http://www.stern.nyu.edu/~jwurgler>.

It then drifted downward in 1997. Hence, the Baker-Wurgler series supports the general perspective provided by the II and AAII series. Between January 1985 and December 1996, the correlation between the II series and Baker-Wurgler series was 41 percent. For the AAII series and Baker-Wurgler series, the correlation was 29 percent. For the call-put ratio and Baker-Wurgler series, the correlation was 19 percent.

As an aside, I should mention that between 1997 and 2005, the correlation between the call-put ratio and Baker-Wurgler series rose to 27 percent. However, this masks an interesting phenomenon. From 2001 to 2005, the correlation was 37 percent. Notably, during the bubble period, January 1999 through March 2001, the correlation was −81 percent. During the bubble period the sentiment of option traders appears to have been extremely bearish. This divergence points to clustered opinions in the tails of investors' return expectations, consistent with the evidence reported in Chapters 6 and 7.

Notably, Baker and Wurgler (2007) note that when sentiment has been high, subsequent market returns have been low. They report that market crashes tend to occur within periods of high sentiment, but emphasize that the timing of such crashes within these periods is difficult to predict. This remark definitely applies to the speculative period in the second half of the 1990s and 2000. Greenspan made his "irrational exuberance" comment in December 1996, yet the bubble did not burst until the turn-of-the century.

22.2   Risk-Neutral Densities and Index Option Prices

Next consider how the heterogeneity in beliefs manifested itself within the prices of index options, implied volatilities, and risk-neutral densities.

The SPX options on the S&P 500 index are traded on the Chicago Board Options Exchange (CBOE). Each contract is for 250 times the value of the index, so these options are mainly traded by institutional investors. The December 1996 options are of particular interest, because they expired about two weeks after Greenspan's "irrational exuberance" remark. This section describes how estimates for the risk-neutral densities can be derived from the prices of these options.

Using Bridge Information Systems, daily data were obtained that permitted estimation of the time series of risk-neutral probabilities for all S&P 500 index options traded from June through December of 1996. For each listed S&P 500 index option, data obtained included the price of the last trade, date and time of last trade, bid price, ask price, trading volume, closing price of the S&P 500 index, and prevailing three-month Treasury bill rate.

Risk-neutral probabilities were estimated using a conventional butterfly position technique.[7] This technique exploits the fact that risk-neutral probabilities are future values of contingent dollar claims, a point made in Chapter 21.[8] To understand why this is so, consider an example using index options that expired in December 1996. Imagine that the current date is November 1, 1996. Let S denote the closing value of the S&P 500 index on December 20, 1996, the expiration date for the December options. Consider three events: $A_L = \{S < 652.5\}$, $A_M = \{652.5 \leq S \leq 657.5\}$, and $A_U = \{S > 657.5\}$. Imagine a security that promises to pay \$1 on December 20, if and only if A_M occurs. Imagine that this security was traded on November 1. The November 1 price of this security is the present value of a December 20 A_M-contingent dollar. Analogously, one may speak of

---

[7] This is a low-tech approach to estimating risk-neutral probability density functions. Much more powerful techniques exist, but the low-tech approach suits the purpose of the exercise. Indeed, some SPX traders also use the butterfly technique to infer risk-neutral probabilities, but smooth the output. I am grateful to SPX options trader Chris Bernard for discussions on this point.

[8] See the proof of Theorem 21.1.

the present value of an A_L-contingent dollar and the present value of an A_U-contingent dollar.

Consider an investor who, on November 1, purchased a package consisting of one unit of each of the preceding three securities. This package would guarantee the investor a one-dollar payoff on December 20. On November 1, the future value of a December 20 dollar is clearly one dollar. Consider the future value of each of the three constituent pieces of the package. The future value of each of these securities is nonnegative, and less than or equal to unity. Moreover, the sum of the three future values must equal unity. Therefore, the three future values have the same properties as probabilities. In fact, they are probabilities, risk-neutral probabilities in particular.

The November 1 price of the three-security package is simply the present value of a December 20 risk-free dollar. If the risk-free rate is 5 percent then, since there are 49 days from November 1 to December 20, the present value of this dollar would be $1.05^{-49/365}$, or \$0.9935. In fact, to obtain the present value of any of the three securities from its future value, one would simply multiply its future value by 0.9935. To obtain the future value from the present value, multiply by the inverse of this figure, 1.0066.

22.2.1 Butterfly Position Technique

Option prices are present values, not future values. However, it was not possible to purchase an A_M security on November 1. At the same time, one can use option prices to estimate the present value of a security that pays one December 20 dollar if event A_M occurs. To do this, form a butterfly position that has almost the same present value; see Breeden and Litzenberger (1978). Suppose that the date is November 1. On this date, the exercise prices of SPX options that were available for trade ranged from 650 to 775.[9] To form the butterfly position, simultaneously purchase one 660 call and one 650 call, and sell two 655 calls. The payoff pattern for this butterfly position is depicted in Figure 22.4. It has the form of the Greek letter Λ, so call the payoff function of this position Λ_B.

Figure 22.4 also depicts the payoff function to a position in which 5 units of the fictitious A_M security are held. Notice that the area under the A_M security is equal to the area under the Λ_B butterfly payoff. Moreover, the two functions have a considerable amount of overlap. This is what enables us to approximate the value of an A_M security with a corresponding butterfly position.

---

[9] Note that options on the S&P 500 index, with exercise prices below 650 and above 775, were also traded, albeit thinly. These are coded by Bridge as SPB, SPZ, and so on. For the sake of this exercise, concentrate on the SPX options alone, since the index stayed well within the range of SPX exercise prices during the time period studied.

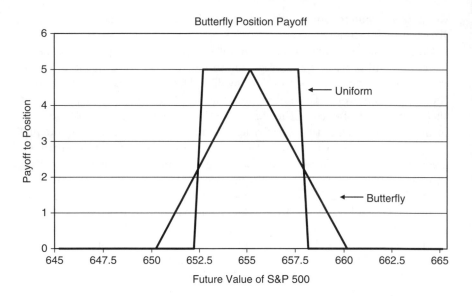

FIGURE 22.4. This figure illustrates the butterfly technique, depicting the payoff function to a position in which 5 units of the fictitious A_M-security are held. Notice that the area under the A_M-security is equal to the area under Λ_B-butterfly payoff.

Think of the risk-neutral probabilities as a density function defined over possible future values of S, the closing value of the S&P 500 on December 20. Option pricing theory tells us that to obtain the future value of any security, we would integrate its payoff function with respect to the risk-neutral density function. Given the extent of overlap between the A_M position and that of the butterfly, we anticipate that for well-behaved risk-neutral density functions, the value of the butterfly position will provide a reasonable approximation to the value of the A_M position.

The previous discussion tells us that the value of five A_M securities is approximately the same as the butterfly position. Now the value of the November 1 butterfly is just the sum of the ask prices for the two long calls minus twice the bid price of the shorted call. This can be written

$$\nu_{\Lambda_B} = ASK_{650} - 2BID_{655} + ASK_{660} \tag{22.1}$$

To remove transaction costs, we can use the bid-ask midpoint in place of the bid and ask prices, to obtain

$$\nu_{\Lambda_B} = 0.5(ASK_{650} + BID_{650}) - (ASK_{655} + BID_{655})$$
$$+ 0.5(ASK_{660} + BID_{660}) \tag{22.2}$$

To obtain an approximate present value for the lower- and upper-bound contingencies, A_L and A_M, we would use a similar procedure. However, instead of a butterfly position, we would use a spread position. For example, the present value of the A_L security is approximated using a position formed from a long December 655 put and a short December 650 put.

The smallest increment in the exercise prices for traded S&P 500 index options is 5. During November and December, the exercise prices for SPX December options ranged from 650 to 775 in increments of 5.[10] Using the procedure described above enables us to estimate the risk-neutral probabilities associated with the events $\{S < 652.5\}$, $\{652.5 \le S \le 657.5\}$, $\{657.5 \le S \le 662.5\},\ldots,\{S > 772.5\}$. Simply compute the present value of the option positions using (22.2), divide by 5, and convert the present values to future values.

There are two points to note about implementing this procedure in practice. First, in theory the present values associated with the events $\{S < 652.5\}$, $\{652.5 \le S \le 657.5\}$, $\{657.5 \le S \le 662.5\},\ldots,\{S > 772.5\}$ should sum to the risk-free discount factor. In practice they do not, so, to transform the present values to future values, normalize the present values by dividing by their actual sum. The estimated future values are then taken to be the normalized present values. Second, the identical butterfly position can be formed with put options instead of calls; one might expect that the call-based butterfly and put-based butterfly should have roughly the same market value, but note that this is not always the case.

22.3   Continuation, Reversal, and Option Prices

Consider next how index option prices reflected the degree of heterogeneity during November and December 1996. Keep in mind that the S&P 500 steadily increased during November, climbing from 703 to 757. Begin by looking at the volatility charts, Figures 22.5 and 22.6. These figures describe the volatilities for call and put options respectively, based on the ask prices. The strength of the smile effect indicates the strength with which traders hold their beliefs. During an up-trend, if bulls become even more bullish and bears become even more bearish in respect to both first and second-moments, the smile effect will intensify. That is, implied volatility patterns reflect sentiment.

Consider six dates during this period, spaced roughly one week apart. Look at what happened to the smile pattern as November progressed. The

---

[10] These were for options that Bridge specifically designated by the symbol SPX. Bridge used other symbols for options on the S&P 500 that were less frequently traded.

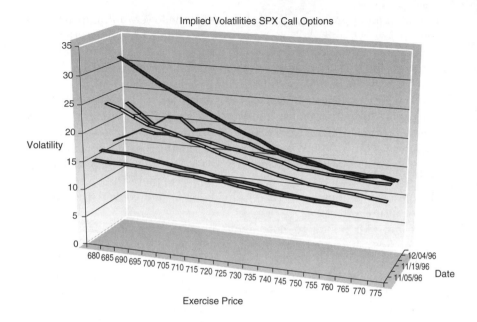

FIGURE 22.5. This figure describes the implied volatilities (IVF) for call options, based on the ask prices during the sample period.

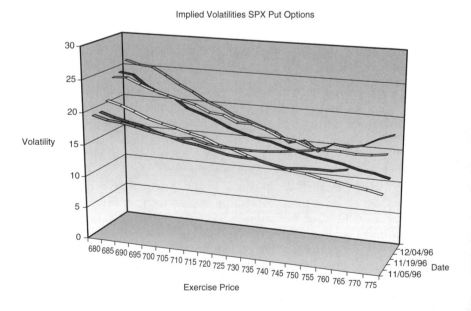

FIGURE 22.6. This figure describes the implied volatilities (IVF) for put options, based on the ask prices during the sample period.

smile pattern did intensify, especially at the lower exercise prices. The most dramatic departure from a horizontal pattern occurred just prior to Greenspan's December 5 remark. This pattern suggests that the bears, those predicting reversal, became much more bearish as November progressed. As for at-the-money (put-implied) volatility, it varied between 13.3 and 17.3 during November, and moved to 15.4 on December 4.

The risk-neutral densities tell a similar story, though more quantitatively, and with additional complexity. In option pricing theory, the risk-neutral expected return to the S&P 500 is always the risk-free rate. What does this imply about the expected value of the index with respect to the risk-neutral probabilities? To answer this question, suppose that the S&P 500 paid no dividends. Imagine that on November 1 we were to invest the value of the S&P 500 in Treasury bills. Then, expected value under the risk-neutral density would simply be the value of this position on December 20. However, since the S&P 500 does pay dividends, we need to adjust the expectation to take into account that the December 20 value of the index will be ex dividend.

By applying the butterfly approximation technique to the daily option price data, obtain a daily series for the risk-neutral probabilities associated with the December expiration date. Consider the expected value of the index with respect to these probabilities.[11] For the moment, do not adjust for dividends. Suppose we were to plot this expected value series, together with the future December 20 value of the daily S&P 500 index. Then, one would expect that the expected value series would lie below the S&P 500 series, with the magnitude of the difference being the accumulated dividend payments.

Figure 22.7 portrays three series. One series is the value of the December S&P 500 futures contract. The second series provides the future values for the S&P 500 index on the expiration date of the December SPX options. The third series is the risk-neutral expected value of the index, when the risk-neutral probabilities are obtained by averaging the values of call-based butterfly positions with put-based butterfly positions. In theory, the futures price series and expected value series should be the same, but the future value series should be somewhat different because of dividends.

In practice, all three differ. There are several reasons why this is the case. These reasons stem from the approximation described in Figure 22.4, bid-ask price considerations, and call-put disparity issues. One reason involves the fact that equity markets close in New York 15 minutes earlier

---

[11] Since we only have a step function approximation to the density function, use the standard step function summation technique to approximate the integral.

FIGURE 22.7. This figure displays the time series of the December S&P 500 futures contract, the future values for the S&P 500 index, and the expected value of the S&P 500 under the risk-neutral measure, between October 21, 1996 and December 11, 1996.

than do option markets in Chicago.[12] Therefore, it is better to use the price of the S&P futures contract, since that market closes at the same time as the options market. Use of the futures price also avoids the computations associated with dividend payouts and interest rate adjustments.

From June 1996 to October 1996, the future value of the S&P 500 and expected value of the index were typically within a half percent of one another. But this changed during November, when the expected value series fell below the other two series by between 2 and 3 percent.

Consider the portion of Figure 22.7 that portrays the two weeks prior to December 5. Notably, the expected value of the index fell well below

---

[12] Although arbitrage does enforce a link between the cash market and the options, up to 3:00 P.M. CST, when the cash market closes in New York, the options market does not close until 3:15. Therefore, for 15 minutes there is no link between the cash market and the options market. For this reason one also wants to use the price of the S&P 500 futures contract, which trades until 3:15 P.M.; it has a much smaller bid-offer differential. I thank SPX trader Rick Angell for pointing this out. He also mentioned that the S&P 500 futures market responds more quickly to changes in sentiment than the cash market.

the future value during this period. On November 20, the closing value of the S&P 500 was 743.95, and the Treasury bill rate was 5.15 percent. An investment of $743.95 at 5.15 percent would have earned $3.07 from November 20 through December 20, the date the December options expired. Hence, the future value of the index was $747.02. The closing price for the December futures contract was $746.15. On November 20, the expected risk-neutral value of the December 20 S&P 500 was 734.73. The difference between the November 20 value of the S&P 500 and the risk-neutral expected December 20 value was 12.30. In theory, this difference would need to be accounted for by dividend payouts. However, the difference was much larger than the dividend payouts of stocks in the S&P 500 during the fourth quarter of 1996. Bridge Information Systems reports that for the fourth quarter, dividends on the S&P 500 were 3.79. The discrepancy in respect to the futures price and future value of the index is even greater.

Notably, the difference between the actual value of the S&P 500 and the expected value under the risk-neutral probabilities rose to a maximum of 27.36 on November 25, and declined to 6.19 on December 5. Greenspan's remark came on the evening of December 5, after U.S. markets had closed. On December 6, the difference fell to 4.28.

It is worth noting that during this period, the probabilities derived from calls were markedly different from the probabilities derived from puts. The put values led to a much lower expected value between November 25 and December 5.[13] During this period the expected value implied by call options was about 10 less than the index, whereas the expected value implied by put options was 30 less than the index. Although it is common for put volatilities to be higher than call volatilities, the magnitude of the difference was unusual. On November 26 and 27, the difference between call-based expected values and put-based expected values peaked, rising more than 3.5 standard deviations from its historic mean of 0.26 percent.[14] That difference did not retreat to within a single standard deviation until December 2. Figure 22.8 displays the volatility view of this phenomenon, showing the difference between call and put volatilities for the December SPX options, on November 27.[15]

---

[13] Note that November SPX options expired on November 16, well before this particular episode.

[14] This variable is computed by subtracting the put-based expected value from the call-based expected value, and dividing the difference by the average of the two expected values.

[15] As a result, the value of Bates' (1991) implicit skewness factor $SK(x)$ (crash premium) is positive for options that are ITM by an amount of 5. In this case, the value of Bates $1 + x$, the ratio of the call premium to the index, is 1.0067. For most distributional hypotheses, $SK(x) = x$. However, here $SK(x) = 0.056$, which is clearly larger than 0.0067.

FIGURE 22.8. This figure displays the volatility view of this phenomenon, showing the difference between call and put volatilities for the December SPX options, on November 27.

As was discussed in Chapter 10, trading volume reflects not disagreement per se, but *changes* in disagreement. In this respect, consider the relationship among overconfidence, prices, and volume during November 1996. In Subsection 22.1.1, evidence was presented that as the market soared in November, the predominant prediction of newsletter writers and individual investors was for continuation. In addition, the call-put ratio drifted downward from November 11 on, meaning that option traders were moving into puts. Notably, as these events unfolded, the volatility pattern for SPX options was *changing*. This change can clearly be seen in the left-hand side of Figures 22.5 and 22.6.

Theory predicts that both prices and volume reflect overconfidence. As the II and AAII sentiment indicators were peaking between November 22 and November 29, the gap between the actual value of the S&P 500 and the expected future value under the risk-neutral density reached its peak. Remember that the expected value associated with put options was much smaller than it was for calls. Was this feature reflected in trading volume? Yes indeed: Puts were much more actively traded than calls during this period. For example, on November 27 there were 3.65 times as many SPX puts traded as SPX calls, whereas on November 4 the corresponding figure was only 1.27. On November 27, the S&P traded between 753 and 757, closing at 755. Over 73 percent of the put options traded that day featured exercise prices at 730 or below.

22.4   Price Pressure: Was Arbitrage Fully Carried Out?

There is reason to suspect that smile effects reflect mispricing stemming from heterogeneous beliefs.[16] According to the efficient market view, the volatility smile simply reflects the fact that the underlying return distribution is not log-normal. Efficient market proponents would remind us that tests of efficiency are joint tests of both efficiency and an asset pricing model, such as Black–Scholes. Smile effects might lead to rejection of Black–Scholes, but not efficiency per se.

Is there a way to test whether smile effects could stem from mispricing, without specifying a specific underlying asset pricing theory? Indeed there is, by using the risk-neutral density to compute the expected value of the underlying asset at the expiration date of the option. The expected value should equal the futures value of the index. This test assumes nothing about log-normality. Rather, it is derived from the definition of the risk-neutral density, and arbitrage-based pricing. As was indicated in the previous section, the difference between the expected value series and futures value series grew quite large during the latter part of November 1996.

Figlewski (1997) notes that arbitrage is not always carried out. He points out that in many markets it is difficult to execute the required trades, and doing so is typically not as profitable as, but riskier than, a simple market-making strategy that reacts to market events, maximizes order flow, and earns the bid-ask spread (as a profit).

If the expected return to the index under the risk-neutral density does not equal the risk-free rate, then in theory arbitrage profits are possible. Here is an example of how those profits might have been earned. On November 27, the closing value of the index was 755. Consider the December 750 call option. This particular option was actively traded on that day and is slightly in-the-money (ITM). Since the expected value of the index under the risk-neutral density lay below the actual value of the index, this option may have been overpriced, in that too much weight was assigned to index values between 750 and 755.

The November 27 bid price on this option was $14.25 at the close, with the last trade having taken place at $14.75 that day. The bid volatility was 11.7, the ask volatility was 12.7, and the implied volatilities were roughly the same for exercise prices between 745 and 755. Consider a dynamic hedge, involving a short position in the December 750 call, and a long position in the index in the amount *delta*, financed by borrowing at the Treasury bill rate. Notably, this option was actively traded on November 27,

---

[16] In theory, arbitrage is supposed to prevent option prices from conveying sentiment, beyond that embodied in the S&P 500 index and interest rate.

with volume of 1043 contracts. Using daily *delta* values based on the ask volatilities displayed by Bridge, update the index position daily at the close of trade to the new value of *delta*.[17] At expiration, the hedge would have earned a theoretical profit of $2.87 per option, which is roughly 20 percent of the option premium.

The arbitrage issue is quite important. If assets are priced in accordance with an SDF, then no nonzero arbitrage profits are possible. To this point, the assumption has been that although market prices might deviate from fundamental values, investors were unable to earn arbitrage profits. The state of affairs just described raises the question of whether this assumption is valid. To be sure, there may have been transaction costs to take into account. If so, that might make clear that arbitrage profits could not be earned. However, even if so, it still might not be the case that assets were priced in accordance with an SDF.

22.5   Heterogeneous Beliefs

Chapters 6 and 7 described the reasons why individual investors are vulnerable to extrapolation bias and why professional investors are vulnerable to gambler's fallacy. The sentiment data presented in this chapter suggest that the views of individual investors and newsletter writers exhibited extrapolation bias in November 1996. The smile patterns in index options during November 1996 suggested that the views of professional investors exhibited gambler's fallacy in November 1996.

Consider Figure 22.9, which depicts the co-movement of II, AAII, and a rescaled value of the difference between the risk-neutral expected future value of the S&P 500 and its future value. Notice that as a general matter, the difference variable moves in the opposite direction from the II and AAII. This pattern suggests that SPX option traders act as if they view the II and AAII as contrarian indicators, at least in this case. However, what seems more likely is that SPX traders, being professional investors, succumbed to gambler's fallacy in the face of an uptrend in the market.

22.6   General Evidence on the Mispricing of Options

Consider how the discussion in this chapter relates to broader issues. In a world where options are priced in accordance with the Black–Scholes

---

[17]Although the computation does not involve an adjusted *delta* to reflect the expected dividend yield, such an adjustment does not alter the calculated values in a substantive way.

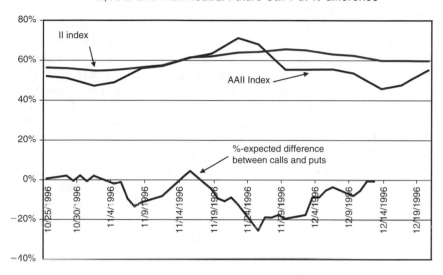

FIGURE 22.9. This figure displays the co-movement of II, AAII, and a rescaled value of the difference between the risk-neutral expected future value of the S&P 500 and its future value.

formula, the IVF is flat. Rubinstein (1994) and Jackwerth and Rubinstein (1996) examined the IVF for SPX options between the time that exchange-based trading began, in April 1986, and the stock market crash of 1987. They report that the IVF was moderately declining during this period, reflecting a mild smile. These authors also examined how the shape of the IVF changed after the crash of 1987, and report that it became much more pronounced and downward sloping, a pattern that came to be called the "volatility skew."

The Black-Scholes framework is based on a log-normality is respect to the risk-neutral distribution. Jackwerth and Rubinstein (1996) report that the risk-neutral distribution was close to lognormal before the October 1987 crash. However, after the crash, the distribution became systematically skewed to the left. This finding led them to ask whether SPX options were correctly priced both before and after the crash. In particular, they wondered whether options prices being consistent with the Black-Scholes formula before the crash indicates that at the time investors underestimated the probability of a crash. Specifically, they wondered whether investors were using a risk-neutral distribution that was lognormal, when the correct distribution was negatively skewed. In other words, they asked whether sentiment was non-zero.

Constantinides, Jackwerth, and Perrakis (forthcoming) examine possible mispricing of SPX options for the periods 1988–1995 and 1997–2002. Their analysis contains some novel elements, specifically the inclusion of transaction costs. Notably, they ask whether market prices were such that in any month of their study, an investor with objectively correct beliefs could have increased his expected utility by engaging in a zero-net-cost trade. They find that there were many months when this would have been possible, thereby leading them to conclude that SPX options were mispriced over time. In particular, they note that mispricing was pronounced for out-of-the-money call options. Interestingly, they suggest that before the crash, option traders might have naïvely used the Black–Scholes formula, when it did not apply. Doing so corresponds to the use of the formula as a heuristic.

The analysis in Constantinides, Jackwerth, and Perrakis implies that the pricing of SPX options cannot be explained in terms of a neoclassical representative investor holding correct beliefs. This analysis neither makes explicit use of sentiment, nor takes into account how sentiment injects oscillation into the shape of the SDF. Nevertheless, the authors acknowledge the sentiment-based explanations provided in the first edition of this book. The next chapter discusses the empirical evidence for a sentiment-based explanation of option prices, and by extension of all assets.

22.7   Summary

This chapter explained how sentiment stemming from heterogeneous beliefs can, and does, cause markets to be inefficient. The chapter argued that option markets are particularly vulnerable in this respect. When there are sharp differences of opinion about the future direction of the market, bulls tend to take long positions in calls, while bears take long positions in index puts. However, because of the large positions required in the index option market, individual investors tend not to use index options. Notably, heterogeneous beliefs give rise to volatility smile effects; The sharper the differences of opinion, the stronger the smile.

The chapter focused on the events in the weeks prior to December 5, 1996, when Alan Greenspan, the chair of the Federal Reserve Board, used the term "irrational exuberance" to describe stock market sentiment. Traditional sentiment index data described the extent of bullish and bearish sentiment among individual investors, writers of advisory newsletters, and option traders during this period. Those data showed that individual investors and newletter writers became increasingly bullish during November 1996. As this occurred, volatility smile effects intensified.

Moreover, one of the fundamental properties of risk-neutral densities appears to have failed, leading to the possibility of unexploited arbitrage opportunities. This property pertains to the expected value of the index at expiration. The expected value should lie above the current value of the index, but in practice it fell significantly below for some of the period.

23

Empirical Evidence in Support of Behavioral SDF

In traditional models, the SDF is a decreasing function. Yet the empirical SDF appears to oscillate instead. Jackwerth (2004) refers to this phenomenon as the "pricing kernel puzzle." This chapter suggests that the oscillating pattern in the empirical SDF stems from sentiment, a natural implication of Theorem 16.1 and the properties of the sentiment function discussed in Chapter 16. That is, the SDF is behavioral.

Option data provide data suitable to estimate state prices and the SDF. The present chapter discusses a series of works that are especially relevant to the character of the empirical SDF. Taken together, these works provide strong support for the position that the empirical SDF is driven by nonzero sentiment as well as fundamentals. All of these works extend the discussion of behavioral option pricing in the previous two chapters. Some of these works provide direct evidence that the shape of the empirical SDF is behavioral.

The first work is the analysis by Bollen and Whaley (2004) of the impact of price pressure on smile patterns in the implied volatility function (IVF). The second work is an analysis by Han (forthcoming) relating option prices and sentiment data. The third work is by David and Veronesi (1999), who analyze overreaction and underreaction in options prices. The fourth work, by Jackwerth, estimates market risk aversion. The fifth work is by Aït-Sahalia and Lo (2000). They also estimate market risk aversion. However, in addition they use option data to estimate the empirical SDF. The sixth work is by Rosenberg and Engle (2002), who also use option data to estimate the empirical SDF. Notably, Rosenberg and Engle conduct an inadvertent test of whether the empirical SDF has the traditional neoclassical shape or a behavioral shape. The seventh work is by Harvey and Siddique (2000) on coskewness. Their empirical analysis supports the theoretical issues involving coskewness developed in Chapter 17. The final work discussed in the chapter is by Blackburn and Ukhov (2006). Their analysis provides an opportunity to estimate the shape of sentiment functions for individual stocks. All of these works provide important insights into the impact of sentiment on prices.

Taken together this series of work tells an interesting story. Bollen–Whaley indicate that most index options are indeed traded by professional investors who use out-of-the-money puts to insure their portfolios. They demonstrate that herding behavior among professional investors and limits to arbitrage among market makers lead to price pressure in these options, thereby producing smiles. Han demonstrates that the trading of professional investors is related to various indexes of sentiment. David–Veronesi relate the shape of the option smile to investors' beliefs, which has implications for the impact of gambler's fallacy. Jackwerth (2000) uses index option data to estimate market risk aversion. His findings indicate that since 1987, risk aversion is partially negative and partially increasing in wealth. Aït-Sahalia–Lo were the first to find that the SDF features the oscillating behavioral shape, the signature of sentiment. Their finding is reinforced by Rosenberg–Engle, who report that the oscillating shape fits the data better than the traditional neoclassical shape. Consistent with the theory developed in Chapter 17 on behavioral mean-variance theory, the work of Harvey–Siddique establishes that coskewness is an important explanatory variable for risk premiums. Finally, the analysis of Blackburn–Ukhov offers a glimpse into the structure of sentiment functions for individual stocks. These appear to have shapes similar to Figure 15.4 and Figure 15.8.[1]

23.1   Bollen–Whaley: Price Pressure Drives Smiles

Bollen–Whaley (2004) establish that price pressure and violations of arbitrage pricing were not unique to December 1996. They are common phenomena, and very closely linked to option smile patterns.

---

[1] Options data provide additional support for behavioral effects discussed in Chapter 18. In this respect, Poteshman (2001a) finds that options traders exhibit short-horizon underreaction to daily information, but long-horizon overreaction to extended periods of mostly similar daily information. Moreover, these misreactions increase as a function of the quantity of previous information that is similar. These findings are not directly related to the issues addressed in this chapter, and so will not be discussed further.

23.1.1   Data

Bollen–Whaley study both index option prices and the prices of options on individual stocks. The index options are for the S&P 500. These are traded on the Chicago Board Options Exchange (CBOE), and Bollen–Whaley focus on the period June 1988 through December 2000. Index options on the S&P 500 are European-style. They expire on the third Friday of the contract month.

Bollen–Whaley also analyze options on individual stocks. These data comprise trades and quotes of CBOE options on 20 individual stocks over the period January 1995 through December 2000. Individual stock options are American-style. They expire on the Saturday following the third Friday of the contract month.

In order to focus on smile effects, Bollen–Whaley separate options by exercise price, using five categories defined by moneyness. For call options, the five categories are (1) deep in-the-money calls (DITM), (2) in-the-money calls (ITM), (3) at-the-money calls (ATM), (4) out-of-the-money calls (OTM), and (5) deep out-of-the-money calls (DOTM). Notably, deep out-of-the-money puts correspond to deep in-the-money calls, so the categories are reversed.

23.1.2   Trading Patterns

Bollen–Whaley study net buying pressure for these different categories of options. They define net buying pressure by dividing transactions into two groups. The first group comprises contracts traded during the day at prices higher than the prevailing bid/ask quote midpoint. They call these buyer-motivated trades. The second group comprises contracts traded during the day at prices below the prevailing bid/ask quote midpoint. They call these seller-motivated trades. Bollen–Whaley compute a difference, the number of contracts in the buyer group minus the number of contracts in the seller group.[2]

Bollen–Whaley document that for index options, the most actively traded calls are the ATM and OTM categories. These are roughly equal in terms of number of contracts, and roughly twice as large as ITM and DOTM categories. DITM calls feature a much smaller number of contracts. The situation with index puts is different. The most contracts for puts are for DOTM, OTM, and ATM options.

For index calls, net buying pressure is positive for only one category: DOTM options. As for index puts, net buying pressure is greatest for DOTM puts and OTM puts. Net buying pressure is positive, but smaller,

---

[2] In order to express demand in stock/index equivalent units, they then multiply the difference by the absolute value of the option delta, and scale by the total trading volume across all option series in the class on that day.

for ATM puts, and negative for ITM puts and DITM puts. These patterns strongly suggest that net buying pressure stems from the use of index options for portfolio insurance, or in the case of DOTM calls stems from increasing the risk in positions.

The patterns for options on individual stocks are different from the pattern for index options. Contracts for calls are highest for ATM options, and decline symmetrically in distance from zero moneyness (that is, ATM). Contracts for puts are highest for OTM puts and ATM puts, and smaller for the other categories.

As for net buying pressure in respect to options on individual stocks, it is negative for DITM and ITM calls, and positive for ATM, OTM, and DOTM calls. Net buying pressure is highest for ATM calls, with the second-highest category being DOTM calls. This pattern is very interesting, and is discussed further in connection with Chapter 27 on behavioral portfolio theory. For put options, net buying pressure is negative for ATM and ITM puts, but positive for the other categories. Buying pressure is greatest for DOTM puts.

23.1.3 Buying Pressure and Smile Effects

Consider the relationship between buying pressure and the shapes of the IVFs, both for index options and for options on individual stocks. Notably, the shapes of the IVFs for the S&P 500 and the individual stocks are dissimilar. Although the slope of the IVF for the index is negative and steep, the slopes of the IVFs for individual stocks are not. Rather, the shape of the IVF for a typical individual stock is closer to flat, and more symmetric than that of the IVF for index options.

The point to notice is that the shapes of the IVFs are closely related to the pattern of buying pressure. For index puts, buying pressure for DOTM and OTM options is associated with the implied volatilities for these options being greatest. Since implied volatility is an increasing function of price (meaning premium), option prices are highest when net buying pressure is highest.

As was mentioned earlier, index puts are traded mostly by institutional investors, as a form of portfolio insurance. These investors may herd in respect to being net demanders for put options. That is what it means for net buying pressure to be positive for this category of options. In such a case, market makers will have to take the other side of these trades, meaning that they will have to hold a nonbalanced position and be exposed to risk. Now market makers may believe that DOTM index puts are overpriced. That is, they may perceive that DOTM index puts are not being priced in accordance with an SDF. However, they may not find it in their interest to exploit the mispricing. Why? For the same reason described in Chapters 9 and 15: the additional expected return is insufficient to offset the additional risk. Market prices have reached the limits of arbitrage.

Bollen–Whaley regress the change in implied volatility on net buying pressure, while controlling for return and trading volume on the underlying asset, and lagged changes in implied volatility. The findings are striking. Net buying pressure for index puts that are in the DOTM and OTM categories drives implied volatility for those categories. The coefficients for net buying pressure associated with both OTM puts and ATM puts are significant and positive.

Net buying pressure for OTM and DOTM index puts drives implied volatilities for index calls that are ITM and DITM, but not vice versa. In the preceding regression, if net buying pressure for ATM index puts is replaced by net buying pressure for ATM index calls, the coefficient for the ATM calls is insignificant. Yet, the coefficient for OTM puts remains positive and significant. For regressions involving the change in implied volatility of OTM index calls, holding constant the net buying pressure of index puts, the net buying pressure of index calls has no discernable impact on implied volatility.

Bollen–Whaley undertake similar regressions for other index option categories and also for options on individual stocks. They find similar patterns for ATM index options as for OTM index options. Changes in ATM implied volatility, for both puts and calls, are driven by net buying pressure from puts, not net buying pressure from calls. However, for options on individual stocks, the situation is reversed. For most individual stocks, net buying pressure for calls, rather than puts, drives implied volatility.

23.1.4 Price Pressure or Learning?

Bollen–Whaley ask whether the steeply sloped IVF for index options might reflect information and learning rather than price pressure. In this respect, perhaps the steep slope simply reflects investors' beliefs. In the context of the framework developed in earlier chapters, the steep slope would emerge in conjunction with the representative investor's probability density function, P_R, which aggregates the views of investors. In this case, the IVF would simply conform to an SDF associated with P_R.

If information and learning drive the smile effect for index options, then Bollen–Whaley suggest there should be no serial correlation in changes in implied volatility. The information associated with a change in implied volatility will be fully absorbed by the market, with subsequent changes in volatility being unpredictable. In contrast, the "limits of arbitrage" hypothesis predicts that changes in implied volatility will reverse, at least in part, as the market maker has the opportunity to rebalance his portfolio.

In order to address the issue in question, Bollen–Whaley include in their regressions the lagged change in volatility as an explanatory variable. The coefficient is negative and statistically significant, both for index options and for options on individual stocks. This suggests that prices reverse.

Approximately 15 percent of the change in index option volatility today will get reversed tomorrow.

23.1.5   Arbitrage Profits

One source of potential arbitrage opportunities stems from differences in the pricing of individual stocks and the pricing of the S&P 500. Consider the empirical return distributions for both the S&P 500 and the individual stocks. These turn out to be quite similar to each other. Yet, as was mentioned earlier, the shapes of the IVFs for the S&P 500 and the individual stocks are dissimilar. Although the slopes of the IVFs for index options are negative and steep, the slopes of the IVFs for individual stocks are not. Rather, the shape of the IVFs for individual stocks is flatter and more symmetric than for index options.

In addition, option-implied volatilities deviate from historical estimates of volatility. For all categories of moneyness, option-implied volatility for index options exceeds historical volatility. The difference is largest for DOTM puts. Green and Figlewski (1999) call this phenomenon a "volatility markup." For options on individual stocks, implied volatility lies above realized volatility for both DOTM and DITM categories, but below realized volatility for ATM options. The average difference between implied volatility across options is less than one percentage point.

Are arbitrage profits possible, at least in theory? Whaley (1986) argued that abnormal profits could have been earned through writing OTM puts during their first year of trading on the Chicago Mercantile Exchange. Bondarenko (2001) concluded that the market for OTM puts on S&P futures was inefficient in the period 1988–2000. Bollen–Whaley investigate several trading strategies and conclude that potential abnormal returns appear to be large, and persistent. For the category that includes DOTM index puts, they report a geometric mean annual return of 105 percent! Moreover, they point out that abnormal returns do not appear to be disappearing with time.

23.2   Han: Smile Effects, Sentiment, and Gambler's Fallacy

The analysis in Bollen–Whaley focuses on the impact of price pressure on the change in implied volatility. Han (forthcoming) investigates the impact of sentiment on the slope of the IVF. His data are for S&P index options, during the period January 1988 through June 1997.

Han points out that the empirical distribution of monthly stock index returns is nearly symmetric. Define risk-neutral skewness as the slope of the

IVF. Notably, risk-neutral skewness associated with index returns reflects the relative weight that the SDF accords to downward movements in the stock index vis-a-vis upward movements. According to the arguments presented in Chapters 16, 21, and 22, risk-neutral skewness should change to reflect changes in market sentiment. *Ceteris paribus*, when some investors become more pessimistic, the representative investor assigns higher probabilities to the downside states, and thus the index return becomes more negatively skewed under the risk-neutral measure. That is exactly what Han finds, a significant relation between investor sentiment and risk-neutral skewness.

To measure price pressure, Han uses the ratio of open interest for OTM index puts to the open interest of OTM index calls. Call this the *open interest ratio*. As to sentiment indexes, he focuses on the II index and the AAII index mentioned in Chapter 22. Han also investigates the relationship between the slope of the IVF and the extent to which the S&P 500 index is mispriced relative to a traditional valuation measure.

23.2.1 Price Pressure

Han presents a series of findings. His first finding is that a higher value in the open interest ratio is associated with a more steeply sloped IVF. That is, consistent with Bollen–Whaley, price pressure appears to result in a more pronounced smile effect. Smile effects are associated with skewness in the underlying risk-neutral measure. Han reports that, *ceteris paribus*, a one–standard deviation increase in the open interest ratio is associated with an increase in risk-neutral skewness of 0.28 standard deviations.

Interestingly, Han reports that the relation between sentiment and risk-neutral skewness is robust to controlling for the put-call ratio of option open interest. Therefore, he concludes that sentiment, not just price pressure, drives risk-neutral skewness.

23.2.2 Impact of a Market Drop: Gambler's Fallacy

Han reports two findings that taken together suggest interesting behavior on the part of option market makers and professional investors. First, the open interest ratio falls after a decrease in the value of the S&P 500. Second, after a recent drop in the value of the S&P 500, the IVF becomes more steeply sloped, and risk-neutral skewness becomes more negative. The combination of these two findings suggests that after a decrease in the S&P 500, market makers mark up the price of put options, in the same way that an insurance firm increases policy premiums after major claims. The higher price results in reduced demand for insurance (that is, put options).

Han's finding that index option put-call ratio of open interest is significantly and positively related to past index return is consistent with the tendency of investors who trade index options to be subject to gambler's fallacy. This finding is consistent with the evidence presented in Chapter 7.

23.2.3   Impact of Sentiment

As to sentiment, the open interest ratio is negatively related to the II, but not to the AAII. Recall that the II measures the sentiment expressed in financial newsletters. Han finds a strong relationship between the II and the slope of the IVF. An increase in bearish sentiment, as measured by the II, is associated with a more steeply sloped IVF. An increase of one standard deviation in the II is associated with a change of 0.17 standard deviations in risk-neutral skewness.

Han also looks at data collected by the Commodity Futures Trading Commission (CFTC) that provide a gauge of sentiment for professional investors. The measure is the Commitment of Traders (COT). The CFTC requires that large traders who hold a position above a specified level must report their positions on a daily basis. The open interest of large traders is separated into "commercial" and "noncommercial" categories. Noncommercial traders include market makers in the index options market.

Han reports that the short position of noncommercial traders is associated with a more steeply sloped IVF. That is, when market makers become more bearish, the relative price of index puts rises.

Han also finds that when institutional investors become more bearish, the S&P 500 index is more undervalued. In the language of Theorem 16.2, the sentiment premium on the S&P 500 increases when institutional investors become more bearish.

23.2.4   Time-Varying Uncertainty

The CBOE Volatility Index (VIX) is viewed as a measure of investors' forecast of future volatility. In order to measure daily volatility in the VIX, Han computes a variable *VolVol* based on the high and low daily values achieved by the VIX. He finds that an increase in *VolVol* is associated with a more steeply sloped IVF. Han interprets an increase in *VolVol* as increased uncertainty about future volatility. He suggests that option market makers react to such uncertainty by increasing the relative price of put options.

Han investigates one last issue. He asks whether the extent of mispricing in the S&P 500 affects the slope of the IVF. He finds that when the S&P 500 appears to be overpriced relative to fundamentals (using a measure developed by Sharpe (2002), the slope of the IVF becomes less steep. Therefore, if the mispricing is associated with excessive optimism on the part of professional investors, then the demand for portfolio insurance will decline. The resulting decline in price pressure will lead the IVF to become flatter.

23.3   David–Veronesi: Gambler's Fallacy and Negative Skewness

The David–Veronesi (1999) study is for S&P 500 index options during the period April 1986 through May 1996. They postulate a model whereby dividends evolve according to a diffusion process whose drift rate is unknown to investors. In particular, the drift rate might be constant, or it might itself evolve according to a known stochastic process. Investors form expectations for the drift rate, and also establish associated confidence intervals for their forecasts. In the David–Veronesi theoretical framework, the change in investor uncertainty over time in response to events leads to stochastic changes in return volatility, and the covariance between returns and volatility.

The covariance between returns and volatility can be negative or positive. David–Veronesi point out that this volatility can explain why the slope of the IVF is sometimes negative and sometimes positive. To see why, consider a run of down-moves that correspond to negative realized drift. As a result, returns are negative. In addition, if investors' uncertainty increases, then volatility increases. Taken together, the result contributes to negative covariance between returns and volatility. However, the covariance between returns and volatility can also be positive. This can happen if investors expect low dividend growth but realized dividend growth is high. The resulting increase in volatility occurs in conjunction with high realized returns.

David–Veronesi suggest that the features that they highlight imply the possibility that option prices misreact to changes in stock prices. In some cases option prices may overreact, while in other cases option prices may underreact. They point out that a down-move that reduces the stock price may simultaneously increase investors' perceived volatility. Therefore, call option prices will be impacted in two ways. The first way is through the price of the S&P 500 index, which declines. The second way is through the impact on perceived volatility, which increases. If the volatility impact is larger than the index price impact, then call option prices may rise, even as the index falls.

The estimation of investors' collective beliefs is accomplished through a maximum likelihood procedure for a two-state regime switching model. Beliefs are over high and low growth states. David–Veronesi report that for 70 percent of the time, the covariance between returns and volatility is negative. That is, when returns go up, investors appear to increase their forecasts of future volatility. In consequence, their state return density process is negatively skewed when returns are high and positively skewed when returns are low. They report that option prices support the notion that returns and volatility are negatively related, and that option prices appear to misreact to changes in the index.

Although David–Veronesi use a maximum-likelihood procedure, their approach has the same general implications when investors who trade index options are vulnerable to gambler's fallacy. After an increase in the index, these investors act as if they increase the probability mass they attach to low growth states in the future. This pattern conforms to the findings by Han just discussed, and to those of De Bondt discussed in Chapter 5.

Work by Shimko (1993) finds a two-humped state price distribution for options on the S&P 100 index (OEX) during the late 1980s. This finding conforms to the manner in which the representative investor's probability density function aggregates the individual investors' probability density functions. (See Chapters 14 and 16.)

23.4   Jackwerth and Aït-Sahalia-Lo: Estimating Market Risk Aversion

Jackwerth (2000) conducted a study to estimate risk aversion functions from S&P 500 index option prices. His data pertain to the period April 2, 1986 through December 29, 1995. Methodologically, Jackwerth used a model featuring a traditional representative investor who maximizes expected utility subject to a wealth constraint, and in equilibrium holds the market portfolio.

Recall from discussion in Sections 21.2.1 and 22.2 that a risk-neutral probability (21.1) is a future price of a contingent claim. Therefore, the risk-neutral density can be used to compute the future value of the representative investor's portfolio, which can then be discounted back to obtain his wealth. The first order condition to the representative investor's expected utility maximization links his subjective probability, his marginal utility, and the risk-neutral probability. As discussed below, by differentiating marginal utility with respect to consumption, Jackwerth computes the representative investor's Arrow–Pratt coefficient of relative risk aversion, and links this to the representative investor's probability density and the risk-neutral density.

Jackwerth assumes that the representative investor holds objectively correct beliefs Π. He uses index option data to estimate the risk-neutral density function. Therefore, he combines estimates of the objective probability density function and estimates of the risk-neutral density to infer the representative investor's risk aversion as a function of wealth.

Jackwerth found that prior to the stock market crash of 1987, marginal utility declined as a function of wealth. However, after the crash, risk aversion functions were not constant across return states, but instead were highly variable. In particular, Jackwerth found negative risk aversion for returns around zero, and that risk averse functions rise for returns greater than −1 percent. This led him to conclude that risk aversion functions cannot be reconciled with a representative investor. He calls this finding the "pricing kernel puzzle."

23.4.1 Behavioral Risk-Neutral Density

Equation (14.7) implies that the risk-neutral density function has the form

$$\eta(x_1) = P_R(x_1)\frac{g(x_1)^{-\gamma_R(x_1)}}{E_R[g(x_1)^{-\gamma_R(x_1)}|x_0]} \tag{23.1}$$

Notice the manner in which the representative investor's probabilities P_R enter the equation for the risk-neutral probability. In particular, notice the manner in which sentiment, embodied within P_R, is transmitted to the risk-neutral density function η. Figure 23.1 displays a risk-neutral density function from a heterogeneous investor model. This density function corresponds to Figure 8.2, where the degree of heterogeneity has been exaggerated in order to highlight its impact. Notice that the risk-neutral density function is bimodal in this example. Were prices efficient, meaning $P_R = \Pi$, then Π would be the probability density function underlying (23.1).

The procedure employed by Jackwerth (2000) imputes the market risk aversion function on the basis of the estimated risk-neutral density and the

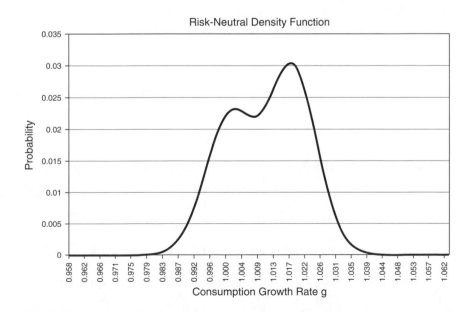

FIGURE 23.1. The figure displays a risk-neutral density function from a heterogeneous investor model.

estimated objective probability density function. Consider the methodology. Jackwerth uses a continuous state model. Therefore his expected utility function and associated budget constraint are integrals rather than sums. In his framework the Lagrangean associated with the representative investor's expected utility maximization has the form

$$\int u(W)\Pi(W)dW - \lambda(1+i)^{-t}\int (\eta(W)WdW - 1) \qquad (23.2)$$

where the 1 in the constraint refers to initial wealth so that future wealth levels connote returns. The first order condition associated with this maximum has the form

$$u' = \lambda(1+i)^{-t}\eta'/\Pi' \qquad (23.3)$$

Differentiating (23.3) to obtain u'', and dividing u'' by u' yields the coefficient of absolute risk aversion $r_{AP} = -u''/u'$. The resulting equation is

$$r_{AP} = \Pi'/\Pi - \eta'/\eta \qquad (23.4)$$

Notice that because Jackwerth uses Π for his expected utility function, he implicitly assumes that prices are efficient. In general, the probability density function (pdf) that appears in (23.2) should be P_R, not Π. This means that the appropriate pdf to use in equations (23.2)–(23.4) should be P_R. In particular, the following equation should replace (23.4):

$$r_{AP} = P_R'/P_R - \eta'/\eta \qquad (23.5)$$

Equation (16.3) connects P_R and Π through the function

$$\Phi = \frac{P_R\delta_R}{\Pi\delta_{R,\Pi}}$$

Let $\Psi = \Phi\delta_{R,\Pi}/\delta_R$. It follows that $P_R = \Psi\Pi$, $P_R' = \Psi'\Pi + \Psi\Pi'$ and

$$P_R'/P_R = \Psi'/\Psi + \Pi'/\Pi \qquad (23.6)$$

Substituting for P_R and P_R' in equation (23.5) yields

$$r_{AP} = \Pi'/\Pi - \eta'/\eta + \Psi'/\Psi = \Pi'/\Pi - \eta'/\eta + \Phi'/\Phi \qquad (23.7)$$

Sentiment Λ is defined as $ln(\Phi)$. Therefore, (23.7) can be expressed as

$$r_{AP} = \Pi'/\Pi - \eta'/\eta + \Lambda' \qquad (23.8)$$

Jackwerth estimates r_{AP} using equation (23.4), with empirical estimates of both Π and η. Estimates of Π are based on index return data, while estimates of η are based on index option prices. However, equation (23.8) indicates that the representative investor's coefficient of absolute risk aversion is given, not by (23.4), but by (23.8). Therefore, using (23.4) results in an omitted variable, namely Λ'.

Jackwerth points out that after 1987 the shape of the absolute risk aversion function, which he estimates for the market, is not monotone declining and time invariant, as traditional theory would suggest. Instead, it tends mostly to be U-shaped and time varying. Moreover, points along the r_{AP}-function vary widely and unrealistically, from below -15 to more than 20, depending on the time period.

Recall the discussion in Subsection 16.3.3 involving Figure 16.3. That discussion identified the risk aversion function necessary to generate the SDF, when Π was erroneously used in place of P_R, and $P_R \neq \Pi$. As can be seen in Figure 16.3, the risk aversion function is exotic, increasing in one region and assuming negative values in another. These are also properties of the risk aversion function estimated by Jackwerth. Of course, the risk aversion function in Figure 16.3 is not the true risk aversion function. In the example used to generate Figure 16.3, the true $\gamma_R = 1$. The distortion in Figure 16.3 arises because Π was erroneously used in place of P_R.

Jackwerth concluded that risk aversion functions cannot be reconciled with a representative investor. However, his conclusion might be restated to say that if sentiment is assumed to be zero when prices are inefficient, then the associated risk aversion function cannot be reconciled with a representative investor.

Aït-Sahalia and Lo (2000) also use index option data to measure the representative investor's coefficient of relative risk aversion. Like Jackwerth's, their estimates also appear to be unrealistic. The Aït-Sahalia-Lo range for CRRA is 1 to 60.

The analysis in Aït-Sahalia and Lo is notable in one other respect. They estimate the empirical SDF. The general shape of the SDF function turned out to be given by the oscillating behavioral shape in Figure 16.2. As was mentioned in Chapter 17, Dittmar (2002) estimated the SDF and found it to be U-shaped. Notably, I argue that both the oscillating pattern and U-shaped pattern stem from sentiment. The next section is notable, in that it discusses a free-form analysis which does not impose prior restrictions on the shape of the SDF. As will be seen, the conclusion that emerges is that the empirical SDF features an oscillating behavioral shape.

23.5   Rosenberg–Engle: Signature of Sentiment in the SDF

Rosenberg–Engle (2002) use S&P 500 index option data for the period 1991–1995 to estimate what they call an empirical asset pricing kernel

(EPK). The EPK is an SDF, or more precisely the projection of an SDF onto the returns to the S&P 500, the counterpart to the risk-neutral density described in Chapter 22. That risk-neutral density measures the value of a contingent claim in terms of future dollars, where the contingent events are particular future values of the S&P 500 index. In contrast, the SDF projection is the present value of a contingent claim, per unit (objective) probability.

23.5.1   Two Approaches to Estimating the EPK

Rosenberg–Engle take two approaches to arriving at an EPK. The first approach is to assume a representative investor model, where the representative investor has CRRA utility and objectively correct beliefs. The second approach is to use a less restrictive model based on the method of Chebyshev polynomials.

Both approaches use the empirical probability density function for the equity index return. Both approaches assume an asymmetric GARCH model. The GARCH model involves two equations. In the first equation, the log of the index change is the sum of a time invariant mean and a disturbance term. The mean of the disturbance term is zero, and its variance (volatility) is a linear function of the square of the prior disturbance, the lagged volatility, and an asymmetric function of the past disturbance.

23.5.2   Estimating Market Risk Aversion

After estimating the EPK, Rosenberg–Engle follow Jackwerth (2000) and compute the coefficient of relative risk aversion in the market. As discussed in Chapter 15, when the representative investor has CRRA utility and objectively correct beliefs, the SDF has the form $\delta_R g^{-\gamma_R}$, where γ_R is the coefficient of relative risk aversion. The log-SDF is $ln(\delta_R) - \gamma_R ln(g)$. Therefore the first derivative of the log-SDF with respect to $ln(g)$ is just $-\gamma_R$. Rosenberg–Engle use this relationship to estimate γ_R from their EPK.

23.5.3   Empirical Results: Estimates of SDF

The downward-sloping functions in Figure 23.2 depict the EPK using the CRRA approach, in conjunction with objectively correct probabilities. The oscillating functions in Figure 23.2 depict the EPK using the Chebyshev polynomial approach. Rosenberg–Engle note that the Chebyshev approach provides the better fit. Notice the upward-sloping portion in the oscillating functions depicted in Figure 23.2. A similar feature is obtained by Aït-Sahalia and Lo (2000).

FIGURE 23.2. The figure depicts the EPK using the CRRA-approach, (average power pricing kernel) and Chebyshev polynomial (average orthogonal polynomial pricing kernel), in conjunction with objectively correct probabilities.

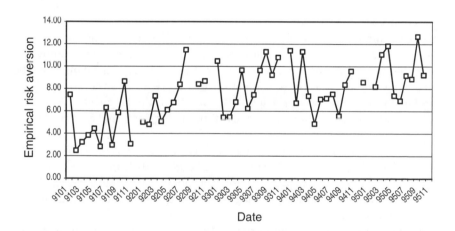

FIGURE 23.3. The figure shows the time series for Rosenberg–Engle estimate of γ_R.

23.5.4   Estimates of Risk Aversion

Figure 23.3 shows that the Rosenberg–Engle estimate of γ_R is highly unstable over time, dipping down as low as 2 and rising above 12. As was the case with the analysis in Jackwerth, the point is that restricting the representative investor to having objectively correct beliefs forces sentiment through the γ_R function. Similar to the point made in Subsection 23.5.1, when sentiment is nonzero, using a model that defines sentiment to be zero by assigning objective beliefs to the representative investor leads to a highly volatile γ_R function.

Recall that the models that combine heterogeneous beliefs and heterogeneous risk tolerance parameters do feature time-varying γ_R. However, those models do not suggest that γ_R will feature the kind of volatility portrayed in Figure 23.3.

23.6   Comparing the Behavioral SDF and Empirical SDF

The behavioral theory of asset pricing presented in this book is centered on the SDF. The cornerstone theoretical result in the book is that the SDF is driven by two components, a fundamental component and sentiment. Given the empirical evidence on investor errors, the theory suggests a particular oscillating shape for the graph of the SDF. In this respect, estimating the empirical SDF is where the rubber meets the road. What is the shape of the empirical SDF or EPK?

Recall Figure 16.2, which contrasted the SDF in an efficient market with a behavioral SDF. Notice that the downward-sloping function in Figure 23.2 is similar in form to the efficient SDF in Figure 16.2. This should not be surprising, in that the bottom function in Figure 16.2 is the graph of the fundamental component of a log-SDF based on CRRA utility. As usual, it is monotone decreasing, to reflect diminishing marginal utility for the representative investor.

The oscillating function is similar in form to the sentiment-based SDF depicted in Figure 16.2. Recall that Theorem 16.1 indicates that the log-SDF is the sum of a fundamental component and sentiment Λ. That is what Figure 16.2 depicts, the log-SDF being the sum of a fundamental component and sentiment.

As was emphasized in Chapter 16, a behavioral SDF need not be monotone decreasing. Excessive optimism on the part of a group of investors who are sufficiently wealthy can cause the SDF to be increasing through part of its range. And excessive pessimism by some investors can cause the SDF to be more steeply sloped in the left-hand portion of its range.

A sentiment-based interpretation of Rosenberg–Engle's Figure 23.2 is that pessimism caused the SDF to be overpriced in the range -7.8 percent to -1.8 percent, and above 5 percent. By the same token, sentiment caused the SDF to be overpriced in the range -1 percent to 5 percent.

I suggest that Figure 23.2 provides an estimate of the sentiment function Λ. To see why, consider the difference between the two SDF functions displayed in Figure 23.2. In view of the discussion in Chapter 16, the fundamental component in equation (16.5) corresponds to the neoclassical estimate of the SDF. For similar reasons, the oscillating shape in Figure 23.2 corresponds to the SDF itself. Now apply Theorem 16.1: The theorem indicates that the difference between the oscillating free-form function and the downward-sloping neoclassical restricted function corresponds to an estimate of the sentiment function Λ.

Notice that in Figure 23.2, the value for the SDF corresponding to a market return of -9.8% is 2.5 for the neoclassical restricted function, but 5.0 for the free-form estimate. The log difference between the two values is 80% ($= \log(5.0/2.5) = 1.61 - 0.81$). That is, the value of market sentiment associated with a market return of -9.8% is 80%. In rough terms, if we take $\delta_R \cong \delta_\Pi$, then we can infer that the market overestimates the probability density associated with a return of -9.8% by 80%.

Chapter 17 describes the pricing of risk in terms of a behavioral mean-variance efficient frontier, meaning a frontier that incorporates sentiment. A mean-variance efficient portfolio features augmented positive returns in regions where the SDF is underpriced, but the augmentation is negative in regions where the SDF is overpriced. In terms of Figure 23.2, a mean-variance efficient portfolio will underperform when the return to the S&P 500 is less than -8 percent, or between -1 percent and 5 percent.

Rosenberg–Engle note that the Chebyshev approach provides a better fit than the CRRA approach. This suggests that sentiment was nonzero during their estimation period.

Is it reasonable to interpret the similar patterns in Figures 16.2 and 23.2 as implying that the SDF is behavioral, and that the oscillations identify loci of mispricing? In order to answer this question, recall the discussion from Chapter 16 about the conditions that underlie the shapes of Figures 16.2 and 1.1.

The shape in Figure 16.2 emerges from a two-investor model where the optimistic investor overestimates expected returns and underestimates volatility, while the pessimistic investor underestimates expected returns and overestimates volatility. The shape in Figure 1.1 emerges from a three-investor model where a small group of super bullish investors are added. Empirically, the question is whether investors tend to cluster in respect to their beliefs, so that it is reasonable to model the market by dividing investors into a few distinct groups.

23.6.1   Empirical Evidence for Clustering: Mode in the Left Tail Reflecting Pessimism

Figure 15.11 provides evidence of clustering for the period 1998–2001. However, Rosenberg–Engle study the period 1991–1995. Of the four main data sets discussed in Chapters 6 and 7 that measure expected returns, two cover the period 1991–1995. The two are the *Wall $treet Week* panelists' predictions and the Livingston survey.

Subsection 7.4.2 discussed the fact that these investors were pessimistic, while Subsection 7.4.3 discussed the fact that during the period 1988–1994 they overestimated volatility. In this regard, the predictions of the *Wall $treet Week* panelists conform to the assumptions about pessimistic investors used to generate Figure 16.2.

Pessimism on the part of professional investors is a key issue. In this respect, Figure 23.4 displays the mean forecasts of the change in the Dow Jones Industrial Average by the panelists on *Wall $treet Week with Louis Rukeyser*, for the period 1984–2002. The forecasts were issued 12 months earlier. For example, the forecast for 1984 was made at the end of December 1983.

Figure 23.4 displays the forecasts for the high value, low value, and closing value of the Dow, along with the actual change for the year. Notice that the actual trajectory lies above the high forecast for more than half of the period. Indeed, the actual trajectory lies well above the forecasted trajectory for most of the period, suggesting that *W$W* panelists were pessimistic during this period. Over the 18-year sample period, the mean forecasted change in the Dow was 6.2 percent, far less than the actual value of 11.4 percent.

Notice too that the mean end-of-year forecast does not lie midway between the low and high values, but instead lies closer to the high value. The interval is negatively skewed, suggesting that panelists perceived there

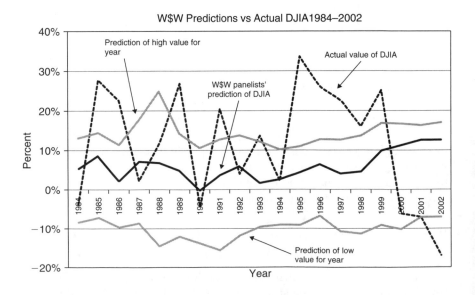

FIGURE 23.4. The figure displays the mean forecasts of the change in the Dow Jones Industrial Average by the panelists on *Wall $treet Week with Louis Rukeyser*, for the period 1984–2002.

to be greater downside potential than upside potential. The mean fore-casted high for the Dow was 14.5 percent, and the mean forecasted low for the Dow was −9.9 percent. The midpoint of the high and low forecasts is 2.3 percent, considerably lower than the 6.2 percent forecasted for the close. This is similar to the De Bondt experimental evidence reported in Chapter 5.

23.6.2 Investors and Predictions of Continuation

Turning next to individual investors, UBS/Gallup did not survey individ-ual investors during the period (1991–1995) that Rosenberg–Engle study in respect to the empirical SDF. Nevertheless, a proxy for the UBS data is the AAII data described in Chapters 6 and 22. Both series are avail-able after September 1998. Figure 23.5 displays the movement of the UBS mean expected return and the eight-week moving average of the AAII series during the period September 1998 through April 2003. The correlation coefficient between the two series is 43 percent.

Consider how the AAII series co-evolved with the forecasts of the *Wall Street Week* panelists' predictions during the period 1991 through 1995. The correlation coefficient between the two series is −0.3. The negative

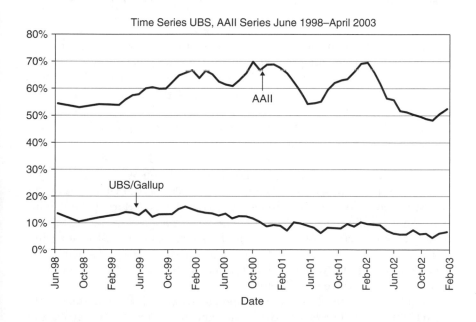

FIGURE 23.5. The figure displays the movement of the UBS mean expected return and the eight-week moving average of the AAII series during the period September 1998 through April 2003.

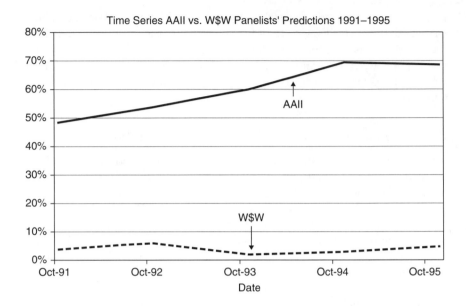

FIGURE 23.6. The figure displays the movement of the year-end AAII series with the *Wall $treet Week* panelists' predictions for the period 1991–1995.

sign is consistent with the general tendency of individual investors to predict continuation and of professional investors to predict reversals. The negative relationship provides further evidence for clustering. Figure 23.6 displays the movement of the year-end AAII series with the *Wall $treet Week* panelists' predictions for the period 1991–1995.

Corroboration for the negative relationship between the reactions of individual investors and the reactions of institutional investors comes from a series of confidence surveys conducted by Robert Shiller.[3] From October 1989 on, Shiller surveyed institutional investors on a six-month basis. One of the questions he asks in his survey calls for the change that the investor expects for the Dow Jones Industrial Average during the coming year. Shiller defines his *one-year confidence index* as the percentage of respondents expecting an increase in the Dow. Using the October value in place of year-end, the correlation between the Shiller one-year confidence index and the year-end AAII value is −0.41. Again, the negative relationship is consistent with clustering.

Notably, the Livingston survey respondents were optimistic during the period 1991–1995. The mean arithmetic expected return for this group was

---

[3] There are four Shiller indexes, which pertain respectively to (1) expected returns, (2) buying on dips, (3) fear of a crash, and (4) whether stocks are fairly valued.

11.2 percent, well above the 3.9 percent that *Wall $treet Week* panelists predicted. In this respect, the Livingston respondents behaved more like individual investors during this period. Indeed, the correlation between the Livingston expected returns and the AAII index was 0.22. Shiller has a valuation confidence index that measures the percentage of investors who believe that stock prices in the United States are not too high. Between 1991 and 1995, the correlation between this index and the Livingston expected returns was 0.48, whereas for the *Wall $treet Week* panelists it was 0.01.[4]

23.6.3   Mode in the Left Tail and Crashophobia

Recall that Figure 15.11 suggests that the distribution of investors' expected returns is either bimodal or trimodal, with one mode being associated with negative returns. The mode in the left tail is key. Additional evidence in respect to a mode in the left tail comes from the evidence presented in the work of Bollen–Whaley and Han. Recall that this evidence indicates that it is institutional investors who actively trade index options, not individual investors. Therefore, the downward-sloping smile pattern in the IVF is driven largely by the purchase of deep out-of-the-money put options. Jackwerth–Rubinstein (1996) refer to this effect as "crashophobia."

In this respect, Shiller provides another confidence index, directly related to the fear of a crash. He asks investors for the probability they attach to a stock market crash in the next six months. Shiller defines his *crash confi dence index* as the percentage of investors who assign less than a 10 percent probability to a crash.

Figure 23.7 displays the time series for the percentage of investors who attached more than a 10 percent probability to a crash in the next six months. Notice that the percentage lies between 60 percent and 80 percent for most of the time. This provides additional support for a left-tail mode.

One of the weaknesses of the UBS survey is that it excludes a category for negative returns. However, Shiller's one-year confidence index provides this information. Figure 23.8 provides additional support for the importance of the left tail in the period 1998–2001. The figure shows the percentage of

---

[4] The Livingston survey data are known to be imperfect. For this reason the survey is used as a secondary source, rather than a primary source. For example, despite the optimism mentioned, the Livingston expected returns feature higher correlations with the *Wall $treet Week* panelists' expected returns (0.5). This suggests that although the level of Livingston expected returns was too high, their changes over time were more like the changes in the *Wall $treet Week* panelists' expectations than the changes in the AAII index.

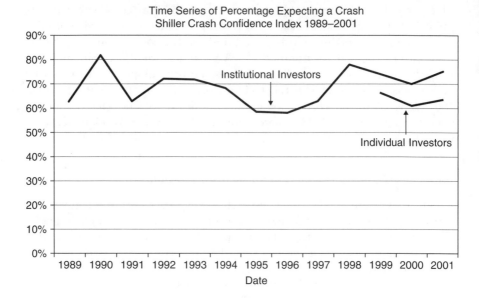

FIGURE 23.7. The figure displays the time series for the percentage of investors who attached more than a 10 percent probability to a crash in the next six months.

institutional investors who expected a decline in the Dow Jones Industrial Average for the next year.

Additional insights can be gleaned by examining the correlation coefficient between Shiller's confidence indices. His one-year confidence index measures the percent of the population expecting an increase in the Dow Jones Industrial Average during the coming year. The correlation coefficient between the one-year index and the crash confidence index is 55 percent. Shiller's valuation index measures the percent of the population who think that "the value of the market is not too high." The correlation coefficient between the valuation index and the crash confidence index is 60 percent. Both correlations point to a positive relationship between optimism and overconfidence. Such a relationship is consistent with the notion of a cluster of underconfident pessimists co-existing with a cluster of overconfident optimists.

23.6.4   Time Variation in the SDF

Figure 23.9 shows the percentage of institutional investors expecting a decline in the Dow Jones Industrial Average for the next year, over the period October 1989 through April 2004. This figure suggests that there is

Weight in Left Tail Shiller One-Year Index

FIGURE 23.8. The figure shows the percentage of institutional investors and individual investors who expected a decline in the Dow Jones Industrial Average for the next year for the period 1998–2001.

considerable time variation in the relative weight in the left tail. Figure 23.7 also displays considerable time variation.

It is important to note that the behavioral theory of the SDF does not necessarily imply that the shape of the SDF will be given by Figure 16.2. If pessimistic investors are overconfident and underestimate the probability of a crash, then the sentiment function could have the inverted U-shape depicted in Figure 15.7. In this case, this shape would be transmitted to the SDF rather than the oscillating shape depicted in Figure 15.8.

Figures 22.5 and 22.6 demonstrate that the IVF exhibits time variation, and the IVF does not always have the same shape. Han's findings demonstrate that the IVF reflects sentiment as well as price pressure. The point is that sentiment affects both the shape of the IVF and the shape of the SDF. And to the extent that sentiment is time varying, so too will be the shapes of the IVF and SDF.

The fact that *Wall $treet Week* panelists underestimated volatility after 1995, combined with the declining pattern in Figure 23.9, suggests that the shape of the SDF might well have been different after 1995. Shiller's crash confidence index shows that the percentage of institutional investors who attached more than a 10 percent probability to a crash (in the subsequent

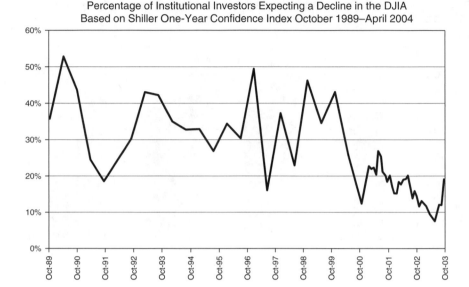

FIGURE 23.9. The figure shows the percentage of institutional investors expecting a decline in the Dow Jones Industrial Average for the next year, over the period October 1989 through April 2004.

six months) generally fell between December 2001 and April 2004: It fell from about 80 percent to the 50–65 percent range. Still, 50 percent is substantial, and does not suggest that the mode at the left tail would have collapsed.[5]

23.7 Heterogeneous Perspectives

How have traditional asset pricing theorists reacted to the preceding argument suggesting that the SDF is behavioral? Typical responses seek to defend the traditional approach by appeal to rational expectations models, such as the habit-formation model discussed in Chapter 28, by suggesting that the behavioral framework offers no testable hypotheses,

---

[5] Shiller has a fourth confidence index, which measures investors' beliefs about short-term return reversals. He calls this index "buying on dips." This index features an upward trend on the part of institutional investors between 1989 and 2004. The same is true for individual investors between October 2000 and April 2004. Indeed the index was generally higher for individual investors than for institutional investors during this period.

or by criticizing the assumptions used in the behavioral model of the SDF.[6]

Jackwerth has stated that he has a difficult time believing that the world is populated only by bulls and bears, who consistently get their means and variances wrong over 10-year periods. He points out that the preceding behavioral argument misses the moderates whose expectations are approximately correct. In this respect, he suggests that he is happier with a model that assumes many moderates to have correct views, with some extremists on either side. With these assumptions, he contends, the argument that the empirical SDF is behavioral does not work. He makes similar remarks (2004) in connection with a paper by Ziegler (2003) about investor heterogeneity.

If sentiment does not drive the oscillating patterns in Jackwerth's risk aversion function and in Rosenberg–Engle's SDF, then what type of rational-based assumptions could? Brown and Jackwerth (2004) argue that the oscillating shapes can be generated in a rational expectations framework with two factors, the index level and volatility. The resulting process features high volatility at the extremes and low volatility in the mid-range. As a result, the risk aversion function has an upward-sloping portion that results from integrating out the volatility dimension of a two-factor SDF.[7]

Jackwerth's comments are critical of the assumptions that underlie the examples developed in Chapter 16. At the time he made the comments he was not familiar with the empirical evidence presented in Chapters 6, 7, and 15, and Section 23.7. However, his perspective is typical of traditionalists, especially the view that investors would not make systematic errors over 10-year periods. That position is one of the main issues that divide traditional asset pricing theorists and behavioral asset pricing theorists. Traditional asset pricing theorists assume that investors will quickly learn from experience. Behavioral asset pricing theorists assume that investors are generally slow learners. In this respect, look again at Figure 23.4. Look how long it took for *Wall $treet Week* panelists to begin to increase their expected returns. Moreover, look at the environment in which those increases finally happened. Look again at Figure 7.7, depicting Frank Cappiello's predictions over an 18-year period. Quick learners they are not.

---

[6] This section deals with the third reaction, concerning the nature of the assumptions. Issues involving the habit-formation model are discussed in Chapter 28. As for the "no testable hypotheses" claim, recall that the shape depicted in Figure 16.2 occurs only in respect to particular assumptions. Other shapes for the SDF are possible.

[7] Brown–Jackwerth point out that they are unable to generate the empirical patterns observed using realistic parameters.

A key point of Chapters 6 and 7 is that investors rely on representativeness-based heuristics that predispose them to extreme predictions, in one direction or the other.[8] As Chapters 2 and 3 emphasized, these heuristics do not conform to Bayes rule. Therefore their use is not consistent with efficient learning. Evidence based on experiments performed by psychologists, experiments performed by economists, and field data such as those presented in Chapters 6 and 7, all point to the conclusion that people are much poorer at learning than traditional asset pricing theorists assume.

The evidence, imperfect though it may be, suggests that the empirical SDF has the shape that it does because of investor sentiment. Is there any evidence at all that suggests that investors hold homogeneous beliefs about returns' being driven by a two-factor model where the factors are index level and volatility? All available evidence points to investors' having heterogeneous beliefs that feature wide dispersion. The evidence suggests that investors use simple heuristics that predispose them to bias. As for having rational expectations about a two-factor process, as Figure 6.7 demonstrates, even financial economists hold widely differing views. If indeed there is a correct model, most do not have it.

23.8   Evidence Pertaining to the Cross-Section

Chapters 16 and 17 discussed what the behavioral SDF-approach implies about the risk premiums of individual securities. Chapter 18 described the key empirical findings about the cross-section of equity returns, suggesting that representativeness is a key determinant of the cross-sectional pattern. In concluding the present chapter, I make two connections between the earlier discussion and empirical work that relates to the findings about the shape of the empirical SDF. The first connection pertains to coskewness with the market portfolio. The second connection pertains to the shape of the sentiment function for individual stocks.

23.8.1   Coskewness

Coskewness is directly connected to the shape of the empirical SDF, the subject of the present chapter. Theorem 17.2 describes the relationship between the SDF and mean-variance return functions. Broadly speaking, the mean-variance function and the SDF are mirror images of each other. Chapter 17 describes why coskewness with respect to the market portfolio

---

[8] Section 6.2 pointed out that academic economists are not immune, even those who view themselves as experts in asset pricing theory.

emerges as a consequence of the behavioral shape of the mean-variance return function. Therefore, the relevance of coskewness is an implication of the SDF having either a U-shape or an oscillating shape.

Harvey and Siddique (2000) study coskewness using a four-factor model, where the factors respectively correspond to the market return, size, book-to-market equity, and momentum. Harvey and Siddique find a correlation of -0.71 between coskewness and mean returns of portfolios sorted by size, book-to-market equity, and momentum. This means that plausibly, coskewness generates much of the explanatory power of size, book-to-market equity, and momentum in the returns of individual stocks.

Harvey and Siddique point out that the market factor by itself explains only 3.5 percent of cross-sectional returns. However, the combination of the market factor and coskewness explains 68.1 percent of cross-sectional returns. This value rivals the 71.8 percent associated with the use of the market factor, size, and book-to-market equity. For momentum, recent winners feature lower coskewness than that of recent losers. All of these findings are consistent with MV portfolio returns having the shape depicted in Figure 17.1.

23.8.2   Sentiment Functions for Individual Securities

The impact of sentiment on individual stock returns can be inferred from the analysis of Blackburn and Ukhov (2006a). Blackburn and Ukhov use Jackwerth's equation (23.4) to estimate the absolute risk aversion for the 30 stocks making up the Dow Jones Industrial Average. They find risk aversion patterns which appear exotic from a neoclassical perspective, and suggest that these patterns might have a behavioral basis involving preferences. Because the risk aversion patterns vary from stock to stock, the preference interpretation suggests different representative investors for different stocks. In contrast, the SDF approach features a single representative investor whose preferences serve to price all assets.

In applying Jackwerth's technique, Blackburn and Ukhov assume that their representative investors have correct beliefs. In this respect, the issues about absolute risk aversion being given by equation (23.8) instead of equation (23.4) also apply to their analysis. However, equation (23.8) can also be used with Blackburn and Ukhov's data in order to gain some insight into the shape of the sentiment functions associated with different stocks.

To apply equation (23.8), assume that the representative investor has CRRA utility. In this case the absolute risk aversion function $r_{AP}(x)$ is equal to γ/x, where γ is the coefficient of relative risk aversion. For the moment, fix the value of γ, so that the function $r_{AP}(x)$ is specified. Notably, equation (23.8) provides an equation for Λ', which can be integrated to yield the sentiment function.

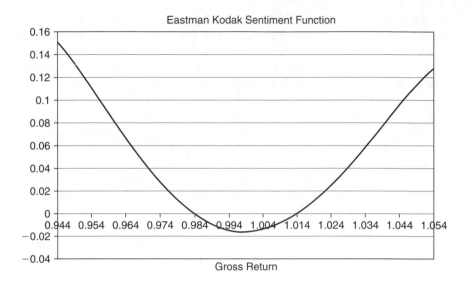

FIGURE 23.10. Shape of Sentiment Function Projection for Kodak Stock. The sentiment function for Kodak stock is derived from the analysis in Blackburn and Ukhov (2006a).

The associated function for Λ, achieved through integration, features two unknown parameters. The first is the constant of integration. The second is the value of γ. The constant of integration does not impact the shape of the sentiment function. The value of γ does impact the exact shape of the sentiment function, but not its general shape, at least not in the range of estimated values discussed in Chapter 13.

Figures 23.10 and 23.11 illustrate the shape of sentiment function for the stocks of Kodak and Chevron respectively, derived from data used by Blackburn and Ukhov (2006a). Notice that the sentiment function for Kodak's stock is U-shaped, while the sentiment function for Chevron stock is oscillating. These correspond to the behavioral shapes depicted in Figures 15.4 and 15.8. Most of the sentiment functions derived from Blackburn–Ukhov's analysis tend to feature one of these two shapes.

Focus on Figure 23.11. This graph has the same interpretation as Figure 15.8. Consider the positive region at the left of Figure 23.10. Positive values in this region mean that the market density P_R has overestimated the probability that the return to Chevron stock would be very low. Negative values at the right mean that the market density P_R underestimated the probability that the return to Chevron stock would be very high. As with Figure 23.8, this pattern suggests a mixture of investor types trading Chevron stock, with significant clusters of both underconfident bears and overconfident bulls.

FIGURE 23.11. Shape of Sentiment Function Projection for Chevron Stock. The sentiment function for Chevron stock is derived from the analysis in Blackburn and Ukhov (2006a).

23.9 Summary

This chapter discussed five empirical studies involving index options that provide evidence supporting the behavioral approach to the SDF and risk-neutral density function. Taken together the five studies tell an interesting story.

Bollen–Whaley indicate that most index options are indeed traded by professional investors who use out-of-the-money puts to insure their portfolios. They demonstrate that herding behavior among professional investors and limits of arbitrage among market makers, lead to price pressure in these options, thereby producing smiles. Han demonstrates that the trading of professional investors is related to various indexes of sentiment, and that sentiment, not just price pressure, impacts the slope of the IVF. David–Veronesi relate the shape of the option smile to investors' beliefs, which has implications for the impact of gambler's fallacy. Jackwerth finds that the empirical risk aversion function appears to have negative segments and upward-sloping segments. Aït-Sahalia-Lo and Rosenberg–Engle use index option price data to estimate the (projection of the) SDF. Their estimates reveal the trademark signature of sentiment: oscillation in the graph of the SDF, along with excessively volatile estimates of market risk aversion.

The chapter concludes with a discussion suggesting that the shape of the empirical SDF is consistent with both behavioral asset pricing theory and the empirical evidence involving the sentiment process. Additional empirical support comes from the analysis of cross-sectional returns, in respect to both coskewness (Harvey–Siddique) and the shapes of sentiment functions for individual stocks (Blackburn–Ukhov).

Part VII

Behavioral Preferences

24

Prospect Theory: Introduction

Two features distinguish the behavioral approach to asset pricing from the traditional neoclassical approach to asset pricing. The first feature is sentiment. Proponents of behavioral finance treat sentiment as a major determinant of market prices, stemming from systematic errors committed by investors. Proponents of neoclassical finance treat sentiment as minor. Instead, they assume that investors by and large are free from bias in their use of available information. Whereas behavioral asset pricing theorists attribute observed pricing phenomena to sentiment, traditional asset pricing theorists attribute observed pricing phenomena to fundamental risk or time varying risk aversion.

The second feature that distinguishes the behavioral approach and traditional approach is the assumption of expected utility. Traditional asset pricing theorists assume that investors seek to maximize expected utility. There is good reason to do so, in that expected utility is a rationality-based framework. Indeed, up to this point, the expected utility assumption has been central to the analysis. However, proponents of behavioral finance are critical of expected utility as a descriptive theory. They suggest that people generally behave in ways that are inconsistent with expected utility theory. Instead, they suggest that people behave more in accordance with a psychologically based theory, such as *prospect theory*. Prospect theory was developed by Kahneman and Tversky (1979).

Prospect theory integrated a series of insights due to Markowitz (1952) and Allais (1953). The latter authors suggested that people do not behave in accordance with the tenets of neoclassically-based theory for describing choice among risky alternatives: expected utility with a concave utility function. Prospect theory combined these insights into a new rich framework with additional implications and insights.

Four main features distinguish prospect theory from the expected utility approach. First, whereas expected utility theory postulates that the carriers of value are final wealth, prospect theory postulates that the carriers of value are gains and losses relative to a reference point. Second, whereas expected utility theory postulates that people's tolerance for risk is reasonably uniform, prospect theory postulates that tolerance for risk is different when people perceive themselves to be in the domain of gains than it is when people perceive themselves to be in the domain of losses. Third, whereas expected utility theory postulates that people weight probabilities correctly, prospect theory postulates that people overweight some probabilities and underweight others. Fourth, whereas expected utility theory postulates that people are immune to the manner in which decision tasks are described or framed, prospect theory postulates that framing can influence the decisions that people make.

Prospect theory is a theoretical framework that Kahneman and Tversky (1979) designed to capture the four features described above. In this respect, prospect theory is a descriptive framework, meaning that its purpose is to describe actual choice patterns. By no means is prospect theory intended to be a normative theory, which would be a theory of how people should make choices. Indeed, one of the aims of prospect theory is to explain why people are prone to making inferior choices.

Prospect theory is the subject of this chapter. The chapter describes elements of the studies that Kahneman-Tversky used to develop their theory. The evidence is both rich and compelling. In this respect, it is important for readers to distinguish between the experimental evidence that Kahneman and Tversky report, and the theoretical framework which they use to explain the evidence. Although the evidence motivated the structure of the theory, the theory is not unique.

Chapter 26 introduces an alternative theory, called SP/A theory, developed by psychologist Lola Lopes. SP/A theory possesses some advantages over prospect theory, both in its descriptive power and in its modeling features.

The focus of Part VII of the book is behavioral preferences. Chapter 25 develops portfolio implications associated with prospect theory preferences. However, portfolio selection is not the main topic of the book. Asset pricing is the main topic of the book. Chapters 28 and 29 discuss the implications of behavioral preferences for asset pricing. The core question in the book involves the impact of behavioral phenomena on the SDF. The main result in the book is the decomposition of the log-SDF into sentiment and a fundamental component. In Chapter 28, I demonstrate that this result extends to the case when investor preferences are behavioral. Notably, the extension encompasses the general case featuring both behavioral beliefs and behavioral preferences. In this respect, it represents a unifying result for the entire approach in the book.

24.1 Subcertainty, Expected Utility, and the Common Consequence Effect

Kahneman–Tversky relied on a series of small experiments to identify the manner in which people make choices in the face of risk. In their experiments they posed questions to subjects in order to identify behavioral traits. These experiments were structured as a series of binary choices, and some of the key choices appear below. The discussion of these choices is divided into subsections. Each subsection begins with one or two choice questions.

24.1.1 Common Ratio Effect

1. Imagine that you have an opportunity to play one of two gambles described below. The gambles are denoted 1A and 1B. If you had to make a choice between the two, which would you choose, 1A or 1B?

   1A: 90% chance of winning $2000, 10% chance of $0.

   1B: 45% chance of winning $4000, 55% chance of $0.

2. Imagine that you have an opportunity to play one of two gambles described below. The gambles are denoted 2A and 2B. If you had to make a choice between the two, which would you choose, 2A or 2B?

   2A: $2000 with probability .002, $0 with probability .998

   2B: $4000 with probability .001, $0 with probability .999

   Typically, the majority of subjects choose 1A over 1B, and almost everyone chooses 2B over 2A. The point of the exercise is that this pattern of choice is not consistent with expected utility theory. To see why, suppose that a person has a utility function $u(x)$, where x denotes the outcome of the gamble. Without loss of generality, $u(0)$ can be set at 0, and $u(4000)$ can be set at 1. Write $u(2000)$ for the utility attached to receiving $2000. Notice that in choosing 1A over 1B, an expected utility maximizing individual reveals that the expected utility he attaches to 1A is greater than or equal to the expected utility he attaches to 1B. That is,

$$0.9u(2000) + 0.1u(0) = 0.9u(2000) \tag{24.1}$$

$$\geq 0.45u(4000) + 0.55u(0) = 0.45u(4000) \tag{24.2}$$

which implies

$$u(2000) \geq 0.5u(4000) \tag{24.3}$$

However, in choosing 2B over 2A, an expected utility maximizing individual reveals that the expected utility he attaches to 2B is greater than or equal to the expected utility he attaches to 2A. That is,

$$0.001u(4000) + 0.999u(0) = 0.001u(4000) \tag{24.4}$$

$$\geq 0.002u(2000) + 0.998u(0) = 0.002u(2000) \tag{24.5}$$

which implies

$$u(2000) \leq 0.5u(4000) \tag{24.6}$$

Unless the individual is indifferent, equations (24.3) and (24.6) cannot hold simultaneously. That is, this pattern of choice cannot be consistent with expected utility theory. Under expected utility theory, if a person chooses 1A over 1B, then he must also choose 2A over 2B.

The key feature of the preceding discussion involves the ratio of the probabilities attached to $4000 and $2000 respectively in the two decision tasks. In choice 1, the ratio is $0.45/0.9 = 0.5$. In choice 2, the ratio is $0.001/0.002 = 0.5$. Expected utility theory implies that choice is invariant to common ratios. Yet, in practice, people often violate this principle, giving rise to what has come to be called the *common ratio effect*.

For Kahneman–Tversky, the issue is only partly whether the choices that people make are inconsistent with expected utility theory. They also seek to understand the factors that drive people's choices. In this regard, the responses from choices 1 and 2 relate to the role of small probabilities. Notice that choice 2 features small probabilities, while choice 1 does not. Kahneman–Tversky suggest that the choice pattern suggests that people are prone to underweight the difference between a probability of 0.002 and 0.001. They propose that this tendency stems from over-weighting small probabilities in general, with the degree of over-weighting being larger for smaller probabilities.

24.1.2   *Subcertainty and Expected Utility*

3. Imagine that you have an opportunity to play one of two gambles described below. The gambles are denoted 3A and 3B. If you had to make a choice between the two, which would you choose, 3A or 3B?

3A: 20% chance of $4000, 80% chance of $0

3B: 25% chance of $3000, 75% chance of $0

4. Imagine that you have an opportunity to play one of two gambles described below. The gambles are denoted 4A and 4B. If you had to make a choice between the two, which would you choose, 4A or 4B?

   4A: 80% chance of $4000, 20% chance of $0

   4B: sure chance of $3000

5. What would the probability of winning $4000 in 4A have to be in order that you be exactly indifferent between 4A (with the new odds) and 4B (a sure $3000)?

The majority of subjects choose 3A over 3B and 4B over 4A. Notice that the common ratio effect applies to choices 3 and 4, in that the likelihood ratio associated with $4000 and $3000 is 0.8 in both problems.

As before, the issue for Kahneman–Tversky is to identify the factors that appear to drive this choice pattern. They suggest that for this pair of choices, the main factor is certainty in choice 4. In particular, they suggest that certainty is accorded additional weight, and call the phenomenon *subcertainty*. (Subcertainty is discussed formally in the next section.)

The typical responses to choices 3 and 4 illustrate a property called the *common consequence effect*. Suppose that a person prefers a sure outcome x to a risky one y. Under expected utility, mixing first x and then y with some other z having probabilities p and $1 - p$ respectively, leads the x-mixture to be preferred to the y-mixture. Under the common consequence effect, this property is violated. In choices 3 and 4, x is the sure $3000 (4B), y is the risky 4A, z is a sure $0, and p is 0.75. Therefore, the x-mixture is 3B and the y-mixture is 3A.

Question 5 highlights the core principle of expected utility. The expected payoff in gamble 4 is $3200. A person who prefers to accept a sure $3000 would presumably want a higher probability of receiving $4000 in order to gamble. The question posed is how much higher?

Suppose a person answers "90 percent" to the question. In an expected utility framework, that person would be said to assign a utility of 0.9 to receiving $3000. The worst outcome ($0) is assigned a utility of 0. The best outcome ($4000) is assigned a utility of 1. In consequence the expected utility of the gamble in which $4000 is received with probability 90 percent and $0 is received with probability 10 percent is just 0.9. With $u(3000) = 0.9$, indifference corresponds to equality between the expected utility of the gamble and the utility of the sure outcome.

24.1.3 Allais Paradox and the Independence Axiom

Economist Maurice Allais was the first to recognize that expected utility theory is not descriptive of how people generally make choices. Two of the questions he used to demonstrate choice patterns that violate the predictions of expected utility appear here. Consider the following choices, and choose between 6A and 6B, and then between 7A and 7B.

6A: sure chance of $1 million
6B: 10% chance of $5 million, 89% chance of $1 million, 1% chance of $0

7A: 10% chance of $5 million, 90% chance of $0
7B: 11% chance of $1 million, 89% chance of $0

In 1953, Allais presented choices 6 and 7 to a group of economists and decision theorists who were pioneering the development of expected utility theory. The majority chose 6A over 6B and 7A over 7B. Assign utilities $u(0) = 0$, and $u(5) = 1$, and leave $u(1)$ unspecified, where the values are in millions of dollars. In an expected utility framework, choosing 6A over 6B implies $u(1) \geq 0.1 + 0.89u(1)$, which implies that $u(1) \geq 0.1/0.11$. Choosing 7A over 7B implies that $0.1 \geq 0.11u(1)$, which implies that $u(1) \leq 0.1/0.11$. Hence, the two inequalities conflict, except in the case of indifference: this choice pattern is inconsistent with expected utility.

Allais' example brings out the importance of the independence axiom of expected utility. The independence axiom can be stated in several ways. One way is to ask the following two questions of a decision maker.

Question 1: What utility would you assign to receiving $1 million? The meaning of this question is the same as above, namely: What would the probability of winning $5 million have to be in order that you be indifferent between playing an "all or nothing" gamble where you won either $5 million or $0, and accepting $1 million for sure?

Suppose the decision maker answers $u(1) = 0.93$, meaning that he would require a probability of 93 percent in the "all or nothing" gamble.

Question 2: Consider gamble 6B. Suppose that you were to play this gamble and win $1 million. Would you be willing, at that stage, to exchange the $1 million for an opportunity to play an "all or nothing" gamble where the probability of winning $5 million is 93 percent?

If the independence axiom of expected utility holds, then the decision maker will always answer "yes" to question 2, as long as the probability used coincides with the response he provides to question 1.

Suppose that the decision maker is willing to agree to the exchange. In that case, what is the probability of playing the modified version of gamble 6B, meaning the version with the substitution? To answer this question, notice that there are two ways to win $5 million, the direct way and the indirect way. The probability attached to the direct way is 10 percent. The indirect way is to first win $1 million, exchange it for an "all or nothing" gamble, and then win \$5 million in that gamble. The probability attached to the indirect way is $0.89 \times 0.93 = 0.828$, and to either the direct way or indirect way is 0.928.

Now the probability of winning \$5 million in the modified 6B corresponds to the expected utility of playing gamble 6B, $0.1 + 0.89u(1) = 0.1 + (0.89 \times 0.93) = 0.928$. That is, the mechanics of computing expected utility provide the same computation for computing the probability of winning \$5 million in the modified 6B.

Think about the implications associated with the equality just described. Effectively, the independence axiom allows any two gambles to be modified into indifferent "all or nothing" gambles. The probability of winning \$5 million in the indifference-modified 6A is 93 percent. The probability of winning \$5 million in the indifference-modified 6B is 92.8 percent. A decision maker who prefers more to less would choose the dominant gamble, and therefore would choose the indifference-modified 6A over the indifference-modified 6B. But given the implicit indifference between the gambles and their indifference modifications, transitivity of preferences implies that the decision maker would choose 6A over 6B in this case. Given that expected utility corresponds to the probability of winning \$5 million in a modified gamble, the discussion implies that the decision maker chooses the gamble with the higher expected utility.

Answering "yes" to the second of the two questions associated with the independence axiom would seem to be reasonable. Indeed, a compelling argument can be advanced that rational behavior requires that people obey the independence axiom. After all, violating the independence axiom implies that people act as if they are choosing gambles that are first order stochastically dominated.

Be that as it may, people do not regularly ask themselves such questions when choosing among risky alternatives. Instead, they use other thought processes, processes that apparently conflict with the independence axiom. In choice 6, people appear to favor the certainty of the \$1 million. In choice 7, where the certainty is absent, the difference in payoff (\$5 million − \$4 million) exerts a stronger influence than the difference in probability (11% − 10%).

24.1.4   The Isolation Effect

Kahneman–Tversky use the term *framing* to denote the manner in which a decision problem is described. The traditional approach assumes that framing is irrelevant to how people make choices. For instance, the traditional approach indicates that people will act *as if* they framed choices involving risk by asking themselves the two questions associated with the independence axiom. If individuals did so, and avoided making stochastically dominated choices, then their behavior would conform to the maximization of expected utility.

8. Suppose that you are paid $1000 to participate in a survey that presents participants with choices such as the following.

    8A. a sure $500

    8B. a 50% chance of winning $1000, a 50% chance of $0

9. Suppose that you are paid $2000 to participate in a survey that presents participants with choices such as the following.

    9A. a sure $500 loss

    9B. a 50% chance of losing $1000, a 50% chance of $0

The most common choices in the two situations just described are 8A (accept the sure $500) and 9B (gamble instead of accepting a sure loss).

From these responses, Kahneman–Tversky conclude that people act as if they are risk averse when only gains are involved, but become risk seeking when they perceive themselves to be facing the possibility of loss. In choice 8, most people prefer a sure $500 over an uncertain expected $500. In choice 9, most people prefer an expected uncertain $500 loss to a sure $500 loss.

In addition, Kahneman–Tversky point out that people tend to focus on gains and losses, as framed in the decision choice, isolating these from other variables that are germane. In this respect, compare choices 8 and 9 when the survey participation fee is included. In both situations, participants are asked to choose between a net gain of $1500 and a 50–50 gamble between winning net amounts of $1000 and $2000. The point is that when the choice is framed in the domain of gains, people respond as if they are risk averse. When the choice is framed in the domain of losses, people respond as if they are risk seeking.

Choices 6A and 8A are sure outcomes that people tend to select over their risky alternatives 6B and 8B respectively. These choice patterns are related to a common consequence effect involving violations of expected utility when alternative choices feature common consequences.[1]

Technically, the preceding choice is between a sure gain of $1500 and an expected uncertain $1500. Therefore, either choice is consistent with risk neutrality. In this respect, Kahneman–Tversky also pose choices such as:

    10A: a sure loss of $3000

    10B: an 80% chance of losing $4000, a 20% chance of $0

---

[1] Suppose a person prefers a sure outcome x to a risky one y. Under expected utility, mixing first x and then y with some other z with probabilities p and $1 - p$ respectively, leads the x-mixture to be preferred to the y-mixture. Under the common consequence effect, this property is violated.

In choice 10, most people prefer an expected uncertain $3200 loss to a sure $3000 loss. That choice reflects risk seeking behavior, not risk-neutral behavior. Kahneman–Tversky refer to this situation as *aversion to a sure loss.*

Kahneman–Tversky conclude that people analyze choices in isolation from the other aspects of their financial situations. That is, they appear to establish a separate *mental account* for each choice, but not tie these mental accounts together. Moreover, because mental accounts are framed as gains and losses, these gains and losses need to be defined in terms of a benchmark, or *reference point.*

24.1.5   Isolation and the Independence Axiom

11. Imagine that you are registering to participate in a lottery. The person who is registering you explains the rules of the lottery, and indicates that you need to answer a question before becoming eligible to win. The structure of the lottery is as follows: The probability of winning a prize in this lottery is 2/900 (that is, .00222222222...). If you win the lottery, you get to choose one of the following as your prize:

   11A. a lottery ticket to play 1A.

   11B. a lottery ticket to play 1B.

   The question you need to answer at the time you register is this: If you win, will you want the prize to be for 1A or for 1B?

Most people make the same choice here as they do in choice task 1. If they selected choice 1A when asked directly, then they select 1A as their contingent prize in choice task 11. However, in choice task 11, they may not win: the odds of winning are only 2 in 900.

Effectively, the compound probability of winning $2000 in choice task 11, given selection 1A, is 0.002, in that $0.002 = (0.9 \times 2/900)$. Notice that 0.002 is the probability of winning $2000 in choice task 2. In fact, when we frame the choice in compound probabilities, the decision problem can be expressed as choice task 2. When the question is framed as choice task 2, most people choose B. When it is framed in conditional probabilities, most people choose A.

24.1.6   Loss Aversion

Consider the following choice:

   12A. a sure $0

   12B. a 50% chance to win $10, a 50% chance to lose $10

Most people find 12A unattractive and choose 12B. Taken together with the typical behavior patterns described in subsection 24.1.4, the choice pattern for choice task 12 suggests that people are risk averse in the domain of gains, and risk seeking in the domain of losses, and that losses loom larger than gains of the same magnitude.

Kahneman–Tversky use the term *loss aversion* to describe the observation that for most people, losses loom larger than gains.

24.1.7 Ambiguity

The following three questions involve valuation rather than choice.

13. An urn contains 100 balls, of which some are red and others are blue. The proportion of balls of each color is unknown. Consider a lottery ticket that pays $5,000 if a red ball is drawn. How much would you be willing to pay to own the lottery ticket?

14. An urn contains 100 balls, of which some are red and others are blue. The proportion of balls of each color is unknown. Consider a lottery ticket that pays $5,000 if a blue ball is drawn. How much would you be willing to pay to own the lottery ticket?

15. An urn contains 100 balls, 50 red and 50 blue. Consider a lottery ticket that pays $5,000 if a red ball is drawn. How much would you be willing to pay to own the lottery ticket?

Most people provide the same value in answering question 13 as in answering question 14. That is, given the symmetry in the problem, they place the same value on the occurrence of red or blue.

The interesting comparison involves their responses to questions 13 and 15. Most people provide a lower value in answering question 13 than in answering question 15. This means that they view not knowing the proportion of balls (in question 13) as being different from facing a situation where they know the probabilities to be 50–50. The situation with unknown probabilities is said to feature *ambiguity*. The lower response to question 15 than to question 13 indicates that people are averse to ambiguity. Questions 13–15 were first proposed by Daniel Ellsberg, and the results just described came to be known as the *Ellsberg Paradox*.

Ambiguity declines in situations where people are familiar with the underlying situation. Even though the following problems about the Dow Jones Industrial Average (DJIA) do not specify particular probabilities, professional investors are familiar with the DJIA, so they will be illustrative.

Consider the closing value of the Dow Jones Industrial Average on two future days, namely the Tuesday and the Thursday of next week. The following choices pertain to the difference d defined as the Thursday closing value minus the Tuesday closing value. Imagine a series of gambles, defined relative to the value d. The amounts referred to in the gambles pay off on the Friday of next week.

16. Choose between 16A and 16B below.

    16A. $2,500 with certainty, meaning irrespective of the value of d.

    16B. $2,500 if d is strictly less than 30 points, $0 if d is between 30 and 35, $7,500 if d is strictly greater than 35 points.

17. Choose between 17A and 17B below.

    17A. $0 if d is strictly less than 30 points, $2,500 if d is 30 points or more.

    17B. $0 if d is 35 points or less, $7,500 if d is strictly greater than 35 points.

The preceding questions set the stage for the theoretical section that follows.

24.2 Theory

Formally, prospect theory consists of a specification of mental accounts to capture framing effects, a utility function defined over gains and losses (known as a value function), and a probability weighting function.

24.2.1 The Weighting Function

Consider questions 16 and 17. When people are not given the underlying objective probabilities, they may use uncertainty weights that resemble subjective probabilities. However, unlike subjective probabilities, uncertainty weights need not sum to unity across events. This property is known as *subcertainty*.

About half of respondents choose 16A over 16B. Most choose 17B over 17A. Consider the implications of this choice configuration. Without loss of generality, let $u(0) = 0$ and $u(7500) = 1$. Define $v(E)$ to be the uncertainty weight attached to event E. The choice of 16A over 16B implies that

$$u(2500) \geq u(2500)v(d < 30) + v(d > 35)$$

Rewrite this expression to read

$$u(2500)(1 - v(d < 30)) \geq v(d > 35)$$

The choice of 17B over 17A implies

$$v(d > 35) \geq u(2500)v(d \geq 30)$$

Combining these two inequalities leads to the expression

$$1 - v(d < 30) \geq v(d \geq 30)$$

If either of the two choices is strictly preferred rather than their being indifferent, then it must be that

$$1 - v(d < 30) > v(d \geq 30)$$

in which case

$$v(d < 30) + v(d \geq 30) < 1$$

Subcertainty can explain the different valuations for questions 13 and 15 above. In answering a question such as 13, a person might assign the same uncertainty weights to the drawing of a red ball as to the drawing of a blue ball. However, in order to reflect ambiguity, those weights may only sum to 0.75 instead of 1. That is why replacing probabilities with uncertainty weights in an expected value calculation leads to a lower valuation in question 13 (with uncertain probabilities) than in question 15 (with known probabilities).

Formally, the subcertainty property entails the result's being strictly less than 1 when uncertainty weights across mutually exclusive and exhaustive events are summed. Notably, weights can also be used when probabilities are given, but note that they would then be called probability weights instead of uncertainty weights. For example, Kahneman–Tversky suggest that subcertainty in the case of probability weights explains why people choose the sure outcome in choice 4 but the gamble in choice 3.

Kahneman–Tversky (1979) proposed a weighting function π on the interval $[0, 1]$ that was continuous and convex in the open interval $(0, 1)$, lying above the 45-degree line in a neighborhood of 0, and lying below the 45-degree line for most of its range. They set $\pi(0) = 0$ and $\pi(1) = 1$, thereby giving rise to discontinuities at both ends of the unit interval.

In order to clean up some technical inconsistencies, Tversky–Kahneman (1993) made some minor modifications to the scheme. First, they proposed using the cumulative distribution function as the basis for weights. Second, they proposed a modified weighting function. Tversky-Kahneman called their modified framework cumulative prospect theory (CPT). A formal comparison of original prospect theory (OPT) and CPT is provided in section 24.3.

In regard to the cumulative representation, one starts by ordering outcome gains (x_k) from worst to best, with the worst outcome indexed by 1 and the best outcome indexed by n. Losses (x_{-k}) are indexed by $-k$, where the most favorable loss is indexed by -1 and the least favorable loss is indexed by $-m$. The index $k = 0$ denotes the zero outcome, meaning no gain or loss.

Tversky-Kahneman define a weighting function w^+ on the domain of decumulative probabilities for gains and a weighting function w^- on the domain of cumulative probabilities for losses. The functions $w^+(D^c)$ and $w^-(D^c)$ are themselves defined to be cumulative and decumulative probabilities. Therefore w^+ and w^- give rise to probability densities, denoted respectively by v^+ and v^-. It is v^+ and v^- which are the actual decision weights used in CPT.

As to the functional forms for w^+ and w^-, Tversky-Kahneman propose that

$$w^+(D) = \frac{D^\gamma}{(D^\gamma + (1 - D)^\gamma)^{1/\gamma}} \tag{24.7}$$

which is the ratio of a power function to a Hölder average. The functional form for w^- is the same as (24.7) except that δ is used in place of γ. Based on experimental evidence Tversky-Kahneman report estimates of 0.61 for γ and 0.63 for δ. Figure 24.1 displays the shape of the weighting function w^+. Notice that the function overweights probability mass associated with extreme gains, whose decumulative probabilties are small. Likewise, the function w^- overweights probability mass associated with extreme losses, whose cumulative probabilties are small.

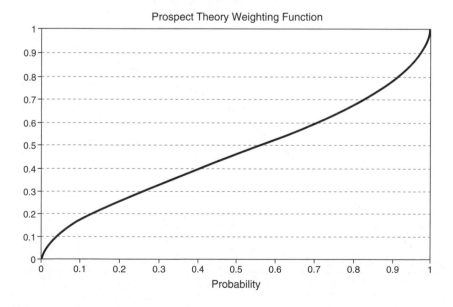

FIGURE 24.1. This figure illustrates the prospect theory weighting function v.

24.2.2   Value Function

The value function is a utility function defined over gains and losses. The function is concave in the domain of gains to reflect risk aversion, and convex in the domain of losses to reflect risk seeking. There is a point of nondifferentiability at the origin, and the function is more steeply sloped to the left of the origin than to the right.

Tversky–Kahneman propose that

$$u(x) = x^\alpha \tag{24.8}$$

if $x \geq 0$ and

$$u(x) = -\lambda(-x^\beta) \tag{24.9}$$

if $x < 0$. Figure 24.2 illustrates the u function. (The notation here corresponds to Tversky-Kahneman (1992); the variables $\alpha, \beta, \gamma, \delta,$ and λ have different meanings in other parts of the book.)

The CPT valuation function essentially has the form $\Sigma_i v_i u(x_i)$. An example is provided in section 24.3, using the median parameter values reported by Tversky-Kahneman. The values they report for α and β are 0.88. This means that the utility function is close to being linear. For gains, the linear function in (24.8) is just $u(x) = x$. A value of 0.88 for α is equivalent

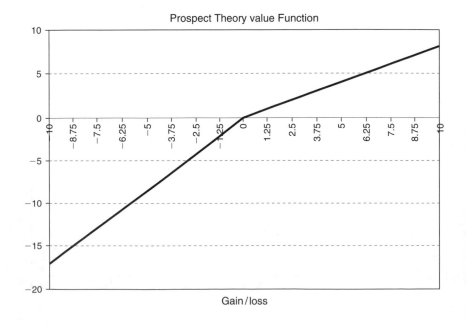

FIGURE 24.2. This figure illustrates the prospect theory value function u.

to a coefficient of relative risk aversion of 0.12. Recall that in the CRRA framework, the exponent in the utility function is $1 - \gamma$, where γ is the coefficient of relative risk aversion. Of course, for losses the coefficient of relative risk aversion is negative.

The parameter λ represents how a loss is psychologically experienced relative to a gain of the same magnitude. A typical parameter value for λ is 2.5. One way to measuring λ is to administer a question such as 18, which follows.

18. Imagine a 50–50 gamble where you lose $50 if the coin toss comes up tails, but win some amount if the coin toss turns up heads. What is the lowest amount you would have to win in this gamble in order to accept the gamble?

A typical response to this question is $125. That is, in order to accept a 50–50 gamble, people typically ask for a gain to be at least 2.5 times the size of a loss.

24.2.3   Interaction Between Value Function and Weighting Function

As a general matter, the shape of the prospect theory value function (see equations (24.8) and (24.9)) implies that people are risk averse in the domain of gains and risk seeking in the domain of losses. However, there is an important qualification that relates to the value function.

Based on the responses to question 2, Kahneman–Tversky (1979) suggest that the overweighting of low probabilities can induce risk aversion in the domain of losses and risk seeking in the domain of gains. As an example of the first, they point out that people are willing to pay actuarially unfair premiums to insure themselves against low probability events (such as airline crashes). As an example of the second, they point out that people are willing to pay actuarially unfair prices to purchase lottery tickets. Notice that these two behavior patterns are opposite to the general patterns previously emphasized in connection with the value function.

Kahneman and Tversky suggest that a single principle underlies the shapes of the weighting function in Figure 24.1 and value function in Figure 24.2. The principle is *psychophysics*, and reflects diminishing sensitivity from a particular reference point. In the case of the value function, a person becomes increasingly less sensitive to marginal gains, as the overall gain increases relative to the reference point. This feature is captured by the concavity of the value function in the domain of gains. Likewise, a person becomes increasingly less sensitive to marginal losses, as the overall loss increases (in absolute value) relative to the reference point. This feature is captured by the convexity of the value function in the domain of losses.

As to the weighting function, there are two reference points, 0 and 1. These correspond to the cases of complete certainty, where an event either must occur or cannot occur at all. The concave feature at the left of the inverse S-shaped weighting function reflects diminishing sensitivity to increases in probability as probability increases relative to 0. The convex feature at the right of the inverse S-shaped weighting function reflects diminishing sensitivity to decreases in probability as probability decreases relative to 1.

24.2.4 Framing

Modeling the weighting function and utility function is less challenging than modeling framing. In this respect, framing appears to be less salient as a part of prospect theory than the other two components. Yet, framing can be quite critical. In order to see why, consider the following choice problem, which appears in Tversky–Kahneman (1986).

19. Imagine that you face the following pair of concurrent decisions. Think of making your choices in the morning, with the outcome to the first decision being determined in the afternoon, and the outcome of the second decision being determined in the evening. Imagine that the current time is morning. First examine both decisions, and then indicate the alternative you prefer.

    First decision:

    19A. a sure gain of $2,400
    19B. 25% chance to gain $10,000 and 75% chance to gain nothing.

    Second decision:

    19C. a sure loss of $7,500
    19D. 75% chance to lose $10,000 and 25% chance to lose nothing

Most people choose 19A over 19B and 19D over 19C. That is, they act as if they are risk averse when choosing between 19A and 19B, and they act as if they are risk seeking when choosing between 19C and 19D.

Observe that the choices in this question are concurrent. The combination of 19A and 19D produces a gamble featuring a probability of 25 percent of winning $2400 and a probability of 75 percent of losing $7600. However, notice that the combination of 19B and 19C results in a gamble featuring a probability of 25 percent of winning $2500 and a probability of 75 percent of losing $7500. Therefore, the combination of 19B and 19C stochastically dominates the combination of 19A and 19D.

When the problem is framed in terms of combinations, most people reject the combination of 19A and 19D. But people are not efficient at reframing. Therefore, framing affects choice.

The frame involving combinations features a single mental account. Choosing the preferred combination involves computing the value of $\sum_{k=-m}^{n} v_k u(x_k)$ for all possible combinations and selecting the combination with the highest value. The frame as presented involves two mental accounts, one for the choice of 19A or 19B, and the other for the choice of 19C or 19D. The point is that choices are made on the basis of one mental account at a time.

24.3 Original Prospect Theory and Cumulative Prospect Theory

The most important difference between the original version of prospect theory (OPT) introduced by Kahneman and Tversky (1979) and the cumulative version (CPT) introduced in Tversky and Kahneman (1992) involves the weighting function.

24.3.1 Original Prospect Theory

In OPT, the probability weighting function has the form $\pi(p)$, where p denotes probability. Therefore, the weight attached to a particular outcome depends only on the probability associated with that outcome, and is independent of the probabilities associated with other outcomes. In CPT, the use of rank dependence implies that the independence property just described generally fails.

Figure 24.3 displays the shape of the $\pi(p)$ function used in OPT, along with the 45-degree line. Notice that $\pi(p) > p$ for low values of p, while $\pi(p) < p$ for higher values of p. In addition $\pi(p) + \pi(1-p) < 1$ for $0 < p < 1$: this property reflects subcertainty.

Unless $\pi(p) = p$ for all p, the subcertainty property in OPT implies that in some circumstances, a stochastically dominant alternative will have a higher prospect theory value than an alternative it stochastically dominates. To see why, consider two prospects. The first prospect pays X with probability p and Y with probability $1 - p$. Assume $X > Y$. The second prospect pays X with probability $p + \Delta p$ and Y with probability $1 - p - \Delta p$, where $\Delta p > 0$. In OPT, the value of the first prospect is

$$\pi(p)u(X) + \pi(1 - p)u(Y) \tag{24.10}$$

and the value of the second prospect is

$$\pi(p + \Delta p)u(X) + \pi(1 - p - \Delta p)u(Y) \tag{24.11}$$

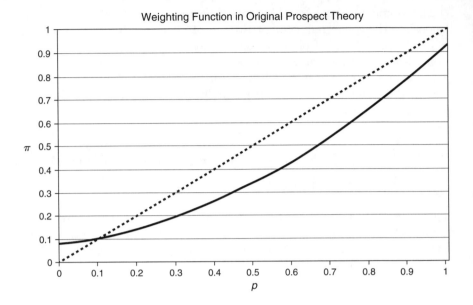

FIGURE 24.3. Weighting function in original propect theory, Kahneman–Tversky (1979). The figure displays the shape of the weighting function $\pi(p)$ in the original version of prospect theory.

Define $\Delta\pi(p) = \pi(p + \Delta p) - \pi(p)$ and $\Delta\pi(1 - p) = \pi(1 - p - \Delta p) - \pi(1 - p)$. Then the value of the second prospect can be expressed as:

$$\pi(p)u(X) + \pi(1 - p)u(Y) + \Delta\pi(p)u(X) + \Delta\pi(1 - p)u(Y) \qquad (24.12)$$

Because $X > Y$ and $\Delta p > 0$, the second prospect stochastically dominates the first prospect. However, by (24.10) and (24.12), the second prospect will only have a higher value than the first prospect if

$$\Delta\pi(p)u(X) + \Delta\pi(1 - p)u(Y) > 0$$

or

$$\Delta\pi(p)u(X) > -\Delta\pi(1 - p)u(Y) \qquad (24.13)$$

If p is low, then by the shape of the weighting function in OPT, $\Delta\pi(1 - p)$ might be much larger in absolute value than $\Delta\pi(p)$. In this case, for X and Y sufficiently close, (24.13) will fail to hold, even though the second prospect stochastically dominates the first prospect. Parenthetically, notice that if $\pi(p) = p$, the expected utility assumption, then (24.13) is automatically satisfied.

Kahneman and Tversky (1979) argue that when the stochastic dominance is transparent, people do not knowingly choose the dominated prospect. They suggest instead that when the above two prospects are evaluated, the prospects are framed as receiving Y for sure, and the possibility of receiving an additional amount $X - Y$. The value of the first prospect is then expressed as

$$u(Y) + \pi(p)(u(X) - u(Y)) \tag{24.14}$$

and the value of the second prospect is expressed as

$$u(Y) + \pi(p + \Delta p)(u(X) - u(Y)) \tag{24.15}$$

Because $\pi(p + \Delta p) > \pi(p)$ and $u(X) > u(Y)$, (24.14) and (24.15) imply that the value of the dominating prospect exceeds that of the dominated prospect.

Kahneman and Tversky argue that people will avoid choosing dominated alternatives when the choice is transparent, but might choose dominated alternatives when the choice is opaque. A pertinent example is choice task 19.

Choice task 19 is a bit complex. Here is a simpler choice task which Tversky and Kahneman (1986) developed to illustrate the issue of stochastic dominance, opaqueness, and transparency.

Imagine an urn containing a mixture of colored balls: white, red, green, etc. A single ball is to be drawn from the urn, and that will determine your prize. Consider the choices 20 and 21 below.

If you were asked to make a choice between 20A and 20B, which alternative would you choose?

20A.	90% white	6% red	1% green	3% yellow
	$0	win $45	win $30	lose $15
20B.	90% white	7% red	1% green	2% yellow
	$0	win $45	lose $10	lose $15

If you were asked to make a choice between 21A and 21B, which alternative would you choose?

21A.	90% white	6% red	1% green	1% blue	2% yellow
	$0	win $45	win $30	lose $15	lose $15
21B.	90% white	6% red	1% green	1% blue	2 % yellow
	$0	win $45	win $45	lose $10	lose $15

Almost everyone chooses 21B over 21A. This is because 21B stochastically dominates 21A in a way that is transparent. In 21A and 21B, the probabilities are the same for the drawing of any colored ball from the urn. The amounts for white, red, and yellow are also the same for the two choices. However, the amounts for green and blue are different. In both cases, the payoffs for 21B are higher than for 21A, no matter which colored ball is drawn.

In choice 20, the stochastic dominance property is not transparent. The probabilities for red and yellow are different in 20A than they are in 20B. If green is drawn, the amounts are different in 20A than they are in 20B. Here people are more mixed in their response to their choices between 20A and 20B. More people find it difficult to see that 20B stochastically dominates 20A; and some choose 20A over 20B. What most people perceive is that 20A is better than 20B in case a green ball is drawn, and 20B offers better probabilities for the red ball and the yellow ball. Most people fail to see that 20A is stochastically identical to 21A and that 20B is stochastically identical to 21B.

To see the stochastic equivalence between choices 20 and 21, compare the probabilities of receiving the four distinct outcomes in 20 with those of 21. For example, the outcome of 21B is $45 if either a red ball or green ball is drawn. Because the probability of a red ball is 6 percent and the probability of a green ball is 1 percent, the probability attached to $45 is the sum, 7 percent. Next, observe that the outcome of 20B is $45 if a red ball is drawn, the probability of which is 7 percent. That is, the probability of receiving $45 in 20B and 21B is exactly the same. A similar argument applies to all the other outcomes.

To repeat, the point of choices 20 and 21 is that people will avoid stochastically dominated alternative when the stochastic dominance property is transparent, but might choose a stochastically dominated alternative when the stochastic dominance property is opaque.

24.3.2   Comparing Original Prospect Theory and Cumulative Prospect Theory

Despite Kahneman and Tversky's use of framing to deal with the violation of transparent stochastic dominance, OPT came to be criticized for requiring what some viewed as an ad hoc procedure. See Gonzalez and Wu (1999). Therefore, Tversky and Kahneman (1992) modified prospect theory to incorporate the rank dependent utility property developed by Quiggen (1982) and Yaari (1987). In the rank dependent utility framework, decision makers do not knowingly choose stochastically dominated prospects.

Tables 24.1 and 24.2 illustrate the difference between OPT and CPT. Table 24.1 provides the prospect theory parameters for the illustration. The functional form for CPT is described in subsections 24.2.1 and 24.2.2. The functional form for $\pi(p)$ is taken to be $\pi(p) = a_0 + a_1 p + a_2 p^2$.

TABLE 24.1. Parameter values for prospect theory example. CPT stands for cumulative prospect theory, and OPT stands for original prospect theory.

Prospect Theory Parameters	
Parameters for value function u	
α	0.88
β	0.88
λ	2.25
CPT parameters for $w-$, $w+$	
γ	0.61
δ	0.69
OPT Parameters for π	
a0	0.08
a1	0.20
a2	0.65

TABLE 24.2. This table displays two evaluations of the prospect displayed in the columns labeled Payoff and Probability p. One evaluation pertains to OPT and the second to CPT. The value function values are displayed in the column labeled Value u. The weighting function in OPT is displayed next. The column labeled $D-$ is the cumulative distribution function for the domain of losses. The column labeled $D+$ is the decumulative distribution function for the domain of gains. The values of the weighting function for the domain of losses are displayed in the column $w-$, and the values of the weighting function for the domain of gains are displayed in the column $w+$. The weighting function values are for transformed cumulative and decumulative values. The weights attached to payoffs are given in the columns labeled $v-$ and $v+$ respectively. The value of the prospect under OPT is -47.5, while under CPT it is -61.9, the sum of -109.1 (the loss component) and 47.2 (the gain component).

Payoff	Probability p	Value u	π	$D-$	$D+$	$w-$	$w+$	$v-$	$v+$
-300	0.143	-340.4	0.122	0.143		0.21		0.21	
-200	0.143	-238.3	0.122	0.286		0.32		0.11	
-100	0.143	-129.5	0.122	0.429		0.41		0.09	
0	0.143	0.0	0.122	0.571	0.571	0.50	0.46	0.09	0.07
100	0.143	57.5	0.122		0.429		0.38		0.07
200	0.143	105.9	0.122		0.286		0.31		0.09
300	0.143	151.3	0.122		0.143		0.22		0.22
Value of loss/gain subfunctionals in CPT								-109.1	47.2
Value of prospect theory functional		-47.9							-61.9

Table 24.2 illustrates the evaluation of a prospect developed in Lopes (1993). The payoffs are displayed in the column labeled "Payoff," whose associated probabilities are displayed in the column labeled "Probability p." Utility values are displayed in the column labeled "Value u," and OPT-probability weights are displayed in the column labeled "π." The value of the prospect is the sum $\Sigma_i \pi(p_i) u(x_i)$, which turns out to be -47.9.

The evaluation under CPT uses the same value function as OPT but different decision weights. Recall that CPT involves two weighting functions, one for gains (w^+) and one for losses (w^-). The function w^- takes as its argument the cumulative probabilities D^-. For example, the cumulative probability attached to the payoff -300 is $D^-(-300) = Pr\{x \leq -300\} = 0.143$. This is because the worst outcome (largest loss) is -300, and the probability attached to the event $\{x = -300\}$ is 0.143. The cumulative probability attached to the payoff -200 is

$$Pr\{x \leq -200\} = Pr\{x = -300\} + Pr\{x = -200\} = 0.286.$$

For gains, the weighting function w+ takes as its argument decumulative probabilities. For example, the decumulative probability $D^+(100) = Pr(x \geq 100) = 0.429$.

The transformed cumulative and decumulative weights w^- and w^+ are computed using equation (24.7). The decision weights attached to the payoffs are given by v^- and v^+. These are the probabilities that apply, respectively, when the cumulative distribution function for losses is given by D^- and the decumulative function for gains is given by D^+.

Define $v_i = v_i^+$ when the payoff is a gain, and v_i^- when the payoff is a loss. Under CPT, the value of the prospect is $\Sigma_i v_i u(x_i)$. In the example, $\Sigma_i v_i u(x_i)$ is the sum of the contributions -109.1 and 47.2 displayed in Table 24.2.

In the example, $\Sigma_i v_i = 0.96 < 1$, which reflects the property of subcertainty. As was discussed above, subcertainty is the culprit associated with violations of stochastic dominance. Notably, in CPT subcertainty can hold for risky alternatives that feature a mix of gains and losses. However, because w^+ and w^- are themselves decumulative/cumulative distribution functions, decision weights for alternatives that respectively involve only gains, or only losses, will not feature subcertainty. As a result, in CPT, the preference pattern described in connection with choices 3 and 4 cannot be attributed to subcertainty. Instead the explanation must involve the shape of the weighting function portrayed in Figure 24.1. The shape at the extreme right, for high decumulative probabilities, must support the sure 4B over the risky 4A, whereas the shape at the extreme left, for low decumulative probabilities, must support the risky 3A over the risky 3B.

Fennema and Wakker (1997) used the prospect described in Table 2.4 to test the two versions of prospect theory against each other. In their study, they provided subjects with the opportunity to shift probability mass of 1/21 from any outcome to the adjacent higher outcome. Under OPT, the maximizing shift is associated with the outcomes -100 and 0. This is because the utility value difference is greatest for these two outcomes. Under CPT, the weights v^- and v^+ are exaggerated at extreme losses and gains: See Table 24.1 where the weights at the extremes are 0.21 and 0.22 respectively, compared to 0.09 and 0.07 near the zero gain/loss payoff. Because of the weighting stemming from rank dependence, CPT features the maximizing shift being associated with -300 and -200.

Fennema and Wakker find that the majority of subjects favor shifting probability weight in the manner predicted by CPT than OPT. They conclude that rank dependent utility is germane and that CPT is the more descriptive framework.

Payne (2006) discusses a modification to the Fennema-Wakker study whereby subjects choose an outcome to which they can augment the payoff by a fixed amount.

The findings of his study are better explained by OPT than CPT. However, Payne's conclusions actually suggest that a theory such as SP/A, which I introduce in Chapter 26, is more descriptive than either version of prospect theory. SP/A theory does not feature subcertainty, and therefore does not support the choice of stochastically dominated outcomes when those choices are transparent.

24.4   Subtle Aspects Associated with Risk Aversion

Imagine that an investor is offered an opportunity to face the following 50–50 gamble, which she can accept or reject.

22. 50% probability to win \$11, 50% probability to lose \$10

This choice problem is similar to choice task 12, but a bit more favorable. Even so, most people reject the gamble. The decision to reject may well be rational. Consider an investor with initial wealth equal to \$500. Suppose that she is an expected utility maximizer, and has CRRA utility with coefficient of relative risk aversion equal to 5. After computing and comparing the respective expected utilities of the decision to accept the gamble and the decision to reject the gamble, she will choose to reject. Next, consider the following gamble.

23. 50% probability to win \$100 million, 50% probability to lose \$100

Remember that the investor has initial wealth equal to \$500. A loss of \$100 will bring her wealth down to \$400, which is considerably lower, but well above zero. Despite the enormous expected gain associated with choice task 23, the investor will choose to reject it. In fact, Rabin and Thaler (2001) show that there is no positive gain high enough to induce the investor to accept this gamble.

The argument developed by Rabin is insightful. Suppose the investor has initial wealth of W, and that she rejects the gamble in choice task 22. Then it must be that

$$0.5u(W + 11) + 0.5u(W - 10) < u(W)$$

which implies

$$u(W + 11) - u(W) < u(W) - u(W - 10)$$

Multiply the left hand side by $11/11$ and the right hand side by $10/10$. Then rearrange to obtain

$$\frac{(u(W + 11) - u(W))/11}{(u(W) - u(W - 10))/10} < \frac{10}{11} \tag{24.16}$$

Inequality (24.16) states that if the investor rejects the gamble in choice task 22, then the average value (utility) of a dollar in the range $[W, W + 11]$ is worth less than $10/11$ of the average value (utility) of a dollar in the range $[W - 10, W]$.

By concavity, this implies that she values the $W + 11$th dollar by at most $10/11$ of the value she places on the $W - 10$th dollar.

If the investor were to accept the gamble, and win, then her new wealth position would be $W + 11$. Now take the sum of the absolute gain and loss, that is, $21 = 11 + 10$. Imagine that the investor had initial wealth of $W + 21$ and accepted the gamble, but lost. Then her new wealth position would be $W + 11$.

Suppose that the investor has the same aversion to accepting gamble 19 when her wealth is $W + 21$ as when her wealth is W. Notice that this is an *assumption* about behavior that corresponds to the effects of isolating choices discussed in subsection 24.1.4. In this case she values dollar $W + 21 + 11 = W + 32$ by at most $10/11$ of the value she places on dollar $W + 21 - 10 = W + 11$. This means that she values dollar $W + 32$ by at most $10/11 \times 10/11 \approx 5/6$ as much as dollar $W - 10$. Continuing in this manner, she will value dollar $W + 20 \times 11$ by at most $(10/11)^{20} \approx 0.149$ as much as dollar $W - 10$, dollar $W + 80 \times 11$ by at most $(10/11)^{80} \approx 0.0005$ as much as dollar $W - 10$, and so on.

The point here is that if the gamble in choice task 22 is viewed unfavorably at higher levels of wealth, then the principle of diminishing marginal utility forces the marginal utility of wealth to decline dramatically. The decline is so dramatic that the incremental utility associated with a gain of $100 million is still too small to compensate for the pain of a $100 loss.

24.4.1   Caveats

There are a few important caveats to understand in connection with the Rabin–Thaler example. First, if the investor's initial wealth is $1000 instead of $500, then she will accept the gamble in choice task 22. In this respect, she will also accept the gamble in choice task 23.

Second, even with her initial wealth at $500, if her coefficient of relative risk aversion were less than 4.5, she would accept the gamble in choice task 19. In other words, the premise is a bit special.

Third, if the investor has coefficient of relative risk aversion equal to 4.5, then she will accept the gamble in choice task 22, but reject the gamble in choice task 23. The loss of $100 is too painful relative to the gain. She can tolerate a loss of $10 much more easily than a loss of $100.

The key issue raised by Rabin–Thaler is whether the choice patterns implied by the combination of expected utility and risk aversion is realistic. They suggest that most people who reject the gamble in choice task 22 would accept the gamble in choice task 23 (featuring a gain of $100 million). Implicitly, they also assume that the isolation effect holds, meaning that the investor behaves the same way in respect to the two gambles, no matter what her initial wealth. In this regard, they argue that prospect theory predicts that people will behave in ways that seem to be more realistic. Loss aversion, the steep slope of the loss portion of the utility function around the origin, leads people to reject the gamble in choice task 22 (and choice task 12). However, because the function is convex in the domain of losses, the pain of larger losses declines. Therefore, the argument advanced earlier for concave utility does not carry over. Rejecting the gamble in choice task 22 does not prevent a prospect theory investor from accepting the gamble in choice task 23.

24.5   Generalized Utility Theories

Prospect theory is not the only alternative to expected utility theory. Machina (1987) puts forth a general framework for describing generalized theories of choice under uncertainty. He begins by noting that the expected utility function $\sum_i p_i u(c_i)$ is linear: here p denotes probability and u is the utility function.

Fix the consumption plan c. Then $u = [u(c_i)]$ is also fixed. Consider the level lines of the expected utility function $\sum_i p_i u(c_i)$ in probability space.

The level lines are indifference curves. Since the expected function is linear in p, the indifference curves will also be linear. Notably, the independence axiom discussed in subsection 24.1.3 requires that indifference curves be not only linear, but parallel to each other.

The discussion in subsection 24.1.1 on the common ratio effect traces out the consistency implications associated with expected utility theory. Essentially these consistency conditions stem from the theory's parallel, linear indifference curves. In this respect, notice that the weighting function (24.7) implies that the indifference curves associated with prospect theory are nonparallel and nonlinear. Explaining the common ratio effect requires that indifference curves be nonparallel. Similar remarks apply to the common consequence effect and Allais paradox.

Generalized utility functions relax the assumption that indifference curves in probability space must be linear and parallel. For example, Machina (1982) proposes a "fanning out hypothesis" whereby the graph of indifference curves conforms to the shape of a fan. He demonstrates that his fanning out hypothesis can rationalize the Allais paradox, common consequence effect, and common ratio effect.

There are other generalized theories that can rationalize these effects. Examples include Chew and MacCrimmon's (1979) weighted utility theory, Chew's (1983) implicit utility, the regret theory of Loomes and Sugden (1982), Epstein and Zin's (1989) dynamic recursive function, Lopes' (1987) SP/A theory, and Becker and Sarin's (1987) lottery dependent utility specification. These postulate yet different shapes for the indifference curves in probability space.

Camerer (1989) evaluated a series of alternative theories of choice under uncertainty. In addition to prospect theory and expected utility theory, he examined Machina's fanning out hypothesis, Chew and MacCrimmon's weighted utility theory, Chew's implicit utility, and Becker and Sarin's lottery dependent utility.

Camerer's general finding is that no single theory can account for the average choice patterns that people typically generate. Indeed, for choices where the probability of all events is positive (anything is possible), expected utility theory appears to do quite well.

There are at least two reasons why Camerer's two general conclusions are worth keeping in mind. First, most of the analysis in this book, and all the analysis prior to this chapter, takes place in an expected utility framework. Camerer tells us that expected utility theory is robust within the interior of choice space. Second, the remainder of this book emphasizes prospect theory. Although prospect theory is rich, it does not uniformly outperform all competing generalized utility theories. Nevertheless, prospect theory is the only theory that emphasizes framing effects. The other theories concentrate on the form of the valuation function, and the shapes of the indifference curves to which these give rise.

24.6   Summary

Prospect theory is a descriptive framework of choice in the face of risk. The theory has three components, a utility function over gains and losses, a weighting function, and a mental accounting structure that includes a reference point from which gains and losses are measured in each account.

People do not typically behave in accordance with expected utility maximization. Rather, they violate expected utility in systematic ways. Some of the major violations are the common ratio effect and the common consequence effect. In addition, the concavity of the utility function implies that people who reject actuarially favorable gambles with small stakes will also reject gambles that combine a modest loss with a huge gain.

25
Prospect Theory Portfolios

Unlike investors with neoclassical preferences, investors whose preferences conform to prospect theory do not select portfolios that are well diversified. The present chapter describes the general properties of prospect theory portfolios. Lack of diversification essentially stems from four features in prospect theory: convex utility in the domain of losses, narrow framing (mental accounts), nonlinear weighting functions, and the kink at the origin of the utility (value) function.

Among the four features just mentioned, the chapter emphasizes the first two, convex utility in the domain of losses and narrow framing into mental accounts. The shapes of the weighting functions impact portfolio selection in respect to distortions for extreme events (in cumulative prospect theory) or small probabilities (in original prospect theory). This is because the weighting function can induce risk averse behavior in the domain of losses and risk seeking behavior in the domain of gains, a phenomenon analyzed in Friedman and Savage (1948).

Formally, the impact of the probability weighting function is the same as that of investor error. In the case of error, the investor misjudges the probability density function. In the case of behavioral weighting, the investor applies a nonlinear operator to the probabilities he perceives.

As a general matter, the value function, the weighting function, and investor errors simultaneously affect investor decisions. In some instances, these behavioral effects will pull in different directions. For example, over-confidence leads investors to underweight the probabilities attached to tail events. However, the weighting function operates in the opposite direction.

25.1   Theory

Consider a financial market in which $T = 1$, so that $t = 0$ serves as the only trading date. At $t = 1$, one of n possible events, x_1, will occur. Let events at $t = 1$ be indexed by i.

25.1.1   Prospect Theory: Decision Weights

Focus attention on a particular investor, j, with probability density function P_j. In view of the discussion in the previous chapter, j will use a decision weighting function v_j which reflects P_j and c_j through equation (24.7). As in previous chapters, investor j has initial wealth W_j. Define j's consumption at $t = 0$ by $c_{j,0}$ and j's consumption at $t = 1$ by $c_j(x_1)$. The vector $c_j = [c_{j,0}, c_j(x_1)]$ is called j's consumption plan.

25.1.2   Utility Function

Gains and losses are defined relative to a reference point. For simplicity, let the reference point for consumption at $t = 0$ be set at 0. Denote by $\rho_j(x_1)$ the reference point from which gains or losses at $t = 1$ are recognized in event x_t by j. Therefore, investor j experiences gain or loss $c_j(x_1) - \rho_j(x_1)$ (or breaks even if the difference is zero).

25.1.3   Prospect Theory Functional

In prospect theory, gains and losses, rather than final consumption, are the carriers of utility. Assume that investor j's preferences are represented by the functional

$$V_j(c_j) = u_j(c_{j,0}(x_0)) + \delta_j \sum_{x_1} v_j(x_1) u_j(c_j(x_1) - \rho_j(x_1)) \qquad (25.1)$$

where u_j conforms to the properties of a prospect theory value function, (24.8) and (24.9), described in the previous chapter.

25.2   Prospect Theory: Indifference Map

As a first step in developing a portfolio choice framework based on prospect theory, consider the indifference map of an investor whose preferences are represented by V_j in (25.1). For this purpose, focus on the case of two states ($n = 2$).

In the traditional expected utility framework, a concave utility function reflects aversion to risk, a linear utility function reflects risk neutrality, and a convex utility function reflects risk seeking. The "better point set" $B(c)$ associated with any consumption plan is the set of consumption plans that are at least as good as c. Any better point set is bounded by an indifference curve. When the utility function is strictly concave, then the better point sets will be convex from below when projected into consumption space, and linear when projected into probability space. When the utility function is linear, then the better point sets will be linear when projected into consumption space, and also linear when projected into probability space. When the utility function is strictly convex, then the better point sets will be concave from below when projected into consumption space, and linear when projected into probability space.

Consider the indifference map associated with prospect theory. A set of indifference curves in gain/loss space is depicted in Figure 25.1. This particular figure is based on the assumption of equal weights (v) for the two events at $t = 1$. In the upper right-hand corner is an indifference curve with the traditional shape associated with risk aversion. This curve corresponds to situations that feature only gains. Because prospect theory features concave utility in the domain of gains, the better point sets associated with the domain of gains will all be convex from below.

Subcertainty gives rise to a discontinuity in the indifference map along a 45-degree line passing through the origin. The indifference curves associated with points along the 45-degree line actually lie above those points,

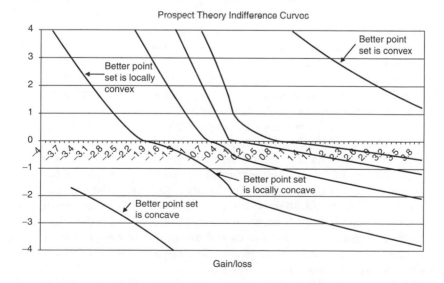

FIGURE 25.1. This figure displays a set of prospect theory indifference curves in gains/loss space for the case of equal weights.

reflecting the idea that certain gain/loss outcomes carry extra probability weight relative to risky outcomes. The character of the arguments in this chapter and the next is not significantly impacted by the presence of the discontinuity, and therefore subcertainty is ignored for the purpose of these arguments.

The bottom-left portion of the figure depicts an indifference curve associated with the investor experiencing only losses at $t = 1$. Because prospect theory features convex utility in the domain of losses, the better point sets associated with the domain of losses will all be concave from below.

The indifference curves that lie between the two extremes reflect the effects of both gains and losses. Notice that some of these indifference curves feature both concave and convex segments. Notably, the indifference curve that passes through the origin has a kink at the origin (meaning a point of nondifferentiability). The kink in the indifference curve corresponds to the kink in the utility function itself, at the origin.

The indifference map in Figure 25.1 pertains to the space of gains and losses, not consumption. The corresponding indifference map for consumption space simply involves a translation of origin, with the translation vector being $\rho_j = [\rho_j(x_1)]$.

25.3 Portfolio Choice: Single Mental Account

Prospect theory is a descriptive theory, postulating that in comparing alternatives, investor j will choose the alternative that makes V_j as high as possible. To study the manner in which the elements of prospect theory affect portfolio choice, consider the case where the entire portfolio decision is framed in terms of a single mental account.

Recall that ν is the vector of state prices. In respect to portfolio choice, investor j chooses a consumption plan c_j to maximize V_j subject to the budget constraint $\nu \cdot c_j \leq W_j$. Given beliefs P_j, and therefore weighting vector v_j, investor j effectively seeks to achieve the highest indifference curve subject to his budget constraint.

Call the component of c_j associated with $t = 1$ investor j's portfolio (payoff) at the end of $t = 0$. The nature of investor j's portfolio depends on the position of his budget constraint relative to his indifference map. For example, if j has high initial wealth, and a low reference point vector, then the relevant portion of his consumption map lies in the upper right-hand portion of Figure 25.1. This situation corresponds to the traditional case of a risk averse investor. That is, in this situation j acts as an expected utility maximizer who is averse to risk.

Consider a very different case, one where the reference vector is high, but wealth is low. In this case the relevant portion of the indifference map is the lower left-hand portion of Figure 25.1, the portion that is concave from below. In this region, investors choose corner solutions in which consumption is only positive in one event. If the two state prices are unequal, investor j will choose positive consumption in the state (event) associated with the lower state price. That is, in this situation j perceives himself to be in the domain of losses, and chooses a portfolio that features an "all or nothing" outcome.

In respect to Figure 25.1, the budget constraint goes through the indifference curve at the origin. If the slope of the budget constraint is close to -1, the investor will choose the kink as his portfolio. The kink corresponds to the reference vector. That is, in this situation j finds that not trading is a superior choice to any budget-feasible trade.

The other cases feature a mixture of concave and convex regions (from below). Tangency point solutions occur only in regions that are convex from below. Otherwise, the choices are made at the boundary.

A loss state is a state in which consumption lies below the reference point. The projection of the better point set onto a subspace associated with loss states is concave, as in the lower portion of Figure 25.1. This implies a boundary solution for such a subspace. Therefore, the maximizing portfolio of a prospect theory investor can feature positive consumption in at most one loss state. This statement is important, and also recorded in Theorem 28.1 which appears later in the text.

25.3.1   Exposure to Loss: Single Mental Account

The kink at the origin in Figure 25.1 supports a portfolio that leads the investor not to experience any gain or loss, no matter what the outcome. Because of the kink, small changes in the slope of the budget constraint around -1 lead to the same choice outcome. However, a large enough change would induce j to engage in trade.

For example, suppose that the parameters of (24.8) and (24.9) are as follows: $\gamma = 0.75$, $\delta = 0.9$, and $\lambda = 2$. Let the probability weight attached to an up-move be 0.75 and the probability weight attached to a down-move be 0.25. Let the state price associated with a down-move be 1.25, and the state price of an up-move be 1. (Prices are relative: Here the price of an up-move serves as numeraire.)

In this example, the investor deliberates about how much loss exposure to tolerate if the down-state occurs, in exchange for a possible gain in the up-state. Given the parameters just stated, the optimal trade-off occurs by his choosing a gain of 16.9 in exchange for a loss of 13.5 (technically, -13.5).

In this example, the combination of concave utility in the domain of gains and convex utility in the domain of losses produces a better point set that is convex from below. Other parameters can produce a better point set that is concave from below, thereby leading to a corner solution. For instance, if the value of γ_L is changed to 0.75, and λ_L is changed to 2.5, then some simple calculation will show that a corner solution results.

The Excel file *Chapter 25 Example 1.xls* describes the optimizing solution that underlies the example in this subsection.

25.3.2   Portfolio Payoff Return: Single Mental Account

In the Kahneman–Tversky framework, the reference point is the same for all future payoffs. That is, $\rho(x_1)$ takes the same value for all x_t. For the remainder of this chapter, assume that the reference point is the same for all states.

In the binomial example, the return pattern for an investor whose choices are governed by prospect theory depends on the location of his reference point vector. An investor who is guaranteed to experience the future outcome as a gain will choose a different pattern of portfolio payoffs than an investor who risks ending up in the domain of losses.

In the binomial example, there can be at most two states where the investor experiences a loss. As mentioned previously, the investor will choose a positive payoff in at most one of those states. In a more general setting where the number n of events at $t = 1$ exceeds 2, a similar statement applies. An investor whose choices are governed by prospect theory would choose a positive payoff in at most one state that he would experience as a loss. The investor would choose zero consumption in all the other states that would be experienced as losses.

The earlier binomial example features a single mental account, as does the general statement made in the preceding paragraph about the case of n events. The "single mental account" assumption is maintained for the remainder of this section.

Consider the variable $\nu(x_1)/v_j(x_1)$. This variable measures the state price per unit (probability) weight, and corresponds to the SDF. Suppose that states are rank ordered according to $\nu(x_1)/v_j(x_1)$. Maximization of V_j implies that j would choose positive consumption in a state for which $\nu(x_1)/v_j(x_1)$ is lowest. If j were to choose zero consumption in some state, the state in question would feature the highest value for $\nu(x_1)/v_j(x_1)$. That is, j would choose to hold the claims that were cheapest, and sell the claims that were the most expensive.

It follows that across states ordered by $\nu(x_1)/v_j(x_1)$, the payoff to j's portfolio will be increasing. It may be 0 in the most expensive states, those where j experiences a loss, and will be positive in at most one state where j experiences a loss. This particular property sharply differentiates the character of prospect theory portfolios from the diversified portfolios associated with neoclassical theory. For states where j experiences a gain, the payoff will be monotonically rising as $\nu(x_1)/v_j(x_1)$ declines.

25.4   Multiple Mental Accounts: Example

Prospect theory is a quasi-maximizing framework, in that the investor is assumed to select among alternatives the choice that features the highest weighted sum V_j. However, as the examples in the previous chapter made clear, quasi-maximization may be at odds with full maximization. In particular, framing effects associated with mental accounting, such as isolation, exert important effects on the manner in which people make choices in the face of risk.

This section presents an example to illustrate the impact of mental accounting on portfolio choice. As in the preceding discussion, the example involves a binomial framework, with an up-state and a down-state occurring at every t. Suppose that at each t, the probability of an up-state is 70 percent. At $t = 0$, state prices are 0.46 for the up state and 0.52 for the down-state. The associated one-period interest rate is 2 percent.

Consider a risky security that returns 10 percent in the event of an up-state and −5 percent in the event of a down-state. Because this is a binomial framework, the risky security and risk-free security together span the range of possible outcomes. In traditional portfolio theory, and in the single mental accounting framework above, there is no need to have more than two securities. Any other securities are redundant, in that they can be formed as convex combinations of the risky and risk-free securities.

In the multiple mental accounting framework, spanning does not render other securities irrelevant. For example, consider two additional securities. One, to be called the conservative security, is formed from a 50–50 combination of the risky security and risk-free security. The other, to be called the aggressive security, is formed by the investors taking a leveraged position, with weights 1.3 and −0.3 respectively attached to the risky and risk-free securities. As will shortly be seen, an investor who evaluates every security in its own mental account will not necessarily view these additional securities as redundant.

Suppose that the investor's utility function has the following parameters: $\gamma = 0.75$, $\delta = 0.9$, and $\lambda = 2$. Let the probability weight attached to an up-move be 0.7 and the probability weight attached to a down-move be 0.3. Notably, the investor who frames each security in its own mental account evaluates the outcomes independently from each other.

To illustrate the point, consider the conservative security. The return to the conservative security is 6 percent in the event of an up-state, and −2.5 percent in the event of a down-state: These returns are just a 50–50 combination of the returns to the risky and risk-free security respectively. An investor who purchases $1 of the conservative security will use the purchase price as a natural reference point, and assign a value of $0.7u(0.06) + 0.3u(-0.025)$, where u is the prospect theory utility function.

By the same token, the return to the aggressive security is 12.4 percent in the event of an up-state and -7.1 percent in the event of a down-state. The associated evaluation is $0.7u(0.124) + 0.3u(-0.071)$.

The above evaluations pertain to investments of \$1 in each security. However, the actual evaluations depend on the amount invested in each security. In this respect, consider investor j who begins with initial wealth $W_j = 1$ at $t = 0$, and faces the problem of dividing his wealth among current consumption $(t = 0)$ and amounts invested in each of the four securities. Suppose that investor j uses a reference point of 0 for consumption at $t = 0$, so that consumption is experienced as a gain. Furthermore, let the value of δ_j in (25.1) be 10: The high value is necessary to render the utility associated with current consumption comparable to the prospect theory valuations associated with the four securities.

The example is worked out in the file *Chapter 25 Example 2.xls*. Computation reveals that in this situation, the investor will choose to consume 0.38 at $t = 0$, and will form a portfolio in which he assigns 0.21 to the risky security, 0.03 to the risk-free security, 0.11 to the conservative security, and 0.27 to the aggressive security. Further computation shows that shifting portfolio weights to the conservative security from the risky security and risk-free security, in 50–50 proportions, makes the investor feel worse off. Of course, given that the conservative security is formed as a 50–50 mix of the risky and risk-free security, the overall return distribution is unaffected. However, the investor does not evaluate the portfolio as a whole. Instead, he evaluates his portfolio one security at a time.

The investor does engage in quasi-maximization. From his perspective, a marginal penny spent on consumption brings the same value as a marginal penny spent on buying any security.

Next, consider the situation at $t = 1$. Let $T > 1$, so the terminal date occurs after $t = 1$. For sake of discussion, let the same one-period state prices continue to prevail at $t = 1$ as prevailed at $t = 0$.

Suppose that an up-state occurs at $t = 1$. How does the investor react? Notably, he registers gains in all four securities in his portfolio. The spirit of prospect theory involves binary comparisons. For example, should the investor sell his holdings of the risk-free security? If he realizes the gain, he receives a rate of return of 2 percent on his \$0.03 investment, which he can consume or reinvest as he wishes. If he continues to hold, he anticipates a sure 2 percent gain at $t = 2$. That is, this particular choice is framed as experiencing a sure gain either at $t = 1$ or at $t = 2$. The decision in this case depends only on the time value of money. Moreover, notice that the isolation effect is implicitly at work here. Neither level of consumption at the two dates enters into the decision, nor does the exact magnitude of the amount invested in the risk-free security.

For the risky securities, all have experienced gains. Relative to the reference point associated with the original purchase price at $t = 0$, the investor must compare the value of a realized gain of 10 percent with a 70–30 chance of extending that gain to 21 percent (if another up-move occurs at $t = 2$) or seeing the gain drop to 4.5 percent (if a down-move occurs at $t = 2$). Given that the future gamble takes place in the domain of gains, the question is whether the perceived risk premium, including the time value of money, is large enough to compensate for passing on the sure experience of a 10 percent gain. In this example, the answer turns out to be yes, and so the investor continues to hold the risky security. Time discounting aside, $0.7u(0.21) + 0.3u(-0.045) > u(0.1)$.

If a down-move occurs, the investor experiences a sure loss of 5 percent if he sells the security at $t = 1$. He could instead take a 70–30 chance that he would escape with a gain of 4.5 percent if an up-move occurs at $t = 2$, but incur an even larger loss (-9.75 percent) if a down-move occurs at $t = 2$. Calculation reveals that $0.7u(0.045) + 0.3u(-0.0975) > u(-0.05)$. The investor would prefer to hold on to the risky security.

25.4.1 General Comments About Multiple Mental Accounts

Typically, portfolio selection with multiple mental accounts involves a sequence of suboptimization problems rather than a single global optimization. In this regard, an investor might examine the mental accounts that already hold assets, in order to decide whether or not to sell the associated asset. This would be done on an account-by-account basis, in a process that does not generally produce well-diversified portfolios. In this process, the reference point becomes critical, in that it determines the extent to which the investor perceives himself to be in the domain of gains or losses.

When assets are sold, the cash received can be deposited into a cash mental account. The cash account serves to determine the value of asset purchases and consumption for the current date.

Recall that prospect theory decisions tend to feature boundary solutions. Either the investor sells the risky security at $t = 1$ or he holds the security. The decision is binary. If he sells, the associated value becomes a resource to be either consumed or saved. If saved, there is a portfolio decision to be made.

In addition, there is the issue of nonconvex preferences. If an investor sets his reference point for consumption at $t = 0$ equal to total wealth, so that consumption is experienced in the domain of losses, then loss aversion tends to force savings to zero: again, a boundary solution.

If the probabilities are replaced with their weights $v(0.7)$ and $v(0.3)$, then the fact that $v(0.7) + v(0.3) < 1$ tends to favor the selection of sure outcomes over risky outcomes. This is the subcertainty property. Subcertainty encourages the realization of gains, but discourages holding on to losers.

For multiperiod horizons, the choices at early dates impact the reference points at later dates. This feature makes for complex modeling. However, keep in mind that prospect theory is a theory about investors who over-simplify. Assuming that investors are sophisticated enough to perceive the link between their current choices and future reference points is something of a stretch. Remember, prospect theory is a framework for understanding why people routinely make choices that are stochastically dominated, and in their role as investors choose undiversified portfolios.

25.5   Summary

This chapter describes the general nature of portfolio choice when investors' preferences are governed by prospect theory. These portfolios tend to be undiversified because of the nature of the indifference map depicted in Figure 25.1 along with narrow framing into mental accounts.

26
SP/A Theory: Introduction

This chapter introduces SP/A theory, a psychologically-based theory of choice among risky alternatives. SP/A theory was proposed by Lola Lopes (1987), and further developed in Lopes and Oden (1999).

SP/A theory shares many important features with cumulative prospect theory, such as an inverse S-shaped weighting function and a reference point. However, SP/A theory's psychological underpinnings are quite different from those of prospect theory. Whereas prospect theory emphasizes psychophysics as a unifying principle underlying the shapes of the utility (value) function and weighting functions, SP/A theory emphasizes the impact of emotions such as fear and hope.

In the next few chapters, I suggest the SP/A theory possesses important advantages over prospect theory that lead it to be better suited for developing both behavioral portfolio theory and behavioral asset pricing theory.[1] Some of these advantages relate to greater explanatory power for how people make choices. Other advantages are structural. For example, cumulative prospect theory uses a transformed decumulative distribution function for the domain of gains and a transformed cumulative distribution function for the domain of losses. In contrast, SP/A theory is more parsimonious in that it only uses a decumulative distribution function.

---

[1] Daniel Kahneman suggested that SP/A theory might provide a cleaner approach to explaining the tendency for behavioral portfolios to mix very safe and very risky assets.

SP/A theory also has features in common with the safety-first portfolio model in the finance literature. In SP/A theory, the S stands for security, the P for potential, and the A for aspiration. Lopes' notion of "security" is analogous to "safety" in "safety-first," in that it addresses a general concern about avoiding low levels of wealth. This has the effect of reducing the degree to which the investor chooses zero consumption in states where she will experience losses. Lopes' notion of aspiration relates to a reference point, and generalizes the safety-first concept of reaching a specific target value. There is no counterpart to "potential" in the safety-first framework. Potential relates to a general desire to reach high levels of wealth.

26.1   The Basic Model

Lopes (1987) and Lopes and Oden (1999) take $u(c)$ to be linear, and uses the weighting function to capture attitude toward risk. In SP/A theory, the objective function is a weighted sum of consumption, akin to the expected value of consumption. This expected value has the form $SP = \sum_i v_i c_i$, where SP stands for security-potential. The variable v_i is determined by a transformed decumulative distribution function $h(D)$; v_i has the form $h(D_i) - h(D_{i+1})$. In this regard, D_i is defined as $p_i + \cdots + p_n$, where n is the most favorable outcome in the outcome ranking. Lopes stresses that in her approach decision makers focus on the probability of receiving at least amount x, for different x. In essence, she contends that the emotion of fear operates by overweighting the probabilities attached to the worst outcomes relative to the best outcomes. As a result, fear leads people to act as if they are using a downward-biased value for the expected value of consumption. By the same token, hope leads people to do the reverse: to overweight the probability of the best outcomes relative to the worst outcomes, thereby using an upward-biased estimate for expected consumption.

Formally, fear and hope are represented in the SP/A framework through the transformation function h, a technique developed by Quiggen (1982, 1993) and Yaari (1987). Figure 26.1 displays three functions. The convex function $h1(D)$ represents the emotion of fear through the overweighting of probabilities associated with the most unfavorable outcomes. To see why, notice that the slope of $h1$ achieves its maximum at the extreme right of Figure 26.1. Because v_i is a difference in successive values of h, it is the slope of h that gives rise to the values v_i. Because D is a decumulative distribution, the probabilities attached to the most unfavorable outcomes are associated with values of D in the neighborhood of unity. Moving down the $h1$ function towards the origin leads to successively smaller weights for

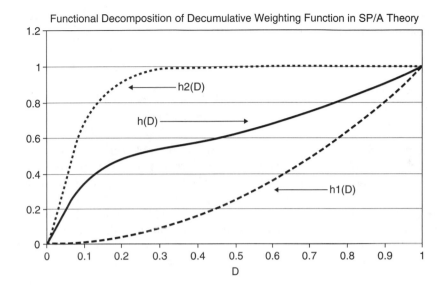

FIGURE 26.1. Decomposition of decumulative weighting function in SP/A theory. The weighting function in SP/A theory is given by the function $h(D)$. $h(D)$ is a convex combination of the two functions $h1(D)$, reflecting fear and $h2(D)$ reflecting hope. The dominance of $h2$ at the left side reflects hope associated with the most favorable outcomes. The dominance of $h1$ at the right side reflects fear associated with the most unfavorable outcomes.

more favorable outcomes. Hence, fear leads to unfavorable outcomes being overweighted relative to favorable outcomes.

The concave function $h2(D)$ represents the emotion of hope. Notice that the slope of $h2$ achieves its maximum at the extreme left of Figure 26.1. The extreme left is associated with the most favorable outcomes, and therefore $h2$ leads the probabilities of the most favorable outcomes to be overweighted. Hence, hope leads to favorable outcomes being overweighted relative to unfavorable outcomes.

In SP/A theory, h is a convex combination of functions $h1$ and $h2$, and is displayed in Figure 26.1. Lopes describes this particular shape of h, concave at the left and convex at the right, as "cautious optimism." Gonzalez and Wu (1999) point out that the function Lopes' h-function in Figure 26.1 has the same general inverse-S shape as Tversky-Kahneman's w-function in Figure 24.1. Gonzalez-Wu also point out that the two functions represent different psychological phenomena. Lopes' function reflects the emotions of fear and hope. Tversky-Kahneman's function reflects psychophysics.

Formally, $h1$ is a power function of D, while $h2$ is 1 minus a power function in $(1 - D)$. Specifically,

$$h1(D) = D^{1+q1}$$

$$h2(D) = 1 - (1 - D)^{1+q2}$$

$$h(D) = wh1(D) + (1 - w)h2(D)$$

Here $q1$ and $q2$ are both nonnegative, and w lies between 0 and 1.

Lopes postulates that risky outcomes are evaluated in terms of two variables. The first variable is SP, the expected value of consumption based on the decision weights associated with v. The second variable is $A = D^c(\rho)$, the probability that consumption will be ρ or higher. In fact, the criterion function used to evaluate alternative risky outcomes is a monotone increasing function $U_j(SP_j, A_j)$ that j seeks to maximize. It is the arguments of U that provide SP/A theory with its name.

26.2   An Example to Illustrate How SP/A Theory Works

Lopes developed SP/A theory as a multi-outcome framework. Her experimental work has focused on the manner in which subjects make choices from a particular set of six risky alternatives. The shapes of the associated probability distributions are displayed in Figures 26.2 through 26.7. Lopes used undergraduate students as subjects, and the amounts were scaled by one-eleventh of those displayed in the figures. Lopes' subjects were presented with pairs of alternatives from this set and asked to indicate which of the pair they regarded as superior. Figures 26.2 through 26.7 display the names of the alternatives, such as Risk Floor, Short Shot, and Long Shot. Notably, all six alternatives feature the same expected payoff $(\sum_i p_i c_i)$. The Risk Floor and the Short Shot have the same standard deviation. The standard deviations of the other alternatives are higher, increasing monotonically from Peaked through the Long Shot.

Recall that in SP/A theory, a decision maker evaluates each alternative by computing two values. The first is the value of $SP = \sum_i v_i c_i$. The second value is the probability of meeting or exceeding the aspiration point ρ, $\text{Prob}\{c \geq \rho\}$. The SP/A valuation functional U has two arguments, SP and $\text{Prob}\{c \geq \rho\}$, and is monotone increasing in both. As shown below, decision makers might find that they have to trade off one of these arguments against the other.

Consider an example in which the parameters of h are $q1 = 4, q2 = 4$, and $w = 0.6$. In this case, the SP values for the Risk Floor and the Short

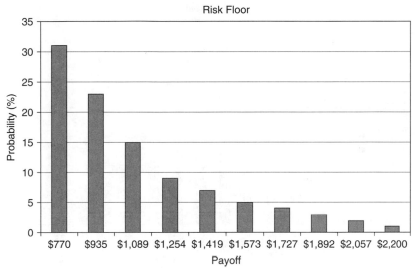

FIGURE 26.2. Risk floor risk alternative used in Lopes (1987) and Lopes-Oden (1999). This alternative (rescaled) features a minimum payoff of $770, and a maximum payoff of $2,200, with a high probability that the payoff will be $1,089 or less.

FIGURE 26.3. Short shot risk alternative used in Lopes (1987) and Lopes-Oden (1999). This alternative (rescaled) features a minimum payoff of $0, a maximum payoff of $1,430, with a high probability that the payoff will be at least $1,111.

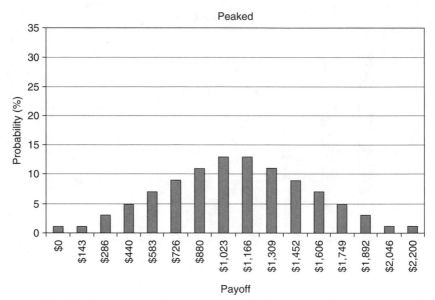

FIGURE 26.4. Peaked risk alternative used in Lopes (1987) and Lopes-Oden (1999). This alternative (rescaled) features a minimum payoff of $0, a maximum payoff of $2,200, with the most likely payoff being between $1,023 and $1,166.

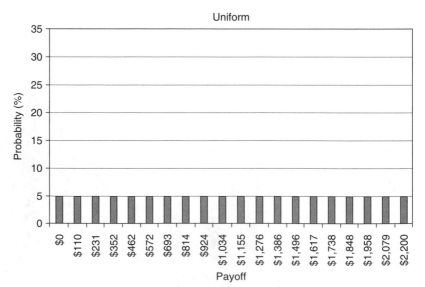

FIGURE 26.5. Uniform risk alternative used in Lopes (1987) and Lopes-Oden (1999). This alternative (rescaled) features a minimum payoff of $0, a maximum payoff of $2,200, with the outcomes being equiprobable.

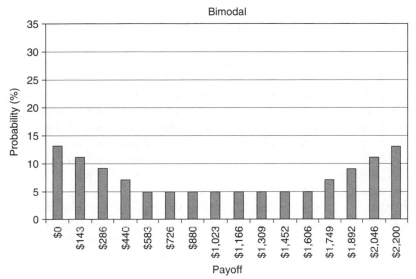

FIGURE 26.6. Bimodal risk alternative used in Lopes (1987) and Lopes-Oden (1999). This alternative (rescaled) features a minimum payoff of $0, a maximum payoff of $2,200, with the most likely payoff being near $0 or near the maximum.

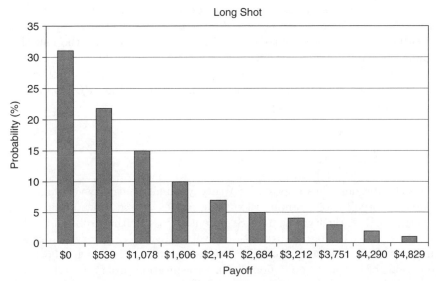

FIGURE 26.7. Long shot risk alternative used in Lopes (1987) and Lopes-Oden (1999). This alternative (rescaled) features a minimum payoff of $0, and a maximum payoff of $4,829, with a high probability that the payoff will be $1,078 or less.

Shot are 1, 144 and 944 respectively. That the Risk Floor has a higher value of SP than the Short Shot is quite intuitive. The Risk Floor does better at both the left and the right extremes than the Short Shot, and therefore does a better job of meeting the needs associated with both fear and hope. If $\rho = 0$, then Prob$\{c \geq \rho\} = 1$ for both the Risk Floor and the Short Shot. In this situation, the Risk Floor is superior to the Short Shot because it features a higher value of SP and the same value for Prob$\{c \geq \rho\}$.

Next consider what happens when $\rho = 1000$. In this case, Prob$\{c \geq \rho\} = 0.46$ for the Risk Floor and 0.69 for the Short Shot. Therefore, if meeting or exceeding this aspiration point is sufficiently important for the decision maker, relative to the value of SP, then the Short Shot will be judged as being superior to the Risk Floor.

In this example, the Risk Floor has the highest SP-value among all six alternatives. When $\rho = 1000$, the Short Shot has the highest value of Prob$\{c \geq \rho\}$ among all six alternatives. As we increase the value of ρ, Prob$\{c \geq \rho\}$ will successively achieve its maximum at the Bimodal and the Long Shot.

The Short Shot has the second smallest SP-value among the six alternatives. Only the Bimodal has a lower value for SP. In their experimental work, Lopes and Oden (1999) find that the Short Shot is judged to be the worst among the six alternatives. In contrast, when I replicate Lopes' study with MBA students, Ph.D. students, and professional investors, I find that the Short Shot is judged to be the most preferred alternative, with the Risk Floor emerging as a close second. In private correspondence with Lopes, she suggests that this difference may stem from the fact that undergraduate students set very low aspiration points: They just want to win something. In contrast, older subjects may well set higher aspiration points, thereby making the aspiration component in the SP/A evaluation functional U much more important.

26.3   Summary

This chapter describes Lopes' SP/A theory, an alternative psychologically-based theory of choice among risky alternatives. Three concepts lie at the heart of SP/A theory: security S, potential P, and the probability A of meeting or exceeding an aspiration level ρ. In SP/A theory, a decision maker's choice is based upon an evaluation function SP, which reflects the emotions of fear and hope, along with an aspiration probability A.

27

SP/A-Based Behavioral Portfolio Theory

SP/A theory provides a parsimonious behaviorally-based framework for portfolio selection. Notably, this theory is especially well suited to the asset pricing approach developed in this book. In particular, it lends itself easily to an asset pricing framework which combines behavioral beliefs and behavioral preferences.

SP/A theory builds on the work of Friedman and Savage (1948), which analyzed the tendency for people to act as if they are risk averse in some of their choices and risk-seeking in their other choices. A key feature of SP/A-based behavioral portfolio theory is bipolarity, in that investors form portfolios which combine very safe securities with very risky securities. The last portion of this chapter presents empirical evidence supporting the bipolarity property.

27.1 SP/A Efficient Frontier

The cornerstone of mean-variance theory is the mean-variance efficient frontier in (μ, σ) space. The behavioral counterpart is in $(SP, 1 - A)$ space. In both cases, investors prefer higher μ and higher SP, but lower σ and lower $1 - A$. Hence, the mean-variance frontier is obtained by minimizing σ for fixed μ, and the behavioral frontier is obtained by minimizing $1 - A$ for fixed SP.

To simplify notation in the discussion that follows, use the index i to denote events x_1. For example, $v(x_1)/v(x_1)$ will be written as v_i/v_i.

Consider a market in contingent claims at $t = 0$, where a state-i contingent claim pays one unit of consumption at $t = 1$ if state i occurs at date 1, and zero otherwise. Let the price of a state-i claim be v_i, and imagine that the states are ordered so that state prices per unit probability, v_i/v_i, are monotonically decreasing in i. Suppose that an investor has wealth W at $t = 0$, and seeks to maximize $SP(c)$ at date 1 subject to a safety-first constraint, by purchasing a bundle of date 1 contingent claims, c, whose market value $\sum_{i=1}^{n} v_i c_i$ does not exceed W.

27.2   Example

Theorem 27.1 (which follows) characterizes the structure of a single mental accounting SP/A portfolio. In order to describe the intuition that underlies the result, consider three simplifying assumptions. First, the weights v are probabilities. Second, states are equiprobable.[1] Third, the (gross) risk-free rate of interest is 1. Notice that because v is the probability density, v_i/v_i is the SDF.

An example with eight states is provided in Table 27.1. Consider an investor with initial wealth of \$1 who faces the state prices displayed in the table. Suppose that the investor establishes an aspiration point for safety equal to \$0.90 at $t = 1$, and seeks to maximize expected consumption subject to the constraint that the probability of achieving her aspiration must be at least 0.125. What portfolio will she choose?

Notice from Table 27.1 that states are ordered from most expensive to cheapest, with state 1 being the most expensive (highest state price) and state 8 being the cheapest (lowest state price). In order to maximize SP (expected consumption) in an unconstrained problem, the investor would only purchase claims that pay off in the cheapest state (8). This is because with all states being equiprobable, a unit of consumption in any state contributes equally to the value of expected consumption. However, a \$1 expenditure spent on claims to the cheapest state results in more units of consumption received.

Notice that the investor who spends all of her wealth purchasing claims to the cheapest state will automatically satisfy the safety-first constraint, since the probability that the cheapest state occurs is 0.125 in the example.

Consider what would happen if the investor wanted the probability of achieving her aspiration to be at least 0.25. In this case, she could

---

[1] That is, $v = P$, and $v_i = v_k$ for all i and k.

TABLE 27.1. Example of behavioral portfolio in SP/A framework.

This table presents an example of a optimal behavioral portfolio in an SP/A framework. The investor maximizes expected consumption, subject to the constraint that the probability her consumption meets her aspiration level of 0.9 is unity.

State	Price	Probability	SDF	Safety-first Portfolio
1	0.372044	0.125	2.976348658	0.9
2	0.186022	0.125	1.488174329	0.9
3	0.124015	0.125	0.992116219	0.9
4	0.093011	0.125	0.744087164	0.9
5	0.074409	0.125	0.595269732	0.9
6	0.062007	0.125	0.49605811	0.9
7	0.053149	0.125	0.425192665	0.9
8	0.035344	0.125	0.282753123	3.729

not allocate all of her wealth to purchasing claims to the cheapest state. Instead she would have to purchase at least 0.9 claims to some other state. And what might that other state be? In order to maximize expected consumption, the investor should purchase 0.9 units of claims to state 7, the second-cheapest state.

For this example, the least-cost way of satisfying the safety-first constraint is to purchase 0.9 units in as few states as necessary, following a pecking order that begins with the cheapest state (8), and proceeds to more expensive states sequentially.

Suppose that the investor wanted to guarantee that she would achieve her aspiration level. In this case, she would buy claims to 0.9 units in all eight states, thereby spending $0.90 of her $1 of wealth. In order to maximize expected consumption, she would then spend the remaining $0.10 on the cheapest claims (state 8), since these give her "the biggest bang for her dime."

Think about the character of her portfolio. In purchasing 0.9 units in all states, she effectively purchases a risk-free security. In allocating the remainder of her wealth to the cheapest state, she effectively purchases a lottery ticket. That is, she forms her portfolio by combining a very safe asset and a very risky asset.

The Excel file *Chapter 27 Example 2.xls* illustrates the above example. The file also demonstrates that the behavioral portfolio just described is not mean-variance efficient. Demonstrating the failure of mean-variance efficiency is accomplished by identifying a portfolio with the same expected return but a lower return standard deviation.

27.3   Formal Analysis

The theorem below applies to the case of fixed probability weights v_i. Section 27.4 provides additional comments about the considerations that stem from rank-dependent values of v_i. The implications for maximizing the function $U(\text{SP}, \text{A})$ are discussed in Section 27.5, Subsection 27.5.1.

Theorem 27.1 *i) Any solution $c_1, \ldots, c_n$ that maximizes*

$$SP(c) = \sum_{i=1}^{n} v_i c_i$$

subject to

$$Prob\{c_i \geq \rho\} \geq A$$

$$\sum_{i=1}^{n} \nu_i c_i \leq W$$

has the following form. There is a subset S_L of states excluding the n-th, such that

$$c_i = 0 \text{ for } i \notin S_L \cup \{s_n\}$$

$$c_i = \rho \text{ for } i \in S_L$$

$$c_n = (W - \sum_{i=1}^{n-1} \nu_i c_i)/\nu_n$$

Moreover, the following property holds: Either

a) $Prob\{S_L\} \geq A$, and if S'_L is a proper subset of S_L then $Prob\{S_L\} < A$;
or
b) $Prob\{S_L\} < A, Prob\{S_L \cup \{s_n\}\} \geq A$, and $c_n \geq \rho$.

ii) If all states are equiprobable, then there is a critical state i_c such that the maximizing portfolio has the following form:

$$c_i = 0 \text{ for } i < i_c$$

$$c_i = \rho \text{ for } i_c \leq i < n$$

$$c_n = (W - \sum_{i=1}^{n-1} \nu_i c_i)/\nu_n$$

where i_c is the lowest integer for which $\sum_{i>ic} p_i \geq A$.

Proof of Theorem Note that $SP(c)$ is a sum of products $v_i c_i$. Consider the unconstrained maximization of SP. To maximize the sum of these products, focus on the state that features the lowest price per unit weight (ν/v), for purchasing contingent wealth. By construction, this will be state n. That is,

$$\nu_n/v_n = min_i\{\nu_i/v_i\}$$

An unconstrained solution for the SP-maximization is the corner solution $c_n = W/\nu_n$ with $c_i = 0$ for all other i. In the special case when $p_n \geq A$, the unconstrained maximum will also be a constrained maximum.

By definition, the maximizing c specified in the statement of the theorem satisfies the constraint Prob$\{c_i \geq \rho\} \geq A$. To establish that it is indeed maximizing, assume the contrary. Suppose that some other candidate c' is proposed for the maximum. Then c' must satisfy Prob$\{c'_i \geq \rho\} \geq A$. Because $c' \neq c$, there must be some state $k \neq n$ for which either $0 < c_k < \rho$ or $c_k > \rho$. Otherwise, $c' = c$. Observe that for c' it is possible to shift finite wealth from expenditure on claims for state k to expenditure on claims for state n without violating the aspiration constraint. Such a shift will increase the value of $SP(c')$ for the same reason that the unconstrained maximum involves all wealth being expended on claims to state n.

If all states are equiprobable, the minimum number of states required to achieve the constraint Prob$\{c_i \geq \rho\} \geq A$ is the maximum i_c such that $\sum p_i \geq A$, where the summation runs from $i_c + 1$ to n. Because the ratio ν_i/v_i declines with i, the maximization of $SP_j(c)$ involves allocating as much of wealth as possible to purchase claims that pay off in state n. Therefore, c_i will be set to ρ for all i in the interval $i_c < i < n$. ∎

27.4   Additional Comments About Theorem 27.1

27.4.1   Non-Uniform Probability Distribution

Theorem 27.1 characterizes an efficient behavioral portfolio BPT-SA solution for a single mental account. Be aware that for sufficiently high values of either A or ρ, it will be impossible to satisfy the probability constraint, and therefore no optimal solution will exist.

What is the role of equal weights? If unequal, consider a three-state case where the weights are $v_1 = 0.6$, $v_2 = 0.2$, $v_3 = 0.2$, and $A = 0.55$. In this case, it is impossible to satisfy the constraint without featuring positive consumption in state s_1. But this means that it is not necessary to have positive consumption in state s_2.

Part ii of Theorem 27.1 pertains to the special case of uniform probabilities. This case avoids technical issues of the sort just described. When there are many states, and probability is not massed in respect to any particular state, then the portfolio return pattern will have the property described in Part ii of Theorem 27.1.

27.4.2   Rank Dependence

Theorem 27.1 describes the SP/A frontier in an environment with fixed decision weights v_i. However, the SP/A framework features rank dependence, with the decision weight for state i being a function of its rank. In order to understand the formal role played by rank-dependent utility, consider the shape of the indifference map in SP/A theory.

Take an arbitrary consumption stream c having distinct components. Associated with c is a specific rank ordering. Consider a neighborhood of c in which all elements also have distinct components. Then all elements of this neighborhood involve the same rank ordering as c, and are therefore associated with the same decision weights as c. Because the SP-function is based on a linear utility function, the indifference map for SP will be linear in this neighborhood.

When c features at least two components with the same values, then the rank ordering is not constant in any neighborhood of c. Specifically, any neighborhood of c will contain two elements in which the ranks of c_i and c_j are interchanged, for some i and j. If these are the only two states whose rankings are changed, then these two states are adjacent in the rank ordering. In this case, the exchange in ranks will be associated with a shift in probability weighting between these two states alone. In particular, the projection of the indifference map onto the (c_i, c_j) subspace will be piecewise linear in this neighborhood.

Figures 27.1 and 27.2 illustrate two such indifference curve projections for the case when variations in consumption levels do not alter the ranks associated with any states other than i and j. Consider the case in which the true probability distribution is uniform. This assumption gives rise to symmetry in these figures. Figure 27.1 illustrates the case when the state with the higher consumption is associated with the higher decision weight. This situation corresponds to the case of hope, which is formally equivalent to excessive optimism. Figure 27.2 illustrates the case when the state with the higher consumption is associated with the lower decision weight. This situation corresponds to the case of fear, which is formally equivalent to excessive pessimism.

Piecewise linearity has some interesting implications. The better point set associated with the indifference curve projection depicted in Figure 27.1 is nonconvex. Therefore, the unconstrained maximization of SP subject to a budget constraint will involve a boundary solution along this projection. Intuitively, this is not surprising. A hopeful investor acts like an excessively optimistic risk-neutral investor. For him, the cheapest states also appear

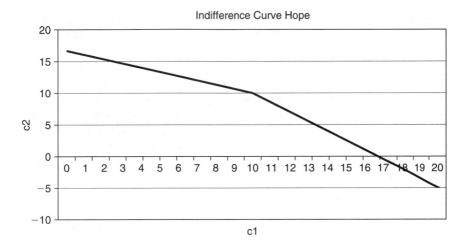

FIGURE 27.1. Rank-dependent utility indifference curve for a hopeful investor. The better point sets for indifference curves associated with a hopeful investor are nonconvex.

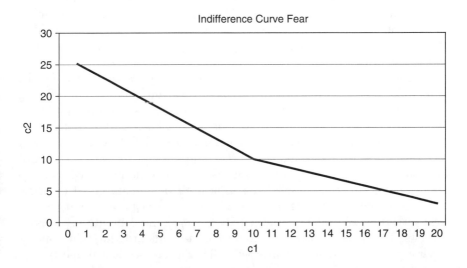

FIGURE 27.2. Rank-dependent utility indifference curve for a fearful investor. The better point sets for indifference curves associated with a fearful investor are convex.

to be the most likely states. Therefore, he maximizes SP by purchasing state claims that only pay off in the cheapest states.

The better point set associated with the indifference curve projection depicted in Figure 27.2 is convex. For budget lines which are sufficiently close to minus 45 degrees, the unconstrained SP maximum occurs at the 45-degree line for consumption. In other words, a small risk premium will induce the investor to choose a flat consumption profile (risk-free solution) along this projection. However, when the slope of the budget line is equal to the slope of either piecewise segment of the indifference curves, the investor will become indifferent between a solution along the 45-degree line and a solution at the boundary. If the slope of the price line is less than the slopes of either piecewise segment, or above the slopes of either piecewise segment, then the investor will choose a boundary solution. Intuitively, a high enough risk premium will induce a fearful investor to take on risk.

The kinked indifference curve property is endemic to rank dependence in a discrete state framework. Movements along an indifference curve projection can impact the rankings of states besides i and j. For example, increasing c_i while decreasing c_j might well lead the rank of state i to increase relative to some other state, say k. In this case, the probability weight associated with c_i might change. As a result, the slope of the indifference curve can change. Notably, this leads to more than just another kink, but a discontinuous break in the indifference curve. Such discontinuities introduce the technical possibility that no maximum SP-solution exists. Cumulative prospect theory features the same technical possibility, because it too involves rank-dependent preferences. The subsequent analysis deals with cases when a maximum solution does exist.

Pragmatically, the search for an SP-maximum involves identifying the rank ordering in consumption. The natural starting point is the ordering induced by ν/P_j, the ratio of a state price to investor $j's$ subjective probability. In a model with fixed decision weights, it is this ratio which determines the rank ordering. The next step is to compute the rank-dependent decision weights v_j based on the ranking by ν/P_j. Suppose that the rank ordering of the solution based on ν/v_j is the same as the rank ordering based on ν/P_j. Then we can proceed to search for a local SP-maximum based on these decision weights. If not, then the next step is to begin an iterative process with the rank ordering associated with ν/v_j and compute its decision weights. The objective here is to find an initial rank ordering that remains invariant to SP-maximization process. This invariance is a property of a local SP-maximum.

27.5   CRRA-Based SP/A Theory

The SP/A framework developed above employs the Lopes-Oden (1999) assumption of a linear utility function, with risk tolerance being completely captured by the decision weights. Although useful for analytical tractability, linearity implies zero consumption in date-event pairs for which consumption falls below the aspiration level. This feature is also implied by prospect theory and is unrealistic for many investors.

Lopes and Oden (1999) point out that they view the utility function in SP/A theory as exhibiting mild concavity, but use linearity to emphasize the role played by the transformed decumulative probability distribution function. Consider a version of SP/A theory in which the linear utility function is replaced by a CRRA utility function. This modification represents a more general version of the theory, in that linear utility is the special case of CRRA when $\gamma = 0$. Notably, risk tolerance in this more general version will be captured by both the curvature of the utility function and the probability weighting function. In the more general setting, the investor maximizes a function $U(SP(c), D^c(\rho))$, where $SP(c)$ is the expected utility of the consumption plan c under CRRA-utility using decision weights v, and $D^c(\rho)$ is the probability A of meeting or exceeding aspiration level ρ.

Formally, an SP/A-portfolio is a constrained expected utility (EU) maximizing portfolio, with decision weights playing the role of subjective probabilities. Other than the budget constraint, the constraints in question pertain to the requirement that consumption be greater than or equal to the aspiration point in particular date-event pairs.

The difference between concave utility and linear utility is most dramatic in date-event pairs with strictly positive probability for which consumption lies below the aspiration level. In this case, the marginal expected utility SP can be very high. When $\gamma \geq 1$, marginal utility approaches infinity as consumption approaches zero. In this case, SP-maximization with concave utility produces nonzero consumption in below-aspiration date-event pairs.

Figure 27.3 displays the character of an SP/A consumption plan assuming linear utility. This figure features three distinct regions, beginning from the left. In the first region, consumption is zero. In the second region, consumption is equal to the aspiration level. In the third region, consumption exceeds aspiration in the state associated with the lowest price-probability ratio. Figure 27.3 illustrates part ii of Theorem 27.1.

Figure 27.4 displays the character of an SP/A consumption plan with concave utility. In Figure 27.4, the regions are similar to those in Figure 27.3. To the left are the date-event pairs in which consumption falls below aspiration. Notice that in contrast to Figure 27.3, in Figure 27.4 returns below aspiration are nonzero. In the middle are the date-event pairs in which consumption is set equal to the aspiration level. At the far right are date-event pairs for which consumption exceeds aspiration.

Additional insight into the character of generalized SP/A portfolios can be gleaned by considering how these portfolios respond to changes in both the aspiration level ρ and the probability threshold A of meeting the aspiration level. When both ρ and A are low, the SP/A-consumption plan is effectively an unconstrained SP-maximum, in that the aspiration constraint

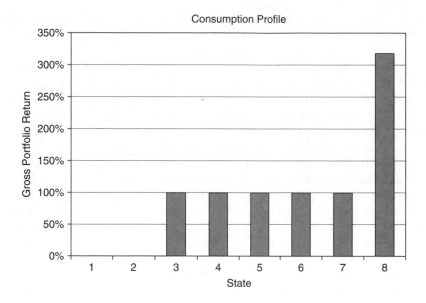

FIGURE 27.3. Portfolio return pattern for an SP/A investor with linear utility. In this figure, the gross portfolio return takes on one of three distinct values: zero, the aspiration level ρ, and a large return at the right.

automatically holds. For any given aspiration level, the unconstrained SP-maximum has an associated probability of meeting or exceeding aspiration. Increasing ρ and A induces the aspiration constraint to begin to bite, thereby forcing consumption in some low consumption date-event pair to increase relative to the unconstrained solution. This increase is funded by decreased consumption in date-event pairs in which consumption is not equal to the aspiration level.

When both the aspiration level ρ and probability threshold A of achieving the aspiration level are high, the middle region will tend to be wide. In Figure 27.5, consumption at the left end will tend to be low. Consumption in the middle region will equal aspiration. Consumption at the right end will equal or exceed aspiration.

In order for consumption to exceed aspiration in the right-most region, wealth must be high enough to allow marginal expected utility SP per dollar to be equal for the highest consumption date-event pair and the lowest consumption date-event pair. If this condition is not met, then marginal expected utility per dollar will be higher for the low consumption date-event pair, thereby forcing maximum consumption to be equal to the aspiration level, rather than exceed the aspiration level. In this case, the right-most region effectively vanishes.

Consider the case of there being only two regions. As the probability threshold A of achieving aspiration continues to increase, the right region

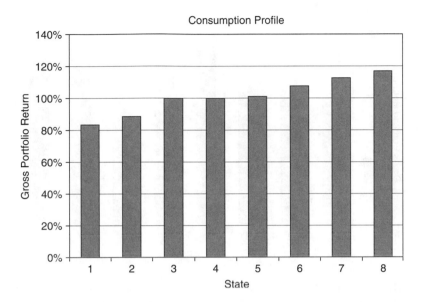

FIGURE 27.4. Portfolio return pattern for an SP/A investor with concave utility. In this figure, the gross portfolio return features three distinct regions: returns below the aspiration level ρ, returns equal to the aspiration level ρ, and returns above the aspiration level ρ. Except for the middle region, the return values are distinct. This contrasts with the case of linear utility. In contrast to Figure 27.3, all returns are positive, including returns below the aspiration level.

will grow, the left region will shrink, and consumption at the extreme left, below aspiration, will fall.

27.5.1 SP/A Portfolio Frontiers and U-Maximization

Figure 27.6 illustrates the concept of SP/A portfolio frontiers. Each frontier involves a trade-off between the two arguments of the evaluation function U, SP and A. The figure depicts two frontiers, one corresponding to the aspiration level $\rho = 1.0$ and the other corresponding to the aspiration level $\rho = 1.1$. The worse point sets associated with both frontiers are convex. Moreover, as A increases, the maximum possible value of SP (weakly) declines. The latter property reflects the fact that as A increases, the aspiration constraint increasingly becomes more binding.

Figure 27.6 also demonstrates the impact of increasing the aspiration level ρ. At any given value of A, increasing ρ serves to weakly reduce the maximum possible value of SP that can be achieved. The latter property reflects the fact that as ρ increases, the aspiration constraint increasingly becomes more binding. In this regard, the insets at the bottom of Figure 27.6

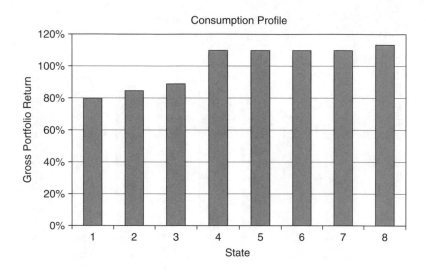

FIGURE 27.5. Portfolio return pattern for an SP/A investor with concave utility, featuring a high probability threshold of achieving the aspiration level. In this figure, the portfolio return features three distinct regions: returns below the aspiration level ρ, returns equal to the aspiration level ρ, and returns above the aspiration level ρ. By setting a high probability of achieving aspiration, the investor tolerates very low returns when she fails to achieve her aspiration level. She also forgoes some return in the most favorable date-event pairs.

describe how the portfolio return pattern across date-event pairs changes as a function of A and ρ.

Notice that the frontier associated with $\rho = 1.1$ does not extend all the way to $A = 100$ percent. This is because there is no feasible way to achieve $A = 100$ percent when $\rho = 1.1$. Notice also that at the left of Figure 27.6, both frontiers are flat for values of A less than 50 percent. This is because the unconstrained solution features $A = 50$ percent for both aspiration levels.

In addition to the two frontiers shown, Figure 27.6 also displays an indifference curve for the valuation function U. Higher indifference curves correspond to higher values of U. An SP/A investor chooses his portfolio by maximizing $U(SP, A)$ along a given frontier. The frontier already reflects the imbedded aspiration level ρ, the range of possible aspiration threshold probabilities A, and the budget constraint. The steeper the indifference curve, the more SP the investor is willing to sacrifice in order to obtain additional A. In other words, the slope of the indifference curve measures the relative value that the investor attaches to achieving a high threshold probability.

Figure 27.6 suggests that when $\rho = 1.0$, the investor maximizes U by choosing a portfolio for which $A = 87.5$ percent. The figure also suggests that

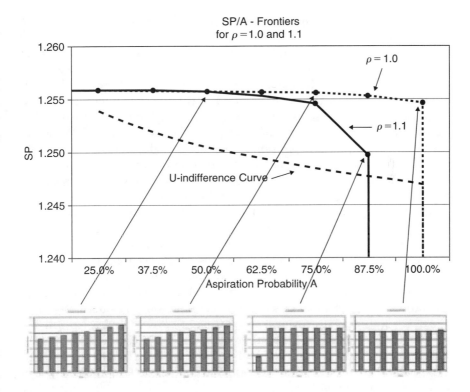

FIGURE 27.6. Two SP/A frontiers corresponding to two aspiration level and a U-indifference curve. Two frontiers are depicted in A-SP space, one corresponding to the aspiration level $\rho = 1.0$ and the other corresponding to the aspiration level $\rho = 1.1$. The figure illustrates the point that SP is monotone nonincreasing in both A and ρ. The indifference curve is a level set for the function $U(SP, A)$, which is taken to be Cobb-Douglas. The insets at the bottom of the figure depict portfolio returns associated with various points on the frontiers.

when $\rho = 1.1$, the investor maximizes U by choosing a portfolio for which $A = 75$ percent. Keep in mind that in both cases, the maximizing solutions for U are at discrete points because both frontiers are a finite set of points. The connecting lines are included only to suggest the underlying structure as the number of states gets large and converges to the continuous case.

27.6   Mental Accounts

The SP/A model developed above features a single mental account for the investor's portfolio. Shefrin and Statman (2000) describe how to extend the model to feature multiple mental accounts, each with its own aspiration level and probability threshold. The simplest extension involves an investor establishing two mental accounts, one with a low aspiration level and the second with a high aspiration level.

The low aspiration level reflects the need for security, while the high aspiration level reflects the need for potential. What provides an aspiration level ρ with its bite is the magnitude of the probability threshold level A. Keep in mind that in the SP/A framework, the emotion of fear is modeled as pessimism, and pessimism increases the attractiveness of consumption at the extreme left. As a result, the portfolio associated with a mental account featuring a low aspiration level ρ and a high probability threshold A will feature a relatively flat payoff across date-event pairs. In terms of Figure 27.4, the middle region will be large. Effectively, such a portfolio features a high concentration of the risk-free security.

The high aspiration level reflects the need for potential. The consumption profile associated with a high aspiration level ρ and a high probability threshold A will feature a mixture of very high consumption at the right and low consumption at the left. The second inset from the right in Figure 27.6 conveys the general idea. Keep in mind that the probability threshold A is endogenous and emerges as part of the SP/A-maximization. When the aspiration level and probability of achieving aspiration are sufficiently high, the right-most region featuring consumption in excess of aspiration will disappear, and consumption will either lie at the aspiration level or lie well below it. In this case, the marginal utility per dollar in the lowest consumption event will exceed the marginal utility per dollar for consumption equal to the aspiration level.

An investor with multiple mental accounts will have a subutility function associated with each such account, along with an overall utility function whose arguments are the subutilities. The investor with multiple mental accounts has the task of allocating wealth across mental accounts in order to maximize overall utility.

Notably, the multiple mental account formulation also serves to generalize the number of dates from 2 to T. In this case, each x_{t-1} generates a mental account in respect to consumption at its successor date-event pairs $\{x_t\}$. Just as we can structure different mental accounts with different aspiration levels (low and high), each x_{t-1} would be associated with its own aspiration level $\rho(x_{t-1})$.

The extension to multiple dates is straightforward when $\rho(x_{t-1})$ is fixed. However, when $\rho(x_{t-1})$ depends on past consumption levels, the nature of the maximizing solution is more complicated. This is because the choice of $c(x_{t-1})$ impacts not only the values of $SP(x_{t-1})$ and $A(x_{t-1})$ but also the SP/A frontiers at dates after $t - 1$. For example, increasing consumption at date $t - 1$ might increase ρ at date t from 1.0 to 1.1. In this case, utility U at t might well decline, as indicated by Figure 27.6. Therefore, the investor would have to take into account the impact of higher consumption at $t - 1$ on utilities at both $t - 1$ and at t.

27.7 Implications of Accentuated Security and Potential

The discussion about Figures 27.3–27.6 focused on the role played by aspiration in SP/A theory, and its interaction with the SP component. For purposes of exposition, this discussion used a linear weighting function h. Such an assumption effectively relegates to the back burner the impact which fear and hope have on portfolio returns.

To complete the discussion, consider how the nonlinear weighting function depicted in Figure 26.1 impacts the character of portfolio returns. Begin with Figure 27.4, and suppose that an SP/A's investor's needs for both security S and potential P increase. Figure 27.7 provides an example of the resulting impact. In comparison to Figure 27.4, Figure 27.7 features higher returns in both the most unfavorable states (because of fear) and the most favorable

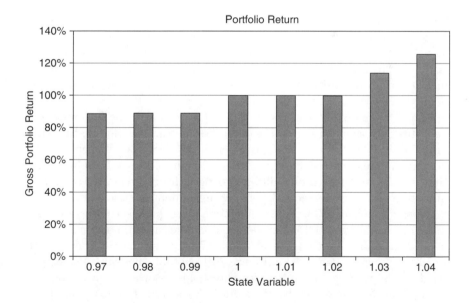

FIGURE 27.7. Portfolio return pattern with accentuated values for S and P. In contrast to Figure 27.4, returns in both the most unfavorable and most favorable states are higher in this figure. Rank dependence tends to induce a flattening of the return pattern in the most unfavorable states. The aspiration constraint tends to induce flattening of the return pattern in intermediate states where consumption exactly equals the aspiration level. Potential serves to induce a lottery-like payoff in the most favorable states. In the limit, as the number of states increases, the return function generally exhibits a discontinuity at the demarcation point separating the left-most region and intermediate region.

states (because of hope). The cost of achieving these higher returns comes from having to incur lower returns in the intermediate states.

Notice in Figure 27.7 that rank dependence tends to raise and flatten the return pattern in the most unfavorable states. This flattening reflects the issue depicted in Figure 27.2. Notably, the impact of fear pertains to the lowest ranked consumption states precisely because those states are associated with lowest ranked consumption. In this regard, fear does not alter the relative ranking of these states.

The aspiration constraint tends to induce some lower returns in intermediate states. Potential serves both to increase and accentuate the return pattern in the most favorable states, thereby inducing a lottery-like payoff pattern.

27.8   Comparison of SP/A Theory with Cumulative Prospect Theory

Four structural features distinguish cumulative prospect theory (CPT) from its neoclassical counterpart, expected utility theory. First, gains and losses are the carriers of value, not wealth. Second, the utility function is concave in gains and convex in losses. Third, decision weights are used in place of probabilities, with the weighting function featuring an inverse S-shape. Fourth, framing is germane to choice.

One of the main implications of CPT is that risk attitude features can be described in terms of a fourfold pattern. For alternatives that feature small probabilities of extreme events, prospect theory predicts risk seeking in the domain of gains and risk aversion in the domain of losses. For alternatives that feature moderate probabilities, prospect theory predicts risk aversion in the domain of gains and risk seeking in the domain of losses.

Lopes developed SP/A theory at a time when prospect theory was still in its original form (OPT). Her work emphasized the importance of rank-dependent utility as a structural issue, and focused on the shape of the weighting function displayed in Figure 26.1. Notably, her work also emphasized the importance of probability thresholds associated with aspiration levels. One of the main implications of SP/A theory is that decision makers are prone to mix very safe and very risky alternatives.

CPT and SP/A share many features in common. The weighting function in both features an inverse S-shape. Central to both theories is the notion of a particular level, the reference point in CPT and the aspiration point in SP/A. In addition, SP/A implicitly defines outcomes in terms of gains and losses, and is consistent with the framing effects emphasized by CPT.

That said, psychologically, the two theories operate differently. In CPT, the inverse S-shape of the weighting function is interpreted in terms of psychophysics: diminished sensitivity relative to 0 and 1. In SP/A, the inverse S-shape of the weighting function reflects cautious hope, a mix of the emotions hope and fear. There is a formal difference as well. Whereas cumulative prospect theory uses two weighting functions, each involving a Hölder average in their respective denominators, SP/A theory uses a single weighting function having the form of a convex combination of power functions.

The two theories also model attitude to risk differently. In CPT, attitude to risk is captured by the curvature of the utility function, whereas in SP/A theory, utility is linear and attitude to risk is captured by the weighting function. Here the contrast is quite marked. Unlike CPT, the utility function in SP/A has no kink, let alone a change from strict convexity to strict concavity at the kink. That said, in CPT, the degree of curvature to the utility function is mild, both in the domain of gains and in the domain of losses. Although Lopes and Oden (1999) develop SP/A using a linear utility function, they state that they do so for convenience, and indicate that in practice, utility functions exhibit mild concavity.

SP/A can accommodate the fourfold pattern that is central to CPT. Here is an example. Consider a decision maker who faces a choice between accepting a sure loss of $3000, or facing a risk which features an 80 percent chance of losing $4000 and 20 percent chance of losing $0. These alternatives correspond to Choice 10 in Chapter 24. In SP/A, these alternatives are evaluated using SP and A, which are combined in the evaluation function U. Consider the values for A. If the aspiration level is $0, then A is 0 for the certain alternative and 20 percent for the risky alternative. Therefore, the risky alternative is preferred to the certain alternative on the A-criterion. Consider the values for SP. Here, the $4000 loss is the most extreme outcome. Therefore, its probability, 80 percent, will be overweighted by the inverse S-shaped weighting function. Even if properly weighted, the risky alternative would be judged inferior to the sure loss on the basis of SP. This is because–$3200, the expected value of the risky alternative is less than–$3000, the expected loss of the certain alternative. Therefore, SP and A rank the two alternatives in opposite directions. If A carries more weight in the U-function than SP, then the decision maker will act in a risk-seeking manner, and choose the risky alternative.

Consider a slight modification to the above example. Suppose that the risky alternative offered a 20 percent chance of losing $100, instead of losing $0. In this case, the value of A associated with the risky alternative would be 0. Therefore, the risky alternative would not dominate the certain alternative on the basis of A, in which case the choice would be determined by SP. In this modified example, the decision maker would choose to accept the certain loss.

The above two paragraphs provide an illustration of two circumstances, one in which a decision maker acts in a risk-seeking manner and another when she acts in a risk averse manner. Both patterns are consistent with

SP/A and CPT. However, the psychological mechanisms are different. CPT relies on probability weighting to explain risk averse choice in the domain of losses: Small probabilities are overweighted, thereby offsetting the effect of convexity in the utility function. SP/A theory relies on the aspiration point and associated probability threshold.

Analogous remarks apply in the domain of gains. Think about the issues associated with the Short Shot, as discussed in Section 26.2. The point there was that the aspiration probability can trump the value of SP. Consider a decision maker who has an aspiration level that corresponds to the status quo, meaning zero gain/zero loss. Imagine that the decision maker faces a choice between a sure $50 and a 50–50 chance of winning $100 or winning $0. The two alternatives have the same expected payoff, but because of cautious hope, the riskier alternative may well have the higher value of SP. However, suppose that a decision maker places great importance on the aspiration probability A relative to the value of SP. Such a decision maker would be inclined to favor the certain gain over the risky gain, because a value of $A = 100$ percent is decidedly superior to a value of $A = 50$ percent.

In their experiments, Lopes and Oden (1999) find that individuals do prefer a sure $50 over a 50–50 chance of winning either $100 or $0. In accordance with the discussion above, they attribute this pattern to the importance of aspiration probability A in the SP/A evaluation function U. To be sure, this pattern is also predicted by CPT, using the median parameters reported by Tversky-Kahneman (1992).

Notably, Lopes and Oden (1999) then identify an important issue that separates SP/A and CPT. They suggest adding $50 to all outcomes in the choice described above. In this case, the decision maker now chooses between a sure $100 and a 50–50 chance of winning either $150 or $50. A simple computation shows that CPT predicts that the individual will choose the sure $100 over the risky alternative. However, SP/A theory predicts that hopeful individuals will choose the risky alternative over the sure alternative. This is because the addition of the $50 has increased the probability of meeting or exceeding aspiration from 50 percent to 100 percent. Doing so leads both alternatives to feature a 100 percent probability of meeting or exceeding aspiration. Hopeful individuals assign a higher value of SP to the risky alternative than the sure alternative.

Payne (2005) reinforces the findings in Lopes-Oden (1999). He reports on several experiments involving equiprobable alternatives in which individuals were allowed to choose an outcome to which value was to be added. One of these involves the prospect described in Section 24.3. He finds that individuals prefer to add value to outcomes that increase the probability of achieving a positive gain. Payne concludes that psychological theories of risk need to incorporate aspiration probabilities into their evaluation functions.

In terms of behavioral portfolio theory, the CRRA version of SP/A offers advantages over both the linear utility version of SP/A and CPT. As documented in Theorem 27.1, the linear utility version of SP/A features a gross return of 0 when the return falls below aspiration. As documented in Section 25.3, CPT features positive gross returns in at most one loss state. These zero return properties are highly unrealistic. In contrast, the CRRA version of SP/A does not exhibit this unrealistic property. As will be seen in the next chapter, the CRRA version of SP/A is also analytically more suitable to asset pricing analysis than both the linear version of SP/A and CPT.

27.9   Real-World Portfolios and Securities

The general character of behavioral portfolios is that they feature a combination of securities that are very safe with securities that are very risky, with the overall portfolio failing to be well diversified.

27.9.1   Empirical Evidence

Two important papers that build on the framework for behavioral portfolio theory developed by Shefrin-Statman (2000) are Polkovnichenko (2005) and Kumar (2007).

Polkovnichenko's paper extends the rank-dependent utility approach along both theoretical and empirical dimensions. His empirical analysis uses data from the Survey of Consumer Finances to document how diversification and portfolio risk vary across wealth levels for individual investors. Kumar's paper focuses on investor preferences for stocks that possess lottery-like characteristics.

Polkovnichenko's study divides investor wealth into the following four categories:

1. Below $10,000

2. Between $10,000 and $100,000

3. Between $100,000 and $1 million

4. Above $1 million

He investigates variations in portfolio composition both across wealth categories and within wealth categories. In particular, he focuses on portfolio weights for direct equity (investors actually holding the stocks) and indirect equity (investors holding mutual funds and pension plans). He also analyzed number of individual stocks held in these portfolios.

In a behavioral framework, the combination of heterogeneous beliefs and heterogeneous preferences gives rise to heterogeneous portfolio composition. Typically, behavioral portfolios are not fully diversified. Polkovnichenko reports that individual investors' portfolios vary widely and are not fully diversified. For example, only 25 percent of investors in the lowest wealth group have historically held equity, whereas 100 percent of investors in the highest wealth group have held equity. However, even within wealth groups there has been considerable variation. For the group with the highest wealth, 18 percent held no direct equity. For the middle two groups, the corresponding figures have been 72 percent and 91 percent.

As to the form in which equity has been held, the wealthiest investors have historically held a bit more direct equity than indirect equity. In contrast, the ratio of indirect equity to direct equity for the other investor groups is in the neighborhood of two-to-one. Investors have also varied in respect to number of stocks held. For investors in the highest wealth group holding direct stock, the typical portfolio has contained 15 stocks. For the other wealth groups, the corresponding number has been between 2 and 3 stocks. In 1998, 75 percent of direct investors holding direct equity had 5 or fewer individual stocks in their portfolios. Interestingly, at least half of investors who owned only one stock owned stock in the company they worked for. That corresponds to 30 percent of direct stockholders. Notably, between 1983 and 2001 the fraction of financial assets in employer stock declined from 18 percent to 9 percent.

Consider Polkovnichenko's finding that most wealthy held individual stocks on top of indirect equity which, by nature, is more diversified. Why would they have done so? Part of the answer might be that investors attempted to buy individual stocks which they perceived to be undervalued. Part of the answer might also reflect SP/A preferences which favor the holding of highly risky securities.

In the theoretical portion of his paper, Polkovnichenko uses a simulation-based example to illustrate how both rank-dependent utility (effectively a CRRA version of SP) and cumulative prospect theory give rise to the empirical patterns he documents. He discusses how the different patterns he documents can stem from variation in the curvature of the weighting function as well as the curvature of the utility function.

Investors with some parameter values choose to hold individual stocks alongside diversified funds. They do so, because they place great importance on achieving very high returns, which is more likely to result from holding an individual stock than a diversified equity fund. Investors with other parameter values avoid equities altogether. These investors place great importance on avoiding losses. As noted above, Polkovnichenko effectively analyzes the SP portion of SP/A theory. However, his analysis does not include the A component.

Polkovnichenko emphasizes that no assumptions on the utility function, including assumptions about its third derivative to reflect a preference for positive skewness, enable expected utility theory to explain the empirical findings he reports. Instead, he contends that rank-dependent utility is required to explain those findings.

Kumar (2007) provides additional insight into the decision to hold individual stocks alongside diversified equity funds. Kumar investigates the extent to which individual investors hold stocks with lottery-like characteristics. Real lotteries offer a low probability of a high payoff (positive skewness), feature low prices per ticket, and have negative expected returns. Lottery-like stocks feature positively skewed return distributions, low prices per share, and possibly negative expected returns.

After classifying stocks into lottery stocks and nonlottery stocks, Kumar presents an interesting comparison. He forms a portfolio benchmark in which the portfolio weights are determined by a random assignment. He then displays how individual investors' portfolio weights differ from those in the random benchmark. Kumar points out that a random assignment would allocate 0.74 percent of the portfolio to lottery stocks. However, on average, individual investors allocate a disproportionate 8.3 percent of their portfolios to lottery stocks. Kumar also reports that even the wealthiest individual investors allocate 7.7 percent of their portfolios to lottery stocks. This point is related to the issue of why the wealthiest investors hold about the same proportion of direct equity as indirect equity. By way of contrast, institutional investors allocate only 0.28 percent of their portfolios to lottery stocks.

At the opposite end of the spectrum lie stocks which are the mirror image of lottery stocks. These stocks feature low volatility, less positive skewness, higher prices per share, and higher expected returns than lottery stocks. The random assignment would allocate 54 percent of a portfolio to stocks that are diametrically opposite to lottery stocks. In contrast, the weight assigned by individual investors is 33 percent, and the weight assigned by institutional investors is 59 percent.

Kumar's findings constitute strong support in favor of behavioral portfolio theory. Just as Polkovnichenko finds that the wealthiest group of investors hold almost the same amount in direct equity as indirect equity, Kumar reports that investors who hold larger mutual fund portfolios invest more in lottery stocks. Kumar also finds that the highest turnover is associated with buyers of lottery stocks.

In line with risk-seeking behavior in the domain of losses, Kumar finds that when economic conditions deteriorate, people increase their allocations to lottery stocks. He finds that on a risk-adjusted basis, those who invest in lottery stocks earn 5.9 percent a year less than those who do not. Those who invest heavily in lottery stocks earn 8.9 percent less than those who invest moderately in lottery stocks. The 8.9 percent actually corresponds to 13.1 percent on a risk-adjusted basis.

In related work, Mitton and Vorkink (2007), Boyer, Mitton, and Vorkink (2008) study the relationship between diversification and skewness in the portfolios of individual investors. Their analysis supports previous results that some investors hold undiversifed portfolios and that some investors seek skewed return distributions. However, what is especially intriguing about Mitton-Vorkink is the finding that investors who are underdiversified intentionally select stocks that feature greater exposure to skewness.

27.9.2   Examples

Swedish lottery bonds and U.K. "premium bonds" possess the features of a security that is suitable for a mental account with a low-aspiration point. Lottery bonds were described by Green and Rydqvist (1999). Premium bonds were described by Shefrin and Statman (2000) whose portfolio framework emphasizes the roles placed by downside protection and upside potential. Holders of lottery bonds receive lottery tickets in place of interest coupons. All bondholders receive the bonds' face value at maturity, but lottery winners receive much more than a usual coupon payment, while losers receive a zero coupon payment.

Lottery bonds with one coupon to maturity resemble the optimal security for a low-aspiration account where the aspiration level is equal to the face value of the bond. Bondholders receive neither coupons nor face value in some low states where the Swedish government goes bankrupt. Beyond these are states where bondholders lose the lottery and receive only the face value of their bonds. Last, there is a high state where the face value of the bond is augmented by a lottery payoff.

Investors do not necessarily need the government to design lottery bonds; many investors design lottery bonds on their own. Some investors buy both bonds and lottery tickets. Others combine money market funds with call options. McConnell and Schwartz (1992) describe the insight of Lee Cole, an Options Marketing Manager at Merrill Lynch, who discovered that many investors who held money market funds used the interest payments to buy call options.

Bollen–Whaley (2004) document considerable trading activity for deep out-of-the-money call options on individual stocks. Call options are different from lotteries that offer single-size prizes. Call options offer many "prizes," low prizes when they are slightly in-the-money at expiration and high prizes when they are deep in-the-money. One can think of call options as securities designed to appeal to many investors with different aspiration levels. Call options do not match the precise aspiration level of any particular investor, but they match approximately the aspiration levels of many investors.

SP/A theory provides important insights into the attraction and design of structured products. Cole's observation led to the construction of LYONs, securities that combine the security of bonds with the potential of call options. The same observation led many brokerage firms and insurance companies to offer Equity Participation Notes, securities that combine a secure floor, usually equal to the amount of the initial investment, with some potential linked to an index, such as the S&P 500 index.

Treasury bills are for investors with very low aspiration levels, while Equity Participation Notes are appropriate for investors with higher aspiration levels. Investors with even higher aspiration levels choose stocks, and those with even higher aspiration levels choose out-of-the-money call options and lottery tickets. Stocks, call options, and lottery tickets feature many states with zero payoffs, but they also feature states with payoffs that meet high, even exceedingly high, aspiration levels.

Cash, bonds, and stocks are the most common elements of portfolios; they are the elements of the portfolio puzzle discussed by Canner, Mankiw, and Weil (CMW, 1997). CMW note that investment advisors recommend that investors increase the ratio of stocks to bonds if they want to increase the aggressiveness of their portfolios. This recommendation is puzzling within the CAPM, since it violates two-fund separation. Two-fund separation theory states that all CAPM-efficient portfolios share a common ratio of stocks to bonds, and that attitudes toward risk are reflected only in the proportion allocated to the risk-free asset.

The portfolio advice of the mutual fund companies illustrates the CMW puzzle. As Fisher and Statman (1997) note, mutual fund companies often recommend that investors construct portfolios as pyramids of assets, cash in the bottom layer, bonds in the middle layer, and stocks in the top layer. Investors increase the aggressiveness of their portfolios by increasing the proportion allocated to stocks without necessarily changing the proportion allocated to bonds.

27.10 Summary

The present chapter developed the implications of SP/A preferences for portfolio selection. The most important trait described in the chapter is the tendency to combine very safe securities with very risky securities, with the overall portfolio failing to be well diversified. Empirical tests of the hypotheses associated with behavioral portfolio theory have found strong support for its general features.

28

Equilibrium with Behavioral Preferences

Chapter 25 describes a portfolio selection model with prospect theory preferences, and Chapter 26 does the same for SP/A theory preferences. The present chapter analyzes the impact of behavioral preferences on asset prices.

Both prospect theory and SP/A theory feature probability weighting. In most respects, probability weighting is akin to erroneous beliefs, and is therefore captured by the framework developed in the earlier part of the book. Therefore, most novel features that stem from behavioral preferences stem from such features as S-shaped utility in prospect theory and aspiration in the SP/A theory.

The first part of the chapter examines equilibrium pricing issues associated with prospect theory. The S-shaped utility function in prospect theory presents some serious challenges for equilibrium analysis. This is because the prospect theory better point preference map is not convex, and non-convexity can prevent the existence of equilibrium prices. For this reason, most of the analysis in this chapter features the caveat "assuming that equilibrium exists." The chapter provides a series of examples to illustrate structural issues, involving the manner in which equilibrium prices reflect S-shaped utility and the location of investors' reference points. One of the examples shows how prospect theory preferences impact the nature of mean-variance returns for an economy featuring some investors with traditional concave utility functions and some investors with S-shaped utility functions.

The second part of the chapter examines how SP/A theory portfolios impact equilibrium prices. This discussion demonstrates how the main results in the book, such as the aggregation theorem (Theorem 14.1) and the decomposition of the log-SDF (Theorem 16.1) can be generalized to accommodate both behavioral beliefs and behavioral preferences. In this regard, it provides a unifying structure for the SDF approach to behavioral asset pricing.

When it comes to portfolio selection, Chapter 27 describes some important empirical advantages that SP/A theory has over prospect theory. These advantages carry over to asset pricing. SP/A theory is more parsimonious than prospect theory in so far as constructing a general framework to accommodate mixtures involving behavioral preferences, behavioral beliefs, neoclassical preferences, and neoclassical beliefs.

28.1   The Model

Consider a financial market in which $T = 1$, so that the first date serves as the only trading date. During the second date, one of n possible states will occur. The probability attached to state s_i is denoted by Π_i. For the moment, assume that all investors have correct beliefs in that $P_j = \Pi$ for all j.

Let there be J investors. As in previous chapters, the model is first described in terms of contingent claims. Investor j possesses an endowment vector ω_j with $\omega_{j,0}$ representing j's endowment of the consumption good at $t = 0$ and portfolio $\omega_{j,i} = \omega_j(s_i)$ representing j's endowment of the consumption good at $t = 1$ if state s_i should occur. Analogously, define j's excess demand $z_{j,0}$ and $z_{j,i}$, and j's consumption $c_{j,0}$ and $c_{j,i}$. Then j's consumption vector $c_j = [c_{j,0}, c_{j,i}, \ldots, c_{j,n}]$ results from the summing of his endowment vector and net trade vector z_j. Assume that $c_j \geq 0$: Consumption cannot be negative.

Consider the components of the endowment vector $\omega = \sum_j \omega_j$ that are associated with $t = 1$. For ease of exposition, assume that these components ω are distinct and monotonically increasing in i. That is, state 1 features the lowest rate of consumption growth g, and state n features the highest rate of consumption growth.

An investor who behaves in accordance with prospect theory is assumed to satisfy the conditions described in Chapters 24 and 25. In this respect, gains and losses are understood to constitute incremental value beyond some reference point. Denote by $\rho_{j,i}$ the reference point from which gains or losses are recorded in state s_i by investor j. If $c_j = [c_{j,i}]$ is investor j's final portfolio, then j's gain (or loss) in state s_i is $c_{j,i} - \rho_{j,i}$. For the purpose of this chapter, each reference vector ρ_j will be exogenous.

Let every investor hold correct beliefs, meaning that $P_j = \Pi$ for all j. For the moment, assume that the weighting function v conforms to original prospect theory. The extension to cumulative prospect theory will be discussed later. Assume that j's preferences over consumption are represented by the functional

$$V_j = u_j(c_0) + \sum_{i=1}^{n} u_j(c_i) v_{j,i}(\Pi) \tag{28.1}$$

where $v_{j,i}(\Pi)$ is the probability weight determined in accordance with Figure 24.3 and u_j is a utility function that is additively separable over time and states. That is, realized utility takes the form

$$u_j(c_0) + u_j(c_i) \tag{28.2}$$

where u_j is parameterized by ρ_j and satisfies (24.8) and (24.9).

28.2   Simple Example

Consider a simple model involving two investors in a two-date model. At date 1 one of two equally likely states can transpire. Initially, investor 1 views state 1 as a good state, but investor 2 views state 1 as a bad state. Investor 1's initial date 0 portfolio pays investor 1 exactly 3 units of consumption if state 1 occurs and 1 unit of consumption if state 2 occurs. The reverse is true for investor 2. Investor 2's initial date 0 portfolio pays investor 2 exactly 1 unit of consumption if state 1 occurs and 3 units of consumption if state 2 occurs.

Notice that there is no aggregate risk in this example. The total amount of consumption available in either state is 4 units.

28.2.1   Neoclassical Case

Suppose that both investors are risk averse expected utility maximizers with identical preferences, and know that the two states are equally likely. What will the equilibrium at $t = 0$ look like?

The equilibrium will involve both investors' choosing final portfolios that pay exactly 2 units of consumption no matter which state occurs. That is, both investors will choose to hold risk-free portfolios, and this will be possible because the economy contains no aggregate risk. The state price associated with each contingent claim will be the same for the two states, say $0.50. Investor 1 will sell 1 unit of state-1 consumption from his endowment for $0.50, and use that $0.50 to purchase 1 unit of state-2 consumption. Investor 2 will do the reverse.

In this example, the two investors begin with undiversified portfolios that feature idiosyncratic risk. They trade to diversify.

28.2.2   Prospect Theory Investors

Suppose that the investors have prospect theory preferences, as represented for example by Figure 25.1, here reproduced as Figure 28.1.

How is equilibrium impacted when investors have prospect theory preferences? Consider some cases. Associated with each case is an Edgeworth Box diagram. The diagrams are color coded to make them easy to follow and can be found in the accompanying Excel file *Chapter 28 Edgeworth Box Diagrams.xls.*

Case 1: Both investors use a reference point that is zero consumption (for both states). Then the prospect theory indifference curves will all correspond to the shape of the curve in the upper-right portion of Figure 28.1. In this situation, equilibrium will be the same as the neoclassical equilibrium, because all investors have risk averse preferences in respect to final asset position. That is so because gains and final asset position are identical when investors use zero reference points.

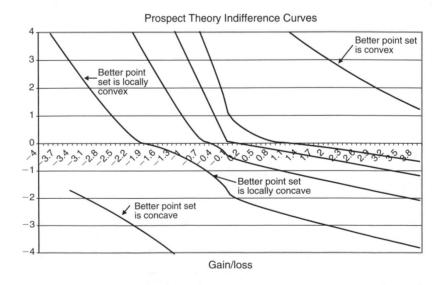

FIGURE 28.1. This figure displays a set of prospect theory indifference curves in gains/loss space for the case of equal weights.

Case 2: If both investors set themselves very high reference points for consumption, such as 4 units, then they are bound to perceive themselves in the domain of losses no matter what the outcome. In this case, the relevant indifference curves will have the shape depicted in the lower-left portion of Figure 28.1.

In this case, there is an equilibrium of sorts, with the same prices as before, $0.50 per state. However, the equilibrium portfolios are completely different. Both investors begin with portfolios worth $2 (the value of 3 claims in one state and 1 claim in the other). They could trade to the risk-free portfolio. Suppose they did so. Would they be content? The answer is no. Because of their high reference points, both investors are risk seeking, not risk averse. So what they will do is move to a corner solution. For example, investor 1 will buy all the claims to state 1, and investor 2 will buy all the claims to state 2. One of them, and only one of them, will avoid a loss at $t = 1$. They both prefer to go "all or nothing." That is the equilibrium solution.

This case, involving only losses, is akin to going "double or nothing" after having lost a bet. Both investors choose this route. In the context of stock trading, a trader who has lost money on a stock, but still believes in the stock, will want to go double or nothing. If the investor has cash, or can sell a winner to get cash, he or she will choose to do so. However, an investor without cash, or with no winners to sell, will simply hold the stock. In this regard, Odean (1999) demonstrates that investors tend to purchase additional shares of stocks on which they have taken a loss.

There is an implicit framing issue in this example. In a rational framework, investors ignore sunk costs. A prospect theory investor who ignores sunk costs accepts losses incurred on previous trades, and resets her reference point. A prospect theory investor who does not accept past losses maintains the purchase price as a reference point and perceives himself to be in the domain of losses. The financial positions of the two investors might be identical. They might even share the same utility function and weighting functions. However, they differ in their reference points. The issue is framing: *Framing can affect portfolio choice.*

Case 3: Suppose that both investors establish their reference points at their initial portfolio positions. This results in a no-trade equilibrium. The reason is that if investor 1 trades to the risk-free position, then he experiences a loss of 1 if state 1 occurs, and a gain of 1 if state 2 occurs. (Here, the reference point is different in the two states, it really being a reference portfolio rather than a true reference point.) Now if losses loom larger than gains, then loss aversion will lead investor 1 to prefer not to trade than to trade to the risk-free position.

Formally, consider the shape of the indifference curve that passes through the endowment point. In Figure 28.1, this curve is the fourth indifference curve up from the lower left. Notice the kink in the indifference curve at the origin. The kink stems from the kink in the value function at the origin of that function.

A budget line with a slope of -1 will support the last indifference curve, so that investor 1 will see this indifference curve as his highest attainable indifference curve. The same remark applies to investor 2. Therefore, the prices of $0.50 in each state are equilibrium prices. But the investors choose not to trade.

In case 3, both investors hold initial portfolios that are undiversified. However, their preferences are based on portfolio changes, not final position. The "isolation" property in prospect theory leads them to ignore issues of diversification in arriving at their portfolios. For both investors, the expected gains from trade are less than the expected pain from their losses, no matter what the trade. As a result, they prefer to hold their initial portfolios.

Case 4: Consider the third indifference curve from the lower left in Figure 28.1. This curve reflects one region of only losses, and another region of mixed gains and losses. Consider the better point set associated with the indifference curve. At the upper left, the better point set is locally convex. In moving down the indifference curve, the better point set will turn locally concave where the outcomes involve losses no matter which state occurs. Continuing into the bottom-right region, the better point set will again become locally convex, as the region is associated with mixed gains and losses.

The regions involving mixed gains and losses are convex, and so in theory could support a traditional interior portfolio choice, rather than a corner solution as in case 2, or a kink solution as in case 3. In theory, the indifference curve just described can support an interior equilibrium, when the reference point is not the endowment point.

The easiest way to illustrate an equilibrium with mixed gains and losses is to set the reference point at the risk-free allocation $(2,2)$. In this case, the no trade allocation involves investor 1 registering a gain of 1 if state 1 occurs, and a loss of 1 if state 2 occurs. Trading from the endowment point to the risk-free allocation allows investor 1 to avoid registering a loss. Instead, the risk-free allocation enables him to register a net gain of 0 regardless of which state occurs.

Because of loss aversion, investor 1 prefers holding the risk-free portfolio $(2,2)$ to endowment portfolio $(3,1)$. Moreover, investor 1's indifference curve through $(2,2)$ features a kink. Therefore, investor 1 prefers this trade to any other budget-feasible trade. Similar statements apply to investor 2. Therefore, the combination of price vector $(0.5, 0.5)$ and risk-free allocation satisfies the conditions for an equilibrium.

Notice in case 4 that if investor 1's reference vector lies in a small neighborhood of the risk-free allocation, then investor 1's preferred allocation will lie not at a kink, but at a tangency point. If the reference vector lies strictly below the risk-free allocation, then the tangency point will lie close to the risk-free allocation. Suppose that the reference vector lies above the risk-free allocation. Then because of local non-convexity, there may be multiple tangency points which lie on both sides of the risk-free allocation.

Notably, case 2 also features two equilibria, which lie at opposite corners of an Edgeworth box. However, the nonuniqueness property in case 2 is not particularly robust. To see why, consider a marginal increase ϵ in investor 2's endowment of the state 1 commodity. Notice that the market endowment, $(4 + \epsilon, 4)$ features risk. Consider the price vector $(0.5, 0.5)$. At these prices, investor 1 is willing to choose the allocation $(0, 4)$, and investor 2 is willing to choose the allocation $(4 + \epsilon, 0)$. Notably, both investors' allocations are budget feasible. Therefore, these choices satisfy the maximizing conditions associated with equilibrium. However, the allocation at the opposite corner, where investor 1 chooses $(4 + \epsilon, 0)$, is not budget feasible. This is because investor 1 can only afford $(4, 0)$, not $(4 + \epsilon, 0)$. Therefore, as case 2 requires that an equilibrium lie at a corner solution, the equilibrium must be unique.

The various cases highlight the different motivations underlying trade, or as in case 3 no trade. In case 2, investors' motive for trade is to go double or nothing. In case 1, no investor experiences losses; no matter what the state, they experience only gains. And trade occurs because investors experience all outcomes as either larger or smaller gains. In case 4, investors can experience a mix of gains and losses. Trade results because of a framing effect associated with the location of the reference point.

Case 5: Investors might have heterogeneous beliefs rather than heterogeneous reference portfolios. Suppose that investor 1 believes that the probability of state 2 is 75 percent, while investor 1 believes that the probability of state 1 is 75 percent.

Let both investors have as their reference portfolios their initial portfolios. In case 3, this led to a no-trade equilibrium. However, case 3 involved homogeneous beliefs. In case 5, if investors trade to the risk-free portfolio, investor 1 perceives an expected gain of 0.75 consumption units and an expected loss of 0.25 consumption units. Notice that the ratio of the expected gain to the expected loss is 3 to 1 for both investors, where 3 is to be compared to 2.5, the coefficient of loss aversion. Therefore, both investors would be willing to trade away from their initial (reference) portfolios. Loss aversion might mitigate the extent of trade, but it does not prevent trade.

Formally, probability beliefs in the model operate by rotating the indifference map. Applying Figure 28.1, if an investor believes that state 2 (vertical axis) is more likely than state 1 (horizontal axis), then he will be willing to accept less state 2 consumption as compensation if asked to sacrifice a single unit of state 1 consumption. That is, his indifference curves will become flatter. In an Edgeworth box model, investors are reluctant to trade when the indifference curves associated with their initial portfolios touch but do not intersect. Rotation through a change in beliefs can lead to intersection, thereby generating trade. Of course, the reverse can also happen. Investors' initial indifference curves might intersect, but a rotation generated by a belief change can lead to a no-trade equilibrium.

28.3   Boundary Value Property

A loss state for a prospect theory investor j is a state in which j consumes less than his reference point. The following proposition is central and follows directly from the nonconvex region of the better point sets in respect to losses.

Theorem 28.1 *i) The maximizing portfolio of a prospect theory investor features positive claims in at most one loss state.*
ii) Let $v_i(\Pi) = \Pi_i$. If there are two loss states s_i and s_k, and ν exhibits risk neutrality, then j will choose nonzero consumption in the least likely loss state.
iii) Let $v_i(\Pi) = \Pi_i$. If two loss states s_i and s_k occur with the same probability, and $\nu_i < \nu_k$, then j chooses $c_j(s_k) = 0$.

   Proof of Theorem   Part i of Theorem 28.1 was established in section 25.3. Part ii of Theorem 28.1 is valid for the following reason. Consider two gambles. The first pays zero in s_i and c_k in s_k, while the second pays zero in s_k and c_i in s_i. Now let c_i and c_k each represent a dollar expenditure on contingent claims: that is, $c_i = 1/\nu_i$ and $c_k = 1/\nu_k$. Because ν exhibits risk neutrality, the expected payoff of these two gambles is the same. That is, $\Pi_i c_i = \Pi_k c_k$ and $\nu_i c_i = \nu_k c_k$. Let $\Pi_i < \Pi_k$. Then $\nu_i < \nu_k$, because ν exhibits risk neutrality. Hence, $c_i > c_k$, and so the second gamble is riskier than the first. Because of nonconvexity of preferences in the domain of losses, the second gamble is preferable to the first. A similar argument establishes part iii of the theorem.   ∎
   As was mentioned in Chapter 25, the behavioral pattern identified by Theorem 28.1 is a fundamental feature of prospect theory. Although the pattern is not especially realistic, it is important to trace through its theoretical implications. However, the last part of the chapter analyzes the CRRA-version of SP/A theory, for which Theorem 28.1 does not hold.

28.4   Equilibrium Pricing

Theorem 28.1 describes a key feature about the portfolio choices of prospect theory investors. This section discusses some of the implications this property holds for the shape of the SDF.

Imagine a market in which all investors have prospect theory preferences, as described in section 28.1. To simplify the analysis, consider the special case in which investors are identical in terms of wealth, utility function, and the weighting function, which is taken to be $v_{j,i}(\Pi) = \Pi_i$ for all j. In addition, take the reference point for each investor to be date 0 per capita consumption.

Theorem 28.1 implies that every investor is willing to hold positive claims in only one loss state. Given the setting, the key question is how Theorem 28.1 impacts equilibrium prices. At issue is the fact that all investors might shun claims to all but one loss state, thereby preventing markets from clearing. Of course, as case 1 in subsection 28.2.2 makes clear, there need not be any loss states. However as was explained in the rest of the subsection, case 1 is special, not general.

In order to analyze the pricing implications of Theorem 28.1, consider a candidate price vector ν' for which the corresponding SDF $M = \nu'/\Pi$ is flat (uniform across states). Consider the excess demand function associated with ν'. The sign of excess demand in each state provides some guidance as to the direction in which prices need to adjust in order to achieve equilibrium.

Theorem 28.1 indicates that if there are at least two loss states, and the SDF is flat, then every investor will choose to hold positive claims only in the loss state which is least likely. Therefore, excess demand associated with ν' will be negative for all loss states but the least likely. This suggests that a move towards equilibrium will require that relative to the least likely loss state, the prices of all other loss states decline.

Theorem 28.1 implies that in this example, all prospect theory investors are willing to hold claims in exactly one state. However, equilibrium requires that excess demand be zero for all states. Therefore, two conditions must hold simultaneously. First, prices need to adjust in order that investors are willing to hold the supply of claims to every loss state. Second, each individual investor must hold positive claims to losses in at most one loss state.

Consider two loss states s_i and s_k. Prices must be such that some investor i is willing to hold claims in s_i and incur a loss in s_i at the same time as some investor k is willing to hold claims in s_k and incur a loss in s_k. Given common beliefs and homothetic preferences, if prices lead one investor to have a strict preference to hold s_i over s_k, then so will all investors. Therefore, equilibrium prices, if they exist, must induce all investors to be indifferent to holding concentrated claims in either s_i or s_k. This will enable at least one investor to hold positive claims only in s_i, and for some other investor

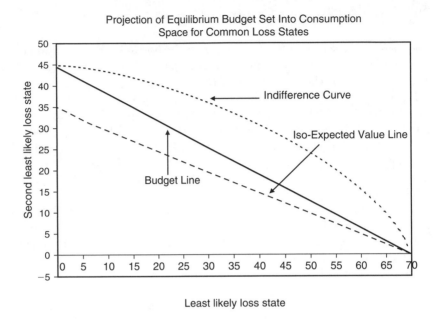

FIGURE 28.2. This figure depicts the equilibrium condition determining the relative prices of common loss states. The equilibrium budget line is steeper than the iso-expected value line, indicating that the SDF for claims to the least likely loss state is higher than the corresponding value for the second least likely loss state.

to hold positive claims only in s_k. Figure 28.2 illustrates such a situation for common loss states, meaning states in which all investors incur a loss.

Suppose that s_i is less likely to occur than s_k. Theorem 28.1 implies that in equilibrium, the price of s_i will be higher than the price of s_k. Therefore, for loss states, the ordering of the components in the SDF will be based on relative likelihood. For loss states, the SDF will be monotone decreasing in likelihood. If loss states which are less likely also feature lower aggregate consumption growth, then the SDF will monotonically decline (weakly) throughout its range.

In the special case when loss states are equiprobable, symmetry implies that the shape of the SDF in the region of common loss states will be flat, not declining. If this were not the case, aggregate demand for the loss state with the highest SDF-value would be zero, and the market would not clear. For an illustration of equilibrium when loss state probabilities are uniform, see case 2 in section 28.2.2. The cases in this subsection effectively portray projections when the number of states exceeds two.

28.4.1 Additional Insights Regarding Convexity and Existence

Given nonconvex preferences associated with loss states, strict restrictions on the distribution of initial endowment portfolios are required in order that equilibrium exist. This is because the concentrated demand pattern across loss states must exactly match the supply (aggregate consumption). Effectively, loss states partition investors into groups, according to the single loss state for which each is willing to hold a positive claim. Ceteris paribus, increasing aggregate consumption growth in state s_i must lead to an increase in the initial portfolio wealth of the group of investors that are willing to hold positive claims to s_i. The fewer the number of investors relative to the number of loss states, the more stringent this restriction becomes.

For an illustration of the point described in the previous paragraph, consider the discussion about $\epsilon > 0$ following case 4 in section 28.2.2. That discussion assumes that investor 1's endowment portfolio is invariant to the magnitude of ϵ, as is the supply of claims to s_2. This property is required for equilibrium to exist, because in equilibrium investor 1 holds all claims to s_2. Unfortunately, this implies that the set of initial endowment portfolios consistent with the existence of equilibrium is very small. In addition, notice that in this example, the equilibrium price vector $(0.5, 0.5)$ is not a function of ϵ. This illustrates the general feature described above that the relative prices of claims to loss states depend on relative probability weights, but not relative aggregate consumption growth.

28.4.2 Weighting and Heterogeneous Beliefs

For sake of exposition, the example in this section has assumed that $v_{j,i}(\Pi) = \Pi_i$ for all j. Notably, the general conclusions are unchanged if v_j conforms to the structure of original prospect theory, so long as v_j is common across investors. What is key is that investors be indifferent between the alternative loss state boundary solutions portrayed in Figure 28.2. Although probability weighting does not alter the general conclusions, it does affect the character of the conclusions. This is because weighting distorts probabilities. Therefore, the weighting will typically accentuate the steepness of the SDF in the region of losses.

Cumulative prospect theory adds a complicating wrinkle in that weights depend on the ranking of states, with the most distortion at the extremes. In equilibrium, investors' rank orderings must differ across states, and therefore so must the weights. This introduces the possibility of heterogeneous weighting, even in the presence of homogenous beliefs. As a result, equilibrium might not require that prospect theory investors be indifferent across boundary solutions. They only need to prefer the boundary solution they choose over others. In addition, rank dependence introduces a kink into indifference curves, as explained in connection with Figure 27.1 and Figure 27.2.

It is heterogeneous weights rather than the kink which is central. Heterogeneous weights are like heterogeneous beliefs. As case 5 of subsection 28.2.2 illustrates, the introduction of heterogeneous beliefs adds several features to the framework. Graphically, heterogeneous beliefs impact the degree to which investor 1's indifference curves are steeper (or flatter) than those of investor 2. For situations involving interior equilibria, such as cases 1, 3, or 4, the impact of introducing heterogeneity is reasonably standard. However, for case 2, which features only losses, the situation is less standard, although it is straightforward.

Case 2 involves homogeneous beliefs, an equilibrium price vector $(0.5, 0.5)$ and two allocations, one at the top left corner of the Edgeworth box and the other at the bottom right corner of the Edgeworth box. Consider the top corner allocation of the Edgeworth box, where investor 1 holds only claims to s_2, and investor 1 holds only claims to s_1. Suppose both investors' beliefs are perturbed so that investor 1 views s_2 as more likely than s_1, and vice versa for investor 2. This perturbation will not impact equilibrium prices or the fact that the top left corner is an equilibrium allocation, as the perturbation reinforces both investors' choices. However, it does eliminate the bottom right corner as an equilibrium allocation, since both investors view the latter as strictly inferior to the equilibrium allocation.

Notably, this last example illustrates that with heterogeneous beliefs, equilibrium does not require that investors be indifferent between holding claims to any two loss states. In this respect, relative prices for claims to loss states are not driven by relative probabilities, as was the case for homogeneous beliefs. Of course, it is possible to associate equilibrium beliefs with a representative investor. However, the aggregating weights for common loss states will depend on relative aggregate consumption growth and the endowment portfolios, not the aggregation weights associated with Theorem 14.1.

28.5   Portfolio Insurance

When the SDF is flat in the region of loss states, equilibrium prices are said to exhibit the *portfolio insurance pricing property*. This is an interesting special case. The present section explains why the flat region is associated with portfolio insurance.

Keep in mind that prospect theory investors are willing to accept the risk of zero consumption in (most) common loss states. Intuitively, this means that they are willing to supply deep out of the money index put options to the market, thereby accepting the risk that they will face catastrophic losses in the event those options are exercised.

Formally, suppose that an investor holds a portfolio Z, and purchases an out-of-the-money put option for which Z is the underlying asset. Then the investor is said to insure his portfolio, since the exercise price of the put will serve as a floor for the value of his position. The first part of Chapter 23 discussed the manner in which institutional investors trade index puts. The present chapter is concerned with a different question, whether the actions of prospect theory investors might induce a rational investor to choose portfolio insurance.

Let there be n securities, denoted Z_1 through Z_n, with the matrix $[Z_i, \ldots, Z_n]$ being of full rank, so that the market is complete. Take Z_1 as the risk-free security, where the *risk-free* subspace is given by the "45-degree" line depicting equal payoffs across states. Take Z_2 as the *market portfolio*, meaning that Z_2 lies in the subspace spanned by ω, the endowment vector for the entire economy. For $n > 2$, assume that the remaining securities are put options on the market portfolio. A put option on Z_2 with exercise price K is defined to pay off $\max\{K - Z_2(s_i), 0\}$ in state s_i. Take as exercise prices $K = Z_2(s_i)$ for Z_3, $K = Z_2(s_2)$ for Z_4, etc.

In view of market completeness, all securities are priced in terms of state price ν. Specifically, the date 1 price q_i of security Z_i is $\nu^1 \cdot Z_i$, where ν^1 represents the components of ν that pertain to $t = 1$. The budget constraint for investor j will have the form $(c_{j,0} - \omega_{j,0}) + \nu^1 \cdot z_j \leq 0$. As usual, equilibrium prices ν will be identified with aggregate excess demand $\sum_j z_j = 0$.

Consider the equiprobable loss state case discussed at the conclusion of the preceding section. The connection between the equi-price/probability condition and portfolio insurance is straightforward. As was mentioned earlier, portfolio insurance involves the holding of a put option on the risky portion of one's portfolio. To illustrate this point, consider a risk averse investor j whose date 1 consumption profile (across states) is formed by his holding equal quantities of two securities. One security is Z_ℓ. The other security is a put option Z_p on Z_ℓ with exercise price K. Let $K = Z_\ell(s_i)$, where s_i is a common loss state. Choose s_i such that there is some other common loss state with such that $Z_\ell(s_k) < Z_\ell(s_i)$. Should s_i occur, then the put option is useless (ex post), since it only permits j to sell Z_ℓ at the exercise price that is the same as Z_ℓ's market value. However, suppose that s_k occurs. Then the market value of Z_ℓ is $Z_\ell(s_k)$. But because j holds Z_p, he is entitled to sell Z_ℓ at the higher price $Z_\ell(s_i)$. What Z_p does is insure j against outcomes that are inferior to s_i. The holding of Z_p constitutes portfolio insurance. Hence j's consumption profile features the same level of consumption in all loss states that are no better than s_i.

The portfolio insurance pricing condition entails equal price/probability ratios across common loss states. A risk averse investor's optimal response to a price vector with this property is to choose the same consumption level in all such states. Equal consumption across loss states reflects the limit on losses provided by portfolio insurance.

28.5.1   Testable Prediction

The value of analyzing the portfolio insurance pricing property is primarily to provide insights into the structure of how portfolio theory preferences impact asset prices. It would be nice if it also produced some theoretical implications that were supported by empirical evidence. However, as the following discussion points out, such is not the case.

Chapter 23 presented evidence that professional investors use deep out-of-the-money put options to insure their portfolios. Could such behavior be the result of prospect theory investors inducing the portfolio insurance pricing property? After all, the preceding discussion implies that portfolio insurance is a rational response by rational investors because the SDF flattens out in its leftmost portion.

The portfolio insurance pricing property constitutes a testable prediction. Empirically, does the SDF flatten out in its left-most portion? Figure 23.2 provides the answer, and the answer is no. Rather, the empirical SDF is steeply sloped in its left-most region.

28.6   Risk and Return: Portfolio Insurance in a Mean-Variance Example

Although the portfolio insurance property does not hold empirically, it does provide some theoretical insights into the structure of models featuring a mix of neoclassical preferences and prospect theory preferences. In this regard, consider the character of the mean-variance frontier for the case of portfolio insurance pricing when $v_j = \Pi$. To this end, replace the power function specification of the prospect theory utility (value) function with a quadratic specification. For risk averse investors, this entails standard mean-variance conditions. If the resulting equilibrium prices satisfy the portfolio insurance condition, then we obtain a portfolio insurance version of the capital asset pricing model (CAPM).

To describe the properties of the portfolio insurance CAPM, recall that CAPM involves two-fund separation: Each investor's portfolio can be expressed as a linear combination of the risk-free security and the market portfolio. Given the presence of prospect theory investors, the market portfolio is mean-variance inefficient, so that the risk held by standard investors will not be represented by the market portfolio. In the portfolio insurance CAPM, risk averse investors choose a portfolio consisting of three components: 1) the risk-free security, 2) the market portfolio, and

3) portfolio insurance (meaning put options on their holdings of the market portfolio).

In this mean-variance example, the utility function of each risk averse investor is assumed to have the form

$$u_j(c_i) = \xi c_i - c_i^2 \tag{28.3}$$

where ξ is a positive parameter. As is well known, the expected utility function can be expressed as $\xi\mu - \mu^2 - \sigma^2$, whose arguments are the mean and variance of the distribution over contingent consumption. To obtain the demand function associated with equation (28.3), form the Lagrangean

$$L_j = \sum_i \pi_i u_j(c_i) - \lambda\left(\sum_i \nu_i c_i - W_j\right)$$

Differentiate L_j with respect to c_i to obtain

$$\xi - 2c_i = \lambda \nu_i/\pi_i \tag{28.4}$$

or

$$c_i = (\xi - \lambda\nu_i/\pi_i)/2$$

Multiply c_i by ν_i and sum over i to obtain

$$W_j = \sum_i \nu_i c_i = \left(\xi\sum_i \nu_i - \lambda\sum_i \nu_i^2/\pi_i\right)/2$$

Solve for λ to obtain

$$\lambda = \frac{\xi\sum_i \nu_i - 2W_j}{\sum_i \nu_i^2/\pi_i}$$

Substitute for λ into the expression for c_i to obtain

$$c_i = \left[\frac{\xi}{2} - \frac{(\nu_i/2\pi_i)\xi\sum_k \nu_k}{\sum_k \nu_k^2/\pi_k}\right] + \frac{(\nu_i/\pi_i)W_j}{\sum \nu_k^2/\pi_k} \tag{28.5}$$

It follows that (28.5) also defines the set of mean-variance efficient portfolios. This is because the Lagrangean attached to the maximization of μ subject to fixed σ and the budget constraint has the same form as the maximization of expected quadratic utility subject to the budget constraint.

Viewed as a vector equation, (28.5) implies that every investor forms his portfolio by combining two assets, where each asset corresponds to one of the terms in (28.5). However, equation (28.5) has the Gorman polar form. That is, for each state s_i, the demand function is a linear function with an intercept term, and a slope term that multiplies wealth. Notably, the slope term is the same for all investors. Moreover, the intercept term differs across investors only in respect to ξ. Therefore, investors form their portfolios using the same two assets. This property is known as the *two-fund separation property*.[1] By a change of basis, the two assets can be selected to be the risk-free security and a risky security.

The prospect theory value function is given by (24.8) and (24.9). Consider now a modification whereby a modified quadratic form is used as a prospect theory analogue to (28.3). In this case, the utility function over gains and losses is given by

$$u_j(c_i) = \xi(c_i - \rho_i) - (c_i - \rho_i)^2 \qquad (28.6)$$

if $(c_i - \rho_i) \geq 0$ and

$$u_j(c_i) = \kappa[\xi(c_i - \rho_i) + (c_i - \rho_i)^2] \qquad (28.7)$$

if $(c_i - \rho_i) < 0$. Here, ρ is the reference point, $\kappa > 1$, and ξ is a positive parameter. For suitably small ξ, this functional form gives rise to an S-shaped prospect theory utility function (in a compact region).

In this model, one can think of a prospect theory investor as forming his portfolio in two stages. In the first stage, he purchases his reference vector ρ, the value of which is $\nu \cdot \rho$. He then spends his residual income $W_j - \nu \cdot \rho$ to maximize his (prospect theory) objective function. Note that when $W_j < \nu \cdot \rho$, the investor perceives himself in the domain of losses. In this respect, his choice variables, the change from the reference vector, lie in the negative quadrant. In addition, the consumption vector c, the sum of the reference vector and the change relative to the reference vector, must be nonnegative.

The main properties of this example will be briefly described shortly. Focus on the second stage, the maximization based on expenditure $W_j - \nu \cdot \rho$ in gain–loss space. Begin by focusing on the projection of the consumption plan onto the gain states. For a prospect theory investor with utility function (28.6), this projection can be expressed in the form (28.5), the demand vector for risk averse investors. The underlying reason for this property

---

[1] The nonhomothetic polar form function is known to violate nonnegative demand somewhere in its range. By choice of ξ, one can ensure an internal solution to the expected utility maximization.

is that the marginal rate of substitution between consumption levels in any two gain states derives from a quadratic utility function, evaluated at the value of the gains (relative to the reference vector), not the level of consumption itself.

Consider the case when ρ_i is the same for all i. In this case ρ is risk-free. By definition, the consumption vector c is the sum of the reference vector and the vector of gains-losses. Notably, the vector of gains and losses is mean-variance efficient. Hence, equation (28.5) has the two-fund separation property: The consumption vector is expressed as a linear combination of two vectors, and individual investor demands differ from one another only in respect to the weights. Hence, the two-fund separation argument underlying CAPM will apply to this example in connection with gain states. That is, for the projection onto gain states, the consumption profile of all investors will be a linear combination of the risk-free security and market portfolio.

Recall that common loss states are states where every prospect theory investor views himself in the domain of losses. Gain states are states where every prospect theory investor views himself in the domain of gains. Section 28.5 established that the equiprobability condition for common loss states implies the portfolio insurance pricing property. From the preceding discussion, the common loss states are those associated with the highest SDF values, and therefore the lowest consumption levels. A risk averse investor's consumption portfolio will feature equal (low) consumption over common loss states. Therefore, the overall portfolio consumption for a risk averse investor displays the CAPM pattern of a risk-free security and market portfolio combination in gain states, and constant consumption in loss states, regardless of how the market portfolio is performing.

Suppose that every loss state is a common loss state, this being a special case of the example. Then the consumption pattern just described can be achieved through the holding of a combination of the risk-free portfolio, the market portfolio, and a put option on the market portfolio with a suitable exercise price. This is the case of full portfolio insurance. Because of (28.3), all mean-variance efficient portfolios can be expressed as a linear combination of the risk-free security and the fully insured market portfolio. In terms of asset pricing, this means that the "insured market portfolio" plays the same role in this example as the market portfolio does in CAPM. Specifically:

1. The beta of a security is replaced with the return covariance of that security with the insured market portfolio.

2. The risk premium is the difference between the expected return of the insured market portfolio and the risk-free security.

In the traditional CAPM, equilibrium can be associated with a conventional representative investor having quadratic utility and consuming the aggregate consumption growth trajectory. In this case, the SDF will be linear in the rate of aggregate consumption growth: see (28.4). In the portfolio insurance property variation, the SDF is piecewise linear. It is linear in consumption growth for gains states, with a negative slope, and is linear with a zero slope in loss states.

Portfolio insurance pricing is also manifest in the relative prices of particular put options. Consider those put options on the market portfolio whose exercise prices lie below the exercise price of the put option associated with the mean-variance efficient level of portfolio insurance. It is not difficult to establish that for this example, the relative market prices of two such options Z_i and Z_k equal the ratio of their expected payouts, that is, $q_i/q_k = EZ_i/EZ_k$. What this equality reflects is a zero relative risk premium within common loss states.

The ratio of put option prices relative to the ratio of expected payoffs provides a way of assessing how the premium for risk varies over the distribution of possible outcomes. If the premium for risk were positive (negative) rather than zero, and Z_i had the lower exercise price, then the price ratio would exceed the ratio of expected payoffs. This is because a positive premium for risk is captured by a higher value of the SDF for less favorable states.

28.7   Heterogeneous Preferences and Heterogeneous Beliefs: Equilibrium with a Mix of SP/A Investors and EU-Investors

The examples developed in this chapter permit a mix of investors with behavioral preferences and traditional expected utility preferences. The key to understanding the structure of these models involves the indifference maps of the investors, which allow us to identify where investors choose internal solutions and where they choose boundary solutions. Notably, the internal solutions for prospect theory investors have the same form as those for expected utility investors.

Turning next to SP/A theory, the present section describes the structure of equilibrium in a market featuring a mix of investors, some with generalized SP/A preferences and others with expected utility (EU) preferences. This discussion deals with the general issue of modeling both heterogeneous preferences and heterogeneous beliefs. The CRRA-based SP/A structure is particularly well suited to the general approach, in that it allows the use of both Theorem 14.1, the main aggregation result in the book, and the key behavioral traits described in earlier chapters. The main point of this section is simply this: The log-SDF decomposition derived in Chapter 16 can be generalized to accommodate SP/A preferences.

Consider a model featuring a mix of investors. Some investors have EU preferences with CRRA-utility. The other investors have SP/A preferences based on CRRA-utility, as described in section 27.5. No condition is imposed requiring investors to share the same beliefs. The purpose of this section is to demonstrate how Theorem 14.1 can be used to characterize the representative investor for a market with a mix of EU and SP/A investors.

For the moment, focus on investors with SP/A preferences where the h-function in SP/A theory is the identity function. Let j be such an investor. Equation (12.23) implies that in date-event pair x_{t-1} investor j can use the ratio $P_j(x_t)/\nu(x_t)$ to rank order how expensive are claims to date–event pairs in successor nodes $\{x_t\}$. Let $\rho_j(x_{t-1})$ be investor j's aspiration level for the date t payoffs in successor date–event pairs to x_{t-1}. In equilibrium, each x_t will have associated with it a group of SP/A investors for whom $c_j(x_t) = \rho_j(x_{t-1})$. Call this set of investors $A(x_t)$. Define

$$c_A(x_t) = \sum_{j \in A(x_t)} c_j(x_t)$$

$c_A(x_t)$ is the total aspiration-constrained consumption for (SP/A) investors as a group. The variable

$$\omega_A(x_t) = \omega(x_t) - c_A(x_t)$$

is the value of equilibrium aggregate x_t-consumption that is not aspiration-constrained. As a general matter, let the subscript A refer to the modified market variables in which the endowment is ω_A instead of ω. For example, g_A denotes the aggregate consumption growth rate for ω_A.

In order to identify the representative investor for the mixed market, define for each SP/A investor j a fictitious EU-counterpart $k(j)$ having discounted probabilities as follows:

$$D_k(x_t) = \begin{cases} D_j(x_t) & \text{if } c_j(x_t) \neq \rho_j(x_{t-1}) \\ 0 & \text{if } c_j(x_t) = \rho_j(x_{t-1}) \end{cases}$$

Effectively, $k(j)$ assigns zero probability to date–event pairs where j is aspiration-constrained. In principle, one might wish to renormalize D_k because zeroing some probabilities prevents the remaining probabilities from summing to unity. While possible for interpretative purposes, this is formally unnecessary, as a single scale adjustment will have no impact on the relevant marginal conditions for maximization. However, the construction for k does introduce the possibility that time preference becomes state-dependent, not just time-dependent, and that $k(j)$-beliefs violate Bayes rule.

Define

$$c_k(x_t) = \begin{cases} c_j(x_t) & \text{if } c_j(x_t) \neq \rho_j(x_{t-1}) \\ 0 & \text{if } c_j(x_t) = \rho_j(x_{t-1}) \end{cases}$$

Suppose that investor $k(j)$ has discounted probability beliefs given by D_k, and shares the same CRRA value γ as investor j. Furthermore, let investor $k(j)$'s initial portfolio be given by c_k.

Imagine that in the market populated by a mix of the original EU-investors and SP/A investors we substitute for j its EU-counterpart $k(j)$. Furthermore, suppose that the EU-investors' initial portfolios are their final equilibrium portfolios. In this case, the equilibrium prices for the original mixed market will also be equilibrium prices in the modified market (with $k(j)$ replacing j for all SP/A investors j). The $k(j)$ EU-investors face the same budget sets and therefore make the same optimal choices as their j-generators whenever $c_j \neq \rho_j$. Each $k(j)$-investor chooses the same value of $c_j(x_t)$, as long as $c_j(x_t) \neq \rho_j(x_{t-1})$. This is because the first order conditions for $k(j)$ are exactly the same as for j in all date–event pairs that are not aspiration-constrained. Moreover, $k(j)$ has lower wealth than does j, and exhausts his wealth purchasing non-aspiration-constrained consumption claims. Investor $k(j)$ has no interest in purchasing claims to consumption in date–event pairs where j is aspiration-constrained because he, $k(j)$, attaches zero discounted probability to those date–event pairs.

The modified market is composed of investors whose structure conforms to the assumptions underlying Theorem 14.1, the main aggregation theorem in the book. Therefore, Theorem 14.1 can be used to identify a representative investor to characterize the equilibrium, and associated SDF.

There are a few subtleties to keep in mind when making use of the modified market. Keep in mind that aggregate consumption is different in the modified market than the original market. This is because aggregate consumption in the modified market is given by ω_A, not ω. As a result, the growth rate of aggregate consumption can be different in the modified market than the original market. Notably, growth rates for date–event pairs that are severely aspiration-constrained will typically be lower in the modified market than the original market. Similarly, probability weight attached to date–event pairs that are severely aspiration-constrained will be lower in the modified market than the original market, because $k(j)$ investors assign these date–event pairs zero probability.

The features described in the preceding paragraph give rise to values for δ_R and P_R from Theorem 14.1 that require additional transformation in order to be properly interpreted as discount factors and probabilities.

Recall that the subscript A refers to the modified market. Define

$$Q_R(x_t) = P_{R,A}(x_t) \, g(x_t)/g_A(x_t)$$
$$P_R(x_t) = Q_R(x_t)/\sum Q_R(y_t)$$

where y_t denotes a typical date–event pair at date t, and the summation is over y_t. Define

$$\delta_R(t) = \delta_{R,A}(t) \sum Q_R(y_t)$$
$$\gamma_R(x_t) = \gamma_{R,A}(x_t)$$

With these transformations, the representative investor for a market featuring a mix of traditional CRRA preferences and behavioral SP/A preferences can be described by γ_R, δ_R, and P_R. In this respect, Theorem 16.1, the decomposition result for the log-SDF continues to hold.

Consider one final technical point. The preceding argument took the h-function in SP/A theory to be the identity function. When h is not the identity function, then rank dependence might introduce a pseudo-constraint in the left-hand-region of the consumption graph, as displayed in Figure 27.7. For the analysis developed in this section, the addition of a pseudo-constraint in this region is treated in the same way as the aspiration constraint for the intermediate region of consumption.

28.7.1 Behavioral Preferences and the Signature of Sentiment

There are two ways that SP/A preferences impact the SDF through the sentiment variable Λ. The first way is through the decision weights v_j, which formally play the same role as P_j in Theorem 14.1. The impact on the SDF, particularly its shape, reflects the degree to which v_j deviates from the objective process Π. What Lopes calls cautious hope involves the overweighting of probabilities associated with both very favorable events and very unfavorable events. In this respect, the sentiment function associated with an individual SP/A investor has the same general U-shape as the market sentiment function displayed in Figure 15.4.

The second way that SP/A preferences impact the SDF is through the aspiration constraint and possible rank-dependent quasi-constraint. This occurs through the differences between g_A and g, and between $P_{R,A}$ and P_R. The accompanying Excel file *Chapter 28 SDF Equilibrium Example.xls* demonstrates the second point in a simple two-investor example. Here the true probabilities are uniform, and h is linear, but the effect of aspiration-constrained consumption is to increase the representative investor's probabilities for the aspiration-constrained states, making them appear more likely than is actually the case.

Recall that in SP/A theory, it is the aspiration variable A which gives rise to risk-seeking behavior in the domain of losses. The risk which SP/A investors face is reflected in low demand for consumption claims in states for which consumption falls below aspiration. The aspiration variable also impacts investors' preference for positively skewed returns, as reflected in their demand for lottery-type stocks.

Both the weighting function effect and the aspiration constraint effect contribute towards an SDF that features an upward-sloping portion, the signature of sentiment. Notably, it is the weighting function and aspiration constraint, not the utility function, which produces the upward sloping-portion property.

In the general case involving both behavioral preferences and behavioral beliefs, sentiment Λ reflects the impact of both. As a result, the fundamental component in Theorem 15.1 now has a different interpretation than in the earlier parts of the book. In this case, the fundamental component in the log-SDF decomposition corresponds to the case when all investors have both EU-preferences and correct beliefs. That is, the fundamental component is neoclassical in respect to both preferences and beliefs.

Neither investors with EU-preferences nor investors with SP/A preferences take explicit account of the shape of the SDF. Rather, both types of investors simply focus on the prices attached to state claims. In the case of EU-investors, comparisons are made on a state price per subjective probability basis, ν/P_j. In the case of an SP/A investor, comparisons are made on the basis of ν/P_j for achieving aspiration, and on a state price per uncertainty weight basis, ν/v_j, for the SP-portion. Neither the EU-investors nor the SP/A investors are directly concerned with whether or not the ordering of states by aggregate consumption growth differs from the ordering by the SDF.

28.7.2   Further Remarks on Skewness and Coskewness

Lopes and Oden (1999) employ a linear utility function in their framework for tractability, and suggest that in practice, the appropriate utility function is mildly concave. In this regard, recall Polkovnichenko's point discussed in section 27.9.1 that rank-dependent utility is required to explain his empirical finding about investors' portfolios featuring a preference for positive skewness. This implies that the upward sloping portion of the SDF stems from its sentiment component, not its fundamental component.

Polkovnichenko's remarks relate to the discussion in Harvey and Siddique (2000). Harvey–Siddique explain their empirical coskewness finding in terms of an SDF which is quadratic in the market return. In their frame-work, the SDF has only a fundamental component, whose quadratic component Harvey–Siddique attribute to the third derivative of the rep-resentative investor's utility function. Polkovnichenko points out that the effect of the third derivative is small relative to the effect of the weight-ing function. In contrast, the Harvey–Siddique model is based on expected utility preferences where the weights are probabilities.

Similar remarks apply to the manner in which CPT preferences impact the shape of the SDF function. See Barberis and Huang (2007). As in the discussion above, it is the weighting functions that exert the most influence. The prospect theory utility (value) function is mildly concave in the domain of gains and mildly convex in the domain of losses. From a neoclassical perspective, a positively sloped SDF corresponds to negative risk aversion; that is, risk-seeking behavior. However, as can be seen from the analysis in Sections 28.4 through 28.6, convexity in the domain of losses does not imply an upward-sloping portion in connection with the SDF. A similar point is made by Blackburn and Ukhov (2006b). See also Post and Levy (2005) who analyze how asset prices are impacted by risk-seeking preferences, embodied either within the utility function or the weighting function.

Skewness and coskewness are both germane to pricing. However, they are distinct concepts. They can be related to each other, but the nature of the relationship can be subtle. Skewness is a property of investors' portfolio return distributions, and it is subjective. In SP/A theory, potential P and high aspiration A lead an investor to choose a portfolio return distribution which displays positively skewed returns; this is from a subjective per-spective. From an objective perspective, beliefs also impact the degree to which portfolio returns are skewed. Investors who are excessively optimistic tend to favor positively skewed returns, while investors who are excessively pessimistic tend to favor negatively skewed returns.

Coskewness is a statistical property which reflects covariation with the square of the market return. Its role as a factor in the pricing of risk is reflected in the shape of the SDF function (at a given point in time). Chapter 17 discusses why a mix of excessively optimistic investors and excessively pessimistic investors results in coskewness being a priced factor. Notably, the pricing of coskewness reflects the degree to which the SDF function oscillates, with the U-shape being a special case.

The discussion in Chapter 17 pointed out that a mean-variance investor with objectively correct beliefs does not intrinsically value skewness. How-ever, he does value coskewness when it is a priced factor, in which case his portfolio return distribution will be skewed. When coskewness features a negative premium, the mean-variance investor's portfolio will be negatively skewed. Erroneous beliefs and behavioral preferences serve to modify and often reverse the impact of coskewness on investors' portfolios. In particular, excessive optimism, potential P, and high aspiration levels all serve to induce portfolio return distributions that are positively skewed.

Keep in mind that when the SDF function is quadratic in its state variable, aggregate consumption growth, the market return and coskewness are the only two priced risk factors. However, if the SDF assumes a more complex oscillating shape, as in Figure 16.2, then other risk factors will also be priced. This is the case with the situation depicted in Figure 17.1.

The above discussion provides some context for interpreting the findings of Mitton and Vorkink (2007). Mitton–Vorkink report that the portfolio returns of underdiversified investors are more positively skewed than the portfolio returns of diversified investors. They report that much of this skewness is idiosyncratic, meaning that its associated risk premium is zero, and that the undiversified investors choose stocks whose return distributions are positively skewed. In this respect, Mitton–Vorkink suggest that underdiversified investors sacrifice mean-variance efficiency in exchange for increased skewness. Finally, they report that asset prices are impacted by idiosyncratic skewness, not just coskewness.

All of the findings described above conform to an equilibrium featuring a behavioral SDF whose shape conforms to Figure 16.2. However, Mitton–Vorkink's theoretical framework is actually neoclassical. It assumes the existence of two types of investors, those with mean-variance preferences and those whose utility functions feature a preference for skewness.

Brunnermeier, Gollier, and Parker (2007) suggest that a combination of beliefs and preferences underlies the findings about the preference for skewness. The combination is manifest in the concept of "optimal beliefs." Optimal beliefs combine beliefs and preferences, in that investors hold beliefs that make them happy at the moment, even if their beliefs are objectively incorrect. Brunnermeier, Gollier, and Parker cite the work of Zhang (2005) who found that assets whose return distributions are positively skewed tend to have lower returns.

28.8   Summary

The portfolio of a prospect theory investor is sensitive to the location of the reference point. For low reference points, prospect theory investors choose traditional portfolios. Higher reference points induce risk-seeking behavior, or the reluctance to engage in trade.

Prospect theory preferences primarily impact the SDF in the region of loss states. The shape of the SDF is determined by both the utility (value) function and weighting function(s). In particular, convex utility in the domain of losses leads probabilities, rather than aggregate consumption growth, to determine the shape of the SDF in the region of loss states. A special case is portfolio insurance pricing. In this case, risk averse investors are induced to purchase put options on their risky assets in order to limit possible losses.

The relationship between risk and return under portfolio insurance pricing is explored within a mean-variance example. In the example, an "insured market portfolio" plays the role of the market portfolio in the CAPM. In equilibrium, traditional risk averse expected utility maximizing investors choose to hold put options that insure their holdings of the market portfolio.

Theorem 28.1 indicates that a prospect theory investor would prefer zero consumption in all loss states, with perhaps one exception. This behavior is not descriptive of the portfolio choices of most investors. Notably, this behavior pattern gives rise to implications for the shape of the SDF which are not supported by the empirical evidence.

Chapter 27 pointed out that a behavioral portfolio framework built on SP/A theory instead of prospect theory can preserve many of the desirable features of prospect theory and avoid the undesirable features just described.

The last section of the present chapter develops a unified behavioral theory, involving multiple time periods, heterogeneous beliefs and heterogeneous behavioral preferences. The key result in the section is that the log-SDF decomposition developed in Theorem 16.1 carries over to the general model. Notably, with a mix of both neoclassical beliefs and preferences, sentiment is to be interpreted as a difference relative to a market featuring only objective beliefs and neoclassical preferences.

29

The Disposition Effect: Trading Behavior and Pricing

In Shefrin and Statman (1985), Meir Statman and I suggested that investors are disposed to sell their winners too early and to ride their losers too long. We identified a series of psychological phenomena that we believed explained the disposition effect, presented data consistent with the effect, and proposed some testable hypotheses. The disposition effect is now one of the most, if not the most, studied behavioral patterns in finance. A literature on the disposition effect has developed to test the hypotheses we developed and extend the focus of discussion from investor behavior to pricing and to trading volume. The present chapter surveys the evidence pertaining to the disposition effect.

Strictly speaking, the disposition effect pertains to the combination of preferences and beliefs. Conditional on beliefs, the disposition effect indicates that behavioral preferences predispose investors to sell winners earlier and ride losers longer than occurs when preferences are neoclassical. To be sure, a strong belief in return reversals can also induce investors to sell winners quickly, but delay selling losers.

29.1 Psychological Basis for the Disposition Effect

The "disposition effect" is a shorthand term for investors' predisposition to sell winners too quickly and ride losers too long. In 1985, Statman and

I coined the term, based on the intriguing empirical study of individual investor behavior by Lease, Lewellen, and Schlarbaum (1976). We suggested that the following four psychological factors underlie the disposition effect:

1. prospect theory;

2. mental accounting operations;

3. regret

4. self-control

Beginning with prospect theory, Statman and I reasoned that investors might code gains and losses in their stock trades relative to original purchase prices. In doing so, an investor would classify a winning stock as one whose current market price lies above the original purchase price. Likewise, a losing stock is one whose current market price lies below the original purchase price.

Look back at the decision task 19 described in subsection 24.2.4. Consider how that task can be given an investment interpretation. For ease of exposition, scale down the value in that task by 100, so that $2,400 becomes $24, etc.

Suppose that on a Monday, an investor read a newspaper article which led him to purchase the stock of a biotechnology firm for $110 a share. The article discussed the fact that the firm has a patent application pending with the Food and Drug Administration (FDA) for a new product X. The article also pointed out that an advisory panel for the FDA is expected to issue a recommendation on the subsequent Wednesday. Suppose that on Tuesday, the biotechnology firm issues a press release reporting favorable results for one of its other products Y which is currently under development, and chemically related to X. As a result of the announcement, the price of its stock jumps to $134, reflecting increased odds that the FDA panel will issue a positive recommendation. Nevertheless, based on similar circumstances in the past, the odds that on Wednesday the FDA panel actually will recommend approval is only 25 percent. If the panel recommends approval, the stock price will rise to $210. If the panel recommends rejection, the stock price will fall back to $110. After the stock has risen on Tuesday, the investor has a choice: Sell the stock for a gain of $24 or wait for the panel's decision on Wednesday. That is effectively the choice between 19A and 19B in the Tversky-Kahneman decision task described in subsection 24.2.4.

A similar analogy can be drawn for the choice between 19C and 19D. Suppose that on a Monday, an investor read a newspaper article which led him to purchase the stock of a biotechnology firm for $110 a share. The article discussed the fact that the firm has a patent application pending with the Food and Drug Administration (FDA) for a new product X. On Tuesday, one of the clinical investigators studying the drug presents a negative report involving product X's side effects. In response to the story, the firm's stock price declines to $35. Before the market closes on Tuesday, the firm's management announces that they will investigate the issue and issue a press release as soon as they are in a position to evaluate the full evidence. If the side effect is serious, the stock price will decline to $10. If the side effect is not serious, the stock price will revert to $110. The probability that the side effect is serious is 75 percent. After the stock has declined on Tuesday, the investor has a choice: Sell the stock for a loss of $75 or wait for the firm's press release. That is effectively the choice between 19C and 19D in the decision task.

The manner in which most people behave in the Tversky-Kahneman decision task suggests that in the analogous stock situation, most investors are predisposed to sell their winners but ride their losers.

Statman and I suggested that although prospect theory is a useful starting point for studying the disposition effect, it does not provide a complete explanation of the disposition effect for individual investors. Our explanation involved taxes and optimal realization policy developed by Constantinides (1983, 1984). Long-term gains usually are taxed at a lower rate than short-term gains. Therefore, individual investors pay a higher tax rate if they sell a winner when it is classified as a short-term gain rather than a long-term gain. Therefore the disposition to sell winners too early is typically costly.

What about the disposition to ride losers too long? Under the U.S. tax code, individual investors can use realized capital losses to offset realized capital gains by $3,000. An investor who is in a position to take advantage of this provision can sell a losing position, and, if he wishes to maintain the same risk profile in his portfolio, replace the stock sold with another stock having the same risk-return profile. This leaves the investor's risk-return combination unchanged, but it provides additional wealth in the form of lower taxes. Looked at this way, the decision to ride losers by avoiding tax-loss selling is akin to throwing away money. Implicit in this discussion is the assumption that the predictable component to returns is zero. If returns featured strong positive autocorrelation, then the task of finding a substitute security for the one being sold becomes more difficult.

Prospect theory does not explain why individual investors would knowingly pay more taxes than necessary, thereby throwing away money. As was discussed in Chapter 24, Kahneman and Tversky structured prospect theory to avoid the choice of stochastically dominated alternatives.

At the same time, prospect theory does explain why some people might unknowingly throw away money. For example, in the Tversky-Kahneman decision task 19 in Chapter 24, the combination of A and D is equivalent to choosing the combination of B and C, and then throwing away $100 no matter what the outcome.

Remember that A and D is the combination most frequently chosen in the example. Virtually everyone who chooses A and D does so without realizing they are acting as if they want to burn $1. Instead most people mentally frame the A vs. B decision and the C vs. D decision into separate mental accounts, which record only the gains and losses associated with a portion of the decision task being faced. However, because most people fail to pool these two mental accounts, they unknowingly choose combination A and D instead of the superior combination of B and C.

To be sure, some individual investors fail to grasp the value of tax-loss selling. However, many individual investors do understand tax-loss selling but find it psychologically difficult to realize a loss. Statman and I suggested that there are two reasons why this might be so, both lying outside the scope of prospect theory. The first reason is that realizing a loss entails a particular mental operation, closing a mental account at a loss. We emphasized that much of the pain associated with the loss is triggered by this operation.

The second reason involves the emotion of regret. Regret is the third psychological factor underlying the disposition effect. In psychological terms, regret is the emotion a person experiences when a past decision that he or she has taken turns out badly, and it is easy for that person to imagine having taken a different decision that would have turned out well (see Kahneman and Tversky, 1982). Shefrin and Statman (1985) also discuss the polar opposite of regret: the pride that comes from selling a stock at a gain.

Statman and I suggested that regret is particularly pronounced if the person feels responsible for a decision. In the case of a losing stock, regret is experienced most acutely when the stock is sold. Selling a stock at a loss involves the admission of a mistake. Therefore, investors will be disposed to hold onto losers in order to postpone regret, or they will avoid it completely if the stock eventually moves into the domain of gains. Notably, the effect of regret can delay the sale of winners when investors track stocks they have sold in the past. Some investors might delay selling their winners for fear they will subsequently perform extremely well, thereby generating regret.

Recall that self-control is the fourth psychological factor underlying the disposition effect. At a conscious level many investors understand that in the long-run they might injure themselves by riding losers too long or selling winners too early. Yet avoiding the disposition effect can be challenging. Regret and pride loom large.

Regret explains the source of immediate pain. Aversion to regret explains why a person might be disposed to making choices to reduce that pain.

However, neither prospect theory nor regret theory addresses how people come to terms with internal conflicts when their dispositions are at odds with their judgments about what is in their own best long-run interests. Addressing such conflicts requires an appreciation of self-control.

A person who is predisposed to riding losers but wishes to counter this disposition typically will need to engage in some form of self-control. Exercising self-control is not always easy. Some investors deal with this particular issue by using some form of stop-loss order, be it formal or informal. Professional investors often use the term discipline to mean the exercise of self-control in order to cut losses early.

Self-control is more challenging in some circumstances than in others. Constantinides' optimal policy calls for loss realization as early as is feasible in light of transaction costs. However, when it comes to tax-loss selling, many individual investors lack the self-control to realize losses quickly. Instead, they wait until December. Of course, they need not wait this long. They have the option of realizing losses during the year, and can do so at the same time that they realize gains. Instead of waiting until next April to receive the associated tax benefit, investors even can adjust their income tax withholdings to capture the effect immediately.

Shefrin and Statman (1985) suggest that in December investors find it easier to exert the self-control necessary to realize a loss because in December, attention gets focused on tax reduction. Some investors might use rules about realizing losses in December. Others might view the tax savings as a silver lining that mitigates the pain of loss realization, thereby reducing the psychological obstacle that prevents loss realization.

In concluding this section, I would mention that much of the literature on the disposition effect emphasizes the role of prospect theory but downplays or ignores the other psychological issues discussed in Shefrin and Statman (1985). For example, Odean (1998) draws on the discussion about prospect theory in Shefrin and Statman (1985), and mentions self-control in respect to December but says little about regret.

Recent theoretical works by Hens and Vlcek (2005) and Barberis and Xiong (2006) also fail to mention regret and self-control. These papers do assert that prospect theory is unable to provide a complete explanation for the disposition effect, but for reasons different from those that appear in Shefrin and Statman (1985). Hens-Vlcek point out that in a two-date optimizing model, the disposition effect is inconsistent with the initial decision to have purchased the stock. Barberis-Xiong develop a multi-date optimizing model in which the disposition effect occurs for some choice of parameters but not others. They also analyze the case in which utility depends, not just on financial gains and losses, but on whether realization of those gains and losses takes place. They find that this feature strengthens the disposition effect, thereby reinforcing one of the central points in Shefrin and Statman (1985).

Empirically, the psychological aspects of closing mental accounts, regret, and self-control are important. Using Finnish data, Lehenkari (2007) provides intriguing evidence that investors are more prone to the disposition effect for stocks they purchased than for stocks they received as gifts or as part of an inheritance. This distinction is important. The emotion of regret is much more closely associated with a stock which an investor decided to purchase than with a stock the investor did not decide to purchase, but instead received as a gift or through inheritance. Recent experimental evidence by Fogel and Berry (2006) strongly supports the importance of regret in explaining the disposition effect, particularly when it comes to riding losers. In this regard, the paper by Barber, Lee, Liu, and Odean (2006) includes an explicit discussion of regret.

The impact of regret has also been studied in a formal framework. Muermann and Volkmann (2007) develop a theoretical model to study the impact of regret on the disposition effect. Their work provides some insight into the different manner in which regret impacts an investor's decisions. As was mentioned above, on the one hand, regret (and its counterpart pride) act to encourage disposition behavior. On the other hand, for investors who continue to track stocks they have sold in the past, regret can also serve to mitigate disposition behavior.

As to self-control, Feng and Seasholes (2005) find that susceptibility to the disposition effect declines by 72 percent with sophistication and experience, especially in connection with riding losses. Dhar and Zhu (2006) report a similar finding, as do Seru, Shumway, and Stoffman (2006) who indicate that after a year of trading experience, the disposition of the median investor improves by 4 percent.

29.2   Evidence for the Disposition Effect

A seminal empirical study by Terry Odean (1998) tested the main predictions associated with the disposition effect. The data for the study came from 10,000 customer accounts at a nationwide discount brokerage house during the period January 1987 through December 1993. For each investor and trading day, Odean identified which stocks were winners and which were losers, based on original purchase price. He considered the value of all the stock positions that were classified as capital gains and called the fraction of all gains sold on that day the proportion of gains realized (PGR). Analogously, he defined for losses the proportion of losses realized (PLR). PGR is the ratio of realized gains to the sum of realized gains and paper gains. PLR is the ratio of realized losses to the sum of realized losses and paper losses.

The disposition effect, as introduced by Shefrin and Statman (1985), states that for all months but December, individual investors fail to minimize taxes when they sell winners too quickly and ride losers too long. However, in December, individual investors are less prone to exhibit the disposition effect. Odean (1998) operationalized the disposition effect through the inequality PGR > PLR in all months but December, with the difference PGR − PLR being lowest in December.

Odean found that for most of the year, on average a stock that was up in value was almost 60 percent more likely to be sold than a stock that was down in value. Outside of December, PGR was about 14.8 percent, while PLR was 9.8 percent. However, the pattern reversed in December, when losses were realized at a more rapid rate than gains: PGR fell to 10.8 percent while PLR rose to 12.8 percent. See Table 29.1. The t-statistics indicate that Odean's findings are highly significant, although Odean is careful to mention that independence of observations is an issue. In addition, Odean reports that his findings are robust across time, and across frequent traders and infrequent traders.

Table 29.2 documents the average returns for the categories Odean uses. Notice that realized losses have higher returns than paper losses, while

TABLE 29.1. Percentage of Gains and Losses Realized

This table presents the main findings in Odean (1998a) concerning PGR, PLR, and PGR − PLR.

	Entire Year	December	Jan–Nov
PGR	0.148	0.108	0.152
PLR	0.098	0.128	0.094
Difference in Proportions	0.050	−0.020	0.058
t-statistic (for Difference)	35	−4.3	38

TABLE 29.2. Average Returns

This table presents the main findings in Odean (1998a) concerning average returns to the four categories.

	Entire Year	December	Jan–Nov
Return on Realized Gains	0.277	0.316	0.275
Return on Paper Gains	0.466	0.500	0.463
Return on Realized Losses	−0.228	−0.366	−0.208
Return on Paper Losses	−0.393	−0.417	−0.391

TABLE 29.3. Average Returns Post Realization

This table presents the main findings in Odean (1999) concerning average returns to stocks purchased and sold.

	Number of Transactions	84 Trading Days, Later	252 Trading Days, Later	504 Trading Days, Later
Purchases	49,948	1.83	5.69	24.00
Sales	47,535	3.19	9.00	27.32
Difference		−1.36	−3.31	−3.32

realized gains are smaller than paper gains. Interestingly, realized losses in December are much higher than realized losses in other months, reinforcing the suggestion of a strong tax-loss selling motive.

Is the disposition effect rational? Odean's analysis suggests not. The loser stocks that investors sell display subsequent superior performance, outperforming the stocks that they purchase. Unlike the losers they sell, the losers they continue to hold do not display superior performance. See Table 29.3, which is also discussed in Section 29.3.

The disposition effect is not confined to individual investors in the United States. Shapira and Venezia (2001) study Israeli investors. They find that the average duration of losers is significantly longer than that of winners. For winners, the average length of a round trip is about 22 days, but for losers the average length of round trip is about 58 days.

Grinblatt and Keloharju (2001) use data from the Finnish Central Securities Depository. They define extreme capital losses as capital losses that feature more than a 30 percent reduction in value. Grinblatt and Keloharju (2001) find that on average an extreme capital loss reduces the probability of a sale by 32 percent. For moderate capital losses, the corresponding probability reduction is 21 percent. Interestingly, in December investors are 36 percent more likely to sell extreme losers than they are during the rest of the year. However, most investors delay selling extreme losers until the last eight trading days of the year. The effect for moderate losses is very small. Analysis of Finnish data by Seru, Shumway, and Stoffman (2006) finds that the cost of the disposition effect, in terms of returns, lies between 3.2 percent and 5.7 percent for the average investor.

Feng and Seasholes (2005) find that investors in China exhibit the disposition effect. Their study uses data from January 1999 through December 2000. As mentioned above, Feng and Seasholes find that investors holding more stocks, who are plausibly more sophisticated than investors who hold fewer stocks, are less prone to exhibiting the disposition effect. Specifically, a sophisticated investor is 67 percent less prone to the disposition effect than the average investor.

Investors in Taiwan also exhibit the disposition effect. Using data from 1995 through 1999, Barber, Lee, Liu, and Odean (2006) report that Taiwanese investors are approximately twice as likely to sell winners relative to losers. In addition, 85 percent of the investors in their sample sell winners at a faster rate than losers. Their study focuses on both individual investors and investment professionals. Barber et al. find that individual investors, corporations, and dealers, who dominate the market, are reluctant to realize losses. In contrast, mutual funds and foreigners are not reluctant to realize losses.

Markku Kaustia (2004) uses trading volume for initial public offerings (IPOs) to study the disposition effect. He suggests that the IPO offer price is the most likely reference point. Consistent with the disposition effect, Kaustia finds that volume for initial losers is lower than it is for initial winners. Volume jumps when a stock becomes a loser right after the IPO, and subsequently the stock price exceeds the corresponding offer price for first time,. Not all of Kaustia's findings support the disposition effect. For example, he found that volume also increases when the stock price first dips below the offer price.

In our 1985 article, Statman and I discussed some of the literature on self-control techniques which some investment professionals use to mitigate the disposition effect. What might be most surprising about the disposition effect is the extent to which it impacts investment professionals as well as individual investors.

Frazzini (2006) studies the disposition effect associated with mutual fund managers. He finds that on balance, mutual fund managers exhibit the disposition effect, though to a lesser degree than individual investors. At the same time, underperforming (loser) funds are 1.7 times more likely to realize a paper gain than a paper loss. That is, underperforming managers appear to be as prone to the disposition effect as individual investors. The findings in Wermers (2003) also suggest that mutual fund managers are prone to the disposition effect.

Jin and Scherbina (2005) employ a novel approach to conclude that mutual fund managers are subject to the disposition effect. Their study points out that when a mutual fund replaces one manager with another, the new manager sells losers from the portfolio at a faster rate than did the prior manager. Why? The new fund manager has no responsibility for having selected the losing stocks; therefore no regret to experience, and no regret to defer or avoid by selling losers.

Coval and Shumway (2005) study the disposition effect using Treasury bond futures. These contracts are traded on the Chicago Board of Trade. Coval and Shumway (2005) find that traders associated with more than $200 million in contracts per day are more likely to take additional risk in the afternoon after experiencing morning losses as opposed to morning gains. The probability of taking above average afternoon risk is 31 percent after morning losses, but only 27 percent chance after morning gains. Coval and Shumway's study is broader than the disposition effect. However, their main finding is that the disposition effect is the strongest behavioral bias they identify, and that the most applicable reference point is original purchase price.

Methodologically, both Coval-Shumway (2005) and Feng-Seasholes (2005) use survival analysis to analyze how long a stock is likely to survive in an investor's portfolio before being sold. Feng-Seasholes discuss the advantages of using survival analysis over the PGR/PLR approach for studying behavior at the level of the individual.

Locke and Mann (2005) provide strong evidence that commodity and currency traders exhibit the disposition effect in the sense of riding their losers. Relative to traders who do not exhibit the disposition effect, traders who do

- pass up more opportunities to realize losses than gains

- hold larger positions when facing losses

- expose themselves to bigger potential losses than to potential gains.

In commodity and currency markets, round trips tend to be short: Ten minutes is a long time to hold a position. Consider a ranking of traders by trading income. For average holding times less than ten minutes, the lowest ranked traders earn revenues that are roughly comparable to more successful traders. However, trades held longer than ten minutes for unsuccessful traders are particularly unprofitable.

The strongest evidence presented by Locke and Mann involves the relationship between a proxy for riding losers and risk-adjusted performance (RAP). Their study uses two proxies for disposition effect behavior, namely length of holding times for positions and maximum potential losses for positions held longer than ten minutes.

RAP is the ratio of daily trading income to value at risk (VaR). VaR is based on maximum potential loss over a one-hundred-day period, and it is measured ex post. Locke and Mann define ex post VaR as the fifth-largest potential loss, corresponding to the ninety-fifth percentile. RAP is average daily income divided by VaR. An RAP equal to 0.2 means that a trader risks five times his or her daily trading income about once every twenty days. There is considerable variability in RAP. Median RAP for the lowest RAP quartile typically is negative. Median RAP for the highest RAP quartile is about 0.42.

Locke and Mann focus on the division of a year into its first and second halves. They use the first half of the year to characterize traders by their susceptibility to the disposition effect. They then correlate the degree of susceptibility to trading success in the second half of the year. They find that the more disposition-prone a trader, the lower his/her RAP value. That is, disposition-prone traders tend to take on much more risk to achieve trading profits. In the majority of cases, being disposition prone is negatively correlated with future income. However, the results are not as strong for trading income as they are for RAP.

O'Connell and Teo (forthcoming) also study the behavior of currency traders. In contrast to the traders studied by Locke and Mann who trade for their own accounts, those studied by O'Connell and Teo are institutional investors who manage other investors' money. Notably, O'Connell and Teo report that the investors they study do not exhibit the disposition effect. Instead, institutions aggressively reduce risk after losses and mildly increase risk after gains.

29.3   Investor Beliefs

Portfolio choices are influenced by a combination of beliefs and preferences, where preferences are understood to reflect psychological phenomena such as aversion to a sure loss.

29.3.1   Odean's Findings

For purchases, the features of prospect theory that are most important are loss aversion and mental accounting. Loss aversion imparts status quo bias, leading investors to be reluctant to trade unless they hold bold beliefs.

The characteristics of stocks that individual investors purchase provide a strong indicator of their beliefs. Odean (1999) documents that individual investors tend to purchase smaller, growth stocks. Specifically, individual investors appear to favor stocks that have been recent winners, in that they have outperformed the CRSP value weighted index by about 25 percent over the preceding two years. In this respect they act as if they are trend followers who predict continuation, a feature that is consistent with the general results reported in Chapter 6. In addition, individual investors tend to purchase small cap stocks, with an average size decile of about 8.65.

The disposition effect does not imply that investors never accept a sure loss. Given a choice between accepting a sure $7,500 loss and facing a gamble that features a 99.9999 percent chance of losing $10,000 and a 0.0001 percent chance of losing nothing, most people choose to accept the sure loss. Even though investors might be risk seeking in the domain of losses, the probability of avoiding a sure loss needs to be high enough to make the gamble worthwhile. Therefore, the disposition effect does not stipulate that investors never sell losers, or only sell losers in the month of December for tax-loss reasons. Beliefs and preferences together determine behavior. That is why the disposition effect hypothesizes that the combination of beliefs and preferences implies that, except in December, investors realize their winners more frequently than their losers.

In general, the characteristics of stocks that individual investors sell are fairly similar to those of the stocks they purchase. Stocks sold performed well over the preceding year; in fact, almost as well as the stocks purchased. A striking difference between the two groups is that stocks sold rose more sharply in the months preceding the sale than did stocks purchased. However, unlike stocks purchased, which registered positive abnormal returns for the preceding two years, stocks sold began to register positive abnormal returns only about a year before the sale.

Needless to say, not every stock that individual investors purchase is a small stock that has recently outperformed the market. Indeed, investors who add to their holdings of stocks on which they have lost money apparently hold bold beliefs that these stocks will do well in the future. In this respect, Odean reports that investors are prone to make additional purchases of stocks already in their portfolios that are losers. Among their existing losers to which investors could potentially purchase additional shares, investors actually made purchases in 13.5 percent of cases. In contrast, for existing winners, the corresponding percentage was only 9.4 percent.

Table 29.3 displays Odean's findings for all transactions. The general pattern is astonishing. The stocks that investors sold subsequently outperformed the stocks that they purchased for a time horizon as long as 504 trading days. Specifically, the stocks that individual investors sold outperformed the stocks that they purchased by 3.32 percent over the subsequent 504 trading days. Notably, the returns in question are raw returns. Odean reports, though, that the results for market-adjusted returns are similar.

29.3.2   A Size Effect

Ranguelova (2001) provides additional intriguing evidence about the trading behavior of individual investors. She reports that the disposition effect is increasing in the market capitalization of the underlying stocks. Moreover, for stocks at the bottom 40 percent of the market capitalization distribution, investors keep their winners and sell their losers. Among stocks at the bottom 20 percent of the market capitalization distribution, individuals tend to realize on average 20 percent of all available losses and only 10.6 percent of all available gains. However, investors in the overall sample do sell a higher fraction of winners than losers, although this behavior varies strongly with firm size.[1]

Ranguelova's findings are based on the daily trading records of 78,000 clients of a major US discount brokerage house over a period of six years. She partitions the sample by market capitalization quintiles, and finds that investors systematically sell a large fraction of their large-cap gains and small-cap losses. In particular, the proportion of gains realized out of all available gains in the corresponding size quintile is monotonically increasing in the quintile number. Moreover, the proportion of losses realized out of all available losses in the corresponding size quintile is monotonically decreasing with the size quintile number.

29.3.3   A Volume Effect

A study by Statman, Thorley, and Vorkink (2006) suggests that the disposition effect also affects trading volume. Statman–Thorley–Vorkink use a vector autoregression model to examine the impact of past turnover, past stock returns, the past return on the market, and volatility on future turnover and returns.

Trading volume is driven by at least two forces. The first is changes in heterogeneity of beliefs, the subject of Sections 10.3 and 10.4. The second is the disposition effect. Investors trade on the basis of differences of opinion, which are amplified by overconfidence. They also trade, or refrain from trade, as a result of the manner in which they frame their current positions.

Formally, the context for the Statman–Thorley–Vorkink analysis consists of Cases 3 and 5 discussed in Subsection 28.2.2. Case 3 is the no-trade equilibrium. When all investors perceive themselves to be in the domain of losses, and hold common beliefs, they become reluctant to trade, even when their portfolios are highly undiversified. Case 5 involves the conjunction of loss aversion and heterogeneous beliefs. When investors hold heterogeneous beliefs, then the differences in those beliefs can be large enough to overcome loss aversion. Overconfidence serves to amplify the impact of heterogeneous beliefs. Statman–Thorley–Vorkink study the impact of overconfidence and the disposition effect on trading volume.

The Statman–Thorley–Vorkink database consists of monthly observations on all NYSE–AMEX common stocks, excluding closed-end funds, REITs, and ADRs, from August 1962 to December 2002. They also study NASDAQ stocks and report that the latter stocks exhibit results that are similar to those for the smallest three size quintiles of the NYSE–AMEX database.

---

[1] The point here is that beliefs as well as preferences impact behavior. Chapter 6 emphasizes that individual investors are prone to predicting continuation. In addition, individual investors' share of trade is larger in small cap stocks than in large cap stocks.

Statman–Thorley–Vorkink find that individual security turnover is positively related to both lagged security returns and lagged market returns. When a security has recently increased in price, trading in that security increases. That is, investors trade more after the securities that they hold have gone up. However, trading also increases after the market has gone up.

Statman–Thorley–Vorkink interpret the positive security turnover response to own lagged return as being consistent with the disposition effect. That is, investors begin to sell their winners after their stocks have gone up, but hold their losers after their stocks have gone down.[2]

At the same time, when the overall market has recently gone up, trading volume increases across the board. Statman–Thorley–Vorkink interpret the positive turnover response to lagged market returns as evidence of investor overconfidence. They note as striking the relatively pronounced dependence of security turnover on lagged market returns in a regression that also includes lagged security turnover and returns.

Keep in mind that Cases 3 and 5 previously discussed also imply that the positive relationship between individual security turnover and lagged market returns is associated with the disposition effect as well as overconfidence. When the market has gone down, investors become reluctant to sell their holdings, and this dampens their ability to purchase new securities. However, after the market has gone up, investors become more willing to sell their holdings, thereby generating the funds required to purchase new securities for their portfolios.

Statman–Thorley–Vorkink also find that the lead–lag relationship between security returns and turnover is stronger in small capitalization stocks and in earlier time periods. They hypothesize that this finding relates to the relatively larger role of individual investor volume versus institutional and arbitrage-based trading volume in small stocks and earlier time periods.

29.4   Momentum and the Disposition Effect

There are two important points to make about the findings that Odean reports in respect to the post-realization performance of stocks. First, stock price movements appear to have a predictable component related to

---

[2] A similar pattern holds in real estate markets. When real estate markets experience a downturn, sellers become reluctant to lower their asking prices below the price they originally paid for their homes. See Genesove and Mayer (2001). As a result, the ratio of asking price to market price increases in down markets. The net effect is for sales volume to decline, even though inventory might remain high.

the trading behavior of individual investors. Second, individual investors appear to make adverse use of the information, in that the stocks they sell subsequently outperform the stocks they purchase.

29.4.1 Theoretical Hypotheses

Why might stock returns feature a predictable component that is related to the realization behavior of individual investors? Grinblatt and Han (2004) offer an intriguing hypothesis, which they proceed to test.

Consider the intuition underlying their argument. The disposition effect stipulates that investors sell their winners early but ride their losers. Proponents of behavioral finance suggest that market prices eventually move to fundamental values, but contend that because of the limits to arbitrage, the speed of adjustment can be slow. If stock prices move toward fundamental value eventually, then the disposition effect will cause the speed of adjustment to slow. If investors rush to sell stocks on good news, then the selling pressure will dampen the upward adjustment of price to fundamental value. If investors are reluctant to sell stocks on bad news, then the absence of selling pressure likewise will dampen the downward adjustment of price to fundamental value. In either case, the result will be short-term momentum, because the disposition effect impedes the speed of adjustment of price to fundamental value.

Grinblatt–Han's formal argument is based on two observations. First, in the Shefrin–Statman multiple mental accounting framework, the reference point distribution is time varying. In theory, every mental account holding a stock has a reference point determined by the purchase price. Therefore, each stock has associated with it a distribution of mental accounts, with each account featuring a reference point and number of shares. As "old" investors sell their holdings of a particular stock, and "new" investors purchase that stock, the mean reference point moves in the direction of the current stock price.

Second, the disposition effect encourages investors to sell their winners more frequently than their losers. For recent winners associated with good news, the disposition effect–induced sale of these stocks will produce price pressure that dampens any price rise. That is, price movements will appear to be anchored by the reference point distribution, and since the stock is a winner for most investors, the mean reference point will lie below the current price. For losers, the opposite effect holds. Investors who are reluctant to sell, or as was mentioned earlier, who continue to purchase more stock, generate price pressure that retards any downward movement in price. Here, too, the price movement will appear anchored by the reference point distribution, but with the stock being a loser for most investors, the mean reference point will lie above the current price.

Consider how the two Grinblatt–Han observations work together. The reference point distribution tends to revert to the current price. Yet, the current price is anchored by the reference point distribution. For winners, this interplay leads the current price to feature upward drift. For losers, the interplay leads to downward drift. In other words, the disposition effect causes momentum in security prices. More precisely, during the months January through November, investors sell winners more frequently than losers, and so stock prices feature drift during subsequent months. At year-end investors realize losers more frequently than winners, and so the hypothesis would be that stock prices do not feature drift at this time.

29.4.2 *Empirical Evidence*

In order to test their hypotheses, Grinblatt–Han estimate the mean of the reference point distribution. The mean of the reference point distribution is estimated as a weighted average of past prices, with the weights determined by turnover rates. The weight associated with a given price is the turnover rate probability that a share was last purchased at a particular past date, and has not been traded since that time.

Grinblatt–Han identify a stock as a winner if the current price exceeds the mean reference point. They define the difference between current price and mean reference point, per dollar, as the capital gains overhang. That is, the capital gains overhang is the difference between the current price and the mean reference point, divided by the current price. For past winners, the capital gains overhang is positive. For past losers, the capital gains overhang is negative.

Notice that stocks associated with high turnover rates tend to feature low capital gains overhang. This is because for these stocks, mean reference points tend to lie close to the current price.

The data set includes all ordinary common shares traded on the NYSE and AMEX exchanges. NASDAQ firms are excluded because of multiple counting of dealer trades. The sample period, from July 1962 to December 1996, consists of 1,799 weeks, which is the extent of the weekly data sample.

Grinblatt–Han test their theory by regressing stock returns on a series of variables. Specifically they regress the week t return of stock k on past cumulative returns (one month, twelve months, thirty-six months), market capitalization, average weekly turnover, and the capital gains overhang. Average weekly turnover refers to the 52 weeks prior to week t (measured by weekly trading volume divided by the number of outstanding shares).

Grinblatt–Han report that a regression which excludes the capital gains overhang produces statistically significant coefficients consistent with the momentum effect: continuation in returns at the intermediate horizon of one year, with reversals at the short and long horizons. Remarkably, a regression for the full year that includes the capital gains overhang produces an insignificant coefficient for returns at the intermediate horizon but a highly significant coefficient for the capital gains overhang.

As for the turn-of-the-year, the last regression, when run for December alone, results in a larger, statistically significant coefficient for the capital gains overhang. However, the same regression, run for January alone when the momentum effect reverses, produces a sign change for the capital gains overhang coefficient, and this coefficient remains statistically significant.

Notably, the estimated average coefficient (0.004) for the capital gain variable from weekly cross-sectional regressions is consistent with the finding of Jegadeesh and Titman (1993) that momentum strategies generate profits of about 1 percent per month. Given that the median difference between the 90th and 10th percentile of capital gains is about 60 percent, this implies that recent winners outperform recent losers by about $0.004 \times 0.60 = 0.0024$ per week, or 12.5 percent per year.

29.4.3 Extensions

Frazzini (2006) extends Grinblatt and Han's analysis. For each stock held by mutual funds, Frazzini focuses on the capital gains overhang associated with these holdings. The capital gains overhang for a stock at a point in time is the ratio of a price-cost basis differential for a stock to its current price.

The cost basis for a stock is computed as follows. Assign every stock purchased by a mutual fund to its own mental account, and set the reference point for that account to the purchase price. Therefore, a mutual fund which makes repeated purchases of a particular stock will have multiple mental accounts for that stock. Assume that when a mutual fund manager sells a stock, and has multiple mental accounts, the manager uses first in, first out accounting (FIFO). At a point in time, the cost basis for a stock is the weighted average of all mental accounting reference points for that stock, with the weight attached to an account being the proportion of shares held in that account.

Frazzini (2006) suggests a trading strategy in which investors go long in good-news stocks with the largest fund overhang values, suggesting that these would feature the largest expected future return drift. Analogously, Frazzini recommends shorting bad-news stocks with the most negative fund overhang values, meaning paper losses. He defines news events as earnings surprises, which he measures using market model cumulative abnormal returns around earnings announcements.

Frazzini (2006) structures his portfolios using a double sort procedure. At the end of each month he creates twenty-five portfolios (five times five) where the sorting criteria are magnitude of earnings surprise and magnitude of capital gains overhang. He weights all stocks in his portfolios equally and then rebalances monthly, resetting to equal weights.

Notably, Frazzini (2006) reports that his long/short trading strategy would have generated a spread of 2.4 percent a month. In addition, he investigated how the trading strategy would have worked had he reversed the roles of paper gains and losses, replacing stocks featuring paper gains with stocks featuring paper losses and vice-versa. This reverse situation is called negative overhang. Frazzini found that the spread for negative overhang is 0. It is straightforward to understand why this should be so. For good-news stocks featuring a negative overhang, disposition-prone investors do not rush to sell on the good news, so the speed of adjustment to that good news is rapid. For bad-news stocks featuring a positive overhang, disposition-prone investors readily sell on the bad news, so the speed of adjustment to that bad news is rapid.

Shumway and Wu (2006) use data from the Shanghai Stock Exchange to study whether the disposition effect is related to momentum in Chinese stocks. They find that a large majority of Chinese investors exhibit the disposition effect. Sorting stocks by the unrealized gains of disposition-prone investors generates a momentum winner/loser spread of 7 percent per year.

While evidence based upon data from the Shanghai Exchange supports the Grinblatt–Han argument, evidence from Taiwan does not. Barber, Lee, Liu, and Odean (2006) conclude that the disposition effect in Taiwan does not lead to momentum.

29.5   Summary

Investor trading behavior is driven by a combination of preferences and beliefs. Behavioral phenomena predispose investors to sell their winners more frequently than their losers. Representativeness leads individual investors to be trend followers predicting continuation. This chapter describes the main empirical work that documents the disposition effect, and describes how the disposition effect causes momentum in security markets. Although there are other explanations for the momentum effect, such as underreaction, the disposition effect alone appears to address why momentum tends to reverse itself at the turn-of-the-year.

30
Reflections on the Equity Premium Puzzle

Campbell (2000) describes three interrelated asset pricing puzzles. One puzzle pertains to the equity premium, a second to stock volatility, and the third to the interest rate. The puzzles involve why the equity premium in U.S. markets has historically been high, why equity markets are much more volatile than consumption growth, and why historical U.S. interest rates have been low.

This chapter discusses the nature of these puzzles from both a traditional perspective and a behavioral perspective. The behavioral perspective is centered on both preferences and beliefs.

30.1   Basis for Puzzles in Traditional Framework

The traditional framework features a single expected utility maximizing investor with CRRA utility, coefficient of relative risk aversion γ, and rate of time preference δ. In addition, consumption growth is assumed to be conditionally log-normally distributed and homoskedastic. The representative investor is assumed to hold correct beliefs.

30.1.1   Brief Review

In order to describe the manner in which the three puzzles emerge in the traditional framework, consider a brief review of the key asset pricing relationships.

1. Let $r(Z)$ denote the (gross) return vector for security Z. Recall from Chapter 16 that the SDF M_t satisfies $E_t(M_{t+1}r_{t+1}(Z)) = 1$.

2. The gross interest rate i_1 satisfies $1/i_1 = E_t(M_{t+1})$.

3. The risk premium on any security Z is given by $-i_1 cov(r(Z), M)$.

4. The maximum Sharpe ratio in the market is bounded from above by the coefficient of variation of the SDF.

$$\frac{\sigma(M_{t+1})}{E_t(M_{t+1})} \geq \frac{E_t(r_{t+1}(Z) - r_{t+1}(F))}{\sigma_t(r_{t+1}(Z) - r_{t+1}(F))}. \tag{30.1}$$

Given CRRA utility and rational expectations, the following relationships hold:

5. The SDF satisfies $ln(M) = ln(\delta) - \gamma ln(g)$.

6. The discount factors that define the term structure of interest rates have the form

$$(1/i_t)^t = \delta^t E\{g(x_t)^{-\gamma}|x_0\}. \tag{30.2}$$

7. The return $r_\omega(x_1)$ to holding the market portfolio from x_0 to the beginning of x_1 is

$$r_\omega(x_1) = \frac{g(x_1)}{\delta_{R,1}} \frac{\sum_1^T E_R\{\delta_{R,1}^t g(x_t)^{1-\gamma R(x_t)}|x_1\}}{\sum_1^T E_R\{\delta_{R,0}^{t'} g(x_t)^{1-\gamma R(x_t)}|x_0\}} \tag{30.3}$$

where $\delta^{t'}$ is defined in Section 11.5.2. See (17.10), where the base from which growth is measured in the numerator is $w(x_1)$, whereas in the denominator the base is $w(x_0)$.

The assumptions about log-normality and homoskedasticity imply a series of relationships to be described shortly. In these relationships, all variables should be understood as being the logarithms of gross rates. For example, r is really $ln(r)$, c is really $ln(c)$, and g is really $ln(g)$. The relationships feature variances and covariances, variables that enter because log-normality involves the relationship $ln(E[X]) = E[ln(X)] + (1/2)Var(X)$. Here, σ is used for variances and covariances, with the subscripts indicating the variables in question. Specifically, σ_i denotes the return standard deviation associated with security i, σ_c denotes the standard deviation associated with aggregate consumption, and σ_{ic} denotes the covariance between the return to security i and consumption c.

8. The expected return on any security i is given by

$$E_t[r_{i,t+1}] = -ln(\delta) + \gamma E_t[\triangle c_{t+1}] - (1/2)[\sigma_i^2 + \gamma^2 \sigma_c^2 - 2\gamma\sigma_{ic}]. \quad (30.4)$$

9. The log risk-free rate is given by

$$r_{f,t+1} = -ln(\delta) - (1/2)\gamma^2\sigma_c^2 + \gamma E_t[\triangle c_{t+1}] \quad (30.5)$$

10. The risk premium on security i is given by

$$E_t[r_{i,t+1} - r_{f,t+1}] = \gamma\sigma_{ic} - \sigma_i^2/2 \quad (30.6)$$

30.1.2 Attaching Numbers to Equations

Table 30.1 contains historical data for U.S. consumption growth, stock returns, and returns to commercial paper. Commercial paper rates are used here as proxies for risk-free rates. These data are taken from Campbell, Lo, and MacKinlay (1997). Consider what the data suggest about the underlying parameters, particularly the coefficient of relative risk aversion γ.

Suppose that the representative investor has log utility (a coefficient of relative risk aversion equal to 1) and a time preference parameter equal to 1. Given the data in Table 30.1, Equation (30.5) implies that the long-term risk-free rate of interest is equal to 1.67 percent per year. This value is just a bit less than the historical 1.83 percent given in Table 30.1. In fact, if the representative investor has a coefficient of relative risk aversion equal to 1.11, then Equation (30.5) implies that the long-term risk-free rate of interest is actually equal to 1.83 percent.

TABLE 30.1. Consumption Growth and Asset Returns, 1889–1994

The data in this table are from Campbell, Lo, and MacKinlay (1997).

	Mean	Standard deviation	Correlation with consumption growth	Covariance with consumption growth
Consumption growth	0.0172	0.0328	1.0000	0.0011
Return on stocks	0.0601	0.1674	0.4902	0.0027
Return on commercial paper (CP)	0.0183	0.0544	−0.1157	−0.0002
Equity premium (stocks relative to CP)	0.0418	0.1744	0.4979	0.0029

Chapter 13 documents the empirical evidence about the distribution of risk aversion, γ, in the general population. Well over 60 percent of the population have a coefficient of relative risk aversion in excess of 2. When $\gamma = 2$, $r_{f,t+1} = 0.032$ per year. When $\gamma = 4$, $r_{f,t+1} = 0.06$ per year. When $\gamma = 8$, $r_{f,t+1} = 0.103$ per year.

The basic conclusion is that given the evidence about risk aversion in the population, the model implies too high an interest rate relative to the historical average.

Of course, the preceding discussion fixed the rate of time preference δ equal to 1. This is plausible, given the evidence presented in Chapter 13 that most people favor a flat consumption stream. However, Equation (30.5) implies that the interest rate is a decreasing function of δ. Suppose that γ were equal to 4. What value of δ would have produced a value of 1.83 percent for $r_{f,t+1}$ in the model? The answer is $\delta = 1.043$. Therefore, a mild negative time preference would have generated a reasonable value for the historical risk-free real interest rate. Why is such a value reasonable? The discussion in Chapter 13 indicated that the second favored choice of consumption stream featured a moderately increasing pattern. In addition, the combination of aggregation bias described in Chapters 12, 14, and 16, and the near-linear features in the utility functions of prospect theory and SP/A theory, give rise to negative time preference ($\delta_R > 1$).

Next, consider the expected return on equities. With $\gamma = 8$ and $\delta = 1.043$, Equation (30.4) implies that the expected return on equities will be 1.5 percent, well below the historical value of 6.01 percent. The resulting equity premium in the model will therefore be negative.

Mehra and Prescott (1985) provided the original analysis of the equity premium puzzle. The reason why the model gives such a low equity premium can be seen by thorough examination of Equation (30.6). Notice that the risk premium is an increasing function of the product of γ and the covariance between returns and consumption growth. From Table 30.1, this covariance is seen to be 0.003, a small number. It is a small number because consumption growth is relatively smooth, with a standard deviation of 3.3 percent. Therefore, a high equity premium in this model requires a high value for γ. In this model, a value of about 20 for γ is needed to produce an equity premium equal to the historical value of 4.2 percent.

The equity premium puzzle is that the value of risk aversion required for the model to produce the historical equity premium is unrealistically high. The associated interest rate puzzle is that using a high rate of risk aversion like 20 requires an associated rate of time preference equal to 1.15, a value not consistent with empirical evidence.

The volatility puzzle described by Campbell (2000) is based on the fact that stock returns are five times more volatile than consumption growth, and yet the consumption stream effectively comprises the dividend stream. Campbell (2000) points out that the volatility of the SDF appears to be puzzlingly high for a variable that is bounded below by zero and whose mean is unity. His observation is based on the fact that the coefficient of variation of the SDF is bounded from below by the maximum Sharpe ratio across securities. See Equation (30.1).

As can be seen in Table 30.1, stocks had a return standard deviation of 18 percent, and a mean of 6 percent. Taking the real (gross) risk-free interest rate to be about 1, (30.1) implies that the standard deviation of the SDF is at least $0.06/0.17 = 0.36$. Recall that in the traditional framework, the SDF M satisfies $ln(M) = ln(\delta) - \gamma ln(g)$. Therefore, $Var(M_{t+1}) \approx Var(ln(M_{t+1})) = \gamma^2 Var(\triangle c_{t+1})$. The variance of consumption growth is about 0.001; this implies that γ must be about 19.

In order to understand what a value of $\gamma = 20$ implies, consider the following question that was discussed in Chapter 13. Suppose that you are the only income earner in your family, and you have a good job guaranteed to give you your current (family) income every year for life. You are given the opportunity to take a new and equally good job, with a 50–50 chance that it will double your (family) income and a 50–50 chance that it will cut your (family) income by a percentage x. Indicate exactly what the percentage cut x would be that would leave you indifferent between keeping your current job or taking the new job and facing a 50–50 chance of doubling your income or cutting it by x percent.

The answer to the preceding question would be about 3.6 percent, for a person whose coefficient of relative risk aversion is 20. By way of contrast, the answer to the preceding question would be about 9.4 percent for a person whose coefficient of relative risk aversion is 8, and 24.5 percent for a person whose coefficient of relative risk aversion is 3.

30.2   Erroneous Beliefs

Traditional asset pricing models such as Mehra–Prescott implicitly assume that investors hold correct beliefs, so asset prices are based on correct probabilities. Indeed, the arguments advanced by most traditional asset pricing theorists about the level of risk aversion and the magnitude of the equity premium basically assume that investors know the correct values for the means, variances, and covariances of all the key variables.

This section makes two points. First, the assumption that investors hold correct beliefs is not supported by the data. Second, the extent to which beliefs are biased can explain the equity premium puzzle.

30.2.1   Livingston Data

Consider the three puzzles relating to the equity premium, interest rate, and volatility. What if investors underestimate returns and overestimate risk? Notably, this combination could give rise to a low expected equity premium but a high actual equity premium. The combination could also produce low real interest rates. Chapters 17 and 20 emphasize that nonzero sentiment injects volatility into mean-variance returns and the term structure of interest rates. Figure 17.1 makes this point vividly for mean-variance returns. Moreover, as Chapters 15 and 23 discuss, the sentiment function is time-varying. Therefore, in theory, sentiment plays a role in respect to all three puzzles.

Cecchetti, Lam, and Mark (2000) and Abel (1988, 2002) develop sentiment-based models of the equity premium puzzle which feature time-varying pessimism. Is there empirical evidence that investors underestimate returns and overestimate risk? Chapter 7 focuses on the beliefs of professional investors. Among the data sets discussed are the Livingston data. These data provide forecasts of the S&P 500, interest rates and gross domestic product (GDP). The GDP forecasts serve as a reasonable proxy for real personal consumption expenditures (PCE). Data involving forecasts of the S&P 500 are available from December 1990, and so attention is focused on the period 1991–2003.

The most important data relates to investors' subjective estimates of the items in Table 30.1, these being the key variables in the Mehra–Prescott framework. Do investors appear to hold beliefs that are relatively unbiased? Or do they instead hold biased beliefs that give rise to the kind of equity premium observed in the U.S. data?

Notably, aggregate consumption growth and gross domestic product are very closely related over time. The correlation coefficient between the two series over the period 1947–2002 is 0.99. Therefore it is plausible to use the GDP forecast as a proxy for the aggregate consumption growth forecast.

The Livingston data set includes forecasts for Treasury bill rates and 30-year Treasury bond rates (beginning June 1992). The Treasury bill forecasts and current Treasury bill rates can be juxtaposed with the forecasts for the S&P 500 forecasts to estimate capital gains portion of the expected equity premium.

Figure 30.1 displays the time series showing the forecasted change in the S&P 500, the forecasted equity premium, and forecasted growth in real GDP. All forecasts are made in the same month and are for a period of one year. The Livingston survey respondents were pessimistic about both GDP growth (proxying for consumption growth) and equity appreciation. During the period 1991 through 2003, the mean GDP forecast was 2.9 percent and the mean forecast for S&P 500 appreciation was 6 percent.[1] Both estimates were biased downwards. The mean of actual real GDP growth was 3.1 percent, and the mean for actual S&P 500 appreciation

---

[1] Between 1991 and 2003, the mean coefficient of variation for annual GDP growth was 25 percent.

FIGURE 30.1. This figure displays the time series for the Livingston data set forecasts of the annual change in GDP, the annual change in the S&P 500, and the capital gains portion of the forecasted equity premium.

was 9.2 percent. Dividend yields during the 1980s had been about 3.5 percent, but fell below 2 percent during the 1990s, and averaged about 1.5 percent between 1992 and 2003. Therefore, investors appear to have held downwardly biased estimates of the total return to the S&P 500.

Next, consider volatility. The Livingston survey does not contain direct estimates of volatility. However, the time variation of the forecasts provides considerable insight. The Livingston survey respondents' forecasts for both equity appreciation and GDP growth appear to be excessively volatile. Annual GDP growth is close to being *i.i.d.*, as is annual S&P 500 equity appreciation. Therefore, rational forecasts of these variables should display very little, if any, volatility. Yet, the standard deviations of the annual mean forecasts for these variables were 3.3 percent for GDP growth and 6.4 percent for S&P 500 appreciation. These are astonishingly high. Notably, the actual standard deviations were 1.6 percent for GDP and 16.6 percent for the S&P 500. Notice that the mean GDP forecast series was actually more volatile than the actual GDP series. This is quite striking, in that a rational forecast should be less volatile than the variable being forecast.

In the Mehra–Prescott analysis, the critical risk measure in respect to the equity premium is the covariance between consumption growth and the equity premium. Between December 1990 and June 2003, the correlation between forecasts for real GDP growth and the equity premium was 0.34. The covariance between these forecasts was 0.0003.

Bear in mind that the Livingston covariance involves forecasted values, not realized values. Efficient forecasts are less variable than the variables being forecast. Investors appear to have believed that the real economy was more volatile than was actually the case, and might have had an upwardly biased estimate of the covariance between consumption growth and the equity premium. Therefore, investors might have overestimated the systematic risk associated with equity returns.

The models in Cecchetti, Lam and Mark (2000) and Abel (2002) model pessimism as a downward shift in the true distribution. In contrast to the sentiment functions displayed in Figures 15.4 and 15.8, which have both upward- and downward-sloping segments, sentiment functions that feature uniform pessimism are monotone decreasing. See Figure 15.2. This is because pure pessimism overweights the probabilities attached to unfavorable consumption growth rates and underweights the probabilities attached to favorable consumption growth rates. However, the evidence discussed in Chapter 23 suggests that market sentiment is neither monotone increasing nor monotone decreasing. Rather, sentiment simultaneously exhibits both optimism and pessimism.

30.2.2 The Market and the Economy: Upwardly Biased Covariance Estimate

Investors who overestimate the volatility in the real economy and who believe that the relationship between market returns and the real economy is strong may well overestimate the covariance between the equity premium and consumption growth. In this respect, recall the comments of Frank Cappiello, quoted in Chapter 7. Those comments are typical of how many investors think about the strength of the relationship between the macroeconomy and the returns to stocks. These passages are consistent with the notion that investors overestimate the covariance between consumption growth and equity returns.

The extent of overestimation in respect to the consumption-return covariance is critical for the Mehra–Prescott analysis. If investors overestimate the covariance, then the implied value of γ can drop significantly. For example, if investors overestimate the consumption-return covariance by a factor of 5, then the value of γ implied by (30.6) will decrease by about a fifth. To be sure, the volatilities of forecasts for GDP growth and equity returns are consistent with a bias of this magnitude.

In the traditional asset pricing model, if the representative investor is unduly pessimistic, then the real interest rate will be low, and for realistic values of relative risk aversion, the expected equity premium will be low. However, excessive pessimism in respect to both returns and volatility will lead the objective expected equity premium to be higher than the equity premium that investors expect.[2]

Does the empirical SDF reflect investor sentiment? There is reason to suspect so. Chapter 23 describes the Rosenberg–Engle empirical SDF analysis. Rosenberg–Engle used a power utility model to estimate the degree time-varying risk aversion, and they interpreted the slope of the function in their analysis to be the estimate of risk aversion. Recall from Chapter 23 that their analysis showed the coefficient of relative risk aversion varying in the range of 2 to 13, and featuring a mean value of 7.6. At the same time, (as Chapter 16 explained), in the sentiment-based SDF framework, the graph of the SDF under pessimism looks like a traditional SDF with very high risk aversion. The more pessimistic investors are, the more steeply sloped the graph of the SDF will be. Therefore, the Livingston data suggest that the estimates of time-varying risk aversion found by Rosenberg–Engle may stem largely from time-varying pessimism.

30.3   Alternative Rationality-Based Models

In the main, traditional asset pricing theorists have clung to the assumption that the representative investor holds correct beliefs, and have concentrated their efforts on explaining the equity premium puzzle through arguments involving preferences. For that matter, the same statement applies to behavioral asset pricing theorists. The remainder of the chapter describes the preference-based arguments of both traditional asset pricing theorists and behavioral asset pricing theorists.

By itself, the interest rate puzzle is not much of a puzzle. It is not difficult to find reasonable parameters such that the model produces a risk-free rate that is in line with the historical rate. The equity premium puzzle and volatility puzzles are entirely different.

The traditional response to the puzzle trilogy has been to modify the preferences of the representative investor. One such route involves using the Epstein–Zin (1989) generalized utility function. Unlike the CRRA utility, which forces $1/\gamma$ to serve as both the coefficient of risk tolerance and the intertemporal elasticity of substitution, Epstein–Zin use a separate parameter for each. The additional parameter allows the risk tolerance

---

[2] Ghysels–Juergens (2004) do estimate a consumption-based model with errors stemming from analyst forecasts. However, their model produces an estimate of risk aversion that is about 400, well above the Mehra–Prescott value. Analyst forecasts are known to be inherently optimistic until just before earnings announcements, in contrast to the data presented in Chapter 7.

parameter to be used to solve the equity premium puzzle, and the elasticity of intertemporal substitution parameter to be used to solve the interest rate puzzle. See Epstein–Zin (1990, 1991).

Unfortunately, Epstein–Zin cannot change the fact that the consumption stream is smooth, and therefore that its covariance with equity returns is low. Hence, solving the equity premium puzzle still requires a high coefficient of risk aversion.

30.3.1 Habit Formation

A second response to the equity premium puzzle involves habit formation. Habit formation recognizes that the coefficient of relative risk aversion is time-varying, and at times may be high. If it is high often enough, then it is possible to rationalize the equity premium puzzle. In addition, the time-variation in risk aversion will inject an additional source of volatility, thereby rationalizing the volatility puzzle as well.

There are several habit-formation models. Consider the model proposed by Campbell and Cochrane (1999). They define a reference consumption level h_t known as the habit level. The utility function is a power function with exponent γ, whose argument is the difference $c_t - h_t$ between consumption c_t and habit h_t. Campbell–Cochrane define a variable they call the surplus consumption ratio as $S_t = (c_t - h_t)/c_t$.

Recall from Chapter 12 that the local coefficient of relative risk aversion is the product of c and the Arrow–Pratt measure $-u''/u'$. Since u is a power function in $c_t - h_t$, $-u''/u' = \gamma/(c_t - h_t)$. By the definition of S_t, $c_t = (c_t - h_t)/S_t$. Therefore, $-c_t u''/u' = \gamma/S_t$. That is, varying c_t with h_t held constant leads to a local coefficient of relative risk aversion equal to γ/S_t.

The Campbell–Cochrane model produces high coefficients of relative risk aversion when consumption is close to habit. For example, if $\gamma = 2$ but consumption lies within 10 percent of habit, the local coefficient of relative risk aversion will be 20 ($= 2/0.10$). If the habit level evolves so that consumption is close to habit for much of the time, then low values of γ will produce high coefficients of (local) relative risk aversion.

30.3.2 Habit Formation SDF

Campbell–Cochrane assume that $s_t = ln(S_t)$ evolves according to an AR(1) process

$$s_{t+1} = (1 - \phi)\bar{s} + \phi s_t + \lambda(s_t)\epsilon_{c,t+1} \tag{30.7}$$

where ϕ is a parameter governing the persistence of habit, and λ controls the sensitivity of s_{t+1} to innovations in consumption growth. Appropriate selection of the parameters in Equation (30.7) ensures that the consumption level c_t always lies above the habit level h_t.

In a representative investor model, relative state prices are determined by the ratio of the representative investor's marginal expected utilities. Therefore, the SDF M_{t+1} is equal to $\delta u'(c_{t+1})/u'(c_t)$. In the Campbell–Cochrane model, $u'(c) = (1 - \gamma)(c - h)^{-\gamma}$. Since $c_t - h_t = S_t c_t$, it follows that

$$M_{t+1} = \delta(S_{t+1}/S_t)^{-\gamma}(c_{t+1}/c_t)^{-\gamma} \qquad (30.8)$$

Consider the shape of the log-SDF, when plotted against the consumption growth rate g. The log-SDF m_{t+1} is the sum of $ln(\delta)$, $-\gamma ln(g)$, and $-\gamma ln(S_{t+1}/S_t)$. The first two terms in this sum are conventional; it is the third term that constitutes the innovation associated with habit formation. Notably, $-\gamma ln(S_{t+1}/S_t)$ is correlated with consumption growth through the last term in (30.7). Since s_t is given at date t, $\lambda(s_t)$ is constant. Therefore, both $ln(g)$ and $ln(S_{t+1}/S_t)$ are increasing functions of g. It follows that m_{t+1} is a monotone decreasing function of g for $\gamma > 0$. However, the function is time-varying. When consumption moves closer to habit, the SDF function shifts down. When consumption moves away from habit, the SDF function shifts up.

The real interest rate in the Campbell–Cochrane model is determined through the interaction between two forces. A decrease in the surplus consumption ratio S_t induces the representative investor to increase borrowing from the future. However, the resulting increase in volatility leads the investor to save more for precautionary reasons. Campbell–Cochrane choose the parameters in their model so that these two forces effectively cancel, and the real interest rate stays constant.

30.3.3   Habit Formation SDF Versus the Empirical SDF

There is a striking formal similarity between the Campbell–Cochrane SDF and the sentiment-based SDF. Both have the same general form, a consumption growth-based term multiplied by another function. However, whereas the empirical evidence supports the existence of sentiment, there is no clear evidence to support a habit-formation model of the sort proposed by Campbell–Cochrane. This is not to suggest that risk aversion is not time-varying. Indeed, heterogeneity leads the coefficient of relative risk aversion to be stochastic in the sentiment-based model.

Chapter 23 presented the Rosenberg–Engle results on the empirical SDF. Recall that the empirical SDF features an oscillating pattern. However, the Campbell–Cochrane SDF is monotone decreasing in consumption growth. In other words, habit formation does not explain why the empirical SDF has the shape that it does.

Recall that Rosenberg–Engle also compute the time series estimates for the coefficient of relative risk aversion. They do so by estimating a CRRA-based model, and allowing γ to be time-varying. As was discussed in Chapter 23, their estimates of relative risk aversion vary between 2 and 13, and feature a mean value of 7.6. They note that their findings are consistent with the Campbell–Cochrane habit formation model.

Now, 7.6 is high for a coefficient of relative risk aversion, but not as unreasonable as 20. Moreover, even the maximum value for the coefficient of relative risk aversion is still well below the value necessary to rationalize the equity premium puzzle.

The upward-sloping portion of the empirical SDF is associated with the region where the S&P 500 return lay between −4 percent and 2 percent. In view of the fact that these are monthly returns, the S&P 500 returns lay in this region about 58 percent of the time during the Rosenberg–Engle sample period. In other words, for 58 percent of the time, the EPK appears to be upward sloping when evaluated at realized returns.

30.4   Behavioral Preferences and the Equity Premium

Shlomo Benartzi and Richard Thaler (1995) proposed the first behaviorally based explanation for the equity premium puzzle. Their approach involved prospect theory. Benartzi–Thaler suggest that investors frame their portfolio decisions using short-time horizons for evaluation purposes. They point out that short horizon evaluation periods emphasize loss aversion, and that loss aversion leads investors to require a high equity premium.

Barberis, Huang, and Santos (2001) extended the Benartzi–Thaler approach to an equilibrium framework, and sought conditions under which their equilibrium model produced magnitudes for the equity premium, interest rate, and level of volatility observed in practice.

This section reviews the main features of both Benartzi–Thaler and Barberis–Huang–Santos. While the two approaches rely on finding parameter values to produce the result, the discussion to follow focuses on intuition and the general framework rather than on the precise values of the parameters. One additional point: Both Benartzi–Thaler and Barberis–Huang–Santos assume that investors hold correct beliefs.

30.4.1   Myopic Loss Aversion

Benartzi–Thaler consider a representative investor, with prospect theory preferences and correct beliefs, who chooses a portfolio consisting of two assets, low-risk bonds and high-risk stocks. In respect to preferences, the representative investor has the value function (24.8), (24.9), and has the weighting function (24.7).

The explanation of the equity premium puzzle offered by Benartzi–Thaler focuses on intolerance for risk. They suggest that the reason that investors act as if they are averse to risk in equity markets is not habit formation, but framing.

In order to communicate the key issues studied by Benartzi–Thaler, consider two stylized decision tasks. In the first task, an investor is presented with an opportunity to accept or reject a risky alternative exactly once. The risky alternative features 50–50 odds of either winning $200 or losing $100. The majority of people choose to reject the risky alternative when given the choice.

In the second decision task problem, the risky alternative entails facing two consecutive independent rounds of play. With two rounds, the investor might win $400 with probability 0.25, lose $200 with probability 0.25, or win $100 with probability 0.5. The majority of people choose to accept the risky alternative when given the choice to play two rounds.

Samuelson (1963) established that an expected utility maximizing, risk averse investor who accepts the risky alternative when played twice will also accept the single-round alternative. Therefore, the choice pattern just described is not expected utility maximizing for risk averse investors. Nevertheless, the pattern is typical.

An investor whose preferences conform to prospect theory may well accept the two-round risky alternative, but reject the single-round version. The reason is easy to see. In the single-round version, the potential gain of $200 is only twice the magnitude of the potential loss of $100. With 50–50 odds, and a typical loss aversion coefficient of 2.5, the potential gain would need to be at least 2.5 times the amount of the potential loss. However, in the two-round version, the potential loss of $100 occurs with probability 0.25, and is counterbalanced with potential gains of $100 and $400. The maximum potential gain of $400 occurs with the same probability (0.25) as the potential loss of $100, but is 4 times as great. That is, the maximum potential gain is more than 2.5 times as great as the potential loss. In addition, a smaller gain of $100 is possible, occurring with probability 0.5.

Consider the same two decision problems, slightly recast. Imagine an investor whose time horizon consists of two years. The investor has the opportunity to invest in two securities. One is a risk-free security that features a zero rate of interest. The second is a risky security that requires the investor to contribute $100 per year. In return, the investor has a 50–50 chance of receiving either $300 (gross) or $0 (gross) each year.

An investor considering whether to invest in the risk-free security or the risky security might frame the decision using a one-period evaluation horizon or a full two-period evaluation horizon. The investor who uses a one-year horizon takes a myopic view, and considers the potential gain to be $200 and the potential loss to be $100. That is, the myopic view involves an evaluation horizon that is shorter than the investment horizon. An investor who is not myopic would use a two-year evaluation horizon.

Benartzi–Thaler argue that the evaluation horizon reflects how investors experience risk psychologically. Myopic investors experience the risk by focusing on a series of short-term movements. In doing so, they frame their decision problems in a way that maximizes the impact of loss aversion. Benartzi–Thaler suggest that myopic investors will be more inclined to act conservatively than investors who are less myopic. Using the long-term historical return distributions for stocks and bonds, they suggest that investors who use a one-year evaluation horizon will tend to be indifferent between holding stocks and bonds. Investors using evaluation horizons that are less than one year will prefer bonds over stocks, and investors using evaluation horizons that are more than one year will prefer stocks over bonds.

The conclusion offered by Benartzi–Thaler is that the equity premium puzzle stems from the fact that too many investors are myopic and evaluate their portfolios more than once a year. By doing so, they act as if they overweight short-term movements; thus they are led to be excessively averse to risk. As a result, stocks are priced as if investors are very risk averse.

30.4.2   Transaction Utility

Like Benartzi–Thaler, Barberis–Huang–Santos (2001) use prospect theory to explain the role of risk aversion in determining the equity premium. However, Barberis–Huang–Santos use prospect theory somewhat differently than Benartzi–Thaler. In particular, they distinguish between two sources of utility. First is the utility a person derives as a consumer, this being the utility u_c derived directly from consumption. Call this "consumption utility." Second is the utility, derived as an investor, from experiencing increases and decreases in the value of one's portfolio. Call this "transaction utility" u_t.

In order to understand the character of transaction utility in Barberis–Huang–Santos, consider the following decision tasks. Imagine two groups of investors, A and B. The first group of investors (A) is presented with the following two decision tasks.

Choice 1A. You can accept a risk-free $1,500 or choose a risky alternative. If you choose the risky alternative, you will receive either $1,950 with probability 0.5 or $1,050 with probability 0.5.

Choice 2A. You can accept a guaranteed loss of $750 or choose a risky alternative. If you choose the risky alternative, you will lose either $525 with probability 0.5 or $975 with probability 0.5.

The second group of investors (B) is presented with the following two decision problems.

Choice 1B. Imagine that you have just won $1,500 and have the opportunity to participate in a second risky alternative. If you choose the second risky alternative, you will win $450 with probability 0.5 or lose $450 with probability 0.5.

Choice 2B. Imagine that you have just lost $750 and have the opportunity to participate in a second risky alternative. If you choose the second risky alternative, you will win $225 with probability 0.5 or lose $225 with probability 0.5.

The net gains and losses in the decisions faced by groups A and B are the same. Choice 1 (both 1A and 1B) involves gains that are either $1,050, $1,500, or $1,950. Choice 2 (both 2A and 2B) involves losses that are either $525, $750, or $975. Yet, people tend to choose differently depending on whether the decision problem is described in the A version or the B version.

People who face the A version tend to take the risk-free alternative in choice task 1, and the risk-seeking alternative in choice task 2. People who face the B version tend to take the risky alternative in choice task 1, and the risk-free alternative in choice task 2.

Typically, loss aversion leads people to reject a 50–50 choice between winning $450 and losing $450. Yet the prior gain of $1,500 leads people to be willing to face the risky alternative. Why is this the case? And why do people treat the two problems differently?

Thaler and Johnson (1990), who document the finding just described, suggest that people in group B do not adjust their reference points immediately after receiving a gain or loss. They suggest that a person who has just won $1,500 and then incurs a second gain of $450 will savor the two gains separately, enjoying them more than a single gain of $1,950. However, someone who incurs the smaller loss of $450 after a larger gain of $1,500 will choose to net the two together, thereby experiencing a net gain of $1,050. Notably, loss aversion induces the majority of people in group A to choose the risk-free alternative. However, for group B, the opportunity to savor the two gains separately leads the majority of people in that group to choose the risky alternative.

Thaler–Johnson coined the term "house money effect" to describe the phenomenon just described. They suggest that prior gains can be considered as akin to house money, meaning gambling chips that casinos provide to gamblers free of charge. Losing some house money, the argument goes, is experienced differently than losing money considered to be one's own. Specifically, losing only house money is experienced simply as a smaller gain, not as a loss.

An analogous argument applies to choice task 2. The experimental evidence suggests that after prior losses, people become even more sensitive to future losses. Therefore, prior losses induce people to become more reluctant to accept the risk of future losses. That is why people in group B tend to act more conservatively in choice task 2 than those in group A.

Barberis–Huang–Santos suggest that during up-markets investors do not adjust their reference points immediately to accommodate prior gains and losses. According to this line of thought, after recent gains investors become more tolerant of risk, and after recent losses they become less tolerant of risk. In this sense, Barberis–Huang–Santos provide a behaviorally based analogue of the Campbell–Cochrane habit-formation explanation of the equity premium puzzle. As in the habit-formation framework, endogenous changes in risk aversion give rise to an additional source of return volatility.

The Barberis–Huang–Santos framework features two securities, a risk-free security and a risky security. Notably, the risky security has associated with it transaction utility. However, the risk-free security does not. As a result, the prospect theory component of preferences explains equity volatility and the equity premium, but does not force the interest rate to be excessively high.

In this respect, the Euler equation for the risky security in the Barberis–Huang–Santos framework is novel. Recall from (16.11) that the traditional Euler equation has the form

$$1 = \delta E_{x_0} \left[\left(\frac{c(x_0)}{c(x_1)} \right)^\gamma r(x_1) \right] \qquad (30.9)$$

Barberis–Huang–Santos assume that utility is additive in consumption utility and transaction utility, taking the form $u = u_c + u_t$, where u_c is the traditional power function. For this reason, Barberis–Huang–Santos establish that Euler equation for the risky security has an extra term:

$$1 = \delta E_{x_0} \left[\left(\frac{c(x_0)}{c(x_1)} \right)^\gamma r(x_1) \right] + \delta E_{x_0}[f(r(x_1))] \qquad (30.10)$$

However, the Euler equation for the risk-free security has the conventional form (16.11).[3]

Consider some final comments about the Barberis–Huang–Santos approach in relation to other works. First, the prospect theory transaction utility component is piecewise linear. Therefore, the assumptions in

---

[3] The different Euler equations for the two securities would imply the existence of arbitrage opportunities in a complete market. Notably, Barberis–Huang–Santos assume that markets are incomplete, consisting of just two securities.

Barberis–Huang–Santos run counter to the disposition effect. Yet, as was discussed in Chapter 29, evidence supporting the disposition effect is strong, and the effect appears to be related to momentum.

30.5 Risks, Small and Large

Some traditional theorists are wary of relying on the type of experimental evidence used in connection with prospect theory. They suggest that in the real world, investors face much larger risks than are reflected in the experiments. In particular, they point out that experiments can be used to discover the factors that influence decisions on small scales, but urge caution in extrapolating these results to larger scales, especially in regard to measuring risk aversion.

The comment about risk aversion is fair. Tversky–Kahneman (1992) conclude from their experiments that people tend to experience losses 2.5 times as intensely as they do gains. At the same time, the evidence presented in Subsection 13.1.1 based on the RHS surveys indicates that 65 percent of respondents have a coefficient of relative risk aversion greater than 3.76. Based on the question used to elicit risk aversion, a coefficient of risk aversion equal to 4 implies that the loss involved in that setting is experienced 5.3 times as intensely as the comparable gain.[4] Only if the coefficient of risk aversion were equal to 1.5 would the loss be experienced at 2.5 times the intensity of a comparable gain.

As for general patterns identified in experiments, Chapter 29 makes the point that evidence based on the behavior of real investors, who face real risks, supports the disposition effect hypothesis stemming from prospect theory. As for the issue of myopic loss aversion described earlier, Galai and Sade (2004) provide evidence that some investors are willing to choose securities that impose longer evaluation horizons. Galai–Sade document that yields on less liquid, longer-term fixed income securities tend to be smaller than on more liquid, shorter-term fixed income securities. They suggest that investors could choose to hold the more liquid, shorter-term securities, but avoid doing so in order not to have to use shorter evaluation horizons.

---

[4] The size of the gain is the respondent's wealth. The size of the loss is determined by the size of cut to which the respondent is indifferent. A coefficient of risk aversion equal to 4 implies that the loss involved in that setting is experienced 5.3 times as intensely as the comparable gain. A coefficient of risk aversion equal to 20 implies that the loss involved in that setting is experienced 28 times as intensely as the comparable gain. The ratio of the gain to the loss is the counterpart of the 2.5 parameter.

30.6   Summary

Conventional explanations for the equity premium puzzle center on time-varying risk tolerance, and why risk aversion increases dramatically in down markets. Notably, these explanations assume that investors are error-free. This chapter presented evidence about investor errors that provides support for the equity premium puzzle's being a manifestation of investor errors. To be sure, behavioral preferences reflecting prospect theory and myopic loss aversion may well play a role in shaping investors' attitudes toward risk. However, the evidence that investors commit systematic errors is substantial, and that evidence is consistent with errors being part of the explanation behind the equity premium puzzle.

Part VIII

Future Directions and Closing Comments

31
Continuous Time Behavioral Equilibrium Models

A key message of this book is that future advances in asset pricing will combine the SDF methods favored by neoclassical asset pricing theorists with the psychological assumptions favored by behavioral asset pricing theorists. The present chapter describes progress on this front, and offers some comments about the future direction of asset pricing research.

Heterogeneity is a ubiquitous property of the results of both the experimental studies and survey data described in this book. For this reason, the approach in the book emphasizes the importance of understanding how markets aggregate heterogeneous beliefs and preferences. The theory developed in this book is part of an ongoing literature in aggregation. Section 14.1 surveys some of this literature.

In the main, the aggregation literature is essentially silent about why investors hold heterogeneous beliefs and especially silent about whether those beliefs reflect errors whose source is psychological. Shefrin and Statman (1994) was the first paper to develop an aggregation model where the source of the heterogeneity is psychologically-based.

Much of the recent advances in the aggregation literature use continuous time models. Examples are Calvet, Grandmont, and Lemaire (2004), Basak (2005), Yong-Ou (2005), and Weinbaum (2001, 2006). This chapter focuses on three particular contributions: 1) Jouini and Napp (2007a); 2) Dumas, Kurshev, and Uppal (forthcoming); and 3) Bakshi and Wu (2006). All three contributions serve to advance the application of continuous time methods to the study of behavioral asset pricing.

Jouini-Napp build on Calvet, Grandmont, and Lemaire (2004). Although Jouini-Napp contribute to the aggregation literature, the paper touches on behavioral issues, and in their other work the authors study behavioral questions. Dumas, Kurshev, and Uppal specifically incorporate behavioral features into their model. Bakshi-Wu's paper is not part of the aggregation literature. However, it uses a continuous time framework to address explicit behavioral issues.

In order to highlight the value added of each contribution, this chapter first reviews key ideas developed earlier in the book, and indeed in the first edition. These reviews appear at the beginning of each major section. In addition, the general layout of the chapter describes new insights associated with the extension from discrete time to continuous time, from a single Brownian motion model featuring no public signal to a dual Brownian motion model featuring a public signal, and from a diffusion framework to a mixed framework featuring both diffusion and jumps. Some remarks about the future direction of asset pricing research appear at the end of the chapter.

31.1   General Structure

Lying at the heart of this book is the observation that investors differ from each other in terms of beliefs, risk tolerance, and time preference. Therefore, it is important to understand how this multidimensional heterogeneity aggregates to impact asset prices. The key aggregation theorem is 14.1, which describes the structure of a hypothetical representative investor. Notably, the representative investor's beliefs evolve over time as a generalized Hölder average of the individual investors' beliefs, where the weights pertain either to consumption or to income.

Theorem 14.1 provides the basis for equation (15.2) which defines market sentiment. Sentiment captures the manner in which investors' beliefs distort market prices. Equation (15.2) demonstrates that sentiment has two components. The first component is the logarithm of a change of measure. This log-change of measure constitutes the deviation of the representative investor's beliefs from objectively correct beliefs. The second component constitutes aggregation bias in the representative investor's time preference function. Theorem 16.1 is the central result in the book. It demonstrates how the SDF decomposes into a neoclassical fundamental component and market sentiment.

Elyès Jouini and Clotilde Napp, Jouini-Napp (2007a) have developed a continuous time analogue to the discrete time framework presented in this book. Their work is absolutely fundamental to the behavioral continuous time approach, demonstrating that the features described above for the discrete time framework carry over to the continuous time framework.

31.1.1 Continuous Time Analogue

The continuous time analogue of the discrete time uncertainty tree with nodes $\{x_t\}$ for $t = 0, 1, \ldots, T$ and objective probability density function Π is a filtrated probability space $(\Omega, (F_t)_{t \in [0,T]}, P)$. Ω corresponds to the set of terminal nodes of the uncertainty tree, F_t to the subset of terminal nodes to which a given x_t is an ancestor-node, and P corresponds to Π. To preserve continuity of notation, the present chapter uses discrete time symbols wherever possible. For example, in this chapter Π will be used instead of P.

The Jouini-Napp framework features J investors. Investor j has subjective beliefs P_j, with P_j being a probability measure equivalent to Π. Investor j has an instantaneous utility function $u_j(t, c_j(t))$ and maximizes the expected utility functional $E[\int u_j(t, c_j(t))dt]$ where the range of integration is $t = 0$ to T and the expectation is taken with respect to P_j. Denote the change of measure $dP_j/d\Pi$ by N_j, and write investor j's expected utility function as $E_\Pi[\int N_j(t)u_j(t, c_j(t))dt]$. Here the notation indicates that the expectation is taken with respect to Π. Henceforth, unless otherwise specified, the range of integration over time for all integrals is taken to be 0 to T.

Notably $c_j(t)$ is assumed to be adapted to x_t, meaning that consumption at time t only depends on information available at t. In the discrete time framework, this assumption is embedded in the notation $c_j(x_t)$.

Jouini-Napp impose a series of assumptions on the class of investor utility functions. For example, utility functions must be concave, continuous, and have continuous first derivatives. This class includes CRRA and CARA utility functions.

Investor j's budget constraint is expressed as an integral in terms of the SDF $M(t)$, namely $E_\Pi[\int M(t)(c_j(t) - \omega_j(t)) \, dt] \leq 0$. Here, $\omega(t)$ is aggregate consumption available at time t, and $\omega_j(t)$ is investor j's initial share of that aggregate consumption. That is, $\sum_j \omega_j(t) = \omega(t)$. As with $c_j(t), \omega_j(t)$ and $M(t)$ are adapted processes. In addition, $E_\Pi[\int |c_j(t)| \, dt] < \infty$. The first order condition associated with budget constrained expected utility maximization is $N_j(t) \, u_j'(t, c_j(t)) = \lambda_j \, M(t)$, where λ_j is a Lagrange multiplier.

In equilibrium, every investor j chooses an expected utility maximizing consumption plan $c_j()$ subject to the budget constraint associated with SDF M, and aggregate demand $\sum_j c_j(t)$ equals aggregate supply $\omega(t)$.

Jouini-Napp describe two types of representative investors. The first type is derived from a transformed economy in which all investors share a common change of measure $N_j = N_R$. Here N_R can be interpreted as the change of measure for the representative investor. Two requirements make the construction of the first type of representative investor meaningful. The first requirement is that the transformed economy must have the same equilibrium SDF as the original economy. The second requirement is that wealth is reallocated so that every investor's marginal valuation is the same in the transformed economy as the original economy. That is, $N_j u'_j(t, c_j(t)) = N_R u'_j(t, c_{j,R}(t))$ where $c_{j,R}(t)$ is investor j's consumption at time t in the transformed economy. This condition serves to preserve the value of the individual investors' Lagrange multipliers.

The second type of representative investor does not involve wealth transfers, and therefore does not require the condition that for all j and t, $N_j(t)u'_j(t, c_j(t)) = N_R u'_j(t, c_{j,R}(t))$. Therefore, the individual investors' Lagrange multipliers will typically take on different values in the transformed economy than the original economy.

The second representative investor's utility function is based on the unweighted sum $\sum_j u_j(t, c(t))/\lambda_j$, where λ_j is the Lagrange multiplier for the transformed economy with no wealth transfers. For each value of aggregate consumption $c(t)$, the representative investor distributes $c(t)$ across the J investors in order to maximize $\sum_j u_j(t, c(t))/\lambda_j$. This gives rise to a representative investor utility function $u_R(c(t))$. A representative investor has a change of measure N_R, and maximizes expected utility $E_\Pi[\int N_R(t)u_R(t, c_R(t))dt]$ subject to the budget constraint $E_\Pi[\int M(t)(c(t) - \omega(t))dt] \leq 0$.

Jouini-Napp present an argument establishing that in general, the representative investor's change of measure N_R emerges as an average of the individual investors' change of measures $\{N_j\}$. The argument proceeds by developing expressions for investor j's marginal utility.

The first type of representative investor rearranges consumption to preserve the Lagrange multiplier values for all investors. Therefore, $N_j(t)u'_j(t, c_j(t)) = N_R u'_j(t, c_{j,R}(t))$, which implies that $u'_j(t, c_j(t)) = (N_R/N_j)u'_j(t, c_{j,R}(t))$.

Investor j's consumption maps to marginal utility. The inverse map goes from marginal utility to investor j's consumption. The sum of the inverse marginal utility maps is aggregate consumption.

N_R must average the values of $\{N_j\}$. If it did not, then N_R would either lie above all the $\{N_j\}$ or below all the $\{N_j\}$. Suppose that $N_R > N_j$ for all j, and focus on the first type of representative investor economy. Add up all the inverse maps for $u'_j(t, c_j(t)) = (N_R/N_j)u'_j(t, c_{j,R}(t))$. But with $N_R > N_j$ for all j, the marginal utility $(N_R/N_j)u'_j(t, c_{j,R}(t))$ for each investor j is increased. Therefore, the sum of inverse map values falls below $\omega(t)$. But this contradicts the condition that aggregate demand be equal to aggregate supply. Therefore, N_R averages the $\{N_j\}$.

Insight into the aggregating weights for the $\{N_j\}$ can be gleaned from the second type of representative investor economy. At the margin, the second type of representative investor values an increment $d\omega(t)$ as being worth $N_R u'_R(t, \omega(t)) d\omega(t)$. Given that u_R is constructed as a weighted average of the u_j-functions, the representative investor does not care which investor receives the increment $d\omega(t)$ to consume. The value which the representative investor places on investor j consuming the increment $d\omega(t)$ is $(N_j u'_j(t, c_j(t))/\lambda_j) d\omega(t)$. The two different expressions for incremental value imply that $u'_j(t, c_j(t)) = (1/\lambda_j)(N_R/N_i) u'_R(t, \omega(t))$.

As in the first type of representative investor economy, the sum of the inverse marginal utility maps is aggregate consumption. The weight attached to N_R/N_i is $(1/\lambda_j) u'_R(t, \omega(t))$. Only $(1/\lambda_j)$ varies from investor to investor. Therefore, λ_j drives the weight associated with N_R/N_i.

31.1.2   Linear Risk-Tolerance Utility Function

Most of the examples in Jouini-Napp involve functions that exhibit linear risk tolerance, which combine the properties of CRRA and CARA. Specifically, risk tolerance, the inverse of the Arrow-Pratt measure of risk aversion, has the form $\theta + \eta x$ where θ and η are parameters and x is the argument of the utility function.

Consider two special cases. In the first case, each investor j has a CARA risk tolerance value of θ_j. Define $\theta_R = \sum_j \theta_j$. Then the representative investor has a CARA risk tolerance value of θ_R and a change of measure N_R equal to the product of terms $(N_j)^{\theta_i/\theta_R}$ for $j = 1, \dots, J$. Moreover, the equilibrium SDF M is given by the product of N_R and $\exp(-(\omega(t) - \omega(0))/\theta_R)$. The expressions for N_R and M generalize the discussion in Section 12.8 for discrete time.

In the second special case, $u'_j(t, c_t)$ has the form $b_j e^{-\rho t}(\theta_j + \eta c_j)^{-1/\eta}$, so that investor j's risk tolerance is given by $\theta_j + \eta c_j$. Here the representative investor's marginal utility function has the form $u'_R(\omega_t) = b(\theta_R + \eta \omega_t)^{-1/\eta}$ and the change of measure N_R has the form $N_R = [\sum_j \gamma_j(N_j)^\eta]^{1/\eta}$. In the expressions for u'_R and N_R, $b = (\theta_R + \eta \omega_0)^{-1/\eta}$ and $\gamma_j = (b_j \lambda_j^{-\eta})/\sum_k(b_k \lambda_k^{-\eta})$.[1] Moreover, the equilibrium SDF M can be expressed as the product of N_R and $b e^{\rho t}((\theta_R + \eta \omega_t)/(\theta_R + \eta \omega_0))^{-1/\eta}$.

The expression $N_R = [\sum_j \gamma_j(N_j)^\eta]^{1/\eta}$ is the counterpart to equation (12.27) for CRRA utility, which is defined in terms of (12.25) and (12.26). Both the discrete time equation and continuous time equation have the form of a weighted harmonic (Hölder) average, with the weights based on Lagrange multipliers. Notably, equation (12.19) indicates that the Lagrange-based weights are proportional to investor wealth. By (12.20),

---

[1] Jouini and Napp also demonstrate that N_R can be expressed using absolute risk-tolerance weights instead of Lagrange multipliers, except that the exponents reverse, with η replaced by $1/\eta$ and vice-versa.

consumption is proportional to wealth, and in equations (12.25) through (12.27), the weights are stated in terms of relative consumption. For the case of CRRA ($\theta_R = 0$), the expression for the continuous time SDF M corresponds to equation (16.4) in the discrete time framework.

31.1.3   Dynamics Driven by a Single Brownian Motion

When the dynamics of the key variables in the model are governed by a single Brownian motion, explicit expressions can be derived to provide insight into both the general character of the model and specific functional forms for such variables as the prices and volatility of different asset prices, market price of risk, and risk-free rate.

Jouini-Napp develop a model with five key variables: aggregate consumption growth c, individual investors' change of measure functions N_j, individual investors' consumption growth c_j, the weighted Hölder average H_R, and the SDF M. In each case, the proportional change dy/y for each variable y evolves as the sum of a time-varying drift term $\alpha_t(y)$ plus the product $\sigma_t(y)dW_t$, where $\sigma_t(y)$ measures volatility and W is a Brownian motion process. The notation should be understood to mean that $\alpha_t(y)$ and $\sigma_t(y)$ are associated with the variable y, but not its value. Jouini-Napp assume that $\sigma_t(c) > 0, \alpha_t(N_j) = 0, N_{j,0} = 1$, and $E[\exp \int \sigma_t(H_R^2)dt] < \infty$.

Section 12.7.1 pointed out that when the CRRA is not unity, the weighted Hölder average will not sum to unity, thereby leading to a distortion in the representative investor's rate of time preference. This property is formally captured in equation (15.2) for market sentiment Λ, which combines the market log-change of measure and the adjustment to the discount function for aggregation bias. In the stochastic differential equation specification, these properties are manifest in the following expression for the SDF:

$$N_{R,t} B_t \, u'_R(t, \omega_t) = M_t \tag{31.1}$$

where B_t captures the impact of the aggregation bias. The equations for B_t and the representative investor's change of measure are as follows:

$$B_t = \exp \int_0^t \alpha_t(H) \, ds, \tag{31.2}$$

$$N_{R,t} = \exp \left[\int_0^t \sigma_s(H)dW_s - 1/2 \int_0^t \sigma_s^2(H) \, ds \right] \tag{31.3}$$

Equation (31.1) for the SDF corresponds to equation (16.4). Equation (16.4) pertains to the case of constant relative risk aversion. When the utility functions are assumed to feature linear risk tolerance with a common value for η, then $\alpha_t(H)$ and $\sigma_t(H)$ have special forms. These forms are defined using convex weights $\tau_j, j = 1, \ldots, J$, where τ_j is investor j's absolute risk tolerance value divided by the sum of all investors' values of absolute risk tolerance. The equations for $\alpha_t(H)$ and $\sigma_t(H)$ are as follows:

$$\alpha_t(H) = 1/2(\eta - 1)\text{Var}^\tau[\sigma_t(N_j, t)] \tag{31.4}$$

$$\sigma_t(H) = E^\tau[\sigma_t(N_j, t)] \tag{31.5}$$

The notation E^τ and Var^τ refer to the mean and variance taken with respect to the variables $\tau_j, j = 1, \ldots, J$, which are nonnegative and sum to unity.

Equation (31.4) indicates that the impact of the Brownian disturbance on the weighted Hölder average defining the representative investor's beliefs is a convex combination of the analogous coefficients for the individual investors. For CRRA, equation (12.13) indicates that the weights correspond to wealth, as absolute risk aversion is wealth divided by relative risk aversion.

Equation (31.4) indicates that for CRRA, $\alpha_t(H) < 0$ when investors' common coefficient of relative risk aversion is greater than unity. Equation (31.2) for B_t implies that when investors are more risk averse than log-utility, B_t is nonincreasing in t. In view of (31.1), the effect is to produce increased time discounting. When investors are less risk averse than log-utility, B_t is nondecreasing in t, which implies negative time discounting. Moreover, (31.4) implies that the more dispersion of beliefs $(\sigma_t(N_j, t))$ and absolute risk tolerance (which is proportional to wealth), the more intense is the time discounting that stems from aggregation bias.

In this model specification, there is a single Brownian motion which impacts both fundamentals (aggregate consumption growth) and the sentiments of the individual investors. This feature corresponds to the discrete time framework where the stochastic process for aggregate consumption growth g and the stochastic process for sentiment Λ both have Π as their underlying probabilities.

In the continuous time model, the disturbance dW_t causes investor j's change of measure N_j to experience a proportional change of magnitude $\sigma_t(N_j)dW_t$. Suppose that $dW_t > 0$. In this case, the proportionate change in aggregate consumption growth, dc/c, experiences a positive transitory shock in the amount $\sigma_t(c)dW_t$.

Chapter 15 defines investor j's sentiment as the logarithm of his change of measure relative to the objective density. In the above model, this variable corresponds to $\ln(N_j(t))$. The variable dN_j/N_j measures how investor j's sentiment evolves over time. If $\sigma_t(N_j) > 0$, then a positive stochastic innovation to aggregate consumption growth leads to an increase in investor

j's error. That is, investor j becomes more optimistic. If $\sigma_t(N_j) < 0$, then a positive stochastic innovation to aggregate consumption growth leads to a decrease in investor j's error. That is, investor j becomes more pessimistic.

In the discrete time framework, investor j is optimistic when his sentiment function is upward sloping, as in Figure 15.2. Investor j is pessimistic when his sentiment function is downward sloping, as in Figure 15.3.

As for the SDF, in (31.1), market optimism is expressed by the condition that $\sigma_t(H) > 0$ and market pessimism by the condition that $\sigma_t(H) < 0$. As was mentioned above, in (31.1) B_t reflects aggregation bias.

A very nice feature of the continuous time framework is that it features a series of simple equations to capture the impact of sentiment on market prices, volatility, asset prices, and risk premiums. In this respect, consider the comparison between two economies, the efficient prices economy in which the sentiment of all investors is zero, and the inefficient prices economy in which market sentiment is nonzero. As in the rest of the book, the symbol Π is used to denote the situation when prices are efficient.

The following equations indicate the manner in which sentiment impacts the drift and volatility of the SDF:

$$\alpha_t(M) = \alpha_{\Pi,t}(M) + \alpha_t(H) + \sigma_t(H)\sigma_t(M) \tag{31.6}$$

$$\sigma_t(M) = \sigma_{\Pi,t}(M) + \sigma_t(H) \tag{31.7}$$

Sentiment causes the drift $\alpha_t(M)$ to be the sum of three terms: (1) its efficient price counterpart $\alpha_{\Pi,t}(M)$; (2) $\alpha_t(H)$ which adjusts for aggregation bias; and (3) the product $\sigma_t(H)\sigma_t(M)$. When prices are efficient, the latter two terms are zero, in which case $\alpha_t(M) = \alpha_{\Pi,t}(M)$. Sentiment causes the volatility $\sigma_t(M)$ to be the sum of two terms: its efficient price counterpart $\sigma_{\Pi,t}(M)$ and $\sigma_t(H)$. When prices are efficient, the second term is zero in which case $\sigma_t(M) = \sigma_{\Pi,t}(M)$. In particular, notice that the excessive optimism and pessimism reflected in the volatility $\sigma_t(H)$ are transmitted to both the drift and volatility of the SDF.

In the neoclassical framework, the market price of risk is measured in terms of a Sharpe ratio (risk premium divided by return standard deviation). Equation (31.7) implies that sentiment causes the market risk premium to be lower by $\sigma_t(H)$. For example, if sentiment is excessively optimistic, then $\sigma_t(H) > 0$, which implies that sentiment lowers the market premium for risk.

Sentiment causes the risk-free rate to change by the sum of two terms. The first term is the impact of a change in overall optimism or pessimism. It is measured as the product of the representative investor's absolute risk aversion, $\sigma_t(H)$, $\sigma_t(c)$, and c. The second term is simply $-\alpha_t(H)$, the term which adjusts for aggregation bias. Recall that when the common coefficient of relative risk aversion is greater than unity, $\alpha_t(H) < 0$.

In the case of CRRA, the first term simplifies to the expression $\sigma_t(H)\sigma_t(c)/\eta$. Notice that optimism is reflected in the inequality $\sigma_t(H) > 0$. Therefore, optimistic market sentiment serves to increase the risk-free rate. Aggregation bias also serves to increase the risk-free rate, as its effect is akin to making investors less patient. Less patient investors require a higher risk-free rate to induce them to be willing to hold claims on future consumption.

The impact of sentiment on the value of the market portfolio also involves two effects, one due to the degree of market optimism or pessimism and one due to aggregation bias. These effects can be seen in the general expression for the value of the market portfolio at time t, $E_t[\int_t^T (M_s/M_t)c_s\, ds]$, where the expectation is taken with respect to Π. This is equal to

$$u_t'(c)^{-1}E_t\left[\int_t^T B_s/B_t\, u_s'(c_s)c_s\, ds\right] \tag{31.8}$$

where the expectation is taken with respect to $N_R\Pi$. If prices are efficient, then $B_t = 1$ and $N_R = 1$. In the CRRA case with relative risk aversion greater than unity, the effect of B_t is to decrease the value of the market portfolio, as claims to the future are more heavily discounted. The effect of optimistic or pessimistic sentiment operates through the integral $E_t[\int_t^T u_s'(c_s)c_s\, ds]$. Under the assumption that investors' utility functions satisfy CRRA, the function being integrated has the form $c^{1-1/\eta}$.

When $\eta = 1$ investors have log-utility. In this case, optimism or pessimism have no impact on $E_t[\int_t^T u_s'(c_s)c_s\, ds]$ because $u_s'(c_s)c_s = c^{1-1/\eta} = 1$ for all c_s and s. When $\eta < 1$ investors are more risk-averse that investors with log-utility. In this case, pessimistic beliefs place more weight on lower values of c_s, and these are associated with higher values of $c^{1-1/\eta}$. Therefore, the Jouini-Napp argument establishes that pessimism raises the price of the market portfolio. In turn, this higher price generates lower subsequent returns than would otherwise occur. Similar arguments can be made to characterize the impact on the price of the market portfolio both from optimism and from η being greater than 1.

Finally, Jouini-Napp compute an expression establishing the impact of sentiment on the risk premium. Sentiment changes the risk premium by the product of the return standard deviation and $-\sigma(H)$.

31.2   Analyzing the Impact of a Public Signal

In Section 31.1, sentiment and fundamentals were jointly driven by a single Brownian motion. This section discusses how the economic character of continuous time models is impacted by the introduction of an additional Brownian motion that represents a signal.

In economic terms, the presence of a single Brownian motion to drive sentiment and fundamentals means that investors only base their beliefs about the future growth of aggregate consumption on the past history of aggregate consumption. Therefore, the consumption history completely determines the errors committed by individual investors, and therefore market sentiment.

31.2.1   Two-Investor Example When One Investor Holds Objectively Correct Beliefs

For purposes of illustration, consider the two-investor example of the log-utility model developed in Chapters 8 through 11, in which one investor holds erroneous beliefs and the other investor holds objectively correct beliefs. Let investor 1 hold incorrect beliefs ($P_1 \neq \Pi$) and investor 2 hold correct beliefs ($P_2 = \Pi$). In addition, assume that under Π, consumption growth evolves as an $i.i.d.$ process. The continuous time analogue of the $i.i.d.$ assumption for discrete time is that consumption growth dc/c be equal to $\alpha(c)dt + \sigma(c)dW_t(c)$, where $W_t(c)$ is a Brownian motion. As above, the notation indicates that α and σ are specific to the variable c, not that they depend on the exact value taken by c.

Equations (8.15) and (8.22) together imply that investor 2's errors must render market prices inefficient relative to the publicly available information x_t. However, equations (10.11) through (10.13) imply that these errors do not impact the process governing the evolution of the price or return of the market portfolio. Therefore, investor 2's errors do not impact investor 1's beliefs about the evolution of the price or return of the market portfolio.

Nevertheless, by equation (10.15), investor 1's errors do impact the risk-free rate. Therefore, investor 1's errors impact the risk premium on the market portfolio. Consider the binomial example developed in Chapter 10. In the binomial case, when the risk-free rate declines, the market risk premium increases, and investor 2 increases his holdings of the market portfolio. When the risk-free rate increases, the market risk premium decreases, and investor 2 decreases his holdings of the market portfolio. Indeed, the example in Chapter 10 illustrates a situation when the market risk premium is negative, with investor 2 shorting the market portfolio.

When investor 1 holds objectively correct beliefs, like investor 2, then the risk-free rate will be invariant over time. This follows from equation (10.15). When investor 1's beliefs are erroneous, the risk-free rate will become time-varying, and with it the market risk premium. In other words, investor 1's errors cause asset prices to become excessively volatile. This occurs because the representative investor's beliefs vary over time, as wealth shifts between the two investors based on the outcome of trade.

By the entropy arguments discussed in Chapters 11 and 16, over time, market inefficiency will cause investor 2 to take advantage of investor 1, whose share of consumption will decline as a result. This occurs as investor 2 takes advantage of investor 1 by shifting portfolio weight from the market portfolio to the risk-free security when investor 1 becomes excessively optimistic, and by doing the reverse when investor 1 become excessively pessimistic.

31.2.2   Signal Structure: General Issues

Chapter 4 provides an example of how a public signal can be incorporated into the model. The key feature of the example is that prior to the true value of aggregate consumption growth g being revealed, investors receive a noisy public signal s about its value, and are then free to trade. The example features binomial consumption growth, but the signal can assume seven different values. Recall that there were two different formulations of the signal model. In the first case, there is a market for claims contingent on the occurrence of (s, g). In the second formulation, s precedes g, and there is a market in claims contingent on g, conditional on the revealed value of s.

Fischer Black (1986) defined noise traders as traders who trade on noise as if it were information. In the signal model, this notion of noise trader can be modeled by assuming that the signal s contains no information about future values of g. That is, the probabilities for g conditional on s are simply the unconditional probabilities. Call this case "Black noise." If investor 1 erroneously believes that s is informative about g, when it is not, then investor 1 is a noise trader in the sense described by Black. In this case, realizations of s will still impact prices, since investor 1's beliefs will impact the representative investor's beliefs and inject excessive volatility into the risk-free rate and market risk premium.

One way to think about the signal in a Black noise economy is that the signal reflects the forecasts of financial strategists. As discussed in Chapter 7, the forecasts of analysts and strategists typically exhibit gambler's fallacy and are less predictive of future market returns than a simple rule based only on past market returns. Yet, some investors appear to qualify as noise traders by heeding the predictions of analysts and strategists.

31.2.3   Continuous Time Signal Structure

Dumas, Kurshev, and Uppal (2006) (DKU) develop a model featuring two investors, one with incorrect beliefs and the other with objectively correct beliefs. In their model, aggregate consumption growth varies randomly around a current drift term, which is itself mean-reverting. When the drift term is above its long-run average value, consumption tends to grow at an above average rate, but with shocks which can be either positive or negative. An analogous statement applies when the drift term is below its long-term average value.

Intuitively, think of consumption growth as economic growth. Economic growth depends on the underlying structural strength of the economy, but it also depends on the effects of random disturbances like weather. In addition, the underlying structural strength of the economy tends to move in cycles. At some times, economic fundamentals lie above the historical average, and at other times the economic fundamentals lie below the historical average. Over time, economic fundamentals tend to revert to the historical average, but also face random disturbances like union strikes and political events that affect the availability of energy on global markets.

Imagine that investors cannot directly observe the strength of the underlying fundamentals in the economy. All they can do is draw inferences about it from the information they have at their disposal. This information includes the actual rate of economic growth. In addition, financial analysts and strategists engage in research and produce reports about their assessment of what the underlying economic fundamentals might be. Think of these reports as a signal. If financial analysts and strategists are brilliant, they are able to identify the underlying fundamentals exactly. If financial strategists and analysts are simply full of bluster, their reports contain no information about the underlying fundamentals. The intermediate case lies in between: The reports are partially informative about the underlying fundamentals.

In DKU, financial analysts and strategists are full of bluster. Some investors understand this to be the case and pay no heed to their reports. However, other investors believe that the reports are partially informative about the underlying strength of the economy. DKU analyze how the magnitude of investors' errors impacts trading strategies and asset prices.

Formally, aggregate consumption growth dc/c satisfies

$$dc/c = \alpha_t(c)\, dt + \sigma(c)dW_t(c) \tag{31.9}$$

where $\alpha_t(c)$ is itself time varying, satisfying

$$d\alpha_t(c) = \zeta(\alpha_t(c) - \mu_\alpha)\, dt + \sigma(\alpha)dW_t(\alpha) \tag{31.10}$$

Equation (31.10) indicates the consumption drift follows a mean reverting Ornstein-Uhlenbeck process. Neither investor has direct knowledge of the current drift $\alpha_t(c)$. However, investors do observe a public signal s_t, upon whose value they can condition their beliefs. DKU assume that the signal evolves according to $ds_t/s_t = \sigma(s)dW_t(s)$. DKU assume that investors estimate (or filter out) the current and future values of α_t from their observations of c and s.

DKU make the Black noise assumption. They assume that s contains no information about consumption growth. They apply a signal-based model developed by Scheinkman and Xiong (2003). Specifically, investor 1 erroneously believes that s is informative about the current value of the change in drift term $d\alpha_t(c)$. In particular, investor 1 believes that the Brownian disturbance for s is a linear combination of two terms. The two terms are $\phi dW_t(\alpha)$ and $\sqrt{(1-\phi^2)}dW_t(s)$. The magnitude of investor 1's error is measured by ϕ. When $\phi = 0$, investor 1 holds objectively correct beliefs, since the Brownian disturbance for s is indeed $dW_t(s)$. The larger is ϕ, the greater is investor 1's belief that s is informative about $\alpha(c)$.

The filtering rule which the two investors apply to their respective beliefs is especially insightful. DKU show that investor 2, who holds objectively correct beliefs, estimates future (instantaneous) consumption growth using equation (31.9) with his (efficient) estimate of the current (unknown) drift $\alpha_t(c)$, and a Brownian disturbance term specific to c, scaled by the known standard deviation $\sigma(c)$. Investor 2 also uses equation (31.10) to estimate the change in drift by using his own estimate of the current drift in place of the true drift, which is then adjusted by investor 2's forecast error for consumption growth. The forecast error is the difference between actual consumption growth and estimated consumption growth. The coefficient applied to the forecast error for estimating (31.10) is $\gamma(2)/\sigma^2(c)$. Here $\gamma(2)$ measures investor 2's estimate of the stationary (long-run) volatility of consumption growth drift.

Investor 1's estimate of the change in drift is similar to that of investor 1, but with three differences. First, investor 1 uses his own estimates of the drift, not the estimate of investor 2. Second, investor 1 uses his own estimate $\gamma(1)$ of the long-run standard deviation of the drift, not that of investor 2. Third, investor 1 adds the term $\phi(\sigma(\alpha)/\sigma(c))\,ds_t$ to his estimate of the change in drift. This third term adjusts for investor 1's belief that the signal provides information about the Brownian disturbance to the change in drift.

Investor 2 holds objectively correct beliefs, and so his estimates are statistically efficient. In contrast, investor 1 is error-prone. In particular, investor 1's error ϕ generally leads him to form a different estimate of the current drift term for aggregate consumption growth. Let investor 1's estimate of the current drift be equal to investor 2's estimate plus Δ. Think of Δ as investor 1's degree of excessive optimism. DKU establish that $d\Delta$ is given by a linear combination involving Δ and two Brownian motions, one pertaining to c and the other pertaining to s.

The coefficients in this linear combination are as follows. The coefficient multiplying Δ is $\zeta + (\gamma(1)/\sigma^2(c))$. The coefficient multiplying the Brownian for c is $(\gamma(1) - \gamma(2))/\sigma(c))$. The coefficient multiplying the Brownian for s is $\phi\sigma(c)$.

Consider the signs of these coefficients. The sign of the coefficient multiplying Δ is made up of positive terms and is therefore itself positive. Similarly, the sign of the coefficient multiplying the Brownian for s is positive.

The sign of the coefficient multiplying the Brownian for c depends on which of two terms is larger, $\gamma(1)$ or $\gamma(2)$. The analysis in Scheinkman-Xiong (2003) implies that the sign of the coefficient is nonpositive because $\gamma(1) \leq \gamma(2)$. This inequality stipulates that investor 1 believes that consumption growth drift has a higher stationary (long-run) volatility than does investor 2. The reason for this is that investor 1 erroneously believes that the value of ds_t provides information about the Brownian disturbance to consumption drift. When investor 1's error $\phi = 1$, investor 1 actually believes that he can always perfectly infer the value of the Brownian consumption drift disturbance. In this special case, $\gamma(1) = 0$.

The difference $\gamma(2) - \gamma(1)$ measures the extent to which investor 1 is overconfident. When $\phi = 0, \gamma(2) = \gamma(1)$ and so investor 1 is not overconfident. When $\phi = 1, \gamma(2) - \gamma(1) = \gamma(2)$ and so investor 1 is maximally overconfident.

The fact that the sign of the coefficient on Δ in the equation for $d\Delta$ is positive indicates that when investor 1 is excessively optimistic, his optimism will continue to rise. This statement applies in the absence of innovations to consumption growth and the signal.

The fact that the sign of the coefficient multiplying the Brownian for c is negative implies that positive innovations in consumption growth will lead the overconfident investor 1 to become less optimistic. This property stems from the manner in which both investors interpret positive innovations in consumption growth. Both investors respond to a positive innovation in consumption growth by revising upwards their estimates of the drift term. However, the adjustment which investor 1 makes to his estimate of the drift reflects both sources of information, as he perceives them: the innovation in consumption growth and the innovation in the signal. Investor 2's adjustment only reflects the innovation in consumption growth. Moreover, the sensitivity of the adjustment to each investor's estimate of the drift is directly proportional to their respective long-run volatilities $\gamma(j)$. Therefore, if the innovation in the signal is zero, investor 1 will tend to adjust his estimate of the drift by a smaller amount than investor 2. As a result, investor 1 will become less optimistic.

The fact that the coefficient multiplying the Brownian for s is positive implies that positive innovations in the signal will lead the overconfident investor 1 to become more optimistic. Of course, when investor 1's overconfidence is zero, his beliefs will coincide with those of investor 1, and so his optimism Δ will also be zero.

As in Section 31.1, each investor j's beliefs relative to Π are represented by a change of measure N_j. When $\Delta > 0$, investor 1 is excessively optimistic. This means that his estimate of consumption drift is upwardly biased, and as a result he attaches higher probability to positive innovations in consumption growth than is warranted. This higher probability is captured by j's change of measure N_j. In DKU's model, Girsanov's Theorem implies that dN_j/N_j is equal to the product of $\Delta/\sigma(c)$ and the Brownian motion associated with c in the expression for $d\Delta$.

DKU assume that both investors maximize expected utility $E_\Pi[\int N_j(t)u_j(t, c_j(t))dt]$ subject to the budget constraint $E_\Pi[\int M(t)(c_j(t) - \omega_j(t))dt] \leq 0$. Here $u_j(t, c_j(t))$ is time-discounted CRRA which is the same for both investors. The time horizon is 0 to ∞. Each investor is initially endowed with a fraction of the market portfolio $\omega_j(t)) = \theta_j\omega(t)$.

The first order conditions for the investors' maximization have the same structure as (12.18). Moreover, the equilibrium SDF conforms to (16.4), with the representative investor's change of measure based on the Hölder average in (12.25)–(12.27).

The SDF in DKU is more complex than the SDF discussed in Section 31.1. This is because the DKU model involves a public signal. In the model of Section 31.1, sentiment is driven by consumption growth alone. In the DKU model, sentiment is driven by both consumption growth and the signal. Formally, this dual driver property is captured by two features. First, investor j's optimism Δ scales the variation dN_j/N_j of his change of measure. Second, $d\Delta$ is driven by two Brownian motions, one for consumption c and one for the signal s.

In the discrete time signal framework, x_t connotes both a consumption growth history and a signal history. Beliefs pertain to the conditional distribution $\text{Prob}\{x_\tau|x_t\}$ for $\tau > t$. For $\tau = t+1$, and descendants x_{t+1} of x_t, investor j's consumption $c_j(x_{t+1})$ can vary across both aggregate consumption growth $g(x_{t+1})$ and the signal $s(x_{t+1})$. This dual dependence is the discrete time analogue of the point made in the preceding paragraph.

In the discrete time framework, it is easy to see that each investor j can bet both on the future value of consumption growth and the future signal. In this regard, $s(x_t)$ is a conditioning variable for both $g(x_{t+1})$ and $s(x_{t+1})$. Therefore, variation across both $g(x_{t+1})$ and $s(x_{t+1})$ is endemic to the following series of variables: each investor's change of measure N_j, the representative investor's change of measure N_R, the objective density Π, state prices, and the SDF M.

For fixed x_t, consider how the representative investor's change of measure N_1 varies across $g(x_{t+1})$ and $s(x_{t+1})$. For fixed $s(x_{t+1})$, if investor 1 is excessively optimistic about consumption growth, then N_1 will be upward sloping. Conversely, if investor 1 is excessively pessimistic, then N_1 will be downward sloping about consumption growth. For fixed $g(x_{t+1})$, the shape of the variation in N_1 with respect to $s(x_{t+1})$ depends on how predictable investor 1 believes that the future signal is, conditional on x_t, meaning the past histories of consumption growth and the signal. If investor 1 believes that future signals are unpredictable, then N_1 will be a flat function of $s(x_{t+1})$, for fixed $g(x_{t+1})$. If investor 1 believes that future signals are predictable, then the value of N_1 will vary across future signals.

Saying that future signals are unpredictable implies that $g(x_{t+1})$ and $s(x_{t+1})$ are uncorrelated. This is different from saying that $g(x_{t+1})$ and $s(x_t)$ are uncorrelated. In the DKU framework, investor 1's perceived correlation between $g(x_{t+1})$ and $s(x_t)$ lies at the heart of his error. Fixing $g(x_t), g(x_{t+1})$ and $s(x_{t+1})$, but varying $s(x_t)$ leads to variation in N_1. The shape of this function is likely to be single peaked, as one particular signal is most predictive of $g(x_{t+1})$ and $s(x_{t+1})$, and the probability associated with the occurrence of this event drops off in moving to different signals.

A distinguishing feature of this signal-based model is that investor 1's trading error leads him to overweight claims to particular combinations of $s(x_t)$ and $g(x_{t+1})$ because he falsely believes that $s(x_t)$ is predictive of $g(x_{t+1})$. It is this behavior pattern that drives the results in the signal-based noise trader framework. A similar property holds in the example developed in Chapter 4, except that in that example it is representativeness which leads to the overweighting of particular pairings of signal and consumption growth.

The properties of N_1 will carry over to N_R and to the SDF. This is because N_R is a Hölder average of N_1 and N_2. Now $N_2 = 1$ because investor 2 holds objectively correct beliefs. Therefore, N_R is simply a weaker version of N_1.

As for the SDF, it reflects Theorem 16.1, the decomposition result, and therefore includes both the neoclassical fundamental component and sentiment. Sentiment has two components. The first is due to the representative investor's log-change of measure N_R. The second is due to the time preference adjustment for aggregation bias. The impact from N_R reflects investor 1's bias, be it optimism or pessimism in respect to consumption growth, and the degree to which future signal values are predictable.

Chapter 14 established the following expression for the growth rate of investor j's consumption.

$$c_j(x_t)/c_j(x_0) = g(x_t)^{\gamma_R/\gamma_j}(D_j(x_t)/D_R(x_t))^{1/\gamma_j} \tag{31.11}$$

where $D_R(x_t)$ is the representative investor's discounted probability (14.21). In the DKU model, both investors share the same coefficient of relative risk aversion, so the first term on the right-side of (31.11) is just $g(x_t)$. The second term is the relative likelihood of j's change of measure N_j to that of the representative investor. Equation (31.11) indicates that investor 1's share of consumption grows in states where he is more optimistic than the representative investor, and therefore more optimistic than investor 2. DKU show that this feature carries through to continuous time.

Consider the number of securities required for trade. In the special case where investor 1 holds objectively correct beliefs, then there is no basis for trade and both investors are content to hold their initial allocations of the market portfolio. Therefore, only one security is required in this case. In general, market completeness in the DKU framework requires that securities be structured to allow investors to bet on two Brownian innovations, one pertaining to consumption growth and the other to the signal. This can be accomplished by allowing trade in three particular securities at each t. DKU use the instantaneous risk-free security, the market portfolio, and a consol bond (with no risk of default). As is the case in the discrete time framework, where investors bet on consumption-signal pairs, investor 1's error ϕ creates excess volatility in asset prices. DKU analyze a series of cases that make this point. They report that as a general matter, investor sentiment increases the volatility associated with the market portfolio, the consol bond, and the correlation between them.

In most ways, discrete time behavioral models and continuous time behavioral models share the same general features. The choice of which one to use is often a matter of convenience. Discrete time models typically involve fewer technical conditions. Continuous time models typically offer more tractable closed form solutions, with fewer securities required to achieve market completeness. In this respect, DKU's analysis provides important insights into the nature of investor 2's portfolio strategy, and the manner in which his wealth is impacted by particular changes. For example, when investor 1's optimism $\Delta(t)$ is zero at time t, investor 2 will hold a lower equity position than investor 1. In addition, investor 2 will sell bonds. Moreover, a positive increase $d\Delta$ will lower investor 2's wealth. Notably, investor 1's marginal optimism will lead him to increase his exposure to the market portfolio, with investor 2 taking the opposite position.

Sentiment impacts the market premium for risk. Consider the two-investor version of the log-utility model developed in Chapters 8 through 11, with consumption growth being $i.i.d.$ If both investors hold objectively correct beliefs, then the risk premium associated with the market portfolio will be time-invariant. Denote the value of this premium by MRP_Π. If investor 1 is a noise trader and investor 2 holds objectively correct beliefs, then the risk premium associated with the market portfolio will rise and fall with the noise trader's degree of optimism. For any x_t, denote its value by $MRP(x_t)$.

The difference $MRP(x_t) - MRP_\Pi$ constitutes a risk premium for sentiment. In this case, the risk premium $MRP(x_t)$ can be decomposed into the fundamental premium MRP_Π and the sentiment premium. When noise traders are optimistic, the sentiment premium is negative. When noise traders are pessimistic, the sentiment premium is positive. When the sentiment premium is negative, the investor with objectively correct beliefs reduces his holdings of the market portfolio relative to the noise trader. When the risk premium on the market portfolio is actually negative, the investor with objectively correct beliefs takes a short position in the market portfolio.

DKU identify the determinants of the long-run price of risk. They show that the long-run price of risk can be decomposed into a series of components. These components relate to the short-term rate of risk, short-term sentiment, and a measure of the future change in the noise trader's degree of optimism. They also examine the relationship between dividend yield and future returns; see Section 22.1. In DKU's model, the sign of this relationship is negative in some circumstances, but positive in others.

31.3   Jump Processes and Stochastic Volatility

Section 31.1 discussed a continuous time behavioral model with a single Brownian motion. Section 31.2 discussed a continuous time behavioral model with two Brownian motions. This section discusses the study of a behavioral issue using a continuous time model with stochastic volatility and jumps to study key behavioral issues associated with the Nasdaq bubble of 1999–2000.

Figure 9.1 illustrates the time series of three stock market indexes, including the Nasdaq Composite Index between 1988 and 2004. The bubble period is evident in the figure. Figure 15.11 shows how investors' return expectations became increasingly optimistic between 1998 and 2000. Figures 23.7 and 23.8 display the change in investors' beliefs about the probability associated with negative returns.

Consider how the combination of increasing optimism and increased concern about a crash would be reflected in the dynamics of the sentiment function. Figure 31.1 provides a hypothetical illustration. The sentiment function depicted in thick black represents the period prior to the bubble. This shape is consistent with the findings reported in Aït-Sahalia and Lo (2000) and Rosenberg and Engle (2002). The dashed sentiment function pertains to the bubble period itself.

Notice that the dashed function lies above the solid function at both right and left extremes, and lies below it in the middle section. At the right, irrational exuberance among bullish investors pushes up the probability that the market (meaning P_M) attaches to very favorable events (continuation of a strong bull market). At the left, bearish institutional investors concerned about a crash push up the probability that the market attaches to very unfavorable events (bursting of bubble or crash). The increased absolute values of the slopes at the extremes of Figure 31.1

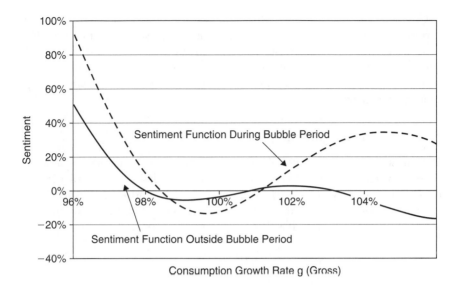

FIGURE 31.1. Illustration of the sentiment functions during and outside the Nasdaq bubble period. The two functions depicted in this figure are hypothetical constructions whose shapes depict how sentiment evolved during the bubble.

connote the strength of unrealistic optimism by bulls and unrealistic pessimism (by bears). Given that the bubble burst, the pessimism of the bears might have been warranted. In that case, the prices of index put options might well have been efficient, in which case sentiment would actually have moved towards zero at the left extreme, not away from zero as Figure 31.1 depicts.

Bakshi and Wu (2006) develop a model to estimate the dynamics for the price of risk in order to study the extent to which the Nasdaq bubble featured nonzero sentiment, particularly irrational exuberance. Lying at the heart of their analysis is the risk premium ηV_t, the product of risk V_t and the premium per unit risk. Bakshi and Wu analyze the behavior of both components during the bubble period. Their findings are generally consistent with the dynamics depicted in Figure 31.1.

The SDF Decomposition Theorem 16.1 indicates that when sentiment is zero, the premium per unit risk stems from the representative investor's degree of relative risk aversion. As the discussion following Theorem 14.1 indicates, wealth shifts from trade cause this variable to be stochastic. Notably, when sentiment is zero, the SDF is independent of the underlying probability density Π. However, nonzero sentiment will cause the premium per unit risk to become volatile, varying over time as wealth shifts back and forth among investors with different degrees of risk aversion.

Compared to the case in which sentiment is zero, nonzero sentiment typically injects much greater volatility into the premium per unit risk. Bakshi-Wu provide important insights into the time series variation of the premium per unit risk. Their findings are more consistent with the time series reflecting nonzero and shifting sentiment than a situation in which sentiment is zero.

31.3.1   Theoretical Framework

Bakshi-Wu's model has the following structure. The asset price is assumed to be governed by dS/S that is the sum of a drift term α, a diffusion process W_t, two jump processes J_t^+ and J_t^- (up and down respectively), minus a time-varying term T_t. All stochastic components are assumed to be adapted to an underlying filtered probability space. Formally,

$$dS/S = \alpha + W_t + J_t^+ + J_t^- - T_t \qquad (31.12)$$

Bakshi-Wu model dS/S as following a time-changed Lévy process, with the jump terms modeled in terms of Lévy densities $\lambda \exp(-\beta x)x^{-2}$. The two jump processes are each assumed to have their own β-parameters. (See Bakshi-Wu for additional details). The notation used in this section is specific to this section. For example, λ as used here is a Lévy density parameter, not a Lagrange multiplier as in the earlier sections of the chapter.

T_t is equal to the cumulative function $\int V_u \, du$ where V_u is instantaneous volatility and the range of integration is 0 to t. V_t is assumed to evolve as a square root process

$$dV_t = \kappa(\theta - V_t) + \omega\sqrt{V_t}dW_t^\nu \qquad (31.13)$$

where W_t^ν is a Brownian motion that is correlated with the Brownian motion W_t associated with the evolution of S_t. The symbol ρ denotes the correlation between the two processes. κ and ω are parameters.

Bakshi-Wu model the pricing kernel as a product of two exponential terms $\exp(-rt)$ and $\exp(L)$. Here $\exp(-rt)$ is an exponential time discount term and L is a linear combination of all the stochastic components in equation (31.11) for dS/S along with W_t^ν. The respective coefficients in L are denoted by γ, subscripted by its associated variable. Notably, $\exp(L)$ is an exponential Martingale that provides the change of measure from the objective probability measure to the risk-neutral measure.

Premiums for risk are embedded in the risk-neutral density. Denote the price of risk by a function ηV_t with η denoting the risk premium per unit risk. Bakshi-Wu prove that η decomposes into three components: one associated with the diffusion process W_t, one associated with the up jump J_t^+, and one associated with the down jump J_t^-.

Each component in the risk premium decomposition conforms to a specific functional form associated with the Lévy structure. The expression for the diffusion risk premium has the form $\gamma_W + \gamma_\nu \rho$. For each jump process J, the expression for the risk premium is a sum of variables $k_J[u] = \ln(E(\exp(uJ_t)))/t$, for values of u equal respectively to $1, 1 - \gamma_J$, and $-\gamma_J$ respectively. Notably, the presence of ρ in the term for diffusion risk reflects a risk premium associated with stochastic volatility.

Bakshi-Wu suggest that irrational exuberance will manifest itself in the diffusion component of the price of risk, which is to say in the sum $\gamma_W + \gamma_\nu \rho$. Keep in mind that this term reflects both the direct effect on dS/S and the indirect effect of stochastic volatility. They suggest that the price of jump risk reflects investors' beliefs about positive jumps and especially negative jumps, associated with the collapse of the bubble.

31.3.2   Empirical Procedure

The estimation procedure which Bakshi and Wu use combines return distribution estimates based on historical data with risk-neutral density information inferred from option prices. The data in their study comprise weekly observations between March 17, 1999 and March 19, 2003. The source of their options data is OptionMetrics. Their sample covers 206 weeks, and 20,160 options with maturities from one week to one year.

Bakshi-Wu study whether the relationship between risk and return was the same during the bubble period as it had been outside the bubble period. In doing so, they address the following three questions. First, how did the dynamics of return risk V_t vary around the bubble period? Second, on average, how were the different sources of risk priced? Third, how did the market prices for various sources of risk vary around the bubble period?

Empirically, Bakshi-Wu use a procedure that involves a Kalman filter technique to estimate the unobservable volatility V_t. The procedure selects the values of the model's parameters to maximize a conditional log-likelihood function based on the time series for historical option prices and returns. The key parameters are the coefficients in (31.12) for volatility dynamics, the variables λ and β for the two jump processes, and the γ-coefficients of the risk-neutral measure.

The key findings from the Bakshi-Wu study pertain to the fact that the risk-return relationship was different during the bubble period than it had been outside the bubble period.

The analysis confirms a finding that had already been documented in the literature, namely that return variance rate V_t started at a relatively low level in March 1999, but increased steadily as the Nasdaq 100 index rose in value. In addition, return volatility remained high even after the bubble burst in March 2000.

As for the risk premium components, outside the bubble period, all risk premium components were positive. The diffusion component of the premium per unit risk is $\gamma_W + \gamma_\nu \rho$. Bakshi-Wu report that the correlation ρ between the diffusion W for dS/S and the diffusion W_ν for stochastic volatility was -0.89. They also report that γ_ν was negative at the beginning of their study period and on average remained negative. It follows that the product $\gamma_\nu \rho > 0$ in the expression for the diffusion component of the price per unit risk. This implies that investors disliked exposure to volatility risk. However, in late 1999 as the Nasdaq 100 rose dramatically, γ_ν experienced an upward spike, even turning positive for a brief period of time.

As to the overall diffusion risk premium $\gamma_W + \gamma_\nu \rho$, Bakshi-Wu report that its value prior to the bubble was slightly below 2. However, in late 1999, its value turned negative. After the bubble burst, the diffusion return risk premium per unit risk turned strongly positive.

A negative diffusion risk premium might imply that investors were risk-seeking in respect to stochastic volatility. However, the survey evidence on return expectations presented in Chapters 7 and 15 suggests that a more likely explanation is irrational exuberance. Indeed Bakshi-Wu report that after the bubble burst, investors' dislike for volatility risk reached a historic high.

Next, consider Bakshi-Wu's findings about the premiums for jump risk. They point out that the difference $\beta^+ - \beta^-$ serves as a measure of excess demand for out-of-the-money put options, which provide insurance against a crash. Their analysis suggests that as the Nasdaq 100 rose in value, the value of $\beta^+ - \beta^-$ rose with it. However, after the bubble burst, the value of $\beta^+ - \beta^-$ declined to its pre-bubble levels. Notably, during the bubble period, both open interest and volume for put options rose dramatically relative to open interest and volume for call options.

31.4   Issues Pertaining to Future Directions

The concluding chapter of the first edition of this book provided some notes of caution about the application of continuous time stochastic models to behavioral phenomena. In respect to future directions and the advances discussed above, this section highlights a few key issues.

The first edition of the book contained only one continuous time model, namely Chapter 21, "Behavioral Black-Scholes." Section 21.3 develops a behavioral option pricing equation in which volatility is constant, and all investors agree about its underlying value. The chapter establishes that implied option volatility smiles are possible in such a model. However, the smile patterns associated with the constant volatility model are driven by time variation in the term structure of interest rates.

Notably, smile patterns inherently relate to return volatility in respect to the underlying asset, not the term structure. A more general version of the behavioral Black-Scholes formula is developed in Section 21.4. Here, investors can disagree about the process governing the evolution of volatility; and the smile patterns are much richer because they are driven by differences of opinion about volatility instead of the term structure.

It is important that the future direction of asset pricing research focus on heterogeneous beliefs about volatility. As the discussion in Chapters 15, 16 and 23 emphasizes, the behavioral explanation for the oscillating SDF estimated in the empirical work of Aït-Sahalia and Lo (2000) and Rosenberg and Engle (2002) stems from the joint distribution of errors in respect to both first and second moments. In this regard, the situation depicted in Figures 16.1 and 16.2 reflects the interactions between overconfident bulls and underconfident bears.

The assumption of heterogeneous beliefs about volatility presents issues for continuous time models. In the diffusion models described in Sections 31.1 and 31.2, volatility is constant, and all investors agree about its value. Because of the Girsanov Theorem, the use of equivalent measures in a continuous time approach is problematic for modeling heterogeneous beliefs about volatility. In this regard, the discrete time methods developed in this book might be better suited to studying the impact of disagreement about volatility.

Jouini and Napp (2006) develop a discrete time version of their continuous time approach, in which they focus on the impact of pessimism and overconfidence on asset prices. Notably, they model overconfidence as a shift in probability weight between the tails and the middle of the distribution. As in Chapter 15, this approach to overconfidence involves beliefs about volatility.

The key economic issues which Jouini and Napp address in their work are behavioral. For example, Jouini and Napp (2006) extends the representative investor models of Cecchetti, Lam and Mark (2000) and Abel (2002) by demonstrating how pessimistic sentiment emerges as an aggregate of the pessimistic beliefs of individual investors. They demonstrate that relative to zero sentiment, pessimistic sentiment leads to a higher market price of risk and a lower risk free rate. They also demonstrate that a positive correlation between risk tolerance and pessimism induces a higher market price of risk. In complementary work, Jouini and Napp (2007b) study the correlation between risk tolerance and pessimism, while Ben Mansour, Jouini, and Napp (2006) report experimental evidence supporting pessimistic beliefs in an *i.i.d.* setting.

Wealth shifts resulting from trade can lead to stochastic return volatility, just as they can lead to stochastic risk aversion and stochastic time preference. See Chapter 14. Stochastic volatility is a key feature in the jump process model described in Section 31.3. The focus of attention in that model is time variation in the premium per unit of risk, as reflected in the risk-neutral process. Bakshi-Wu's analysis reports that this premium declined and turned negative during the bubble period.

The pricing kernel in Bakshi-Wu has the form $\exp(-rt)\exp(L)$, where r is a time invariant instantaneous rate of interest and L is a linear combination of the components in (31.11). This form is neoclassical, and can capture the impact of sentiment on risk premiums without modeling sentiment directly. The risk-neutral pricing method effectively captures positive risk premiums by replacing the objective density Π with a density that reflects more pessimism; that is, by shifting probability mass to more unfavorable outcomes. Negative risk premiums are captured by replacing the objective density Π with a density that reflects more optimism. Equation (21.2) illustrates the application of risk-neutral pricing to options.

By decomposing returns into diffusion and jump components, Bakshi-Wu move in the direction of an oscillating SDF as depicted in Figure 31.1, where bullish investors largely impact the shape of the SDF in the region of high returns and bearish investors impact the shape of the SDF in the region of low returns. In their model, diffusion risk and the risk associated with the two jump processes are priced separately. However, their analysis does not model sentiment directly. It is important for the future direction of asset pricing research that models formally incorporate sentiment. This will permit the study of whether, for example, the shape of the SDF changed during the bubble period in the manner depicted in Figure 31.1.

The earlier discussion in the book discusses how sentiment impacts the risk-neutral density. In particular, equations (21.1) and (23.1) describe the structure of a behavioral risk-neutral density which directly incorporates the impact of sentiment. The discussion in Sections 16.3.3 and 23.4 points out that if sentiment is an omitted variable, its impact will largely be reflected through the variables capturing risk aversion. In particular, the impact of irrational exuberance will be captured as low aversion to risk, which can cross over into the negative domain (risk-seeking). In addition, the discussion in Chapters 20 and 21 pointed out that the presence of sentiment renders the term structure of interest rates stochastic, which of course includes the instantaneous rate. It is important that the future direction of asset pricing research incorporate the impact of sentiment on the joint dynamics of the term structure and volatility.

Models that permit SDF processes of the sort depicted in Figure 31.1 feature heterogeneous beliefs about volatility. The SDF processes in the models described in Sections 31.1 and 31.2 tend to be simpler than those depicted in Figure 31.1. For example, consider the model described in Section 31.2. At a given moment in time, the noise trader will almost surely commit an error, and be either excessively optimistic or excessively pessimistic. As a result, the representative investor will be either excessively optimistic or excessively pessimistic. Pretty much ruled out are more complex situations that result in SDF functions which are either U-shaped or feature oscillations.

Another way of making the last point is to note that in typical asset pricing models a Radon-Nikodym derivative has log-linear structure. That is, the logarithm of the Radon-Nikodym derivative is linear. Figures 15.2 and 15.3 serve as examples. However, Figures 15.4 through 15.8 illustrate Radon-Nikodym measures that are both more complex and more realistic. It is important that future research in asset pricing focus on Radon-Nikodym derivatives whose logarithms are both nonlinear and more realistic.

A related issue with the model developed in Section 31.2 is that it focuses on interactions between only two types of investors, one being a noise trader and the other, holding objectively correct beliefs. This structure involves two unrealistic assumptions. The first assumption is that noise traders commit only one type of error. This rules out the more complex U-shaped SDF functions.

The second assumption is that there exist investors who hold objectively correct beliefs. This assumption is common in the behavioral finance literature. See Shefrin and Statman (1994) and Shleifer (2000). To be sure, some investors are smarter than others. However, the notion that there exists an investor with objectively correct beliefs is extreme. Indeed, most of the arguments in this book do not rely on the existence of an investor with objectively correct beliefs. Instead, the issues of interest are how asset prices are set when all investors are prone to erroneous judgments, with some errors being more serious than others. It is important that the future direction of behavioral asset pricing focus on the impact of different investor error processes rather than the interaction between noise traders and investors who hold objectively correct beliefs.

Turning to a different issue, consider heterogeneity in investors' degree of risk aversion and time preference. The main theorems developed in this book apply to the case of heterogeneous risk aversion for CRRA utility and heterogeneous time preference. In contrast, the models described in Sections 31.1 and 31.2 assume homogeneous risk tolerance in the case of CRRA utility, and homogeneous time preference.

Notably, the models described in Sections 31.1 and 31.2 feature expected utility maximizing investors. However, Part VII of the book surveys evidence and implications stemming from behavioral preferences. It is important that the future direction of asset pricing research focus on behavioral preferences as well as behavioral beliefs.

31.5 Summary

This chapter has focused on three contributions that advance the application of continuous time stochastic models to behavioral asset pricing theory. These contributions establish that key results in the discrete time framework extend to continuous time.

Section 31.1 discusses a continuous time model featuring a single Brownian motion. Section 31.2 discusses the implications of adding a second Brownian motion to capture the introduction of a public signal. Section 31.3 discusses the application of a mixed diffusion-jump process model to study the dynamics of the premium for risk around the bubble period. Finally, Section 31.4 discusses some subtle issues involving the restrictions in some of the assumptions used in these models.

32
Conclusion

Traditional asset pricing theory and behavioral asset pricing theory share a common framework. The stochastic discount factor (SDF) constitutes the core concept in both approaches. The features that distinguish the two approaches are the differing assumptions and results.

Traditional asset pricing theory assumes that prices are set as if investors hold correct beliefs about the underlying stochastic process governing returns, and have preferences that conform to expected utility theory. In contrast, behavioral asset pricing theory assumes that investors are subject to systematic psychologically induced errors, and have preferences that violate the assumptions of expected utility theory.

32.1   Recapitulating the Main Points

The behavioral decision literature identifies a rich set of systematic errors to which people are vulnerable. Of these, the most important for asset pricing theory is representativeness. Chapters 6 and 7 present empirical evidence relating to the impact of representativeness on investors. Representativeness induces naive individual investors to succumb to extrapolation bias, and predict unwarranted continuation. Representativeness induces experienced professional investors to succumb to gambler's fallacy, and predict unwarranted reversals. Overconfidence amplifies representativeness-based errors, and also induces investors to underestimate risk.

A common finding in behavioral studies is that people are heterogeneous. People hold different beliefs, differ in their tolerance for risk, and differ in their levels of patience. These differences can be important and affect both prices and trading volume. Individual differences are typically large.

Representativeness causes heterogeneity to have a time-varying structure. The extent to which investors disagree has a predictable component. Differences of opinion widen after extreme market movements. Notably, changes in the heterogeneity have implications for volume as well as pricing.

If there is a central concept in the book, it is sentiment. Sentiment is a stochastic process that describes the overall market error. Sentiment sometimes has a simple structure, as when investors are uniformly optimistic or pessimistic. However, when investors exhibit considerable heterogeneity, sentiment is typically complex.

If there is a central result in the book, it is that the log-SDF decomposes into the sum of a fundamental component and a sentiment component. When sentiment is zero, prices reflect fundamentals alone. When sentiment is nonzero, the prices of some assets deviate from their fundamental values.

Theoretically, a behavioral SDF can assume a variety of shapes. If all investors are irrationally exuberant, the SDF is upward sloping. If all investors are unduly pessimistic, the SDF is downward sloping. If some investors are irrationally exuberant and other investors are unduly pessimistic, the SDF typically has a shape that features oscillation. Possible shapes are a sine wave with negative trend, a U, and an inverted U.

Behavioral asset pricing theory does not predict a single shape for the SDF. Rather, the theory predicts a relationship between the distribution of investors' errors and the shape of the SDF. For example, the theory predicts that if investors cluster per their beliefs into optimists and pessimists, with the optimists underestimating volatility and the pessimists overestimating volatility, then the shape of the SDF will resemble a sine wave with negative trend. The theory also predicts that if sentiment is time varying, then the SDF will also be time varying.

Empirical studies conclude that during the period 1991–1995, the SDF was not a monotone declining function, as neoclassical theory would suggest, but instead was an oscillating function. This finding is consistent with the empirical evidence pertaining to investors' errors during this period. The predictions of institutional investors featured unwarranted reversals, downward-biased estimates of returns, and upward-biased estimates of volatility. The predictions of individual investors featured the opposite patterns.

The log-SDF decomposition theorem is one of several decomposition results in the book. All the decomposition results stem from a single theorem, Theorem 14.1, which establishes the characteristics of a representative investor who sets equilibrium prices. The risk premium decomposition theorem establishes that the risk premium associated with each asset is the sum of a fundamental component and a sentiment premium. The beta decomposition theorem establishes that the beta of each asset is the sum of a fundamental component and a sentiment component. The return to a mean-variance efficient portfolio decomposes into a fundamental component and a sentiment component. In this respect, the shape of a behavioral mean-variance return function oscillates, reflecting the oscillation in the SDF.

Nonzero sentiment generates asset pricing patterns that are different than the case when sentiment is zero. Nonzero sentiment introduces additional volatility into asset prices, affects the slope of the yield curve, induces smile patterns in the implied volatility function for options, and alters the character of the mean-variance frontier that underlies systematic risk. In this respect, sentiment appears to manifest itself within cross-sectional returns through a factor structure. This structure expresses itself through coskewness with the market portfolio. Indeed when sentiment is U-shaped and the SDF is approximately quadratic, the factors correspond to the market portfolio and the squared market portfolio.

To repeat a point made in the introduction, there is a unified thread in the examples presented in Chapters 15 through 23, one that has sentiment as its core. The oscillating shape of the sentiment function underlies the oscillating structure of the mean-variance efficient frontier discussed in Chapter 20, the fat-tailed character of risk-neutral density functions discussed in Chapter 21, and the downward-sloping smile patterns in the implied volatility functions for index options discussed in Chapter 21. In other words, these features are different facets of a single sentiment-based theory, not a disparate collection of unrelated phenomena.

Option markets are important to the study of the SDF, in that options can be combined to produce positions that approximate state claims. In this regard, there is a growing body of work aimed at identifying behavioral features in option prices. The most important application of option data for the approach in this book is the estimate of the empirical SDF. However, option prices also reflect traditional proxies for sentiment and behavioral biases such as gambler's fallacy.

Asset pricing theory features puzzles such as the equity premium puzzle, interest rate puzzle, volatility puzzle, and violation of the expectations hypothesis for the term structure of interest rates. Typically, asset pricing theorists seek to explain these puzzles within models that assume that investors hold correct beliefs. The present approach suggests that at least part of the explanation for the features that underlie these puzzles stems from investor errors.

Behavioral asset pricing theorists have proposed explanations for some of the puzzles, especially the equity premium puzzle. These explanations are based on prospect theory, rather than investor errors. At this stage there is no reason to assume that a full explanation of the equity premium will rest on only one behavioral dimension (that is, prospect theory), rather than a combination of preference effects and investor errors.

Prices adjust as investors alter the holdings in their portfolios. Prospect theory (like other behavioral choice theories) suggests that investors will hold different portfolios than the portfolios associated with traditional mean-variance theory. Behavioral portfolios are typically undiversified and bipolar, featuring a mix of very safe and very risky securities.

Prospect theory also affects the manner in which investors alter their portfolios in reaction to events. Notably, prospect theory induces investors to sell their winners more quickly than their losers. This behavior appears to affect asset prices by inducing a momentum effect.

The behavioral framework developed in this book does not bring closure to the implications of behavioral finance for asset pricing. There is much work to be done in studying the nature of the SDF from the perspective of multiple markets, not just the S&P 500. Indeed, the empirical findings from studies of option markets suggest the existence of arbitrage opportunities, which are after all inconsistent with pricing in terms of an SDF.

32.2   Current and Future Directions

The ideas in this book are intended to describe new approaches to thinking about asset prices, not resolution to all the puzzles in asset pricing, let alone closure to a debate.

The framework presented here is but one stage in a process. The point is that progress is made through refinement, modification, and extension. The behavioral asset pricing framework presented in this book is an extension of the traditional approach. The behavioral SDF is an extension of the traditional SDF. Future work should refine, modify, and extend the framework presented in this book. For example, studies might examine the relationship between investor errors and the shape of the SDF in other markets and other time periods than those discussed in the book. The model might be modified to incorporate multiple mental accounts and incomplete markets.

32.2.1   Issues Involving Investor Benefits

The most important new concept in the book is the stochastic process for sentiment, and its role as a component of the SDF. Some traditional neoclassical asset pricing theorists, such as Cecchetti, Lam and Mark (2000) and Abel (2002), have incorporated behavioral elements into SDF-based models. However, historically most have been reluctant to introduce sentiment into their models. Some, as typified by Jackwerth (2004), maintain the assumption of a representative investor with rational expectations.

Others, such as Detemple–Murthy (1994), Basak (2000), and Weinbaum (2001), introduce heterogeneous beliefs into their models, but stop short of attributing the heterogeneity to investor errors. In addition, they tend to use the weakest notion of market efficiency, namely the absence of risk-free arbitrage. In contrast, proponents of behavioral finance favor defining market efficiency as the coincidence of market prices and fundamental values.

A key message in this book for traditional asset pricing theorists is that they should begin to incorporate explicit sentiment stochastic processes into their models. In doing so, traditional asset pricing theorists should be careful to remember the lessons about aggregation: The market error may not bear a close likeness to those of any of the individual investors. That is, sentiment is an amalgam.

A major message of the book is that the future of asset pricing research involves the introduction of behavioral assumptions into the traditional SDF framework. Since the publication of the first edition of this book, a number of neoclassical asset pricing theorists have indeed begun to develop models which incorporate behavioral assumptions. Chapter 31 surveys three important contributions along these lines. Notably, all three contributions involve continuous time methods.

The last part of Chapter 31 suggests important future directions for the application of continuous time behavioral asset pricing models. Chapter 31 mentioned extending the assumptions about investor heterogeneity to reflect different degrees of relative risk aversion, introducing disagreement about underlying volatility, and incorporating behavioral preferences.

The opportunities to apply behavioral concepts and techniques to asset pricing are rich. An example of future research involves identifying the projection of sentiment for individual assets, such as stocks. Another example is to study whether during the first decade of the 21st century the Chinese equity market and the U.S. real estate market experienced bubbles. Examples of future research on bubbles might involve estimating the time series for market risk premiums (as in the study of the Nasdaq 100 by Bakshi and Wu [2006]), and the investigation of trading by investment professionals, (as in the study by Brunnermeier and Nagel [2004] of hedge fund strategies during the Nasdaq bubble).

32.2.2   Issues Involving Behavioral Preferences

The discussion in Chapter 25 suggests that SP/A theory is well suited to serve as the basis for behavioral preferences. It is solidly grounded in the psychology literature, well structured from a modeling perspective, and leads to hypotheses about portfolio selection for which there is support in the empirical literature.

Chapter 25 points out that SP/A theory has important advantages over prospect theory. One advantage concerns the issue of aspiration. Chapter 25 describes experimental evidence which indicates that prospect theory fails to capture the aspiration component of SP/A theory. In addition, the formal structure of SP/A theory is more convenient for modeling purposes than that of prospect theory. However, readers should not jump to the conclusion that these points imply that prospect theory is to be abandoned entirely. Rather, the idea is to understand prospect theory's weak points, and work around them.

Historically, prospect theory has served as the basis for the behavioral approach to investor preferences. In this respect, prospect theory has many rich features. It proposes a reference point from which gains and losses are measured and emphasizes that gains and losses are the carriers of value, not wealth. It emphasizes that because of psychophysics, the value function will have the shape of an S and the weighting function will have the shape of an inverse S. Prospect theory also features a property known as loss aversion: At the origin, the value function is more steeply sloped in the domain of losses than in the domain of gains. In addition, prospect theory proposes that people engage in editing, a process featuring mental accounting (or narrow framing).

The first edition of this book suggested that at least one feature of prospect theory is highly unrealistic. Theorem 26.1 establishes that the convex shape of the value function in the domain of losses will lead investors to expose themselves to severe boundary risk in states where they incur losses. In particular, prospect theory implies that investors will choose to hold positive claims in at most one loss state. Their claims in all other loss states will be zero.

Over time, scholars have raised a number of issues about prospect theory. In their paper introducing the disposition effect, Shefrin and Statman (1985) point out that by itself, prospect theory is incapable of explaining why individual investors fail to implement an optimal tax-loss selling strategy. Using a two-period model, Hens and Vlcek (2005) point out that prospect theory cannot jointly explain why investors would both purchase a stock and subsequently exhibit the disposition effect. Using a multiperiod model, Barberis–Xiong (2006) develop conditions for prospect theory preferences to generate disposition effect behavior. They emphasize that under quite reasonable conditions, prospect theory does not imply the disposition effect.

The disposition effect has been the most actively researched behavioral phenomenon involving the trading activity of individual and professional investors. The empirical evidence documenting the strength of the disposition effect is significant, robust, and beyond dispute. Therefore, if there is a conflict between prospect theory and the empirical evidence pertaining to the disposition effect, it is prospect theory that comes out the loser.

The analysis in Barberis–Xiong indicates that prospect theory is at odds with broader features of real-world investor behavior. In calibrating the parameter values of their model, Barberis–Xiong use estimates reported in Tversky–Kahneman (1992). The heart of the Barberis–Xiong analysis involves a prospect theory investor making partial adjustments to highly leveraged positions. There are two features here, one pertaining to leveraged positions, and the other pertaining to partial adjustments. Both features are unrealistic.

First, most real-world investors do not hold leveraged positions. Margin debt as a function of the value of stock outstanding is typically around 1.5 percent. The ratio reached a recent peak during the dot-com bubble, but this peak did not exceed 3 percent. Second, most individual investors sell entire positions, not partial positions. In this respect, approximately three quarters of the transactions in Odean (1998) involve the sale of entire positions, as opposed to partial positions.

Despite its weaknesses, prospect theory encapsulates the complex nature of attitude towards risk. A key feature of prospect theory is its articulation of a four-fold pattern in respect to risk attitude. The typical pattern involves risk aversion in the domain of gains and risk seeking in the domain of losses. However, when very small probabilities of extreme events are involved, the pattern might reverse: risk seeking in the domain of gains and risk aversion in the domain of losses. In terms of the latter pattern, Barberis and Huang (2007) apply the small probability overweighting feature of prospect theory to study the preference for skewness. Although Barberis–Huang address many of the issues discussed in Chapters 17, 23, 25, and 28, they miss some of the key connections to the existing behavioral literature on the preference for skewed portfolio returns and lottery stocks.

Kahneman and Tversky developed prospect theory in an attempt to reconcile a collection of empirical observations such as the four-fold pattern for attitude towards risk. It is important to distinguish between the general empirical patterns and a theory that was developed in order to explain those patterns. The patterns are documented. The theory is another matter, in that some of its implications are contradicted by evidence. As noted above, the predictions of prospect theory are at odds with the empirical evidence in respect to boundary solutions, the disposition effect, the reluctance to hold leveraged positions, and the tendency to trade whole positions. As was discussed in Chapters 24 and 25, prospect theory also fails to capture the effect of altering the probability of achieving an aspiration level.

In contrast to prospect theory, SP/A theory is tailor made to deal with aspiration issues and the preference for skewness. When used in conjunction with concave utility, SP/A solutions avoid the boundary solution property. In addition, choice based on SP/A preferences can be structured as a constrained CRRA maximization. As a result, the CRRA approach developed in the book extends naturally to accommodate behavioral preferences. The extension to accommodate prospect theory is more involved. Prospect theory features two weighting functions, not one, convex utility in the domain of losses, and a kink at the origin of the value function.

With its dual focus on fear and hope, SP/A theory provides important insights into why investors' portfolios feature bipolarity, combining very safe and very risky securities. In this regard, SP/A theory explains the attraction of structured products, premium bonds, lottery bonds, and lottery stocks. At the same time, it is important to understand that like prospect theory, SP/A theory does not fully explain the disposition effect. This is because SP/A theory does not involve regret and self-control, two key determinants of the disposition effect. In addition, the reluctance to use direct leverage and the tendency to liquidate entire positions also relates to features outside SP/A theory.

There are many potential avenues for future research involving the application of SP/A theory to portfolio choice. Among these are developing frameworks which combine SP/A features with other psychological phenomena, and identifying dynamic solutions when aspiration levels are endogenous.

32.2.3   Issues Involving Behavioral Beliefs and Behavioral Preferences

The approach presented in this book represents a unified behavioral approach to asset pricing, featuring both behavioral beliefs and behavioral preferences. The key result in the book is that in the presence of either or both features, the log-SDF can be decomposed into sentiment and a fundamental component. In this respect, sentiment is a function that explains how prices deviate from a neoclassical market in which all investors have correct beliefs and expected utility maximizing preferences (involving power utility).

A key message in this book for behavioral asset pricing theorists is that they should develop SDF-based models that explicitly incorporate the manner in which markets aggregate investor errors and preferences. Behavioral asset pricing theorists are prone to build representative investor models that do incorporate sentiment. See Barberis, Shleifer, and Vishny (1998). However, the representative investor in these models does not aggregate heterogeneity across the investor population. Instead these behavioral representative investors commit typical errors identified in the behavioral decision literature. The point of developing the concept of sentiment as a stochastic process is to capture the complexities generated by the coexistence of different behavioral errors on the part of the investing public. A key message for behavioral asset pricing theorists is that they should begin to incorporate into their models sentiment stochastic processes that reflect multiple coexisting investor errors.

Behavioral asset pricing theorists are also prone to build representative investor models where the representative investor has prospect theory preferences and holds objectively correct beliefs. The papers by Barberis and Huang (2007) and Barberis and Xiong (2006) serve as examples. This approach is subject to the same general criticism as building representative investor models featuring typical errors. It misses the impact of how market prices aggregate investor heterogeneity. In addition, the approach treats sentiment as being zero, thereby by failing to capture the interactions between behavioral errors and behavioral preferences.

Coskewness and skewness feature prominently in behavioral asset pricing. Chapter 17 points out conditions under which sentiment leads coskewness to emerge as a priced risk factor. Notably, the pricing of coskewness is reflected in the shape of the SDF function. Chapters 25 and 28 discuss why both behavioral preferences and behavioral beliefs underlie the preference for skewness. As was discussed in Chapter 28, although coskewness and skewness might relate to each other, they are distinct concepts.

Some pricing effects are driven largely by investor errors. Other pricing effects are driven largely by investor preferences. Yet other pricing effects are driven by a combination of both errors and preferences. The early debate between proponents of market efficiency and proponents of behavioral finance focused on the role of investor errors.

Statman (1999) predicted that future debates would focus on preferences. One of the most compelling aspects of his article is a discussion about value expressive investing. Future research will study the role of value expressiveness in terms of both portfolio selection and asset pricing. Statman emphasizes that many investors hold stocks that are consistent with their values. Socially responsible investing is a prime example of value expressive investing; however, it is not the only example. Some investors might invest in technology stocks because of what their decisions say about their values.

Statman draws an analogy between the stocks people buy in their role as individual investors and the watches they buy in their role as consumers. He suggests that functionally speaking, an inexpensive watch will tell time just as well as a very expensive watch. However, many people buy very expensive watches, for the signal the watch sends about their demographic characteristics. In addition to telling time, the watches they wear serve as conspicuous consumption. Statman suggests that investors behave in similar ways when they purchase assets. In addition to generating returns, the assets they hold can also serve as conspicuous consumption. Fama–French (2004) develop a model that features heterogeneous beliefs, explicit investor errors, and nontraditional preferences. Fama–French suggest that it might not be possible to disentangle the effects of preferences from the effects of errors. This issue generally applies to models that feature both behavioral beliefs and behavioral preferences. For example, SP/A theory models the emotion of hope as if it were optimism. Doing so raises the question of how to distinguish between hope and true optimism? I suggest that disentangling the effects is possible, by making use of the growing evidence about the systematic structure of investor errors. That is the main general point made in Chapters 6 and 7.

Historically, those who work in traditional asset pricing have tended to mistrust evidence that derives from surveys. However, some of the evidence about ex ante expectations comes from analysts and strategists whose predictions are a part of their professional responsibilities. This evidence clearly identifies errors consistent with representativeness.

One of the main areas where behavioral preference arguments have been advanced is in attempting to explain the equity premium puzzle. As was mentioned in Chapter 30, the equity premium puzzle might well reflect a combination of investor errors and investor preferences. In this respect, Barberis–Huang–Santos (2001) put forward a behavioral explanation based only on preferences, applying prospect theory to explain the puzzle.

There is one feature in Barberis–Huang–Santos (2001) that merits special attention. These authors assume that the state prices underlying SDF used to price bonds is different from the SDF used to price stocks. The basis for their assumption is that prospect theory affects transaction utility for stocks but not for bonds. This is an important assumption, one that could be a significant feature in future models. Notably, the assumption implies that prices might not be efficient even according to the weak definition of no risk-free arbitrage. As discussed in Chapters 22 and 23, evidence suggests that index option prices frequently violate the assumption that all options are priced in accordance with a common risk-neutral density function.

Future work might well develop the idea of multiple SDF functions that reflect psychic components of utility. Such developments naturally lead into models that feature incomplete markets. The models developed in this book all assume market completeness. There is a large literature on the economics of the second-best, establishing that economists' intuition often fails when markets are incomplete. For an example involving the entropy concept discussed in Chapters 11 and 16, see Blume–Easley (2004).

32.3   Final Comments

I have the same message for traditional neoclassical asset pricing theorists as for behavioral asset pricing theorists. The future of asset pricing theory lies in bringing together the powerful SDF-based tools favored by neoclassical theorists with the psychologically based assumptions favored by behavioral theorists.

I remind asset pricing theorists about two related issues. The first issue involves recognizing the degree of investor heterogeneity that is typical of real-world markets. When it comes to beliefs, investors widely disagree with one another. As the discussion in Chapter 6 about Ivo Welch's surveys demonstrates, even financial economists express widely different opinions about the future equity premium. In fact, those surveys show that even asset pricing theorists express widely different opinions.

The second issue pertains to the representative investor. Heterogeneity is typically incompatible with the existence of representative investor who shares the features of some average investor in the market. This statement applies equally to neoclassical expected utility maximizing investors who are error free as to behavioral investors with prospect theory value functions, SP/A utility, decision weighting functions, and erroneous beliefs.

My point is that asset pricing theorists of both stripes, neoclassical and behavioral, need to consider abandoning the common representative investor assumption. Instead they need to replace that assumption with a representative investor whose characteristics reflect the manner in which market prices aggregate heterogeneity. This means building models in which equilibrium prices aggregate probability density functions as Hölder averages. It means building models in which the representative investor's coefficient of relative risk aversion is stochastic. It means building models in which the representative investor's time discount factor is nonexponential.

In building models involving a representative investor with exotic characteristics, the objective is not to generate behavioral equilibria with peculiar features. The direction of causality is not from the representative investor to equilibrium prices. It is the other way around. The representative investor is simply a device for helping to understand the character of equilibrium prices.

Modern asset pricing theory is built on an SDF-foundation. John Cochrane's (2001) excellent book *Asset Pricing* has transformed the way that asset pricing is taught around the world. Behavioral asset pricing theorists have tended to build their models outside the SDF framework as if the SDF framework is neoclassical and therefore incompatible with behavioral phenomena. The point of this book is to demonstrate that the SDF framework is flexible enough and rich enough to accommodate behavioral phenomena.

My last point also applies to neoclassical asset pricing theorists who believe that the SDF framework is only for neoclassical assumptions. As fine a book as John Cochrane's is, virtually all of the assumptions he makes are neoclassical. Those assumptions are overly restrictive. For example, consider the theorem that the maximum Sharpe ratio in the market is bounded above by the coefficient of variation of the SDF. The variation in a neoclassical SDF stems from fundamentals alone. As a result, the neoclassical SDF does not exhibit the volatility necessary to explain the high Sharpe ratios we observe in real markets. In contrast, a behavioral SDF can be much more volatile than its neoclassical counterpart. This is because a behavioral SDF is the sum of its neoclassical counterpart and sentiment. If there is one thing we should know from financial market history, it is that sentiment can be highly volatile.

In summary, where does the future of asset pricing lie? It lies in a union that marries the SDF framework favored by neoclassical asset pricing theorists and the behavioral assumptions favored by behavioral theorists.

References

Abel, A., 1988. "Stock Prices Under Time Varying Dividend Risk, An Exact Solution in an Infinite-Horizon General Equilibrium Model," *Journal of Monetary Economics*, 22, 375–393.

Abel, A., 2002. "An Exploration of the Effects of Pessimism and Doubt on Asset Returns," *Journal of Economic Dynamics and Control*, 26, 7–8, 1075–1092.

Aït-Sahalia, Y., and A. Lo, 2000. "Nonparametric Risk Management and Implied Risk Aversion," *Journal of Econometrics*, 94, 9–51.

Allais, M., 1953. "Le Comportement de L'homme Rationnel Devant le Risque: Critique des Postulats et Axiomes de L'ecole Americane," *Econometrica*, 21, 503–546.

Allais, M., 1979. "The Foundations of a Positive Theory of Choice Involving Risk and a Criticism of the Postulates and Axioms of the American School." In M. Allais and O. Hagen (eds.), *Expected Utility Hypotheses and the Allais Paradox*, Dordrecht: Reidel (original work published 1952), 27–145.

Allen, F., and D. Gale, 1987. "Optimal Security Design," *Review of Financial Studies*, 1, 229–263.

Andersen, T., L. Benzoni, and J. Lund, 2002. "An Empirical Investigation of Continuous-Time Equity Return Models," *The Journal of Finance*, Vol. 57, No. 2, 1239–1284.

Anderson, E., E. Ghysels, and J. Juergens, 2005. "Do Heterogeneous Beliefs Matter for Asset Pricing?" *Review of Financial Studies*, 18, 875–924.

Anginer, D., K. Fisher, and M. Statman, 2007. "Stocks of Admired Companies and Despised Ones," Working paper, Santa Clara University.

Arrow, K. J., and F. H. Hahn, 1971. *General Competitive Analysis*, San Francisco: Holden-Day, Inc.

Arzac, E., 1974. "Utility Analysis of Chance-Constrained," *Journal of Financial and Quantitative Analysis*, Vol. IX, No. 6, 993–1007.

Arzac, E., and V. Bawa, 1977. "Portfolio Choice and Equilibrium in Capital Markets with Safety-First Investors," *Journal of Financial Economics*, 4, 277–288.

Backus, D., S. Foresi, A. Mozumdar, and L. Wu, 1997. "Predictable Changes in Yields and Forward Rates," Working paper, Stern School of Business, New York University.

Baker, M., and J. Wurgler, 2006. "Investor Sentiment and the Cross-Section of Stock Returns," *Journal of Finance*, 61, 1645–1680.

Baker, M., and J. Wurgler, 2007. "Investor Sentiment in the Stock Market," *Journal of Economics Perspectives*, 21, 2, 129–151.

Bakshi, G., C. Cao, and Z. Chen, 1997. "Empirical Performance of Alternative Option Pricing Models," *Journal of Finance*, 52, 2003–2049.

Bakshi, G., and L. Wu, 2006. "Investor Irrationality and the Nasdaq Bubble," Working paper, University of Maryland.

Balduzzi, P., E. Elton, and T. Green, 2001. "Economic News and the Yield Curve: Evidence from the U.S. Treasury Market." *Journal of Financial and Quantitative Analysis*, 36, 523–543.

Bange, M., 2000. "Do the Portfolios of Small Investors Reflect Positive Feedback Trading?" *Journal of Financial and Quantitative Analysis*, 35(2), 239–255.

Bange, M., and T. Miller, 2004. "Return Momentum and Global Portfolio Allocations," *Journal of Empirical Finance*, Vol. 11, No. 4, 429–459.

Barber, B., R. Lehavy, M. McNichols, and B. Trueman, 2001. "Can Investors Profit from the Prophets? Security Analyst Recommendations and Stock Returns," *Journal of Finance*, 56, 2, 531–563.

Barber, B., and T. Odean, 2008. "All That Glitters: The Effect of Attention and News on the Buying Behavior of Individual and Institutional Investors," *The Review of Financial Studies*, 21, 785–818.

Barber, B., and T. Odean, 2000a. "Too Many Cooks Spoil the Profits: The Performance of Investment Clubs," *Financial Analyst Journal*, January/February, 17–25.

Barber, B., and T. Odean, 2000b. "Trading Is Hazardous to Your Wealth: The Common Stock Investment Performance of Individual Investors," *Journal of Finance*, 55, 2, 773–806.

Barber, B., T. Odean, and N. Zhu, 2006. "Do Noise Traders Move Markets?" Working paper, University of California.

Barber, B. M., Y-T. Lee, Y-J. Liu, and T. Odean, 2006. "Is the Aggregate Investor Reluctant to Realize Losses? Evidence from Taiwan," Working paper, Graduate School of Management, University of California, Davis.

Barberis, N., and M. Huang, forthcoming. "Stocks as Lotteries: The Implications of Probability Weighting for Security Prices." *American Economic Review*.

Barberis, N., M. Huang, and T. Santos, 2001. "Prospect Theory and Asset Prices," *Quarterly Journal of Economics*, 116, 1, 1–53.

Barberis, N., A. Shleifer, and R. Vishny, 1998. "A Model of Investor Sentiment," *Journal of Financial Economics*, 49, 3, 307–344.

Barberis, N., and R. Thaler, 2003. "A Survey of Behavioral Finance." In G. Constantinides, M. Harris, and R. Stulz (eds.), *Handbook of the Economics of Finance* (Vol. 1, part 2, 1052–1090). Amsterdam: North-Holland.

Barberis, N., and W. Xiong. 2006. "What Drives the Disposition Effect? An Analysis of a Long-Standing Preference-Based Explanation," *Journal of Finance*.

Barsky, R., F. T. Juster, M. Kimball, and M. Shapiro, 1997. "Preference Parameters and Behavioral Heterogeneity: An Experimental Approach in the Health and Retirement Survey," *Quarterly Journal of Economics*, 107, 537–579.

Basak, S., 2000. "A Model of Dynamic Equilibrium Asset Pricing with Heterogeneous Beliefs and Extraneous Risk," *Journal of Economic Dynamics and Control*, 24, 63–95.

Basak, S., 2005. "Asset Pricing with Heterogeneous Beliefs," *Journal of Banking and Finance*, 29, 2849–2881.

Bates, D., 1991. "The Crash of '87: Was It Expected? The Evidence from Options Markets," *Journal of Finance*, 46, 1009–1044.

Bates, D., 1996. "Testing Option Pricing Models." In G. S. Maddala and C. R. Rao (eds.), *Statistical Methods in Finance/Handbook of Statistics* (567–611). Amsterdam: Elsevier.

Bates, D., 2000. "Post-'87 Crash Fears in S&P 500 Futures Options," *Journal of Econometrics*, 94, 181–238.

Becker, J., and R. Sarin, 1987. "Lottery Dependent Utility," *Management Science*, 33, 1367–1382.

Beja, A., 1978. "State Preference and the Riskless Interest Rate: A Markov Model of Capital Markets," *Review of Economic Studies*, 46, 435–446.

Bell, D. E., 1982. "Regret in Decision Making Under Uncertainty," *Operations Research*, 30, 961–981.

Benartzi, S., and R. Thaler, 1995. "Myopic Loss Aversion and the Equity Premium Puzzle," *Quarterly Journal of Economics*, 110.1, 73–92.

Ben Mansour, S., E. Jouini, and C. Napp, 2006. "Is There a 'Pessimistic Bias' in Individual Beliefs? Evidence from a Simple Survey," Working paper, Université Paris Dauphine.

Benninga, S., and J. Mayshar, 1993. "Dynamic Wealth Redistribution, Trade, and Asset Pricing." Working paper 8–93, Wharton School.

Benninga, S., and J. Mayshar, 2000. "Heterogeneity and Option Pricing," *Review of Derivatives Research*, 4, 1, 7–27.

Benninga, S., and A. Protopapadakis, 1983. "Real and Nominal Interest Rates Under Uncertainty: The Fisher Theorem and the Term Structure," *Journal of Political Economy*, 91, 5, 856–867.

Bick, A., 1987. "On the Consistency of the Black–Scholes Model with a General Equilibrium Framework," *Journal of Financial and Quantitative Analysis*, 22, 3, 259–275.

Black, F., 1986. "Noise," *Journal of Finance*, 41, 3, 529–543.

Blackburn, D., and A. Ukhov, 2006a. "Estimating Preferences Toward Risk: Evidence from Dow Jones," Working paper, Indiana University.

Blackburn, D., and A. Ukhov, 2006b. "Equilibrium Risk Premia for Risk Seekers," Working paper, Indiana University.

Blume, L., and D. Easley, 1992. "Evolution and Market Behavior," *Journal of Economic Theory*, 58, 1, 9–40.

Blume, L., and D. Easley, 2004. "If You're So Smart, Why Aren't You Rich? Belief Selection in Complete and Incomplete Markets." Working paper, Cornell University.

Bollen, N., and R. Whaley, 2004. "Does Net Buying Pressure Affect the Shape of Implied Volatility Functions?" *Journal of Finance*, 59, 711–753.

Bondarenko, O., 2001. "On Market Efficiency and Joint Hypothesis." Working paper, University of Illinois at Chicago.

Boyer, B., T. Mitton, and K. Vorkink, 2008. "Expected Idiosyncratic Skewness," Working paper, Brigham Young University.

Brav, A., and J. B. Heaton, 2002. "Competing Theories of Financial Anomalies," *Review of Economic Studies*, 15, 2, 575–606.

Brav, A., R. Lehavy, and Roni Michaely, 2005. "Using Expectations to Test Asset Pricing Models," *Financial Management*, 34(3), 31–64.

Breeden, D., and R. Litzenberger, 1978. "Prices of State-Contingent Claims Implicit in Option Prices," *Journal of Business*, 51, 621–651.

Brennan, M., 1979. "The Pricing of Contingent Claims in Discrete Time Models," *Journal of Finance*, 24, 1, 53–68.

Brennan, M., and A. Kraus, 1978. "Necessary Conditions for Aggregation in Securities Markets," *Journal of Financial and Quantitative Analysis*, 13, 3, 407–418.

Brown, D., and J. C. Jackwerth, 2004. "The Pricing Kernel Puzzle: Reconciling Index Option Data and Economic Theory." Working paper, University of Konstanz.

Brown, R., and S. Schaefer, 1994. "The Term Structure of Real Interest Rates and the Cox, Ingersoll, and Ross Model," *Journal of Financial Economics*, 35, 3–42.

Brunnermeier, M., Gollier, C., and J. Parker, 2007. "Optimal Beliefs, Asset Prices, and the Preference for Skewed Returns," *American Economic Review* (Papers and Proceedings), 97, 2, 159–165.

Brunnermeier, M., and S. Nagel, 2004. "Do Wealth Fluctuations Generate Time-Varying Risk Aversion? Micro-Evidence on Individuals' Asset Allocation," *American Economic Review.*

Calvet, L., J. M. Grandmont, and I. Lemaire, 2004. "Aggregation of Heterogeneous Beliefs and Asset Pricing in Complete Financial Markets," Working Paper, CREST.

Camerer, C., 1989. "An Experimental Test of Several Generalized Utility Theories," *Journal of Risk and Uncertainty*, 2, 61–104.

Campbell, J., 1995. "Some Lessons from the Yield Curve," *Journal of Economics Perspectives*, 129–152.

Campbell, J., 2000. "Asset Prices at the Millennium," *Journal of Finance*, 55, 1515–1568.

Campbell, J., and J. Cochrane, 1999. "By Force of Habit: A Consumption-Based Explanation of Aggregate Stock Market Behavior," *Journal of Political Economy*, 107, 205–251.

Campbell, J., and J. Cochrane, 2000. "Explaining the Poor Performance of Consumption-Based Asset Pricing Models," *Journal of Finance*, 55, 6, 2863–2878.

Campbell, J., A. Lo, and A. C. MacKinlay, 1997. *The Econometrics of Financial Markets*, Princeton, NJ: Princeton University Press.

Campbell, J., and R. Shiller, 1984. "A Simple Account of the Behavior of Long Term Interest Rates," *American Economic Review*, 74, 44–48.

Campbell, J., and R. Shiller, 1991. "Yield Spreads and Interest Rate Movements: A Bird's Eye View," *Review of Economic Studies*, 58, 495–514.

Campbell, J., and R. Shiller, 1998. "Valuation Ratios and the Long-Run Market Outlook," *Journal of Portfolio Management*, 24, 2, 11–26.

Canner, N., N. G. Mankiw, and D. Weil, 1997. "An Asset Allocation Puzzle," *American Economic Review*, 87, 1, 181–191.

Cao, C., H. Li, and F. Yu, 2000. "The Economic Significance of Investor Misreactions in the Options Market," Working paper, Pennsylvania State University.

Carhart, M., 1997. "On Persistence in Mutual Fund Performance," *Journal of Finance*, 52, 1, 57–82.

Carr, P., and D. Madan, 2001. "Optimal Positioning in Derivatives," *Quantitative Finance*, 1, 1, 19–37.

Cecchetti, S. G., P. Lam, and N. Mark, 2000. "Asset Pricing with Distorted Beliefs: Are Equity Returns Too Good to Be True?" *American Economic Review*, 90, 787–805.

Chen, H-L., and W. De Bondt, 2004. "Style Momentum Within the S&P-500 Index," *Journal of Empirical Finance*, 11, 483–507.

Chen, J., H. Hong, and J. Stein, 2000. "Breadth of Ownership and Stock Returns," Working paper, Stanford University.

Chew, S. H., 1983. "A Generalization of the Quasilinear Mean with Applications to the Measurement of Income Inequality and Decision Theory Resolving the Allais Paradox," *Econometrica*, 51, 1065–1092.

Chew, S. H., and K. MacCrimmon, 1979. "Alpha-nu Choice Theory: An Axiomatization of Expected Utility Theory." Working paper, University of British Columbia.

Chopra, N., C. M. K. Lee, A. Shleifer, and R. H. Thaler, 1993. "Yes, Discounts on Closed-End Funds Are a Sentiment Index," *Journal of Finance*, 48, 801–808; and "Summing Up," 811–812.

Clarke, R. G., and M. Statman, 1998. "Bullish or Bearish? The Patterns of Investor Forecasts," *Financial Analysts Journal*, May/June, 63–72.

Cochrane, J., 2005. *Asset Pricing*, Princeton: Princeton University Press.

Constantinides, G., J. Jackwerth, and S. Perrakis, forthcoming, "Mispricing of S&P 500 Index Options," *Review of Financial Studies*.

Constantinides, G., 1983. "Capital Market Equilibrium with Personal Tax," *Econometrica*, 51, 3 (May): 611–636.

Constantinides, G., 1984. "Optimal Stock Trading with Personal Taxes: Implications for Prices and the Abnormal January Returns," *Journal of Financial Economics*, 13, 1, 65–89.

Coval, J., and T. Shumway, 2005. "Do Behavioral Biases Affect Prices?" *Journal of Finance*, 60, 1 (February): 1–34.

Cox, J., J. E. Ingersoll, and S. Ross, 1985. "A Theory of the Term Structure of Interest Rates," *Econometrica*, 53, 385–407.

Cox, J. C., S. A. Ross, and M. Rubinstein, 1979. "Option Pricing: A Simplified Approach." *Journal of Financial Economics*, 7, 229–263.

Cuoco, D., and H. He, 1994a. "Dynamic Equilibrium in Infinite-Dimensional Economies with Incomplete Information." Working paper, Wharton School, University of Pennsylvania.

Cuoco, D., and H. He, 1994b. "Dynamic Aggregation and Computation of Equilibria in Finite-Dimensional Economies with Incomplete Financial Markets Equilibrium." Working paper, Wharton School, University of Pennsylvania.

Daniel, K., D. Hirshleifer, and A. Subrahmanyam, 1998. "A Theory of Overconfidence, Self-Attribution, and Security Market Under- and Over-Reactions," *Journal of Finance*, 53, 1839–1886.

Daniel, K., D. Hirshleifer, and A. Subrahmanyam, 2001. "Overconfidence, Arbitrage, and Equilibrium Asset Pricing," *Journal of Finance*, 56(3), 921–965.

Das, S., and R. Sundaram, 1999. "Of Smiles and Smirks: A Term Structure Perspective," *Journal of Quantitative and Financial Analysis*, 34, 211–240.

David, A., and P. Veronesi, 1999. "Option Prices with Uncertain Fundamentals." Working paper, Board of Governors of the Federal Reserve System.

De Bondt, W., 1991. "What Do Economists Know About the Stock Market?" *Journal of Portfolio Management*, 17, 2, 84–91.

De Bondt, W., and R. Thaler, 1985. "Does the Stock Market Overreact?" *Journal of Finance*, 40, 793–805.

De Bondt, W., and R. Thaler, 1987. "Further Evidence on Investor Overreaction and Stock Market Seasonality," *Journal of Finance*, 42, 793–805.

De Bondt, W. F. M., 1992. *Earnings Forecasts and Share Price Reversals*, Charlottesville, VA: The Research Foundation of the Institute of Chartered Financial Analysts.

De Bondt, W. F. M., 1993. "Betting on Trends: Intuitive Forecasts of Financial Risk and Return," *International Journal of Forecasting*, 9, 355–371.

Derman, E., and I. Kani, 1994. "Riding on a Smile," *Risk*, 7, 32–39.

Detemple, J., and S. Murthy, 1994. "Intertemporal Asset Pricing with Heterogeneous Beliefs," *Journal of Economic Theory*, 62, 294–320.

Detemple, J., and S. Murthy, 1997. "Equilibrium Asset Prices and No-Arbitrage with Portfolio Constraints." Working paper, McGill University/Rutgers University.

Dhar, R., and N. Zhu, 2006. "Up Close and Personal: Investor Sophistication and the Disposition Effect," *Management Science*, 52(5) 726-740.

Diamond, D., and R. Verrecchia, 1981. "Information Aggregation in a Noisy Rational Expectations Economy," *Journal of Financial Economics*, 9, 221–235.

Diether, K., C. Malloy, and A. Scherbina, 2002. "Differences of Opinion and the Cross-Section of Stock Returns," *Journal of Finance*, 57, 5 (October): 2113–2141.

Dittmar, R., 2002. "Nonlinear Pricing Kernels, Kurtosis Preference, and Evidence from the Cross Section of Equity Returns," *Journal of Finance*, 57, 1, 369–403.

Diz, F., and T. J. Finucane, 1993. "Do the Options Markets Really Overreact?" *Journal of Futures Markets*, 13, 298–312.

Dumas, B., 1989. "Two-Person Dynamic Equilibrium in the Capital Market," *Review of Financial Studies*, 1, 377–401.

Dumas, B., J. Fleming and R. E. Whaley, 1998. "Implied Volatility Smiles: an Empirical Investigation," *The Journal of Finance*, 53:6, 2059-2106.

Dumas, B., A. Kurshev, and R. Uppal, forthcoming. "What Can Rational Investors Do About Excessive Volatility and Sentiment Fluctuations?" *Journal of Finance*.

Dupire, B., 1994. "Pricing with a Smile," *Risk*, 7, 18–20.

Dybvig, P., and J. Ingersoll, 1982. "Mean-Variance Theory in Complete Markets," *Journal of Business*, 55, 2, 233–251.

Edwards, W., 1968. "Conservatism in Human Information Processing." In B. Kleinmuntz (ed.), *Formal Representation of Human Judgment*. New York: John Wiley and Sons, 17–52.

Edwards, W., 1982. "Conservatism in Human Information Processing." In D. Kahneman, P. Slovic, and A. Tversky (eds.), *Judgment Under Uncertainty: Heuristics and Biases.* Cambridge, MA: Cambridge University Press. 359–369.

Emmanuel, D.C., and J. D. MacBeth, 1982. "Further Tests on the Constant Elasticity of Variance Option Pricing Model," *Journal of Financial and Quantitative Analysis,* 17, 533–554.

Epstein, L., and S. Zin, 1989. "Substitution, Risk Aversion, and the Temporal Behavior of Consumption and Asset Returns: A Theoretical Framework," *Econometrica,* 57, 937–969.

Epstein, L., and S. Zin, 1990. "First-Order Risk Aversion and the Equity Premium Puzzle," *Journal of Monetary Economics,* 26, 387–407.

Epstein, L., and S. Zin, 1991. "Substitution, Risk Aversion, and the Temporal Behavior of Consumption and Asset Returns: An Empirical Investigation," *Journal of Political Economy,* 99, 263–286.

Fama, E., 1965. "Random Walks in Stock Market Prices," *Financial Analysts Journal,* Vol. 21, No. 5, September/October, 55–59.

Fama, E. R., and K. R. French, 1992. "The Cross-Section of Expected Stock Returns," *Journal of Finance,* 47, 427–465.

Fama, E. R., and K. R. French, 1996. "Multifactor Explanations of Asset Pricing Anomalies," *Journal of Finance,* 51, 1 (March): 55–84.

Fama, E. R., and K. R. French, 2002. "The Equity Premium," *Journal of Finance,* 57, 637–659.

Fama, E. R., and K. R. French, 2004. "Disagreement, Tastes and Asset Prices." Working paper, University of Chicago.

Feiger, G., 1978. "Divergent Rational Expectations Equilibrium in a Dynamic Model of a Futures Market," *Journal of Economic Theory,* 17, 2, 164–178.

Feng, L., and M. Seasholes, 2005. "Do Investor Sophistication and Trading Experience Eliminate Behavioral Biases in Finance Markets?" *Review of Finance,* 9, 3 (September): 305–351.

Fennema, H., and P. Wakker, 1997. "Original and Cumulative Prospect Theory: A Discussion of Empirical Differences," *Journal of Behavioral Decision Making* 10, 53–64.

Ferson, W., and D. Locke, 1998. "Estimating the Cost of Capital Through Time: An Analysis of the Sources of Error," *Management Science*, 44, 4, 485–500.

Figlewski, S., 1978. "Market 'Efficiency' in a Market with Heterogeneous Information." *Journal of Political Economy*, 86, 581–597.

Figlewski, S., 1997. *Forecasting Volatility. Financial Markets, Institutions, and Instruments*, Vol. 6, No. 1. Boston MA: Blackwell Publishers.

Finucane, M., 2003. "Mad Cows, Mad Corn, and Mad Money," *The Journal of Psychology and Financial Markets*, 3, 4, 236–243.

Finucane, M., A. Alhakami, P. Slovic, and S. Johnson, 2000. "The Affect Heuristic in Judgments of Risks and Benefits," *Journal of Behavioral Decision Making*, 13, 1–17.

Fisher, K., and M. Statman, 1997. "Investment Advice from Mutual Fund Companies," *Journal of Portfolio Management*, Fall, 9–25.

Fogel, S. O., and T. Berry, 2006. "The Disposition Effect and Individual Investor Decisions: The Roles of Regret and Counterfactual Alternatives," *Journal of Behavioral Finance*, 7, 2, 107–116.

Frazzini, A., 2006. "The Disposition Effect and Underreaction to News," *Journal of Finance*, 41, 6 (August): 2017–2046.

Friedman, M., and L. J. Savage, 1948. "The Utility Analysis of Choices Involving Risk," *Journal of Political Economy*, 56, 279–304.

Galai, D., and O. Sade, 2006. "The "Ostrich Effect" and the Relationship Between the Liquidity and Yields of Financial Assets." *Journal of Business*, 79(5), 2741–2759.

Ganzach, Y., 2000. "Judging Risk and Return of Financial Assets," *Organizational Behavior and Human Decision Processes*, 83, 353–370.

Genesove, D., and C. Mayer, 2001. "Loss Aversion and Seller Behavior: Evidence from the Housing Market." *Quarterly Journal of Economics*, Vol. 116(4), 1233–1260.

Gibbons, M., and W. Ferson, 1985. "Testing Asset Pricing Models with Changing Expectations and an Unobservable Market Portfolio," *Journal of Financial Economics*, 14, 217–236.

Gilovich, T., R. Vallone, and A. Tversky, 1985. "The Hot Hand in Basketball: On the Misperception of Random Sequences," *Cognitive Psychology*, 17, 295–314.

Glassman, J., and K. Hassett, 1999. *Dow 36,000: The New Strategy for Profiting from the Coming Rise in the Stock Market*, New York: Times Books.

Goetzmann, W., and A. Kumar, 2004. "Why Do Individual Investors Hold Undiversified Portfolios?" National Bureau of Economic Research Working Paper 8686.

Goetzmann, W. N., and R. G. Ibbotson, 1994. "Do Winners Repeat?" *Journal of Portfolio Management*, 20, 2 (Winter): 9–18.

Gonz'alez de la Mota, A., 2000a. "Essays on Asset Pricing and Risk Management Under Endogenous Uncertainty: The Infinite Dimensional Case." Working paper, Stanford University.

Gonz'alez de la Mota, A., 2000b. "The Relevance of the Market Price of Risk and Multi-Scale Stochastic Volatility for the Dynamics of Smile Curves: Insights from Endogenous Uncertainty and Heterogeneous Beliefs." Working paper, Stanford University.

Gonzalez, R., and G. Wu, 1999. "On the Shape of the Probability Weighting Function," *Cognitive Psychology* 38, 129–166.

Gorman, W., 1953. "Community Preference Fields," *Econometrica*, 21, 63–80.

Graham, J., and C. Harvey, 2002. "Expectations of Equity Risk Premia, Volatility, and Asymmetry: From a Corporate Finance Perspective." Working paper, Fuqua School of Business, Duke University.

Green, T.C., and S. Figlewski, 1999. "Market Risk and Model Risk for a Financial Institution Writing Options," *Journal of Finance*, Vol. 54(4), 1465–1499.

Green, R., and K. Rydqvist, 1999. "Ex-Day Behavior with Dividend Preference and Limitations to Short-Term Arbitrage: The Case of Swedish Lottery Bonds," *Journal of Financial Economics*, 53, 2, 145–187.

Greenspan, A., 1996-12-05, "The Challenge of Central Banking in a Democratic Society," speech delivered at American Enterprise Institute.

Grether, D., 1980. "Bayes Rule as a Descriptive Model: The Representativeness Heuristic," *Quarterly Journal of Economics*, 95, 537–557.

Griffin, D., and A. Tversky, 1992. "The Weighing of Evidence and the Determinants of Confidence." *Cognitive Psychology*, 24, 411–435.

Grinblatt, M., and B. Han, 2004. "The Disposition Effect and Momentum." Working paper, UCLA.

Grinblatt, M., and M. Keloharju, 2001. "What Makes Investors Trade?" *Journal of Finance*, 56, 2, 589–616.

Han, B., 2004. "Limits of Arbitrage, Sentiment and Pricing Kernel: Evidences from Index Options." Working paper, Ohio State University.

Han, B., 2008. "Investor Sentiment and Option Prices," *Review of Financial Studies*, forthcoming.

Harris, M., and A. Raviv, 1991. "Differences of Opinion Make a Horserace," *Review of Financial Studies*, 6, 3, 473–506.

Harvey, C., and A. Siddique, 2000. "Conditional Skewness in Asset Pricing Tests," *Journal of Finance*, 55, 1263–1295.

Hausman, J., 1979. "Individual Discount Rates and the Purchase and Utilization of Energy-Using Durables," *Bell Journal of Economics*, 10, 33–54.

He, H., 1990. "Convergence from Discrete to Continuous-Time Contingent Claims Prices," *Review of Financial Studies*, Volume 3, number 4, 523–546.

Heineke, J., and H. Shefrin, 1988. "Exact Aggregation and the Finite Basis Property," *International Economic Review*, 29, 3, 525–538.

Hens, T., and M. Vlcek, 2005. "Does Prospect Theory Explain the Disposition Effect?" (December 22). NHH Dept. of Finance and Management Science Discussion Paper No. 18/2005. Available at SSRN: http://ssrn.com/abstract=970450.

Heston, S., 1993. "A Closed Form Solution of Options with Stochastic Volatility with Applications to Bond and Currency Options," *Review of Financial Studies*, 6, 327–343.

Hong, H., T. Lim, and J. Stein, 1999. "Bad News Travels Slowly: Size, Analyst Coverage, and the Profitability of Momentum Strategies," *Journal of Finance*, 55, 1, 265–295.

Hong, H., and J. Stein, 1999. "A Unified Theory of Underreaction, Momentum Trading, and Overreaction in Asset Markets," *Journal of Finance*, 54, 6, 2143–2184.

Hong, H., and J. Stein, 2007. "Disagreement and the Stock Market," *Journal of Economics Perspectives*, 21, 2, 109–128.

Hull, J., 2004. *Options, Futures, and Other Derivatives*, Englewood Cliffs, NJ: Prentice-Hall.

Ingersoll, J., 1987. *Theory of Financial Decision Making*, Totawa, NJ: Rowman and Littlefield.

Jackwerth, J. C., 2000. "Recovering Risk Aversion from Option Prices and Realized Returns," *Review of Financial Studies*, 13, 433–451.

Jackwerth, J. C., 2004. *Option-Implied Risk-Neutral Distributions and Risk Aversion*, Charlottesville, VA: Research Foundation of AIMR.

Jackwerth, J. C., and M. Rubinstein, 1996. "Recovering Probability Distributions from Contemporaneous Security Prices," *Journal of Finance*, 51, 5, 1611–1631.

Jaffe, J., and R. Winkler, 1976. "Optimal Speculation Against an Efficient Market," *Journal of Finance*, 39, 49–61.

Jegadeesh, N., and S. Titman, 1993. "Returns to Buying Winners and Selling Losers: Implications for Stock Market Efficiency," *Journal of Finance*, 48, 65–91.

Jegadeesh, N., and S. Titman, 2001. "Profitability of Momentum Strategies: An Evaluation of Alternative Strategies," *Journal of Finance*, 56, 2 (April): 699–720.

Jin, L., and A. Scherbina, 2005. "Change Is Good or the Disposition Effect Among Mutual Fund Managers. Working paper, Harvard Business School.

Jorion, P., 1994. "Mean-Variance Analysis of Currency Overlays," *Financial Analysts Journal*, May/June, 48–56.

Jouini, E., and C. Napp, 2006. "Heterogeneous Beliefs and Asset Pricing in Discrete Time: An Analysis of Pessimism and Doubt," *Journal of Economic Dynamics and Control*, Volume 30, Issue 7, 1233–1260.

Jouini, E., and C. Napp, 2007a, "Are More Risk Averse Agents More Optimistic? Insights from a Rational Expectations Model," Working paper, Université Paris Dauphine.

Jouini, E., and C. Napp, 2007b. "Consensus Consumer and Intertemporal Asset Pricing with Heterogeneous Beliefs," *Review of Economic Studies*, 74, 1149-1174.

Kahneman, D., 2002. untitled PowerPoint presentation for lecture at Northwestern University.

Kahneman, D., and A. Tversky, 1972. "Subjective Probability: A Judgment of Representativeness," *Cognitive Psychology*, 3, 430–454.

Kahneman, D., and A. Tversky, 1973. "On the Psychology of Prediction," *Psychological Review*, 80, 237–251.

Kahneman, D., and A. Tversky, 1979. "Prospect Theory: An Analysis of Decision Making Under Risk," *Econometrica*, 263–291.

Kahneman, D., and A. Tversky, 1982. "The Psychology of Preferences," *Scientific American*, 246, 160–173.

Kandel, E., and N. Pearson, 1995. "Differential Interpretation of Public Signals and Trade in Speculative Markets," *Journal of Political Economy*, 103, 4, 831–872.

Karolyi, G. A., 1993. "A Bayesian Approach to Modelling Stock Return Volatility for Option Evaluation," *Journal of Financial and Quantitative Analysis*, 28, 579–594.

Kaustia, M., 2004. "Market-Wide Impact of the Disposition Effect: Evidence from IPO Trading Volume," *Journal of Financial Markets*, 7, 2 (February): 207–235.

Knutson, B., G. E. Wimmer, C. Kuhnen, and P. Winkielman, 2008. "Nucleus Accumbens Activation Mediates the Influence of Reward Dues on Financial Risk Taking," *NeuroReport*, Vol. 19, No. 5, 509–513.

Kosowski, R., A. Timmermann, R. Wermers, and H. White, 2006. "Can Mutual Fund Stars Really Pick Stocks? New Evidence from a Bootstrap Analysis," *Journal of Finance*, 61, 6 (December): 2551–2595.

Kumar, A., 2007. "Who Gambles in the Stock Market?" Working paper, University of Texas.

Kurz, M., 1997. *Endogenous Economic Fluctuations: Studies in the Theory of Rational Beliefs*. Studies in Economic Theory No. 6, Berlin and New York: Springer-Verlag.

Kurz, M., R. Spiegelman, and R. West, 1973. "The Experimental Horizon and the Rate of Time-Preference for the Seattle and Denver Income Maintenance Experiments: A Preliminary Study." Menlo Park, CA: SRI International Research Memorandum, No. 21.

Lakonishok, J., A. Shleifer, and R. Vishny, 1994. "Contrarian Investment, Extrapolation, and Risk," *Journal of Finance*, 49, 5, 1541–1578.

Lakonishok, J., A. Shleifer, and R. W. Vishny, 1992. "Brookings Papers on Economic Activity," *Microeconomics*, 32, 339–391.

La Porta, R., 1996. "Expectations and the Cross-Section of Stock Returns," *Journal of Finance*, 51, 5, 1715–1742.

Lease, R. C., W. Lewellen, and G. Schlarbaum. 1976. "Market Segmentation: Evidence on the Individual Investor," *Financial Analysts Journal*, 32, 5 (September/October): 53–60.

Lehenkari, M., 2007. "The Disposition Effect: Underlying Mechanisms and Implications for Individual Investors," Working paper, University of Oulu, Finland.

Leland, H., 1999. "Beyond Mean-Variance: Performance Measurement in an Nonsymmetrical World," *Financial Analysts Journal*, January/February, 27–36.

Lintner, J., 1969. "The Aggregation of Investors' Diverse Judgements and Preferences in Pure Competitive Markets," *Journal of Financial and Quantitative Analysis*, 4, 347–400.

Lo, A., 2001, "Risk Management for Hedge Funds: Introduction and Overview," *Financial Analysts Journal*, 57, 16–33.

Locke, P., and S. Mann, 2005. "Professional Trader Discipline and Trade Disposition," *Journal of Financial Economics*, 76, 2 (May): 401–444.

Loomes, G., and R. Sugden, 1982. "Regret Theory: An Alternative Theory of Rational Choice Under Uncertainty," *Economic Journal*, 92, 805–824.

Loomes, G., and R. Sugden, 1983. "A Rationale for Preference Reversal," *American Economic Review*, 73, 3 (June): 428–432.

Loomes, G., and R. Sugden, 1987. "Some Implications of a More General Form of Regret Theory," *Journal of Economic Theory*, 41, 2 (April): 270–287.

Lopes, L., 1987. "Between Hope and Fear: The Psychology of Risk," *Advances in Experimental Social Psychology*, 20, 255–295.

Lopes, L., 1993. "Reasons and Resources: The Human Side of Risk Taking." In N. J. Bell and R. W. Bell (eds.), *Adolescent Risk Taking*. Lubbock, TX: Sage, 29–54.

Lopes, L. L., and G. C. Oden, 1999. "The Role of Aspiration Level in Risk Choice: A Comparison of Cumulative Prospect Theory and SP/A Theory," *Journal of Mathematical Psychology*, 43, 286–313.

Lucas, R., 1978. "Asset Pricing in an Exchange Economy," *Econometrica*, 46, 1429–1445.

MacBeth, J. D., and L. Merville, 1980. "Tests of the Black–Scholes and Cox Call Option Valuation Models," *Journal of Finance*, 35, 285–301.

MacGregor, D., P. Slovic, D. Dreman, and M. Berry, 2000. "Imagery, Affect, and Financial Judgment," *Journal of Psychology and Financial Markets*, 1, 2, 104–110.

Machina, M., 1982. "Expected Utility Analysis Without the Independence Axiom," *Econometrica*, 50, 277–323.

Machina, M., 1987. "Choice Under Uncertainty: Problems Solved and Unsolved," *Journal of Economic Perspectives*, 1, 121–154.

Madan, D., F. Milne, and H. Shefrin, 1989. "The Multinomial Option Pricing Model and Its Brownian and Poisson Limits," *Review of Financial Studies*, 2, 251–265.

Malkiel, B., 2000-12-28. "Are Markets Efficient? No, Arbitrage Is Inherently Risky," *The Wall Street Journal*.

Malmendier, U., and D. Shanthikumar, 2003. "Are Investors Naive About Incentives?" Working paper, Stanford University.

Markowitz, H., 1952a. "Portfolio Selection," *Journal of Finance*, 6, 77–91.

Markowitz, H., 1952b. "The Utility of Wealth." *Journal of Political Economy*, 60, 151–158.

Markowitz, H., 1999. "The Early History of Portfolio Theory: 1600–1960," *Financial Analysts Journal*, July/August, 5–16.

Mayers, T. A., 1989, 1994. *The Technical Analysis Course*, Chicago: Irwin.

Mayshar, J., 1983. "On Divergence of Opinion and Imperfections in Capital Markets," *American Economic Review*, 73, 114–128.

McConnell, J., and E. Schwartz, 1992. "The Origin of LYONs: A Case Study in Financial Innovation," *Journal of Applied Corporate Finance*, Summer, 40–47.

Mehra, R., and E. C. Prescott, 1985. "The Equity Premium Puzzle," *Journal of Monetary Economics*, 40, 2, 145–161.

Meyer, D., and J. Meyer, 2005. "Relative Risk Aversion: What Do We Know?" *The Journal of Risk and Uncertainty*, 31, 3, 243–262.

Meyer, D., and J. Meyer, 2006. "Measuring Risk Aversion," *Foundations and Trends in Microeconomics*, 2, 2, 107–203.

Miller, E., 1977. "Risk, Uncertainty, and Divergence of Opinion," *Journal of Finance*, 32, 1151–1168.

Milne, F., and S. Turnbull, 1996. "Theoretical Methods for Security Pricing." Working paper, Queen's University.

Mitton, T., and K. Vorkink, 2007. "Equilibrium Underdiversification and the Preference for Skewness," *Review of Financial Studies*, Volume 20, Issue 4, 1255–1288.

Moskowitz, T., and M. Grinblatt, 1999. "Do Industries Explain Momentum?" *Journal of Finance*, 54, 4 (August): 1249–1290.

Muermann, A., and J. M. Volkman, 2007. "Regret, Pride, and the Disposition Effect," Working paper, University of Pennsylvania.

Naik, V., and M. H. Lee, 1990. "General Equilibrium Pricing of Options on the Market Portfolio with Discontinuous Returns," *Review of Financial Studies*, 3, 493–522.

O'Connell, P., and M. Teo, forthcoming. "Institutional Investors, Past Performance, and Dynamic Loss Aversion," *Journal of Financial and Quantitative Finance*.

Odean, T., 1998a. "Are Investors Reluctant to Realize Their Losses?" *Journal of Finance*, 53, 1775–1798.

Odean, T., 1998b. "Volume, Volatility, Price, and Profit When All Traders Are Above Average," *Journal of Finance*, 53, 1887–1934.

Odean, T., 1999. "Do Investors Trade Too Much?" *American Economic Review*, Vol. 89, 1279–1298.

Ou, J., and S. Penman, 1989. "Financial Statement Analysis and the Prediction of Stock Returns," *Journal of Accounting and Economics*, 11, 295–329.

Ou-Yang, H., 2005. "An Equilibrium Model of Asset Pricing and Moral Hazard," *Review of Financial Studies*, 18:4, 1253–1303.

Pan, J., 2002. "The Jump-Risk Premia Implicit in Options: Evidence from an Integrated Time-Series Study," *Journal of Financial Economics*, 63, 3–50.

Payne, J., 2005. "It Is Whether You Win or Lose: The Importance of the Overall Probabilities of Winning or Losing in Risky Choice," *The Journal of Risk and Uncertainty*, 30:1, 5–19.

Polkovnichenko, V., 2005. "Household Portfolio Diversification: A Case for Rank-Dependent Preferences," *The Review of Financial Studies*, 18, 4, 1467–1501.

Post, T., and H. Levy, 2005. "Does Risk Seeking Drive Stock Prices? A Stochastic Dominance Analysis of Aggregate Investor Preferences and Beliefs," *Review of Financial Studies*, 18, 3, 925–953.

Poteshman, A., 2001a. "Underreaction, Overreaction and the Increasing Misreaction to Information in the Option Market," *Journal of Finance*, 56, 3, 851–876.

Poteshman, A., 2001b. "Forecasting Future Volatility from Option Prices." Working paper, University of Illinois at Urbana-Champaign.

Poti, V., 2006. "The Coskewness Puzzle in the Cross-Section of Industry Portfolio Returns," Working paper, Dublin City University Business School.

Quiggin, J., 1982. "A Theory of Anticipated Utility," *Journal of Economic and Behavioral Organization*, 3, 323–343.

Quiggin, J., 1993. *Generalized Expected Utility Theory: The Rank-Dependent Model*, Boston: Kluwer Academic Publishers.

Rabin, M., and R. Thaler, 2001. "Risk Aversion," *Journal of Economics Perspectives*, 15, 1, 219–232.

Ranguelova, E., 2001. "Disposition Effect and Firm Size: New Evidence on Individual Investor Trading Activity," Working paper, Harvard University.

Ritter, J., 1988. "The Buying and Selling Behavior of Individual Investors at the Turn of the Year," *Journal of Finance*, 43, 3, 701–717.

Roberds, W., and C. Whiteman, 1997. "Endogenous Term Premia and Anomalies in the Term Structure of Interest Rates: Explaining the Predictability Smile." Working paper, Federal Reserve Bank of Atlanta.

Rosenberg, B., Reid K., and R. Lanstein, 1985. "Persuasive Evidence of Market Inefficiency," *Journal of Portfolio Management*, Spring, 9–16.

Rosenberg, J., and R. Engle, 2002. "Empirical Pricing Kernels," *Journal of Financial Economics*, 64, 3, 341–372.

Rouwenhorst, K. G., 1998. "International Momentum Strategies," *Journal of Finance*, 53, 1, 267–284.

Roy, A.D., 1952. "Safety-First and the Holding of Assets," *Econometrica*, 20, 3, 431–449.

Rubinstein, M., 1973. "The Fundamental Theorem of Parameter Preference Security Valuation," *Journal of Financial and Quantitative Analysis*, 8, 61–69.

Rubinstein, M., 1974. "An Aggregation Theorem for Security Markets," *Journal of Financial Economics*, 1, 3, 225–244.

Rubinstein, M., 1976. "The Valuation of Uncertain Income Streams and the Pricing of Options," *Bell Journal of Economics*, 7, 407–425.

Rubinstein, M., 1985. "Nonparametric Tests of Alternative Option Pricing Models Using All Reported Trades and Quotes on the 30 Most Active CBOE Option Classes from August 23, 1976 Through August 31, 1978," *Journal of Finance*, 40, 455–480.

Rubinstein, M., 1994. "Implied Binomial Trees," *Journal of Finance*, 49, 771–818.

Samuelson, P., 1963. "Risk and Uncertainty: A Fallacy of Large Numbers," *Scientia*, 98, 108–113.

San, G., 2007. *The Dynamics of Institutional and Individual Trading Activity*, Ph.D. dissertation, Tel Aviv University.

Sandroni, A., 2000. "Do Markets Favor Agents Able to Make Accurate Predictions?" *Econometrica*, 68, 6, 1303–1342.

Scheinkman, J. A., and W. Xiong, 2003, "Overconfidence and Speculative Bubbles," *Journal of Political Economy*, 111, 1183–1219.

Scherbina, A., 2003. "Analyst Disagreement, Forecast Bias and Stock Returns." Working paper, Harvard Business School.

Seru, A., T. Shumway, and N. Stoffman., 2006. "Learning by Trading." Working paper, University of Michigan.

Shapira, Z., and I. Venezia., 2001. "Patterns of Behavior of Professionally Managed and Independent Investors," *Journal of Banking and Finance*, 25, 1573–1587.

Sharpe, S., 2002. "Reexamining Stock Valuation and Initiation: The Implication of Analysts' Earnings Forecasts," *The Review of Economics and Statistics*, 84, 4, 632–648.

Shefrin, H., 1984. "Inferior Forecasters, Cycles, and the Efficient Markets Hypothesis: A Comment," *Journal of Political Economy*, 92, 156–161.

Shefrin, H., 1999a. "Irrational Exuberance and Option Smiles." *Financial Analysts Journal*, November/December, 91–103.

Shefrin, H., 1999b. *Beyond Greed and Fear: Understanding Behavioral Finance and the Psychology of Investing*, Boston: Harvard Business School Press.

Shefrin, H., 2001a. "Do Investors Expect Higher Returns from Safer Stocks Than from Riskier Stocks?" *Journal of Psychology and Financial Markets*, 2, 4, 176–181.

Shefrin, H., 2001b. "On Kernels and Sentiment." Paper available at http://papers.ssrn.com.

Shefrin, H., 2001c. *Behavioral Finance: A Three Volume Edited Collection*, London: Edward Elgar.

Shefrin, H., 2006. *Behavioral Corporate Finance*, New York: McGraw-Hill/Irwin.

Shefrin, H., and M. Statman, 1985. "The Disposition to Sell Winners Too Early and Ride Losers Too Long: Theory and Evidence." *Journal of Finance*, 40 (July): 777–790.

Shefrin, H., and M. Statman, 1989. "Introducing Prospect Theory into General Equilibrium: Implications for CAPM and Portfolio Insurance." Working paper, Santa Clara University.

Shefrin, H., and M. Statman, 1994. "Behavioral Capital Asset Pricing Theory," *Journal of Financial and Quantitative Analysis*, 29, 323–349.

Shefrin, H., and M. Statman, 1995. "Making Sense of Beta, Size, and Book-to-Market," *The Journal of Portfolio Management*, Winter, 21, 2, 26–34.

Shefrin, H., and M. Statman, 2000a. "Behavioral Portfolio Theory," *Journal of Financial and Quantitative Analysis*, 35, 127–151.

Shefrin, H., and M. Statman, 2003. "The Style of Investor Expectations." in T. Coggin and F. Fabozzi (eds.), *The Handbook of Equity Style Management.*

Shiller, R., 1981. "Do Stock Prices Move Too Much to Be Justified by Subsequent Changes in Dividends," reprinted as Ch. 4 in R. Thaler (ed.), *Advances in Behavioral Finance,* New York: Russell Sage Foundation.

Shiller, R., 1990. "The Term Structure of Interest Rates." In B. Friedman and F. Hahn (eds.), *Handbook of Monetary Economics* (Vol. 1, 627–722). Amsterdam: North Holland.

Shiller, R., 2000. *Irrational Exuberance,* Princeton: Princeton University Press.

Shimko, D., 1993. "Bounds of Probability" *Risk,* 6, 33–37.

Shleifer, A., 2000. *Inefficient Markets,* New York: Oxford University Press.

Shleifer, A., 2000-12-28. "Are Markets Efficient? "No, Arbitrage Is Inherently Risky," *The Wall Street Journal.*

Shumway, T., and G. Wu, 2006. "Does Disposition Drive Momentum?" Working paper, University of Michigan.

Sias, R., and L. Starks, 1997. "Institutions, Individuals and the Turn-of-the Year." *Journal of Finance,* 52, 1543–1562.

Siegal, J., and R. Thaler, 1997. "The Equity Premium Puzzle," *Journal of Economics Perspectives,* 11, 1, 191–200.

Slovic, P., 1987. "Perception of Risk," *Science,* 236, 280–285.

Statman, M., 1999. "Behavioral Finance: Past Battles and Future Engagements," *Financial Analysts,* 55, 6 (November/December): 18–27.

Statman, M., 2002. "Lottery Players/Stock Traders," *Financial Analysts Journal,* 58, 14–21.

Statman, M., S. Thorley, and K. Vorkink, 2006. "Investor Overconfidence and Trading Volume," *Review of Financial Studies* Volume 19, 1531–1565.

Stein, J., 1989. "Overreactions in the Options Market," *Journal of Finance,* 44, 1011–1023.

Thaler, R., and E. Johnson, 1991. "Gambling with the House Money and Trying to Break Even: The Effects of Prior Outcomes on Risky

Choice." In Richard H. Thaler (ed.), *Quasi-Rational Economics*, 48–73. New York: Russell Sage Foundation.

Treynor, J., 1998. "Bulls, Bears, and Market Bubbles," *Financial Analysts Journal*, 54, 2, 69–74.

Treynor, J., 2001. "The Canonical Market Bubble," mimeo. Treynor Capital Management.

Tversky, A., and D. Kahneman, 1971. "Belief in the Law of Small Numbers," *Psychological Bulletin*, 76, 105–110.

Tversky, A., and D. Kahneman, 1974. "Judgment Under Uncertainty: Heuristics and Biases," *Science*, 185, 1124–1131.

Tversky, A., and D. Kahneman, 1986. "Rational Choice and the Framing of Decisions," *Journal of Business*, 59, 4, 2, S251–S278.

Tversky, A., and D. Kahneman 1992. "Advances in Prospect Theory: Cumulative Representation of Uncertainty." *Journal of Risk and Uncertainty*. 5:4, 297–323.

Vissing-Jorgensen, A., 2004. "Perspectives on Behavioral Finance: Does 'Irrationality' Disappear with Wealth? Evidence from Expectations and Actions," *NBER Macroeconomics Annual 2003*.

Wang, J., 1996. "The Term Structure of Interest Rates in a Pure Exchange Economy with Heterogeneous Investors," *Journal of Financial Economics*, 41, 75–110.

Weber, M., and C. Camerer, 1998. "The Disposition Effect in Securities Trading: An Experimental Analysis," *Journal of Economic Behavior and Organization*, 33, 2, 167–184.

Weinbaum, D., 2001. "Investor Heterogeneity and the Demand for Options in a Dynamic General Equilibrium," Working paper, New York University.

Weitzman, M., 2001. "Gamma Discounting," *American Economic Review*, 91, 1, 260–271.

Welch, I., 2000. "Views of Financial Economists on the Equity Premium and on Professional Controversies," *Journal of Business*, 73, 4, 501–537.

Welch, I., 2001. "The Equity Premium Consensus Forecast Revisited," Working paper, Yale University.

Wermers, R., 2003. "Is Money Really 'Smart'? New Evidence on the Relation Between Mutual Fund Flows, Manager Behavior, and Performance Persistence." Working paper, University of Maryland.

Whaley, R. E., 1986. "Valuation of American Futures Options: Theory and Empirical Tests," *Journal of Finance*, 41 (March): 127–150.

Whitelaw, R., 2000. "Stock Market Risk and Return: An Equilibrium Approach," *Review of Financial Studies*, 13, 3, 521–547.

Yaari, M. E., 1987, "The Dual Theory of Choice Under Risk," *Econometrica*, 55, 95–115.

Yong-Ou, H., 2005. "An EEquilibrium Model of Asset Pricing and Moral Hazard," *Review of Financial Studies*, 18:4, 1253–1303.

Zhang, Y., 2005. "Individual Skewness and the Cross-Section of Average Stock Returns." Unpublished.

Ziegler, A., 2003. "Why Does Implied Risk Aversion Smile?" Working paper, Ecole des HEC, BFSH 1, University of Lausanne and FAME.

Index